RESEARCH HANDBOOK ON ISLAMIC LAW AND SOCIETY

Research Handbook on Islamic Law and Society

Edited by

Nadirsyah Hosen

Senior Lecturer, Faculty of Law, Monash University, Australia

Edward Elgar PUBLISHING

Cheltenham, UK • Northampton, MA, USA

Published by
Edward Elgar Publishing Limited
The Lypiatts
15 Lansdown Road
Cheltenham
Glos GL50 2JA
UK

Edward Elgar Publishing, Inc.
William Pratt House
9 Dewey Court
Northampton
Massachusetts 01060
USA

A catalogue record for this book
is available from the British Library

Library of Congress Control Number: 2018943995

This book is available electronically in the **Elgar**online
Law subject collection
DOI 10.4337/9781781003060

MIX
Paper from
responsible sources
FSC
www.fsc.org
FSC® C013056

ISBN 978 1 78100 305 3 (cased)
ISBN 978 1 78100 306 0 (eBook)

Typeset by Columns Design XML Ltd, Reading

Printed and bound in Great Britain by TJ International Ltd, Padstow, Cornwall

Contents

List of contributors vii
Acknowledgements x

Introduction: Islamic law in action 1
Nadirsyah Hosen

PART 1 FAMILY LAW AND COURTS

1 Colonial legacies: family laws in Singapore and Australia 13
Ann Black
2 The application of *kafala* in the West 48
Kieran Mclean Eadie
3 'The best interests of the child': critical analysis of the Libyan High Court decision 77
Ali Omar Ali Mesrati
4 ADR and Islamic law: the cases of the UK and Singapore 120
Arif A. Jamal

PART 2 PROPERTY AND BUSINESS

5 Corporate social responsibility and workplace casualties in Bangladesh: an appraisal of Islamic principles as a potential solution 141
S. M. Solaiman
6 Business in Islam: revisiting Islamic banking practices in Bangladesh 159
Afroza Begum
7 Property law and trusts (*waqf*) in Iran 178
Hossein Esmaeili

PART 3 CRIMINAL LAW AND JUSTICE

8 Corporate criminal liability in Saudi Arabia 201
Mohammed Fahad Aljiday Alsubaie

9 Blasphemy and apostasy laws in the Muslim world: a critical analysis 217
Faisal Kutty

10 Restorative justice in Islamic law: application in Malaysian legal history and the criminal justice system 250
Hanifah Haydar Ali Tajuddin, Nasimah Hussin and Majdah Zawawi

PART 4 ETHICS, HEALTH AND SCIENCES

11 Genetic engineering and ethics in Muslim communities: case studies from Tunisia and Saudi Arabia 273
Nurussyariah Hammado

12 Collective *ijtihad* on health issues in Indonesia 289
Nadirsyah Hosen

13 Halal and other codes: can religion, science and ethics guide legal regulation? 307
Richard Mohr

PART 5 ARTS AND EDUCATION

14 Finding the Islam in Islamic art: the relationship between Islamic law and artistic practice 331
Mia Corbett

15 The lawfulness of music in contemporary Indonesian debate 350
Neneng Yanti Khozanatu Lahpan

16 Educational rights for women in Saudi Arabia 371
Maan Abdul Haq Khutani

PART 6 COMMUNITY AND PUBLIC SPHERES

17 Progressive Islam in Europe: a critical analysis of the unique nature of Bosnia and Hercegovina's Islamic practice 405
Richard Burgess

18 *Khutbahs* and *fatwas* in colonial Indonesia and Malaya 428
Muhamad Ali

Index 453

Contributors

Muhamad Ali is an Associate Professor of Islamic Studies at the Religious Studies Department, University of California, Riverside. His most recent book is *Islam and Colonialism: Becoming Modern in Indonesia and Malaya* (Edinburgh University Press, 2015). His research interests are Islam in Southeast Asia, Qur'anic and Hadith Studies, Muslim politics and society, religious pluralism, and Islam and contemporary issues.

Mohammed Fahad Aljiday Alsubaie was awarded a PhD in Law from the University of Wollongong with a special commendation of his PhD thesis. He is a former Professor in the Institute of Public Administration, Dar al-'Uloom University and a legal consultant of a military Judge in Saudi Arabia.

Afroza Begum is a Professor of Law at the Islamic University, Bangladesh. Currently, she is on leave and working as a sessional academic at the University of Wollongong and at Macquarie University, Australia. Her teaching and research interest predominantly lies in international business law, corporations law and public law.

Ann Black is an Associate Professor and Reader at the TC Beirne School of Law, University of Queensland, Australia. She is the Deputy Director of the Centre for Public International and Comparative Law. Her books include *Modern Perspectives on Islamic Law* (co-written with Nadirsyah Hosen and Hossein Esmaeili, 2013).

Richard Burgess is an alumnus of the University of Wollongong where he graduated with Honours in both European Studies and Law. He practises contract and construction law at firm Herbert Smith Freehills, where he advises on major infrastructure projects across Australian and international jurisdictions.

Mia Corbett is an Australian solicitor who advises international clients in the field of media and gambling law. Mia actively pursues her interest in contemporary art practice by presenting guided tours of exhibitions in regional Australian galleries.

Kieran Mclean Eadie has been employed with the Australian government since 1999. During this period, Kieran has spent more than five years living and working in the Middle East and South Asia regions in his official capacity. He holds a Masters Degree in Politics and Public Policy (Macquarie), a first-class Honours Degree in Law (UOW) and a BA in History and Politics (NTU).

Hossein Esmaeili is an Associate Professor of Law at Flinders University, Adelaide, Australia. He is a Co-rapporteur of International Law Association's Committee on Islamic Law and International Law. His most recent book is *The Rule of Law, Freedom of Expression and Islamic Law* (Hart Publishing, 2017, co-authored with Irmgard Marboe and Javaid Rehman).

Nurussyariah Hammado is a medical doctor, neuroscientist and clinical exercise scientist who teaches at the Universitas Negeri Makassar (UNM), Indonesia. She has special interest in exploring the neuroscience basis of religious behaviour. She obtained her degrees from the Universitas Hasanuddin, the University of Queensland and the Australian National University.

Nadirsyah Hosen has been working as a Senior Lecturer at the Faculty of Law, Monash University since 20 July 2015. Prior to this role, Nadir was an Associate Professor at the School of Law, University of Wollongong. He has written and/or edited 13 books on the issues of Islam, constitution, law and religion.

Nasimah Hussin is an Associate Professor at the Ahmad Ibrahim Kullliyyah of Law, International Islamic University Malaysia (IIUM). She has extensively researched areas relating to Shari'ah law, Islamic criminal law, victimology, social sciences and restorative justice. She is also actively involved with government and university projects in developing Shari'ah law of Malaysia.

Arif A. Jamal is an Associate Professor in the Faculty of Law, National University of Singapore (NUS Law). He serves on the Executive Committee of the Centre for Asian Legal Studies (CALS) at NUS Law and as an Editor with the *Asian Journal of Comparative Law*. His research and teaching interests include legal and political theory, law and religion, and law in Muslim contexts. His most recent book is *Islam, Law and the Modern State: (Re)imagining Liberal Theory in Muslim Contexts* (Routledge, 2018).

Maan Abdul Haq Khutani is a lawyer, with a PhD in Islamic law and international human rights law. He works in Jeddah, Saudi Arabia.

Faisal Kutty is an Associate Professor of Law and Director of the International LL.M. program at Valparaiso University Law School in Indiana and an Adjunct Professor of Law at Osgoode Hall Law School of York University in Toronto. He also serves as counsel to Kutty Law, a Toronto-based law firm. He is currently on the executive committee of the Association of American Law School Section on Islamic Law.

Neneng Yanti Khozanatu Lahpan is a Senior Lecturer at ISBI (*Institut Seni Budaya Indonesia*) Bandung, Indonesia. She completed her doctoral degree in anthropology at Monash University, with the thesis entitled 'Negotiating Ethnicity and Islam in Musical Performances in West Java, Indonesia' (2015).

Ali Omar Ali Mesrati is an Assistant Professor of International Law at the College of Law, University of Bahrain. He is the founder and director of the University of Bahrain's Human Rights Legal Clinic. His interest is in education relating to international human rights and he has played a significant role in introducing a wide variety of human rights courses in Bahrain.

Richard Mohr is a sociologist (PhD UNSW) specialising in legal and urban issues. He is Director of Social Research, Policy and Planning, incorporated in Australia. He edited *Law and Religion in Public Life: The Contemporary Debate* with Nadirsyah Hosen (Routledge, 2013).

S. M. Solaiman is an Associate Professor of Law, University of Wollongong, Australia. He has extensively published on corporate regulation and stakeholder protection in leading law journals around the world, mostly in the United Kingdom, the United States, Continental Europe and Australia.

Hanifah Haydar Ali Tajuddin is a Senior Officer at the Shariah Judiciary Department of Malaysia. Throughout her career, she has had experiences in the Syariah prosecution unit and in the research unit of her department. She is currently a PhD candidate at the International Islamic University Malaysia (IIUM) in the area of comparative criminal law.

Majdah Zawawi is an Associate Professor at the Ahmad Ibrahim Kullliyyah of Law, International Islamic University Malaysia (IIUM). Her research background has been a mixture of Islamic law, jurisprudence, biosafety law and the halal industry. She has also been actively involved in university and government projects in developing Shari'ah law and the halal industry of Malaysia.

Acknowledgements

The book is a product of a collective effort from many people involved in the early stages until readers have this book in their hands. Therefore, I would like to acknowledge and thank them. First of all, I would like to thank Mr Edward Elgar, who encouraged me to write or edit books on Islamic law when I met him in Sydney around 2010. As a result, I produced *Modern Perspectives on Islamic Law* (co-written with Ann Black and Hossein Esmaeili), published by Edward Elgar Publishing in 2013. Unfortunately, it took me a long time to edit this volume of the *Research Handbook on Islamic Law and Society*, owing to circumstances both at work and at home. I thank Mr Edward Elgar and his team (Laura, Ben and others) who kept encouraging me to complete the task. With the help of his team, I am glad that the edited collection has finally been published.

Secondly, this book was edited during my transition to the Faculty of Law, Monash University in mid-2015. It is not easy to move to a different workplace and new city. I would like to thank Professor Stephen Barkoczy, a great mentor, and also our Dean, Professor Bryan Horrigan. Their guidance made my move as smooth as possible. I also thank all of my colleagues in Monash for their collegiality, and my students (LLB, JD and PhD programmes) for the interesting discussions.

Thirdly, this book could not be completed were it not for the 20 contributors. I thank each of the authors for devoting his/her time and efforts in contributing to this book. Reading and editing your works for this book has given me great pleasure in that I, as the editor, learnt many things from your chapters. I am sure the readers will feel the same way.

Fourthly, life without friends would be an empty one. I thank all my Nahdlatul Ulama (NU) friends whom I frequently visit in Indonesia, Australia, New Zealand and all over the world. Their vision, discussions and commitment to serving Muslim communities inspire me, reminding me that there is so much to life outside the academic world. I also thank Rick Mohr and Ian Usman Lewis for their wise advice, mentorship and, most importantly, their friendship.

Finally, my family deserves special thanks. It sounds like a cliché, but it is true that without your continuing support, it would be hard to imagine that all the late night work, perspiration, tiredness, sickness and thousands of cups of coffee could be transformed into a solid edited volume like this. I must also mention both my late father (2001) and mother (2017): their spirit remains the fuel that makes everything is possible with my life at work, in the community and at home. *Shallu 'alan Nabi!*

Melbourne, January 2018
Nadirsyah Hosen

Introduction: Islamic law in action

Nadirsyah Hosen

This book examines the role of Islamic law, not just as it exists in the Holy texts (*Qur'an* and *Hadith*), but as it is actually applied in society, through legislation, *fatwa*, court cases, *khutbah* (sermon), media, or scholarly debate. By considering its larger social, political, economic and cultural contexts, all the contributors in the book evaluate when and how actors and institutions turn to Islamic law to find the answers to problems faced by Islamic society.

Modern problems are complex and require explanation from different perspectives before one may find the right answers. Most of the time, what we perceive as the 'right' answers should be understood in a local, temporal and debatable context. This indicates that the 'right' answers in Saudi Arabian, Bangladeshi or Australian societies might not be considered to be the 'right' solutions in other Muslim societies. However, the main approach of this edited collection is not to discuss development and progress in Muslim countries and non-Muslim countries where Muslim live. In other words, it is not a country report. The approach taken in the book is based on issues; rather than countries. At the same time, some case studies are needed to illustrate the application and interaction of Islamic law in societies.

The idea of the way Islamic law responds to problems in society is nothing new. It seems 'new' because there has been propaganda by the Islamist movement of 'back to the *Qur'an* and *Hadith*' coined by Muhammad bin Abdul Wahab (1703–1792). Wahab, within the context of the Muslim response to the increasing influence of Europe and to the subjugation of the Arab world by the non-Arab Ottoman Turks, was convinced that Muslims had departed from pure Islam and needed to return to its original beliefs and practices. His interpretation of Islam is also referred to as Salafist –the first 300 years of the practice and the interpretation of the *Qur'an* and the *Hadith* which Wahab considered as the pure and correct form of Islam.[1]

[1] John Esposito, *Islam and Politics* (Syracuse, NY: Syracuse University Press, 1998) 33–4.

How could Muslims face the challenges of the twenty-first century by returning to the practice and interpretation of the Qur'an and the Hadith appropriate to the sixth–ninth centuries? According to Wahabism, the answers to all problems have been provided by the *Salaf al-Shalihin* (early Muslim scholars). Muslims had to go back to their own traditions in the past, and to reject what Wahab regarded as *Bid'ah* (innovation) and *Shirk* (idolatry). The way in which Wahab read and interpreted the *Qur'an* and the *Hadith* has influenced many Muslims, who call him a reformer and a modernist, whereas those who are against him label him a puritanist and Wahabist.

Amongst the Islamist movements influenced by Wahab's reading of the Holy texts, there has been a view that Islamic teaching is immutable, because the authoritarian, divine and absolute concept of revelation in Islam does not allow any change in Islamic teachings and institutions. The *Qur'an* and the *Hadith* are considered immutable, regardless of history, time, culture and location. Muslims may change, but Islam will not. This means that the rulings pronounced by Shari'ah are held to be static, final, eternal, absolute and unalterable. In other words, Islam's idealistic nature, religious nature, rigidity and casuistic nature lead to the immutability of Islamic teaching.[2] For Textualists, it is the *Qur'an* that should guide Muslims, rather than any so-called modern 'needs'. They consider the meaning of the *Qur'an* to be fixed and universal in its application.[3]

However, the view above is only one side of the coin. Islamic teaching is, in fact, the product of a very slow and gradual process of interpretation of the *Qur'an*, and the collection, verification and interpretation of the *Hadith*, during the first three centuries of Islam (the seventh to the ninth centuries AD). This process took place amongst scholars and jurist who developed their own methodology for the classification of sources, derivation of specific rules from general principles, and so forth.[4] The *Qur'an* and the *Hadith* must involve human interpretation. The *Qur'an* and the *Hadith* cannot be understood nor have any influence on human behaviour except through the efforts of (fallible) human beings. Therefore, even though Islam is based on the revelations of God, it cannot possibly be drawn up except through human understanding, which means

---

[2] See the discussion in Muhammad Khalid Masud, *Shatibi's Philosophy of Islamic Law* (Pakistan: Islamic Research Institute, 1995) 17.

[3] Abdullah Saeed, *Interpreting the Qur'an: Towards a Contemporary Approach* (New York: Routledge, 2006) 3.

[4] Robert Gleave, *Islam and Literalism: Literal Meaning and Interpretation in Islamic Legal Theory* (Edinburgh: Edinburgh University Press, 2012).

both the inevitability of differences of opinion and the possibilities of error, whether amongst scholars or the community in general.

Whilst the *Qur'an* contains a variety of elements, such as stories, moral injunctions and general (as well as specific) legal principles, it should be noted that the *Qur'an* prescribes only those details which are essential. It thus leaves considerable room for development, and safeguards against restrictive rigidity. The contextualists argue for a high degree of freedom for the modern Muslim scholar in determining what is mutable (changeable) and immutable (unchangeable) in the area of socio-ethico-legal content.[5] The clash of the literalist and the contextualist is a huge source of debate between Islamic scholars and jurists, and is arguably the main reason that there are multiple schools of thought within Islam.

The diversity of Islamic Law has been further deepened with the development of Muslim nation-states during the era of empires, because each nation established its own Islamic legal system according to its needs and understandings.[6] As a result, a wide range of different constitutional systems emerged, some of them separating 'mosque and state', others implementing a theocratic system.[7] This constitutional diversity set different starting points for the further application and interpretation of Islamic law, establishing different practices in different Muslim countries.

Islamic jurists and ordinary Muslims hold diverse opinions about how Shari'ah applies to certain aspects of a Muslim individual's life in the modern world. Some aspects, including marriage, divorce and the custody of children, are mainly regulated by what can be precisely labelled as Islamic law. In an Islamic state, other aspects are subject to provisions which are not Islamic law, although they also may not necessarily contradict Islamic law. While principles of Islamic law govern family law, inheritance, trusts, contract and, in some Islamic states, criminal law, it can be seen that modern regulations govern matters such as corporations, broadcasting law, health law, food production, travel, immigration and the environment. Things will be different in non-Islamic state, where Muslims live as the minority and have to obey the law of the land, and

---

[5] Saeed, above n3, 3.

[6] L. Ali Khan and Hisham M. Ramadan, *Contemporary Ijtihad: Limits and Controversies* (Edinburgh: Edinburgh University Press, 2011) 7.

[7] Ibid., 7–8.

where Shari'ah is practised only at the private level. Today the opinions and practices in the Muslim world vary widely.[8]

This edited collection is an effort to demonstrate how differently Islamic law in different areas has been practised, in different contexts and circumstances. There are 18 chapters, divided into six themes, covering around 22 countries, presented in this volume. The 20 contributors are a mix of established and emerging scholars, and also practitioners, consultants and government officials. The book has been designed for scholars and postgraduate researchers in the field, but at the same time, the general reader will also find the edited collection a lively debate and an inspiration to shape future research.

FAMILY LAW AND COURTS

The themes discussed in these chapters provide an understanding of how Islamic family law has been applied both in, as well as outside, the court systems, in both Muslim and non-Muslim countries. It starts with Ann Black's chapter examining how Islamic family law can be applied in Singapore and Australia where, in both nations, there is a significant and recognisable Muslim minority: 3 per cent in Australia and 15 per cent in Singapore. She points out that Singapore and Australia were colonised by Britain two centuries ago, thereby becoming inheritors of the common law legal system, with its attendant institutions, methodology and principles. Yet despite this common legal heritage and a government-endorsed policy of multiculturalism, only Singapore has adopted and endorsed a form of formal legal pluralism. In Australia, a different approach was taken, known as 'one law for all'. There are neither separate courts nor Islamic personal status laws enacted or applied to Muslim Australians, nor for any other religious or ethnic group.

Arif Jamal explores Alternative Dispute Resolution (ADR) in Singapore and compares it with the system in the United Kingdom (UK). This examination shows that Islamic law is applied more formally in Singapore than in the UK. However, the implications in the ADR context are interesting. Drawing upon literature about religious-based ADR, he argues that the informal system in the UK may be more facilitative of Islamic ADR than the more formal system of Singapore.

Kieran Eadie reviews the issues of *kafala*, of providing support for orphans, but this becomes controversial, as it involves the issues of child

---

[8] Jamila Hussain, *Islam, Its Law and Society*, 3rd ed. (Leichhardt: The Federation Press, 2011), 48.

adoption for migration purposes to Western countries. He discusses the practice and focuses on the difficulties with meeting all the requirements provided by Shari'ah, immigration law and international law. It requires a careful approach to ensure the government's policy is based on the best interest of child. The topic of the best interests of the child is also discussed in Ali Mesrati's chapter. He critically evaluates how the Libyan court has made decisions on guardianship, and whether those decisions are in line with the requirements of the Convention on the Rights of the Child (CROC). He provides analysis from both Shari'ah and international human rights perspectives.

PROPERTY AND BUSINESS

In Iran, land ownership and interests in land are regulated by the Iranian Civil Code, which has adopted modern principles of European land law blended with principles of Shari'ah. However, the law of *waqf* (trust law) is almost entirely based on Islamic law. Hossein Esmaeili argues in his chapter that both Islamic law and Iranian law have recognised and protected private ownership of land and other property interests. His chapter finds a compatibility between Iranian and Islamic laws.

The incompatibility issues arise in Afroza Begum's examination of Islamic banking practices in Bangladesh. Shari'ah prohibits interest-based transactions and discourages monopolistic, deceptive and restrictive trade practices. Bangladesh embraced Islamic banking via the establishment of the Islamic Bank (IB) in 1983 and became the first nation in Southeast Asia to introduce it. Afroza Begum's work investigates Shari'ah compliance in devising 'modes of financing', and she argues that the way in which IB functions in Bangladesh is fundamentally flawed and needs to be reviewed to achieve the pertinent goals of Shari'ah.

S. M. Solaiman highlights an important point that, although Shari'ah is not part of the domestic or positive law of Bangladesh governing employment relationships, a vast majority of its people respect and voluntarily adhere to the rights and obligations enunciated in Islam. His chapter examines the safety rights of workers and the corresponding obligation of their employers under the principles of Islamic law. He draws the conclusion that employers evidently fail to comply with their religious obligations to protect workers. This is in addition to their failures under municipal law.

The chapters on this theme give us an insight into the compatibility or incompatibility of Islamic law and domestic law. Western influence has dominated the areas of trade and finance in the Muslim world. Traditional Islamic contracts and financial instruments have been replaced by Western financial instruments and institutions, through either colonialism or capitalism. On the other hands, many Muslim countries are trying to 'Islamize' their property, trade and commercial laws. This could be one of the most challenging issues faced by Muslim societies.

CRIMINAL LAW AND JUSTICE

The discourse of criminal law in modern Islamic states goes beyond traditional *hudud* (ranging from public lashing to publicly stoning to death, amputation of hands and crucifixion). This because what we consider to be a 'crime' is no longer restricted to personal issue, but can also involve corporations. Corporate criminal liability is one of the significant tools governments can use to prevent corporate crimes. Mohammed Alsubaie specifically examines the situation in the Kingdom of Saudi Arabia and takes the position that not only should the Saudi law be amended to reflect new developments in the area of corporate crimes, but also that Saudi Arabia must create independent and specialised commercial courts, with qualified and trained judges and prosecutors, to hear only commercial cases. He suggests that the database of corporate cases and statistics should be published, as this would help judges, investors, companies, lawyers and researchers.

The next chapter under this theme is written by three scholars (Hanifah Haydar Ali Tajuddin, Nasimah Hussin and Majdah Zawawi) and focuses on Shari'ah, criminal law and restorative justice in Malaysia. The authors highlight some of the issues with the current practices, in particular that they have yet to include laws permitting offenders to take responsibility and restore losses which they have caused personally to victims, other than by paying some small amount of compensation.

Moving to a different but still controversial issue, Faisal Kutty reviews the laws of apostasy and blasphemy in the Muslim world, by looking particularly at Pakistani and Malaysian cases. He strongly argues that the death penalty in the laws of apostasy and blasphemy is untenable in the modern period. He demonstrates in his chapter that these laws conflict with a variety of foundational teachings of Islam, and with the current ethos of human rights, in particular the freedom to choose one's religion and the freedom to express oneself.

ETHICS, HEALTH AND SCIENCES

Nurussyariah Hammado explores areas of Islamic law affecting the reproductive and health issues of Muslim women, such as adoption, medically assisted reproduction, abortion, child marriage and female genital mutilation. She compares the situation in two different countries: one with strongly religious sentiments (Saudi Arabia), and another one where more liberalist views prevail (Tunisia). Having compared those issues in Saudi Arabia and Tunisia, she observes that Islam is not the source of all discriminatory treatment of women, but rather that it stems from the traditional cultural and social norms of a particular society. However, as religion informs and shapes cultures, such practices are the indirect consequences of a particular Islamic interpretation.

My own chapter provides an example of how Muslim scholars are responding to the issue of modernity. I evaluate new developments such as collective *ijtihad* in the Muslim world as a group effort to find answers. This is different to the early formation of Islamic schools of thought (*maddhab*) when individual scholars interpreted the Holy Books. I provide examples of Indonesian collective *fatwa* on health issues such as organ transplant, vasectomy and IUDs (Intra-Uterine Devices). It can safely be stated that the institution of collective *ijtihad* is a viable tool through which a society can adjust itself to internal and external social, political and economic change.

Richard Mohr in his chapter goes beyond the issues of modernity. He questions whether halal certificates, along with science and ethics, could together provide legal guides for consumers. He outlines that religious requirements may be regulated by a religious council; food safety is monitored by government and industry bodies; while consumer and animal rights organisations may be involved in demands for particular standards and the reliability of various claims for food. Using a case study in Sydney (Australia), he argues that there is continuous negotiation between government, industry, religious or ethical bodies and consumer advocates over labelling and other regulations.

ARTS AND EDUCATION

Mia Corbett admits in her chapter that the relationship between law and art in Islam varies greatly between temporal, geographical and political boundaries. She points out that the lack of figurative representation in Islamic art is often also subjected to the Western understanding of art, as a cultural movement toward the most accurate representation of the human figure, which is considered to parallel the development of civilisation. As a result, there is a perception that Islamic law and civilisation is primitive and backward for its perceived aversion to the development of the figurative style. She argues that the reality is that Muslims are constantly changing and evolving their understanding and relationship with religious law, like any other culture.

The next chapter, written by Neneng Lahpan, is on the lawfulness of music in contemporary Indonesian discourse. There has long been a debate among Muslim scholars on this issue, but she goes further by looking at the Indonesian local context in West Java, where ethnicity and politics play their parts. What we consider to be 'Islamic' music does not need to be in the Arabic language nor to employ Arabic songs and instruments.

Maan Khutani conducts research on the rights of Saudi women to pursue education at university level. This is one of the hot topics in the Islamic world. His chapter reveals the structural gaps in institutions concerned with women's education in Saudi Arabia. He believes that there is a necessity to review all philosophical and social basics and domestic laws relating to women's education in the Kingdom. He further argues that its objectives need to be reviewed; and its suitability examined in regard to the modern changes which have altered a woman's vision of herself and also society's vision of her. This, in turn, requires radical change in educational and vocational services in Saudi Arabia, opening them up to women, in order to increase their opportunities and to create future strategies for investment of female ability and power in economic and educational activities.

COMMUNITY AND PUBLIC SPHERES

Richard Burgess evaluates the practices of Islam in Bosnia and Hercegovina. He believes that it is both compatible and sustainable within a Christian and laic Europe. As a result, he reveals that there are national communities where (among other things) the social participation of women is expected and inter-faith dialogue is endorsed. While domestically serious tensions regarding national identity remain, he takes the view that the Bosnian model rests as an example as to how the faith may be practised throughout Europe.

Finally, Muhamad Ali examines sermons (*khutbah*) and edicts (*fatwas*), and the extent to which colonial contexts shaped their characteristics and development in colonial Indonesia, particularly in South Sulawesi, and in Malaysia, particularly Kelantan. His chapter analyses how various *ulama* (clergy) constructed sermons and edicts, what sources and languages they used, and what problems and issues they faced. In such an analysis, the flexibility of religious knowledge and the contending interpretations of the religious texts reveal some of the tensions, as well as the compromises, that characterise the production of such knowledge. He argues that the sermons and the edicts are textual and contextual, persistent and changing, according to the *ulama*'s interpretations and socio-cultural and political circumstances.

CONCLUDING REMARKS

All 18 chapters in this volume demonstrate that Islamic law is changeable according to the requirements of different places and times, and therefore suits the values shared by Muslim societies. This is in contrast with the common assumption that Shari'ah law is a medieval and unchangeable legal code which reflects the seventh-century, Arabian desert-living practices of Muhammad (peace be upon him).

Islamic teaching today may be based on the original two primary sources (the *Qur'an* and *Hadith*) but the majority of rules which apply were developed over 15 centuries of juristic interpretation, scholarly work and occasional pronouncements by authorities. Therefore, some rules and principles are based on facts and circumstances in existence many centuries ago. In this sense, contemporary Muslim scholars must find a way to determine which principles should be maintained, and which ones should be adjusted, in response to social changes. This volume has revealed how Islamic law has engaged with contemporary issues beyond what has been prescribed in the *Qur'an* and *Hadith*. It involves a dynamic interpretation and also responses to the challenges faced by Muslim societies. In other words, what we offer in this volume is Islamic law in action.

PART 1

FAMILY LAW AND COURTS

1. Colonial legacies: family laws in Singapore and Australia

Ann Black

I. INTRODUCTION

Situated on the Asia-Pacific rim, the two island states of Singapore and Australia are each home to approximately half a million Muslims. In both nations there is a significant and recognisable Muslim minority: 3 per cent in Australia and 15 per cent in Singapore. In both, Islam is the religion with the third largest number of faith adherents after Christianity and Buddhism, with Hinduism fourth. Australia and Singapore also have a large number of citizens who have no religious affiliation, around 20 per cent. Both are secular states, with neither Constitution proclaiming a state religion. Each nation is proud of its multi-ethnic, multi-religious and multicultural polity, and both triumph in the respective ways by which they have maintained overall national cohesion. Singapore's Chief Justice Chan Sek Keong describes multiculturalism as Singapore's 'way to a harmonious society'.[1] It creates Singapore's identity and builds a cohesive society from the different racial communities through belief in shared values and then 'sharing those common values in their daily lives'.[2] Former Prime Minister Gillard described Australia's multiculturalism as more than the ability to maintain diverse backgrounds and cultures, saying that it acts as a 'meeting place of rights and responsibilities' including 'non-negotiable respect for our foundational values of democracy and the rule of law'.[3]

Both share a common legal heritage. Singapore and Australia were colonised by Britain two centuries ago, thereby becoming inheritors of the common law legal system with its attending institutions, methodology

[1] Chan Sek Keong, 'Multiculturalism in Singapore: the Way to a Harmonious Society' (2013) 25 *Singapore Academy Law Journal* 84. This was from his Audrey Ducroux Memorial Lecture given in 2012.

[2] Ibid., 85.

[3] Julia Gillard, Speech to the Multicultural Council of Australia, Parliament House Canberra, 19 September 2012. Available at: www.theage.com.au/national/gillard-defends-nations-diversity-20120919-267d7.html#ixzz2UHUfh6SM.

and principles. Yet, despite this common legal heritage and a government endorsed policy of multiculturalism, only Singapore has adopted and endorsed a form of formal legal pluralism; today more aptly described as legal dualism. Muslim citizens in Singapore are legally required to apply Shari'ah personal status laws and to have family and inheritance matters arising from those laws resolved in a separate Shari'ah Court system. The Shari'ah Court operates exclusively for Singapore's Muslim population and is separately administered and fully government funded. Singapore's model of legal dualism is well accepted by the nation's Muslim and non-Muslim communities. The model is promoted as a workable, on-going and respectful manifestation of legal coexistence based on 'the mutual respect the Muslim and the non-Muslim community have for each other'.[4] In Australia, a different approach was taken, known as 'one law for all'. There are neither separate courts nor Islamic personal status laws enacted for or applied to Muslim Australians, nor for any other religious or ethnic group. In the Australian 'one law for all' approach, Muslims are free to adhere to Islamic law in their personal lives, but it always remains a matter of self-choice taken in accordance with one's religious conviction and personal conscience. Muslims' commitment to Islamic law is evident in their use of a wide array of informal forms of Islamic arbitration and dispute resolution to resolve any family or community matters that arise. This is accepted by Australian law provided the outcome is not in conflict with, or contrary to, it.

This chapter will provide a theoretical and practical analysis of these two distinctive approaches: the legal dualism of Singapore and the legal monism in Australia. The first section will look at the historical setting in which these approaches arose during the time of British colonisation to explain why, right from inception, a different course was chartered in each country and how that direction was affirmed at independence. The second section will consider the practical aspects of how both systems operate today though the two key life events of marriage and divorce, and the consequences for Muslims and non-Muslims in both instances. Lastly, there will be comparative analysis of philosophical basis for both approaches by highlighting the ways in which the two systems diverge today.

---

[4] Ahmad Nizam bin Abbas, 'The Islamic Legal System in Singapore' (2012) 21(1) *Pacific Rim Law and Policy Journal* 163, 187.

II. HISTORICAL CONTEXT AND ITS CONSEQUENCES

In the late nineteenth century, when the British arrived in Singapore and Australia, they found inhabitants whose prior settlement and control over the land was identified through terms such as 'native', 'indigenous' or 'Aboriginal' peoples. In Singapore, these were the Malays with a handful of Chinese 'living along the banks engaged in pepper and gambier planting'.[5] The religion of the Malays since the fourteenth and fifteenth centuries had been Islam. The British had earlier encountered Islamic law in India when Warren Hastings, as Governor–General (1773–84), recognised its importance to Muslim Indians. He created a hybrid known as 'Anglo-Mohammadan Law' which was a compilation and later a codification of Islamic texts and practices which incorporated some aspects of English law, including concepts of case law and precedent. In this way, Islamic personal status law could be administered by British judges in India's common law courts or in separate Shari'ah Courts. Based on the experiences from India, it was not surprising that a similar pluralistic model was adopted by the British in the 1820s in colonial Singapore[6] in which, depending on one's ethnicity or religion, separate legal orders for personal law[7] operated. This was not just for the Malays. In addition to 'Mohammadan' law for Malays, Chinese customary law of marriage and family coexisted with the religious laws of the Hindus, Sikhs and Jews. English Christian-derived marriage and family law was of course applied to its own expatriate community. However it was of significance that in Sir Stanford Raffles' negotiations with Sultan Hussein Muhammad Shah[8] for the island of Singapore, a condition was that a special legal status for Muslim Malays must be maintained. It was agreed that in all cases

---

[5] Keong, n1, 84, 96.

[6] Singapore was founded by Sir Stanford Raffles in 1819 through the British East India Company. With Penang and Malacca, Singapore became part of the Straits Settlements in 1825. In 1866 the Settlements came under the direct control of the Colonial Office in London and were disbanded after World War II. In 1946, Singapore became a Crown colony.

[7] Leong Wai Kum, *Elements of Family Law in Singapore* (Singapore: Lexis-Nexis 2007) 885–7. The Mohammedan Marriage Ordinance of 1880 allowed for the establishment of Kathi courts.

[8] Singapore was under the control of the Sultan of Johore, and Sultan Hussein was supported in that position by Raffles. On the founding of Singapore, see Kevin Y. L. Tan, 'Singapore: A Statist Legal Laboratory' in E. Ann Black and Gary F. Bell (eds), *Law and Legal Institutions of Asia: Traditions, Adaptations and Innovations* (Cambridge, UK: Cambridge University Press 2011) 331.

involving Malays in ceremonies of religion, marriages and inheritance, 'the law and custom of the Malays will be respected' unless 'contrary to reason, justice or humanity'.[9] From the outset, Islamic law was separately recognised and the Singaporean legal system evolved pluralistically.

In contrast, there was no Muslim presence in Australia when colonisation took place. The British could find neither a recognisable religion nor a legal system. The colonial categorisation of Australia as '*terra nullius*' (land belonging to no one)[10] stands in contrast to the process in Singapore and other parts of South East Asia where the British found a religion, laws and a form of governance they recognised. These discoveries enabled negotiations and treaties to be signed with the various South East Asian Sultans. There was no treaty negotiated in Australia nor was there any formal recognition of the indigenous beliefs, customary laws and dispute resolution process of the Australian Aborigines. When Captain Arthur Phillip hoisted the Union Jack at Sydney Cove in 1788 and proclaimed the continent for King George III, the Aboriginal people became subject to the laws of England and its courts. Legal monism had its genesis in this time. Although in recent decades there has been legal recognition of native title[11] and special sentencing courts, known as Murri or Koori Courts, set up in some states for indigenous Australians who plead guilty to minor offences, separate legal recognition of Aboriginal laws and customs pertaining to family, inheritance and other personal status issues has never been accorded. These different historical foundations have led to a distinctive legal trajectory for both nations.

At the time when the six British colonies[12] federated in 1901, the Australian Constitution omitted any recognition or acknowledgement of the first peoples of Australia.[13] Although in 1901 Christians made up over

---

[9] Cited by Noor Aisha Abdul Rahman, 'Muslim Personal Law within the Singapore Legal System: History, Prospects and Challenges' (2009) 29(1) *Journal of Muslim Minority Affairs* 109–126.

[10] This was justified on the basis of the legal concept of *terra nullius* in international law. The validity of *terra nullius* in Australia was not considered by the High Court of Australia until 1992 in *Mabo v Queensland* (No.2) (1992) 175 *CLR* 1.

[11] The decision in *Mabo v Queensland* (No.2) (1992) 175 *CLR* 1 was given legislative effect by the Native Title Act 1993 (Cth) with the National Native Title Tribunal established to determine claimant applications.

[12] New South Wales, Victoria, Queensland, South Australia, Tasmania and Western Australia.

[13] Currently, there is debate on how best to redress this omission. To give recognition of Aboriginal and Torres Strait Islander peoples in the Australian

98 per cent of the population, the Constitution did not establish Christianity or one of its denominations (for example, Church of England, Roman Catholicism or Presbyterianism) as the state religion, opting instead for a de-establishment provision. Section 116 makes it unconstitutional for any religious test to be required as a qualification for any office or public trust under the Commonwealth. The Constitution guaranteed freedom to practise one's religion. Muslims living in Australia in those early days of settlement were able to practise Islam and to establish mosques, Islamic schools and community centres. Whilst anti-sectarianism informed Australia's secularism[14] the Australian secular system did allow each and every religion and spiritual tradition to have its own place of worship and for followers to apply voluntarily any religious law with the proviso that it did not transgress any national or state law. As a consequence, many of Australia's religions have kept alive their own religious laws especially dealing with matters of marriage, including the validity or invalidity of inter-faith marriage, and matters of divorce and the care of children. These remain internal to the religion and are quite separate from government or judicial control. Each religion, sect or faith tradition is able to establish processes to address compliance with its religious and legal requirements and to set up informal courts, boards or tribunals to deal with issues that arise.[15] As adherence to Shari'ah is voluntary, Australian Muslims are able to accept or reject any decrees or rulings pertaining to Shari'ah law given by sheiks, imams or boards. Decisions are unofficial and are not legally enforceable, nor are they reviewable by Australian courts.

By contrast, Muslims in Singapore are legally required to have personal status matters resolved by the Shari'ah Court and in accordance with the Administration of Muslim Law Act 1966 (Cap 3)[16] (hereinafter AMLA). This separate avenue was entrenched and well accepted at the time of Singapore's independence in 1965. AMLA replaced the Muslims' Ordinance (1957) which was a revision of the earlier Mohammadan

---

Constitution is seen as an important step towards building a nation based on mutual respect and understanding.

[14] These views are expanded by Malcolm Voyce and Adam Possamai, 'Legal Pluralism, Family Personal Laws and the Rejection of Shari'ah in Australia: A Case of Multiple or Clashing Modernities' (2011) 7 *Democracy and Security* 339, 343.

[15] The Roman Catholic Church has ecclesiastical courts, Jews have the Beth Din, a rabbinical court, and Muslims have Shari'ah councils (*majlis*).

[16] Administration of Muslim Law Act 1966, Act 27 of 1966, 2009 Rev. Ed. Sing. [hereinafter AMLA].

Marriage Ordinance (1880), which was the first legislative enactment of the laws and regulations to be exclusively applied to Muslims in Singapore. From 1961, all non-Muslims in Singapore – whether Hindu, Buddhist, Christian or Sikh – were governed by the Women's Charter. It was called a Charter not an Act because it was to be the Charter for women's rights and has been credited with changing the family law landscape for non-Muslims through its commitment to monogamy and by working towards the legal and economic equality of married women.[17] It ended Singapore's era of legal pluralism in favour of dualism, as the only exception to this law was for persons of the Islamic faith. Prior to independence, Singapore also had established courts with exclusive jurisdiction over Muslims which from 1955 onwards were designated as Shari'ah Courts. These continued post-independence. In addition, Singapore had had many decades of separate administrative bodies for Muslims. The Muslim Advisory Board was established in 1946 to advise the government on Muslim issues and matters pertaining to Islam. Under AMLA these functions were subsumed and strengthened by the *Majlis Ugama Islam Singapura* (hereinafter MUIS). To legitimise a separate legal regime for its Muslim citizens, the Constitution of Singapore was drafted to recognise Malays as 'the indigenous people of Singapore',[18] thus justifying the grant of special legal status to Muslims. In so doing, it also honoured the original agreement between Raffles and Sultan Hussein Muhammad Shah. Section 153 of the Constitution provides that the legislature can make laws 'regulating Muslim religious affairs' and can constitute a Council to 'advise the President in matters relating to the Muslim religion'. Section 12 of the Constitution excludes the regulation of Muslim personal law from the constitutional guarantees to its citizens of 'equality before the law' and 'equal protection'.

Due to the accumulation of these precursors, Ahmad Nizam believes that at the time of independence in 1965, the right for Muslims in Singapore to adhere to Islamic law was so entrenched that AMLA merely facilitated rather than created 'a new jurisprudence of law'.[19] As AMLA was applied by the Shari'ah Court, the family law system of Singapore became a dual, not plural system. It was based on religious identification only in so far as Muslim or non-Muslim identity.

---

[17] Chan Wing Cheong, Leong Wai Kum and Debbie Ong Siew Ling, 'Editorial' (2011) July *Singapore Journal of Legal Studies* x–xii.

[18] Constitution section 152.

[19] Ahmad Nizam bin Abbas, 'Overview of Islamic Judicial Structure in Singapore', unpublished.

III. PRACTICAL CONSEQUENCES OF LEGAL DUALISM AND MONISM IN THE APPLICATION OF SHARI'AH FAMILY LAW TODAY IN AUSTRALIA AND SINGAPORE

A. Marriage

When Muslims marry,[20] most will do so in accordance with the Shari'ah. In approaching important life events, Muslims, even non-observant ones, seek to 'get it right' by using traditional practices that accord with their religious and moral obligations.[21] In both Singapore and Australia, Muslim couples marrying in accordance with Islam will need to meet the form requirements of a valid Islamic marriage which include a *nikah* (marriage contract) with offer and acceptance, witnesses and *maskahwin/mahr* (dowry) provisions; the contract may also contain valid contractual *taklik* (conditions). The conditions were included to give certainty and security to a wife, and her *maskahwin/mahr* was the traditional legal means for protecting and empowering her for the duration of the marriage. It was an important resource by which a wife could finance her post-marriage period of life. Also, for the marriage to be valid in Islamic law, it must not violate any of the permanent or temporary prohibitions laid down by the Shari'ah.[22]

For Singaporean Muslims, the specific requirements and form for marriage are found in AMLA augmented by local Malay customs and traditions. In a dual legal system, the applicable marriage law depends on the religion of the parties to the marriage. For Muslims the laws on marriage are contained in Part VI of AMLA, whilst for all other Singaporeans these laws are in the Women's Charter.[23] In the Charter, the marriageable age is 21 years although 18-, 19- and 20-year-olds can marry with parental consent; in AMLA, the marriageable age is now

---

[20] Marriage is seen as desirable, even an obligation on Muslims.

[21] Julie Macfarlane, 'Islamic Divorce in North America' in Anna C. Korteweg and Jennifer A. Selby (eds), *Debating Sharia: Islam, Gender Politics and Family Law Arbitration* (Toronto: University of Toronto 2012) 40. It notes that the number of North America Muslims who marry with a *nikah* is far higher than those who attend prayers or consider themselves to be observant.

[22] Ann Black, Hossein Esmaeili and Nadirsyah Hosen, *Modern Perspectives on Islamic Law* (Cheltenham: Edward Elgar 2013) 111–21.

[23] Cap 353, 2009 Rev. Ed. Sing.

18 years.[24] One of the differences between the two laws is that AMLA specifies and codifies the role of the *wali*, who is defined in AMLA section 2 as 'the lawful guardian according to Muslim law for purposes of marriage of a woman who is to be married'. In practice, the *wali* is the bride's birth father, her paternal grandfather, brother, paternal uncle or any male relative from her paternal side.[25] AMLA has provisions, however, for a *kadi* (Islamic judge) to intervene in cases where a woman has no *wali*, or where the *wali* refuses to consent to the marriage.[26] Where the bride is the only Muslim convert in her family, a *wali* is not required. Another significant point of differentiation is that polygamous marriages are lawful for Muslim men in Singapore (the maximum is four wives at a time), although an application for each additional wife must be made to the *kadi*, who will conduct interviews prior to allowing or disallowing the marriage.[27] For Singapore's non-Muslims, polygamy is prohibited by section 4 of the Charter, rendering any subsequent marriage void.

Registration of marriage also comes under a dual system. The Registry of Muslim Marriages (ROMM) has exclusive jurisdiction to register marriages where both parties are Muslim,[28] whilst the Registry of Marriages (ROM) registers all other Singaporean marriages including marriages between a Muslim and a non-Muslim. This is the case even where the non-Muslim woman is a Christian or Jew. In some schools and traditions of Islam, such a marriage could be lawful because of the *kitabiyah* (person of the Book)[29] categorisation. For Shia and Muslims who adhere to the Hanafi school of Islam, marriage between a Muslim man and *kitabiyah* woman is lawful,[30] although it is generally regarded as undesirable. However, Singapore follows the Shafi'i school in this and most matters. Shafi'i employs a narrow interpretation which requires the woman to establish

---

[24] Amended in 2009 from 16 years by section 19 of the Administration of Muslim Law (Amendment) Act 2008 (Act 29 of 2008).

[25] http://app.romm.gov.sg/about_marriage/romm_wali.asp.

[26] Section 95, Administration of Muslim Law Act 1966, Act 27 of 1966, 2009 Rev. Ed. Sing.

[27] http://app.romm.gov.sg/about_marriage/romm_polygyny.asp.

[28] Section 89, Administration of Muslim Law Act 1966, Act 27 of 1966, 2009 Rev. Ed. Sing.

[29] The term the 'book' refers to revealed law through the lawgivers in the Abrahamic tradition. See generally Maznah Mohamad, 'Islam and Family Legal Contests in Malaysia: Hegemonizing Ethnic over Gender and Civil Rights' Asia Research Institute Working Paper series No.109, The National University of Singapore, 8.

[30] The Prophet married a Christian and also a Jewish woman.

she is a descendant from a lineage that was Christian before the time of the Prophet Muhammad, or Jewish before the time of the Prophet Isa – conditions that are almost impossible to fulfil. Consequentially, in practical terms this amounts to a de facto not *de jure* prohibition on this type of inter-faith marriage. For this reason, the marriage would need to be registered under ROM, unless there was a prior conversion to Islam.

In secular Australia, there are no equivalent restrictions on religious grounds on whom one can marry. Under the Marriage Act 1961 (Cth), marriages between Muslims and non-Muslims present no legal obstacle; however, as most Muslims prefer to marry within their faith tradition, imams who conduct Islamic marriage ceremonies can refuse to marry the couple until the non-Muslim party converts. For this reason it is not uncommon for a conversion ceremony to precede a marriage ceremony, although distinguishing between the two events can be difficult in some cases and require court determination.[31] Also, where one party is not Muslim, this fact may be kept secret from both the imam and the Muslim spouse's family and friends. When there is deception of this type, it can unravel later, as was seen in *H v H* [2003] FMCAfam 31 where the imam and the bride's Lebanese family were unaware that the man she was marrying in the Islamic ceremony was a Maronite Christian.

Australia's Marriage Act 1961 (Cth) is accommodating of Islamic marriage. It provides that Islamic marriage ceremonies can be performed and the marriage registered with the relevant state government office for births, deaths and marriages. However, to be registered, the marriage must meet the requirements of the Act including that the parties are of marriageable age and have freely given consent, there is an absence of consanguinity and the ceremony must have been conducted by a recognised marriage celebrant or minister of religion. For Muslims this will usually be an imam or sheik from their mosque. The result is that marriages between Muslims can be simultaneously valid under Islamic law and Australian law. Some Muslims will choose to just have the marriage contract (*nikah*) and an Islamic ceremony making their union a lawful Islamic marriage without registering the marriage in accordance with the Australian legislation. There are several reasons for this, ranging

---

31 *Wold v Kleppier* [2009] FamCA 178 [note the names of the parties in Family Court cases are a pseudonym given by the court to protect identification]. The Court had to decide whether a ceremony performed by an Imam was an Islamic marriage ceremony or merely one converting the woman with whom he lived to Islam. Kleppir, the husband, claimed that the ceremony was a conversion to Islam ceremony whilst the wife claimed that it was a marriage.

from a conscious rejection of secular requirements in deference to a purely religious union (*nikah*) to inadvertence or lack of knowledge of the law. Non-registration can occur because the couple plan to return to a Muslim nation where only the Islamic *nikah* will have application, rendering the Australian certification obsolete. It can also occur as an oversight or from an erroneous belief that the Islamic marriage is automatically a state marriage, or because one or both of the spouses believe that the marriage is going to be registered but the imam fails to do so.[32] In some cases it is because the person who performs the ceremony is not qualified or registered as a marriage celebrant,[33] or because the marriage does not meet Australian requirements for a lawful marriage. If one or both are under the lawful age for marriage (which is 18 years)[34] it will be unlawful and also an offence under section 95 of the Marriage Act 1961 (Cth).[35] Imams have indicated that with underage marriages, they encourage the couple to register the marriage when both attain lawful marriage age. If the marriage is polygamous, it is also unlawful and constitutes the criminal offence of bigamy.[36] There is no accurate way of knowing the extent of underage and polygamous marriages. Sheikh Chami of Lakemba Mosque argues that it is not difficult for a man wanting to take a second wife to find 'someone' with Muslim credentials to approve it, on the basis that 'if I don't want to do it, another imam will do it'.[37]

---

[32] *Oltman & Harper* (No.2) [2010] FamCA 1360.

[33] Marriage Act 1961 (Cth) section 5(a) a minister of religion registered under Subdivision A of Division 1 of Part IV; or (b) a person authorised to solemnise marriages by virtue of Subdivision B of Division 1 of Part IV; or (c) a marriage celebrant.

[34] Marriage Act 1961 (Cth) section 1: 'Subject to section 12, a person is of marriageable age if the person has attained the age of 18 years.' Section 12 allows a person who has attained the age of 16 years but has not attained the age of 18 years to apply to a Judge or magistrate for an order authorising him or her to marry a particular person of marriageable age. The judge will require the circumstances of the case to be exceptional and unusual as to justify the making of the order.

[35] It is a defence to a prosecution under section 95 for the defendant to prove that he or she believed on reasonable grounds that the person with whom he or she went through the form or ceremony of marriage was of marriageable age, or had previously been married, or had the consent of the court to do so in accordance with the Act.

[36] Marriage Act 1961 (Cth) section 94.

[37] Quoted in an interview with Sally Neighbour, in 'The Way to the Watering Hole: Sharia Law', *The Monthly*, December 2010, www.themonthly.com.au/issue/2010/december/1294083136/sally-neighbour/way-watering-hole.

Some Muslim marriages may not be registered because in Australia they would be deemed a 'forced' or 'servile' marriage. These are distinct from arranged or facilitated marriages, which are lawful as both parties have given full and informed consent.[38] Whilst it is more typical for the victim of a forced marriage to be taken overseas to wed under the national law of another country, marriages where there has been physical, emotional or financial duress or deception do take place in Australia. Forced marriage is, of course, contrary to Islamic law but Muslim sheiks and Imams do officiate over such marriages, possibly in the misguided belief that the Muslim parents who seek these are 'protecting their child or preserving cultural or religious traditions'.[39] The Australian government believes that cases of forced marriage are widely under-reported and in 2011–12 conducted an enquiry into the problem.[40] The Crimes Legislation Amendment (Slavery, Slavery-like Conditions and People Trafficking) Act was enacted in 2013 and criminalizes forced marriage, imposing a seven-year maximum imprisonment term for any person who attempts to force a vulnerable person into marriage.[41] Giving evidence in the case of *Wold v Kleppier* ([2009] FamCA 178, the imam who performed the ceremony but did not register the Islamic marriage explained that Islamic marriages are 'very, very quick to perform' as the one-month notice period of intention to marry is not required,[42] nor are birth certificates and other forms of identity required.[43] A final ground for not registering an Islamic marriage is that it will allow a husband a quicker and easier divorce by *talak/talaq* divorce (unilateral right of a

---

[38] Such marriages performed under duress also occur in mainly South Asian and Middle-Eastern ethnic communities, and are not confined to Muslim adherents. Coptic and some other Christian sects, Hindu and 'traveller' families also engage in the practice.

[39] Attorney-General's Department, Discussion Paper: Forced and Servile Marriages, www.ag.gov.au/Consultations/Documents/Consultationonforcedandservilemarriage/Discussion%20Paper%20for%20Public%20Release%20forced%20and%20servile%20marriage.pdf.

[40] The report estimated that there are 1000 forced marriages occurring annually.

[41] The Crimes Legislation Amendment (Slavery, Slavery-like Conditions and People Trafficking) Bill 2012 was introduced on 12 April 2012 and passed by both Houses of Parliament in February 2013.

[42] The Marriage Act 1961 (Cth) section 42 requires written notice of the intended marriage to be received not later than one month before the date of the marriage.

[43] *Wold v Kleppier* [2009] FamCA 178: para 30.

husband to divorce by pronouncement) should he want to end the marriage at any time.

Another difference between the two countries is that in Australia, a couple also has the choice to cohabit without marrying, as a de facto couple, in which case they will receive legal protections akin to a married couple. The latter attracts no penalty, whereas in Singapore such cohabitation could be a criminal offence (section 134 AMLA), attracting possible fines and/or imprisonment. AMLA also makes it an offence to entice an unmarried woman away from her *wali* (male guardian). However, as Singapore does not have religious police, it is generally acknowledged that this provision is rarely enforced. However, it acts as a deterrent and educative principle. Furthermore, in 2017, Australia enacted legislation to allow same-sex or homosexual marriage under the Marriage Amendment (Definition and Religious Freedoms) Act, and no longer has any criminal sanctions for homosexual acts between consenting adults (over the age of 18 years). Whilst no one has been recently prosecuted, section 377A of Singapore's Penal Code does make acts of 'gross indecency' between men a crime, with a two-year imprisonment term. The constitutionality of this section was upheld by Singapore's High Court in 2013.

In summary, in Australia's 'one law for all' approach there is one Act regulating marriage with religious affiliation playing no role in marriage validity or its registration. Complete freedom is given to the individual to follow his or her religious or non-religious traditions for marriage, which, provided there is compliance with each component of the Act, can be lawfully registered. In Singapore, the main difference is that there is a dual system with separate legal pathways provided for Muslims and other Singaporeans. Muslim marriage is governed exclusively by AMLA with separate registration, from which a range of legal consequences flow should the marriage end by divorce or when one of the spouses dies.

Who is a Muslim for the purposes of the Women's Charter and for the application of AMLA? Section 2 of AMLA gives little guidance, as it provides simply that a Muslim is 'a person who professes the religion of Islam' and states that the court's jurisdiction is for actions and proceedings in which 'all the parties are Muslim or where the parties were married under the provisions of Muslim law'.[44] There is acceptance that a child born to a Muslim parent is by birth Muslim, as is a person who formally converts to Islam and registers the conversion with ROMM.

---

[44] Section 55(2), Administration of Muslim Law Act 1966, Act 27 of 1966, 2009 Rev. Ed. Sing.

Although the issue of 'who is Muslim' does not frequently arise, jurisdiction can be relevant in cases of mixed religious marriages or in situations of conversion, whether into or out of, Islam especially for marriage validity[45] and for inheritance distribution,[46] as the estate of a Muslim must be distributed in accordance with Islamic inheritance laws.[47]

B. Divorce

Islamic law has always allowed for divorce by either the husband or the wife. It has been widely disliked but the message in the Quran is clear: couples need not stay in unhappy or destructive marriages. Instead they should part 'with kindness'. The avenues for divorce differ for husbands and wives. As already mentioned, husbands can divorce by *talak/talaq* (pronouncement),[48] and there are several forms of divorce generally accepted as available to wives including *mubarat*, mutual agreement; *taklik/ta'liq*, breach of a marriage condition; *talaq-i-tafwid*, a delegated divorce; *fasakh*, annulment or fault divorce; *khuluk/khula*, no-fault divorce but where a wife dislikes her husband and returns her *maskahwin/mahr*; *dharar*, dissolution because of the husband's cruelty; and divorce by conversion of one spouse to another religion.

In keeping with its 'one law for all' commitment, Australia also takes a monist stance on divorce with one law, the Family Law Act 1975 (Cth) governing divorce and all ancillary matter including the care of children, property and financial issues flowing from the divorce. Under s48 of the Family Law Act (Cth), the only ground for divorce in Australia is 'irretrievable' breakdown of the marriage proven by 12 months' separation. Fault is irrelevant. As the law applies equally with the same procedure required for husbands and for wives, and as the court is unconcerned about the cause of the marriage breakdown, both dimensions place Australian divorce law at odds with the principles and processes of Islamic divorce. Because of the gender complexity in Islamic divorce, there cannot be simultaneously a valid Australian (that

---

45 *Noor Azizan bte Colony (alias Noor Azizan bte Mohammad Noor) v Tan Lip Chin (alias Izak Tan)* [2006] 3 *Singapore Law Reports* 707.

46 *Re Mohammad Said Nabi, decd* (1965) 31 *Malayan Law Journal* 121.

47 Sections 111 and 112 of Administration of Muslim Law Act 1966, Act 27 of 1966, 2009 Rev. Ed. Sing.

48 This term and the divorce terms that follow are transliterated in Singapore as *talak*, whilst *talaq* is more commonly used in Australia. For this reason, both have been included in this section.

is, secular) divorce which also serves as an Islamic one. For example, a *talak/talaq* divorce proclaimed by a husband in Australia has no formal legal status, although he may hold it to be lawful under Islam and it may be seen as such in the eyes of his family and the Muslim community to which he belongs, including its religious leaders. Although *talak/talaq* has no legal consequences under Australian law, it may be used to mark the commencement of the required 12-month separation period needed to establish 'irretrievable' breakdown of the marriage. In the same way, a divorce decree (absolute) under Australian secular law will not generally be recognised as also ending the religious Islamic marriage.

However, as with marriage, a Muslim couple can comply with both Shari'ah and Australian divorce law, but they are two separate events. The Australian divorce is overseen by the Family Law Act and the Family Courts, but Islamic (or other religious) divorce is relegated to an informal and unofficial regulatory process governed by the rules and processes of the religion itself.

Without a formal Shari'ah Court, a wife seeking a Shari'ah divorce in Australia has to find a person or organisation that she believes can grant her a divorce in accordance with Islamic law. This is not always easy, especially for recent immigrants, or for couples with tenuous links to a mosque or a Muslim community. However, obtaining an Islamic divorce remains of considerable importance. Krayem Ghena explains that 'regardless of their religiosity, even if they have never walked into a mosque in their lives, and don't really pray or do any outwardly religious things, when it comes to marriage and divorce they think it's important to go to a mosque or imam'.[49] In the Australian context, much will hinge on the imam or group of scholars to whom the wife turns. As there are no religious qualifications prescribed by the government, nor are religious functionaries appointed by the government (unlike in Singapore), it is a system resting on self-assertion of expertise or Muslim community recognition of a person's religious authority and standing. The men assuming this role are usually sheikhs or imams, but it could also be undertaken by an individual Shari'ah scholar or group of scholars or imams (*majlis ulama*) who simply put themselves forward as sufficiently learned, pious or authoritative to make family law determinations, especially for the ethnic community with which they are aligned. In determining issues of Islamic divorce they may apply modernist interpretations on matters such as polygamy, divorce, *maskahwin/mahr* rulings, property settlement and child custody, or they may adhere to

---

[49] Krayem Ghena quoted in Sally Neighbour, above n37.

patriarchal, conservative and textualist interpretations that are found in the more conservative parts of the Muslim world. This increases the likelihood of inconsistent outcomes,[50] and also gives rise to concerns of unaccountability and the possibility of error or bias. One tangible consequence is the practice of Imam shopping. When it is known, for example, that certain imams will not grant a *khuluk/khula* divorce (divorce by redemption where the wife forgoes her *mahr* to buy her way out of the marriage) unless the husband first agrees to the divorce,[51] a wife may seek an imam with a more liberal interpretation. Some imams are known to give greater veracity to a husband's statement of facts and accept his over his wife's in cases of *fasakh* (where a wife seeks divorce based on fault). When a conservative approach favours the husband in divorce cases, it can leave Muslim women disadvantaged and vulnerable. This is especially true for recent migrants whose English is limited, and who have little knowledge of additional avenues or contacts outside their immediate Muslim community. The phenomenon known as 'limping' marriages, where a secular divorce is given or is available to a wife, but a religious one is denied, is well documented in Australia[52] and also in the United Kingdom.[53] What isn't known is the number of wives in that

---

50 Inconsistency may be simply a reflection of the diversity within the Australian Muslim population and a confirmation of the diversity of interpretations within 'Islam' itself.

51 There are a range of interpretations on this. In *khula* the wife requests divorce and in return provides her husband with compensation, which is usually the return of part or all of her *mahr*, or if deferred, to forego her rights to it, along with rights to maintenance during her *iddah* (three-month waiting period before a divorce becomes irrevocable). The divorce is irrevocable. If the husband agrees, he will pronounce *talaq* on those terms, or a court will order him to do so once the court has settled the amount of the compensation payable by the wife. There is debate on the matter of whether the husband must agree to this and whether his lack of consent negates *khula*. Jurisprudence developed over many centuries in which the dominant position was that a grant of *khula* was contingent upon the husband's consent. However, in recent times when this issue has been revisited, this fetter has often been removed.

52 Family Law Council of Australia, *Report on Cultural Community Divorce and the Family Law Act 1975* (2001) 4 (Executive Summary 17).

53 Law Commission UK (Law Com. No.48) *Family Law: Report of Jurisdiction in Matrimonial Causes* (1972); Ishan Yilmaz, 'Muslim Alternative Dispute Resolution and Neo-Ijtihad' (2003) 2, 1 *Alternatives* 1; Muslim Arbitration Tribunal, Family Dispute Cases: www.matribunal.com/cases_faimly.html. Also in secular Turkey, see Ishan Yilmaz, 'Non-Recognition of Post-modern Turkish Socio-political Reality and the Predicament of Women' (2003) 30(1) *British Journal of Middle Eastern Studies* 25–41.

position. Macfarlane estimates that 20 per cent of Muslim women in Canada who seek a Shari'ah-sanctioned divorce do not obtain one.[54] President of the Australian Federation of Islamic Councils Iqbal Patel sees limping marriages as a significant issue which warrants government intervention to deal with 'the difficulties some divorced Muslim women experienced in persuading their former husbands to grant them a religious divorce. If that doesn't happen, she is in limbo – she cannot move on.'[55]

In Singapore, limping marriages do not arise. As there is no avenue for a Muslim to go the civil court and use the divorce procedures under the Charter, it is not possible to have a secular divorce and be denied a religious one. If you married under AMLA then you are required to divorce under AMLA. As with marriage, in Singapore there is a dual system for divorce. One's divorce pathway depends solely on religious affiliation. For Muslims, only the Shari'ah Court has authority to hear and determine a divorce application. AMLA recognises many of the classic Shari'ah divorce avenues: *talak/talaq* for the husband, although the court has the power to appoint arbitrators to bring out a reconciliation (section 50), but as the divorce takes effect from the time of pronouncement this is not a significant limitation. Referral for arbitration and counselling can also be ordered when a wife requests divorce by *khuluk/khula* (section 46), *taklik/ta'liq* (section 48) and *fasakh* (section 49). Whilst the grounds for *fasakh* are quite specific, the law on divorce in AMLA is not a comprehensive codification and the court's general jurisdiction to apply Muslim law continues, which can be varied where applicable by 'Malay custom'.[56] The court therefore can turn to primary sources of law, the Quran and Sunnah, as well as the writings of classic jurists and scholars for elaboration and interpretation.[57] In this way the court has the jurisprudential licence to invoke interpretations of Islamic family law that resonate with family life in contemporary Singapore. Yet Abdul Rahman has found that the court accepts and does not question what it sees as an immutable body of divine and absolute legal rules, but

---

[54] Macfarlane, n21, 60.

[55] Chris Merritt, 'It Was a Mistake to Mention Sharia Law, Admits Islamic Leader' *The Australian*, 17 June 2011. Also, Ismael Essof, 'Divorce in Australia: from an Islamic Perspective' (2011) 36(3) *Alternative Law Journal* 182–6.

[56] Section 35(3) Administration of Muslim Law Act 1966, Act 27 of 1966, 2009 Rev. Ed. Sing.

[57] Noor Aisha bte Abdul Rahman, 'Traditionalism and its Impact on the Administration of Justice: The Case of the Shari'ah Court of Singapore' (2006) 5(3) *Inter-Asia Cultural Studies* 415, 432.

what she describes as 'the rich and diverse body of juristic thought and legal traditions are of little interest or concern'.[58] Whilst AMLA could allow for assimilation of more progressive and egalitarian legal opinions on many aspects of family law, the court in Singapore instinctively adopts what has been described as a traditionalist stance. This is particularly evident in divorce cases, where the Shari'ah Court in Singapore upholds the conservative view that divorce is the 'exclusive preserve of the husband who has an unfettered right to pronounce *talaq* and thereby terminate his marriage without cause'.[59] Abdul Rahman also found that the court makes divorce applications by women procedurally onerous and resists decreeing divorces initiated by wives.[60] *Fasakh*, for example, was found to be confined to a few cases of apostasy and insanity, and the referral to arbitrators appeared merely to lengthen the process, with the added disincentive that further financial costs would be incurred.[61]

The Shari'ah Court's exclusive power to hear and make an order on divorce does not extend to determining all the legal issues that may arise in a divorce case. Matters of spousal maintenance or whether a protection order should be issued must be remitted to the civil court. In some matters the courts have concurrent jurisdiction. Whilst a Muslim couple must have their divorce heard in the Shari'ah Court, applications for child custody, access and distribution of matrimonial property can be made to 'any court', which enables a Muslim party during or after divorce proceedings in the Shari'ah Court to make an ancillary application to the civil Family Court where the civil law will be applied.[62] AMLA requires this to be with the consent of the parties and with the leave of the Shari'ah Court.[63] Although adoptions fall under the jurisdiction of the civil family court,[64] the court takes into account Islamic principles on adoption – for example, to allow the child to keep the name of her birth parents and not that of the adoptive family (Abdul Rahman 2004: 416). Also as the Shari'ah Court lacks powers of enforcement, its orders for

58 Ibid., 417.

59 Ibid., 418.

60 Ibid., 422.

61 Ibid., 425.

62 Section 17A(2) Supreme Court of Judicature Act, Cap 322, 2009 Rev. Ed. Sing.

63 Section 35A, Administration of Muslim Law Act 1966, Act 27 of 1966, 2009 Rev. Ed. Sing.; Supreme Court of Judicature Act, Cap 322, 2009 Rev. Ed. Sing. section 17.

64 Adoption of Children Act, Cap 4, and generally see bin Abbas 2012: 174.

mutaah (compensation),[65] marriage expenses, custody and property division are enforceable (section 53) but not reviewable by the civil court. They are enforced as if they were orders of the District Court. It means that in many areas of family law there is a shared jurisdictional arrangement between the religious and the civil court. This gives rise to one of two views: it is either a working court partnership or a system made notoriously complex.

IV. REFLECTIONS ON MULTICULTURALISM: CONVERGENCE AND DIVERGENCE IN AUSTRALIA AND SINGAPORE

As outlined above, a colonial legacy has meant different practical consequences for Singapore's half a million Muslims than for Australia's Muslims. Both legal systems seek to provide just and fair family and personal law outcomes for all their citizens, but have taken different paths for achieving this goal. In managing its racially and religiously diverse society, the key in Singapore, as elsewhere in South East Asia, is 'that a well-functioning civil society is not nurtured by enforced uniformity, but by tolerance and mutual respect for different racial and religious groups'.[66] If a minority ethnic or religious group feels it is protected by its own laws and has a distinctive place in the legal system, this will 'solidify their commitment to the state and enable them to focus on what is shared, rather than what divides'.[67] For its culturally diverse population, Australia advocates multiculturalism in which that diversity is respected through the 'unifying principles of Australian values, identity and citizenship', but within the existing 'framework of Australian law: it is not a platform for legal pluralism based on religion, culture or ethnicity'.[68] To this end the law must give sufficient scope for people to 'arrange their private affairs according to their own beliefs', providing

---

[65] Payment of compensation to a woman divorced without fault.

[66] Keong, n1, 84, 96.

[67] Li-ann Thio, 'Constitutional Accommodation of the Rights of Ethnic and Religious Minorities in Plural Democracies: Lessons and cautionary tales from South-east Asia' (2010) 22 *Pace International Law Review* 43, 49.

[68] Parliament of the Commonwealth of Australia: Joint Standing Committee on Migration, *Inquiry into Migration and Multiculturalism in Australia*, March 2013, ix.

that this does not conflict with 'obligations enacted by the Australian, and state, Parliaments'.[69]

These divergent views on multiculturalism have meant that the role of Shari'ah law plays out in distinctive ways in each nation. These will now be considered from a comparative perspective, highlighting points of divergence.

A. Indigenous Peoples versus Immigrants

In recognising Malays as the first people of Singapore, the Constitution provides a justification for Islam and Islamic law, to be differentiated and applied separately from the Women's Charter which governs most Singaporeans. The same rationale does not apply in Australia as Australia's indigenous people have the same family law applied, as do all Australians regardless of race or religion. As the spiritual traditions of Aboriginal and Torres Strait Islanders (the first peoples of the continent) receive neither legal priority nor Constitutional recognition, it is more challenging to advocate for another sector of the community to be given special legal status, especially when they are more recent immigrants. El Matrah rejects as 'unethical' the frequently made comparison equating the rights of indigenous Australians with those of Muslim Australians. She writes that Muslims were 'part of the process that dispossessed indigenous Australians', so indigenous entitlements are beyond 'anything a migrant community should appropriately expect'.[70] Additionally, Singapore's dual system was also a continuation of the legal arrangement established in the early nineteenth century; not only does this give it popular acceptance, but also its proven track record is reassuring for non-Muslims. Australians look at the application of Shari'ah law in some other parts of the Muslim world with concern, and are apprehensive about what it could mean for Australia. This is not confined to the non-Muslim population, as some Muslims migrated to Australia willingly leaving behind some components of Shari'ah law that they believed impacted in negative ways upon their lives. It is conceptually more challenging to win support in a democracy for transplanting a new and separate system of family law for Muslims, when many Australians have little knowledge of Islam. Most if not all Muslims who migrate to Australia do so in the knowledge that it is a secular nation. In Singapore it is known that Shari'ah law will be applied to Muslims.

---

[69] Ibid.

[70] Joumanah El Matrah, 'A Sharia Tribunal is a Contradiction of Islam' *The Age*, 20 October 2009.

B. Community Acceptance versus Community Concerns

The longevity of legal pluralism and Constitutional protections afforded to persons of the Islamic faith in Singapore, have meant that having a religious court and different set of family laws for Muslims is accepted and rarely criticised, although though there is acknowledgement by many Singaporeans that this dichotomy remains 'very sensitive'. Ahmad Nizam Abbas, a lawyer, reflects the commonly expressed sentiment that the dual system works for the benefit of Muslim Singaporeans, describing the requirement to use the Shari'ah system as an 'honour' or 'privilege' given only to Muslims,[71] and noting that the Shari'ah system is becoming increasingly more professional in ensuring fairness and justice.[72] Leong Wai Kum, Professor of Law, sees Singapore's dual court system as problematic. He argues that in resolving family law disputes, 'apparent and real conflicts do crop up' which cannot be resolved by 'reference to a simple separation' of jurisdiction of the two court systems.[73] He concludes that as such, conflicts are 'notoriously difficult' to resolve and he awaits 'the eventual integration of the entire family law in Singapore to regulate all Singaporeans'.[74] Abdul Rahman also identifies 'significant problems'[75] in the current system but unlike Professor Leong, she does not favour cessation of the dual system but advocates for greater jurisprudential and legislative reform of the Shari'ah system. The problems that she identifies occur because the 'substantive law on marriage, divorce and ancillary issues is not comprehensively codified' in AMLA, which leaves the interpretation of Shari'ah family law with the judges of the court and with MUIS. She feels the initial spirit of the framers of AMLA, which was attuned to the contemporary needs of women, has been eroded by traditionalism, which she cites as a 'dogmatic attitude that clings firmly to old ways, resisting innovations or accepting them only unwillingly'.[76] This is significant as Muslims are restricted from accessing the civil adjudicative forum for family law matters.

---

71 Abbas, n4, 163.

72 Ibid., 187.

73 Kum, n7, 903 with case examples of jurisdictional conflict given at 903–16.

74 Ibid., 918.

75 Rahman, n57, 415, 416.

76 This is the definition given by Karl Mannheim cited in Rahman, n57, 415, 416. Robert Towler defines it as a 'style of religious belief whose essence is to cherish the entire tradition received as sacred such that if any part is threatened or called into question, it is the whole pattern which is put at risk' in Towler, *The Need for Certainty: a Sociological Study of Conventional Religion.*

In Australia, there is general acceptance of the 'one law for all' approach. There is a level of consensus that social cohesion and unity is best achieved through a single legal order, not multiple ones, to protect 'the principles of equality, legal security, legality, and political unity'.[77] In March 2013, the Australian government re-committed the nation to this approach by endorsing the recommendation of its Parliamentary Inquiry into Migration and Multiculturalism in Australia 'not [to] support legal pluralism'.[78] Instead, the government promotes the 'message that multiculturalism entails both respect for cultural diversity and a commitment to the *framework of Australian laws and values* which underpin social cohesion'[79] (italics added). The Report specifically addressed Islamic law in the context of submissions made to it by Muslim organisations in support of Shari'ah Courts or tribunals, affirming that the 'Australian Government has consistently stated that implementation of Shari'ah law in not being contemplated'.[80] The Inquiry called for submissions. Of the 513 submissions made, 212 raised concerns about Islam in Australia, specifically the levels of ethnic separatism and ghettoization, with 113 objecting to the possibility of introducing legal pluralism to accommodate the requirements of Shari'ah law. Submissions from Muslim groups were also divided on the role for Shari'ah law in Australia. Iqbal Patel, representing AFIC as its President, submitted that 'multiculturalism should lead to legal pluralism', arguing that conflicts should be resolved according to the law and traditions of one's own religion.[81] The AFIC submission challenged Australia's policy of multiculturalism on the ground that by limiting it to culture, religion and language and not extending it to encompass law, Australia was treating Muslims as 'second class citizens' by requiring them to live 'under one law: Western law'. He reasoned that Shari'ah was not immutable but adaptable, and it was possible to have a moderate form that could coexist

---

77 Daniel Bonilla Maldonado, 'Extralegal Property, Legal Monism, and Pluralism' Yale Law Electronic Resource site: www.law.yale.edu/documents/pdf/sela/Bonilla.pdf.

78 Parliament of the Commonwealth of Australia: Joint Standing Committee on Migration, Inquiry into Migration and Multiculturalism in Australia, March 2013, 85: www.aph.gov.au/Parliamentary_Business/Committees/House_of_Representatives_Committees?url=mig/multiculturalism/report.htm.

79 Ibid.

80 Parliament of the Commonwealth of Australia: Joint Standing Committee on Migration, Inquiry into Migration and Multiculturalism in Australia, March 2013, 67.

81 Australia Federation of Islamic Councils; Submission 81: 'Embracing Australian Values – Maintaining the Right to be Different'.

with the Australian legal system through a concept of 'twin tolerations'.[82] However, other submissions from Muslim organisations did not advocate for either Shari'ah Courts or legal pluralism, noting that 'the overwhelming majority of Australian Muslims want nothing more than to get on with their lives and make meaningful contributions' to Australia.[83] The Director of the Islamic Women's Council of Victoria, Joumanah El Matrah, argued against setting up a separate Shari'ah tribunal or court on the ground that it would amount to 'legal ghettoization of Muslims' because 'establishing a parallel system for Muslims does not ensure a culturally appropriate response to justice: it fundamentally locks out Muslims from services they as citizens have a right to access'.[84]

Singapore values its dual system just as Australia values its one law for all. Just as it would be difficult for Singapore to repeal AMLA and bring its Muslims under the jurisdiction of the Charter, it is equally difficult to change the Australian formulae. Muslims see difficult possibilities too. A minority advocated that Muslims should be able to have every aspect of life regulated by Shari'ah,[85] but many more argued that certain aspects of family, inheritance and commerce could be transferred to a Shari'ah entity,[86] whilst others believe the Australian system already meets the higher objective of the Shari'ah with no change needed (Halim Rane quoted in Merritt 2011c).[87] Views are diverse and sometimes divisive amongst Muslims, just as they are amongst non-Muslims. However, there is a desire in the wider Australian society to be inclusive and to counter (or at least reduce) disaffection amongst some sectors of the Muslim community. Whether formal accommodation of the Shari'ah would diminish or aggravate alienation continues to be debated.

---

[82] Ibid.

[83] Islamic Council of Victoria: Submission 13.

[84] Joumanah El Matrah, 'A Sharia Tribunal is a Contradiction of Islam' *The Age*, 20 October 2009.

[85] Sharia4Australia organization.

[86] Abdullah Saeed, 'Reflections on the Establishment of Shari'ah Courts in Australia' in Rex Adhar and Nicholas Aroney (eds), *Shari'ah in the West* (Oxford: Oxford University Press 2010) 231. He also notes at 231 that legal academic Jamila Hussain speculates that most Muslims are happy with Australian law.

[87] See Halim Rane quoted in Merritt 2011, also El Matrah 2009, in which a woman's perspective is given on a Sharia tribunal.

C. Homogeneity versus Heterogeneity

One factor contributing to the lack of Muslim consensus on the role for Shari'ah in Australia is that the Muslim population is Australia is not homogeneous, unlike Singapore, where Malay ethnicity, language and culture and Shafi'i school dominate. Australia has Shia Muslims, Ibadis, Sufis, as well as adherents from each of the four Sunni *madhab*s (schools of law). Australian Muslims comprise 56 different ethnicities and have migrated since the days of first settlement from more than 70 nations. This internal plurality gives a complexity to the Australian situation not replicated in Singapore. This leads to a range of views on the role for Islam in a secular Australia and different ideological commitments to Islam and Shari'ah law. Some Muslims in Australia describe themselves as secular or nominal Muslims. They have an Islamic heritage but have embraced the secular Australian lifestyle – they rarely attend the mosque or observe the five pillars of Islam, they drink alcohol and many have married or are in relationships with non-Muslims. All this is possible and lawful in Australia. Australia also has extremely devout textualist Muslims who desire Shari'ah law to operate in every aspect of their lives and are committed advocates for a Shari'ah Court and laws to be implemented. The plurality that exists across the Muslim world is reflected in Australia where the role for Shari'ah can be informed by models from secular Turkey or theocratic Iran, moderate Indonesia or conservative Saudi Arabia, and viewpoints of new immigrants or fifth-generation Muslim Australians. Such heterogeneity mitigates against dogmatism but also challenges any notion of a Muslim consensus on how Shari'ah should operate in the lives of contemporary Muslims. This stands in contrast to Singapore where the role for the Shari'ah Court and MUIS is not debated, but both are acknowledged as the legitimate custodians and implementers Shari'ah law.

Consensus is also more difficult in a setting where Muslims in Australia are geographically dispersed across a large continent. Singapore has the one Shari'ah Court based at Lengkok Bahru, and *kadis* in districts easily accessible to all Singaporeans. Australia is vast. Although both countries have roughly the same number of adherents, Muslims in Australia are found in every city from Darwin to Hobart and also in many rural areas. Cairns is almost 3000 km from Melbourne, and Perth to Sydney is 4000 km, which is essentially the same distance from Perth to Singapore. Establishing a Shari'ah Court or tribunal system would have logistical consequences, thereby raising equity and access issues given the geographic spread of Muslims across Australia.

D. Mandatory versus Voluntary Jurisdiction

The success of the Singaporean approach rests heavily not only on the homogeneity of its Malay Muslim community, who by and large accept the jurisdiction of the Shari'ah Court, the rulings of MUIS and the application of AMLA, but also on the Shari'ah Court's mandatory jurisdiction. Singapore's Muslims have no choice but to submit to the Shari'ah system (unless they leave Islam). It does necessitate the keeping of a reliable record of who is Muslim. In Singapore this can be through self-identification as section 2 of AMLA defines a Muslim as 'a person professing the religion of Islam', but the more important mechanism is through the separate registration system (ROMM) for Muslim births, conversions and marriage. In Australia, because no legal consequences flow from one's religious affiliation, neither religion nor race is put on official marriage, death or birth registers. In Australia, just as religious marriage ceremonies are optional, so too are other personal milestones. Parents can voluntarily choose to have their child undergo a religious ceremony such as a baptism, bar mitzvah, *aqiqah* (welcoming ceremony for a Muslim baby), christening or other naming service, and similarly choose funeral and burial arrangements in accordance with faith requirements. One's religion is not officially recorded with any government body, which means changing one's religion or becoming atheist remains in the private realm or with the religious bodies' own record-keeping systems.

A Singapore-style system of mandatory jurisdiction for Shari'ah Courts would deny Australian Muslims the same right as other citizens to have cases heard in the common law courts. This would be unlawful discrimination in secular Australia. To deny access to the Federal Circuit Court or the Family Court in Australia based on religious grounds would not be acceptable. Any dual system introduced in Australia would have to be on a voluntary opt-in basis, rather than the mandatory lines of Singapore. Even with an opt-in system, several legal issues would still arise in Australia. The first is that for any government to recognise and cede jurisdiction to a religious court, even on a voluntary basis, constitutional amendments would be needed. Section 116 of the Australian Constitution makes it unconstitutional for any religious test to be required as a qualification for any office or public trust under the Commonwealth. Where a qualification for judicial or arbitral appointment was based on religion, namely Islam, it would be unconstitutional. As already noted, these issues do not arise in Singapore, where Constitution was drafted to entrench legal pluralism not only by creating a special legal status for Muslims[88] but also by specifying that guarantees of 'equality before the law' and 'equal protection' in section 12(3) do not extend to the regulation of personal law. This allows AMLA and the Shari'ah Court to operate in this realm of personal law using personnel appointed and funded by the government. Unlike section 153 of the Singapore Constitution, which provides that the legislature can make laws for 'regulating Muslim religious affairs and for constituting a Council to advise the President in matters relating to the Muslim religion', the Australian government has been given no similar authority. The Australian federal and state governments can (and do) have advisory bodies, such as the Muslim Community Reference Group (MCRG)[89] and the government-funded National Centre of Excellence in Islamic Studies,[90] but these are not offices of the government or under a public trust.

Regardless of the constitutional obstacles, there are other concerns with an opt-in system. One is that such a system could intensify Muslim community pressure, even family or spousal coercion, to follow the 'official' Islamic dispute resolution option. In effect, this could undermine their free choice. The second arises from the internal plurality that exists in Australia's Muslim population. This has already been discussed, but were there a government-run Shari'ah Court option, it could in fact impact adversely on plurality of interpretations of Islam that currently flourish. The third is one of public policy. Where there is divergence between religious law and state law, any adverse outcomes for faith adherents become a matter for the religion, in this case Islam, or one for the Australian government or its courts to address. Earlier the issue of limping marriages was mentioned and the predicament for Muslim women that can ensue is frequently cited as a reason for endorsing some form of formal or official Shari'ah Court or Muslim divorce tribunal.[91] Yet a similar predicament arises in other faith traditions in Australia. Islam is not alone in requiring a religious divorce for its adherents. There are other religions that also do not accept a divorce granted under

---

88 Constitution section 152.

89 MCRG 'Report Building on Social Cohesion, Harmony and Security' (2006): www.immi.gov.au/living-in-australia/a-multicultural-australia/mcrg_report.pdf.

90 This was an initiative of the Howard government that came into operation in 2007. However, the training of Australian imams proved impractical in the Australian University environment and all funding ended in 2011.

91 Family Law Council of Australia, *Report on Cultural Community Divorce and the Family Law Act 1975* (2001) 4 (Executive Summary 17); Essof, n55, 182, 186.

Australian law dissolves a marriage which took place under their own religious law. Roman Catholics and Jews in Australia[92] have an ecclesiastical or rabbinical court to make such determinations. These matters remain internal to the religion and do not involve government funding or endorsing of religious courts, nor oversight or the creation of exceptional rules. To do so for one, or for all religions, would seem an unwarranted intrusion into religious freedom generally. Essof, for example, writes that this is needed for limping marriages because Muslim husbands can distort and abuse the Islamic system, and there may be bias and lack of sensitivity from the imams when making decisions that 'could be long, demeaning and emotionally traumatic'[93] for women. Whilst not refuting the legitimate concerns raised, Islamic jurisprudence does favour interpretations that do not create hardship for Muslims through principles of *maslaha* (public interest). If 'limping marriages' result in hardship for Muslim women because Imams will not grant them an Islamic divorce after they have received a civil one, then *ijtihad* (independent reasoning) with its many juristic techniques should be utilised to ensure fairer interpretations. Otherwise the problem will remain. As we see from the traditionalist interpretations in divorce cases from Singapore's Shari'ah court (section 47 AMLA) which uphold the classic juristic view that the husband must consent to a *khuluk/khula* divorce, the outcome for divorcing wives would remain and the problem not rectified.[94] The presence of a religious court, council or tribunal does not guarantee modernist interpretations, and in practice it could restrict options currently available to Muslim women in Australia's informal system. Currently, if refused a *khuluk/khula* divorce, the wife is now at least able to seek out another scholar who may apply a different interpretation and grant the divorce. And a wife always has the right to obtain a secular divorce which will provide her with a financial and property settlement

---

[92] In Roman Catholic canon law, there is no such thing as divorce, which means there is nothing for the church to recognise when a secular divorce is granted. Under Catholic Canon law, the exercise is not one of untying people from the marriage bond but of asking whether, according to established criteria, there was ever a marriage in the first place, that is, whether in the circumstances of the case was there ever a marriage, *ab initio*. Hence it is an annulment that parties must seek from the Church's tribunal, an ecclesiastical court comprised of priests and lay men and women trained in canon law.

[93] Essof, n55, 182, 186.

[94] In limping marriages, the wife cannot remarry but the husband can, as it is considered lawful for him in Islam to have more than one wife.

and a determination on parenting arrangements irrespective of the religious process. These are legally enforceable. Arguments put forward that the Family Court should not grant divorces until a Muslim wife can prove she already has a religious divorce[95] from an Islamic Council would again be discriminatory and would deny her legitimate legal entitlements.

E. Consistency versus Diversity

In the Australian context, the lack of an official Shari'ah Court or a *Majlis Ugama Islam Singapura* (MUIS) equivalent has meant there is less certainty and predictability in the application of Islamic law. This arises from the informal unofficial status of Shari'ah law and the heterogeneity of Islam in Australia. In Singapore, there is jurisprudential consistency which gives more certainty and predictability in the law. This comes not only from adhering to predominately to Shafi'i tenets,[96] as section 33 AMLA requires both the *Majlis* and the Legal Committee to 'ordinarily follow the tenets of the Shafi'i school of law, unless it is not in the public interest to do so,[97] but also from the supervisory role of MUIS on the application of Shari'ah law through its Appeal Board and also the MUIS Legal Committee. Section 31 of AMLA sets out the composition of the legal committee, namely '(a) the Mufti; (b) two other fit and proper members of the *Majlis*; and (c) not more than two other fit and proper Muslims who are not members of the *Majlis*'. The Mufti of

95 Ibid., n93.

96 Section 33(1) of the Administration of Muslim Law Act specifies that 'the Majlis and the Legal Committee in issuing any ruling shall ordinarily follow the tenets of the Shafi'i school of law' unless that is contrary to public interest. In such situations, section 33(2) states 'the Majlis may follow the tenets of any of the other accepted schools of Muslim law as may be considered appropriate, but in any such ruling the provisions and principles to be followed shall be set out in full detail and with all necessary explanations'.

97 Section 33(1), Administration of Muslim Law Act, Cap 3 2009 Rev. Ed. Sing with section 33(2) stating that 'the tenets of any of the other accepted schools of Muslim law as may be considered appropriate' can be used in such rulings, but that 'the provisions and principles to be followed shall be set out in full detail and with all necessary explanations'. Rulings can also be made when specifically requested 'in accordance with the tenets of [another] particular school of Muslim law'; see Administration of Muslim Law Act, Cap 3 section 33(3).

Singapore is the Chairman of the Committee and the Mufti and Committee members are appointed by the President of Singapore, with the advice of the *Majlis* for the other members.[98]

MUIS also issues fatwas (legal opinions on matters of Islamic law). In keeping with the tradition of *ifta* (the issuing of fatwas) in Islamic law, a question requiring a fatwa on any point of Islamic law can be asked by 'any person',[99] by a court of law, including the Shari'ah Court,[100] and the Committee can 'of its own motion' make and publish any ruling or determination.[101] The process involves making a draft ruling which if it is unanimously approved by the Legal Committee[102] will be issued by the *Majlis*; if it is not unanimously approved, it will be referred to the *Majlis* who will issue the fatwa in 'accordance with the opinion of the majority of its members'.[103] This consensual process furthers consistency in the interpretation of Shari'ah law within Singapore. The role given to the Legal Committee provides not only the Shari'ah Court with an authoritative source for interpretations of Sharia law but fulfils that role also for the civil courts. Although the civil courts are not bound by the ruling of the Legal Committee (unlike the Shari'ah Court), the cases show consideration and respect for the Committee's rulings.[104] That the civil courts have one entity to which they can turn for an Islamic law opinion is a valuable attribute of the Singaporean model. In Australia, who qualifies as an expert in matters of Islamic law can be problematic and has to be established each time to the satisfaction of the court. As with the presentation of other forms of expert evidence, parties can provide their own Shari'ah law expert so the court has to decide between two versions. In the case of *Mohammed Salah & Gastana* [2011] FamCA 440, the parties had contrary expert opinions given by two Muslim scholars. One of the issues in dispute was whether their child's name, given by the mother, was 'blasphemous in the Islamic religion' or not.

98 Section 30, Administration of Muslim Law Act, Cap 3 2009 Rev. Ed. Sing.

99 Section 32(1), Administration of Muslim Law Act, Cap 3 2009 Rev. Ed. Sing.

100 Section 32(8), Administration of Muslim Law Act, Cap 3 2009 Rev. Ed. Sing.

101 Section 32(6), Administration of Muslim Law Act, Cap 3 2009 Rev. Ed. Sing.

102 Section 32(4), Administration of Muslim Law Act, Cap 3 2009 Rev. Ed. Sing. includes those members present and entitled to vote.

103 Section 32(7), Administration of Muslim Law Act, Cap 3 2009 Rev. Ed. Sing.

104 *Saniah Binte Ali & Anors v Abdullah Bin Ali* [1990] 1SLR (R)555.

The component of consistency in the interpretations provided by MUIS can act as a unifying force for Singapore's Muslim community. On the MUIS website some of the more important fatwas are published in Malay or English, or both languages. They include: legal rulings on finance and estate matters; *zakat* (tithe or charity tax); family matters including family planning; the permissibility of certain medical advances including the stem cell research, organ donation and transplantation, bone marrow transplantation, abortion and advanced medical directives; the permissibility of using ethanol as a food additive; and whether a particular group engaged in deviant teachings (on Islam). These questions would also resonate with many Muslim Australians. The role that fatwas fulfil in the Islamic system is not limited to Muslim countries or to ones like Singapore. Fatwas are equally if not more important in countries like Australia with a preponderance of immigrants rather than a long settled cohesive population. In order to accommodate Islamic religious requirements within a secular framework, it can be argued that fatwas are of even greater significance for Australian Muslims,[105] as they can ease transition into a secular society and facilitate compliance with Islam in a new social and regulatory context. Research in Australia and also Europe has found the demand for fatwas in the West appears greater than in Islamic countries.[106]

Without an equivalent of Singapore's MUIS Legal Committee or a government-appointed Mufti, there can be confusion and inconsistency in the legal opinions provided, or alternatively, a plethora of views which reflects the voluntary nature of *ifta* as a tradition and also gives voice to the diversity within the Australian Islamic community. Just as Australian Muslims can select the imam or informal Islamic body of their choice for divorce and other proceedings, Muslims in Australia can turn to a range of sources for fatwas: national organizations such as Australian Federation of Islamic Council (AFIC), the Darulfatwa Islamic High Council, or the National Council of Imams (ANIC); state organizations including

---

[105] Ann Black and Nadirsyah Hosen, 'Fatwas: Their Role in Contemporary Secular Australia' (2009) 18(2) *Griffith Law Review: A Journal of Social and Critical Legal Studies* 405–27; and Ann Black, 'Fatwas and Surgery: How and Why a Fatwa May Inform a Muslim Patient's Surgical Options' (2009) 79(12) *Australian and New Zealand Journal of Surgery* 866–71.

[106] Alexandre Caeiro, 'Transnational Ulama, European Fatwas, and Islamic Authority: A Case Study of the European Council for Fatwa and Research' in Stefano Allievi and Martin van Bruinessen (eds), *Producing Islamic Knowledge: Transmission and Dissemination in Western Europe* (Abingdon: Routledge 2010).

state Islamic Councils and local *majlis ulama*; local sheikhs or imams at their mosque; or a scholar or organization in an overseas country; and last, but importantly, the Internet's many online fatwa sites.[107] The process of searching Islamic websites for a religious ruling has been called 'fatwa shopping' or surfing the 'inter-madhab net'.[108] All sorts of new, alternative and diverse interpretations of Islam can be found online, but traditional or conservative versions appear dominant of some of the most used sites. Some of these overseas Islamic websites[109] have Muslim scholars who may answer the question without necessarily understanding life in Australia. If the question closely relates to life and social interaction in an Australian context, the answer might not be contextually suitable.[110] Of course, Singapore's Muslims can also go online to surf the 'inter-madhab' net, but the presence of a national *ifta* body is a stabilising and unifying force, and fatwas issued by MUIS are cognizant of local conditions.

F. Courts Working Together versus Separately

The longevity of legal pluralism in Singapore has meant that the Shari'ah and civil courts have had to establish a working relationship. The jurisdiction of each is delineated and there is recurring interaction between the two. For example, the Shari'ah Court lacks powers of enforcement, so its orders for maintenance, *mutaah* (compensation)

---

[107] Black and Hosen, n105.

[108] Mohamad Abdalla, 'Do Australian Muslims need a Mufti? Analysing the Institution of Ifta in the Australian Context' in Nadirsyah Hosen and Richard Mohr, *Law and Religion in Public Life* (Abingdon: Routledge 2010) 214, 221.

[109] *Islam on-line*, based in Doha, Qatar with fatwas issued by a committee of scholars headed by Dr Yusuf Qardawi, www.islamonline.net/livefatwa/english/select.asp; *islamtoday*, based in Saudi Arabia with fatwas issued by committee of scholars supervised by Sheikh Salman bin Fahd al-Oadah, www.islamtoday.com/fatwa_archive_main.cfm; *Ask the Imam*, South African site with fatwas issued by Mufti Ebrahim Desai, http://islam.tc/ask-imam/index.php; *Islam Q&A*, based in Saudi Arabia with fatwas issued under supervision of Shaykh Muhammad Saalih al-Munajjid, http://63.175.194.25/index.php?ln=eng; *Fatwa on-line*, Saudi Arabian site designed to give English speaking Muslims access to translations of officially published Arabic fatwas, www.fatwa-online.com.

[110] An example given is the issue of saying 'Merry Christmas'. In Australia this is a cultural practice to mark the season, not a religious observation or one identifying a theological battle between Islam and Christian. Overseas online websites routinely forbid it; for example, the Indonesian website, Shari'ah Online, www.Shari'ahonline.com/new_index.php/id/1/cn/2445 strongly forbids it, as does Islam Q&A: www.islam-qa.com/en/ref/947/Christmas.

marriage expenses, custody and property division are enforceable (section 53 AMLA) but not reviewable, by the civil court: the District Court. These orders are enforced as if they were orders of the District Court. There are also cases in which each court will play a distinct role, for example, in distributing a Muslim's estate, the Islamic laws of inheritance are applied by the Shari'ah Court in order to issue an inheritance certificate,[111] but all grants for probate and letters of administration come from the civil courts.[112] As noted earlier, the Shari'ah Court has exclusive jurisdiction to make a divorce order but does not have the power to determine matters of spousal maintenance or when a protection order should be issued. These must be remitted to the civil court. In some matters the courts have concurrent jurisdiction. Whilst a Muslim couple must have their divorce heard in the Shari'ah Court, applications for child custody, access and distribution of matrimonial property can be made to 'any court'. This enables a Muslim party during or after divorce proceedings in the Shari'ah Court to make an ancillary application to the civil Family Court where the civil law will be applied.[113] AMLA requires this to be with the consent of the parties and with the leave of the Shari'ah Court.[114] Similarly, adoptions fall under the jurisdiction of the civil Family Court,[115] but the Court takes into account Islamic principles on adoption, to allow the child to keep the name of his or her birth parents, and not that of the adoptive family.[116] Similarly, the Shari'ah Court can apply legal principles from the civil law system when the issue is one not covered by Islamic law.[117] Lastly, the criminal offences contained in AMLA Part IX, which include religious offences such as failure to pay *zakat*, cohabitation outside of marriage, enticing an unmarried woman away from her *wali* (male guardian, usually her father) and teaching false doctrines about Islam[118] are heard, determined and sentenced in the civil courts.

---

[111] Section 115, Administration of Muslim Law Act 1966, Act 27 of 1966, 2009 Rev. Ed. Sing.

[112] Probate and Administration Act, Cap 215, 2009 Rev. Ed. Sing.

[113] Section 17A(2), Supreme Court of Judicature Act, Cap 322, 2009 Rev. Ed. Sing.

[114] Section 35A, Administration of Muslim Law Act 1966, Act 27 of 1966, 2009 Rev. Ed. Sing; section 17 Supreme Court of Judicature Act, Cap 322, 2009 Rev. Ed. Sing.

[115] Adoption of Children Act, Cap 4, and generally, Abbas, n4, 163, 174.

[116] Rahman, n57, 415, 416.

[117] Abbas, n115.

[118] Sections 134, 135, 137 and 139, Administration of Muslim Law Act 1966, Act 27 of 1966, 2009 Rev. Ed. Sing.

In Australia, the Family Courts will apply Australian family law to disputes that come before it, regardless of the religion of the parties. When *mahr* provisions are raised in the context of a post-divorce property settlement, the Family Court will treat *mahr* either paid or deferred as part of the combined asset pool to be distributed in line with spousal and child maintenance needs and property distribution. Parties will usually try to work out these matters without recourse to litigation, but some do come to the Family Court for resolution. An interesting development in the intersection of Shari'ah law and common law arose recently when the courts in New South Wales had to determine whether a *mahr* provision should be enforced as a contractual term. The case of *Mohamed v Mohamed* [2012] NSWSC 852 gives insight into how the 'one law for all' approach plays out in Australian judicial thinking. Faced with paying his wife *mahr*, the appellant husband argued from an Australian law perspective that the marriage contract was contrary to Australian law on public policy grounds, or alternatively, that the issues involved the applicability of Islamic law which could only be determined by an Islamic law. The court held that *mahr* agreements could be enforced as long as they complied with the applicable Australian law of contract. The religious component in the contract did not make a case 'non-justiciable',[119] and the $50,000 *mahr* clause was an enforceable term of a contract in circumstances where the husband had initiated the separation and/or the divorce. If the wife initiated the separation or there was mutual agreement to do so, *mahr* was not payable. The court found that on the facts, the husband initiated the separation and he was ordered to make the payment. The case is significant because it shows that Australian courts will apply Australian law of contract, not Shari'ah family law, to decide such issues, even where the marital relationship was 'blessed by Islamic Sharia' – the phrase used in the Mohamed's marriage contract. Whether the outcome would be different if determined by a Shari'ah Court applying relevant Islamic principles was irrelevant. It should be noted, however, that the marriage contract in this case had expressly referred to Australian legislation regarding the couple's assets should their marriage end. If the contract had instead specified Islamic law rather than Australian property law, the outcome might have been different. The husband's submission that the Australian court lacked jurisdiction for matters involving Shari'ah law failed, thereby signalling that Australian courts will not cede jurisdiction because a religious

---

[119] Citing *Marcovitz v Bruker* [2007] 3 SCR 607 at [12–13]. Contra *Kaddoura v Hammoud* [1988] OJ No.5054 [24].

dimension is involved. Harrison AsJ cited Black and Sadiq's view that Shari'ah 'family law cannot be relegated exclusively to a religious tribunal, court or other body to apply and enforce as it is the right of all citizens to bring family matters to the courts of law for determination and have the general law of the land apply'.[120] That Australia does not deny a Muslim spouse the right to have a case heard in the civil court is an important feature of the Australian 'one law for all' system. When interviewed after the judgment, the wife said it was 'important for Muslim women to fight for their rights'.[121] Where a party believes a secular court may provide a better (depending on one's perspective) outcome, then he or she has a right to take that case to the courts for adjudication.

G. Unofficial versus Professional

In contrast to Australia's ad-hoc system, Singapore's model with a government-funded and government-regulated Shari'ah Court creates a professional and transparent body. Trials and hearings are open,[122] with the power given in section 46(2) for the court, if it thinks fit, to hold part or all of the proceeding in camera. This power is frequently exercised. Unlike in the common law courts, Shari'ah Court decisions are not formally reported and published, but there is an internal system of records which can be accessed by the legal representatives of the parties. This has allowed a kind of informal system of precedence to develop which facilitates consistency and predictability. Appeals are also possible. Decisions of both the Shari'ah Court and registrars can be taken on appeal to the Shari'ah Appeal Board.[123] This degree of transparency and appellate review are two important safeguards lacking in Australia's

---

[120] Ann Black and Kerrie Sadiq, 'Good and Bad Sharia: Australia's Mixed Response to Islamic Law' (2011) 17(1) *UNSW Law Journal* 383, 406 cited at *Mohamed v Mohamed* [2012] NSWSC 852 [49].

[121] N. Berkovic, 'NSW Court Tells Man to Pay Islamic Dowry' *The Australian*, 1 August 2012.

[122] Section 32(1), Administration of Muslim Law Act, Cap 3 2009 Rev. Ed. Sing. Sections 32 and 46, with the power given in section 46(2) for the court, if it thinks fit, to hold part or all of the proceeding in camera. This power is frequently exercised.

[123] Section 55, Administration of Muslim Law Act, Cap 3. The minimum number for the Appeal Board is seven. Currently there are 16 members: seven religious teachers, five district judges and four lawyers. Four of the members are women. Abbas, n115, 163, 185.

informal system.[124] In an unofficial system, if an individual or a group of Islamic scholars asserts that they have knowledge and authority to make determination on marriage, inheritance, divorce and financial matters, there are no reliable means to verify this. As hearings take place in private, without lawyers, and without recordings or transcripts, and as there is no formal appeal structure, it is not impossible to know if the reasoning and application of Shari'ah law is fair and accurate. Different outcomes on similar issues can occur. The Singapore model provides a superior system as there is oversight of legal decision making, consistency in application of law, with the added safeguard of an appeal process. Parties are entitled to legal representation 'by advocate or solicitor or by an agent, generally or specially authorized to do so by the Court'.[125] This does not exclude non-Muslim lawyers.[126] The Legal Aid Bureau can grant legal aid to litigants in the Shari'ah Court, when the means and merits requirements are met.

V. CONCLUSION

The legacies of colonial times still direct the nature and form of the legal systems in Singapore and Australia. The template laid down by the British colonial government has proven resilient for two centuries and seemingly retains the support of each government and its citizens. For Muslims in both countries, it has meant quite different things. Muslims in Australia have choices. Muslims in Singapore have certainty. Choice can be empowering but it can lead to uncertainty, vulnerability and disconnection from mainstream Australia. Certainty on the other hand can mean conformity with singular interpretation of Islam which can enhance a shared religious and ethnic identity. Australian Muslims are afforded the same relationship choices as other Australians: the decisions are theirs to make. Whether they marry or divorce according to Shari'ah law or Australian law, or both; whether they marry a non-Muslim, or marry

---

124 See Ann Black, 'Accommodating Shariah law in Australia. Can We? Should We?' (2008) 33(4) *Alternative Law Journal* 214, 217.

125 Sections 32(1) and 39, Administration of Muslim Law Act, Cap 3.

126 AMLA does not specify any qualifications or requirements for Shari'ah legal counsel. Ahmad Nizam Abbas notes that because there are no such mandated requirements or qualifications, legal counsel must find the 'motivation to equip oneself adequately' in Shari'ah law and procedure, and the onus lies with the individual lawyer to engage in self-study, attend courses and seek guidance from experienced practitioners. See Abbas, n115, 163, 181.

without a *wali*'s consent; whether they simply live together and raise a family outside of marriage, or enter a same-sex union; it is their choice. Singapore's Muslims do not have the same choices, but they have the certainty of knowing that the Shari'ah Court and registry are there to guide and sanction the relationships they enter and exit, in the assurance that as Muslims they are following the path laid down by their faith.

Whereas 'traditionalism' has been the hallmark of Singapore's jurisprudence,[127] Australia's eclectic Muslim population holds diverse jurisprudential and doctrinal allegiances ranging from 'liberal, progressive, modernist, reformist, secular at one end through to moderate, traditional, orthodox in the mid-range and to conservative, extremist, radical, literalist, neo-revivalist or fundamentalist at the other end'.[128] Given this pluralistic context, a formalised and officially recognised Shari'ah Court or Council in Australian would face practical obstacles in terms of the jurisprudence to be applied, the interpretative approach adopted, the persons entrusted with the role of adjudication, and how appointment, oversight and enforcement would occur. In Singapore these obstacles do not arise as it is a streamlined, professional, government-endorsed and legislatively sanctioned system.

The Singapore Constitution facilities the application of Shari'ah law whilst the Australian Constitution creates a significant obstacle to implementing a dual or plural regime based on religious affiliation. Governments in Australia continue to endorse the 'one law for all' approach, rejecting notions of legal pluralism or any formal mechanism to apply Shari'ah law, whilst the government in Singapore is committed to its dual system. Each of these multicultural and multi-religious nations is unwavering in support for the route being taken as the best way to bring about social cohesion and fairness for all.

---

[127] Traditionalism is discussed earlier but can be defined as 'a dogmatic attitude that clings firmly to old ways, resisting innovations or accepting them only unwittingly'. See Rahman, n57, 415, 416.

[128] Black and Sadiq, n120, 383, 386.

2. The application of *kafala* in the West

Kieran Mclean Eadie

Despite growing Muslim minority populations in many Western countries, one area where there has traditionally been seen to be a legal disconnect between those populations and their new countries is the area of adoption, or the similar but distinct concept known in Islam as '*kafala*'. The result of this disconnect is that despite the presence of millions of orphans in conflict zones or abject poverty in Muslim majority countries; Muslim minorities, despite their comparatively strong economic position, have not been able to assist to provide a home for these orphans. This inability to assist is due to legal and procedural barriers in relation to migration and perceived religious barriers, most of which are embedded in the historical international and state-based approaches to adoption and *kafala*, respectively.

The number of Muslim orphans in Afghanistan alone was thought to be more than 10 per cent of the population as of 2004,[1] or 1,800,000 people.[2] Based on the current disconnect, these children would be ineligible to be permitted to leave Afghanistan, even to families who are practising Muslims. Although non-government organisations do not regard foreign adoption as a real contributor to poverty in a country,[3] an arrangement permitting this (or a variant of this) would lead to a substantial improvement in the lives of those who were permitted to migrate and, importantly, would permit a minority group to be in a similar position as the broader community in matters of adoption.

This chapter seeks to analyse the current position both internationally and at the state level, and to look for possible areas for reform or international/state based concord to benefit orphans as well as to assess the merits of the idea that there are diametrically opposed views of 'adoption' between Western law and Muslim majority states. In doing so, it is useful to group the approaches to *Kafala* in several Muslim majority

[1] UNICEF, Children on the Brink, *A Joint Report of New Orphan Estimates and a Framework for Action* (2004), www.unicef.org/publications/index_22212.html 9 (accessed 4 May 2018).

[2] Ibid., 31.

[3] Ibid., 18.

states to identify possible states where a bilateral or multilateral approach may succeed whilst protecting all relevant interests and concerns.

This chapter builds upon the paper 'Islamic Law: Adoptions and *Kafalah*',[4] which analysed the then recent European Court of Human Rights decision (in *Harroudj*[5]) and considers recent *ijtihad* ('independent legal reasoning') on *kafala* from the Women's Shura Council to conclude there are possible opportunities for *kafala* in the West. The chapter will also incorporate 2013 developments including the Canadian decision to ban migration for children in *kafala* arrangements from Pakistan[6] and an Australian case.

I. WHAT IS *KAFALA*?

The Prophet, himself an orphan, called for a different approach to orphans than pre-Islamic Arabia, where children of conquered tribes or orphans were routinely taken and their true parentage denied, taking on the name of the new family.[7]

In its simplest form, *kafala* is providing support for an orphan, which can occur without merging the child into the existing family unit or co-residing;[8] the arrangement may be for a limited or unlimited period but in all cases is intended to provide 'all the privileges of being a Musalman'.[9] The issue of *kafala*, as with all aspects of family law, is 'of considerable interest to Islamic legal scholars[10] and there is discussion

---

4 Faisal Kutty, 'Islamic Law, Adoptions and Kafalah' on *Jurist Forum* (6 November 2012), http://jurist.org/forum/2012/11/faisal-kutty-adoption-kafalah.php (accessed 29 November 2013).

5 *Harroudj v France* (2009) 43631 Eur Court HR (Ser A) ('*Harroudj v France*').

6 Canadian Immigration and Citizenship Service Statutory Order, not yet gazetted, issued 1 July 2013, www.cic.gc.ca/english/department/media/notices/2013-07-01.asp (accessed 29 November 2013).

7 *Sahih Al-Bukhari* Hadith 7.25 narrated by Aisha Abu Hudhaifa bin Utba bin Rabi'a bin Abdi Shams. It was the custom in the pre-Islamic period that if somebody adopted a boy, the people would call him the son of the adoptive father and he would be the latter's heir.

8 Jamila Bargach, 'Personalizing it: Adoption, Bastardry, Kinship and Family' in James D Faubion (ed.), *The Ethics of Kinship: Ethnographic Inquiries* (Lanham, MD: Rowman and Littlefield 2001) 80, 81.

9 Ibid., 250.

10 'Family law is the only branch of human transaction which has received maximum attention in the fundamental law of Islam', Alamgiar Muhammad

both from the Qur'an and in Hadith that describe *kafala* as being a noble arrangement.

> If anyone strokes an orphan's head, doing so only for Allah's Sake, he will have blessings for every hair over which his hand passes[11] [and] if anyone treats well an orphan girl or boy under his care, he and I (Prophet Mohamed (saws)) shall be like these two in Paradise [putting two of his fingers together!].[12]

The arrangements are subject to restrictions on the creation of filial bonds or changing names of children,[13] and *kafala* adoptees are generally unable to inherit by right:

> Muslim law does not recognise adoption ... if a Muslim adopts a child in accordance with ... laws ... in ... any other country ... (and) his adopted father leaves assets in a ... Muslim country, he will not be entitled to inherit ... in spite of (the) legal adoption.[14]

Whether the *kafala* 'parent' can purport to enter a permanent arrangement depends on interpretation and varies from state to state. The traditional view is that adoption is anathema as it involves the permanent and absolute transfer of parental rights to adoptive parents, a denial of ancestry and falsifying of bloodlines[15] as well as removal of the child. However, many Muslim majority state-based approaches adopt a more nuanced and purposive approach to the issue of permanency, whilst others take a stricter approach. The challenge arises when approaches are reconciled with Western legal constructs of adoption. The main issues

---

Serajuddin, *Muslim Family Law, Secular Courts and Muslim Women of South Asia: A Study in Judicial Activism* (Pakistan: Oxford University Press 2011) 152.

[11] *Al-Tirmidhi* Hadith 4974, narrated by Abu Umamah, also Sahih Al-Bukhari Hadith 8.34 narrated by Sahl bin Sad.

[12] *Al-Tirmidhi* Hadith 4973, narrated by Abu Hurayrah: 'The best house among the Muslims is one which contains an orphan who is well treated, and the worst house among the Muslims is one which contains an orphan who is badly treated.'

[13] *The Holy Qur'an*, Sura 33.5. Call them (the children you have adopted) after their (real) fathers: doing so is more equitable in the sight of God. If you do not know who their fathers are, then (they are) your brothers in religion and your protégés.

[14] Zulfikarali C. Valiani, *Introduction to Muslim Laws* (Pakistan: Ahmed Brothers Printers, by Khwaja Printers and Publishers 1990) 38.

[15] Kerry O'Halloran, *The Politics of Adoption: International Perspectives on Law, Policy and Practice* (2nd ed.) (Germany: Springer 2009), 381 – Attachment 1.

(although not the only ones) arise due to lack of permanence where parents want to exercise full parental agency[16] and the main legal instruments have this requirement.

On this basis, the key areas of likely conflict with traditional Western constructs arise in the areas of the lawful physical removal of a child to another jurisdiction (migration), permanency (the severance of filial bonds/inability for the natural parent to 'undo' the arrangement), the changing of the child's names (creation of filial bonds) and matters of inheritance.

II. WESTERN CONSTRUCTS OF ADOPTION

The legal frameworks in Australia, France and Canada have been considered in this analysis due to their codified systems of law, sizable Muslim minorities and cases or policies on *kafala*. Pre-1960s adoption in a Western cultural and legal sense bore little analogy with Islamic *kafala*. Adoption was a full and permanent arrangement resulting in severance of ties with the birth family, a name change and withholding information regarding the true parentage. Since the 1960s, Western adoption has, through its own processes and evolution, become more closely aligned to key tenets of Islamic *kafala*. This convergence has not been recognised in state-based or international law approaches, with Muslim minorities largely legally unable to bring children, even orphans, to the West from their country of origin or from other Muslim majority states.

Australia provides a practical example of the changes in the law and conceptions of adoption over the past 30 years. During the 1950s and 1960s, when the number of adoptions in Australia were at their peak, adoptions were generally 'closed'; an adopted child's original birth certificate was sealed forever and an amended birth certificate was issued that established the child's new identity and relationship with their adoptive family.[17] During the 1980s, an adoption reform movement lobbied for and achieved progressive legislative reform across Australian states and territories, including the 'opening' of closed adoption.[18]

---

16 Ibid.

17 Daryl Higgins, 'Adoption: Past Policy, Reform, and its Lingering Effects' (2013) 5 *Australian Social Policy Association Report*, Sydney, 1.

18 Marian Quartly, Shurlee Swain, Denise Cuthbert, Amy Pollard, Kathy Lothian and Nell Musgrove, 'History of Adoption in Australia: A four-year Research Project (2009–12)' (2010) 2 (2) *Australian Journal of Adoption* 1.

The result of this is that Australian family law at present is fairly accommodating of the needs of the Muslim community,[19] and 'this enables Muslims to comply with both Shari'ah and Australian law',[20] with the focus on the best interests of the child;[21] a child's 'given name or names, identity, language and cultural and religious ties should, as far as possible, be identified and preserved'.[22]

Despite the fact that only one Muslim majority country is a signatory to the Hague Convention on Intercountry Adoption, Adoption NSW has engaged in a unique process of community engagement, promoting to Muslim communities that NSW law now permits retention of cultural ties and retention of name. Other Australian jurisdictions now also emphasise the importance of children and young people growing up with a 'clear sense of identity ... through "open" adoption practices (and) some ongoing facilitated contact between adopted children ... and ... their birth family'.[23] Despite these changes, it remains that NSW law does result in severance of the legal relationship between the parent and child, and children will obtain inheritance rights subject to the usual legal processes.[24]

The approach to *kafala* more generally was considered in research conducted by the European Court of Human Rights in relation to the *Harroudj* case. This case categorised the Western approaches based on the choice of law rules applied in relation to adoption and identified four approaches to *kafala* arrangements, including:[25]

- preference to the forum state where adoption takes place;
- preference to the adoptees national law;
- preference to the adopter's national law; or
- a cumulative approach.

---

[19] Ann Black and Kerrie Sadiq, 'Good and Bad Sharia: Australia's Mixed Response to Islamic Law' (2011) 34 (1) *University of New South Wales Law Journal*, Sydney, 398.

[20] 'Muslims in Australia can and do adhere to Sharia in matters of family law' ibid., 398.

[21] Adoption Act 2000 (NSW) s(1)(a).

[22] Ibid., s(1)(e).

[23] Adoption (Amendment) Bill 2009 explanatory statement – Legislative Assembly for the Australian Capital Territory – 2009.

[24] 'Mandatory Written Information on Adoption; Information for Parents of a Child in Out-of-home Care' – NSW Department of Family and Community Services, January 2016, p. 3 – http://www.facs.nsw.gov.au/?a=331619 (accessed 20 April 2018)).

[25] *Harroudj v France* at 22.

Of the 22 states studied, nine states were found to have no theoretical obstacles to recognition of *kafala*;[26] however, some of this group had administrative burdens above and beyond general law on adoption.[27] No Western state sought to draw analogy between *kafala* and adoption, and France, for example, had a system similar to Tunisia and Turkey (and to a lesser extent, Morocco) by permitting care arrangements with a view to permanency and potential for citizenship.[28] Unless a minor is born or usually resides in France, adoption may not take place unless the personal law of the child permits this to occur;[29] this is a system intended to reflect comity between France and Algeria in such matters.[30] These similarities are discussed further below and provide a fertile climate for a revision of the prospects for use of international instruments or comity based bilateral agreements to bring children (particularly orphans) from Muslim-majority countries to reside with minority communities.

This issue arose in 2012 in the European Court of Human Rights when the issues of *kafala* and French domestic law was considered in a case that to deny adoption to a child brought to France under a *kafala* arrangement was to breach article 8 of the Convention[31] (a denial of family life). An Algerian child under a *kafala* arrangement in the care of a French woman of Algerian descent was allowed by Algerian authorities to migrate under the auspices of *kafala* with the child complying with French law upon entry. A primary issue was whether the French courts had been correct in denying a domestic adoption and finding analogy between Algerian Kafala and Adoption. The court applied a broad margin of appreciation in light of the diverse approaches by member states in the aforementioned comparative law study,[32] and found the decision was not contrary to state law or internal public order,[33] accepting *kafala* as a mode of alterative care that did not infringe on the family life of the child. Kutty states the decision meant 'Kafalah was fully accepted in

---

26 Belgium, Denmark, Finland, Greece, Ireland, the Netherlands, the United Kingdom, Sweden and Switzerland (Australia, France and Canada did not form part of the survey).

27 Ibid., n25.

28 Ibid., at 48.

29 Civil Code of the Republic of France 1950 (France) arts 370–3.

30 See n27 at 34.

31 Convention for the Protection of Human Rights and Fundamental Freedoms, open for signature 14 October 1950, CETS 005 (entered into force 03 September 1953).

32 See n27 at 48.

33 *Harroudj v France*.

French law'[34] and that *Harroudj* was 'not deprived of any rights in not being allowed to change the kafalah to adoption'.[35]

Whether this case is truly a watershed is not yet known; however, that comity is relevant, that a wide margin of appreciation is applied and that all considerations will be balanced with the interests of the child affected are important outcomes of the case. Critically the court did not see the child's interests were adversely affected by the arrangement and took the view that such arrangements in accordance with originating state law can be sufficient.

Although the above issues appear to provide a positive impression of the prospects for *kafala*, 2013 interactions between Pakistan and Canada changed the position somewhat. Until June 2013, Canada had considered *kafala* sufficient for migration, with the ability then to convert the arrangement into adoption. In July 2013, Citizenship and Immigration Canada issued a notice discontinuing this practice in relation only to Pakistan:

> Pakistani law allows for guardianship of children, but does not recognise our concept of adoption. Proceeding with further such placements would violate Canada's obligations under The Hague Convention on Protection of Children and Co-operation in Respect of Intercountry Adoption.[36]

The decision was widely criticised by the minority Pakistani Muslim community in Canada.[37] Although the decision turned on the law of Pakistan, it will likely have implications for other *kafala* arrangements not purporting to be analogous to adoption. The Canadian decision was made relying on a combination of comity and international law, namely that:

> … legal and procedural requirements to obtain a guardianship certificate under Pakistan's Guardians and Wards Act do not allow for subsequent adoption in the guardian's country of residence (and) Pakistan applies the Islamic system of Kafala, or guardianship, which neither terminates the birth

---

[34] Kutty, above n4.

[35] Kutty, above n4.

[36] Canadian Statutory Order, above n6.

[37] Glenn Johnson (Immigration spokesman) in Keung, Nicolas 'Canada Ban on Pakistani Adoption Baffles Parents' (2013), *Toronto Star* (5 August 2013), www.thestar.com/news/canada/2013/08/05/canadas_ban_on_pakistani_adoptions_baffles_parents_clerics.html (accessed 4 May 2018).

parent-child relationship nor grants full parental rights to the new guardian. This means that there are … legal incompatibilities.[38]

The Islamic Foundation of Toronto[39] argued differences around adoption are accommodated in Canada with a bequest to an adopted child available and a name change possible as long as there is no lying about the filial bond.[40] Contrary to the French comity-based view, the Canadians have taken the view that the intercountry adoption framework is unable to support *kafala* and demonstrate that a notional lack of permanency can be fatal to the prospects for any proposed solution. Any scope for reform and accommodation will inevitably lie at the periphery of both systems rather than at the strictest degree of approaches.

III. ISLAMIC COUNTRIES, SYSTEMS OF LAW AND TREATMENT OF *KAFALA*

An analysis of *kafala* across the Islamic world is necessarily constrained by uncodified systems of law, widely divergent legal approaches and the necessity to group approaches roughly based on their potential to be amenable to practical arrangements or agreement being put in place. Domestic approaches range from refusal to permit removal of children or recognise analogy between *kafala* and adoption to acceptance of Western conceptions of adoption with safeguards on children drawn from *kafala*: 'most states (apart from Tunisia) continue to disallow disaffiliative legal adoption, although some … regulate the established institution of *Kafala* to formalise and regulate covenants of care.'[41]

The issue and suitability of either international or state based comity solutions are further complicated by the prevalence of informal local arrangements where 'most domestic adoptions are first party informal care arrangements … not necessarily endorsed by court orders',[42] and

---

38 Ibid.

39 Imam Yusuf Badat in Keung, Nicolas 'Canada Ban on Pakistani Adoption Baffles Parents' *Toronto Star* (5 August 2013), www.thestar.com/news/canada/2013/08/05/canadas_ban_on_pakistani_adoptions_baffles_parents_clerics.html (accessed 4 May 2018).

40 Nicolas Keung, 'Canada Ban on Pakistani Adoption Baffles Parents, Clerics' *Toronto Star*, www.thestar.com/news/canada/2013/08/05/canadas_ban_on_pakistani_adoptions_baffles_parents_clerics.html (accessed 4 May 2018).

41 Ibid., 437.

42 O'Halloran, above n15, 397 – Attachment 1.

even formal arrangements are generally with a minimum of formality.[43] This is especially the case in countries with a system of Islamic law (generally strict Shari'ah or Shari'ah-compliant countries) where Saudi Arabia and Afghanistan apply a strict local Shari'ah approach to *kafala*, whilst Egypt, despite codification, has the same ultimate law with minor differences. This strict Shari'ah approach contrasts with other Muslim majority countries such as Turkey and Tunisia, which have intermediate approaches combining elements of traditional *kafala* with Western and international constructs where these are consistent with their purposive or locally appropriate approaches.

There are four categories of Muslim Majority approach to *kafala*:[44]

- strict Shari'ah or Shari'ah-compliant codified model;
- post-colonial pragmatists with varying judicial controls;
- permitting adoption via a purposive approach and influence of *'urf*; and
- signatories with characteristics of the above groups.

In terms of numbers, according to Bargach, at present only Moroccan children are routinely adopted; otherwise, 'the international placement of children under *Kafala* remains rare, or even non-existent, except for nationals living abroad (apart from) individual cases'.[45] However, the evidence does suggest that a number have in the past migrated from Pakistan to Canada (this is now on hold indefinitely).

A. Strict Shari'ah or Shari'ah-compliant Codified Model – No Recognition, No Clarity, No Flexibility

Muslim majority states such as Saudi Arabia and Afghanistan maintain there is no analogy between *kafala* and adoption, and will not permit the removal of the child from the country. Egypt has a similar but slightly more nuanced approach.

---

43 Ibid., 387 – Attachment 1.

44 Jamila Bargach, *Orphans of Islam: Family, Abandonment, and Secret Adoption in Morocco* (USA: Rowman & Littlefield 2002). Bargach grouped approaches to *kafala*; I acknowledge this idea but have developed my own categories based on a different approach and analysis of the categories and current state.

45 Bargach, above n44, 304.

In Saudi Arabia, 'Qur'anic revelation and detailed judicial texts (with an) intend to cover all aspects of life'.[46] Although there is a basic law, the legal system relies upon a 'traditional corpus of Islamic law, Fiqh, to an extent unequalled by any other existing national legal system',[47] permitting only a literalist interpretation of the Qur'an and discouraging 'innovation'. Accordingly, cases and authority on *kafala* is rare. As a result, although there are few cases or works on how laws of *kafala* would be interpreted, this is further complicated by the fact that arrangements are often informal amongst family members. Secondary sources such as foreign missions (for example, the British in the country) have confirmed this strict interpretation (an effective ban on 'adoption') that 'local law does not allow the adoption of children by foreigners'.[48]

In Afghanistan, although civil law is formally present (with *Hanafi Fiqh* filling most gaps[49] except on judicial divorce[50]), in practice a combination of Islamic law mixed with custom (*'urf*) still governs many day-to-day interactions with law 'shaped by … Hanafi law on the one hand and the conservative male dominated tradition of the tribes on the other'.[51]

In matters of *kafala*, the civil law provides for the provision of care with the court to intervene[52] having regard to the interest of the child. Persons providing care for orphaned children do so 'either free(ly) … or give the child to charity',[53] and the care period is per Hanafi

[46] Heidi Hirvonen, *Christian-Muslim Dialogue: Perspectives of Four Lebanese Thinkers* (Leiden: Brill 2012) 256.

[47] Frank E. Vogel 'The Complementarity of Ifta and Qada: Three Saudi Fatwas on Divorce' in Muhammad Khalid Masud, Brinkley Messick and David S. Powers (eds) *Islamic Legal Interpretation: Muftis and Their Fatwas* (1st ed.) (Cambridge, MA: Harvard University Press 1995) 262.

[48] UK Foreign & Commonwealth Office, 'Living in Saudi Arabia the essential regulations, laws and social customs you need to understand when living in Saudi Arabia' (undated), www.gov.uk/living-in-saudi-arabia (accessed 29 November 2013).

[49] Ibid., 158.

[50] Ibid., 158, where *Maliki Fiqh* is dominant due to its relative dynamism.

[51] Mohammad Hashim Kamali, *Law in Afghanistan: A study of the Constitutions, Matrimonial Law and the Judiciary* (Leiden: E.J Brill Publishing 1985) 158.

[52] Civil Code of Afghanistan 5 January 1977 (Afghanistan) [Afghanistan Rule of Law Project, 2006] official Gazette No.353, art. 242.

[53] Ibid., art. 246.

jurisprudence.[54] Importantly, a carer take cannot take a child on any journey.[55]

In Egypt, as in Saudi Arabia and Afghanistan, there is no legal concept of adoption. Instead, *kafala* permits a care arrangement wherein the 'foster parent protects, feeds, clothes, teaches and loves him or her as her own without attributing the child to him but also without giving him the rights which are reserved under Shari'ah for the natural child'.[56]

There has been no publicly available information on legal change following the Arab Spring, but the approach is codified and very conservative,[57] and in the context of other legislative priorities it is unlikely there has been change with the current system, 'a long, labyrinthine process set up by the Ministry of Social Affairs'.[58]

In Egypt, reforms took place in relation to inheritance, permitting an orphan to inherit in the place of their parent should the latter pass away, 'subject to the traditional limit of 1/3'.[59] However, this does not apply to non-related children,[60] who are denied inheritance rights.[61]

In light of this, the system is in many ways less generous than that based on *'urf* (custom), which would have some level of pragmatism at a local level to accommodate circumstances. Egypt's resistance to any form of adoption initially resulted in reservations (now withdrawn) being made to articles 20 and 21 of the Convention on the Rights of the Child, despite that convention permitting and legitimising *kafala*.[62] One interesting deviation from Saudi Arabia and Afghanistan is that Egypt allows

---

54 Ibid., arts 249 and 250.

55 Ibid., art. 253.

56 Kerry O'Halloran, above n15, 385.

57 International Reference Centre for the Rights of Children Deprived of their Family, Fact Sheet number 51, *Kafala*, www.crin.org/docs/Kafalah.BCN.doc (accessed 29 November 2013).

58 Anthony Fontes and Faye Wanchic, 'Beloved Outcasts' (2004) *Cairo Times* (25 March) 25–31.

59 Noel J. Coulson, 'A Comparison of the Law of Succession in the Islamic and British Legal Systems' (1977) 26 (2) *The American Journal of Comparative Law* 232.

60 Ibid.

61 UNIFEM, 'Progress of Arab Women', *Social Security and Social Welfare* (2004), www.wunrn.com/2006/12/progress-of-arab-women-2004 32 (accessed 4 May 2018).

62 International Bureau for Children's Rights, *Making Children's Rights Work in North Africa: Country Profiles on Algeria, Egypt, Libya, Morocco and Tunisia* (March 2007), www.ibcr.org/editor/assets/thematic_report/1/cp_north_africa_rev13august2007_en.pdf 49 ('Making Children's Rights Work in North Africa') (accessed 4 May 2018).

foster parents to change the child's name through the court[63] for foundlings or those of unknown parentage. This is done through a process managed by the Ministry of Social Affairs, which has integrated 2,500 abandoned children into host families.[64]

Although the naming and inheritance issue runs counter to the other strict Shari'ah adherents, and interestingly is rare in Muslim-majority states, the naming is only for those whose names are unknown and inheritance only for relatives. Therefore, on balance, considering that Egypt does not allow the child to go abroad, does not permit an unrelated orphan to inherit and applies a labyrinthine process, that country falls in practical terms into the strict Shari'ah group.

The strict Shari'ah group is characterised by inconsistent application of rules on moving the child outside of the jurisdiction and on matters of permanency, inheritance and name changes (except Egypt, to a limited degree) with some matters decided at the village or local level. This rigidity on one hand and uncertainty on the other hand means that few analogies can be drawn between Western and strict Shari'ah constructs. None of these systems represent a formal or consistent system of law that would be readily analogised with any expectations of the Western system of law, and therefore no agreement, either international or bilateral, is likely to be effective in permitting Muslim minorities to bring a child to the West from these jurisdictions under the auspices of *kafala*.

This fundamental incompatibility is confirmed by US Department of State advice that there is no adoption in Saudi Arabia[65] with US law, as a comparator, requiring the adoption be irrevocable[66] and a purported Saudi 'adoption' considered insufficient for US migration purposes. NGOs working in Egypt have confirmed that the situation is similar in practice,[67] whilst ineffective and inconsistent governance in Afghanistan continues to make any consistent system or rule of law impossible on a national level.

---

63 Above n57, 32.

64 United Nations Office on Drugs and Crime, *Street Children Report* (2001), www.unodc.org/pdf/youthnet/egypt_street_children_ report.pdf 30 (accessed 4 May 2018).

65 Passport USA Inter-country Adoption Information – www.passportsusa.com/family/adoption/country/country_445.html (accessed 29 November 2013).

66 Immigration and Nationality Act 8 USC § 1101 §101(b)(F) (1996).

67 International Reference Centre for the Rights of Children Deprived of their Family, fact sheet number 51, *Kafala*, www.crin.org/docs/Kafalah.BCN.doc (accessed 29 November 2013).

B. Post-colonial Pragmatists

Countries such as Morocco and Pakistan have certain conditions before *kafala* can take place and arguably do not reject international migration outright, so long as it is preceded by a period of care and control in that country, with approaches derived from a combination of custom, Islam and colonial law. The practice (Morocco) and law (Pakistan) is that the child and parent must be the same religion, and the system in both is similar to Western countries, with close safeguards on the care assessment of the attributes of the parents. The dominant concern is the best interests of the child.

The Pakistani system of guardianship represents a legal hybrid between a common law system and Islamic rules through the vehicle of guardianship which permits a solution for orphans within general constructs of traditional *kafala*. Adoption as such is not governed by any law in Pakistan according to the Pakistani government, but it is also not officially prohibited. Despite this, rights apart from inheritance are protected through a *kafala*-style regime via the Guardians and Wards Act 1890.[68] This act may allow a child to be in the permanent care of a family. Article 7 permits any person to be made guardian of a minor[69] and the law overrides Shari'ah.[70] Safeguards intended to protect the key interests of *kafala* include a provision that the court may not appoint a guardian in the cases where the father is alive and not unfit to take on that role.

O'Halloran provides an overview of the judicial process in Pakistan:

> Applicants … seek a guardianship order in respect of an orphan or foundling … will be assessed by government officials (in) the form of a home study report accompanied by the usual references and an assessment of their eligibility and suitability to provide a home environment likely to safeguard

---

[68] Office for the UN High Commissioner of Human Rights. 'Reply to List of Issues: Pakistan: 24 January 1994; article 21', www.unhchr.ch/tbs/doc.nsf/(Symbol)/72953ec731e640b1c1256363004a5c29?Opendocument, attachment 2 (accessed 29 November 2013). It does not mean that adoption is literally prohibited in Pakistan. Children in especial circumstances are placed under the guardianship of their near relatives or suitable person appointed by the court. In that case the children do not automatically adopt the parentage of their guardians. They will legally enjoy all social and economic rights except for inheritance of property from their guardian.

[69] The Guardians and Wards Act 1890 (Pakistan) (no VIII), Attachment 4.

[70] West Pakistan Muslim Personal Law (Shariat) Application Act 1962 (Pakistan) (No.V), s2.

> the welfare of the child … if approved … they will be vested with custody and guardianship rights. If the child's parents are known … they … enter into an irrevocable, bilateral, intra-familial agreement in writing in which the birth parent/s clearly waive any right to reclaim their child.[71]

Such a determination or agreement may include where a child will ordinarily reside.[72]

Regarding the matter of inheritance, once relatively progressive laws permitting orphaned grandchildren a share of an estate came under attack in 2000 from the Pakistani federal Shari'ah court[73] and the current status appears to indicate that laws on inheritance do not permit orphaned grandchildren (and presumably *kafala* children) to inherit.

Kafala matters have, however, been decided in favour of adopting parents in the courts, although precedents are scant and often turned on the facts. In *Mst. Irfana Shaheen v Abid Waheed*,[74] two separate cases of custody of adopted children were considered. In the first case, the spouses 'adopted' a female child, aged a month and a half. After divorce, the foster father forcibly took custody. The foster mother claimed custody as 'the man could have no special or preferential right over the woman to retain custody'. On the face of it this was a custody decision; however, the court went further and observed that 'the welfare of the child at this stage would also demand that he/she should remain in the custody of the female partner of adoption'.[75] The second case pertained to a newborn orphan. The court decided the person who found the adopted child would have 'the exclusive right to … custody … and no private person except the … real parent would have the right to deprive her of its custody'.[76]

The traditional view has been that as long as the child is brought up as a Muslim, the court will agree to such arrangements (*kafala*, knowing it may lead to adoption elsewhere) and will give permission for the child to

---

71 O'Halloran, above n15, 387.

72 *Mst. Irfana Shaheen v Abid Waheed*, PLD 2002 Lah. 283 in Alamgiar Muhammad Serajuddin, above n10, 152: 'the holy Qur'an … has left open to the court to determine and give the status of Wali to a person to secure the welfare of minor in case of dispute.'

73 Lucy Carroll, 'The Pakistan Federal Shariat Court, Section 4 of the Muslim Family Law Ordinance, and the orphaned grandchild' (2001) 9 (1) *Islamic Law and Society Journal* 73–5.

74 *Mst. Irfana Shaheen v Abid Waheed*, PLD 2002 Lah. 283.

75 Serajuddin, above n10, 152.

76 Serajuddin, above n10, 153.

leave the country.[77] So established are the 'guardianship' *kafala* arrangements in the country that 'where there is not enough money to support a child the shortfall may be borne by the Zakat and Asher fund'.[78]

This established system has recently become less certain, with Pakistan raising objections with Canada on the basis that intercountry adoption from Pakistan is inconsistent with the laws of Pakistan.[79] Canada acceded to this request and stopped all visas for Pakistani children under *kafala* arrangements, stating:

> As a signatory to The Hague Convention on Protection of Children and Co-operation in Respect of Intercountry Adoption (Hague Convention), Canada has committed to adhering to principles designed to encourage cooperation between countries and mutual respect for state laws in order to best support the protection of children.[80]

A similar regulation was signed by the then Minister for Immigration and Border Protection in Australia in 2015, with the result that applications for adoption visas from Pakistan cannot be accepted.[81]

Notwithstanding the above, Pakistani law in principle permits the removal of the child as long as the best interests have been taken into account and robust procedures followed to ensure child welfare. Like Western systems, the arrangement can in practice be permanent within country, with the law silent on matters of naming. Inheritance is one issue where there are disconnects between Western and Pakistani requirements, with a *kafala* child not able to inherit their share of the estate.

Although the Pakistani approach gives a theoretical framework for analysis and significant hope for comity-based arrangements as the irrevocable deed is unique in Muslim-majority countries, given the uncertainty of the approach at present in Pakistan between the formal law and the strong views of the government, it would be unwise to commence any arrangement for the removal of children until legal clarity arises

---

77 Werner Menski, in K. O'Halloran, above n15, 385.

78 *Mst. Irfana Shaheen v Abid Waheed*, PLD 2002 Lah. 283 in Alamgiar Muhammad Serajuddin, above n10, 152.

79 Milica New – Ministry of Children and Youth Services 2 July 2013 MEMORANDUM TO: All prospective adoptive parents of children from Pakistan – www.ontarioadoptions.com/DynamicData/AttachedDocs/2013-06-28%20-%20memo%20to%20adoptive%20parents.pdf (accessed 6 July 2014).

80 Ibid.

81 Migration Regulations 1994 – Specification of Arrangements for Child Visa Applications 2015 – IMMI 15/136 – www.legislation.gov.au/Details/F2015L01963 (accessed 9 January 2018).

around the status of such children. In particular, it needs to be clearer whether such removal will be sanctioned through government processes and take place with appropriate safeguards.

Morocco, like Pakistan, represents a melding of the pre-existing colonial era adoption and Islamic precepts. Abandoned children are treated in accordance with the rules of *kafala*[82] and, similar to what happens in Western countries, can be provided with a new family environment and long-term guardians. The court may also permit removal of the child on strict conditions. However, the Moroccan system differs from Western constructs, as it is robust in its rejection of any conception that suggests filial links can be established by any form of legal process or of any analogy between *kafala* and legal adoption,[83] and the rules do not create legal inheritance rights for the child.[84]

Despite some important differences, the codification of *kafala* has provided safeguards for children and clarity to Moroccans and expatriates, particularly from the Moroccan diaspora seeking to enter into a *kafala* arrangement in relation to a child. The Moroccan Ministry of Justice and Freedoms has released a guide explaining the policy precepts and implications. *Kafala* is only available to those who meet strict criteria requiring sound finances and character, with arrangement available for Muslim couples, Muslim women and community institutions.

In practical terms, a non-Moroccan family can present the same dossier to the ministry as a Moroccan family, with requirements as to religion but not nationality. *Kafala* may occur in two situations: either by consent of the parents or by a judicial order for an orphan.[85] There is a time period of around a month and a half from meeting the child to requesting *kafala* and taking the child outside the country.[86] The only requirement in terms of departing is that the child must have the right to enter the other country and there must be an undertaking of care suitable for a Moroccan judge,[87] including that the child will have a stable legal environment in that country.[88]

---

[82] *Making Children's Rights Work in North Africa* above n62, 125.

[83] *Moudawana* [the family code] (Morocco) 5 February 2004, art.149.

[84] *Making Children's Rights Work in North Africa* above n62, 125.

[85] Guernica Facundo Vericat 'Adoption of fostering? The case of Morocco' (speech to the adoption federation, 2006), www.ciimu.org/webs/forum internacional/pdf_ngl_abstract/facundo_ngl.pdf (accessed 29 November 2013).

[86] Ibid.

[87] Ibid., 32.

[88] Ibid., 32–3.

The law was amended in the last decade to conform to obligations under the United Nations Convention on Children's Rights.[89] Morocco has also signed the 'Child Protection Convention'. It was through a similar arrangement (from Algeria) that the *Harroudj* case arose.[90]

Pakistan and Morocco represent a balance between outright rejection of all Western precepts and providing safeguards for the migration of children, including a period of care before arrangements are formalised. Both restrict *kafala* to Muslims and deny inheritance or the establishment of filial links, although this is likely of little consequence, as *kafala* is only available to Muslims who would be likely to adhere to these tenets regardless. Importantly, both reference strongly the best interests of the child, and consider the character and means of the parent with wording similar to the Western system of adoption.

C. Permitting Adoption via a Purposive Approach and Influence of *'Urf*

Tunisia is a Muslim majority state with a codified system of law in relation to *kafala* and a permissive approach to full adoption almost analogous to Western adoption. It is one of the few Islamic-majority countries (with Turkey and Indonesia) to permit disaffiliative adoption in a legal and formal sense. Tunisia is unique in the Islamic world as its tiered approach to adoption arose through a pragmatic approach to economic malaise as well as incorporation of local cultural practice into law (*'urf*).

Originally much of the Islamic family law was derived from *'urf*, with states 'retain(ing) a residual affiliation with pre-Islam(ic) culture and practice which does not always fit comfortably with Islamic law'.[91] Local customs are seen in Hadiths and 'the history of the Islamic legal tradition (is an) encounter between Shari'ah and the different regional customs',[92] 'systematised and Islamicised by ... early scholar-jurists (with) discontinuity and mutation ... necessitated by geographic and temporal

---

89 *Making Children's Rights Work in North Africa* above n62, 109.

90 Ministry of Justice and Freedoms Procedures in Family Justice 2004 (Morocco) [Ministry of Justice and Freedoms], http://adala.justice.gov.ma/production/Guides_Manuels/fr/PlaquetteANG.pdf 32 (accessed 29 November 2013).

91 O'Halloran, above n15, 379.

92 Shabanam Ayman, *Custom in Islamic Law and Legal Theory: The development of the Concepts of 'Urf and 'Adah in the Islamic Legal Tradition* (Palgrave MacMillan Publishing, 1st ed., 2010) 3.

changes'.[93] The acceptance of adoption in the Tunisia can be viewed in this context, with social change and local historical and cultural conditions creating an approach to adoption that differs substantially from other Muslim-majority approaches.

Tunisian adoption law contains no nationality or religious requirements, although judges have held adoptive parents must be Muslim and 'a rational male or female, married, ethical, healthy … and able to look after the affairs of the adoptee (and that) the age difference … must be at least 15 years'.[94] The law 'concerning public guardianship, unofficial tutorship and adoption' was regarded as a cardinal achievement and a major breakthrough for Tunisia,[95] and 'by 1994, three quarters of children leaving orphanages were adopted'.[96]

The law was not a colonial adaptation, but formed organically due to needs of children post-independence in the absence of established care structures. In 1955/56, during an extremely cold winter resulting in the deaths of many children across Tunisia,[97] civil society was activated to respond and infant care became a priority. The decision to permit adoption was made at the time not only considering giving children a better life, but life itself.[98] It was also a combined example of *'urf*, as a local custom that 'families preferred to establish a filial link as a result of the maximalist attitude of families desiring, a real filiative link'.[99] As such, the law not only permitted adoption but emphasised the necessity of treating the adoptee as if they were the actual son or daughter of the adopter. This law has not yet been revoked following the Arab Spring. Chapter 6 of the Tunisian Civil Code states that the adoptee has all the civil rights resulting from lineage, including the adopter's last name and inheritance.[100] Safeguards in the system include a tutorship and care agreement being translated into adoption, permitting a period of trial care prior to formal adoption.

---

93 Ebrahim Moosa, 'Social Change' (2008) in Andrew Rippin (ed.) *Islamic World* (Routledge 2008) 571–2.

94 The Tunisian Civil Code 4 March 1958 (Tunisia) No.58-27, arts 8–16.

95 Committee on the Rights of the Child, *Initial Reports of State Parties, 1994: Tunisia, Intercountry Adoption Information Portfolio* (1 June 1994) UN Doc.CRC/C/11/Add.2., www.unicefirc.org/portfolios/documents/189_tunisia.htm para 130 (accessed 4 May 2018).

96 Ibid., 134.

97 Ibid., 131.

98 Ibid., 132.

99 Ibid., 134–5.

100 Civil Code of Tunisia 4 March 1958 (Tunisia) Law No.58-27, Chapter 6.

Historically, foreigners could adopt, but this was abolished in 1996 when Tunisia signed the United Nations Convention on the Rights of the Child in which article 8 requires 'state parties respect the right of the child to preserve his or her identity, including nationality, name, and family relations as recognised by law'.[101] As will be discussed below, this protection of cultural heritage is now embedded into most Western constructs of adoption.

This is a uniquely local approach to *kafala* which can be distinguished from the colonial pragmatists as it is an organic Tunisian law and reflects local custom, with filial bonds established and a child having full rights of inheritance after a period of *kafala*.

Although Tunisia has banned foreign adoptions based on an interpretation of its international obligations, in practice, many Western countries have substantial safeguards to protect and guard the issues, such as culture and language, that were of concern to Tunisia in banning such adoptions. On this basis, and considering the difference in Tunisia's approach to other Muslim-majority states, there appears to be a high degree of potential for comity-based arrangements to facilitate adoption by the Tunisian diaspora abroad.

D. Signatories – Turkey

Adoption in Turkey is subject to codified law.[102] Unique amongst Muslim-majority countries, Turkey is a signatory to the Hague Intercountry Adoption Convention.[103] Despite this, the Turkish model is not far different from that applied in Morocco, and has similarities to the Tunisian tiered *kafala* to the adoption approach practised by all but the strict Shari'ah adherents. The Turkish approach does not ignore but instead incorporates aspects of *kafala* into an international process.

In terms of process, a legal determination is made on an application[104] for a temporary caring arrangement for one year, with surveillance and

---

[101] Convention on the Rights of the Child, opened for signature 20 November 1989, UNTS 1577 (entered into force 2 September 1990), art. 8.

[102] Turkish Civil Code, 22 November 2001 (Turkey) arts 305–20 and the statute titled 'Execution of Interventions Regarding Adoption' based on Council of Ministers Decision No.2009/14729.

[103] The Hague Intercountry Adoption Convention has also been enforceable in Turkey since 1 September 2004.

[104] The 'General Directorate of Social Services and Protection of Children' (Social Services), Turkish Civil Code dated 22 November 2001 (Turkey), art. 320.

monitoring every three months. After the one-year period, a court will consider the final evaluation from the directorate and may issue a decision[105] permitting adoption. If the applicant is a foreigner from a Convention country, they are required to obtain approval from their competent authority.

As a result of Turkey signing the Convention,[106] the usual procedures under the relevant conventions are available for adoption to Western countries. However, unlike many Western models, Turkey incorporates *kafala* into the initial stages of its domestic adoption process, and permanent adoption occurs only after a *kafala*-like relationship has been established for a period, and with the court's and ministries' approval. Turkey provides an instructive example of the possible alternative approaches for countries around *kafala* to balance internal religious requirements and engage in the relevant international instrumentalities. Although signing the convention is not a practical prospect for many Muslim-majority states, it does provide an instructive example of a palatable set of procedural safeguards that could be emulated.

To sum up, most countries require either in practice or in law for the parents to be Muslim, and most prefer the name to remain the same and do not permit inheritance. Most will permit the removal of the child, and all apart from the strict Shari'ah group refer explicitly to the best interests of the child and the capacity of the parent to maintain the child and the child's care arrangements, and consider if the parents are of good moral character as defined in each state.

Although of the countries analysed only Tunisia and Turkey allow a relationship to be created and inheritance to occur, most Muslim majority states have '(unique) laws (which) regulate the established institution of *Kafala* to formalise and regulate covenants of care'.[107] On this basis, there is considerable scope to identify possible areas for comity-based arrangements. These arrangements seem most promising in states that have adopted a 'post-colonial pragmatist' or 'permitting adoption via a purposive approach and influence of *Urf*" approach to *kafala* where many of the attributes are similar or identical to the approaches for adoption in Western states.

---

105 Turkish Civil Code, 22 November 2001 (Turkey), art. 316.

106 Hague Intercountry Adoption Convention enforceable in Turkey since 1 September 2004.

107 Welchman, below n120, p. 437.

IV. AN INTERNATIONAL LAW SOLUTION?

Any proposal that would look to move children over international borders should first look to the possibilities of using international instrumentalities already in place and adapted to fit, as mentioned above the Canadian example already shows some of the challenges in doing this. At present, there is a clear lack of analogy between *kafala* and adoption in international instrumentalities. Most international instruments require a permanent arrangement with no prospect of severance at a later date, including in relation to inheritance. Few of the current approaches would simply fit this model.

Kafala is recognised as a form of care in some international instruments[108] with the Convention on jurisdiction, applicable law, recognition, enforcement and cooperation in respect of parental responsibility and measures for the protection of children,[109] permitting cooperation in relation to 'recognition and enforcement'[110] and recognising 'care by *Kafala* or an analogous institution'.[111] Other instruments refer to a 'valuable alternative institution ... Kafalah of Islamic Law, which provide substitute care to children'.[112] Despite this recognition, few Muslim-majority states have signed these conventions,[113] and amongst Muslim-majority states the primary instrument providing for adoption – the Convention on the Protection of Children and Co-operation in respect of Intercountry Adoption,[114] which requires a permanent parent-child relationship[115] – has only been signed by Turkey.[116] The idea of codified permanency

---

108 Convention on jurisdiction, applicable law, recognition, enforcement and co-operation in respect of parental responsibility and measures for the protection of children, opened for signature 19 October 1996, CM 8477 (entered into force 1 January 2002) ('The Child Protection Convention') art. 3(e).

109 The Child Protection Convention.

110 The Child Protection Convention, chapter 1, art. 1(d).

111 The Child Protection Convention, chapter 1, art. 3 (e).

112 United Nations Declaration on Social and Legal Principles Relating to the Protection and Welfare of Children, with Special Reference to Foster Placement and Adoption Nationally and Internationally GA Res 41/85, 95th plenary meeting, UN Doc A/RES/41/85 (declaration of 3 December 1986).

113 The Child Protection Convention, signatories listing: www.hcch.net/index_en.php?act=conventions.status&cid=70 (accessed 4 May 2018).

114 Hague Intercountry Adoption Convention.

115 Hague Intercountry Adoption Convention, art. 2(2).

116 Hague Intercountry Adoption Convention (signatory list): www.hcch.net/index_en.php?act=conventions.status&cid=69 (accessed 4 May 2018).

dominates this instrument and controls all movement of children,[117] providing an impediment to international or multilateral agreement.

In terms of instruments that have been signed by Muslim-majority countries, the Convention on the Rights of the Child does provide legitimate care 'could include … *Kafala* of Islamic law',[118] but does not offer cross-jurisdictional recognition or implementation of *kafala*. This divergence has resulted from an Islamic resistance to Western constructs and Western resistance to approaches that do not result in the permanent severance of the parent-child relationship. Another key concern in not signing by Muslim-majority countries is a fairly well-founded view that proposals for signing have been predicated upon Islamic adherence to international norms[119] rather than a negotiated approach to recognise views of Islamic minorities and Shari'ah postulates.[120]

The practical implication is that for Muslims living in non-Muslim-majority countries (apart from Turkey), procedures can be onerous or non-existent, or based on bilateral comity (of which there are no formal examples) rather than international frameworks.

In light of the above, it is unlikely that international conventions will provide a timely solution, as they are historically difficult to change and currently focus on permanency and formal transfer of the child and strict enforceability. Nor is it likely that one will appear that is socially or religiously palatable for many Muslim-majority 'sending' states or for most Western 'receiving' states.

State law and bilateral comity therefore provide the only viable and practical prospect for filling the void.

---

[117] Convention on the Protection of Children and Co-operation in respect of Intercountry Adoption, opened for signature 29 May 1993, 33 ILM 1134 (entered into force 1 May 1995) ('Hague Intercountry Adoption Convention'). This applies only to adoptions that create a permanent parent-child relationship, art. 2(2).

[118] Convention on the Rights of the Child, opened for signature 20 November 1989 (entered into force 2 September 1990) UNTS 1577 3, art. 20(3) ('Convention on the Rights of the Child').

[119] Asifa Quraishi, *Workshop on Islamic Law; Islamic Family Law* (American Society of Comparative Law and Law and Society Association, January 2004), www.aals.org/am2004/islamiclaw/familylaw.htm (accessed 29 November 2013).

[120] Lynn Welchman, 'Women, Family and the Law: The Muslim Personal Status Law Debate in Arab States' in Robert W. Hefner (ed.) *The New Cambridge History of Islam* (Cambridge, MA: Cambridge University Press 2010) 437.

V. PROSPECT FOR CHANGE, ADAPTATION AND RECOGNITION

In the last decade, new approaches to *kafala* in the West have been proposed by Islamic scholars. This revisiting has been driven by the social and legal change around adoption and the realisation that both Western and Islamic legal approaches have similar goals. All of this is bolstered by the approach of the ECHR to the *kafala* arrangement in *Harroudj* and by various intermediate approaches to *kafala* adopted across the Islamic world.

A recent proponent of the view that legal and cultural change in the West has increased analogy with *kafala* is the Muslim Women's Shura Council, which released a report suggesting that adoption can be acceptable as long as 'ethical guidelines are followed',[121] seeking to 'ignor[e] the sophistication and nuances of both Western law and Islamic dictates'[122] and describing *kafala* as an institution that 'closely resembles what is known today as the practice of open adoption'.[123] The report concludes that 'open, legal, ethical adoptions can be preferable to … institutional care and other unstable arrangements'.[124] Controversially, this paper was produced by women who reside as minorities in Western states, and as *ijtihad*, it is inconsistent with the current consensus (*ijma'*) on the issue.[125] This being said, however, it does raise interesting purposive arguments around the similarities in intent and practice of adoption between the West and the Islamic world.

Nurullah Ardic proposes that selective appropriation of Western institutions is warranted, to accommodate 'exigencies of modern life' and prioritise 'social change over textual sources of Islam'.[126] Ingrid Mattson argues that 'flexibility in Islamic law for accommodating local cultures

---

[121] Muslim Women's Shura Council, 'Adoption and the Care of Orphan Children: Islam and the Best Interests of the Child' (2011) *The Digest* (August 2011), www.wisemuslimwomen.org/images/activism/Adoption_%28August_2011%29_Final.pdf (accessed 29 November 2013).

[122] Kutty, above n4.

[123] Muslim Women's Shura Council, above n121, 4.

[124] Ibid.

[125] Kutty, above n4.

[126] Ardic, Nurullah, *Islam and the Politics of Secularism: The Caliphate and Middle Eastern Modernization in the early 20th Century* (1st ed.) (London and New York: Routledge Publishing 2012) 315.

and customs may lead to a solution in … (relation to) adoption';[127] this view appears to be shared by the approach of countries such as Turkey and Tunisia.

Faisal Kutty considers the NSW adoption programme a promising step toward accommodation, which he describes as a two-way street. Kutty argues that key conflicts around filial links and inheritance resulted from a lack of clarity on the differences between Islamic and Western adoption, and a lack of cross-fertilisation between ideas coupled with reluctance to look at the purpose rather than the text (to protect children in pre-Islamic tribal society). In Kutty's view, *kafala* can be reformed where reforms are consistent with the *'maqasid al Shari'ah* (higher objectives of the Shari'ah) provided that the Western legal system accommodation matters are not subject to legal change.[128]

Outside Islamic scholarship, there has been consideration by Western jurists of the future of adoption. Ironically, many of these jurists considered (although did not accept) the option of abolition of adoption at the precise time where the Western conception of adoption had come to be closest to the Islamic conception of *kafala*. In 1997, the NSW Law Reform Commission reviewed adoption.[129] They proposed adoption be maintained but alternative care expanded, and adoption should only apply where circumstances of the particular child dictate it best meets his/her needs.[130] In 1999, the New Zealand Law Reform Commission suggested adaptation of the law with the effect (although not expressly in those words) that it would be closer to Islamic precepts[131] (a modified form of guardianship). The report considered adoption outmoded,[132] as it created legal fictions and reflected the court's increasing preference for guardianship arrangements.[133] It also identified the main impediments as permanency, status and succession.[134] The ultimate option was a tiered

127 Kutty, above n4.

128 Kutty, above n4.

129 New South Wales Law Reform Commission, *Review of the Adoption of Children Act 1965* (1997) – Report 81.

130 Ibid., 2.5.

131 New Zealand Law Reform Commission, *Adoption; Options for Reform Preliminary Paper*, [1999] NZLCPP 38.

132 New Zealand Law Reform Commission, *Adoption; Options for Reform (final paper)*, [1999] NZLCPP 41.

133 Ibid.

134 New Zealand Law Reform Commission [1999] above n132, 43.

approach, with adoption a last resort, and removal of impediments to discovering birth parents.[135]

The final approach of the New Zealand Law Reform Commission was strikingly similar to the approach followed in Tunisia, Morocco and Turkey (and to a lesser extent Pakistan), demonstrative of the substantial similarities that now exist in legal approaches and good prospects for comity-based arrangements on *kafala*.

As mentioned above, the intent and effect of *kafala* and adoption in most Muslim-majority and Western countries is much the same: to establish an arrangement that acts to protect the best interests of the child with safeguards to ensure that the parents are suitable to undertake such a role. Despite this, there remain obvious clashes. Upon comparison, the difficulties in accommodation range from the irreconcilable such as 'strict Shari'ah' adherents, who will not let a child depart, to those where there appear to be few difficulties (and significant commonalities), such as New Zealand and Tunisia.

The fundamental incompatibilities (and solutions) are as follows.

A. Migration and the Permanent Nature

Kafala is, strictly speaking, a non-permanent arrangement in Islam and a permanent arrangement in the West, although some states such as Tunisia, Turkey and Morocco appear to recognise (formally or informally) that the arrangement will ultimately be permanent, in a practical sense. For countries that do not recognise the permanent (or likely permanent) nature of the arrangement, this is a serious disconnect and one which is reconciled only by negotiated approaches and where international instrumentalities do not assist.

To take Australia as an example, the rules around bringing children for migration purposes and are applied through a combination of State and Commonwealth legislation. Section 116 of the Adoption Act[136] permits recognition of adoptions from countries outside of the Convention,[137] but only if the adoptive parent has a superior right to the birth parents[138] and the adoptive parent has lawfully acquired full and permanent parental rights by the adoption[139] via laws relating to

---

[135] New Zealand Law Commission, *Adoption and Its Alternatives: A Different Approach and a New Framework* (September 2000) NZLCR 65, 25.

[136] Adoption Act 2000 (NSW).

[137] Hague Intercountry Adoption Convention.

[138] Adoption Act 2000 (NSW) s116(2)(b).

[139] Migration Regulations 1994 (Cth), regulation 102.211 (d).

adoption of the country in which the child is normally resident.[140] On this basis, many Kafala arrangements would not meet the legal requirements for adoption, even though some Muslim majority states have elements similar; most Muslim majority states would baulk at describing a right superior to the birth parents, even if describing the relationship as permanent. Australia cannot comply with the domestic version of article 2 of the Hague Intercountry Adoption Convention if an arrangement is not permanent.[141]

The legal framework may permit a child visa where the *kafala* relationship already exists via the 'dependant' provisions. In a provision unique to Australia, as long as the child is in an 'arrangement in the nature of adoption' made in accordance with the usual custom of practice of that culture,[142] and the relationship is stronger than between the child and any other person[143] and formal adoption was not available or was not practicable and the relationship is not contrived to circumvent migration requirements,[144] a child could accompany the migrating family. This requirement cannot be complied with where a new arrangement is proposed, or where the *kafala* parents themselves are not applying for migration; therefore a new *kafala* arrangement is unlikely to meet Australia's migration requirements.

In relation to migration and acceptance of foreign law, issues of comity were considered by the High Court in 2012 in the case of *Tahiri*.[145] In this instance, the delegate was asked to decide in relation to child custody and public interest criterion 4015.[146] The delegate considered that Afghan law was relevant in interpreting the migration law of Australia as written in that it referred, *inter alia*, to the 'law of the applicant's home country'. The court held that this was open to the delegate and a proper exercise of power.

The acceptance of the court of such legal requirements which were drafted in response to international obligation does give credit to the idea that a comity- or bilateral-based approach may have promise in relation to *kafala*. The precedent from the *Tahiri* case was that if a bilateral

---

140 Ibid., regulation 102.213.

141 Family law (Hague Convention on Intercountry Adoption) Regulations 1998 (Cth) schedule 1, art. 2(2).

142 Migration Regulations 1994 (Cth), regulation 1.04 (a).

143 Ibid., regulation 1.04 (b).

144 Hague Intercountry Adoption Convention.

145 *Case of Tahiri*.

146 Migration Regulations 1994 (Cth), Schedule 2, Public Interest Criterion 4015.

arrangement was entered into in order to permit *kafala* arrangements for migration purposes and such an arrangement was codified in Australian law, the law of the sending country could be a relevant factor. This may permit different approaches to issues of inheritance and permanency to be put in place, allowing the balancing of the law of the sending and receiving countries with the interests of the child.

B. Inheritance

As outlined above, in the Islamic world it is almost universally accepted that a *kafala* adoptee cannot inherit a share of their adoptive family estate. This is difficult to reconcile with Western conceptions where each child may lay an equal claim to a share of the estate. Valiani considers this critical to the extent that 'even if a child inherits in America (for example) they would not be granted a share in Pakistan or other Muslim lands'.[147] In some states, such as Tunisia, inheritance comes with *kafala*, in others inheritance rights are limited or difficult and in most, inheritance is not permitted. The Tunisian model carries potential for 'double inheritance' whilst other models may deprive a needy child of inheritance. This is a fundamental disconnect and one for which a solution in comity is proposed below.

C. Naming

Whilst changing a name was once expected practice in the case of a Western adoption, open adoptions now permit choice with retention of lineage and a preference for adoption within customs and religions. Although this was once a fundamental disconnect, it is now essentially a resolved issue between most Western and Islamic states, with no obligation of expectation for a name to be changed.

VI. SOLUTIONS NOW AND THE FUTURE

Accommodation of minority groups through special rules and arrangements is a difficult political issue in the West. The most satisfactory approach is a 'compromise between the demands of religion and the

---

[147] Valiani, above n14, 38.

requirements of Australian society and law'[148] and for minority rights to be achieved via a palatable compromise[149] within systems where sufficient similarities can be distilled.

Islamic *kafala* and modern Western adoption have much more in common than might be expected in a superficial analysis. Despite notable conflicts, both focus on open adoptions and the best interests of the child. Further, there is significant overlap between the legal approaches of some Muslim-majority countries and Western states. In particular, the approaches of Tunisia and Morocco (and in principle Pakistan) appear to have sufficiently similar characteristics with Western systems for development of comity-based arrangements. Such arrangements could seek to safeguard the fundamental principles valuable to each community to the benefit of orphans, with procedures grounded in domestic law as occurred in the *Harroudj* and *Tahiri* cases, but with additional safeguards and codification to ensure clarity for minority communities, the *kafala* children and the general public.

Although broad international instruments provide little appeal, the most rational suggestion that flows from the similarities in approaches in both *Harroudj* and *Tahiri* is bilateral comity. Bilateral agreements outside the international framework could permit recognition of *kafala* for migration to Western states, but with substantial and negotiated safeguards as outlined below.

To mitigate the risk and ensure the success of such a programme, arrangements in the initial stages should ideally focus on minimising fraudulent activity and the likelihood of trafficking in persons, as well as respecting fundamental Islamic reservations as to the permanency of an arrangement. This would mean a focus on those whose parents are deceased (as opposed to missing or unable to provide), and permitting an arrangement only through the formal 'adoption or *kafala*' agencies, with a priority on the condition and needs of the child and not on the views of, or relationship to, the prospective *kafala* parent in the Western country.

This arrangement would then be coupled with a compliance regime in country to ensure the child's orphan status to both states' satisfaction, and ensure that the rights of all other relatives have been considered. A certificate could then be issued that permits a legally permanent arrangement from the perspective of a receiving country, confirms that there is no requirement for a name change or denial of a parental right or lineage

---

148 Rex Adhar and Nicholas Aroney, 'The Topography of Shari'ah in the Western Political Landscape' in Rex Adhar and Nicholas Aroney (eds), *Shari'ah in the West* (Oxford: Oxford University Press 2010) 1, 3.

149 Black, above n19, 398.

and provides the right to monitor for a set period. This mitigates the risk of a parent contriving their circumstances to 'reappear' and seek a migration outcome, or a child being abducted or sold. Such verification could take place through a trusted agency such as the Red Cross/Red Crescent.

The most complex matters are those of inheritance, based on the approaches of both the 'post-colonial pragmatists' and 'permitting adoption via a purposive approach and influence of '*Urf*,' potentially if the child is no worse off they could be dealt with under the one-third of inheritance provisions or through voluntary bequest, as currently occurs in Canada. There is also an option for a government to-government agreement for the issuance of a pre-*kafala* inheritance certificate indicating entitlements of a child abroad; these would be taken into account when determining estates upon the death of the parent. Such an arrangement would put members of the Muslim community in the same position as other citizens and on notice as to their possible liabilities with respect to inheritance, but ensure the child is no worse off. This would be a difficult position to negotiate in any agreement.

On the Western side, the target is equality of access to orphans for care but to be cautious not to provide benefits unavailable to the general community. To this end, Western interests could be assured by:

1. limiting numbers to a pilot arrangement;
2. continual revision of arrangements and monitoring at a diplomatic level of procedures for determining *kafala* (as well as access to records of decisions made and the reasons therein);
3. the agreement itself to be revokable with limited notice; or
4. severance of the parental rights for migration of other family, i.e. the parents (to mitigate fraud and encourage genuine arrangements).

The result of comity arrangements are that essential interests of both communities are protected. Note that although the countries were illustrative only (and there would be benefit from a broader analysis), the proposed approach did provide good prospects for successful pilot *kafala* arrangements between Australia, France and Canada with Tunisia and Morocco (and Pakistan if further legal clarity is obtained, allowing applications to be permitted once more).

3. 'The best interests of the child': critical analysis of the Libyan High Court decision

Ali Omar Ali Mesrati

I. INTRODUCTION

Early attempts of international law in identifying the rights of children can be traced to the 1924 Geneva Declaration of the Rights of the Child[1] and the 1959 Declaration of the Rights of the Child.[2] However, it was the adoption of the Convention on the Rights of the Child (CROC)[3] by the United Nations General Assembly on 20 November 1989 that constituted a major development in the identification of and support for children's rights by the international community.[4] The adoption of CROC was followed one year later (29–30 September 1990) by the first World Summit for Children, during which the World Declaration on the Survival, Protection and Development of Children was signed and a Plan of Action adopted for its implementation in the 1990s.[5] World leaders made a commitment to the protection of children's rights to guarantee their survival and development. The Plan of Action was to become the

[1] Geneva Declaration of the Rights of the Child, adopted 26 September 1924, League of Nations OJ Spec Supp 21, at 43 www.un-documents.net/gdrc1924.htm (accessed 11 May 2004).

[2] Declaration of the Rights of the Child, GA res 1386 (XIV), 20 November 1959, 14 UN GAOR Supp. 16, at 19, UN Doc A/4354 (1959).

[3] Convention on the Rights of the Child, opened for signature 20 November 1989, 1577 UNTS 3 (entered into force 2 September 1990).

[4] Munyae M. Mulinge, 'Implementing the 1989 United Nations' Convention on the Rights of the Child in sub-Saharan Africa: The Overlooked Socio-economic and Political Dilemmas' (2002) 26(11) *Child Abuse & Neglect* 1117.

[5] UN GA 55th sess, Agenda Item 151 [Presentation of the texts to the GA by the UN Sec Gen], 18 October 1990, UN Doc A/45/625 (1990). Text of the *World Declaration on the Survival, Protection and Development of Children*, Annex 1–5; *Plan of Action for Implementing the World Declaration on the Survival, Protection and Development of Children in the 1990s*, Annex 7–23.

guiding framework around which international organisations, national governments, non-government organisations (NGOs) and individuals would style their own programmes of activities.[6]

One of the abstract concepts, which has been established in both international and national legal systems, is 'the best interests of the child'.[7] Today, this concept is embedded in international treaties such as the Convention on the Rights of the Child (CROC), where an example of the use of this principle can be found in article 3.[8] This same principal is also emphasised within the Hague Convention on Protection of Children and Co-operation in Respect of International Adoption, article 1.[9]

It is also part of the African Charter on the Rights and Welfare of the Child, which was ratified by Libya and which provides that 'in all actions concerning the child undertaken by any person or authority the *best interests of the child* shall be the primary consideration'.[10]

As a result, modern domestic legal systems adopted the 'best interests' concept into their jurisdictions.[11] Consequently, Acts relating to child welfare were altered accordingly and obligations were imposed on courts to make judgements in accordance with 'the best interests of the child'.

In terms of Libya's participation in international conventions regarding the rights of the child, Libya signed the Convention on the Rights of the Child (CROC) without any reservations on 15 April 1993.

---

[6] Mulinge, above n4.

[7] For some trial definitions see Harvey R. Sorkow, 'Best Interests of the Child: By Whose Definition?' (1990–1991) 18 *Pepperdine Law Review* 383.

[8] Convention on the Rights of the Child, opened for signature 20 November 1989, 1577 UNTS 3, art 3(1) (entered into force 2 September 1990) (emphasis added).

[9] Hague [Hague Conference on Private International Law] Convention on the Protection of Children and Co-operation in Respect of International Adoption, opened for signature 29 May 1993, art 1(a) (entered into force 1 May 1995) (emphasis added). For text, see www.hcch.net/index_en.php?act=conventions.text&cid=69 (accessed 10 August 2009).

[10] Organisation for African Unity (OAU), African Charter on the Rights and Welfare of the Child, opened for signature 11 July 1990, OAU Doc. CAB/LEG/24.9/49 (1990) art 4 (entered into force 29 November 1999) (emphasis added) www.unhcr.org/refworld/docid/3ae6b38c18.html (accessed 5 December 2008).

[11] Amanda Barratt and Sandra Burman, 'Deciding the Best Interests of the Child: An International Perspective on Custody Decision-making' (2001) 118 *The South African Law Journal* 556.

Libya's willingness to participate in international and supranational laws on a number of broad-ranging issues related to the rights of children is indicated in its being a signatory to additional protocols and instruments. Libya ratified the African Charter on the Rights and Welfare of the Child on 23 September 2000. Libya also ratified two optional protocols to the Convention on the Rights of the Child, namely the Optional Protocol on the Sale of Children, Child Prostitution and Child Pornography (on 18 June 2004), and the Optional Protocol on the Involvement of Children in Armed Conflict (on 29 October 2004).

The primary concern raised by the Committee on the Rights of the Child (CRC) in its 2003 response to Libya's Second Periodic Report forms the basis of this chapter. In its response, the CRC concluded that Libya does not 'fully incorporate in legislation and practice, article 3 of the Convention, including in the area of custody of children'.[12] The perceived discrepancy between the Libyan Government's interpretation and consequent implementation of the 'best interests of the child' principle, and the CRC's expectation of Libya's fulfilment as a State party to the Convention on the Rights of the Child (CROC) is at the heart of the concerns of this chapter.

This chapter aims to analyse critically Libyan Legislation 10/1984 and cases adjudicated by the Libyan High Court – Guardianship Jurisdiction (LHC-GJ) in order to determine whether the CRC's concerns are well founded. In order to achieve this goal, a systematic approach will be undertaken. At the outset, detailing the foundations of the Libyan political and legal system will be necessary. This will provide the reader with the necessary context for understanding Libyan law and its influences.

Prior to performing an analysis of cases adjudicated by the LHC-GJ, the relevant articles in the Law of Marriage and Divorce Rules and their Effects (10/1984) will be outlined. This will provide important context for understanding the basis on which decisions are made.

Three factors have determined the selection of cases for analysis in this chapter. Firstly, the cases have been adjudicated by the LHC-GJ, which is the ultimate authority in interpreting Libyan laws. Secondly, cases have been selected to ensure coverage of a broad range of issues within the

---

12 Committee on the Rights of the Child, *Concluding Observations: Libyan Arab Jamahiriya. 04/07/2003* [28], UN Doc CRC/C/15/Add.209 (2003) www.unhchr.ch/TBS/doc.nsf/e121f32fbc58faafc1256a2a0027ba24/8ea5ea3ba958 29a1c1256daa002dbd01?OpenDocument (accessed 18 April 2008).

guardianship jurisdiction. Finally, the analysis focuses on cases that resulted in authoritative interpretations of relevant articles within the Legislation 10/1984, in cases that were subsequently adjudicated on the basis of the same principles.

Applying these factors has resulted in the selection of over 60 cases decided in the 30-year period between 1971 and 2001. The starting date for this time frame is significant, given that the structure of Libyan Legislation 10/1984 has been influenced by Shari'ah, which was introduced to the Libyan system in the early 1970s. This will make it possible to comment on whether the Libyan legal system is truly influenced by its culture, being Islam, and in particular the interpretation of Islam by the *Malikiyah* school of jurisprudence.

II. LIBYAN LEGAL SYSTEM

The Libyan legal system is comprised of Islamic, French and Italian elements of the law.[13] In the early years following the 1969 Revolution, a special committee was established by the RCC (Revolutionary Command Council) to amend personal status laws in order to make them consistent with Islamic law.[14] The RCC issued a declaration recognising Shari'ah as the main source of legislation and establishing a high commission to ensure that all legislation is consistent with Shari'ah principles.[15]

Amendments were made to the 1953 penal code in the early 1970s. Several laws were revised while some new laws based on Shari'ah were

---

[13] Abdullahi Ahmed An-Na'im, *Islamic Family Law in a Changing World: A Global Resource Book* (London: Zed Books 2002) 174; The Law and Religion Program of Emory University website, *Islamic Family Law: Possibilities of Reform through Internal Initiatives* (September 1998–July 1999) www.law.emory.edu/ifl/index2.html (accessed 2 January 2008).

[14] Paul Rozario, *Libya (Countries of the World)* (USA: Gareth Stevens Pub Secondary Lib 2004) 17.

[15] An-Na'im, *Islamic Family Law in a Changing World: A Global Resource Book*, above n13, 175; The Law and Religion Program of Emory University, *Islamic Family Law: Possibilities of Reform Through Internal Initiatives* (September 1998–July 1999) www.law.emory.edu/ifl/index2.html (accessed 2 January 2008).

introduced.[16] In 1984 a new family law was ratified.[17] In article 72 of Legislation 10/1984, Shari'ah law was recognised as the abiding source of law in the absence of explicit provisions in the legislation.

There are four levels of courts within the Libyan legal system: summary courts, courts of first instance, appeal courts and the High Court.[18] Courts of first instance are comprised of several divisions; noteworthy is the personal status division. Both the appeals court and the first instance court are comprised of three-judge panels with final judgements based on a majority decision ruling. Previously, Shari'ah courts of appeal were comprised of Shari'ah judges. However currently, Shari'ah judges sit in regular courts of appeal, specialising in Shari'ah appeals cases. The High Court has five chambers: civil and commercial, criminal, administrative, constitutional and Shari'ah.[19]

Al-Jarida Al-Rasmiya is the official journal in which law reports are published. Furthermore, decisions made in the Libyan High Court (LHC) are published in *Majallat Al-Mahkama Al-Ulya.*[20]

---

16 Related laws are: Law on Protection of Women's Right to Inheritance 1959; Law on Women's Rights in Marriage and Divorce 1972 (Law No. 176 of 1972); Law No. 87 of 1973 (merging civil and shari'ah courts); Law No. 22 of 1991 (amending law relating to polygamy); Law No. 9 of 1994 (amending law relating to polygamy); Wills Act 1994 (Law No. 7 of 1994. See also: Law Forming Committee to Islamize Libyan Legislation 28/10/1970; Law on Offences against Property 1972 (first amendment to Penal Code 1953); Law on Artificial Insemination 1972 (Law No. 175/1972, introducing penalties); Law on Sexual Offences 1973 (Law No. 70/1973, relating to *zina*); Law on Sexual Slander 1973 (Law No. 52/1973, relating to *qadhf*); Law on Prohibition 1973 (relating to alcohol consumption); Law on Homicide 1973 (relating to *qisas*, *diya* and *kaffara*).

17 Law of Marriage and Divorce Rules and their Effects (10/1984).

18 Rozario, above n14, 17.

19 An-Na'im, *Islamic Family Law in a Changing World: A Global Resource Book*, above n13, 176; The Law and Religion Program of Emory University website, *Islamic Family Law: Possibilities of Reform Through Internal Initiatives* (September 1998–July 1999) www.law.emory.edu/ifl/index2.html (accessed 2 January 2008).

20 An-Na'im, *Islamic Family Law in a Changing World: A Global Resource Book*, above n13, 177; The Law and Religion Program of Emory University website, *Islamic Family Law: Possibilities of Reform Through Internal Initiatives* (September 1998–July 1999) www.law.emory.edu/ifl/index2.html (accessed 2 January 2008).

A thorough analysis of the relevant laws and other legal material is required to determine whether the LHC has upheld the requirements stipulated by law. The chapter argues that the interpretation of international human rights in municipal legal systems will inevitably, understandably and legitimately be affected by local cultures. This process of 'translation' is evident in the approach that Libya has taken to implementing 'the best interests of the child', where the influence of Islamic law is also apparent.

Interpretation in a very practical and policy-oriented area of sociolegal research has been adopted in this chapter along with a qualitative research style which involves a more explicit judgement and interpretation.

As stated earlier, over 60 LHC cases have been selected in a time frame of 30 years ending in 2001. This time frame represents a span able to demonstrate the effect of Shari'ah law on the Libyan legal system as it was introduced after the '1969 First of September Revolution'. Topics to be discussed in the context of Libyan law and LHC interpretations of 'the best interests of the child' are as follows: the definition of a child; the definition and ordering of potential guardians; whether the right of guardianship is that of the child or the guardian; guardianship conditions; the place and time of guardianship; the court's responsibility with relation to guardianship issues; how and when guardianship is to be reinstated; and the issue of child and guardian maintenance.

Articles 62–70 of Legislation 10/1984 will be introduced, followed by presentation of LHC decisions prior to and subsequent to the introduction of Legislation 10/1984. Some of the high-level cases will be presented in depth. However, a number of key cases will be analysed in detail in terms of how lower courts and the LHC implement the 'best interests' principle when adjudicating on guardianship issues. Following each issue presented in this chapter, a commentary section will examine whether the theoretical and practical sides of Libyan law are consistent with the main argument presented in this chapter.

III. GUARDIANSHIP: GENERAL PRINCIPLES

A. Definition and the Ordering of Guardians

Definition of the child

In accordance with article 1 of CROC, article 3 of Legislation 17/1992, which is an amendment to the Libyan Civil Code, defines a child as follows:

> A child is a person who has not attained the age of majority. He is either capable or incapable of discernment.
>
> (a) A child incapable of discernment is a child under seven years of age;
> (b) A child capable of discernment is a child who has attained the age of seven years.[21]

Article 9 of the same legislation stipulates that 'The age of majority is 18 years'. Article 17 also stipulates that 'A minor is a person who has not attained the age of majority or who is insane or simpleminded'.

This definition is the Libyan legislature's response to CROC. Prior to this amendment, the Libyan Civil Code had set the age of majority at 21 years. Under this article, it is clear that the Libyan legislature acted in opposition to its own culture because the age of majority under Islamic law is the age of puberty, which is around the age of 15. This attitude can be viewed positively in the context of the 'best interests' principle, since the age extension from 15 to 18 years will inevitably provide further protection to the individual.

Definition of guardianship

Libya's Law of Marriage and Divorce Rules and their Effects (Legislation 10/1984) addresses all aspects of guardianship. Article M62F.A states:

> [c]ustody is a shelter for the child to be nurtured, and cared for, and looked after from their birth until the boy is a man and the girl gets married and sexually interacts with her husband, and all of this is without opposing the right of the sponsor.

Article M62F.B notes that 'during marriage the right of the child's custody is for both parents'. However if separation occurs, then a woman's right to guardianship remains as a wife, in the three-month waiting period after a divorce is declared, and any time after a divorce.[22]

Article M62F.C states that 'the court does not have to be restricted by the order that was mentioned in the last paragraph (except for the child's mother and her mother and the child's father and his mother) and that is in order to fulfil the needs of the child'.

In 1971, in accordance with the definition of guardianship, the LHC observed that 'Legally (according to Islamic law) guardianship is rearing

---

21 *Al-Jrida Al-Rasmiya* (1992) 36/30.

22 Law of Marriage and Divorce Rules and their Effects (10/1984), art M63A.

the child and taking care of him/her and meeting all of the child's needs until a certain age'.[23]

The central legal issue in this case was to clarify the relationship between the rights of the child and the rights of their parents. It created a very significant legal precedent in how these rights can be evaluated. In Case 1/18, 1971, the court elaborated:

> according to Islamic law experts, there are three rights: the right of the child being guarded, the right of the mother or female guardian, and the right of the father or the sponsor; and if all these rights coincide and were capable of being in agreement then the child's rights should be accommodated, and if these rights contradict each other then the right of the child comes first because the aim of guardianship is to benefit, teach, educate and care for the child.[24]

Three years later the court, in decision 2/21, 1974, confirmed its understanding of the legal principles governing custody and guardianship. The LHC reiterated this as follows:

> The aim of custody is to provide a caring environment for the child and to be able to meet the child's needs. The provision of such an environment is mainly assigned to a woman, because a woman typically has more sympathy for the child and is more capable of meeting the child's needs. That is why the mother is given first priority when assigning the custody of the child, as long as there are no impediments to that assignment.[25]

In decision 3/37, 1990, the LHC explained the application of these principles when clearly differentiating between guardianship and *kafalah* (sponsorship). In this particular case, the father of a girl, who left his daughter in the care of his brother before travelling overseas, did not give his brother any right as a guardian but rather as a sponsor for a limited time:

> the child staying with the appellant for a period of time with consent from her father … [the appellant] is considered as a sponsor and [the father] does not

---

23 *Majallat Al-Mahkama Al-'Ulya* 8/1, decision 1/18, 06/06/1971, 93.

24 Ibid. See also Wahbah Al-Zuhaily, *Al-Fiqh Al-Islamiy Wa Adilatuhu*, Vol. 4 (Beirut: Dar al-Fikr 2002) 7297; Sa'id Muhammad al-Julaydi, *Ahkam al-Usrah fi al-Zawaj wa-al-Talaq wa-Atharuhuma: dirasah fiqhiyah muqaranah, ma'a sharh wa-ta'liqat 'alá al-Qanun raqm 10 li-sanat 1984 M* (Misratah: al-Jamahiriyah al-'Arabiyah al-Libiyah al-Sha'biyah al-Ishtirakiyah al-'Uzmá 1986) 271.

25 *Majallat Al-Mahkama Al-'Ulya* 2/11, decision 2/21, 07/11/1974, 20.

> give him any of the criteria needed for guardianship that is mentioned in the stated law.[26]

Prior to Legislation 10/1984 coming into force, the LHC reaffirmed that, according to the *Malikiyah Madhhab*,[27] precedence to the role of guardian is as follows: the mother, maternal grandmother, maternal full aunt, maternal half aunt, maternal aunt of the child's mother, paternal aunt of the child's mother, child's paternal grandmother then the paternal great grandmother. The kinships of the child also have priority over foreigners, while relatives from the mother's side have priority over those on the father's side.[28]

The LHC has confirmed this on many occasions. For example, in one of its decisions, the LHC stated:

> Guardianship is the period of nurturing the child through which the availability of a woman who has a right to raise the child in according to the *Malikiyah Madhhab*, the right of the mother has priority to that of the father and then to his blood relative women as well. So, the measures that were used to consider are that the mother has priority over the father and the mother's kinship has priority over the father's such that the mother of the mother, even if she chose not to accept, has the priority in custody after the child's mother and before the mother of the father. The foundation of guardianship should be compassion, and bloodline kinships are consistent with compassion, so the mother and her parents are the most compassionate towards the child.[29]

Commentary

Libyan Legislation 10/1984 considers guardianship as a right for the child above that of the parents. If the parents are married and living together, it is the responsibility of both the parents to take on the role of guardianship and as long as they are settled together as a social unit (family) they can cooperate and share the caring duty that is given to them.[30]

---

26 *Majallat Al-Mahkama Al-'Ulya* 3/26, decision 3/37, 22/11/1990, 9.

27 One of the Sunni Islamic schools of thought.

28 *Majallat Al-Mahkama Al-'Ulya* 1/8, decision 18/1, 06/06/1971, 93.

29 *Majallat Al-Mahkama Al-'Ulya* 10/2, decision 3/20, 01/11/1973, 25. Twelve years later, Libya's Law of Marriage and Divorce Rules and their Effects (10/1984) was issued where LHC confirmed that 'the guardianship is for the parent during marriage, followed by mother after divorce and then by the maternal grandmother': *Majallat Al-Mahkama Al-'Ulya* 2-1/29, decision 26/42, 04/07/1996, 16.

30 Law of Marriage and Divorce Rules and their Effects (10/1984), art M62FB.

Libyan Legislation 10/1984 relies upon Ibn Rushd's opinion relating to the issue of guardianship, which states that the majority of scholars agree that if the father divorces the mother while the child is still at a young age, then the role of guardian is assigned to the mother. Such opinion is based on the teachings of the Prophet Muhammad (PBUH) when he said that 'whosoever separates a mother from her child Allah shall separate him from his beloved on judgment day'.[31] Furthermore, Ibn Rushd added, 'the ability to transfer guardianship from the mother to someone other than the father is unproven in any way'.[32]

If the circumstance should arise that the mother, father or any of the female blood relatives cannot take on the role and responsibility of guardian, the male relatives are then considered in the following order. First to be considered is the child's brother, if he is an adult and capable of taking on the role. If this option is not feasible, then the paternal grandfather is considered, followed by the child's paternal uncle, if he is an adult and capable of taking on this role. The child's nephew is the last to be considered from the child's male blood relatives for the role of guardian. If the situation arises that the father has passed away and has decreed in his will a specific male relative from those mentioned above to become the guardian, then this request will be respected and granted as long as the request has been made for his sons. If the request has been made for his daughters, the choice of guardian will be considered by a judge first because it is preferred that she be placed in the care of a male relative that she is prohibited to marry. In the circumstance that the requested guardian is not seen as being suitable, the father's request will be overturned.[33]

In all Islamic schools of thought, the mother of a child has the responsibility of care and control of the child for the first few years of the child's life. This is based on the widespread belief that it is beneficial for a small child to remain with its mother. Care in the early years is termed '*Hadanah*'. The age at which *Hadanah* ceases varies between the schools of thought and the gender of the child. For example, in the *Malikiyah*

---

[31] Saying of the Prophet (PBUH) narrated by Al-Tirmidhi, Al-Islam.com website, *Hadith No. 1204* (2007).

[32] Muhammad Ibn Ahmad Ibn Rushd, *Bidayat Al-Mujtahid Wa Nihayatu Al-Muqtasid*, Vol. 2 (n.p., n.d.) 42.

[33] 'Abdusalam al-'Alim, *Al-Zawaj wa al-Talaq fi al-Qanun al-Libiy wa Asaniduh al-Shar'ia* (3rd ed, n.p., 1998) 313.

Madhhab, 'the right of *Hadanah* in relation to a daughter lasts until she is married'.[34]

As quoted above, article M62F.C provides that the court does not have to be restricted by the order that was mentioned in article M62F.A when making decisions on guardianship to fulfil the needs of the child.[35] It is appropriate to emphasise that Libyan law does not take a completely rigid approach in terms of priority and does consider the specific circumstances of the children in question except in the first four prospective guardians. This is not inconsistent with Islamic law because there is no strong evidence to apply the priority of these four over the others except in the case of the mother. This notion of flexibility is in total agreement with CROC, which demands that the factor of 'the best interests of the child' have greater importance than any other factor, including the guardianship hierarchy. To reiterate, the position of this chapter on this matter is that the adjudicator should be assigned greater authority to evaluate the matter on a case-by-case basis to meet the 'best interests' principle as outlined in CROC.

This highlights the importance that the LHC places on the character and lifestyle of the guardian of the child. The court aims to place children in the care of adults whom it deems will care, maintain and cater for 'the best interests of the child'.

Under the interpretations advocated by the *Malikiyah Madhhab*, preferences to the role of guardian continue well beyond the first four outlined above. As mentioned earlier, the priority to guardian will be initially assigned to the child's mother and then to her mother. The father is considered after the maternal grandmother according to Legislation 10/1984. This opinion comes from *Hanabilah Madhhab* and Ibn Rushd from the *Malikiyah Madhhab*. If the grandmother and the father are not able to take on this duty or the maternal grandmother did not request it, guardianship will then be assigned to the paternal grandmother.

After this order of preference, the law provides the adjudicator with full authority to nominate from the available relatives, with preference

---

[34] See also Jamila Hussain, *Islam: Its Law and Society* (2nd ed.) (Sydney: Federation Press 2004) 95.

[35] Law of Marriage and Divorce Rules and their Effects (10/1984) art M62F.C 'The court does not have to be restricted by the order that was mentioned in the last paragraph (except for the child's mother and her mother and the child's father and his mother) and that is in order to fulfil the needs of the child.'

given to the closest female relative over relatives that are male. According to the *Malikiyah Madhhab*, the first female in line after the mother and maternal grandmother is the mother's sister but only if she is her full sister (that is, they have the same mother and father). This condition is based on the teaching of the Prophet Muhammad (PBUH) when he said: 'the mother's sister is like a mother.'[36] If the aunt is not capable of taking on this role, then the great-aunt of the child will be considered for this role and responsibility.[37]

In summary, this ordering which presents the jurisprudence advocated by the *Malikiyah Madhhab* is only a guide. The only strict rules stated in this matter are those related to the first four prospective guardians. If a conflict arises between the mother's and father's side, the mother's blood relatives will have priority over the father's blood relatives.[38] This is because of the compassion found in the mother's kin, and the law has given the judge leverage to alter this ordering as was mentioned in article M62F.B.[39] However, the judge cannot alter the first four preferences (the mother, maternal grandmother, father and paternal grandmother)[40] if the conditions for guardianship exist. These conditions include being an adult, capable, trustworthy, able to care for the child, and being free from transmittable diseases. In the case of other potential guardians, the ordering can be changed by the judge even if the conditions of guardianship exist. Such changes must still be justified on the grounds of 'the best interests of the child'.

B. Is the Right of Guardianship a Right of the Child or a Right of the Guardian?

According to article M62, guardianship is a right of the child, distinct from and above the rights of the parents. If the parents are not considered to be appropriate guardians, then custody will be transferred to the child's unmarriageable kin. If none of them accepts the role, then custody will be transferred to whomsoever the court nominates, whether it is an individual or organisation.[41]

---

36 Saying of the Prophet (PBUH) narrated by Al-Tirmidhi, Al-Islam.com website, *Hadith No. 1826* (2007). See also Al-Kasaniy, *Bada'i al-Sana'i fi Tartib al-Shara'i* (n.d., n.p.) Vol. 2, 208.

37 Sa'id Muhammad al-Julaydy, above n24, 272.

38 Al-'Alim, above n33, 313.

39 Law of Marriage and Divorce Rules and their Effects (10/1984).

40 *Al-Mahkama Al-'Ulya*, decision 19/46, 25/11/1999, GM.

41 Al-'Alim, above n33, 314.

Even though Libyan law grants the mother conditional priority as guardian, provisions are in place for the judge to grant the father custody of the child over the mother if this was viewed to be in the child's best interests. An example where this situation may occur is when a mother leaves her home due to some disagreement with her husband. This is stated in article M63F.A: 'if the mother leaves her husband's house over a disagreement with her husband, she has the right for her children's custody … that is if the court does not see that as being against the children's interests.'[42]

The chapter takes the position that such provisions are against Islamic law because the priority of the mother as a guardian is evident through the Holy *Qur'an* and Sunnah. It may be seen as consistent with CROC because choosing the guardian in this case will be according to 'the best interests of the child' as it will be evaluated by the court. It is not clear why Libyan law in this particular case grants the court the authority to override a mother's preference to guardian, while in the normal preferences line it does not.

LHC decisions

In determining whether the right of guardianship is that of the guardian or the child, the LHC-GJ, has clearly adopted the position, in a 1974 decision, that the right of the child will be its first consideration:

> According to the *Malikiyah Madhhab*, guardianship is incumbent upon three rights which are: the right of the child, the right of the mother/female guardian and the right of the father/male sponsor. If those rights coincided and it was easy to accord between those rights, that should be the path taken, otherwise if there is conflict between those rights, the right of the child becomes worthier than the other rights because it is the strongest.[43]

Since 1971 this approach has consistently been adopted by the LHC[44] except in its decision 15/48, 2001. In this case, the LHC accepted an application from a wife for a divorce from her husband and refused to grant her guardianship, not on the grounds of inability, but rather due to her disagreement with her husband and her consequent attempts to

---

42 Law of Marriage and Divorce Rules and their Effects (10/1984).

43 *Majallat Al-Mahkama Al-'Ulya* 3/10, decision 13/20, 07/02/1974, 28. See also *Al-Mahkama Al-'Ulya*, decision 9/42, 18/04/1996, GM.

44 *Majallat Al-Mahkama Al-'Ulya* 1/8, decision 1/18, 06/06/1971, 93; *Majallat Al-Mahkama Al-'Ulya* 2/7, decision 2/17, 03/01/1971, 56.

blackmail him emotionally. The subsequent judgement clearly illustrates that the right of the father was preferred over the rights of the children.[45]

Commentary

In the case presented above to the LHC (decision 13/20, 1974), the appellant (the father) requested cancellation of his daughter's guardianship by her maternal grandmother because his daughter was behind in her studies at the age of eight, her life with her grandmother was not favourable and he wanted his daughter to live with him in Tripoli. He was willing to provide a house for her and her grandmother, and to pay all expenses for them if they moved to Tripoli.

After the guardian refused the father's offer, he applied to the court in Bany Walyyed (the city in which his daughter resided in with her guardian) to grant him guardianship of his daughter. The court complied with his request.

The grandmother refused to move; she went to the court of appeal and challenged this judgement on the grounds that the father had been inconsiderate towards his daughter for eight years while he knew his daughter lived with her grandmother.

The court of appeal revoked the first judgement because the father had been silent for a long time. The LHC agreed with the court of appeal decision on the grounds that the father's silence meant he was not sincerely concerned with the interests of his daughter. Therefore keeping the girl with her maternal grandmother was seen to be in her best interests.[46]

Shari'ah scholars consider this principle as a precedent in all actions taken regarding a child. For example, when Ibn Qudamah discussed the rights of the child's guardianship, he stated that 'in order to choose the suitable person we have to choose the one who is most kind to the child because the best interests of the child must become the first consideration'.[47]

Therefore, it is clear that there are three interests to be considered when dealing with guardianship: those of the child, the father and the mother. These interests are considered in both Islamic and Libyan law. Libyan law seeks to find a solution that caters to the interests of all three parties. It is believed that the child's best interests will be met even further if the parent's interests are in harmony or protected. However, if

---

45 *Al-Mahkama Al-'Ulya*, decision 15/48, 14/06/2001, GM.

46 *Majallat Al-Mahkama Al-'Ulya* 3/10, decision 13/20, 07/02/1974, 28.

47 Ibn Qudamah al-Maqdisiy, *Al-Sharhu al-Kabir* (ND) 291, 292.

the decision made does not cater to all three interests, then the child's interests will be paramount.[48] Therefore, seeing to the interests of the child is undoubtedly consistent with the 'best interests' principle outlined in CROC.

The 'best interests' principle can also be observed in the case of the guardianship of a new-born baby. According to Libyan Legislation 10/1984, the mother is obliged to take custody and care for her newborn. Protection and care for the newborn by their mother are in 'the best interests of the child'. Libyan Legislation 10/1984 in article M63F.B states that 'if the subject child was a baby then it needs its mother and cannot manage without her, and the mother is obliged to be guardian'. This circumstance cannot be exploited by a woman who wishes to disconcert her baby's father by leaving him and the baby as well, since there is an obligation set out by law to care for the baby. This opinion is taken from the jurisprudence of the *Malikiyah*, who encourage the mother's obligation of guardianship in the case of a newborn. However the *Hanafiyah Madhhab* does not obligate the mother to accept custody unless there is no one else to do the job or if neither the father nor the child has sufficient funds.[49]

Another example that confirms that the right of guardianship belongs to the child under Libyan Legislation 10/1984 is the case where non-Muslim guardians exist. Custody is the right of the mother regardless of whether she is a Muslim or an adherent of another revealed religion.

In summary, according to the case details presented above, Libyan Legislation 10/1984 along with LHC interpretations recognise the right of guardianship based on 'the best interests of the child'. As illustrated in the case brought forward by the father to the Bany Walyyed local court, the judgement was based on the father's interests and the literal meaning of the conditions of guardianship. This judgement was overruled in the LHC since 'the best interests of the child' would require maintaining the subject in the same environment as she had been for the past eight years.

In a situation concerning a newborn, details in Libyan legislation were presented which unambiguously obligate the mother to be guardian of a child once she has separated from the husband.[50] Again the common theme of having the best guardian, in this case the mother, is firmly upheld as being in 'the best interests of the child'.

---

48 Wahbah al-Zuhaily, *Huquq al-Atfal wa al-Musinin* (Beirut: Dar al-Maktabi 2002) 38.

49 Ibn Rushd, above n32, 126.

50 M63F.B, Legislation 10/1984.

Finally, if a situation arises where the mother is a non-Muslim, Libyan legislation clearly advises that custody of the child(ren) will be granted to her. In conclusion, the Bany Walyyed case coupled with the details of Libyan legislation outlining guardianship issues in the case of a newborn and a non-Muslim mother illustrate that the right of guardianship is the right of the child. This understanding is totally consistent with the 'best interests' principle outlined in CROC.

C. Guardianship Conditions

Libyan Legislation 10/1984

As stipulated in article M65, general conditions, along with those for individuals, need to exist when guardianship is granted. Article M65 states that 'the guardian must be an adult, capable, trustworthy, able to bring up the child and free from transmittable diseases'.

The condition that is specific to a potential female guardian is that 'the nursing mother should not be married to a man who is considered to be marriageable to the child' (article M65). It means that the nursing mother's right to guardianship can be cancelled by her marriage, unless the man was unmarriageable to the child.

Conditions for a potential male guardian are also described by article M65: 'the guardian man should be unmarriageable to the girl, and should have a woman who will nurse the child.' The son of the uncle, for example, does not have the right to be a guardian of his female cousin, because he is considered to be of marriageable kin.

Article M66F.A states: 'custody will fail if any of the mentioned conditions in article M65 were invalid.'

Article M66F.B clearly states how guardianship can also lapse: 'the right of guardianship will lapse by the act of silence on the part of the individual who had the right for it for a whole year counted from the date of his/her knowledge, unless it was impossible for the request to be made.' Noteworthy is the term the 'whole year', because this is the defining criteria in this circumstance. In this situation, the issue of granting guardianship is totally dependent on the time when the individual who is requesting to be guardian gained knowledge of their eligibility. If the 'whole year' passes without a request being made, then the individual's eligibility will be deemed invalid in the future.

The law states in article M66F.C that 'guardianship returns to its first owner when its cause disappears, unless the court decides otherwise in order to fulfil the needs of the child'. 'The best interests of the child' is implicit in this article because the priority is the needs of the child.

LHC decisions

In an early case heard by the LHC Case 1/2, 1956, the decision handed down by the sitting panel of judges broadly detailed the required conditions of a prospective guardian:

> According to Islamic legislation, whoever the guardian is, whether it be a male or a female, they must have some required characteristics including; sense and capability to … [meet] the needs of the guarded child/ren, the female guardian must have a safe place where she can protect a teenage girl, loyalty in religion and maturity, lack of transmittable diseases, and the female guardian should not be married … [except] if she was married to a person who was unmarriageable to the guarded girl, or the person who has the right of guardian knew about it and did not ask for it for a whole year without an excuse, so that way his guardianship will be cancelled. However, if it was confirmed in the proceedings that the woman who was appealed against got married four years ago and the appellant did not object or [contradict] this statement, the judgment that has been agreed on which says that the appellant neglected requesting guardianship of his two young brothers from his mother after she got married until the legal period passed away is not against the law and is compatible with the *Malikiyah* school of jurisprudence.[51]

Since this case was presented to the LHC, there has been a continual emphasis on these guardianship conditions in many other cases. Such cases will be discussed in detail along with other cases due to their importance and relevance to this study.

D. Key Cases

In one of the key cases (2/17, 1971), the LHC declared the conditions of granting guardianship of a child for a man or woman and how these conditions must be in accord with the interests of the child:

> According to Islamic legislation, guardianship is meeting the needs of the child in terms of providing food, clothes, …[sleeping accommodation] and it is legally bestowed on women, with its transfer to the male conditional on him being accompanied by a woman who will take care of the child whether she is paid or not. It was debatable whether guardianship was the right of the mother or father in that guardianship is most commonly decided upon the basis of the benefit to the child without taking into account the feelings of either parent. The interest of the child is not to be forbidden … the compassion and care of both parents, so if the child was taken from the mother for a legal excuse and was given to the father, and the father neglected his duties or the excuse disappeared the child will be returned to its divorced

51 *Majallat Al-Mahkama Al-'Ulya* G1/M, decision 1/2, 21/03/1956, 87.

> mother. If the judgment refused the request in returning the child in light of the most commonly held interpretations in this school of jurisprudence and after proof of the father's negligence, then an error has been committed in upholding the law and the judgment must be revoked.[52]

Case 2/17, 1971 was decided upon by the LHC after decisions in a number of lower courts prior to it being presented to the LHC for final adjudication. The court of first instance in Benghazi had previously granted guardianship to the mother of two sons after she and her husband divorced. The husband moved from Benghazi to Darnah, a city 180 miles (300 km) east of Benghazi. Once he had moved, he appealed the custody decision on the condition that, as the father, he can request guardianship of the children if he moves away permanently to a location that is considered to be a long distance from the female guardian. The court fulfilled his request and granted him guardianship of his sons.

The mother appealed this decision to the court in the city of Al-Baydah on the following grounds. Firstly, the father did not inform her about the move or ask her if she wanted to relocate. Secondly, the father's relocation was made under a false pretence and was just a ploy to take the children away from their mother. She also added that the condition that the female guardian must be not far from the *wali* (male guardian) – for their protection and easy access – was not a valid argument due to modern transportation and technology, and given that people are able to move thousands of miles in a few hours. In a further argument made to advance her cause, the mother mentioned that she had already moved to a city called Al-Baydah which was only 60 miles (100 km) west of Darnah, so the father's access to the children was made easier. The court rejected the mother's appeal because it decided that she must live in the same city as her ex-husband. However, the court did grant her visitation rights of only once a month for the whole day at her ex-husband's expense.

Following her initial failure, the mother brought a new case before the Benghazi court of first instance claiming that her ex-husband had moved the children from Darnah to Alexandria in Egypt and left them there with his new wife before he moved back to Tripoli alone. The father claimed that this was in their best interests because they would receive better education. The court responded to this statement as not being true since both Libya and Egypt have the same education system. A report was submitted to the court, authored by the Libyan Counsel-General in Alexandria, Egypt. This report declared that the children were struggling,

[52] *Majallat Al-Mahkama Al-'Ulya* 7/2, decision 2/17, 03/01/1971, 56.

and that their health and emotional status were not good. Unfortunately, the court still refused the mother's request, declaring that she had already lost guardianship and could not regain it. The mother finally took her case to the LHC and based her argument on the following four grounds:

1. The father acquired her right of guardianship under a false pretence when he relocated the children to Darnah. He then moved them to Alexandria and left them under the supervision of his second wife who was not considered a close female guardian and they were without a father, which is against their interest. The mother claimed that he did this because he did not want to pay what he would have been obligated to pay her if they had remained in her custody.
2. The first decision of the court was made on the grounds that the father relocated his children to Egypt on the basis of enhancing their level of education, a claim which had already been rejected by the appeals court in the city of Al-Baydah. Furthermore, when the children were taken away from their mother, the father placed them in a school in Darnah where they were examined. Their examination results were good, which indicated that their education thus far had been fine.
3. Guardianship is supposed to be granted on the basis of the best interests of the child, but unfortunately this principle had not been upheld in this case. The mother claimed that the father had demonstrated neglect, and as a consequence should not be deemed to be a suitable guardian.
4. The first decision was made on the grounds that when the father had moved to Darnah, the mother refused to move with him. This was not true as he had not informed her of his relocation. Therefore, because of this untruth, he had not met the condition of a suitable guardian.

On the grounds detailed above, the LHC decided in favour of the mother and granted her guardianship status over the children. The main points in the judgement detailed the importance of a child's need for compassion from both parents along with the continued monitoring of guardianship conditions, in particular the issue of neglect. As a consequence, the children returned to Benghazi to live with their mother.[53]

This case highlights a number of issues. It details the conditions of the female guardian living nearby to the children's *wali*. Another subject

---

[53] *Majallat Al-Mahkama Al-'Ulya* 2/7, decision 2/17, 03/01/1971, 56.

detailed is that of the male guardian who must provide a female to assist him in taking care of the children, and, finally, the location of guardianship. The details of this case clearly indicate that the father had made various statements to advance his cause. If the statements had been proven, they would have made his case quite plausible. However, in upholding the 'best interests of the child' principle, the LHC sought the facts of the children's current circumstances and made a decision on this basis.

This case is significant on two levels. Firstly, the lower courts had applied the law on a literal basis. Such an approach resulted in the upholding of guardianship conditions, which was viewed as a narrow-sighted approach. The LHC, on the other hand, made its judgement on the complete context on which this case was presented. By this, the LHC had taken into consideration first and foremost 'the best interests of the child' from an Islamic perspective.

Another reason for the significance of this case is that even though the case judgement was handed down in 1971, the LHC had based its decision on the 'best interests' principle at the heart of CROC, which was institutionalised many years later. Therefore, the view taken by this chapter is in total agreement with the decision made by the LHC. In its judgement, the LHC was unambiguous as to the reason why such a decision was sought, and more importantly highlighted the need to uphold 'the best interests of the child'. In particular, the LHC decision supports the main argument of this chapter that the culture affects the interpretation of the 'best interests' principle.

In Case 1/28, 1982, the LHC emphasised guardianship eligibility conditions:

> According to the Imam Malik school of jurisprudence, the conditions of guardianship include: the person eligible for guardianship being conservative religiously and loyal, and if the person lacks those conditions that person can no longer be considered eligible.[54]

In 1985, the LHC had been consistent in stressing the necessity of guardianship conditions in its decision to Case 3/31, 1985:

> The main purpose of guardianship is the protection of the child … Guardianship is also about meeting the child's needs, and guiding the child to the right path in life. It is very important for the guardian to be trustworthy and capable

[54] *Majallat Al-Mahkama Al-'Ulya* 18/3-4, decision 1/28, 13/01/1982, 9.

> of protecting the child. Failing to protect the child encompasses exposing the child to corruption.[55]

In Case (3/31, 1985),[56] the appellant (the girl's father) requested that the court abort the mother's custody of their 13-year-old daughter. The main argument for the appellant's request was that the daughter in question was tending her maternal grandfather's sheep on her own, at a considerable distance from the mother's residence. Her father also claimed that she had failed her exams at school and he argued that this was due to neglect. It was argued that a teenage girl being consistently away from home during the day might result in her involving herself in acts of indecency or in being abused. In handing down its decision, the court decided to approve the request and abort the mother's guardianship of the girl.

When the mother appealed the decision, the court of appeal reinstated the mother's custody of the girl. The reason for the decision was the court's belief that the child should not be deprived of her mother's love and care. However, the appeals court failed to see that the father was seeking protection for his daughter. The decision of the appeals court contradicted Islamic law because one of the purposes of guardianship in Islam is to protect the child from any type of harm.[57] This case illustrates that a court's implementation of guardianship conditions can have a negative effect on a child. This chapter rejects the appeals court opinion, since 'the best interests of the child' would be best served by her remaining in an environment under continuous monitoring and not alone at a location far from any sort of supervision.

E. Other Related Cases

The following LHC decisions demonstrate the court's approach in upholding guardianship conditions with room for flexibility to ensure 'the best interests of the child'. In Case 24/20, 1974, the LHC declared:

> The marriage of the divorced woman to a man … who is not related to the child/ren under her guardianship, does not cancel her right in guardianship if only the contract of marriage has been agreed upon. If marriage was

---

55 *Majallat Al-Mahkama Al-'Ulya* 1-2/25, decision 3/31, 22/05/1985, 9. See also *Al-Mahkama Al-'Ulya*, decision 26/45, 25/02/1999, GM; *Al-Mahkama Al-'Ulya*, decision 27/42, 04/01/1996, GM; *Al-Mahkama Al-'Ulya*, decision 38/47, 03/05/2001, GM.

56 *Majallat Al-Mahkama Al-'Ulya* 1-2/25, decision 3/31, 22/05/1985, 9.

57 Ibid.

> confirmed through sexual intercourse and the female guardian would be then pre-occupied with her newly wed husband, then it is obligatory to cancel her right in guardianship and take the child/ren away from her, *as long as the well-being of the child is not detrimentally affected or the child accepts another guardian*.[58]

Furthermore, the LHC decided in Case 7/20, 1974:

> If a person has the right to custody and did not request it, that right will be cancelled if they were aware of their eligibility; but if they did not know and they did not ask for it, their right will not be eliminated regardless of the period of their silence.[59]

In the above two cases, it is clear that the court, even though emphasising the importance in upholding guardianship conditions, has allowed these conditions to run secondary in situations where the guarded child is not negatively affected and 'the best interests of the child' are protected.

Unlike the above grouping of cases, the following group of LHC decisions have maintained other guardianship conditions as being non-negotiable when present in order to meet 'the best interests of the child'. If such conditions fail, the guarded child(ren) are perceived by the court to be endangered physically, emotionally or in any other undisclosed manner. Therefore such conditions need to be abided by on a strict basis.

Case 14/23, 1977,[60] presented before the LHC, highlights a case where an important prospective guardian condition, namely health, had formed the basis of argument by a father to gain custody over his children. The children were being cared for by their maternal grandmother. The father argued that the grandmother was medically unfit to take care of the children and that this might potentially harm his children. The grandmother had an artificial valve in her heart, yet it was found that this did not prevent her from taking care of both children in her custody. The judge did not grant cancellation of her right to custody over the children because the father of the two children failed to point to a single event where the children were harmed or were neglected due to the grandmother's medical condition. Thus, the guardian was considered capable of taking care of the children and satisfied the health and capability conditions that are legal requirements.[61]

---

[58] *Majallat Al-Mahkama Al-'Ulya* 3/10, decision 24/20, 28/02/1974, 36 (emphasis added).

[59] *Majallat Al-Mahkama Al-'Ulya* 10/3, decision 7/20, 31/01/1974, 13.

[60] *Majallat Al-Mahkama Al-'Ulya* 13/4, decision 14/23, 24/02/1977, 9.

[61] *Majallat Al-Mahkama Al-'Ulya* 13/4, decision 14/23, 24/02/1977, 9.

It should be noted that the grandmother, in her own defence, made mention of the fact that her two daughters were also living with her and the guarded children. In light of the law mentioned above relating to the guardian requiring assistance when they are not fully capable of fulfilling the child's needs, the court would have still made a judgement upholding the status quo on the basis of the aunts' presence.

In the Case 14/24, 1978, the LHC again expressed these conditions in one of its decisions when it stated:

> The whole purpose of guardianship is to care for the child, and part of that is protecting the child from corruption. Some of the conditions that must be satisfied for the establishment of custody is that the guardian must be mentally mature, be able to meet the needs of the child, ensure the safety of the child (especially for girls), be religiously faithful, and be rational. If the guardian was to be a man, then he must make available a woman to care for the child, for example, his wife or a nanny.[62]

Therefore, the above cases unambiguously illustrate the inflexible stance taken by the LHC in cases where failure of prospective guardians to meet the required conditions is deemed to place the guarded child(ren) in some form of danger.

The LHC in the following two case decisions had been consistent in its judgement on issues related to prospective guardians being silent for more than a year. The aim of enforcing this guardian condition is to guarantee the stability of the guarded child(ren) with respect to location, social environment and, most importantly, the guardian themselves. By achieving these goals, 'the best interests of the child' are best achieved.

Case 4/28, 1982 presented to the LHC details of a father's appeal against a ruling which granted custody of his children to the maternal grandmother. The case was based on the claim that the grandmother was too busy to care for the children. The court of appeal was not satisfied that a carer was provided for the children while the grandmother was at work, so the judge upheld the appeal and granted custody of the children to the father.[63]

As a consequence, the case was then appealed by the grandmother, who claimed that the ruling was against the law. She argued that the court of appeals made its ruling based on the petition of the father without considering the investigation that was performed by the court that heard

---

[62] *Majallat Al-Mahkama Al-'Ulya* 3/14, decision 14/24, 19/01/1978, 30.
[63] *Majallat Al-Mahkama Al-'Ulya* 1/19, decision 4/28, 04/04/1982, 12.

the original case. In the original case, the judge had provided the father with two alternatives:

1. to increase the alimony payment that the father was making to allow the grandmother to leave her job, which required her to be away for half of every working day; or
2. to start paying the original amount that was being previously paid to the mother of the children.

Both choices were rejected by the father. The court of appeals had aborted the right of the grandmother to custody of the children despite having no legal reason for such action. The court of appeals had relied solely on the fact that the grandmother was working in a job that she needed desperately without considering the fact that there was someone else caring for the children while the grandmother was at work. That person was the grandmother's maid. Furthermore, the grandmother was also willing to assign the role of carer to her other daughter (the children's maternal aunt). However, the role of guardian could not be interchanged among the carers as they pleased, and therefore the grandmother could not just assign care to her other daughter. The aunt would have to make a claim for custody through the courts.[64]

The final decision handed down was in favour of the grandmother. Having two aunts living in the same house satisfied the LHC that there was enough care for the children while the grandmother was fulfilling her employment duties.

In light of the High Court's decision, a number of points are noteworthy. Firstly, the grandmother was and continues to be the guardian. The presence of the aunts does not eliminate or degrade the grandmother's role or importance in any way. However, it was viewed by the court as assistance to the guardian's role. Another significant factor is that being assigned guardian does not grant the ownership over the role of guardian itself. Therefore, the role is not transferable at the discretion of the guardian.

The decision made by the LHC is supported by this chapter. It should be emphasised that if the LHC had taken a strict approach to determine whether the guardian upheld guardianship conditions, the LHC could have judged in favour of the father's case on the sole basis of the grandmother's absence from the children due to work commitments. However, the LHC had adopted the flexible approach to decision making

---

[64] *Majallat Al-Mahkama Al-'Ulya* 1/19, decision 4/28, 04/04/1982, 12.

as outlined in Libyan law, which upholds the *Malikiyah* version of Islam. The judgement considered the children's current family environment context and made a decision based on the broader picture. Even though CROC was adopted 12 years later, this case is a clear example that the 'best interests' principle as defined by CROC was already embedded in Libyan law because of its inherent Islamic culture.

Therefore, as has been illustrated in the above cases, guardianship under Libyan law has been developed with the guarded child(ren) as its primary concern, such that the child is to be served and cared for, and requires that the guardian be capable of taking care of and protecting the child. These requirements mean that the guardian must be completely dedicated to this role as detailed in the case above. If dedication to other activities leads to the neglect of the guardian's duties towards the child, then their right to custody will be forfeited.

Guardian conditions are based not on emotions but rather on rational grounds. For example if a mother harms her child(ren), she will lose custody of the child even if they are emotionally attached to her. Removing a child in this situation may be difficult emotionally; however, it is perceived as being in 'the best interests of the child'. A similar judgement was handed down by the LHC in Case 3/31, 1985 where a teenage girl had been seen tending to her maternal grandfather's sheep away from her guardian mother. The LHC disagreed with the appeals court decision to return the child to the mother on the grounds of emotionally being attached to her. In its judgement, the LHC emphasised that the well-being of the child, specifically her safety, determined what was in the child's best interests rather than the emotional attachment to her mother.[65]

Another example where the LHC was stringent in upholding the conditions of guardianship was in Case 14/23, 1977. If the guardian or anyone else in the household is proven to be diagnosed with a transmittable disease that could harm the guarded child, the right of the guardian will be cancelled even if the child's needs were being met. If the guardian has a medical condition that is deemed to be non-infectious and not harmful to the child in any way, then guardianship will remain with the allocated female family member.[66]

According to CROC, the purpose of guardianship is to nurture, care for and to meet the child's needs for a specified period of time. In Case 7/28, 1982 a grandmother had been granted custody of both her daughter's

---

65 *Majallat Al-Mahkama Al-'Ulya* 1-2/25, decision 3/31, 22/05/1985, 9.

66 *Majallat Al-Mahkama Al-'Ulya* 4/13, decision 14/23, 24/02/1977, 9.

children. The uncle of the girls' father appealed, arguing that the grandmother's commitment to working by night and sleeping during the day exposed the guarded children to abnormal conditions. The judge rejected the appeal. This decision was based upon the argument that the assistance of two of the children's aunts would be sought when the grandmother was not available. This case was then taken to the High Court on the same grounds. In addition, the uncle argued that the assisting aunts were not mature enough to help with the responsibilities of guardianship without providing any evidence to support this claim. The LHC confirmed the appeals court decision.[67]

According to Libyan Legislation 10/1984, the court has a responsibility to ensure that the guardianship conditions are being fulfilled. One of these conditions is that a prospective guardian needs to be capable of fulfilling the guardianship duties. In light of this fact, this chapter maintains that in Case 7/28, 1982 the court failed to confirm the claim made by the plaintiff that the assisting aunts did not fulfil an important guardian condition – that is, capability. The LHC played a passive role by making a judgement on the evidence presented. It should have been proactive in seeking whether the claims made by the plaintiff were true. It can be concluded that in this case, 'the best interests of the child' as understood by Libyan Legislation 10/1984 were not adequately addressed.

Case 14/24, 1978 presented to the LHC established that the plaintiff (mother) had been working in a government department in order to help her disabled mother meet living expenses. The plaintiff would leave the guarded child along with another daughter, who was 19 years old, during work hours. It was proven, through the testimony of an expert physician, that the mental capacity of the mentioned daughter was that of a 7-year-old child. It was also proven that she was ineligible to be a carer for the child even for a short period of time. In addition, the plaintiff did not deny her mother's disability. This disabled grandmother could not cope with the burden of supervising the child in question as well as the mentally immature 19-year-old girl.[68] It was necessary, in the interests of the child, that the mother care for them. As her work commitments harmed the child's interests, consequentially, the mother's guardianship was made void because it was argued that 'the best interests of the child'

67 *Majallat Al-Mahkama Al-'Ulya* 19/1, decision 7/28, 04/04/1982, 16.
68 *Majallat Al-Mahkama Al-'Ulya* 3, 4/24, decision 2/35, 29/06/1985, 17.

were not being catered for under this arrangement. The ruling to abort her guardianship is seen as proper under the law.[69]

However, through its powers, the LHC should have activated the Social Security Legislation;[70] this would have solved the financial needs of the mother and provided her with some sort of income to enable her to stay at home to take care of her dependents. The decision made here can be seen as being harmful to both parties involved. Both the mother and children would suffer emotionally. Furthermore, although it was based on logic, the court failed to look at the personal interests of those involved.

In Case 1/18, 1971 the LHC confirmed that, 'legally, if the guardian of the child was a man, he must provide a woman to nurse the child, such as a wife, a woman who is of kin, or a nanny'.[71] The decision handed down in Case 14/24, 1978 confirms this point. An appellant declared in a submission to the court that the defendant, her ex-husband, did not have a female carer to take care of the children and therefore was ineligible for custody. However, it became clear that the father had remarried and was therefore eligible to regain custody because the assisting female carer was now available.[72] Therefore, the court ensured that 'the best interests of the child' were catered for because it made certain that there was a female carer with the father. In this case the second wife would care for the children under the supervision of the father. This case shows one of the Islamic cultural influences in guardianship aspects: in the case of a male guardian, 'the best interests of the child' are met when there is a female assisting the male guardian.

The first paragraph of article 66 from the Legislation 10/1984 considers the failure of all or some of the conditions in section 65 as causing the termination of the custody. Case 19/42, 1996 highlights the importance that the LHC places on investigating the conditions of the eligible guardian. The original ruling gave the defendant the right to guardianship of her children, without establishing whether the right conditions for custody existed.[73] This is seen as not being fair to the plaintiff because the court should have investigated both sides of the case and made sure that all necessary steps had been taken. The LHC's ruling that this decision was wrong represents an attempt on the part of the LHC to ensure that 'the best interests of the child' are taken into consideration, by insisting that the court should check the conditions of the guardian

---

69 *Majallat Al-Mahkama Al-'Ulya* 3/14, decision 14/24, 19/01/1978, 30.
70 *Social Security Legislation* (72/1973).
71 *Majallat Al-Mahkama Al-'Ulya* 1/8, decision 1/18, 06/06/1971, 93.
72 *Majallat Al-Mahkama Al-'Ulya* 3/14, decision 14/24, 19/01/1978, 31.
73 *Majallat Al-Mahkama Al-'Ulya* 3-2/30, decision 19/42, 21/03/1996, 18.

properly. Furthermore, the right of guardianship belongs to the child and not the guardian; for this reason, the court should investigate whether a potential guardian is suitable.

As mentioned earlier, the law states in article M66F.C that 'guardianship returns to its first owner when ... cause [for its initial loss] disappears, unless the court decided the opposite in order to establish the interests of the child'. This means that if a reason arises that makes the guardian no longer eligible or renders them unable to fulfil the requirements of guardianship, then the role of guardian will become void. However, once the cause disappears, the right to guardianship will return and the claim for guardianship can be made once again. This is to ensure that 'the best interests of the child' are maintained and that the child is under the care of the best guardian.

For example, if a mother falls sick during guardianship and can no longer care and maintain the child, the child will be taken from her care and placed with another suitable guardian (such as the father). Once she has regained full health, she becomes eligible for guardianship once again and will gain the right to guardianship again once/if she makes her claim.

The *Malikiyah Madhhab* distinguishes between voidable and unvoidable conditions.[74] However, Libyan Legislation 10/1984 does not follow this interpretation and is therefore perceived to rule in contrast to the *Malikiyah* version of Islam because it believes this opinion is contrary to 'the best interests of the child'. Under article M66F.C, if a woman marries a 'stranger', she will lose her right to guardianship. However, if she were to divorce this person, her right to guardianship would return. The *Malikiyah Madhhab* does not take this approach and believes that because the *choice* was made to marry while being aware that as a consequence her guardianship would become void, hence the right to guardianship does not return if divorce is sought. From the perspective of the *Malikiyah*, only on the basis of unavoidable conditions, such as sickness or necessary travel, can the right to guardianship be regained.

Commentary

In cases of parental separation/divorce, the father is obliged to maintain his children during their stay with their mother. No one can remove a child from the custody of their parents unless circumstances demand

[74] Avoidable conditions: where an action has been taken as a matter of choice, e.g. remarry. Unavoidable conditions: where an action has occurred beyond one's control, e.g. sickness.

otherwise. In such a case, the parents or guardians should agree upon a person(s) who they believe can cater for 'the best interests of the child' until a court can adjudicate on the matter. A person who is an eligible guardian must be proactive in requesting custody of the child. Placing the onus on prospective guardians ensures that the child is not neglected for any length of time and that there is someone caring for them at all times.

During the course of litigation for guardianship of the child(ren), the primary concern should always be 'the best interests of the child'. Such litigation should not be perceived as just a formality determining who the next in line on the guardianship hierarchy is, but rather an in-depth examination of the next appropriate person deemed to be responsible and capable of taking care of the child and meeting their needs. Furthermore, an investigation of how the child's best interests can be met should be the overriding concern of any guardianship litigation. This approach was exemplified by the court cases presented to LHC which have been detailed above.

These cases highlight the LHC decisions based on factors that include desirable characteristics of the guardian, a safe place for the child(ren) to reside and the time in which the claim was made for guardianship. These factors illustrate how 'the best interests of the child' were the main concerns for the LHC in its rulings.

In Case 7/30, 1985, the grandmother, who was the most eligible guardian for the child according to the guardianship hierarchy, had her right to guardianship dismissed because she waited over one year to make her claim. As has been mentioned above, silence over a period of one year according to Islamic law and Libyan Legislation 10/1984 is grounds for making void the right to guardianship. It was the view of the LHC that it would be in the child's best interests to keep the child with the grandfather as he had taken care of the child for the whole period of time and taken care of the child's needs, enrolling her in school and caring for her well-being. It would have been unfavourable for the child to be removed from under the care of the grandfather, given that her environment had showed signs of stability.[75]

It is clear that the LHC decisions detailed under the sub-heading 'Guardianship conditions' have consistently been handed down with 'the best interests of the child' as the primary concern. Such a statement can be substantiated because the 'best interests of the child' has been a recurring theme in decisions handed down over a period of 30 years by the LHC.

---

75 *Majallat Al-Mahkama Al-'Ulya* 22/1, decision 7/30, 17/01/1985, 14.

In conclusion, in accordance with guardianship conditions already discussed, Libyan Legislation 10/1984 and its official interpretation through LHC decisions, the cases presented above are clearly consistent with CROC in terms of making 'the best interests of the child' a primary consideration.

F. Upholding Guardianship

Libyan Legislation 10/1984

Article M67F.B states that 'moving with the child inside the country will be allowed by a guardian if it does not harm the child's interests'. Article M67F.C states that:

> The female guardian cannot relocate with the child outside Libya except in the case where permission has been sought from the male sponsor (*Wali*). If permission was refused, then she can raise the matter with the relevant court.

LHC decisions

In cases presented to the LHC concerning the issue relating to the place of guardianship, decisions handed down by the court have differed prior to and after the introduction of Legislation 10/1984. This legislation, unlike a strict *Malikiyah* approach, allowed for flexibility in judging cases relating to this matter. Prior to Legislation 10/1984, a strict 72-mile (116 km) radius was enforced on the female guardian's residence to that of the *wali*. This 72-mile maximum was believed to be in the child's best interests because it was feasible for both male and female guardians to share supervision of the child. With the introduction of Legislation 10/1984, movement by the female guardian to any location within Libya would not result in losing her right to guardianship. However, relocation outside Libya would require the relevant court to decide on whether the female guardian would lose her right to guardianship to maintain 'the best interests of the child'. Such an approach is consistent with the argument advocated by this chapter because it is this flexibility granted to the relevant court which guarantees that 'the best interests of the child' are upheld. This movement from a strict framework to a more relaxed set of guidelines allows Libyan law in relation to guardianship to be more consistent with the 'best interests' principle set out in CROC.

In one of its decisions prior to the introduction of Legislation 10/1984, the LHC in Case 3/10, 1974 decided:

> If the *Wali* moved to a location that is further than seventy two miles from the location of the child on a permanent basis, then this move obliges the

> relocation of the female guardian and the child that is under her custody to the location of the *Wali* in order to obtain the right care and supervision for the child, so if she did move, the child would stay with her and if she did not, her right in custody would be cancelled.[76]

Similarly, in Case 12/24, 1978, which was also decided upon prior to the advent of Legislation 10/1984, the LHC declared:

> It is widely known in the Imam Malik School of jurisprudence ... that the female carer of the child is not allowed to move with the child permanently to a location that is far from the sponsor of the child. Any distance beyond seventy two miles is considered far. The reason is to allow the sponsor of the child to supervise the raising of the child. This religious obligation must be practised, even with the existence of more accessible and faster modes of transportation ... The reason for aborting the mother's right to custody in a case where she moves the mentioned distance away from the sponsor is that the sponsor is ultimately responsible for the supervision of the child's upbringing.

Unlike the above two decisions, Case 6/37, 1990 was presented to the LHC after Legislation 10/1984 was introduced. In its decision, the LHC refused to cancel the mother's guardianship because she travelled outside Libya temporarily to seek treatment for her son while leaving her other children with a friend.[77]

Commentary

Prior to the introduction of Legislation 10/1984, the interpretation provided by the *Malikiyah Madhhab* on the issue of relocation was a dominant factor. Since its introduction, the legislation has provided the judge with flexibility to rule whether a parent can relocate with the child if it is perceived not to be harmful and therefore in 'the best interests of the child'. In the opinion of this chapter's author, the judge has applied the following criteria or guidelines to establish 'the best interests of the child' in handing down the respective judgements.

One of the conditions of custody is trustworthiness. If the guardian wishes to relocate, the guardian may not be allowed to relocate with the child unless they have shown that the relocation is permanent and that the guardian is trustworthy enough to care for the child.

The law has a different perception to relocation within and outside Libya. If the female guardian decides to relocate permanently with a

---

[76] *Majallat Al-Mahkama Al-'Ulya* 13/20, decision 3/10, 07/02/1974, 28.
[77] LHC decision 6/37, 21/12/1990, cited in Al-Julaydi, above n24, 287.

child outside the country, she will lose custody if such relocation is performed without permission from the *wali*.

The mother has the right to see and visit her child even if she has lost her right to guardianship. Time spent with a child by both guardians is perceived to be in 'the best interests of the child'. Libyan law, in this situation, makes it a priority for both parents to think and reassess where they decide to live because they have to consider the other guardian's need to visit and spend time with the child, and therefore meet 'the best interests of the child'.

In cases concerning relocation, Libyan law has been modified to be more flexible in its approach. The opinion adopted by this chapter is that Libyan law goes a step further in maintaining the 'best interests' principle as stipulated in CROC, even though conflict may arise with the opinions advocated by the *Malikiyah Madhhab*. This does not mean that such flexibility is in conflict with Islam itself, since this issue of flexibility and differences in opinion is widely accepted within Islamic jurisprudence.

Regarding relocation of a female guardian, Libyan Legislation 10/1984 does not discriminate on the basis of who the female guardian is. It provides that relocation within the country of Libya, whether temporary or permanent, does not affect guardianship. This comes from the *Zahiriyah Madhhab* and is highlighted in the following statement by Ibn Hazm: 'the mother has the first right to her son's and daughter's custody until they both reach maturity, whether the father has left the country the mother is living in or not, and similarly with the mother.'[78]

This view is against the *Malikiyah* and *Shafi'iyah Madhhab* because they do not allow the female guardian to move with the child to any place without the permission of the *wali* on the basis that 'the best interests of the child' are best served by having a male guardian close by, because of his obligated duty of care and maintenance of the child. It is considered to be difficult for the *wali* to meet his obligations towards the child if they are distant from each other.[79] Although the *Malikiyah Madhhab* is the founding source of Legislation 10/1984, an alternate opinion from another *Madhhab* was used as a reference because it was viewed as being the better option in meeting 'the best interests of the child'.

According to Libyan law, the following three interests need to be considered during guardian relocation: those of the child, the father and the mother. If the interests conflict with each other, then the priority is

---

78 Ali Ibn Ahmad Ibnu Hazm al-Zahiriy, *Al-Muhalla* (ND) 323.

79 Wahbah Al-Zuhaily, *Al-Fiqh Al-Islamiy Wa Adillatuhu*, above n24, 7738.

the child's interests, followed by those of the parents.[80] It is important to recognise the role of the *wali* as decision maker and maintainer of the child, so when guardian relocation occurs, it is important that the *wali* is still able to fulfil his duties.

Legislation 10/1984 clearly forbids the female guardian from travelling with the child outside the country except with the *wali*'s permission. The preference is that permission should be sought early in order to prevent any type of conflict between the guardians.

However, what can be done if the *wali* refuses to grant permission? The answer is that the justice system is the exclusive authority for adjudication. The main focus in such a case should be the evidence presented by the female guardian when justifying the child's relocation. A secondary concern of the justice system is to determine why the *wali* refused to grant permission when it was requested. If relocation outside the country goes ahead without permission, this will result in the forfeit of the female guardian's right to guardianship, even if permanent settlement was not the intention.

This chapter has made it clear that with regards to relocation issues, Libyan law has adopted a flexible approach in decision making. Flexibility is in no way a cause of conflict with Islamic law, but rather reflects the differences in opinion which Islamic jurisprudence allows for. Such an approach provides the respective adjudicator with full authority to assess the circumstances surrounding relocation to ensure that 'the best interests of the child' are being protected. Even though 'the best interests of the child' were being met prior to the introduction of Legislation 10/1984, the flexibility that is now inherent in the legislation ensures more than ever the implementation of Libya's obligations under CROC and in particular the 'best interests' principle.

G. Visitation Rights

Libyan Legislation 10/1984

Article M68 of Legislation 10/1984 states that 'if the child's *Wali* and the guardian disagreed about child visitation rights, the judge has to decide the time and place for such visits, and the matter should be given priority for immediate judgement'.

---

[80] *Majallat Al-Mahkama Al-'Ulya* 30/1, decision 5/41, 16/06/1994, 14.

LHC decisions

In Case 5/41, 1994 the LHC declared that if a dispute occurs between male and female guardians about child visitation, the judge has full authority to decide the time and place of visitation in a manner that removes obstacles on the part of the father and to protect the interests of the child and his/her mother. The LHC stated:

> According to the law, if the guardian and the *Wali* cannot agree on how to organise visits to see the child, then the judge will determine the time, location and duration of such visits. That ruling should be enforced by the power of the law, which ensures that the father of the child will not have any further problems in visiting the child, and further still, the interests of the child and the mother would have been protected.[81]

Commentary

Visitation rights have always been a point of contention between opposing parties with relation to guardianship. The cause of the contention may be an attempt by one party to seek revenge against another. To settle such disputes, article M68, as stated above, declares that 'the judge has to decide the time and place for such visits, and the matter should be given priority for immediate judgement'. Therefore, the court is the only body that can decide the time and place of regular visits. A speedy decision is encouraged in order to prevent further damage and aggravation between the respective parties. The importance of a rapid decision cannot be underestimated because the duties that hinge upon kinship, and which Islam obligates the faithful to observe, strongly encourage unmarriageable kin visitation rights to children and return visits from them. This is especially important when the parents of the child are deceased, lost, kidnapped, in jail, held captive and so on. It is the right of the child's kinships, who are replacing the parents, to visit the child and make sure their needs are being catered for. In light of the above, this chapter encourages a proactive approach by both parties, in being willing to grant visitation rights. Embedded in Libyan culture, visitation rights are extremely important from an Islamic perspective. Therefore, the concept of visitation rights is in total agreement with the 'best interests' principle outlined in CROC.

---

[81] Ibid.

H. Discretion of the High Court

Libyan Legislation 10/1984

Article M63F.C states: '[I]f the one, who is eligible for guardianship, refused or he/she no longer become eligible, the right of guardianship will be transferred to the next person on the guardianship hierarchy. If one is not available, *the court will need to declare one*' (emphasis added).

LHC decisions

In Case 2/11, 1974 the LHC referred to the Court of First Instance in Tripoli which has heard the case of a plaintiff to abort his sister-in-law's right to custody of her children (these being the children of the plaintiff's deceased brother). The plaintiff based his case on the mother's re-marriage to a man who was considered 'a stranger'[82] to the children. On this basis, the court ruled in favour of the plaintiff, consequently handing the plaintiff guardianship of the children.

The mother of the children then appealed this case in the Tripoli Court of Appeal, claiming that she had remarried on the condition that the children live with her and that the new husband pay their expenses and maintenance; as a result, this agreement was a condition recorded in the marriage contract. This marriage condition was explicitly sought by the mother because she did not have any female kin who could have been a prospective guardian and would therefore be granted guardianship. The mother also claimed that the incumbent guardian could not be trusted with the children. To back up her claim, she reported that he took control of the compensation money paid by the driver who accidentally hit and killed her late husband. The mother added that it was better for the children to stay with her being married than to stay with their uncle's wife who was not related to them at all.[83]

However, in his own defence, the incumbent guardian rejected the claim that he received any payment related to his brother's death and that such an argument was used to undermine his case. He also offered to pay the expenses of the minors from his own wealth. The court heard from trustworthy witnesses that the guardian was paid 700 dinars (Libyan currency, about £1,034) as compensation from his brother's killer. Thus, the court concluded from his denial of receiving any payment and the consequent testimony given by witnesses before the court that he was untrustworthy and dishonest. The court then ruled that it was better for

---

82 Meaning 'from marriageable kinship'.

83 *Majallat Al-Mahkama Al-'Ulya* 2/11, decision 2/21, 07/11/1974, 13.

the children to live with their married mother than to stay with their uncle and his wife. Subsequently, the court of appeal disagreed with the judgement made in the court of first instance and as a consequence judged in favour of the mother.[84]

The uncle took the case further to the LHC. At this point, it should be noted that one of the conditions of a female guardian stated by *Malikiyah Madhhab* and confirmed later by Legislation 10/1984 is that marrying kin that is marriageable to the child will result in cancelling the guardianship status in the case of a female guardian. Therefore, it was on this basis – the mother being married to a 'stranger' – that this case was presented to the LHC. The appellant also claimed that it was incorrect to claim that he, the uncle, was untrustworthy as he was still paying the mother 20 dinars (£30) per month as child maintenance, and had helped the mother and the children to receive help from charities. It was also claimed that if the mother was truly committed to her children's care and well-being, she would not have followed her instincts to seek marriage to a stranger.[85]

The important facts presented to the LHC in this case are as follows:

1. The mother's husband, even though being a stranger to the children, declared that he was willing to care for the children and pay their expenses. The uncle argued that this was seen as wrong as it is in conflict with what is known in the *Malikiyah* school of jurisprudence, which holds that the mother's right to custody is aborted as soon as she consummates a marriage to a stranger to the children. The school's philosophy holds that the mother will be preoccupied with her husband, and that her husband will probably not tolerate her children, and so it is not right to leave the children with someone who will not tolerate or be good to them.
2. The untrustworthiness of the appellant was determined based on the claims made by witnesses before the court in relation to the appellant actually receiving money from the killer of the father of the children in question.

Commentary

In relation to guardianship issues, this is a case of major significance. Most noteworthy in this case is the conflict generated by the court of first instance in attempting to achieve 'the best interests of the child' through

---

84 *Majallat Al-Mahkama Al-'Ulya* 2/11, decision 2/21, 07/11/1974, 16.

85 *Majallat Al-Mahkama Al-'Ulya* 2/11, decision 2/21, 07/11/1974, 17.

the literal implementation of the law. What is meant by this is that the court of first instance sought to uphold a guardianship condition (that is, marriage to a stranger) in its belief that 'the best interests of the child' would be protected.

The judgement handed down by the court of appeal reflected the belief that the interests of the children had not been protected. The appeal court revoked the decision made by the court of first instance on the basis that applying the law would ultimately protect the interests of the child(ren). Even though marriage to a stranger would usually cause a woman to forfeit her right to guardianship, in this particular case, the court of appeal believed the interests of the children would surely be protected by granting their mother guardianship because their stepfather had accepted them and was willing to pay their living expenses.

Even though the LHC upheld the court of appeal's decision in favour of the mother, it did so on different grounds. It stated that the children should be left with their mother not because the court believed their interests would be better protected, but rather because the next eligible guardian (in this case the uncle) forfeited his right as guardian due to his lack of trustworthiness. This case clearly shows that there is conflict between the 'best interests' principle, which under CROC was a primary consideration, and the *Malikiyah* understanding on this issue, which later contributed to the formation of Libyan Legislation 10/1984. According to both the *Malikiyah* interpretation of Islam and Libyan legislation, a mother's right to guardianship would be forfeited if she remarries a stranger. Even though the LHC tried to resolve this discrepancy through its discretion in interpreting guardianship conditions, the grounds on which the LHC made its judgement were not the 'best interests of the child' principle, but rather on the basis that there was no alternative eligible guardian. In the opinion of this chapter's author, the law should be amended to make all the guardianship conditions firmly linked with the 'best interests' principle rather than having discrete guidelines which legislation hopes will protect a child's interests. With such legislative amendments, it would be up to the discretion of the respective court to ensure that guardianship conditions will protect 'the best interests of the child'.

On a related issue, if a person who has the right to guardianship but backs down from this right, or is not able to fulfil the obligated duties, then the right of custody will be granted to whoever is nominated by the court.[86] The judge will choose the most appropriate person depending on

---

86 *Al-Mahkama Al-'Ulya*, decision 10/47, 07/12/2000, GM.

the merits of the case. This decision will still be in accordance with the *Malikiyah* jurisprudence.

In light of the case details mentioned above, the discretion of the LHC to adjudicate on guardianship issues is not to be used separately – that is, apart from Libyan legislation – but rather as a tool to reinforce the aims and objectives of the relevant law. It is clear that the LHC utilised discretion in order to protect 'the best interests of the child'.

I. Reinstating the Right of Guardianship

Libyan Legislation 10/1984

The law states in article M66F.C that 'custody returns to its first owner when its cause disappears, unless the court decides otherwise, in order to establish the interests of the child'.

LHC decisions

The LHC in the Case 2/17, 1971 makes it unambiguous the difference between a mother's failure in her role as guardian and the cancellation of this right:

> To declare that the right of guardian that was taken from the mother would not return at all is against the law (the *Malikiyah* school of jurisprudence) because the most accepted interpretation in that school is that failure is different to cancellation, so it would not be returned in the latter, but would in the former. Some of the reasons that may cause failure in guardianship and permit its return are: illness, leaving because of an obligatory trip to Hajj, the relocation of the father or the *Wali* ... So if the cause of guardianship failure disappears, guardianship returns to the mother and is upheld as long as the conditions for guardianship continue to be satisfied.[87]

The LHC confirmed this opinion on another occasion when it stated that 'If the mother of the child had surrendered guardianship of the child to the father for a reason that is later removed, she can then ... [have] that child [returned] to her custody'.[88]

Commentary

With respect to the LHC decision detailed above, if a mother rejected guardianship of her own child, the role of guardian will not return to her. However, if this right was annulled for a reason that was beyond her control, then that right will return as soon as the reason for its annulment

---

87 *Majallat Al-Mahkama Al-'Ulya* 2/7, decision 2/17, 03/01/1971, 57.

88 *Majallat Al-Mahkama Al-'Ulya* 3/10, decision 20/24, 28/02/1974, 36.

is removed. This opinion is derived from the *Malikiyah Madhhab*, which is different from the other schools of Islamic jurisprudence, where no difference exists between failure and cancellation. This chapter supports the opinion advocated by the *Malikiyah Madhhab*, and specifically the relevant Libyan legislation which, as detailed above, has provisions for adjudicators to make ad-hoc decisions which are consistent with the 'best interests' principle as a primary consideration as outlined in CROC. 'The best interests of the child' are undoubtedly upheld with a return of the mother's guardianship when reasons beyond her control previously eliminated this right. In the case where a mother neglected a child or chose to remarry, and the interests of the child(ren) had run second to the mother's decision, the mother would permanently lose her right to guardianship.

J. Expenses for Maintaining the Child and the Guardian

Libyan Legislation 10/1984

Article M69 states:

> the mother does not deserve to be paid for her child's custody while she is still under the bond of marriage to his father, so if they separated, or the female guardian was not the mother, then she deserves to be paid for her care of the child with the child's assets, else the duty of maintenance is placed on the *Wali*.

Article M70FA, B states: 'the divorced woman deserves to live in suitable residence as long as her right in custody is still active. If her custody is terminated, then her right to such residence will fail.'

LHC decisions

In a case related to the maintenance payments during guardianship, a mediation hearing was held prior to the case being presented to the court of instance. An agreement between a man and his divorced wife was reached. Under this agreement, the husband would pay his ex-wife all expenses incurred in caring for the daughter. However, no explicit figure was suggested. Libyan Legislation 10/1984 defines costs of custody in article 22: 'Expenses of custody include the cost of residence, food, clothing, medication and any other expenditure required to maintain a normal life.'

When the case was heard in the appeals court, the father based his case on the fact that even though he agreed to pay for the costs of guardianship, he was not obliged to make any payments since there was no specific amount set under the terms of the mediation agreement. The appeal was rejected because the mediation agreement did not specifically mention any such payments.

Following the appeals court judgement, the mother took the case to the LHC. It ruled in favour of the mother, declaring that even though the existing agreement did not specify the costs of guardianship, such costs were obligated by law and not by any agreement which may have excluded such costs. Therefore the *wali* was now obligated to pay extra to cover the expenses of guardianship. In its decision, the LHC declared that 'the mother who is performing the duties of a guardian deserves to have her expenses paid by the child's father'.[89] In support of this decision, the LHC also stated:

> The text in Article 69, Legislation (10/1984) is concerned with the rules of marriage, divorce and their affect. This section declares that the mother is ineligible for any payments in return for caring for the children as long as she is still married to their father. If, on the other hand, the mother was to be divorced from the father or if the carer of the children was not the mother then she has the right to be paid for the care provided to the children.[90]

Commentary

Islamic law obligates the *wali* to pay the expense of the supported child[91] while a female guardian is responsible for the child's daily needs. In doing so, it upholds 'the best interests of the child' by distributing the duties of the child's care on both guardian and *wali*.

Libyan Legislation 10/1984 considers that caring for the child is a role that must be shared by both parents. The law believes that the mother needs to care for and maintain the everyday needs of the child, while the father needs to support this financially. When both parties fulfil their responsibilities under this arrangement, 'the best interests of the child' are all but guaranteed.

The *Malikiyah Madhhab* emphasises that payments made to the female guardian should be sourced from the *wali*. A decision as to how much should be paid is for the judge to decide, and that depends on the *wali*'s financial situation. In summary, the issue of financial support is clear under Libyan legislation. Regardless of the terms of arrangement set out in a guardianship case, that the financial needs for the guarded child must

---

[89] *Majallat Al-Mahkama Al-'Ulya* 4-3/27, decision 40/18, 13/01/1994, 16; *Majallat Al-Mahkama Al-'Ulya* 4-3/27, decision 40/21, 13/01/1994, 16.

[90] *Al-Mahkama Al-'Ulya*, decision 29/45, 27/05/1999, GM.

[91] Wahbah al-Zuhaily, *Huquq al-Atfal wa al-Musinin*, above n48, 38.

be met is implicit, and therefore the respective *wali* is bound to fulfil that obligation. Such guarantee of financial resources means that the 'best interests' principle as defined in CROC is upheld by Libyan legislation, which is based on *Malikiyah* jurisprudence.

K. Accommodation of the Guardian

Libyan Legislation 10/1984

Article M70FA,B states that: 'the divorced woman deserves to live in suitable residence as long as her right in custody is still active. If her guardianship is terminated, then her right to suitable residence will fail.'

LHC decisions

The LHC in the Case (1/38, 1991) stated:

> According to Article 70/A taken from legislation (10/1984), the sponsor of the guarded children has the duty to supply the suitable residence for the divorced (mother) in order [for her] to live with the guarded children for the period of her guardianship, and the court has no jurisdiction on this right and so cannot contradict it. The court that decided to mention this Article in its ... [ruling] did that in order to protect the divorced mother and the child under her guardianship.[92]

Commentary

If the female guardian does not have a place of residence, the father must provide such suitable shelter. Therefore, a divorcee who has custody of any children is entitled to suitable accommodation for as long as her right to guardianship stands and her entitlement to such accommodation terminates with the termination of guardianship. These rights continue until the child(ren) complete their education and are able to earn a living.[93]

Some amendments were made to article M70FA, by Legislation 9/1994, which details that if a female guardian loses guardianship for one reason or another, she is still eligible to stay in the marital home until she

---

92 *Majallat Al-Mahkama Al-'Ulya* 1-2/26, decision 1/38, 08/05/1991, 15. See also *Majallat Al-Mahkama Al-'Ulya* 4-3/29, decision 8/40, 26/06/1993, 17; *Al-Mahkama Al-'Ulya*, decision 33/44, 29/06/2000, GM; *Al-Mahkama Al-'Ulya*, decision 47/45, 18/11/1999, GM; *Al-Mahkama Al-'Ulya*, decision 52/45, 18/11/1999, GM; *Al-Mahkama Al-'Ulya*, decision 12/47, 07/12/2000, GM.

93 *Law of Marriage and Divorce Rules and their Effects (10/1984)* art 70FA and B. 'Abdusalam al-'Alim, above n33, 327–9.

remarries. The only time this will not apply is if the woman has been convicted of committing adultery.

Originally, article M70FA,B stated that the female guardian would lose her residency once she had lost her guardianship. It is clear that the change to this article is important for a number of reasons. The first reason is that the law is now protecting the mother post guardianship except in the instance mentioned. Secondly, the law highlights the continued link between the mother and child and ensures a safe place for the child when visitation rights are exercised by the mother. Finally, it can be seen that guaranteeing the place of residence keeps some sense of stability in what can be a very turbulent divorce process, thereby reducing the emotional scars on the child.

With regard to accommodation provisions to both the female guardian and guarded child, this chapter argues that under Libyan legislation, 'the best interests of the child' are protected. The provisions outlined regarding accommodation display a concern to maintain solid sense of stability, in particular for the child, in an extremely uncertain phase of their life. Such stability is essential from an Islamic perspective, and consequently ensures the 'best interests' principle defined in CROC.

IV. CONCLUSION

This chapter has clearly identified the LHC as the supreme authority when implementing Libyan legislation and, most importantly, upholding the 'best interests of the child' principle. Many cases presented in this chapter have unambiguously demonstrated that the LHC is fulfilling its role as the ultimate safeguard of the law.

Also unequivocally established is that the 'best interests of the child' principle is embedded in Legislation 10/1984. Examples of articles proving this exact point include: article M62F.C, nominating a guardian after the first four potential guardians in the guardianship hierarchy; article M66F.C, reinstating guardianship if in 'the best interests of the child'; and article M63F.A, that the mother will always be granted guardianship except in the case where it is not in 'the best interests of the child'. These articles all aim to protect 'the best interests of the child'; however, an explicit discrete article detailing the 'best interests' principle does not exist. This may have formed the basis of the concerns expressed by the CRC.

The success of the LHC has been proven in cases relating to guardianship matters where 'the best interests of the child' has been the primary consideration in the decision making process. It has been so successful that in one particular case detailed in this chapter, the LHC utilised its discretion in interpreting the relevant legislation to uphold the 'best interests' principle instead of the legislation's literal application, which would have otherwise prevented the interests of the child from being protected.

Libyan Legislation 10/1984 has clearly defined conditions that need to be met by a prospective guardian. These conditions provide the basic foundations in ensuring 'the best interests of the child'. If any condition is not upheld, then the prospective guardian will forfeit their right to be a guardian, even if that guardian is the mother of the child. These conditions should be tightly coupled with the 'best interests' principle as the primary consideration.

In further highlighting the role of the LHC when dealing with guardianship issues, it has been made clearly evident that flexibility has been utilised to guarantee the child's best interests. Libyan Legislation 10/1984 explicitly provides the court with leverage when determining the next appropriate carer, provided that the conditions of guardianship have been upheld. The flexibility only exists after the first four prospective guardians defined by the guardianship hierarchy. A case that is representative of such an adjudication made by the High Court was presented in this chapter.

It has been demonstrated, after presenting the relevant articles in Legislation 10/1984 and relevant cases, that the official interpretation of the law is influenced by the local culture, specifically the *Malikiyah* 'brand' of Islam. In handing down its decisions, the LHC has made frequent references to the *Malikiyah* interpretations, supporting the chapter statement that the interpretation of international human rights in municipal legal systems will inevitably, understandably and legitimately be affected by local cultures.

4. ADR and Islamic law: the cases of the UK and Singapore

Arif A. Jamal

I. INTRODUCTION

This chapter explores the use of alternative dispute resolution (ADR) within Muslim legal traditions as they are expressed in the UK and in Singapore. In doing so, it addresses two areas of increasing concern in legal scholarship generally – namely ADR and Islamic law. Moreover, within the context of Islamic law, the chapter discusses an issue that currently is gaining attention as ancient Islamic norms, with a grounding in the Quranic text and expressing a preference for negotiated, amicable dispute settlement, are brought into conversation with contemporary ADR discourses.

The chapter proceeds by discussing the classical bases for the use of forms of ADR, including negotiation, mediation and arbitration, in Muslim legal thought, and then proceeds to look at the ways in which ADR operates within Muslim contexts in the UK and in Singapore. This examination will show that Islamic law is applied more formally in Singapore than in the UK. This is well known and not surprising; however, its implications in the ADR context are interesting. Drawing upon literature about religious-based ADR, this chapter will argue that the informal system in the UK may be more facilitative of Islamic ADR than the more formal system of Singapore. Lastly, the chapter will raise some of the challenges that might emerge from this more facilitative environment.

II. ADR AND ISLAM

The bases of ADR in classical Islamic thought and theory are well known and may be found even before the advent of Islam in the practice of pre-Islamic communities in Arabia, in the text of the Qur'an, and in early (as well as contemporary) Muslim practice, inspired in part at least from these bases. In other words, there has developed what one may call an 'ethic of ADR' in Muslim contexts.

In the pre-Islamic milieu, as Toshihiko Izutsu has noted, tribal solidarity was a key virtue.[1] As a result of this value and of the tribal organisation of the society, settlement of disputes through mediated means was encouraged especially within the tribe and in order to maintain the integrity of the tribal framework. Thus, conciliation and peace-making by elders, leaders and those in authority was practised through informal means,[2] and these practices became part of the social ethic. By the time of the emergence of Islam, therefore, both the practice and the ethic of mediated settlement were known and established in the Arabian context.[3]

With the advent of Islam, the values of mediated and amicable settlement were not just validated, but enhanced and reinforced by receiving Quranic sanction and thereby moving from being just pragmatic to participating in a richer notion of justice. The use both of amicable settlement involving mediation (*sulh*) and of arbitration (*takhim*) are noted in the Quran.

For example, the fourth chapter (*sura*) of the Quran, Sura An-Nisa, makes reference to the concept of *sulh*, saying:

> And if a woman fears cruelty or desertion on her husband's part, there is no sin on them both if they make terms of peace between themselves; and making peace (*sulh*) is better.
>
> (Sura An-Nisa (4:128))

Likewise, the Quran also says:

> The believers are nothing else than brothers (in the Islamic religion). So make reconciliation (*sulh*) between your brothers, and fear Allah, that you may receive mercy.
>
> (Sura Al-Hujurat (49:10))

And:

> So fear Allah and adjust (*sulh*) all matters of difference among you.
>
> (Sura Al-Anfal (8:1))

---

1 Toshihiko Izutsu, *Ethico-Religious Concepts in the Qur'an* (Montreal: McGill-Queen's University Press, 2002; first published 1966), chapters IV and V (pp. 55–104).

2 Aseel Al-Ramahi, '*Sulh*: a Crucial Part of Islamic Arbitration' *LSE Law, Society and Economy Working Papers 12/2008* (Law Department, LSE) 3–4.

3 Aida Othman, 'And Amicable Settlement is best: *Sulh* and Dispute Resolution in Islamic Law' (2007) 21(1) *Arab Law Quarterly* 64 at 66.

Sulh therefore is presented as both a legitimate and even desirable form of settlement, and indeed the maxim that 'amicable settlement is best' (*al-sulh khayr*)[4] or that amicable settlement is the best verdict (*al-sulh sayyid al-ahkam*) captures the notion that, as Ann Black et al. have put it, 'Sulh is not only regarded as an accepted method of dispute resolution within the Islamic justice system, but for some is seen as the "ethically and religiously superior" means of settling disputes.'[5]

So, too, the use of arbitrator and arbitration (*takhim*) is mentioned in the Quran. Thus, Sura An-Nisa also says:

> If you fear breach between them (husband and wife) appoint two arbiters, one from his family, and the other from hers. If they wish for peace, Allah will cause their conciliation. For Allah has full knowledge and is acquainted with all things.
>
> (Sura An-Nisa (4:35))

It is important to note that, as one can see in the verse above, the arbitration was not conceived of, as it seems to be in the contemporary context, as distinct and independent from attempts at conciliation. Rather these processes could work simultaneously and in a complementary fashion. This is significant because it keeps to the fore the substantive value that the Islamic tradition gives to mediated arrangements even in the presence of other 'ADR' models of settlement.[6]

The Quranic ethos of amicable settlement was complemented by early practice, including of the Prophet Muhammad himself, of mediation or mediation-cum-arbitration of disputes. Indeed, this too has a Quranic grounding from Quran 4:59, which says:

> O you who believe, obey Allah and obey the Messenger and those charged in authority from amongst you. If you differ in anything among yourselves, refer it to Allah and His Messenger, if you do believe in Allah and the Last Day. This is best and most suitable for final determination.

---

[4] From the above-referenced Quranic verse 4:128 but differently translated as: 'And if a woman fears from her husband contempt or evasion, there is no sin upon them if they make terms of settlement between them – and settlement (*sulh*) is best.'

[5] Ann Black, Hossein Esmail and Nadirsyah Hosen, *Modern Perspectives on Islamic Law* (Cheltenham: Edward Elgar 2013) 157.

[6] Wael Hallaq links this preference to the importance of the structures of the extended family or clan that existed at the time. See Wael Hallaq, *Sharia: Theory, Practice and Transformation* (Cambridge: Cambridge University Press 2009) 159–64.

The Prophet, as well as early leaders of the Muslim community after him, served as mediators for private and public disputes and spoke of the virtue of *sulh*. The limits of amicable settlement were also identified in this early period with the Caliph Umar (the second Caliph after the Prophet) and his view that amicable settlement was fine but it could not agree to make licit the illicit, or illicit the licit.[7] It is useful to note that this practice continues today even in the context of the *qadi* (judges) courts. In his study of these courts in Saudi Arabia, Frank Vogel notes that 'Saudi *qadis* (judges) show great skill as mediators and conciliators' and that 'In Saudi sharia courts, I was often told, "the great majority", or "99 percent" of all civil cases end in reconciliation'.[8]

Mediation, conciliation and arbitration have thus been a fundamental part – and not just a recent addition – of the pre-Islamic and Islamic systems of dispute settlement. They have been sanctioned by past and continuing practice and by the Quranic text and are thus considered virtuous parts of the ethos of the Islamic system of justice.

III. ADR, ISLAM AND THE UK

The UK is broadly accommodating of ADR processes such as conciliation and arbitration, whether of commercial or private disputes, and allows parties to choose the law that they wish to apply to their agreements.

Thus, section 4 (2) of the Arbitration Act 1996[9] allows 'the parties to make their own arrangements by agreement but provides rules which apply in the absence of such agreement'. For this purpose, an applicable law determined in accordance with the parties' agreement, or which is objectively determined in the absence of any express or implied choice (via the Act), shall be treated as chosen by the parties.

The Act also states in sections 4 (4) and (5) that:

> (4) It is immaterial whether or not the law applicable to the parties' agreement is the law of England and Wales or, as the case may be, Northern Ireland.

---

[7] As cited in Frank Vogel, *Islamic Law and Legal System: Studies of Saudi Arabia* (Leiden and Boston, MA: Brill 2000) 153.

[8] Ibid., 155 and 154. One can also see an excellent example of these mediation-cum-adjudication processes in Islamic courts at play in Kim Longinotto and Ziba Mir-Hosseni's documentary film *Divorce Iranian Style* (London: Second Run DVD) 2009.

[9] Arbitration Act 1996 (UK), chapter 23.

(5) The choice of a law other than the law of England and Wales or Northern Ireland as the applicable law in respect of a matter provided for by a non-mandatory provision of this Part is equivalent to an agreement making provision about that matter.

These provisions are accommodating and facilitative of the use of religious norms, including of Muslim legal traditions, in the context of choice of law clauses for arbitration in the UK.

Moreover, as stipulated in the landmark decision of the UK Supreme Court, *Jivraj* v *Haswani*,[10] arbitral agreements can require arbitrators to have a particular religious background or affiliation in UK law, including, as in the *Jivraj* case, to have affiliations to a Muslim background. The Court stated that (at paragraph 61):

> 61. One of the distinguishing features of arbitration that sets it apart from proceedings in national courts is the breadth of discretion left to the parties and the arbitrator to structure the process for resolution of the dispute. This is reflected in section 1 of the 1996 [Arbitration] Act which provides that: 'the parties should be free to agree how their disputes are resolved, subject only to such safeguards as are necessary in the public interest'. The stipulation that an arbitrator be of a particular religion or belief can be relevant to this aspect of arbitration. As the ICC puts in its written argument:
>
> The raison d'être of arbitration is that it provides for final and binding dispute resolution by a tribunal with a procedure that is acceptable to all parties, in circumstances where other fora (in particular national courts) are deemed inappropriate (e.g., because neither party will submit to the courts or their counterpart; or because the available courts are considered insufficiently expert for the particular dispute, or insufficiently sensitive to the parties' positions, culture, or perspectives).

Thus, when the above material is considered as a whole, there is no preclusion to the use of religious, and Islamic, norms in ADR process in the UK, but for normal concerns of natural justice and conformity with public policy. Indeed, this was neatly summarised and one might even say endorsed by Lord Phillips (the then Lord Chief Justice of England and Wales) in a famous speech when he said: 'There is no reason why principles of Sharia Law, or any other religious code should not be the basis for mediation or other forms of alternative dispute resolution.'[11]

There is, however, considerable debate as to whether there is any fundamental inconsistency – or indeed incompatibility – between the

---

[10] [2011] UKSC 40, [2011] WLR 1872.

[11] Speech by Lord Phillips, Lord Chief Justice, 'Equality before the Law', delivered at the East London Muslim Centre, 3 July 2008.

basic norms of Islamic law and justice and of British public policy (or, to the minds of some, even of British natural justice).[12]

Another challenge, highlighted by the well-known case of *Beximco*,[13] is the meaning that an appeal or reference to Islamic legal principles might have at law. In *Beximco*, the agreement stipulated a choice of law clause that said '[s]ubject to the principles of the Glorious Shari'ah, this agreement shall be governed by and construed in accordance with the laws of England'. The challenge for the Court was to make sense of this stipulation, especially the meaning to give to 'the principles of the Glorious Shari'ah'. Lord Justice Potter wrote (at paragraph 52):

> The general reference to principles of Sharia in this case affords no reference to, or identification of, those aspects of Sharia law which are intended to be incorporated into the contract, let alone the terms in which they are framed. It is plainly insufficient for the defendants to contend that the basic rules of the Sharia applicable *in this case* are not controversial. Such 'basic rules' are neither referred to nor identified. Thus the reference to the 'principles of … Sharia' stand unqualified as a reference to the body of Sharia law generally. As such, they are inevitably repugnant to the choice of English law as the law of the contract and render the clause self-contradictory and therefore meaningless.

He added (at paragraph 55):

> Finally, so far as the 'principles of … Sharia' are concerned, it was the evidence of both experts that there are indeed areas of considerable controversy and difficulty arising not only from the need to translate into propositions of modern law texts which centuries ago were set out as religious and moral codes, but because of the existence of a variety of schools of thought with which the court may have to concern itself in any given case before reaching a conclusion upon the principle or rule in dispute.

Hence, the courts in England and Wales have recognised that there is a diversity of opinion within Islamic law and reliance upon these legal traditions will therefore have to take cognisance of challenges arising from this interpretational plurality.

In addition to the use of Islamic law norms in choice of law clauses discussed above, one area that has generated considerable discussion in

---

12 On this matter, see generally Samia Bano, 'Islamic Family Arbitration, Justice and Human Rights in Britain' (2007) (1) *Law, Social Justice and Global Development Journal* (LGD).

13 *Beximco Pharm. Ltd v Shamil Bank of Bahrain EC* [2004] EWCA (Civ) 19, [2004] 1 WLR 1784.

the last few years is the phenomenon of 'sharia courts' in the UK. To be clear, this term is a misnomer as these are not courts in the proper sense of the term inasmuch as they are not formal parts of the judicial system. Rather, the 'courts' are community-based and community-organised mediation and arbitration fora, which employ a framework of Islamic law in mediating disputes or arbitrating, as the case may be. These institutions deal almost exclusively with personal or family law matters that might otherwise go to the mainstream civil courts.

In this context, 'Islamic ADR' is thus a private matter in the UK and has arisen out of a desire amongst Muslims to have their affairs settled or dealt with in accordance with the norms of Islam. The different bodies such as the Muslim Arbitration Tribunal (MAT),[14] the Muslim Law Sharia Council,[15] Islamic Sharia Council,[16] the Sharia Council of Britain and other bodies, in the main, serve, different Muslim communities. They also employ different procedures. The MAT, for example, has its arbitration panels sit with a qualified solicitor. The Ismaili Conciliation and Arbitration Board (CAB) for the UK, which caters to the needs of its community, also seeks to make extensive use of solicitors amongst its members; however, this is not necessarily the case with all the other bodies. Some will rely not so much on qualified solicitors but rather upon those with 'Islamic' credentials, i.e. those learned in the religious law. Most of the bodies will also try to mediate disputes as much as possible using their good offices and moral suasion to seek reconciliation, if possible, or to realise some other form of mutually agreed, amicable settlement. Arbitral determinations are resorted to when such efforts do not succeed.

Procedurally, what takes place at these bodies varies. Some have more elaborated, formal systems, while others may be more amorphous. The greater the involvement of qualified solicitors, with the lawyer's penchant for procedure, the more formal one can expect the processes to be. What is distinctive in these procedures, however, and what gives them their cultural and normative weight, is that they may all seek to combine different varieties of ADR – i.e. negotiation, mediation and arbitration – and to make reference to Islamic legal norms (such as with respect to inheritance or custody or forms of divorce). The processes might then be seen to be both normatively and procedurally 'blended' in drawing upon not just the rules (*hukm*; pl. *ahkam*) of Muslim legal traditions – as these

14 www.matribunal.com.
15 www.shariahcouncil.org.
16 www.islamic-sharia.org.

are understood and interpreted by the communities/community institutions – but also the above-noted emphasis on the methodologies of *sulh*, if possible, and then the use of arbitrators, having in mind the context of the British law and the British courts, because, in all instances the work of the boards or councils takes place either in the context of arbitration and thus the framework of the Arbitration Act 1996 or as part of less formal 'community-based justice'. The work of these entities is, therefore, reviewable by the state courts and they all therefore are conscious, in various degrees, of the fact that they operate in the shadow of state law and the state institutions. John Bowen reported that from work he has done looking at the work of these institutions, 'Today Muslims [in the UK] generally turn to civil courts for custody and financial disputes, as well as for civil divorces, and to the [Islamic] tribunals only for religious divorces. So the situation is largely one of distinct legal worlds with some shadow arbitration and no substitution.'[17]

Overall, what the British approach facilitates, therefore, is a series of things which bear exposition. First, it allows for British Muslim communities to establish bodies that are expressive of 'Islam' and its norms as they understand these. In so doing, the British state does not provide a definition of the relevant norms of Islam; rather, it accommodates the different normative understanding of Islamic law that may exist amongst British Muslim communities. This accommodation is significant because it aligns with the oft-noted interpretational diversity of Islamic law, a diversity that is more plural than just saying that there are four (or five or more) major 'schools' (*maddhabs*) of Islamic law. In turn, the institutional space for the different interpretive traditions means that Islamic norms are understood from the community level up, rather than decided in a top-down manner such that the institutions and their processes are 'Islamic' insofar as they are seen to be so by the communities and individuals who would use them. Second, the British model allows for individual British Muslims, if they so choose, to access these institutions to resolve disputes that might arise in family law (mainly) but also other contexts. This element of choice is significant because it keeps recourse to Islamic bodies a 'voluntary' matter and allows the users to exercise their agency in accessing these fora.[18] Finally, the British framework puts

---

[17] John R. Bowen, 'Private Arrangements: "Recognizing Sharia" in England', *Boston Review*, 1 March 2009 (www.bostonreview.net/john-bowen-private-arrangements-sharia-England).

[18] I use quotation marks here deliberately. Some think that due to family or community pressure turning to community-based institutions is really not all that voluntary, but that people get pressurised to use these institutions because they

the 'sharia courts' regime under the aegis of the general British state legal system, rather than as a standalone or parallel system. With such a set up not only is there normatively the overhanging 'shadow of civil law' as noted above, but in addition, or as part and parcel of this same situation, the civil courts remain as a back-stop to the 'sharia courts', as well as offering the institutional opportunity for appeal.

IV. ADR, ISLAM AND SINGAPORE

Singapore's system of dealing with Islamic law is fundamentally different from that of the UK, and this has an impact on ADR practice amongst Muslims in Singapore. At one level, Islamic law is a formal part of the legal system of Singapore, referenced in the Constitution, implemented in legislation and adjudicated via the existence of a formal Shari'ah (local rendition 'Syariah') Court and Board of Appeal. These formal processes, however, only really deal with family law matters involving marriage, divorce and its financial and custody consequences, and inheritance. In these areas, the ADR processes of negotiation, mediation and arbitration are also variously used, as will be outlined below. In addition, Islamic law may also be the basis of private arbitration, not involving family law matters, under the Arbitration Act,[19] which will also be discussed below.

In terms of the formal, posited system, Article 152 of the Constitution of Singapore addresses the Malay community, which is overwhelmingly Muslim, stating that:

> *Minorities and special position of Malays*
>
> 152.(1) It shall be the responsibility of the Government constantly to care for the interests of the racial and religious minorities in Singapore.
>
> (2) The Government shall exercise its functions in such manner as to recognise the special position of the Malays, who are the indigenous people

---

are viewed as having a greater sense of Islamic credibility – and hence more social legitimacy – than the state courts. While this may be the case in some contexts and for some people (in particular communities perhaps also in certain socio-economic positions), it is difficult to make universal claims. See the discussion of these challenges in Michael A. Helfand, 'The Future of Religious Arbitration in the United States: Looking Through a Pluralist Lens' Pepperdine University School of Law Legal Studies Research Paper Series, Paper Number 2017/15 (forthcoming in Paul Schiff Berman, ed., *Oxford Handbook on Global Legal Pluralism* 2018) 29ff.

[19] Cap 10, Rev. Ed. 2002.

> of Singapore, and accordingly it shall be the responsibility of the Government to protect, safeguard, support, foster and promote their political, educational, *religious*, economic, social and cultural interests and the Malay language. (emphasis added)

To this, Article 153 adds that:

> 153. The Legislature *shall by law make provision for regulating Muslim religious affairs* and for constituting a Council to advise the President in matters relating to the Muslim religion. (emphasis added)

It is on this basis that the Islamic Religious Council of Singapore (generally known by its Malay-language name *Majlis Ugama Islam Singapura* and usually referred to locally by its acronym, MUIS), has been established by the government. MUIS oversees religious affairs such as the maintenance of mosques, halal certification and the provision of religious education and guidance to the Malay, and other, Muslim communities. Furthermore, MUIS is empowered to issue legal opinions (*fatwa*, pl. *fatawa*) through its Legal (Fatwa) Committee.[20] *Fatawa* opinions need not be linked to any legal action in process and it should be noted that these legal opinions are not binding – though they may be persuasive – on the civil courts in Singapore.[21]

The role and impact of MUIS has been characterised by Tim Lindsey and Kerstin Steiner as follows:

> MUIS is involved in a vast array of areas … This deep reach in to the life of Muslims has meant that the inward-looking, traditionalist and state-compliant norms discernible in MUIS' *fatawa* (and so many of its other public statements and programmes) have saturated the official religious culture of Singapore's Muslim community and will probably do so for the foreseeable future.[22]

In addition to the Constitution, Islamic law is also substantially dealt with in Singapore through the Administration of Muslim Law Act (AMLA),[23] which, as its name suggests, provides a structure for the administration of

---

[20] Noor Aisha Abdul Rahman, 'Muslim Personal Law and Citizen's Rights: The Case of Singapore' (2012) 7 *Asian J. of Comparative Law* 127, 133–4.

[21] On this, see the Singapore cases of *Saniah bte Ali v Abdullah bin Ali* [1990] 1 SLR(R) 555, [1990] SGHC 40 (High Court) affirmed in *Shafeeg bin Salim Talib v Fatimah bte Abud bin Talib* [2010] 2 SLR 1123 (Court of Appeal).

[22] Tim Lindsey and Kerstin Steiner, *Islam, Law and the State in Southeast Asia, Volume II: Singapore* (London: I. B. Tauris 2012) 134.

[23] Administration of Muslim Law Act (AMLA), Cap. 3, 2009 Rev. Ed.

Muslim law – including the establishment of MUIS. This Act primarily addresses personal law matters such as marriage, divorce and inheritance, which are the main areas where Muslim legal traditions are expressed in Singapore law. In the main, AMLA leaves the substantive law in these areas to be decided within the context of the Muslim community itself and the Act is concerned principally with administrative procedures. That said, AMLA does provide the broad boundaries, if not the detailed specifics, within which Islamic law operates in Singapore.

Muslim law is also articulated by the operation of a special Shari'ah Court, and a Board of Appeal to hear appeals from the Shari'ah Court. On some matters such as child custody, divorce, and maintenance of a wife and child, the Shari'ah Court has concurrent jurisdiction with the High Court. In addition, AMLA stipulates that in some matters the jurisdiction and authority of the Shari'ah Court and Appeal Board is final and conclusive. Section 35 of AMLA, which discusses the jurisdiction of the Shari'ah Court, thus says:

> 35. (1) The [Shari'ah] Court shall have jurisdiction throughout Singapore.
>
> (2) The Court shall have jurisdiction to hear and determine all actions and proceedings in which all the parties are Muslims or where the parties were married under the provisions of the Muslim law and which involve disputes relating to –
>
> (*a*) marriage;
> (*b*) divorces known in the Muslim law as fasakh, cerai taklik, khuluk and talak;
> (*c*) betrothal, nullity of marriage or judicial separation;
> (*d*) the disposition or division of property on divorce or nullification of marriage; or
> (*e*) the payment of emas kahwin, marriage expenses (hantaran belanja), maintenance and consolatory gifts or mutaah.
>
> (3) In all questions regarding betrothal, marriage, dissolution of marriage, including talak, cerai taklik, khuluk and fasakh, nullity of marriage or judicial separation, the appointment of hakam, the disposition or division of property on divorce or nullification of marriage, the payment of emas kahwin, marriage expenses (hantaran belanja) and consolatory gifts or mutaah and the payment of maintenance on divorce, the rule of decision where the parties are Muslims or were married under the provisions of the Muslim law shall, subject to the provisions of this Act, be the Muslim law, as varied where applicable by Malay custom.

In *Mohamed Yusoff bin Mohd Haniff v Umi Kalsom bte Abas (Attorney-General, non-party)*[24] in discussing the scope of the Shari'ah Court's work, the High Court of Singapore cited section 56A of AMLA and stated (at paragraph 25):

> [a]s s 56A of AMLA provides that subject to the Act, a decision of the Syariah Court or the Appeal Board is final and conclusive and 'no decision or order of the Court or the Appeal Board shall be challenged, appealed against, reviewed, quashed or called into question in any court and shall not be subject to any Quashing Order, Prohibiting Order, Mandatory Order or injunction in any court on any account'.

In addition, under section 35A of AMLA, parties who have commenced proceedings involving disposition or division of property on divorce or custody of children may apply to the Shari'ah Court for leave to commence or to continue proceedings in the civil courts. Thus, while the Shari'ah Court has its own jurisdiction, this is within a limited range created by AMLA versus a general jurisdiction and the Shari'ah Court operates under the general supervision and oversight of the High Court of Singapore.

These jurisdictional matters were recently addressed in the case of *TMO v TMP*.[25] There the Court of Appeal said (at paragraphs 22–25 and 30):

> 22 Whether the Syariah Court has jurisdiction is thus dependent on two conditions. The first is that the parties to the dispute must either be Muslim or have been married under the provisions of Muslim law. The second is that the dispute must relate to the matters identified in ss 35(2)(*a*) to (*e*) of the AMLA. Where the Syariah Court has jurisdiction over a matter that falls within ss 35(2)(*a*), (*b*) or (*c*) of the AMLA, such jurisdiction is *exclusive* and the High Court shall have no jurisdiction over those matters. This is provided for by s 17A(1) of the SCJA [*Supreme Court of Judicature Act*, Cap. 332, Rev Ed 2007], the effect of which is to exclude the jurisdiction vested in the High Court by ss 16 and 17 of the SCJA in cases where the Syariah Court is in a position to exercise jurisdiction under ss 35(2)(*a*), (*b*) or (*c*) of the AMLA [...].
>
> 23 Where the Syariah Court has jurisdiction over a matter that falls within ss 35(2)(*d*) or (*e*) (and incidentally also ss 51 or 52(3)(*c*) or (*d*)) of the AMLA, it shares that jurisdiction *concurrently* with the High Court. This is provided for by s 17A(2) of the SCJA which has been reproduced above.

---

24 [2010] SGHC 114.

25 [2017] SGCA 14.

> 24 Hence, parties who were married under Muslim law and who are then divorced may, during or after the divorce proceedings in the Syariah Court, apply to *either* the Syariah Court *or* the High Court for ancillary relief. But this is subject to the conditions set out in ss 17A(3), (5) and (6) of the SCJA, and in general terms, these contemplate that the jurisdiction of the High Court may be invoked with the consent of the parties to the proceedings or with the leave of the Syariah Court.
>
> 25 Where a matter does *not* fall within the jurisdiction of the Syariah Court, the High Court retains residual jurisdiction over the matter. This is provided for by ss 16 and 17 of the SCJA, which confer upon the High Court 'jurisdiction under any written law relating to divorce and matrimonial causes' where this has not been excluded by any other provision vesting jurisdiction in the Syariah Court [...].
>
> 30 If the dispute is one in respect of which the High Court *shares* jurisdiction *concurrently* with the Syariah Court and if the High Court takes jurisdiction over the matter under s 17A(2) of the SCJA (see above at [23]), s 17A(7) of the SCJA expressly provides that it shall apply the *civil law* [emphasis in the original].

With respect to procedure, AMLA provides that the Shari'ah Court can at its discretion appoint a *hakam* (arbitrator) in a family dispute, and that, in this role, it may appoint 'close relatives of the parties having knowledge of the circumstances of the case'.[26] This is consistent with the Quranic verse cited above[27] that embodies a preference for relatives to be appointed as arbitrators in family disputes.[28] Further, consistent with the traditional notion that arbitrators' decisions should be binding, the same legislation 'confers ... arbitrators with the authority to order for divorce or *khulu*'.[29] Essentially, the arbitrators' ability to pronounce a divorce is dependent on the giving of authority from the parties, but if the arbitrators are of the opinion that the parties should be divorced but he lacks the authority formally to do so, the Court will simply appoint other *hakam* with the requisite authority to effect a divorce.[30] Also, in line with the Islamic ethic, AMLA also provides for *sulh* in requiring the *hakam* to

---

26 Section 50(1) AMLA.

27 Quran 4:35.

28 Mahdi Zahraa and Nora A. Hak, 'Tahkim (Arbitration) in Islamic Law within the Context of Family Disputes' (2006) 20(1) *Arab L.Q.* 2, 21.

29 Ibid., 37, quoting section 48(5) and (6) Malaysian Islamic Family Law (Federal Territories) Act 1984; section 50(6) and (7) of AMLA provides for the same.

30 Section 50(7) AMLA.

'effect ... reconciliation'[31] between the parties prior to arbitration, if it is possible to do so.

Indeed, more generally, the procedure in the Shari'ah Court is like the type discussed in the UK context above in being a blended process involving mediation and arbitration. Thus, in part, the Shari'ah Court is a formal institution whose decisions are reported, but it is also quite normal in the Shari'ah Court, which, recall, is essentially a forum to address family law matters to attempt to reconcile the parties or to find a negotiated settlement be undertaken that the Court may then endorse. In fact, Court officials will often act as informal mediators to attempt to bring about resolution where possible. In so doing, Shari'ah Court operates in a manner consistent with the concept of *sulh* in the Islamic tradition. This flexibility to blend formal processes attempts at *sulh* is facilitated by section 42 of AMLA, which states that 'The Court shall have regard to the law of evidence for the time being in force in Singapore, and shall be guided by the principles thereof, *but shall not be obliged to apply the same strictly*' (emphasis added).

In terms of substantive law, while this is left to the community (via MUIS and the Shari'ah Court) to determine, section 33 of AMLA does direct MUIS ordinarily to follow the tenets of the Shafi'i school of law (*madhhab*), which has historically been the school which predominates in Southeast Asia. Other of the major schools can also be relied upon, however, and provisions relating to these possibilities are also found in the subsections of section 33.[32] Muslim law in Singapore is also variable by 'Malay custom', an acknowledgment of the historical, and still major, role of Malay Muslims in Singapore. Of particular interest is that section 114 of AMLA stipulates that the Court may accept 'as proof of the Muslim law any definite statement on the Muslim law' in a list of seven texts.[33] This is not exactly to preclude reference to other materials, but it

---

[31] Section 50(5) AMLA.

[32] See AMLA, section 33(2) and (3).

[33] The section states:

'114.—(1) In deciding questions of succession and inheritance in the Muslim law, the court shall be at liberty to accept as proof of the Muslim law any definite statement on the Muslim law made in all or any of the following books:

(*a*) The English translation of the *Quaran*, by A. Yusuf Ali or Marmaduke Pickthall;

(*b*) *Mohammedan Law*, by Syed Ameer Ali;

(*c*) *Minhaj et Talibin* by Nawawi, translated by E. C. Howard from the French translation of Van den Berg;

provides a set of materials which are, one might say, 'canonised by legislation' as sources of Muslim law for Singapore.

With respect to private arbitration under the Arbitration Act, the use of Islamic law becomes an option according to section 32(1) of the Act, which says: 'The arbitral tribunal shall decide the dispute in accordance with the law chosen by the parties as applicable to the substance of the dispute.' Thus, Muslims (and of course others) may choose to use Islamic law to govern arbitration proceedings involving commercial or other issues within the scope of the Act.

What is the impact of AMLA, the Shari'ah Court and the Arbitration Act on ADR practices amongst Muslims in Singapore? With respect to arbitration, while in general Singapore does not allow arbitration of family law matters, the institution of the *hakam* that is made available under AMLA means that arbitration in this form and in the context of some family law matters may occur. Outside of AMLA and family law matters, Islamic law norms via choice of law clauses may also be the basis for arbitration, if this is the desire of the affected parties. Indeed, with the growth of Islamic banking and finance and Singapore's efforts have more of this type of work done in the country, Islamic law norms may feature more prominently in financial or commercial arbitration contexts in the future.

When one does turn to family law matters, however, which today represent the majority of issues where Islamic law gets involved in Singapore, the structure of the Shari'ah Court provides a conducive venue for *sulh*-based practice, which is akin to the ADR process of negotiation and mediation. Indeed, particularly in the context of issues like division of property in cases of divorce or in disputes on inheritance, mediation, at and with the support of the Shari'ah Court, is regularly attempted. There are two ways this is practised. Outside of the court structure, mediation may be attempted by family representatives, by counsellors or indeed by lawyers acting for the different parties. At the court, a familiar pattern is for an officer of the Shari'ah Court to attempt informal mediation between the parties, which is actually a mandatory part of divorce proceedings in Singapore. If the mediation takes place under the auspices of the Court, the ultimate agreement can then be verified (as to its conformity with the law) and endorsed (to give it

---

(*d*) *Digest of Moohummudan Law*, by Neil B. E. Baillie;
(*e*) *Anglo-Muhammadan Law*, by Sir Roland Knyvet Wilson, 6th Edition Revised by A. Yusuf Ali;
(*f*) *Outlines of Muhammadan Law*, by A. A. Fyzee;
(*g*) *Muhammadan Law*, by F. B. Tyabji.'

greater legal weight and standing) by the Court. In a divorce case, the mediation agreement would be converted into a court order and then result in the issuance after some time of a divorce certificate. Unlike in the UK, however, one can note that neither MUIS nor any other agency provides an alternative institutional mechanism for family law-based ADR within the general Muslim community in Singapore. Thus, the Sharia Court represents the only 'structured' venue for '*sulh* practice' for the general Muslim community in Singapore. One important matter to note, and a significant difference between Singapore and the UK, is that, in Singapore, the jurisdiction of the Shari'ah Court is not optional: the Shari'ah Court *is* the venue and has compulsory jurisdiction over the range of matters stipulated in section 35(2) of AMLA involving Muslim parties and (a limited range of) matters may only be transferred to the civil courts by leave of the Shari'ah Court under section 35A.

One may say, therefore, that the overall context for Islamic law in Singapore is for its norms and its adjudication to be governed much more heavily by state-influenced or state-defined processes than is the case in the UK. This is done by legislation in which the state defines the scope of Islamic law, the forum for hearing cases involving Islamic law (Shari'ah Court) and the institution of MUIS and especially MUIS' *fatawa*-providing function. This larger role and involvement of the state is a major distinguishing feature of Singapore model vis-à-vis the operation of Islamic legal norms in the UK. And it has implications.

As has already been commented, the Shari'ah Court provides a convenient venue and a conducive institutional structure with physical space and court officers, in which to pursue negotiation-cum-mediation to seek out amicable settlement (*sulh*). Where this fails, the Shari'ah Court can then use arbitrators (*hakam*) in and effect arbitration (*takhim*). But be that as it may, the institutional structure, and its link to MUIS and the stipulations of AMLA, also means that there is a normative, Islamic law overhang in Singapore. Put differently, this is an example of a well-known and easily understood phenomenon of concretisation and some attendant rigidity that comes from taking the highly plural traditions of Islamic law, that emerged classically without the context of the modern state and expressed much interpretational diversity, and fitting them into a contemporary state environment. One might say, of course, that nowadays that context is all but impossible to avoid and that there is as much of a state context in the UK as there is in Singapore because the British state will have its own normative overhangs – based on administrative law, human rights law or other normative bases. That cannot be denied. The salient point for the context of this discussion, however, is that Singapore is palpably more directive about the normative content of

Muslim legal traditions because bodies of the Singapore state are more involved in defining, shaping and implementing these norms than is the case in the UK.

V. CONCLUSION

Amicable settlement (*sulh*) and arbitration (*takhim*) have a long history in pre-Muslim and Muslim contexts. They find sanction in the Quran and in the historical as well as contemporary practices of Muslim communities. These practices are also consistent and sit in happy congruence with what one might term the ethos of contemporary ADR. A key part of this ethos is to let the parties come to their own terms of settlement with limited normative constraints. Both the Islamic systems and 'secular' ADR can, broadly speaking, accept such a framework.

When one looks at the operation of Islamic ADR in the UK and in Singapore, one sees that both jurisdictions allow it to be practised in different ways. In the UK, Muslim legal traditions may be invoked as part of choice of law clauses in arbitral clauses and, in family matters, Muslims may – and as a matter of fact some do – seek to use community-based bodies to deal with matters of (religious) divorce and attendant division of property, amongst other matters. However, these community-based bodies have no formal standing in British law, even though they obviously operate in the 'shadow' of the British legal system – its courts and its legal norms. This shadow operation allows British Muslims as the interested parties and the institutions that they may use to help them to exercise a lot of freedom in the normative frameworks that they choose and the detailed substantive outcomes that they structure.

The situation in Singapore is different. Singapore is also accommodating of mediation and arbitration as part of the practice amongst Muslims in the country. Islamic legal norms are not precluded from arbitral agreements, and in family matters amicable settlement is encouraged and even facilitated. However, all of this work conducted in the context of important state institutions, especially MUIS and the Shari'ah Court, and the framework of AMLA, which structures the understanding of Muslim legal norms. These processes provide greater definition to the context of Islamic law and, along more traditionalist lines, in Singapore, and this in turn can constrain the breadth of the interpretational freedom available to Muslim participants.

Farrah Ahmed and Senwung Luk have written of the possibilities of religious arbitration enhancing personal autonomy.[34] In their piece they explore 'whether there are reasons based on personal autonomy, which count in favour of religious arbitration [including but not limited to Muslim religious arbitration] in family matters'.[35] In short, they highlight the autonomy-enhancing potential of religious arbitration because it facilitates or, it might be said, acts as an expression of, religious practice.[36] Crucially, however, for the autonomy to be realised, the religious practice being promoted must be one that the individual defines for herself or himself. As they say: 'Religious people can use religious arbitration to order and organise their lives according to the religious norms they believe in.' This point is echoed by Michael Helfand, who notes that from the perspective of faith communities, religious tribunals can afford the communities 'the opportunity to resolve disputes in accordance with deeply held and shared religious values'.[37]

In this light, we can return to our two case studies. As between the two structures we have seen in the UK and in Singapore, which is more conducive to the autonomy-enhancing potential of religious arbitration, and, one might add, to religious mediation? The argument that has sought to be presented here is that notwithstanding the status of Muslim legal norms in Singapore, and the institutions of MUIS and the Shari'ah Court with their venues and structures that facilitate and encourage settlement, it is the UK's more loosely structured and privately arranged system that provides Muslims with greater scope for autonomy-enhancing amicable settlement and arbitration of disputes. This is because out of the two systems, the UK is more normatively capacious because it is less directive as to the content and sources of Islamic legal norms, leaving these to be structured more by the parties engaging in the ADR practices.

Of course, one might think that this looser structure raises its own problems. One notable problem is the potential for private arrangements to be (more likely) sites where coercion or inequality of bargaining power hold sway. Relatedly, private arrangements might also lead to dispute settlements that violate important norms of public policy, such as

---

34 Farrah Ahmed and Senwung Luk, 'How Religious Arbitration Could Enhance Personal Autonomy' (2012) 1(2) *Oxford Journal of Law and Religion* 424.

35 Ibid., 426.

36 See ibid., 433ff.

37 Ibid., 433. Michael A. Helfand, 'The Future of Religious Arbitration in the United States: Looking Through a Pluralist Lens' (above, n18) 4 (see also at 10, where this is reiterated).

those related to gender relations or the priority of interests of children.[38] The risk here is that private arrangements might fall 'under the radar' of scrutiny and public accountability. However, the UK system suggests that some of these concerns might be allayed by two factors. The first is that any private arrangements still fall under the shadow of the state system and may be reviewed by this system and its institution. The second is that private arrangements are not forced on parties but entered into voluntarily. The capacity for this voluntariness to be checked by the involvement of officials may in fact commend the Singapore model in this regard. But if the great genius of the ethos of ADR is to give power to the parties themselves to operate freely and if this value – whether called autonomy or something else – is to be paramount, then, on balance, one may still prefer the UK's structure to that of Singapore.

[38] See Ayelet Shachar, '"Privatizing Diversity": A Cautionary Tale for Arbitration in Family Law' (2008) 9 *Theoretical Inquiries in Law* 573.

PART 2

PROPERTY AND BUSINESS

5. Corporate social responsibility and workplace casualties in Bangladesh: an appraisal of Islamic principles as a potential solution

S. M. Solaiman

I. INTRODUCTION

Bangladesh is home to around 6,000 garment factories, which make the industry the second largest apparel manufacturer in the world just behind China. The garment industry as a single sector adds the highest amount of foreign currency[1] to the gross domestic products (GDP) of the country.[2] This sector alone earned more than US$24 billion out of the total export revenue of US$30.17 billion of Bangladesh in the fiscal year 2013–14.[3] However, a Harvard conference lately reveals that India has surpassed Bangladesh by occupying the second position in the aftermath of the recent fatalities in the garment industry that appear to have affected customer loyalty, contributing to this downturn.[4] The industry employs an estimated four million people; about 90 per cent of these are women who come from impoverished, uneducated and untrained backgrounds and who are often teenagers.[5] They have found this work in a demographic scenario where 32 percent of youths in the

---

[1] The garments industry accounts for 78 per cent of the total exports and contributes 17 per cent of the GDP: Md Mahbub Alam Prodip and Fatema Ferdausi, 'How are Women Workers in RMG Sector?' *The Financial Express*, Dhaka (22 June 2014), editorial.

[2] Palash Ghosh, 'Despite Low Pay, Poor Work Conditions, Garment Factories Empowering Millions of Bangladeshi Women' *International Business Times* (25 March 2014), politics.

[3] Jubair Hasan, 'Unrest Feared if RMG Workers Not Paid – $150m Needed in 18 Months for Factory Safety: Alliance' *The Financial Express*, Dhaka (26 July 2014), last page.

[4] Abdullah Shibli, 'Harvard Conference on Bangladesh – Whither Bangladesh Garments Industry?' *The Daily Star*, Dhaka (16 July 2014), Op-Ed.

[5] Palash Ghosh, above n2.

potential labour force are either unemployed or underemployed as revealed from the latest population census of the country, which took place in 2011.[6] Taking advantage of such an awful dearth of job opportunities, garment owners can do almost anything they want to do. Hence, the workers are to work in an exploitative environment that includes safety risk, low salaries, sexual harassment, and both physical and verbal abuse.[7] Employers ignore the safety requirements assumingly with a belief that the law is confined to the books and people are willing to work regardless of safety hazards. As a result, the number of workplace deaths and injuries continues to grow day by day with virtual impunity being granted to the wrongdoers leaving no redress for their victims.[8] The unprecedented fire at Tazreen Fashions Ltd in November 2012 and the horrific collapse of Rana Plaza in April 2013 that claimed more than 1,000 lives and caused serious injuries to many others have galvanised the agonies of garment workers in Bangladesh as discussed in Section IV below. According to the US Committee on Foreign Relations, '[w]hen the Tazreen Fashions factory burned down, it was the worst garment factory accident in Bangladesh's history. When Rana Plaza collapsed, it was the worst garment factory accident in world history.'[9] The Committee adds that 'Bangladesh's garment sector may not be able to withstand another tragedy on the scale of Tazreen and Rana Plaza'.[10]

Despite it being a valuable sector of the national economy, the garment industry until recently received little attention from neither the Government of Bangladesh (GOB) nor the profit-hungry importers of the developed world, who play on 'cheap labour, low production costs and a huge eager workforce'.[11]

An organised religion plays a pivotal role in developing personal values and human behaviour, thus it impacts on different aspects of businesses that are run by people who are generally faithful to a religious

---

6 Staff Correspondent, 'Unemployment the Biggest Challenge – Youths Can be Turned into Assets if Properly Trained' *The Daily Star*, Dhaka (11 July 2014), front page.

7 Prodip and Ferdausi (2014), above n1.

8 The incidents and fatalities are discussed in Section IV in this chapter.

9 Committee on Foreign Relations – United States Senate, 'Worker Safety and Labor Rights in Bangladesh's Garment Sector (22 November 2013), 5.

10 Id., 13.

11 Ghosh (2014) above n2.

belief and practice.[12] Islam is probably the single religion which is declared and acclaimed to be not merely a way of worship for the life hereafter, but a complete code of life encompassing 'an entire legal, economic, social, political, and commercial system' for its believers called Muslims.[13]

As regards the legal system, Bangladesh in practice belongs to the common law family as a former British colony and presently over 88 per cent of its populace are Muslim.[14] The labour law currently in force in the country was enacted in 2006 and amended in 2013 after the aforementioned destructions following enormous pressures from the developed nations and international bodies including the United Nations Organisation (UNO) and International Labour Organisation (ILO). Nevertheless, the labour law still remains flawed, which has been analysed elsewhere.[15] This chapter is concerned with the right of workers to have a safe workplace and corresponding duties of their employers prescribed in the Islamic Law (Shari'ah).[16] The objective of this writing is to show that the provisions of Shari'ah correspond to the labour rights as recognised in the prevailing law of the western world that are explicitly protective of workers' safety. The owners of both Tazreen Fashions and Raza Plaza are Muslim,[17] and most of the workers died and injured are supposedly Muslims as the country's demography implies. Therefore as a Muslim, both the employees and employers (owners of the factories) are subject to the Islamic dictates at least religiously and ethically, if not legally. This research thus endeavours to examine the

---

12 See Geoffrey Williams and John Zinkin, 'Islam and CSR: A Study of the Compatibility between the Tenets of Islam and the UN Global Compact' (209) 91 *Journal of Business Ethics* 519.

13 See J. Michael Taylor, 'Islamic Banking – the Feasibility of Establishing an Islamic Bank in the United States' (2003) 40 *American Business Law Journal* 385, 387; Bernard K. Freamon, 'Slavery, Freedom, and the Doctrine of Consensus in Islamic Jurisprudence' (1998) 11 *Harvard Human Rights Journal* 1, 3 as cited in Radwa S. Elsaman, 'Corporate Social Responsibility in Islamic Law: Labor and Employment' (2011) 2 *Yonsei Law Journal* 64, 66.

14 Board of Investment Bangladesh – Prime Minister's Office, 'Introduction', www.boi.gov.bd/index.php/about-bangladesh/bangladesh-at-a-glance (accessed 23 July 2014).

15 See S. M. Solaiman, 'Unprecedented Factory Fires of Tazreen Fashions in Bangladesh: Revisiting Bangladeshi Labour Laws in Light of Their Equivalents in Australia' (2013) 31(1) *Hofstra Labor & Employment Law Journal* 125.

16 Two terms, 'Islamic law' and 'Shari'ah', are used interchangeably in this chapter.

17 They are Mr. Delwar Hossain and Mr. Shohel Rana, respectively.

safety right of the workers and corresponding obligation of their employers under the principles of Islamic law, and concludes that the latter evidently failed to comply with their religious obligations to protect the former in addition to their failure under the municipal law.

As the discussions progress, Section II demonstrates the justification for this research. Section III briefly explains the legal concept of corporations and the notion of their social responsibility as recognised in Shari'ah. Section IV discusses the concerns for workplace safety or occupational health and safety (OHS) focusing on the principles of Shari'ah, whilst Section V concludes this chapter.

In discussing the OHS under the principles of Shari'ah, brief references to the relevant provisions of the Universal Declaration of Human Rights 1948 (UDHR), the International Covenant on Civil and Political Rights 1966 (ICCPR), the International Covenant on Economic, Social and Cultural Rights 1966 (ICESCR), the Universal Islamic Declaration of Human Rights 1981 (UIDHR) and the Cairo Declaration of Human Rights in Islam 1999 (CDHR) will be made in order to demonstrate the inherent strength of Islamic principles which have come into being much earlier than the man-made instruments for protecting workers.

II. JUSTIFICATION FOR THIS RESEARCH

Although Shari'ah is not part of the domestic or positive law of Bangladesh governing employment relationships,[18] a vast majority of its people respect and voluntarily adhere to the rights and obligations enunciated in Islam concerning various aspects of Muslims, for example, marriage, divorce, inheritance, will of property, etc. Hence, an adequate understanding of rights and obligations under Shari'ah would be likely to stimulate both sides of the employment relation to be respectful towards each other's entitlements and duties. In addition, the justification for this pursuit lies in the fact that the business markets made up of Muslims around the world is significant, which warrants an understanding of corporate social responsibility (CSR) in the Islamic Legal System by both corporations and their stakeholders including employees. Notably, several recent studies demonstrate that some Muslim countries (countries having the majority of their population Muslim) are presently amongst the most wealthy market contributors in global trade and commerce, such

---

[18] In Bangladesh, Shari'ah governs certain social and legal relations between Muslims such as marriage, divorce, inheritance, will of property etc, but not the relationship between an employer and an employee.

as, Saudi Arabia, Turkey and United Arab Emirates.[19] Moreover, the large Muslim populace invite and expect multinational corporations to come into their markets as producers, manufacturers and investors.[20] In response to this reality, several international law firms are now considering an expansion of their professional services to many Muslim countries, for example, Ashurst, a leading law firm, has extended its service network to many countries including United Arab Emirates, Indonesia and Saudi Arabia.[21] More vividly, the intergovernmental Organisation of Islamic Cooperation (OIC) itself has 56 member countries, which have the majority of their population Muslim. Therefore, CSR in Islam has become a vital area of investigation by both academics and professionals. This chapter contributes to such an academic expedition.

III. CORPORATIONS AND CORPORATE SOCIAL RESPONSIBILITY

Everyone in the world is affected by corporations in one way or another, simply because of the fact that the products we consume and services we use are provided by businesses formed predominantly as a company or corporation (these two terms used interchangeably). Today it would be unrealistic, if not impossible, for a person of any standing anywhere on earth to avoid corporation in his or her pursuit of living as a human being. A corporation is legally defined as an entity created by law conferring artificial personality[22] as a veil of individuals who own and operate it for profits or other purposes with perpetuity in its existence and simplicity in its contractual relations. Initially, companies emerged as a division of society and gradually changed to an association of individuals.[23] However, presently a single person can form a company.[24]

---

19 For details, see Radwa S. Elsaman, 'Corporate Social Responsibility in Islamic Law: Labor and Employment' (2012) 18 *New England Journal of International and Comparative Law* 97, 98.

20 John H. Donboli and Farnaz Kashefi, 'Doing Business in the Middle East: A Primer for U.S. Companies' (2005) 38 *Cornell International Law Journal* 413, 414.

21 Ashurst, Locations, www.ashurst.com/office.aspx?id_Content=14 (accessed 12 July 2014).

22 *Salomon v Salomon & Co Ltd* [1897] AC 22.

23 John P. Davis, *Corporations: A Study of the Origin and Development of Great Business Combinations and of Their Relation to the Authority of the State* (1909) New York: B. Franklin, 246.

A corporation as a legal person does have both rights and responsibilities that are conferred and imposed on it with the recognition of a separate entity independent of its owners and managers. One of these obligations is social responsibility owed to the society in which it operates and thereby provides its products and services to the people for consumption. The notion of CSR is founded on the stakeholder theory of the corporation[25] as opposed to the apparently rival stockholder theory of the corporation,[26] whilst the former advances relatively new concepts compared to the latter which is solely devoted to the maximization of shareholders' benefits.[27] A contemporary corporation in general has various responsibilities, such as financial, environmental and social. All these responsibilities have had a legal dimension which may vary between jurisdictions and legal systems. Therefore a single definition of any of these responsibilities is hard to be articulated.

In an effort to define CSR, some commentators argue that it 'is inherently vague and ambiguous, both in theory and practice'.[28] In the absence of any universally accepted definition of CSR and recognition of the fact that any appropriate connotation of this concept (CRS) is problematic,[29] it can be broadly described as being the responsibility to promote good and prevent harms of the society of consumers of products and services of a given corporation.[30] The World Business Council for Sustainable Development defines CSR as 'the continuing commitment by business to behave ethically and contribute to economic development

---

24 For example, in Australia, s114 of the Corporations Act 2001 (Cth) and s123 of the Companies Act 2006 (UK) allow formation of one member companies.

25 See Jill Solomon and Aris Solomon, *Corporate Governance and Accountability* (2004) West Sussex: John Wiley & Sons, 23–9.

26 See Steen Thomsen and Martin Conyon, *Corporate Governance: Mechanisms and Systems* (2012) Berkshire: McGraw-Hill, 111–12.

27 For a discussion of these two competing theories, see Thomas Donaldson and Lee E. Preston, 'The Stakeholder Theory of the Corporation: Concepts, Evidence, and Implications' (1995) 20 (1) *Academy of Management Review* 65–91.

28 P. R. P. Coelho, J. E. McClure, and J. A. Spry, 'The Social Responsibility of Corporate Management: A Classical Critique' (2003) 18(1) *Mid-American Journal of Business* 15.

29 See Mark S. Schwartz, *Corporate Social Responsibility: An Ethical Approach* (2011) Canada: Broadview Press, 15–17.

30 Milton Friedman has given a completely different definition of CSR which is concerned solely with the protection of investor interests: see Milton Friedman, *Capitalism and Freedom* (1962) Chicago: University Press, 133.

while improving the quality of life of the workforce and their families as well as of the local community and society at large'.[31] The World Business Council further states that CSR refers largely to corporate ethical behaviour towards society that particularly requires corporate management to act responsibly in its relationships with stakeholders who have legitimate interests in its business going beyond the interests of stockholders.[32] Amongst the stakeholders, it goes without saying that employees hold a significant stake in their corporation in terms of generating benefit for, and causing harm to, the respective society.

Islam is a religion of peace, harmony, brotherhood and tolerance. The Islamic principles consider business organisations and their responsibilities in a somewhat different way. This is because Islamic scholars in general firmly believe that the holy book of Qur'an is not merely a religious book, but a complete code of life as mentioned earlier. Hence the religious faith and conviction of Muslims considerably influence their everyday decisions including those of business transactions.[33] CSR is integral to the concept of corporate governance. There are as good as six approaches to corporate governance recognised around the globe, an Islamic approach is one of them.[34] As explained by the scholars of Shari'ah, the primary objective of corporate governance in Islam is ensuring 'fairness to all stakeholders to be attained through greater transparency and accountability'.[35] Kay and Silbertson term a large public corporation as a social organisation, and therefore should be governed by 'the concept of trusteeship to sustain its assets' including 'the skills of its employees, the expectations of customers and suppliers, and the company's reputation in the community' would appear to sit

---

[31] World Business Council for Sustainable Development, *Meeting Changing Expectations: Corporate Social Responsibility* (2000) 3.

[32] Ibid.

[33] Nisrine Abiad, *Sharia, Muslim States and International Human Rights Treaty Obligations: A Comparative Study* (2008) London: British Institute of International and Comparative Law (BIICL), 46.

[34] Lewis (1999) identifies six models of corporate governance that include the Anglo-Saxon model, the Germanic model, the Japanese model, the Latinic model, the Confucian model and the Islamic model: M. K. Lewis, 'Corporate Governance and Corporate Financing in Different Cultures' as cited in Mervyn K. Lewis, 'Islamic Corporate Governance' (2005) 9(1) *Review of Islamic Economics* 5, 23–4.

[35] See generally M. Umer Chapra and Habib Admad, *Corporate Governance in Islamic Financial Institutions*. IRTI Publication Management System, Jeddah, www.irtipms.org/PubDetE.asp?pub=93 (accessed 1 August 2014).

comfortably with the Islamic thoughts of corporate governance.[36] In this description of CSR, the skills of employees and corporate reputation in the community do inherently embrace the safety of workers at the workplace, the absence of which must negatively affect both employees' performance and corporate social image.

Further, the Islamic law puts the foremost emphasis on the structure of a commercial transaction in order to determine the presence of any element that may invalidate the profit stemmed from a business deal, and this structural investigation is somewhat similar to that of the secular corporate law which aims to strictly comply with the corporate charter.[37] Any vitiating elements repugnant to the principles of Shari'ah in a transaction would render it illegal *ipso facto*.[38] This is so because Islamic corporate governance is concerned with both the substance as well as the form of the business transaction.[39] When it comes to an employment relationship, Shari'ah requires both the employers and their employees to adhere to the rights and obligations enshrined in the Islamic rules prescribed for maintaining a healthy relation between these two unequal parties with the spirit of brotherhood and harmony. Central to this relationship is the protection of employees at the workplace by their employers. Making money showing disregard for the relevant Islamic dictates should be religiously vitiated, therefore, would be regarded as prohibited for a Muslim employer. Shari'ah contains specific principles for workplace safety that are binding on all Muslims at work.

IV. OCCUPATIONAL HEALTH AND SAFETY

There is little dispute that life is more important than anything else, whilst any occupation is taken up by a person to live his/her life as a human being. However, the garment factories, especially their owners, seem to believe in the opposite, ie, a worker's life has been created for work regardless of the working environment, times and wages. This is so

---

[36] J. Kay and A. Silbertson, 'Corporate Governance' (August 1995) *National Institute Economic Review* 90–91 as cited in Lewis (2005) above n34, 24.

[37] Ali A. Ibrahim, 'Convergence of Corporate Governance and Islamic Financial Services Industry: Toward Islamic Financial Services Securities Market' (2006) *Georgetown University Law Center* http://scholarship.law.georgetown.edu/gps_papers/3 10 (accessed 27 July 2014).

[38] Ibid.

[39] See generally, Mahmoud A. El-Gamal, *Islamic Finance: Law Economics and Practice* (2006) as cited in Ibrahim (2006) above n37.

because, several thousand workers have died at their workplace in Bangladesh over the past decade, but none has been punished for such irreparable losses to date.[40] Despite the enormous significance of the garment sector for the national economy of Bangladesh, the incidents of deaths and fatal injuries used to fall on deaf ears until the collapse of an eight-storey building Rana Plaza in April 2013 which housed five garment factories. The Rana Plaza itself has killed at least 1,142 garment workers and seriously injured more than 2000 others, whilst 160 workers remain missing even after a year of the debacle.[41] It unearthed the infinite miseries of millions of workers and reckless hunger for profits of the traders. The magnitude of the tragedy 'not only shocks the conscience of humankind throughout the world, but also solicits our attention, assaults our moral propriety, and offends our sense of justice'.[42]

To make the situation even worse, fires at garment factories have become almost a normal phenomenon, whilst collapse of the factory buildings occurred several times in the past. Recurrent factory fires have been causing garment workers' deaths for decades without any legal recourse being available to them. The devastating fire at Tazreen Fashions Ltd in November 2012 alone burnt down 130 workers when its nine-storey factory building caught fire originating from an unauthorised cotton store room on the ground floor.[43] It is obviously shocking, but none might look up in surprise in the country, because the Washington-based International Labour Rights Forum (ILRF) found at least 1,000 workers had been killed, whilst 3,000 others were injured in

---

[40] Golam Mortuza, Pranab Bal and Mithhun Chowdhury, 'So Many Loss of Lives – But No One Punished' *The Prothom Alo*, Dhaka (1 December 2012), first page (translated from Bengali).

[41] Monira Munni, 'Rana Plaza Tragedy – BGMEA List Set to Put Missing 160' *The Financial Express*, Dhaka (13 July 2014), last page; 'Rana Plaza Collapse – Primark Begins Paying Compensation' *The Daily Star*, Dhaka (8 June 2013), front page; Hasnat Abdul Hye, 'The Stakeholders in RMG' *The Financial Express*, Dhaka (21 May 2013), editorial; 'Two Accused in Rana Plaza Cases Get Bail' *The Daily Star* (28 January 2014), Business.

[42] M. Rafiqul Islam, 'Savar Tragedy through Legal Prisms – Corporate Greed and Government Inaction' *The Daily Star*, Dhaka (11 May 2013), Law & Our Rights.

[43] Nizam Ahmed, 'Improving Safety in BD RMG Sector – US Labour Department Announces $2.5m Grant' *The Financial Express*, Dhaka (15 June 2013), last page citing the US Labour Department.

more than 275 incidents in garment factories alone in Bangladesh between 1990 and 2012.[44]

The devastations caused by both the breakdown of Rana Plaza and burning down of Tazreen Fashions warrant condemnation in the strongest possible terms. This is because, there were reportedly several warnings from respective authorities of the vulnerability of Rana Plaza preceding the collapse,[45] nonetheless, the owner of the building and the proprietors of factories housed therein compelled the workers to come in and continue their work. Similarly, the middle managers of Tazreen, acting with gross negligence at its best and with reckless culpability at its worst, prevented workers from exiting the building even through the normal doors after it caught the fire, whilst the building did not have any emergency exits which are strictly required by the country's labour law. In addition, the Tazreen building had several deficiencies in respect of workplace safety.[46] Paradoxically, the owner of Tazreen in his initial reaction after the fire expressed his deep concerns about losing business with overseas buyers instead of showing repentance for his workers' loss of invaluable lives.[47] However, he subsequently claimed that no one had told him about the requirement of emergency exits which could have been otherwise easily included in the building.[48]

The international community for the first time woke up following such colossal losses of human lives which are virtually survived by the indefinable miseries of their hapless families. The International Labour

---

44 'EU Worried – Nationwide Factory Inspection Begins' *The Daily Star* (31 January 2013) Dhaka, front page.

45 Zaglul Ahmed Chowdhury, 'News Analysis – Savar Tragedy: Garment Industry Must be Saved, Phasing Out the Errants' *The Financial Express*, Dhaka (5 May 2013), first page; '45 More Bodies Found, Death Toll Now 550' *The Financial Express*, Dhaka (5 May 2013), first page; '38 More Bodies Recovered, Toll 425 – 32 Unclaimed Bodies Buried at Jurain after DNA Test' *The Financial Express*, Dhaka (3 May 2013), first page; Inam Ahmed '9-Storey Building Caves in – Rescue Races against Time' *The Daily Star*, Dhaka (25 April 2013), front page; Nizam Ahmed, 'Savar Tragedy Triggers Outcry Worldwide – RMG Exports Likely to be Affected' *The Financial Express*, Dhaka (26 April 2013), first page.

46 See, for details, Solaiman (2013), above n15.

47 M. Shahidul Islam, 'Conspiracy Theory Lacks Credibility – Deadly Garment Fire Shakes Buyers' Confidence' *The Weekly Holiday*, Dhaka (30 Nov 2012), front page.

48 Refayet Ullah Mirdha and Sarwar A. Chowdhury, 'My Fault, but None Alerted Me – Tazreen MD Tells Star' *The Daily Star*, Dhaka (29 November 2012), front page.

Organisation (ILO) urged the Government of Bangladesh to take appropriate measures to ensure safety of workers and to prevent the recurrence of such 'entirely avoidable workplace tragedies'.[49] The incidents also moved the Secretary-General of the United Nations who expressed his deep sorrow for those deaths, whilst the European Mission visiting Bangladesh to see the devastation themselves also joined others in expressing their shock.[50] The United States, a vital customer of garment products, in its response to the catastrophes asked the government to improve safety conditions at the workplace and took a punitive measure by suspending Bangladesh from the Generalised System of Preferences (GSP) program which has not been restored to date despite repeated requests of government.[51] The continued refusals of the United States to restore the suspended GSP conform to the reports of the British weekly newspaper, The Economist, that no serious effort to improve workplace environment have been taken to bring the safety standard acceptable to the international community.[52] These clearly indicate that the international pressures against the government and factory owners are mounting, and the US Senate Committee prescribes that the 'surest way to guarantee the success of the apparel industry is to avoid another disaster by promoting and protecting labor rights now, while the world's attention is on Bangladesh. The present opportunity to improve working conditions in Bangladesh cannot be squandered.'[53]

The Islamic law regarding corporations sharply contrasts to the 'self-interested agents' model of corporate governance, which is considered to be the most extreme view operating in the 'ruthless economy' with a 'cowered labour force' as Samuelson coins it.[54] This model emphasises maximisation of shareholder value where the market force disciplines and controls the economic actors in a free market economy.[55] The Islamic

---

[49] 'ILO for Quick Action: Ensure Safety to Garment Workers' *The New Nation*, Dhaka (5 May 2013).

[50] Nizam Ahmed, 'UN Chief Condoles Deaths in Savar Bldg Collapse' *The Financial Express*, Dhaka (28 April 2013).

[51] Wasi Ahmed, 'US GSP Suspension and the Worry-Box' *The Financial Express*, Dhaka (30 June 2013), editorial; Rahman Jahangir, 'RMG: Roadblocks versus Roadmap' *The Financial Express*, Dhaka (12 July 2014), editorial.

[52] See 'No Serious Efforts to Improve Factory Safety – *The Economist* Focuses on Rift among Retailers' *The Financial Express*, Dhaka (13 July 2013), last page.

[53] Committee on Foreign Relations (2013) above n9, 13.

[54] P. Samuelson, 'Where do the European and American Models Differ' as cited in Lewis (2005) above n34, 23.

[55] Lewis (2005) above n34, 23.

model rests on largely the stakeholder model of corporate regulation. Shari'ah encourages production of essentials for humans whilst imposes prohibition on financing goods and services that are in conflict with the Islamic values and principles (*haram* activities), such as, producing alcohol, facilitating gambling (*maysir*), engaging in usury (*riba*) and stimulating uncertainty (*gharar*).[56] Further, the Islamic law also fosters the protection of environment, vegetation and even animals.[57] It would be imprudent to argue that such prohibitions have been put in place for nothing. This is because all the prohibited things in business have negative impacts on human health and life.[58] The Qur'an itself explains the justification for such prohibitions whilst it provides that 'In them is great sin, and some benefit for people; but the sin is greater than their benefit'.[59] The concern of this chapter goes far beyond any ordinary harm of humans because it relates to human life and safety.

The right to life is a universally recognised human right. In addition, it is a fundamental right in Bangladesh as enshrined in its Constitution.[60] The Supreme Court of Bangladesh has pronounced on several occasions that the state has binding obligations to protect fundamental rights. For example, the Supreme Court in *Ain O Salish Kendra (ASK) v Government of Bangladesh* held that the state is constitutionally obligated to make effective provisions for securing the right to life, living and livelihood within its economic capacity.[61] Consistently, Shari'ah provides explicit provisions for the protection of life and security of human beings without any discrimination being made based on any consideration as the Holy Qur'an ordains that 'Take not life, which Allah has made sacred except through justice and law'.[62] The importance of life given by the divine book is further evident in its words equating one life with that of the mankind, 'that if anyone slew a person unless it be for murder or for the spreading of mischief in the land – it would be as if he slew the whole people, and if anyone saved a life, it would be as if he had saved the life of the whole people'.[63] Obviously, this prohibition applies to

---

[56] Ibid.

[57] Ibid.

[58] See Williams and Zinkin (2010), 'Islam and CSR: A Study of the Compatibility between the Tenets of Islam and the UN Global Compact' (2010) 91 *Journal of Business Ethics* 519, 523.

[59] The Holy Qur'an, Chapter 2, Verse 219.

[60] Art 32 of the Constitution of Bangladesh.

[61] (1999) 19 BLD (HCD) 488.

[62] The Holy Qur'an, Chapter 6, Verse 151.

[63] The Holy Qur'an, Chapter 5, Verse 32.

everyone without any discrimination against anyone and does 'make it clear that Muslims are obliged to protect life wherever possible, as well as to be careful about how a life should be taken'.[64]

Shari'ah is always in favour of discipline and adherence to the religious norms in every sphere of human life, thus it gives importance to justice and equality of treatment at work, and does permit hierarchies in corporate management. The Islamic law believes in 'freedom, justice and equality' and opposes 'discretion, injustice and inequality in the workplace'.[65] Islam, as a religion, provides guarantee for workplace safety.[66] Shari'ah provides the details of entitlements of employees and their employers that can 'neither be abrogated nor be disregarded'.[67] Regarding workplace in particular, the Qur'an mentions that 'He has raised you in ranks, some above others: that He may try you in that which He has bestowed on you'.[68] So, a clear emphasis on the greater responsibility of a higher position at work is evident in this Qur'anic verse. Labour is well regarded as being dignified human contribution to, or factor of, production in Islam and employment obligations must be properly discharged based on contracts that mirror justice on the part of both employers and their employees.[69] The prohibition on the oppressive conduct of higher officials with their subordinate colleagues is further evidenced by the words of Prophet Muhammad (SM) who asked people to 'help their brothers whether he is the oppressor or the oppressed, i.e. if one is an oppressor another should prevent him from doing it, for that is his help and if one is the oppressed he should be helped (against oppression).[70] Allah has categorically made oppression against one another unlawful.[71]

Regarding compelling a worker to do a certain job, the Qur'an pronounces that 'on no soul doth Allah place a burden greater than it can bear'.[72] Also, workplace safety is required by the Qur'an itself which orders that '... make not your hands contribute to your (own) destruction (by refraining); and do good; indeed, Allah loves the doers of good'.[73]

---

64 Williams and Zinkin (2009) above n12, 525.

65 Rozanah Ab Rahman, 'Protection of Safety, Health and Welfare of Employees at Workplace under Islamic Law' (2006) 14(1) *IIUM Law Journal* 51.

66 Id., 53.

67 Id., 52.

68 The Holy Qur'an, Chapter 6, Verse 165.

69 Rahman (2006), above n65, 52.

70 Shahi Muslim, Book 3, Hadith No. 6246.

71 Sahih Muslim, Book 3 Hadith No. 6254.

72 The Qur'an, Chapter 2, Verse 286.

73 The Qur'an, Chapter 2, Verse 195.

The Qur'an further says, 'You are the best community which has been brought forth for mankind. You command what is right and forbid what is wrong and you believe in Allah.'[74] These Qur'anic orders are reinforced by the words of Prophet Muhammad (SM) who said, 'Do not ask them to do any job that is beyond their abilities and if you have to, then you must help them fulfilling such a work.'[75] He has further advised employers to ensure fair labour practices that:

> Your employees are your brethren upon whom Allah has given you authority. Hence, if one has one's brother under his/her control, one should feed them with the like of what one eats and clothe them with the like of what one wears. Even no workers can be compelled to do more than what they are capable of doing, and the employer is obligated to provide safe workplace. You should not overburden them with what they cannot bear, and if you do so, help them in their job.[76]

Hence, Islamic law requires employers to provide acceptable working conditions to their workers and give them only reasonable kinds of work.[77] All employees must be treated fairly and equitably and no discrimination is permitted in Islam. The Prophet enunciates in his last sermon reinforcing the people's right to be treated equally as Allah has assured everyone's enjoyment of bounties on earth that:

> No Arab has superiority over any non-Arab and no non-Arab has any superiority over an Arab; no dark person has superiority over a white person and no white person has any superiority over a dark person. The criterion of honour in the sight of Allah is righteousness and honest living.[78]

The foregoing discussion demonstrates that the treatment of Islam with workers is well protective of their safety, cooperative and healthy workplace. Prohibitions against forced labour and negligence about safe working environment are categorical and unambiguous. The principles of Shari'ah are in full alignment with the prevailing western law as well as

---

[74] The Qur'an, Chapter 3, Verse 110.

[75] Muhammad Muhsin Khan, *Sah-ih al-Bukh-ar-i* (Dar Al Arabia, 4th ed., 1994), 18.

[76] Sahih al Muslim Book 3: Hadith No. 4093. See also Elsaman (2012) above n19, 112.

[77] Beekun and Gamal A. Badawi, 'Balancing Ethical Responsibility Among Multiple Organizational Stakeholders: The Islamic Perspective' (2005) 60 *Journal of Business Ethics* 131, 138.

[78] The Prophet's Last Sermon, delivered on the Ninth day of Dhul al Hijjah 10 A.H. in the 'Uranah valley of Mount Arafat in 632 A.C.'.

the standards set forth by the international community. Shari'ah seems to be one step ahead of the man-made law in that no other laws explicitly require an employer to be so kind and generous towards his/her employees. This is so because Shari'ah requires employers to feed their employees with the foods they eat, and to provide them with the clothes that they wear as alluded to above. This is certainly distinctive from the conventional laws. This underscores the central thirst of brotherhood and equality in Islam, which disapproves any lack of safety at the workplace and prohibits any prejudicial or deleterious behaviour of the employer with their employees.

Shari'ah principles are applicable to the negligent or reckless conduct of garment factories with their workers. The employers or owners of the garment factories should adhere to these Islamic principles as long as they believe in Islam apart from the potential sanctions against the breach of the pertinent municipal law. But in practice, their conduct directly contradicts the Islamic principles. Tazreen mid managers reportedly compelled factory workers to stay at work despite fires, whilst its owner ignored the responsibility to ensure safe working environment for his workers. On the other hand, the owner of Rana Plaza along with the proprietors of the factories established therein allegedly forced the ill-fated workers to come to work despite the repeated public warnings of life-risk of the occupants.[79] These clearly breach the principles of Shari'ah which impose liability directly on individuals as it does not recognise corporate separate personality unlike the man-made law. Therefore the owners and executives, instead of their corporations, bear the liability for the casualties mentioned earlier.[80] This individual-centric responsibility denotes a significant difference between the concepts of corporate personality under the conventional law and Shari'ah in that 'the corporation is no more than a legal entity that has no responsibilities that can be separated from those of the individuals who make up the organisation' in Islam.[81] Hence owners or employers and their executives have the primary liability for any lack of safety measures at the workplace.

Along the line of Shari'ah, the formulation and operation of several major international efforts to protect human life and workplace safety can

---

79 See the sources cited in above n45.

80 See A. Bhatia, Speech given by Lord Bhatia entitled 'CSR: An Islamic Perspective' at a Conference on 'Singapore/UK Developing Corporate Social Responsibility' at the Shangri La hotel in Singapore on 23 February 2004 as cited in Williams and Zinkin (2009), above n12, 529.

81 Ibid.

be found. The first global instrument on people's rights is the Universal Declaration of Human Rights 1948 (UDHR). Its Article 3 pronounces that 'Everyone has the right to life, liberty and security of person', whilst it begins with Article 1 by reassuring that 'All human beings are born free and equal in dignity and rights. They are endowed with reason and conscience and should act towards one another in a spirit of brotherhood.' So, any negligence or recklessness in protecting workers' lives would breach this charter of the humankind.

Adding legal force to the UDHR, Article 6(1) of the International Covenant on Civil and Political Rights 1966 as ratified by Bangladesh[82] states that 'Every human being has the inherent right to life. This right shall be protected by law. No one shall be arbitrarily deprived of his life.' Likewise, the International Covenant on Economic, Social and Cultural Rights 1966, to which Bangladesh is a state party,[83] contains an explicit provision pertaining to workplace safety. Its Article 7 provides that 'The States Parties to the present Covenant recognise the right of everyone to the enjoyment of just and favourable conditions of work which ensure, in particular: ... (ii) A decent living for themselves and their families in accordance with the provisions of the present Covenant; (b) Safe and healthy working conditions ...'

The Cairo Declaration of Human Rights in Islam 1999, articulated in light of the Islamic principles, contains clear provisions concerning rights of workers. It incorporates, amongst others things, the right to work itself, the right to enjoy safety, security and social guarantee, the right not to be compelled to work beyond one's capacity, and the right not to be subject to any harm. These rights are enshrined in Articles 13 and 14. Article 13 reads:[84]

> Work is a right guaranteed by the State and Society for each person able to work. Everyone shall be free to choose the work that suits him [or her] best and which serves his [or her] interests and those of society. The employee shall have the right to safety and security as well as to all other social guarantees. He [or she] may neither be assigned work beyond his capacity nor be subjected to compulsion or exploited or harmed in any way.

Article 14 adds that 'Everyone shall have the right to legitimate gains without monopolization, deceit or harm to oneself or to others'.

---

82 Bangladesh ratified the ICCPR on 5 October 1998.

83 Bangladesh ratified the ICESCR on 7 September 2000.

84 The Cairo Declaration on Human Rights in Islam 1990, Arts 13–14.

Likewise, the Universal Islamic Declaration of Human Rights 1981 (UIDHR) having regard to the Qur'an and Sunnah categorically abhors slavery and forced labour.[85]

Therefore, the Islamic international documents are clearly in complete agreement with the international law on workplace safety.

V. CONCLUSIONS

Both international secular instruments and the principles of Islamic law strongly assert that maintenance of workplace safety is an essential obligation of employers. CSR does not uphold a concept of charity or philanthropy; rather it denotes the responsibility of corporations as an integral part of the national and international communities to protect those who may be affected by their (corporations) actions or omissions in both short and long terms. As a means of long-term risk management, 'CSR recognises the importance of investing in man-made capital to make the workplace safer, and factories and infrastructure more productive'.[86] It plays a positive role to improve financial performance, enhance brand name and reputation and increase the ability to attract, motivate and retain the best workforce.[87]

Garments owners in Bangladesh appear to be complacent by offering an earning opportunity to millions of unemployed poor youths especially untrained women without adequate safety standards and remuneration. Many workers too are thought to be seemingly happy with whatever they get in exchange for their hard labour believing in the old saying that 'something is better than nothing'. They fear that they may lose whatever they are presently earning, if they want more from their employers. Therefore, they have to continue to work with a calm disappointment for years. The discontent gets worse when it is amplified by safety concerns. Such a workplace environment is not only exploitive, but also unproductive simply because workers' motivation for work is affected by the feeling of unsafety and deprivation. The existence of such an atmosphere at the workplace is not only condemned, but proscribed in Islam. Hence both the owners and workers especially when they are Muslim need to be respectful to each other's rights and obligations for mutual interests in this life, as well as for the divine rewards in the eternal life hereafter

---

85 Preamble g(iii) of the UIDHR.

86 John Zinkin, 'Why Malaysia's Companies Should be Socially Responsible' *Malaysian Business* (1 August 2004), 56–7.

87 Id., 56.

under Islamic teachings. Employers, by virtue of their higher rank, do have a greater responsibility compared to that of their employees to ensure compliance with Shari'ah principles.

The preceding discussions provide evidence of the fact that Islamic principles are by no means in conflict with the spirit of CSR currently prevailing throughout the globe especially in the developed world in the era of 'corporate tyranny'. Rather Shari'ah is unambiguous in imposing responsibility on individuals in exclusion of the entity itself for ignoring workplace safety.[88] Personal liability does work as incentives to comply with regulation which is attached to sanctions.[89]

In response to a potential question as to why the employers in Bangladesh should abide by the CSR principles of Shari'ah, John Zinkin's contention in a Malaysian context could be mentioned that 'it makes good business sense; it is the Islamic way of doing business; and it is good risk management'.[90] Bangladesh is clearly comparable with Malaysia in terms of both religion and business in general, although the former is much stronger than the latter particularly in the garment sector. Bangladesh cannot afford to lose the dominating position of its garment industry at home and abroad in the interest of economic and social well-being of the nation at the very least. Moreover, Islam is a religion which contains the ultimate code of human life; it instructs employers to embrace their workers with due kindness, respect, honour and a sense of brotherhood. All these collectively obligate employers to provide a safe and healthy workplace to their workers.

---

[88] See Williams and Zinkin, (2009), above n12, 520.

[89] See F. Gigler, 'Discussion of an Analysis of Auditor Liability Rules' (1994) 32 *Journal of Accounting Research* 61, 64; R. Schwartz, 'Legal Regime, Audit Quality and Investment' (1997) 72 *Accounting Review* 385, 397–8.

[90] Zinkin (2004), above n86, 56.

6. Business in Islam: revisiting Islamic banking practices in Bangladesh

Afroza Begum

I. INTRODUCTION

Business in Islam is guided by Shari'ah and a set of ethical standards.[1] Some of the core tenets that Islamic business should endorse include divineness, legitimate ways of earning, righteousness, generosity towards consumers and selflessness.[2] Shari'ah prohibits interest-based transactions and discourages monopolistic, deceptive and restrictive trade practices.[3] In sharp contrast with the capitalism, self-centric individualistic and competitive approach, Islamic ethical values build on humanity, compassion, tolerance, fairness and self-reliance.[4] Accordingly, business should conform to some religious and social missions such as fair and responsible treatment of workers, honesty and leniency in business dealing, avoidance of excessive profits and hoarding practices and exploitation of one's ignorance of the market conditions. Arguably

---

[1] Bruce Hearn, 'Islamic Finance and Market Segmentation: Implications for the Cost of Capital' (2012) 21 (1) *International Business Review* at 103.

[2] Umar Esq et al., 'Contractual Forms in Islamic Finance Law and *Islamic Inv. Co. of the Gulf (Bahamas) Ltd. v. Symphony Gems N.V. & Ors*: A First Impression of Islamic Finance' (2003) 27 (1) *Fordham International Law Journal* at 152.

[3] For a detailed discussion about this see, Michael Taylor, 'Islamic Banking – the Feasibility of Establishing an Islamic Bank in the United States' (2003) 40 *American Business Law Journal* at 385; Mahmoud El-Gamal, '"Interest" and the Paradox of Contemporary Islamic Law and Finance' (2003) 27 (1) *Fordham International Law Journal* at 109.

[4] Arafa Mohamed, 'Corruption and Bribery in Islamic Law: Are Islamic Ideals Being Met in Practice?' (2012) 18 *Annual Survey of International & Comparative Law* at 172; Nedal El-Ghattis, 'Islamic Banking's Role in Economic Development: Future Outlook', www.iefpedia.com/english/wp-content/uploads/2010/12/Islamic-Bankings-Role-in-Economic-Development-Future-Nedal-El-Ghattis.pdf; Haider Hamoudi, 'Muhammad's Social Justice or Muslim Cant?: Langdellianism and the Failures of Islamic Finance' (2007) 40 *Cornell Int'l L.J.* at 92.

Islamic banking institution (IBI) is based on these fundamental principles. Various regulatory institutions, including the Accounting and Auditing Organization for Islamic Finance Institutions (AAOIFI) set basic standards for regulating IBI and evaluating their compliance with Shari'ah. These standards focus on a number of areas, including mode of financing, accounting, auditing and supervisory mechanisms.

Bangladesh embraced Islamic banking via the establishment of the Islamic Bank (IB) in 1983 and became the first nation across Southeast Asia to introduce it.[5] This chapter argues that the way in which IB functions in Bangladesh is fundamentally flawed and needs to be reviewed to achieve the pertinent goals of Shari'ah. Given the limited space, this work only investigates the Shari'ah compliance in devising 'modes of financing', especially *Murabaha* (discussed shortly) and the implementing mechanism of IB in Bangladesh. The following discussion begins with a brief exploration of the way in which a business should form and function in Islam.

II. BUSINESS IN ISLAM

The significance of business is deeply entrenched in the Islamic tradition and reaffirmed by *Sunnah*. The Prophet (SWS) urged 'Be involved in business as nine out of ten sources of income lie in business' (*Ihya*).[6] Shari'ah, however, has imposed a range of restrictions that a business should comply with. Foremost among these is the recognition of the fact that God is the creator and ultimate owner of all resources and business must be conducted to satisfy Him and to achieve some philosophical undertakings, including social welfare, satisfaction of the consumer and ensuring 'value-maximization' among relevant stakeholders triggered by equity and social justice.[7] Islam places great emphasis on legitimate ways of earning; many *Qur'anic* verses disapprove the wrongful taking of the property.

---

[5] Akbar Chowdhury, 'Analysing the Islamic banking framework in Bangladesh' 9 May 2014, http://newagebd.net/9712/analysing-the-islamic-banking-framework-in-bangladesh/#sthash.8vCnRtEx.dpbs.

[6] Murray Hunter, 'Integrating the philosophy of Tawhid – an Islamic approach to organization', www.culturaldiplomacy.org/pdf/case-studies/Integrating_Islamic_approach_to-the_organization.pdf.

[7] Nicolas Jacquot, 'Tax Guidelines Boost Islamic Finance in France' (2009) 20 (4) *International Tax Review* at 38.

The *Holy Qur'an* provides: '[do] not devour one another's property wrongfully, nor throw it before the judges in order to devour a portion of other's property sinfully and knowingly.'[8] The Prophet (SWS) said, 'A man's work with his hands, and every legitimate sale.'[9]

Consequently, business must avoid exploitation, 'usury' (Riba[10] or interest), manipulation of the market, taking excessive advancement, speculative selling, and investing in forbidden goods and services such as alcohol, drugs and gambling.[11] Shari'ah strictly condemns all forms of interest since these involve both oppression and exploitation.[12] Providing loans without the condition of interest is rewarding; many *ahadith* (refers to actions and habits of the Prophet Muhammad (pbuh) constituting the major source of guidance for Muslims) stipulate that 'the reward for giving charity is multiplied ten times whereas the reward for giving an interest-free loan is multiplied eighteen times'.[13] By prohibiting interest-based transactions and discouraging speculative economic growth Islamic business not only fosters religious and social goals but also a stable and accountable financial system.[14]

The transition in financial thinking in conformity with Shari'ah heavily influenced the mid-1980s banking policy and framework across nations and became institutionalised via the emergence of Islamic bank (IB) in the late twentieth century. Progressive developments in devising new modes of financing such as *Mudarabah* made IB very profitable, galvanised the economy and arguably injected greater market discipline.[15] In brief, these Shari'ah based modes of financing theoretically aim to stimulate a banking practice in which emphasis is given to

---

8 The Holy Qu'ran, 2:188.

9 *Ahmad*, No. 1576, www.renaissance.com.pk/Mayviewpoint2y5.htm.

10 Riba is the extra amount charged by a lender which a borrower is required to pay off in addition to the initial principal.

11 Jacquot 2009 n7 at 38.

12 '... but Allah hath permitted trade and forbidden usury ...' (Al-Baqurah 2:275). The Prophet (SWS) is reported to have said: 'May Allah send down His curse on the one who devours *Riba* and the one who pays it and on the two witnesses and on the person writing it' See *Ahmad*, No. 624; Esq et al., 2003 n2 at 168.

13 'Business Moral Codes in Islam', www.islamic-laws.com/fiqhofbusiness.htm.

14 See generally M. Chapra, 'The Case Against Interest: Is it Compelling?' (2007) 49 (2) *Thunderbird International Business Review* at 161–81.

15 See for details, Michele Penzer et al., 'Shari'w-Compliant Financings: New Opportunities for the U.S. Market', (2009) 126 *Banking Law Journal* at 59; Dena Elkhatib et al., 'Islamic Finance' (2012) 46 (1) *The International Lawyer* at

developing various projects and trading relationship based on talent, expertise and prospects where returns are not fixed in advance instead are dependent upon the real economic outcome. Some scholars of the West consider the use of Islamic banking more suitable for economic development.[16] The Islamic finance institution has advanced into a significant industry with assets estimated at $1.8 trillion and 'growing at an annual rate of over 20 per cent per year'.[17]

Building on some investment techniques of financing while IB resembling conventional banking (CB) in several key aspects, it is notionally and spiritually different in its objectives and vision.[18] Unlike CB, the participatory and interest-free approaches to business, for example, dominate the production, economic and financial behaviour of IB. Shari'ah compliance, pursuing religious and social goals through empowering the disadvantaged, reliance on the profit-loss sharing (PLS) strategies and the absence of a predetermined rate of interest and collateral, and speculative transactions are some distinguished features of IB.[19] Another distinguished feature of IB is the ownership-oriented selling, that is, an ownership is required to give effect to any transaction; a financier can only sell those products and services that it owns. Financing extended by these Islamic modes can thus expand only in step with the rise of the real economy and thereby help curb excessive credit expansion, which is one of the major causes of instability in the international financial markets.[20] All these provide powerful impetus for changes in investment techniques of IB. Yet, IB in Bangladesh has promoted a different practice, perhaps as elsewhere, which is addressed in the following discussion.

281; Conway Kevin et al., 'Rules Refined to Ensure Shari'ah Compliance' (2010) 21 (4) *International Tax Review* at 42–3.

[16] M. Hassan et al., 'Islamic Finance: A System at the Crossroads?' (2007) 49 (2) *Thunderbird International Business Review* at 151.

[17] Haider Hamoudi, 'Impossible, Highly Desired Islamic Bank' (2014) 5 (1) *William and Mary Business Law Review* at 152; Hamoudi 2007 n4 at 1; Esq et al., 2003 n2 at 151.

[18] Hassan et al., 2007 n16 at 151.

[19] Khaled Qasaymeh, 'Islamic Banking in South Africa: Between the Accumulation of Wealth and the Promotion of Social Prosperity' (2011) 44 (2) *Comparative and International Law Journal of Southern Africa* at 276.

[20] Hamoudi 2007 n4.

III. ISLAMIC BANKS IN BANGLADESH

Islamic banking emerged in Bangladesh in the mid-1980s with the establishment of the first Islamic bank in the capital city, fostering the subsequent formation of another seven full-fledged Islamic banks (IBS).[21] A number of private banks also operate Shari'ah-based banking parallel to their conventional interest-based transactions.[22] Founded on the core spirit of Shari'ah, IBS aimed ideologically at the advancement of a financial system based on equity and social justice.[23] Currently IBS hold 'almost 25 per cent of the total market share in banking sector [and it] experienced a growth of 25.83 per cent compared to 20.58 percent in conventional banks'.[24]

The regulatory framework comprising Bank Companies Act 1991, Bangladesh Bank Order 1972, Securities and Exchange Commission Act 1993, the Income Tax Ordinance 1984 and the Shari'ah while guiding responsible business of IBS allows them to determine their PLS ratios and mark-ups consistent with their own policy and banking environment.[25] This facilitates an independent exercise of Shari'ah principles in adopting various modes of financing and persuades IBS to be competitive with conventional banking.

Bangladesh Bank (BB) is entrusted with the legal authority to supervise IBS' conducts and the enforcement of these laws. BB introduced an internal and Islamic economics division for managing IBS and issued a guideline in 2009 for conducting Islamic finance.[26] Even though, there is no separate Islamic banking law to regulate IBS, unlike other Asian nations, an amendment to the Banking Companies Act 1991 (Act No. 14 of 1991) incorporated a range of provisions relevant to IBS. These require IBS, *inter alia*, to maintain a reserve fund (Statutory Liquidity Reserve), and pursue certain Shari'ah principles in operating their business. The following discussion concentrates on the financing modes and examines whether IBS apply these in line with Shari'ah.

---

[21] Salahuddin Yousuf et al., 'Islamic Banking Scenario of Bangladesh' (2014) 2 (1) *Journal of Islamic Banking and Finance* at 23.

[22] Currently, there are 16 Islamic banking windows of conventional banks. See Chowdhury 204 n5.

[23] Ibid.

[24] Ibid.

[25] Faruq Ahmad et al., 'Regulation and performance of Islamic banking in Bangladesh' (2007) 49 (2) *Thunderbird International Business Review* at 254.

[26] The Government Circular, 9 November 2009 as mentioned in Chowdhury 2014 n5.

A. Modes of Financing

Islamic banking operates through the two major methods of financing: equity based profit-and-loss-sharing (PLS) and debt-based sale-lease transactions (DST).[27] While the first mode is designed to stimulate a cooperative/participatory approach to financing, the second contemplates purchasing and reselling or leasing assets with a marked-up price and a fixed-return.[28] PLS is the most Shari'ah-approved financing mechanism comprising *Musharakah* and *Mudarabah* on which contemporary Islamic economics is fundamentally rooted.[29]

Musharakah and *Mudarabah* typically refer to partnerships or joint ventures (between the bank and the client) in which the bank and the client agreed to launch different projects and share profits based on their mutually agreed proportion.[30] Losses are also shared between the parties in accordance with the ratio of their respective capitals. That is 'only the party providing financial capital in a *mudaraba* bears all the losses'.[31] Since the bank usually provides the capital to develop entrepreneurial projects, it is the bank which has to consume all the resulting losses that makes this mode risky and less attractive. In DST, debts are created via, *inter alia*, *Ijara* and *Murabaha*.[32] *Ijara* transaction involves the bank purchasing an asset and then leasing this to the client on a fixed-term return and a condition that the bank will retain the ownership until the full payment has been made by the client.[33]

In the *Murabaha*[34] transaction the bank first finances the purchase of the goods or asset on behalf of the client and then resells it to him/her

---

27 'International Briefing' (2007) 26 (6) *International Financial Law Review* at 67.

28 Institute of Islamic Banking, 'Islamic Banking', www.islamic-banking.com/profit_and_lose_sharing.aspx.

29 El-Gamal (2003) n3 at 113.

30 Qasaymeh (2011) n19 at 281.

31 Shah Nizami, 'Islamic Finance: The United Kingdom's Drive to Become the Global Islamic Finance Hub and the United States' Irrational Indifference to Islamic Finance' (2011) 34 (1) *Suffolk Transnational Law Review* at 226.

32 Institute of Islamic Banking n28.

33 Kelly Holden, 'Islamic Finance: Legal Hypocrisy Moot Point, Problematic Future Bigger Concern' (2007) 25 (1) *Boston University International Law Journal* at 350.

34 'Murabaha in ancient Islamic connotations referred to a particular kind of simple sale and had no relevance whatsoever with a transaction of financing … in recent times … See Shahid Siddiqui, 'Islamic Banking: True Modes of Financing', www.islamic-banking.com/iarticle_2.aspx.

(the client) by adding a cost-plus price with a fixed return to be paid over a definite time-frame. Hence, there are two transactions involved in the process: the first transaction is made between the bank and the third party from whom the bank purchases, and the second one is between the bank and the client. The whole process is conducted based on an agreement (the pre agreed promise of the client) that the client will buy the same asset from the bank.[35]

One of the distinguished characteristics of PLS (as compared to DST) is that only the profits are distributed in a mutually agreed proportion and the loss is exclusively borne by the financier as mentioned which is what makes the transaction risky. In DST, the payment methods and rate are fixed in advance which ensures a profitable return and is therefore less risky and attractive. While its limited use is accepted by some Islamic scholars,[36] others raise serious objections as it contradicts the fundamental principles of Islamic finance.[37]

B. PLS vis-à-vis DST in Islamic Banks (IBS) in Bangladesh

Several research findings confirm that DST transaction, especially *Murabaha*, heavily dominates IBS' financing in Bangladesh and very little recourse has been made to use PLS approach. One study claims that 'Islami Bank Bangladesh Limited, Al Arafah Bank and Social Investment Bank Limited have used 54%, 76% and 65% respectively of their investment funds by resorting to *Murabaha*'.[38] Another research reveals, '[presently] 60%–70% investments of Islamic banks are made on mark-up basis (Murabaha and Bai-Muajjal etc.). As a result, the ideal modes of investment (Mudaraba and Musharaka) are quite absent in their practices.'[39] More importantly, there has been a genuine allegation that IBS even failed to introduce and practice the truly *Murabaha* transaction. The reports of IBS' *Sharīca* Council from 1984 to 1997 unveiled that

---

[35] Kilian Bälz, 'A *Murabaha* Transaction in an English Court – The London High Court of 13th February 2002 in *Islamic Investment Company of the Gulf (Bahamas) Ltd. v. Symphony Gems N.V. & Ors*' (2004) 11 *Islamic Law & Society* at 120.

[36] See generally El-Gamal (2003) n3 at 113–35.

[37] See for example, Taylor (2003) n3; ibid.

[38] 'Issues and Problems of Islamic Banking', www.islamibankbd.com/abtIBBL/cis_issues_and_problems_of_islamic_banking.php.

[39] Abdul Sarker, 'Islamic Banking in Bangladesh Growth, Structure, and Performance', Proceedings of the Third Harvard University Forum on Islamic Finance: Local Challenges, Global Opportunities Cambridge, Massachusetts. Center for Middle Eastern Studies, Harvard University (1999) at 271–90.

IBS failed to conform to the 'true mechanism of *Bayc-murābaha*' in buying and selling, and a huge amount of '*Bayc*' investment did not follow the guidelines of Shari'ah.[40] Consequently, Abull Sarker recommends, '[thus], their "*Bayc*" practices may be termed "Corrupted *murābaha*" ... An analysis of the activities and reports of all other Islamic Banks' *Sharīca* Councils also reveals a similar situation.'[41]

Quite consistent with the above findings, a recent study of Islamic Banking Institute demonstrates that that predominance of *Murabaha* financing in the portfolio management of investment funds and the utilisation of 'interest rate as a criterion for fixing the profit margin' by IBS of Bangladesh have sparked widespread outcry.[42] One of the major unresolved problems lies within the *Murabaha* framework is the 'technique' of financing based on a fixed and assured return, and IBS have been nurturing 'interest' in its substance under the pretext of a different name by only changing the nomenclature of their transactions.[43] The most controversial aspects of *Murabaha*, is 'mark-up' which has become a common financing practice to raise capital.

Mark-up, as endorsed in *Murabaha* is realised by IBS through a predetermined fixed instalment to be paid by the client over a specific period of time. More fundamentally, the rate of return that gets fixed beforehand is excessive – normally more than the prevailing interest rates charged by their conventional analogues, and is recovered via a deferred-payment method. This prefixed return along with the resulting total payment and their interconnectedness with the wealth creation resemble the characteristics of interest-based transactions practiced by the conventional banks, which essentially contradict and disrespect the divine values of Shari'ah. Any form of interest is prohibited in Islam because of, *inter alia*, to discourage exploitation, undue accumulation of wealth and sustain a system accommodating social development and ethical standards. The proponent of *Murabaha*, however, contends:

> The particular nature of the *Mudaraba* and *Musharaka* is a threat to banking ... A bank cannot finance in an equal chance of making profit or losing capital because it is, after all, a financial intermediary and is engaged in banking business with depositors' money. Moreover, the deposit is payable on

40 Islami Bank Bangladesh Limited, 'Tiaras Council's Reports, 1984–97' as cited in Sarker, ibid.

41 Ibid.

42 'Issues and Problems of Islamic Banking' n38.

43 Sarker (1999) n39.

> demand so it is protected by a banking safety-net, and besides, banks are under obligation to safeguard depositors' money.[44]

By upholding this, Chapra argues that *Murabaha* is different from the conventional interest-oriented banking transactions on a series of accounts.[45] Firstly, in *Murabaha* transaction the bank purchases the asset in reliance on an agreement, and then resells it (real asset) to the same client consistent with Shari'ah which requires 'ownership' to be obtained in order to give effect to any sales transaction. Secondly, in between these two transactions the Bank assumes certain risks, for example, a sudden fall in price may convince the client to change its decision or there may be a delay in payment due to unexpected circumstances. In such a case, the bank assumes vital risks and responsibility for the asset before it is completely transferred to the client. This intermediary risk and extra steps/requirements add to the cost of the transaction.[46] Thirdly, the bank cannot change the original agreed-upon amount if the client fails to make payments by the due date.[47] Fourthly, the rate of return via the deferred payment is mutually agreed and 'it is the price of the good or service sold, not the rate of interest that is stipulated'.[48]

Despite the third point having some merits, for several reasons, the above remaining claims cannot be sustained from a Shari'ah point of view. The first claim fails to satisfy one of the core requirements of selling asset: the seller must own and possess the asset being sold. That is, the asset in question must be in physical possession of the bank before its sale to the client. The bank never possessed this asset in between the two transactions and therefore all the theoretical connections to the asset as claimed are illusory in practice. Although Justice Taqi Usmani recommends that even though there should be a gap between purchasing the commodity and selling it to the customer, in practice, 'there is no gap ... the bank makes the payment almost simultaneously or even after the goods are delivered at the premises of the client'.[49]

The second – regarding potential risks undertaken by the bank – does not have a substantive basis either; since no interim period practically

44 Mahmood Ahmed, 'Feature and Analysis Economics of Profit in Islamic Banking' *Financial Express*, 2 August 2014.

45 Hassan (2007) n16.

46 Id at 155.

47 Ibid.

48 Hassan (2007) n16.

49 Siddiqui n34.

exists in between the two transactions as mentioned, the bank does not actually assume any risk 'including even the risk of the goods'.[50] Even if that is sustained, from another important angle this claim can also be refuted; *Murabaha* is essentially a sales contract between the parties[51] which is legally enforceable. The risks are always highly leveraged (in favour of the seller, i.e., the financier) with all possible strong/legal terms included in the respective contractual arrangements. Read the following part of a *Murabaha* agreement:

> 4.2 When the Seller shall have purchased Supplies, the Purchaser *shall be absolutely, unconditionally and irrevocably obliged to purchase* such Supplies from the Seller and to pay (a) all sums as mentioned in the Acceptance relating to such Supplies and (b) all other sums expressed or agreed to be payable hereunder in respect of such Supplies, in all cases *notwithstanding any defect, deficiency or any loss or any other breach of any Supply contract relating* thereto by the Supplier or any other matter or thing whatsoever.[52]

More relevantly, these conditions were enforced by the court against the buyer (client); the Court in *Islamic Investment Company of the Gulf (Bahamas) Ltd. v. Symphony Gems N.V. & Ors* observed that 'delivery of goods is not a prerequisite to recovery by the seller of the relevant instalments of the sale price from the purchaser'.[53] Even in the 'event of a failure of delivery, the court holds, the defendant remains under the obligation to pay the purchase price'.[54] This simply illustrates how risks are recognised and remedied in *Murabaha* transactions in favour of the seller (the bank).

Moreover, under the legal presumption of any commercial agreement, for example, the burden of proof always lies with the claimant.[55] Thus if such an instance of refusal arises (by the client) after the first transaction, it is the client who needs to prove that it did not intend to buy the asset from the bank. Thus it appears illogical to accept that the bank takes the exclusive risk and cannot enforce the agreement in case of the client's

50 Ibid.

51 See Huda Ahmed, 'Not Interested in Interest – The Case for Equity-Based Financing in U.S. Banking Law' (2007) 2 (1) *Entrepreneurial Business Law Journal* at 489.

52 Esq (2003) n2 at 123. Emphasis added.

53 Esq (2003) n2 at 123.

54 Id at 124.

55 See, for example, John Arthur, 'Damages and Equitable Compensation in a Commercial Setting' www.gordonandjackson.com.au/uploads/documents/seminar-papers/Damages_and_Equitable_Compensation_-_John_Arthur.pdf (accessed 23 August 2014).

subsequent refusal to buy the asset from the bank. Instead, the bank gets a return at a pre-determined fixed rate without taking any effort and risk; this is clearly unacceptable (especially when they are doing Islamic business) and more importantly, is in violation of Shari'ah. For any transaction to have a reward under Shari'ah is required to take the corresponding risks as well.[56] Shahid Siddiqui maintained:

> It does not appeal to the mind that by simply assuming some risks by banks in financing through murabaha and the like during 'shifting of stocks' from the godown of the seller to the entrepreneur (party availing finance from the bank) which can also be practically avoided and ensuring a fixed return on financing while not sharing in the operational losses of the entrepreneur, which is the essence of Islamic banking, the objectives of the Shari'ah are met.[57]

The fourth, the client does not have a choice but to agree the bank's fixed rate simply because he/she could not afford to buy the asset on his/her own but genuinely intends to be submissive to the divine spirit of Islam. The bank exploits this disadvantaged situation and religious conviction of the client to stockpile its own wealth by not only charging higher interest but by grasping unjustified profit with no effort of its own – 'it is the element of oppression and exploitation that Islam forbids'.[58] Obviously, offending religious mind-sets and passion is more damaging and dangerous from ethical and Shari'ah perspectives.

In regards to the second part – the determination of the price of the good or service sold – and how this is made. Understandably, the price is calculated based on a predatory and irrational assumption about the asset's capacity of producing higher future value which is essentially uncertain in principle. In such a case, the client bears the exclusive risk, unlike the bank, as it remains indecisive how much value/prospect the asset would generate in future. Hence it is a sale 'of an uncertain gain for a certain gain' that epitomises a speculative sale which is forbidden in

---

[56] See for example, Peter Maggs, 'Islamic Banking in Kazakhstan Law' (2011) 36 (2oH) *Review of Central and East European Law* 1 at 3.

[57] Siddiqui n34.

[58] 'Mortgage in Islam', www.ukessays.co.uk/essays/accounting/mortgage-in-islam.php#ixzz39hM67a5j; John Donohue, 'Note on the Theory and Practice of Islamic Banking' (1998–99) 5 *Yearbook of Islamic and Middle Eastern Law* at 138.

Islam,[59] and is exploitative in essence despite the fact that the deal was agreed upon.

Nicop–Swartz considered a *Murabaha* transaction 'two sales in one' which is also prohibited in Islam. By referring to Imam Malik, he quoted:

> Imam Malik wrote in his Muwatta: 'Yahya related to me from Malik that he had heard that the Messenger of Allah, may Allah bless him and grant him peace, forbade two sales in one sale.'[60]

These apart, a few issues and the resulting consequences of this transaction need to be resolved, which include: whether mark-up is allowed in Shari'ah; how fair is this agreed fixed and excessive rate; whether this excessive rate is conducive to promoting social and religious dimensions upon which IBS are premised.

Inevitably, the mark-up as entrenched in *Murabaha* is interest in substance, galvanising a back door to institutionalise its practice and to reproduce the similar effect with extended returns and security.[61] Aqdas Ali Kazmi, who has researched the standpoint of Islamic jurists on mark-up during the past three decades, concludes, '[in] its operations, structure and use, mark-up resembles interest ... if the Shari'ah accepts mark-up as valid, it is left with no basis to reject interest ...'[62] Yet the prohibition of interest 'is ordained in Islam in all forms and intent. This prohibition is strict, absolute and unambiguous', and reinforced by a powerful spiritual dictate having 'fixed foundations that admit neither allegorical interpretation, nor modifications'.[63] Accordingly, the fixed returns under the costume of 'mark-up' and being prospered via *Murabaha* by IBS in Bangladesh cannot be permitted.

Nijatullah Siddiqui comments on 'mark-up':

> I would prefer that Bai' Mu'ajjal is removed from the list of permissible methods altogether. Even if we concede its permissibility in legal form, we

---

[59] '... any Shari'ah financing transaction must not be deemed speculative or otherwise uncertain.' See 'International Briefings' (2007) 26 (6) *International Financial Law Review* at 60; Nicop–Swartz, 'Contractus Trinus and Murabaha Offshoots for Usury: A Theoretical and Practical Approach with Regard to Islamic Case Law on Home Loans' (2011) 23 (3) *South African Mercantile Law Journal* at 422; Nizami (2011) n31 at 223.

[60] Nicop–Swartz id at 426–7.

[61] Id at 427–30; Institute of Islamic Banking n28.

[62] Muhammad Ayub, 'Interest, Mark up and Time Value of Money', www.sbp.org.pk/departments/ibd/interest_mark_up.pdf.

[63] Siddiqui n34; El-Gamal (2003) at 113.

> have the overriding legal maxim that anything leading to *something prohibited stands prohibited.* It will be advisable to apply this maxim to Bai'Mu'ajjal in order to save interest-free banking from being sabotaged from within.[64]

Pakistan Council of Islamic Ideology, considered mark-up a 'crude trading practice' approved by some religious scholars (under specified conditions) but seriously condemned by others, and its general use as a technique of financing must never be allowed as it 'does not differ in essence from the interest system'.[65] The similar view has been reflected in a judicial decision in which the Supreme Court of Pakistan held:

> The major condition for the permissibility of a mark-up transaction is that it should not be charged on lending or advancing money. ... By not even gradually enhancing the financing on PLS basis, the basic philosophy of Islamic banking seems to be totally neglected by the Islamic banks.[66]

One of the reasons for the imposition of strict prohibition on the interest by Shari'ah is to ensure unqualified adherence to Islam as it demands by restricting the imbalance creation and distribution of wealth and advancing social welfare. Accordingly, profits can only be legitimatised if it involves some proportionate risks. In *Murabaha* as discussed IBS not only consumes profit without virtually taking any risk but also imposes excessive burden (even more than the conventional banks) on the client. This is not only in breach of Shari'ah but also goes against the core principle of fairness and ethics especially when IBS end results are ideologically embedded to this. This is unfair because IBS' return becomes secured and multiple via the extensive and unyielding use of *Murabaha*, which contributes neither to eradicating injustices arguably entrenched in the interest-based system nor to furthering socio-economic justice in the society as mandated by Shari'ah.[67] Rather, it exacerbates the disadvantaged situation of the client in important ways. It is observed that:

> To begin with, what murabaha does is that it replaces interest with mark-up ... this puts it at a great disadvantage vis-à-vis the interest based conventional finance in circumstances where payment of interest on home finance for the purpose of income tax are deducted. Second, In comparison to conventional home finance where it requires only one transfer of property, murabaha requires two. ... Stamp tax, public notary fees, and registry therefore end up

[64] Siddiqui id. Emphasis added.

[65] Ibid.

[66] Ibid.

[67] See for example, The Holy Qur'an, 2:279.

> being paid twice. As if that is not enough, the mark-up which is included in the price of that particular home facilitates a substantial increase of price at the second sale transaction and consequently a proportional stamp tax increase.[68]

In particular, there are convincing arguments that there is no difference between IBS and conventional banks in regards to financing social aspects. Both are reluctant to extend credit facilities in favour of the underprivileged who need them most; it is the corporate giant who is empowered to seize both of their services because of its privileged position.[69] Nevertheless, in case of IBS, it is more blameworthy because they are operating in order to achieve the true economic objectives of Islamic finance. Furthermore, their current transactions through *Murabaha* 'resulted in persons being burdened with a debt far in excess of what it would have been, had they taken conventional interest-based loans'.[70] Khaled Qasaymeh argued 'Islamic normative rules always intertwine ethical obligations with the compulsory obligations' that encourages empowering of the disadvantaged through an equitable distribution of wealth, eliminating poverty and ensuring social prosperity; yet a significant shift from PLS to *Murabaha* derails IBS from their social purposes and renders their functions questionable.[71] In the 1990s, Homoud stated that IBs must avoid exceeding the prevailing interest rate and exploiting the clients.[72]

Despite these intense criticisms IBS continues to take recourse to a widespread and persistent use of *Murabaha* mode in financing investment. On the other hand, the system to which they are officially embedded 'stands for the furtherance of religious and social goals involving ... economic development, the alleviation of poverty and maximise profit', and advancement of a just society free from exploitation and unfairness. If this conflicting scenario continues to progress unabated different stakeholders will not only lose confidence in the whole system but also question the foundation – that is, IBS' genuineness towards Islam which would be much more detrimental and insulting. El-Gamal observed:

---

68 'Mortgage in Islam' n58.

69 'Issues and Problems of Islamic Banking' n38.

70 Nicop–Swartz (2011) n59 at 430–1.

71 Qasaymeh (2011) n19 at 291–2.

72 Sami Hasan Homoud, 'Progress of Islamic Banking: The Aspirations and the Realities' (1994) 2 (1) *Islamic Economic Studies* at 74–5.

> Islamic finance as it functions bears 'little resemblance' to PLS upon which it was constructed. 'Instead, a fast-growing industry is built on medieval ruses, with which contemporary financial practices are reproduced at a higher cost – to be borne by the industry's captive market of Muslim clients.[73]

Hence a genuine activism is urgently required to rescue the whole financial system from these anomalies and embarrassment and save the users from being financially and religiously deceived, and the sooner the better. Sincere attempts to revive PLS with new vigour and progressive devices may yield positive results. Many Islamic jurists have already echoed this by providing relevant policy recommendations.[74] It is however, important to acknowledge that PLS may produce a series of indisputable risks and even losses;[75] yet these are common to all business transactions and some of PLS challenges can be remedied via short, medium and long-term financing or 'investing in highly liquid, and low return equities'.[76] This mere fact therefore should not deter IBS from pursuing their true economic goals especially when they are consensually and theoretically outfitted and committed to promote spiritual morals of Islam. Moreover, if the PLS-calculation (reached by its inherent risk factors) is not matched with the IBS' plans, then the plans should be abandoned altogether instead of striving for the other whose credibility and authenticity has been seriously questioned. And inevitably, this would be much more benevolent than fostering something under the disguise of Islam which is injurious to the religious spirit of Islam and exploitative in its application.

IV. IMPLEMENTING MECHANISM

The Accounting and Auditing Organization for Islamic Finance Institutions (AAOIFI) requires IBS to have an independent Shari'ah Supervisory Board (SSB) with highly qualified religious leaders equipped with substantial experience of modern business dealings and finance.[77]

---

[73] Hassan (2007) n16.

[74] 'Some scholars believe that the only way to save the industry is to branch away from mimicking conventional finance and rebuild a purely Islamic system that bans techniques like *murabaha*.' See for example Holden (2007) n33; Qasaymeh (2011) n19 at 292.

[75] Hamoudi (2014) n17 at 118.

[76] Institute of Islamic Banking, n32; Hamoud (2007) n4 at 117.

[77] Nizam Yaquby, 'Shariah Requirements for conventional banks', www.islamic-banking.com/iarticle_7.aspx.

Accordingly, the articles of association, prospectuses, or relevant statutes must incorporate a provision outlining the functions and authority of SSB which decisions are binding for the IBS. Its main tasks include, assessing 'Shari'ah compliance' with the IBS' practices, monitoring and providing continued supervision.[78] Also, this provision should mandate that the creation and function of SSB must be concurrent with those of IBS to ensure that it can guide the procedures and operations of all contracts and transactions soon after their inception.

Unfortunately, Bangladesh Bank (BB, the central bank of Bangladesh), neither have a SSB nor a separate department to control and supervise the operation of IBS. IBS' operation and supervision are conducted by BB based on a guidelines developed for the conventional banks.[79] The absence of SSB influenced IBS to form their own Shari'ah Councils (SCS). The SCS comprising members from different backgrounds (such as religion, law, economics and business) functions in accordance with IBS' bylaws and regulations, and serve as consultative rather than supervisory agencies.[80]

While the formation of SCS is an attempt towards the right direction especially in the absence of a SSB, they became inept to dealing with the dynamics and complexities of practical transactions in line with Shari'ah.[81] A research study claims that 'none of the Islamic banks in Bangladesh are full-compliant with Shari'ah governance system of the AAOIFI'.[82] The reasons are manifold. The absence of a specific law regulating IBS, non-cooperation among SCS' members and their conflicting views about IBS financing methods and other related issues, the lack of transparency in issuing financial reports and a binding authority of SCS remain the powerful factors that frustrate the effective operation of IBS and assessment of Shari'ah compliance. Except for the Faysal Islamic Bank of Bahrain, the SCS of other IBS operate as consultative agencies. A series of reports confirm that the lack of SCS' binding authority makes the board and management of IBS reluctant to implement their decisions in due course and on some occasions ignore the

---

78 See for details, Mahmood Ahmed et al., 'The Compliance with *Shariah* Governance System of AAOIFI: A Study on Islamic Banks Bangladesh' (2013) 9 (3) *Journal of Islamic Economics, Banking and Finance* at 177: http://ibtra.com/pdf/journal/v9_n3_article9.pdf; www.aaoifi.com/en/about-aaoifi/about-aaoifi.html.

79 Chowdhury (2014) n5.

80 Sarker (1999) n39.

81 Abdul Sarker, 'Islamic Banking in Bangladesh: Achievements and Challenges', www.financialislam.com/uploads/3/8/5/3/3853592/bangladesh.pdf.

82 Ahmed (2013) n78 at 177.

relevant guidelines.[83] By failing to grant such an important aspect of administration, IBS not only violate AAOIFI' standards but also undermine the significance and objectives of such an institution. Inevitably, the ensuing outcome neither promotes Shari'ah-led good governance nor a positive culture of deterring the actual and potential abusers of the system.

These apart, it has become a practice to elect some members of SCS from inside of IBS which is also a deviation from the AAOIFI standards. This causes or potentially could cause a conflict of interest.[84] In particular, in the absence of a uniform guideline issued by the central authority, different SCS pursue their own laws, procedures, resulting in inconsistent and conflicting decisions. Mahmood Ahmed contends that '[differences] in interpretation of Islamic principles by different schools of thought may mean that identical financial instruments are rejected by one board but accepted by another'.[85] This inconsistency and incompatible judgement is, to some extent, driven by the fact that some SCS members despite having expertise in their relevant fields lack sophisticated knowledge and skills required for a Shari'ah-complaint decision to make. Understandably, this allows an entry of extra religious elements into business which in turn has stimulated a hostile environment that galvanises a very competitive – individualistic and insensitive attitude among IBS, instead of an approach based on interconnectedness, professionalism, compassionate, transparency and cooperation. One study reveals:

> At present, there is no cooperation between the *Sharīca* Councils of the various Islamic banks in Bangladesh. Individual *Sharīca* Councils takes decisions independently. There is no means of mutual discussions and the exchange of views on common issues. Thus the Councils follow their own individual reasoning, which in many cases raises questions about the sanctity of their decisions, particularly in cases where they issue two opposite *fatāwā* on the same issue. This creates confusion among ordinary people who wish to bank with them.[86]

Given the situation there is no alternative but to introduce a SSB with a proper and binding authority to guide, monitor and evaluate IBS' transactions. Such a committee will more likely to promote compliance by mandating all IBS to operate and manage their business in line with

---

83 Sarker, n81.
84 Ahmed (2013) n78.
85 Ibid.
86 Sarker (1999) n39.

Shari'ah and by assisting BB to administer IBS.[87] Independence and accurate expertise of the SSB' members must be ensured and assessed in accordance with the AAOIFI standards via enacting a specific law on IBS. This law will require SSB to develop a uniform and consistent guideline exclusively applicable to IBS. A specific provision can also be made designed to promote coordination among SCS of IBS and a proper disclosure regime of financial methods, reporting and the ways in which they are complying with Shari'ah. This coordination may focus on contentious and governance issues of IBS, especially how these can be dealt with based on contemporary practices developed by other jurisdictions. Such a provision will sensibly advance conformance to Shari'ah by the existing IBS and deter potential abusers from the misuse of the system under the pretext of Islam.

V. CONCLUSION

Islamic banking is premised on some basic tenets and ideologically ingrained in PLS. By adhering to this core approach Bangladesh theoretically endorsed Islamic banking in the mid-1980s and made significant progress in facilitating the investment growth and portfolio diversification. IBS have already established their dominant presence with a substantial share increase in the financial market and a growing acceptance of the people. Yet, the way in which IBS function has fuelled a widespread controversy and raised serious doubt about the genuineness of their Shari'ah-compliance. The foregoing discourse demonstrates that the excessive use of *Murabaha*, pervasive influence of conventional banking on their competitive attitude and disregard of PLS are crucial factors that plague IBS' financial culture which unquestionably undermines the credibility and integrity of the whole financial system of Islamic banking.

In addition, the implementing mechanism of IBS suffers from some important shortcomings. The absences of SSB at the central level with appropriate authority and a specific law on IBS have evidently impaired the effective operation and compliance of IBS in accordance with Shari'ah. This phenomenon is neither supportive of fostering an independent, responsible and transparent IBS governance essential for effectively guiding banking practices nor of sustaining religious and moral values on which these are fundamentally entrenched. Hence this

---

87 Kyle Gaffaney, 'Buying a Home Can Be Difficult for Muslims in the United States' (2009) 20 (4) *Loyola Consumer Law Review* at 562; ibid.

note recommends the reconstruction of IBS in Bangladesh to achieve the true objectives of Islamic banking. The reconstruction can be accomplished via *inter alia,* integrating those key features such as activating PLS as mandated by Shari'ah, the introduction of a SSB with a binding authority at the central level and a specific law exclusively designed to regulate and monitor IBS' practices. Sensibly this will not only liberate Islamic economics from inappropriate/counterfeited business conduct but also save the 'captive' clients from being financially deceived and religiously bankrupted.

7. Property law and trusts (*waqf*) in Iran

Hossein Esmaeili

I. INTRODUCTION

Property law, particularly land law, is one of the classical areas of Islamic law. Basic principles of Islamic property law can be found in the Qur'an and other sources of Islamic law. The legal system of the Muslim world, particularly before the establishment of modern independent nation states in the nineteenth century, was based on general principles of Shari'ah. Indeed, in most modern Muslim countries the principles of land law and the *waqf* are based on Islamic law. In Iran, land ownership and interests in land are regulated by the Iranian Civil Code (1928), which has adopted modern principles of European land law that is blended with principles of Shari'ah. However, the law of *waqf* is almost entirely based on Islamic law.

Private land ownership is well recognised under Islamic law. Further, public ownership of certain land by governments and public institutions is also recognised. A number of land interests recognised in modern legal systems, such as easements, mortgages, restrictive covenants and leases are also recognised and regulated under traditional Islamic law. However, the Iranian legal system has adopted some modern legal principles in relation to these land interests that are arguably consistent with principles of Islamic law.

The main sources of property law and the law of *waqf* in Iran are *fiqh* (Islamic jurisprudence), the Iranian Constitution, the Civil Code of 1928 and other relevant legislation and by-laws. The significance of property law in Iran is a notable distinction between practice and theory. While fundamental sources of property law are based on Islamic jurisprudence texts, the Constitution, and the Civil Code, property law is regulated in practice by a large number of government decrees, local councils (*Shahrdariha*), the Department of Registration (*Sazman Sabt v Asnad*), as well as many other parliamentary acts and decrees of different government departments, including the judiciary. Unlike countries with common law legal systems, case law is not as relevant in Iran. However, in exceptional circumstances when there have been different decisions on similar facts by courts, the Department of the Iranian Judiciary (*Divan Ali Keshvar*) may make a decision that will be binding for all the courts.

Apart from fundamental principles of law based on Shari'ah and *fiqh*, the Constitution and the Civil Code, another significant feature of Iranian law is that other sources of property law, such as decrees of different departments and the judiciary, are not easily and publicly available. Most of these provisions are not subject to much academic discussion, but are known to relevant institutions and departments as well as some practising lawyers who work in the area of property law. Therefore, most of the available literature on property law and commentaries simply discuss some general principles of property law, in *fiqh* and modern law, without investigating and analysing relevant practical issues. In addition to this, the amount of literature on property law is very limited, both on real property and personal property. The available scholarship on Iranian property law is brief, descriptive, theoretical, and lacks any critical analysis.

Further, Islamic jurisprudence has not allocated a distinct area or systematic field to land and property law. In Islamic textbooks on jurisprudence there are sections (known in Arabic as *kitab*) on certain proprietary interests, such as leases, gifts, wills, treasure troves, and land taxes. However, there is no specific chapter on land law or land ownership.

This chapter discusses property law and *waqf* under Iranian law and Islamic law. Given that Iranian law is predominantly based on Islamic law, the first section will analyse concepts of property law, particularly land law, under Islamic law and Islamic jurisprudence (*fiqh*). Protection of private ownership under Islamic law, as well as the nature or public ownership and key concepts of property law, will be analysed. This provides the basis for a discussion on the general principles of property ownership under the Iranian Constitution, as well as the relevant provisions of the Iranian Civil Code, which is almost entirely based on Islamic jurisprudence (*shia*). In addition, some important aspects of property ownership, such as ownership of minerals and intellectual property under Iranian law, will be discussed. Finally, the Islamic institution of *waqf*, known under common law as trust, under Iranian law will be reviewed.

II. BASIC CONCEPTS OF PROPERTY UNDER ISLAMIC LAW

Under Islamic jurisprudence, a number of legal maxims have been provided in relation to propriety interests in goods and in land. These include the principle of *taslit* (control) and *la-dharar* (the principle of no harm). The principle of *taslit* provides that owners of land and personal property have absolute authority and control over using and alienating their proprietary interests. However, based on the principle of *la-dharar*, individuals shall not cause damage or harm to others, or the interests of other people, when using and utilising their property. The use, possession, and alienation of property is well protected under Islamic law, but is the subject of some limitations, particularly based on the principle of no harm, which is a similar principle based in other modern legal systems, such as the common law.

Under Islamic law, there are a number of key concepts of property law that lay down the basic principles of Islamic property law. These include *mal* (concept of property), *milk* (relationship with a thing), *malikiat* (ownership), *mawat* (vacant land) and *rahn* (mortgage).

Mal generally refers to things of real property and its interests, such as land and easements, or personal property, such as jewellery and domestic animals. The word *mal* is Arabic. In legal terms, it can be interpreted as any thing that can be the subject of legitimate ownership in Islam.[1] Islamic jurisprudence texts do not specifically define *mal*; however, examples have been provided for the concept of *mal*. Not everything can become the subject of *mal* under Islamic law; only things that are legitimate, useful, and have commercial value can be defined as *mal*. Many Islamic scholars have left the definition of *mal* to the *urf* (custom) of each society to determine.[2] It is difficult to find an equivalent term or concept under the common law system that corresponds to a similar definition under Islamic law, as property is held not to be a thing under common law, but is instead described as a legal relationship with a thing.[3] Whereas, under Islamic law, *mal* means a thing that can be the subject of legitimate ownership and has commercial value. This means things that cannot be the subject of legitimate ownership, such as wine

[1] Ibn Mandhour, *Lesan Al-Arab* [The Language of Arab, Vol. 11] (Qom: Nashr Adab Howzeh 1984) 636.

[2] Ahmad Naraghi, *Awayed Al-Ayyam* [Earning a living] (1st ed.) (Qom: Maktab Al-Alam Al-Eslami 1996) 113.

[3] *Yanner v Eaton* (1999) 201 CLR 351, [17] – High Court of Australia.

and pork, are not *mal*. Also, things that do not have commercial value, such as a handful of soil, may not be considered as *mal* under Islamic law.

On the other hand, *milk* refers to the control and possession of things by a person. Thus, the term is very similar to the concept of ownership. In other words, any thing that is under the control and possession of a person, even if the thing does not have any commercial value, is considered as *milk*. Perhaps the common law definition of property, as a legal relationship with a thing, as held by the High Court of Australia in *Yanner v Eaton*,[4] is more closely associated with *milk* than with *mal*.

The distinctions between *milk* and *mal* have some practical relevance, particularly in the modern world. For example, people have control and possession over their body parts and, therefore, body parts are considered to be *milk*. However, since selling body parts may not be considered legitimate, the body parts would not be considered as *mal*. Selling and buying body parts is a new topic that is the subject of extensive debates in Islamic jurisprudence (*fiqh*). According to some Islamic jurists, body parts are not *mal* and, hence, cannot be the subject of commercial transactions.[5] However, according to some other Islamic jurists, since people have control over their body parts, consistent with the *urf* of modern societies, they must be able to alienate their body parts for commercial consideration, as long as there is no prohibition under Shari'ah.[6]

III. THE PLACE OF PROPERTY LAW UNDER ISLAMIC JURISPRUDENCE

Islamic law regulates the property rights. In other major legal systems, such as common law and civil law, property, particularly real property, has occupied a significant place in the legal system. In both civil law and common law, as well as Islamic law, property is a principal subject matter of law. Further, the concept of property is considered significant in modern legal theories, such as natural law and positivism. Under natural

---

4 *Yanner v Eaton* (1999) 201 CLR 351.

5 Ahmad Sharaf Al-din, *Al-Ahkam Al-Shari'ah Lil Amal Al-Tabieiah* [The Rules of Sharia] (Kuwait: Al-Majlis Al-Vatani Lil Thaqaf Va Al-Fonoun Va Al-Adab 1982) 94–5.

6 Esmaeil Aghababaei, *Payvan Aza Az Bimaran Fowt Shodah Va Marg Maghzi* [Transplant from deceased brain-dead bodies] (Qom: Pejouhesgah Oloum Va Farhang Eslami 2006) 166.

law theory, property is considered a natural right, and according to legal positivists such as Jeremy Bentham, 'property and law are born together and die together'.[7] Property and land have always generated wealth and been subject to commercial transaction in the West, and to a lesser extent in the Muslim world. However, in recent years, intellectual property is becoming increasingly significant in modern economies and international investment sectors.

Although property ownership and interests in relation to land, including water and minerals, have been subject to legal principles under Islamic law, there is no distinct area of property law under classical Islamic jurisprudence (*fiqh*). Classical Islamic law texts cover chapters and sections on proprietary interests such as *kharaj* (taxes), *hibah* (gifts), *wasyat* (wills), *zakat* (a special tax), *dafinah* (treasure troves) and *sherkat* (partnership). Legal principals relating to personal property and real property can be found in several other areas of law, such as commercial law, inheritance law, Islamic law of partnership, the law of mortgage (*rahn*), and taxation law. In sources of Islamic law, notably the Qur'an and the Sunnah, general principles of Islamic property law can be found. In some classical textbooks on Islamic jurisprudence, ownership of land and other real property interests are discussed under the area of *ahya-mawat* (reviving of dead land).[8] According to some schools of law, such as the Hanbali school of jurisprudence, the area of property law is classified under the category of *siyar*. The *siyar* in this context is taken as the conduct of an Islamic government in its relationship with non-Muslims, which in modern terms, can be considered as some kind of Islamic international relations. Given that at earlier stages of the advent of Islam, Muslim armies conquered large areas of land from non-Muslims in Asia and Africa, land law and taxes relating to property and land became a part of *siyar*.[9]

---

[7] Jeremy Bentham, *Theory of Legislation* (1931, first published 1802) 113.

[8] See, for example, Muhaqiq Helli, Abolqasim Najm al-din Jafar ibn Muhammad ibn al-Hassan, *Sharaye al-Islam* [Laws of Islam, written in thirteenth century] (1983).

[9] See Abu Yusuf, *Kitab al-kharj* [Taxation in Islam] (1969); Majid Khadduri, The Islamic Law of Nations: Shaybani's *Siyar* (Baltimore: Johns Hopkins University Press 1966).

IV. PUBLIC OWNERSHIP v PRIVATE OWNERSHIP UNDER ISLAMIC LAW AND IRANIAN LAW

Islam has recognised the private ownership of land and other types of property. It has also provided commercial benefits for land and property. Although certain types of property, such as pork, alcohol, and other illegal goods, have no proprietary values, property interests in land and goods are generally accepted under Islamic law. With the exception of certain holy places, such as the Shrines of Mecca Medina in Saudi Arabia, and the mosque in Jerusalem (*ghods*) and mosques in other places, land has commercial value and can be subject to business transactions. Although public ownership of certain land, such as jungles, deserts, and other uninhabited and unoccupied land is recognised, private property is also well-established and recognised under Islamic law. The notion of absolute ownership of land by God, and the doctrine of the Islamic state's role in distributing conquered lands and ownership of inhabited land, does not deny private ownership of land and other goods.

Nevertheless, in the history of Islamic societies (particularly Iran), individualism, individual rights and identities were not prevalent compared to the rights of the community. Hence, private ownership is not strong when compared with public ownership by the states and by tribes and communities. As a result, in practice, the private ownership of land in farming and agriculture had not been very strong. States, whether the Caliphate or other governments ruling the Middle East, particularly in Iran, have arbitrarily confiscated lands and disposed it as they wished. Unlike Europe, strong private ownership of land in the Middle East and in Iran did not develop at any stage in history. A few periods were an exception to this, such as during the Samanian dynasty.[10] Major owners of the land included the state, tribal leaders and powerful individuals known as *khans* were the major land holders. Private land owners (tribal leaders and *khans*) did not have independent rights against the arbitrary absolute rulers. However, a hierarchy of land ownership, as seen in the feudal system in Europe, did not emerge in Iran. This was partly due to the frequent change in rulers, and unstable governments and local authorities in Iran.[11] It was only after the Constitutional Revolution that

---

[10] The Saminian dynasty ruled Iran from 819–999.

[11] For a study of land ownership in Iran prior to the 1907 Constitutional Revolution, see Ann K. S. Lambton, *Landlord and Peasant in Persia: A Study of Land Tenure and Land Revenue Administration* (London: I. B. Tauris and Co. Ltd 1991) 283–305; see also, Sadegh Zibakalam, *Ma Chegouneh Ma Shodim,*

private ownership, as acknowledged in Islamic jurisprudence, was officially recognised by the law in Iran and became subject to legal protection.[12]

In recent times, particularly during the late twentieth century, there have been debates and discussion in the Muslim world in relation to the status and limitation of private ownership under Islamic law. During the 1950s and 1960s, when communism, socialism and leftist political views influenced the Muslim world, including countries such as Libya, Algeria, Indonesia, Iraq, Syria and Afghanistan, there were discussions as to the position of Islamic law in relation to the recognition of private and public ownership of property. Some Muslim intellectuals and scholars argued that public ownership of property is the main principle of ownership under Islamic law. They would cite certain principles from original sources of Islamic law, such as the Qur'an and the *Sunnah*, in making their arguments in favour of public ownership of property.[13] Some other Muslim jurists argued that Islam recognised limited private ownership, but rejected the capitalist theory of private ownership.[14]

However, according to the majority of Islamic jurists and scholars, as well as the practice of Islamic states throughout history, Islam has acknowledged and recognised private ownership and has protected property rights of individuals in very strong terms. Private ownership is recognised in various verses of the Qur'an.[15] According to Ghazzali, a famous Muslim jurist of the eleventh–twelfth centuries, the purpose of Shari'ah is to protect the life, private property, mind, religion, and the offspring of people.[16]

Under Islam, there are three types of ownership: absolute ownership of God, public ownership of the state, and private ownership. The absolute ownership of land and property by God does not have many practical

---

Rishehaye Aghabmandegin Dar Iran [How We Became What We Are: The Roots of Underdevelopment in Iran] (18th ed.) (Tehran: Rozaneh Publisher 2011).

12 Hassan Ghazi Moradi, *Dar Piramoun Khodmadari Iranian* [on the Culture of Egoism in Iran] (6th ed.) (Tehran: Ketab Ameh 2010) 23–4.

13 Qur'an, 20:6: 'All the things (property) on Earth and in the heavens, and whatever is underground, belongs to Allah.'

14 See generally, Mohammed Abdul Mannan, *Islamic Economics: Theory and Practice* (Lahore: Sheikh Muhammad Ashraf 1970).

15 See for example, 'All those who believe do not take property of each other except through legitimate transactions with consent …', Qur'an, 4:29. See also, Qur'an, 4:2; 44; 46; 4161 and 9:34.

16 See generally Jasser Auda, *Maqasid Al-Shari'ah as Philosophy of Islamic Law, A Systems Approach* (Surrey: The International Institute of Islamic Thought 2008).

consequences, except some justifications for the state in interfering with private property ownership when this is necessary for public interest reasons. For example, this occurs with the development of schools, roads and public institutions. It should be noted that an Islamic state cannot claim absolute ownership of property or unlimited interference with private ownership and an individual's proprietary interest on behalf of Allah. The Qur'an expressly gives individual rights of owning property on behalf of God. According to the Qur'an, the Earth belongs to Allah and people may inherit the Earth on behalf of Allah.[17] There are also extensive authorities in the *Sunnah* that supports private ownership of property in Islam.[18] The practice of the Islamic state from the early stages of the advent of Islam shows that private property was protected in the Islamic state, and *Caliphs* have paid compensation to individual Muslims for the taking of their property.[19]

The absolute ownership of land and other property by God may resemble the doctrine of tenure that underpins the modern land laws of common law systems, such as Australia. This means that under Islam, the real owner of land is Allah and individuals own land and other property on behalf of God. Therefore, private ownership of property in Islam is similar to common law systems. However, the absolute ownership of property by Allah does not give an Islamic state the same rights of ownership that the Crown had under English common law and Australian common law, based on the doctrine of tenures.[20] Islamic law provides a legal framework for recognition and protection of private property rights and remedies and sanctions for individual proprietary interests.[21]

---

17 Qur'an, 7:127.

18 According to a *hadith*, 'everything that belongs to a Muslim is forbidden to other Muslims: their property, their life, and their honour': Ibn Majah, *Sunan Volume 2* (Houston, TX: Dar-us-Salam 1999) Hadith No. 3933.

19 Siti Mariam Malinumbay S. Salasal, 'The Concept of Land Ownership: Islamic Perspective' (1998) 2(2) *Buletin Geoinformasi, Jld* 285, 292.

20 The doctrine of tenures dates back to medieval era of Feudalism in western Europe. It is linked to the social system of feudalism, where the Crown owned the land and would grant the land to English nobles in return for service. For further discussion, see Peter Butt, *Land Law* (6th ed.) (Sydney: Lawbook Co. 2010) 73–83.

21 Sirah Sait and Hilary Lim, *Land, Law & Islam, Property & Human Rights in the Muslim World* (London: Zed Books 2006) 13.

V. PROPERTY LAW UNDER THE IRANIAN CONSTITUTION

The Iranian Constitution was adopted in 1979[22] by a referendum and was then amended in 1989. The institution that drafted the Constitution consisted of high-ranking Muslim clerics (mainly Shia) and lawyers. It is arguable that the Constitution of Iran is the only written Constitution in the world that is based on theocracy. It provides, under Article 4, that 'all criminal, civil and administrative laws and policies relating to the economy, finance, military, culture, and politics must be based on Islamic principles'. The same Article further provides that the principles of Islam would prevail over all provisions of the Constitution and other laws of the country. It also gives the highest authority and significant powers to the *vali faghih*, who must be a person able to issue fatwas on all matters of Islam.[23]

The issue of ownership is covered in Articles 44, 46, and 47 of the Constitution. These articles recognise three types of ownership: private ownership, co-operative ownership, and state ownership. Article 44 provides that:

> The economy of the Islamic Republic of Iran is to consist of three sectors: state, cooperative, and private, and is to be based on systematic and sound planning. The state sector is to include all large-scale and mother industries, foreign trade, major minerals, banking, insurance, power generation, dams and large-scale irrigation networks, radio and television, post, telegraph and telephone services, aviation, shipping, roads, railroads and the like; all these will be publicly owned and administered by the State. The cooperative sector is to include cooperative companies and enterprises concerned with production and distribution, in urban and rural areas, in accordance with Islamic criteria. The private sector consists of those activities concerned with agriculture, animal husbandry, industry, trade, and services that supplement the economic activities of the state and cooperative sectors. Ownership in each of these three sectors is protected by the laws of the Islamic Republic, in so far as this ownership is in conformity with the other articles of this chapter, does not go beyond the bounds of Islamic law, contributes to the economic growth and progress of the country, and does not harm society. The [precise] scope of each of these sectors, as well as the regulations and conditions governing their operation, will be specified by law.

---

22 The English text of the Iranian Constitution can be found on the website of the Library of Congress at www.loc.gov/law/help/guide/nations/iran.php#constitution.

23 Constitution of the Islamic Republic of Iran, arts 5, 110.

This article of the Constitution outlines of two types of ownership that have been recognised in traditional Islamic law. These are private ownership and public/state ownership. However, the cooperative ownership, although not inconsistent with Islamic principles, is a new category of property ownership that is recognised by the Iranian Constitution. Further, this article gives the ownership of certain major industries, such as banking, insurance, and communications, to the state. The private ownership is considered to be supplementary to the economic activities of the state and cooperative sectors. According to a leading Iranian constitutional lawyer, these provisions in the constitution are similar to the law in socialist countries, such as the constitution of China.[24]

Since the adoption of the Constitution in 1979, the process of privatisation of certain state industries has led to an expansion of the private sector, particularly following the end of the Iran-Iraq war in 1988. The private sector is now involved in foreign trade, mining, banking, aviation and various other industries.

Article 47 provides that private ownership is protected as long as it is legitimate. Article 45 is concerned with public ownership that is known in classical Islamic texts as *anfal*. This article provides that:

> Public wealth and property, such as uncultivated or abandoned land, mineral deposits, seas, lakes, rivers and other public water-ways, mountains, valleys, forests, marshlands, natural forests, unenclosed pastureland, legacies without heirs, property of undetermined ownership, and public property recovered from usurpers, shall be at the disposal of the Islamic government for it to utilise in accordance with the public interest. Law will specify detailed procedures for the utilization of each of the foregoing items.

VI. CIVIL CODE OF IRAN AND PROPERTY INTERESTS

The Iranian Civil Code was adopted initially in 1928 and was amended on many occasions before the Islamic Revolution in 1979, as well as after the Revolution. Part 1 of the Civil Code was concerned with ownership and contracts, which was drafted based on Shia jurisprudence. Other sections were added to this original part in 1935. This later amendment related to citizenship, personal law and evidence, which reflected the

---

[24] S. Mohammad Hachemi, *Hogough Asasi Jomhouri Islam Iran* [The Constitutional Law of Islamic Republic of Iran] (Tehran: Mizan Press 2005) 376–7.

provisions found in the Civil Codes of France, Belgium and Switzerland.[25] The Civil Code covers property law in relative detail in its first part, from Articles 11–182.

A. Classification of Property

This Code does not define property or *amwal* (plural of *mal*). However, it divides *mal* (things that are subject of property) into two categories of *manghoul* (moveable) and *gheir manghoul* (non-removable). This classification is almost the same as the classification of personal property (chattel) and real property (land) under common law systems.

Article 13 of the Civil Code classifies land, buildings and fixtures as *gheir manghoul* (non-removable) or real property, whereas Articles 19–22 outline certain types of property as *manghoul* (moveable) or chattel. A chose in action, such as debt, is defined as moveable property or chattel. Trees, fruits, and crops, as long as they are attached to the land, are considered as part of the land (Articles 15–16). Mirrors, curtains, statues, and tapestries, if they are attached to the land and would cause damage to the land if they were removed, are also considered to be part of the land.[26] Similar to common law systems, leases are considered as personal property, whereas easements are considered real property interests (Article 18).

B. Public Property

Property that does not have a specific owner, such as roads, streets, alleyways, bridges, as well as vacant land, cannot be owned by individuals, except when provided by law. Articles 23–28 of the Civil Code

---

25 Sayed Hassan Amin, *The History of Law in Iran* (Tehran: The Encyclopaedia of Iran Publications 2004) 512.

26 Under Australian common law, there is a body of case law that relates to the nature of land, known as the concept of fixtures. A fixture is an item that has been attached to the land in a way that means the item becomes part of the land in law. There is an old Latin maxim that states: 'quicquid plantatur solo, solo cedit', which translates to 'whatever is affixed to the soil becomes part of the soil'. Given that proprietary interests in land are generally rights in rem (against the whole world), they are strong proprietary interests that can be traced and recovered in kind. Therefore, if items are fixed to the land, known as a fixture, then they are part of the land interests and are subject to those laws. Under common law, a number of legal tests have been developed in order to determine whether an item is a fixture (part of the land) or a chattel (personal property). For further discussion, see Butt, n20, 41–53.

relate to public property. Article 28 provides that property without an owner (treasure troves) must be spent by the state for charitable purposes.

C. Interests in Property

According to the Civil Code, proprietary interests can be divided into three different categories: ownership, *hagh entefa* (the personal right of enjoyment, such as leases and licences) and *hagh ertfagh* (rights to limited rights over another's land such as easements). Ownership is discussed in Articles 30–39. The ownership provisions are almost completely based on Islamic (Shia) jurisprudence. The relevant provisions provide that the owner of a property (whether land or personal property) can use and alienate their property within the boundaries of the law. Similar to common law, Article 38 of the Civil Code provides that the owner of the land owns all the space above it, as well as all the ground below.[27] Under both Iranian law and Australian common law, this principle has been modified to some extent. Australian law, through legislation, precludes minerals from being subject to personal property, even if found on an individual's land, as these are owned by the Crown.[28] Conversely, Iranian law provides that individuals still have some rights to minerals underneath their land. This will be discussed further below.

Hagh entefa, which literally means the 'right to use', is almost the equivalent to leases, licences and profit-à-prendre. It also corresponds with the life estate freehold interests found under common law. Article 41 of the Civil Code states that:

> A Life-Right [Life Estate] is a right of exploitation which has been established by means of a contract entered into by the owner in favour of someone, either for his own lifetime or for the lifetime of the user or for that of a third party.

---

27 This principle is similar to the common law maxim of *cuius est solum*, which means the person who owns the land owns it from the heavens above to the centre of the Earth below. This principle can be traced back to 1285, and was noted in *Bury v Pope* (1586) 78 ER 375. See Butt, n20, 8–18.

28 The first exception under the general principle of common law was introduced in the mid-sixteenth century in the *Case of Mines* (1568) 1 Plow 310; 75 ER 472 (KB). This case established that precious metals (gold and silver) found on private land, belonged to the Crown. Legislation has been introduced in Australia that vests all minerals to the Crown. See, for example: Crown Lands Alienation Act 1861 (NSW) s18; and Mining Act 1971 (SA) s16.

The third proprietary interest, according to the Civil Code, is *hagh ertfagh*. Article 93 of the Civil Code outlines the proprietary interest where a person has an interest in the property of another person. This category of interest is similar to the common law proprietary interest known as an easement. Under common law, an easement is:[29]

> A privilege without profit, which the owner of one neighbouring tenement has of another … by which the servient owner [person who provides an easement to another] is obliged to suffer or not to do something on his own land, for the advantage of the dominant owner [person who benefits from the easement].

This type of interest under Iranian law only applies to non-removable properties, mainly land.[30] This interest can be created by legislation, such as the case of public utility access, or through private contracts. It may also be created as a natural right with adjoining or neighbouring land and buildings, for example, when a building relies on the neighbouring building's structure and foundations to remaining standing. The interest is divided into negative and positive *hagh ertfagh*. It even includes restrictive covenants, we well as negative easements.[31] The *hagh ertfagh* interest can be proved by official documents (registered deeds). However, possession and long use can be an evidence of the existence of this interest without official documents. Although, the long use presumption can be rebutted through the evidence of trespassing.[32] Article 97 of the Civil Code states:

> Whenever a person has for a long time had a water channel running through the house or property of another to his own property or, has had a right in his favour, the owner of that house or land shall not hinder the taking of water nor its passage through his property, and similarly with regard to rights such as holding rights in doors, openwork windows, aqueducts, irrigation channels and so on.

D. Sources of Property Ownership

The Civil Code, in Article 140, provides for four sources of ownership, which are: ownership through cultivation and use of vacant land (*ahya*

---

29 *Concord MD v Coles* (1906) 3 CLR 96, 110 – per Justice Barton of the High Court of Australia.

30 Nasser Katouzian, *Hoqouq Madaini, Amwal wa Malikiat* [Civil Law: Property and Ownership] (11th ed.) (Tehran: Mizan Press 2006) 225.

31 Ibid., 227.

32 Seyyed Hossein Safaei, *Introduction to Civil Law Vol 1* (Tehran: Mizan Press 2012) 308.

mawat); ownership through contracts and assignments; acquisition by priority rights (pre-emption);[33] and ownership through inheritance.

The first source of ownership is known as *ahya mawat*. It means working and cultivating the land; this may include planting trees, producing crops, and building on the land. Fencing, even if it is not substantial building, such as marking by stones around the land, may still create some priority over the land, but does not establish any ownership interests.

Article 143 of the Iranian Constitution explicitly states that 'anybody who cultivates (*ahya*) the dead land with the intention of ownership would obtain ownership of that land'. However, according to some Islamic jurists (*shia*), the ownership of the dead land, even after cultivation by individuals, is subject to the permission of the Imam (the leader).[34] But according to the majority of Islamic jurists (particularly *sunni* jurists), cultivating or *ahya* of the dead land establishes the ownership of the land without the permission of the leader or the state.[35]

The Iranian Civil Code has some relatively detailed provisions in relation to ownership of water, as Articles 146–60 are concerned with ownership of water. The Civil Code recognises private ownership of underground waters, as well as what is known in common law as riparian rights around the rivers. These provisions, in conjunction with Article 45 of the Iranian Constitution, provide that individuals can have private ownership of underground waters, rivers, canals (*ghanat*) and small springs and dams, as well as riparian rights over rivers. However, the state has ownership of lakes, rivers, and other waters not owned by individuals.

---

[33] Art 808 of the Iranian Civil Codes states: 'When real property, capable of being divided, is held jointly by two individuals, and one of them transfers his share to a third person by way of sale, the other joint owner has the right to give the purchaser the price which he has paid for it, and to take possession of the portion sold. This right is known as the right of pre-emption (shuf'eh), and the person who exercises that right is known as a "shafi"'.

[34] Mohaghigh Helli, *Sharaye al-Islam* (Persian Translation by Abolghasim Ibn Ahmad Yazdi) [The Rules of Islam] (Tehran: University of Tehran Press 2004) Vol 3, 1340.

[35] Seyyed Al Sabiq, Fiq Al Sunna [The Sunni Jurisprudence] Vol 3, 393 (1998) 140.

VII. OTHER RELEVANT LEGISLATION

Apart from the Constitution and the Civil Code, numerous other pieces of legislation, by-laws, and policy instruments regulate property law in Iran. These include the Registration of Deeds and Properties Act 1930, which regulates registration of properties, particularly land ownership. However, registration of proprietary interests is not mandatory, except for those interests that have already been registered. In practice, this means that people can have proprietary interests without official registered documents. This means that the traditional Islamic law forms of evidence, such as witnesses, are required to prove proprietary ownership in relation to interests which are not registered. In practice, the majority of properties in modern towns and cities are registered and regulated by the Registration of Deeds and Properties Act 1930 and other similar by-laws. However, there are proprietary interests in rural areas where modern registration documents may not be available.

The Urban Land Act 1987 regulates the ownership of the dead land around cities and towns. According to s6, the dead land around the cities vests with the State of the Islamic Republic of Iran. Since this legislation was adopted, the Ministry of Housing and local governments have granted lands to individuals and corporations and have issued ownership documents for the grantees of those lands.

VIII. OWNERSHIP OF MINERALS

Section 45 of the Constitution provides that the *anfal* (public properties), including minerals, are property of the state. Section 161 of the Constitution provides that minerals found within private property are property of the owner, and can be exploited according to the law. This means that minerals in Iran are subject to both private and public ownership. However, private land ownership is limited by the terrain, which restricts how much land can be privately owned by individuals. Indeed, 49.7 per cent of the land in Iran is mountains and deserts; none of this is useable. Only 10 per cent of the country is used for agriculture, and is owned by farmers in small scales.[36]

The first Mining Act was enacted by the Iranian Parliament in 1938. Section 2 of this Act provided that 'minerals found in private property

---

[36] Sadegh Zibakalam, *Ma Chegouneh Ma Shodim, Rishehaye Aghabmandegin Dar Iran* [How We Became What We Are: The Roots of Underdevelopment in Iran] (18th ed.) (Tehran: Rozaneh Publisher 2011) 94.

belong to the owner of the property'. However, Article 3 gave the right of exploitation of oil and precious materials, such as gold, silver, and diamonds to the government. Nevertheless, the owners of lands where these materials were found were able to enter into an agreement with the government to determine their interests. In 1998, the new Mining Act was enacted, and provided that exploration and exploitation of minerals shall only be permitted by the Ministry of Minerals (Articles 5–16).

IX. INTELLECTUAL PROPERTY

Intellectual property is well-developed under modern legal systems, such as civil law and common law systems. There are also principles in international law based on regional and international treaties concerning intellectual property. Traditional Islamic law does not have specific provisions regarding intellectual property rights. The area of intellectual property law is of recent origin, and has developed in recent decades. However, many Muslim and Middle Eastern countries have joined international treaties relating to intellectual property. Iran was not party to any international treaty relating to copyright and protection of intellectual properties. However, in 2000, the Iranian Parliament enacted legislation allowing the Iranian Government to join the World Intellectual Property Organisation. At the time of writing this chapter, serious discussions are currently being undertaken within the Iranian Government and Parliament to ratify the 1886 Berne Convention for the Protection of Literary and Artistic Works. There are, however, a number of pieces of legislation that protect copyright interests in Iran. The Law of Registration of Trademarks and Inventions 1930 regulates the registration of business and commercial signs and trademarks, as well as inventions and commercial plans. There is also legislation for the protection of copyright, and the protection of artistic works of individuals and artists. The Law of Protection of Copyrights and Rights of Artists was enacted in 1961. According to Article 2 of this Act, books, articles and other written materials, such as poems, songs and musical works, as well as any other architectural and artistic works, are protected. In 2000, the rights of inventors of computer software came under the protection of the Law of Protection of Creators of Computer Software 2000.

X. *WAQF*

Waqf, known in common law systems as a trust, is an important area of property law under Islamic law and Iranian law. While the institution and remedy of trust under the common law covers many commercial and personal transactions, including for charitable purposes, the institution of *waqf* is of a more charitable nature. Historically, under common law, the trust device developed as an innovative legal institution by major land owners to prevent some obstacles in the management of their land interests.[37] By this device the land owners were able to manage their property as they wished, particularly after their death. In common law countries, the institution of 'trusts' has constantly developed and evolved through case law. The law of trusts has acted to address the state intervention in the redistribution and management of wealth by eliminating or reducing taxes, and limiting the government's regulation of an individual's wealth and property.[38]

Under Islamic law, *waqf* is a charitable institution that has acted as a social mechanism to eliminate poverty and support low socio-economic groups in Muslim societies. It is also a device to support and manage certain Islamic institutions, such as mosques, cemeteries, holy shrines, and Islamic schools and religious institutions. The origin of the *waqf* in Islam is based on the *Sunnah* of the Prophet Muhammad, and in a *hadith* (saying) he referred to the continuous charity as a good deed for every Muslim.[39] This continuous charity was developed as *waqf* under Islamic jurisprudence and later became an important institution throughout the history of Islam, particularly during the Ottoman Empire (1299–1923).

Under Islamic law, *waqf* is classified into two main categories: *waqf al ahli* (*waqf* for the family) and *waqf al khayiri* (charitable *waqf*).[40]

---

[37] For a discussion on the historical development of the trust under common law, see Michael Evans, *Equity and Trusts* (3rd ed.) (Chatswood, NSW: LexisNexis 2012) 5–10.

[38] Jeffrey Schoenblum, 'The Role of Legal Doctrine in the Decline of the Islamic Waqf: A Comparison with the Trust' (1999) 32 *Vanderbilt Journal of Transnational Law* 1191, 1203.

[39] It is narrated from the Prophet Muhammad (by Moslem, Abu Daoud, Al-Termadhi and Al-Nisai) that 'When a person dies, they are survived by three things: *sadaqato jariyeh* [continuous charity]', knowledge that benefits society, and their children of good character'. It has been said that *sadaqato jariyeh* means *al-waqf*. See Sheikh Sayyed Sabeeq, Fiqh al-Sunna [Sunni Jurisprudence] Vol 3 (2nd ed., 1998), 268.

[40] Sheikh Sayyed Sahbeq, *Fiqh al-Sunna* [Sunni Jurisprudence] Vol 3 (2nd ed., 1998), 267.

According to some Islamic jurists, including the majority of *shia* scholars, a significant aspect of *waqf* is that the assignment of property for the purpose of *waqf* must be perpetual.[41]

The land subject to *waqf* cannot be alienated, and is not to be gifted, nor to be inherited.[42] However, according to the Hanafi school, the *waqf* property may, under certain circumstance, be sold.[43] The trustee (*mutawali*) may be paid from the benefit and may use the benefit to feed needy and poor people.[44]

Both real property and chattels, including animals, can be the subject of *waqf* except under the Hanafi School, where animals cannot be the subject of *waqf*.[45] *Waqf* for certain non-Muslims who are people of the Book (Christians, Jews and Zoroastrians) is allowed.[46] One of the Prophet's wives, Saphiah, made certain properties *waqf* for her brother who was Jewish.[47] According to some scholars, particularly in the Hanafi School, a person may make *waqf* for himself or herself, and for their children and grandchildren.[48]

Waqf is an important institution under Iranian law and details of *waqf* are covered by the Iranian Civil Code (Articles 55–91). The provisions of the Civil Code in relation to *waqf* are almost entirely based on Islamic jurisprudence (*Shia*). *Waqf* is defined by Article 55 as 'freezing the ownership and allocating the benefits' for charitable purposes. This definition is entirely based on the definition of *waqf* under Islamic jurisprudence.[49] The term '*habs*', which literally means 'detention', does not show whether the ownership transfers to the beneficiary (*mawqoufon*

---

41 See Mohammad Aminian Modarres, *Waqf Az Didgah Hoghough Wa Ehavanin* [Principles of Waqf] (Astan Quds Tazavi, Mashard, Iran: Islamic Research Foundation 2001) 22.

42 Ibid., 269.

43 Ibid.

44 Ibid., 269.

45 Ibid., 271.

46 Mohaqqeq Helli, Sharayeh al-Islam [Farsi translation by Abol Qasim Ibn Ahmad Yazdi] (1995), 347; Zaynodeen bin Ali (Shaheed Thani), *Al-Rodha al-Bahiya fi Sharha al-Loma al-Demeshqiya* [Collection of Legal Sections by Asadollah Lotfi] (2009), 38.

47 Sheikh Sayyed Sahbeq, *Fiqh al-Sunna* [Sunni Jurisprudence] Vol 3 (2nd ed., 1998), 271.

48 Ibid., 271–2.

49 *Waqf* is 'habs al-asl wa tasbil al-thamarah' (freezing the property and using the benefit): Sheikh Sayyed Sahbeq, Fiqh al-Sunna [Sunni Jurisprudence] Vol 3 (2nd ed., 1998), 268; see also Mohaqiq Helli, Sharaye al-Islam [The Laws of Islam] (Tehran: Maktabat al-Islamyyah 1957) 152.

alayhem) or to the trustee (*motavalli*), or stays with the settler or testator (*waqef*). It may mean that the ownership stays with the settler, but the assignment and alienation of the property and its interests are frozen except for the benefit of the beneficiaries. According to the Shafi'i school of jurisprudence, when a property is made *waqf*, the ownership of the property is transferred to God, and therefore the settler, trustee or beneficiary would not have any legal title over the trust property (*mawqouf alayh*).[50] However, according to the Maliki and Hanbali schools of jurisprudence, by creating a *waqf*, the settler or the testator transfers the ownership to the beneficiary.[51]

Under common law, when a trust is created, the legal ownership of the property is assigned to the trustee (*waqef*) but the benefits of the property are transferred to the beneficiary.[52]

Under Article 56 of the Civil Code of Iran, *waqf* is a contract. Therefore there must be an offer made by the settler and acceptance expressed by the beneficiary. In the case of a charitable purpose trust, the state shall accept the offer in order to create the *waqf*.[53] However, according to some *Shia* and *Sunni* scholars, the institution of *waqf*, in certain circumstances such as general charitable trusts for the elimination of poverty, can be created by the intention of the settler only.[54]

Article 71 of the Civil Code provides that the subject of the *waqf* must be certain. Other provisions of the Act such as Articles 57, 58 and 67 provide that the *waqf* property must be certain, too. However, *waqf* for a purpose, as long as the purpose is not unlawful according to the Shari'ah, is valid. This means that under Islamic law and Iranian law, certainties of

---

50 Sheikh Sayyed Sahbeq, Fiqh al-Sunna [Sunni Jurisprudence] Vol 3 (2nd ed., 1998), 270.

51 Ibid.

52 M. W. Bryan and V. J. Vann, *Equity & Trusts in Australia* (Cambridge: Cambridge University Press 2012) 210.

53 Art 56 of the Iranian Civil Code provides: 'An endowment takes place when the donor makes an offer by any form of words which definitely carry this meaning and when the first generation of beneficiaries, or their legal representative if they are limited in number, as in the case of children, accept it or if the beneficiaries are unlimited in number or the endowment be made for the benefit of the public, then the acceptance of the judge is required.'

54 See Mohammad Aminian Modarres, *Waqf Az Didgah Hoghough Wa Ghavanin* [Principles of Waqf] (Astan Quds Tazavi, Mashard, Iran: Islamic Research Foundation 2001) 36.

the object and the subject of the trust (*waqf*) are necessary in order to establish an express trust.[55]

In addition to Islamic jurisprudence (*fiqh*) and the Iranian Civil Code, there are other pieces of legislation and statutory provisions which regulate *waqf* in Iran. The first piece of legislation dealing with *waqf* was enacted in Iran in 1910.[56] Since then, there has always been a statutory body (*Sazman Awqaf*) dealing with *waqf* properties, particularly public and general charitable trusts. In 1983, legislation was enacted and the *Sazman Awqaf* and the relevant *Hajj* (pilgrimage to Mecca) body were merged into one department, known as *Sazman Hajj wa Awqaf wa Omour Kheiriah* (The Department of Hajj, Trusts and Charities).[57] The Department manages public charitable trusts, mosques, holy shrines, old cemeteries, and any other charitable institutions which do not have specific trustees. Given that there are thousands of mosques, shrines and charitable trusts in Iran, the Department is a significant and powerful economic institution in Iran. There are significant trust properties in various parts of Iran, and in some towns and cities; over half of the land is subject of public and charitable trusts.[58]

XI. CONCLUSION

Property law, particularly land law, is an important area of traditional Islamic law, but does not occupy a significant area of legal scholarship under Islamic *fiqh*. It is discussed in areas such as taxation and spoils of war, gifts, treasure troves, partnership, and cultivation of dead land for agricultural purposes.

In principle, both Islamic law and Iranian law have recognised and protected private ownership of land and other property interests. The Iranian Constitution, drafted in 1979 (after the Iranian-Islamic Revolution), has adopted three types of ownership, which are public ownership,

---

[55] Under common law, in order to have an express trust, three certainties are required. These are the certainty of intention to create a trust, the certainty of subject (trust property), and the certainty of objects (the beneficiary). See *Knight v Knight* (1840) 44 ER 58.

[56] *The Law of Knowledge and Trusts* (Awqaf) Ministeries (Qanoun Wezarat Maaref Wa Awqaf) (1910).

[57] The relevant legislation is *Qanoun Tashkilat Wa Ekhtiarat Sazman Awqaf Wa Omour Kheiria* [The Law Relating to the Structure and Powers of Department of Awqaf and Charities] (1983).

[58] See the homepage for *Sazman Hajj wa Awqaf wa Omour Kheiria* [The Department of Hajj, Trusts and Charities]: www.awqaf.ir.

cooperative ownership, and private ownership. The Constitution emphasises that private ownership is supplementary to the public and co-operative ownership. This is probably influenced by socialist principles which were dominant among revolutionaries in the 1970s in the Middle East. However, in practice during the last few decades, privatisation of major companies and resources has increased.

Iranian property law, particularly land law, is largely based on principles of Islamic law with the adoption of some modern legal principles from continental European legal systems, such as the Swiss and French laws. *Waqf*, or trust, is an important charitable institution under Islamic law and Iranian law, which acts as a social security mechanism. Public charitable *waqf* in Iran is subject to extensive statutory provisions and is managed by a centralised department, which owns significant property resources such as mosques, and holy shrines.

PART 3

CRIMINAL LAW AND JUSTICE

8. Corporate criminal liability in Saudi Arabia

Mohammed Fahad Aljiday Alsubaie

I. INTRODUCTION

The Kingdom of Saudi Arabia (KSA) is the largest country in the Middle East and the twelfth largest in the world.[1] With an area of about 2,250,000 km^2 and a population of approximately 32 million people,[2] it occupies most of the Arabian Peninsula.[3] It is the birthplace of Islam and the guardian of the Islamic holy places, Makka and Madinah.[4] The foundation of the Constitution of the KSA, its national laws,[5] and to some extent its foreign policy, are premised on strict Islamic/Shari'ah[6] laws.[7] Despite this, and because of its growing affluence, the KSA has begun embracing a free market economic policy, loosening its controls

[1] Neva Helena Alexander, 'Teaching Leadership to Female Students in Saudi Arabia' (2011) 31 *Advancing Women in Leadership* 199, 199.

[2] This number is based on the latest statistics, which were published in 2017, www.sama.gov.sa/ar-sa/EconomicReports/Pages/YearlyStatistics.aspx.

[3] Wafaa M. El-Ghanim, Loutfy M. Hassan and Adelfattah Badr, 'Floristic Composition and Vegetation Analysis in Hail Region North of Central Saudi Arabia' (2010) 17(2) *Saudi Journal of Biological Sciences* 119; Sajjad M. Jasimuddin, 'Analyzing the Competitive Advantages of Saudi Arabia with Porter's Model' (2001) 16(1) *Journal of Business and Industrial Marketing* 59, 120.

[4] Jan Michiel Otto (ed.), *Sharia Incorporated: A Comparative Overview of the Legal Systems of Twelve Muslim Countries in Past and Present* (Amsterdam: Amsterdam University Press 2010) 145.

[5] State laws in the KSA are called (*Anzimah*/ أنظمة) and law is called (*Nizam*/ نظام).

[6] 'Shari'ah' has a number of spelling variations. The author has selected Shari'ah. Similarly, the author has used the terms KSA, Saudi Arabia and Saudi interchangeably where appropriate.

[7] Janet K. Mullin Marta et al., 'Some Important Factors Underlying Ethical Decisions of Middle-Eastern Marketers' (2004) 21(1) *International Marketing Review* 53, 55.

over certain economic sectors, such as telecommunications and public utilities.[8]

The KSA is a member of the Gulf Cooperation Council (GCC), the Organization of the Petroleum Exporting Countries (OPEC)[9] and the World Trade Organization[10] (WTO).[11] Being a member the KSA is committed to adhering to those organisations' objectives in pushing for substantial economic reforms, including the removal of trade barriers and the promulgation of laws appropriate to such reform in regard to labour and investment.[12] The GCC also prompts further developments as it aims to achieve coordination and interconnection between members in most areas (including economic, commercial, industrial and customs policies, as well as financial and monetary policies, even to eventually securing a joint currency).[13] All of these developments have greatly facilitated the expansion of domestic corporate sectors, as well as attracting foreign investment into the country. More importantly, this policy enables its oil and gas-related industry – the backbone of the Kingdom's economy – to flourish, benefiting private commercial companies[14] and local communities alike.

---

[8] Mohamed Branine and David Pollard, 'Human Resource Management with Islamic Management Principles: A Dialectic for a Reverse Diffusion in Management' (2010) 39(6) *Personnel Review* 712, 715, 716; Nicholas H. D. Foster, 'Islamic Perspectives on the Law of Business Organisations II: The Sharia and Western-Style Business Organisations' (2010) 11(2) *European Business Organization Law Review* 273, 280–2.

[9] For more information (member countries, secretariat, mission etc), see Organization of the Oil Exporting Countries, *About Us*, www.opec.org/opec_web/en/index.htm.

[10] The KSA has been a member of WTO since 11 December 2005.

[11] World Trade Organization, *Understanding the WTO: The Organisation – Members and Observers* (23 July 2008), www.wto.org/english/thewto_e/whatis_e/tif_e/org6_e.htm.

[12] Svitlana Khyeda, 'Foreign Direct Investment in the Middle East: Major Regulatory Restrictions' (2007) 9(2) *Insight Turkey* 73, 74, 83.

[13] For more information (Charter, Economic Agreement, Member States etc), see Cooperation Council for the Arab States of the Gulf Secretariat General website: www.gcc-sg.org/eng/index.html.

[14] The term 'commercial company' is used intentionally as it differentiates a profit-oriented company operating in the business or industrial sector from other non-profit companies or companies incorporated in whole or in part by a Royal Decree. For more detailed definition and further explanation. Later on (unless otherwise indicated), the terms 'company' and 'corporation' shall refer to 'commercial company' as well. So, the study uses terms 'company' and 'corporation', where appropriate, interchangeably.

Significant developments recorded in business and corporate areas have combined to improve the current Saudi Arabian business environment.[15] The KSA, like any other growing economy, has witnessed a number of key developments over the years in its business environment that have played a role in facilitating competition and improving strategies to regulate business operations.

Within the last few years, the expansion of private corporations in the KSA has been clearly evident, as their numbers have substantially increased from tens to hundreds. The latest statistics published in 2017 show that by the end of 2016 the council of Ministers had approved the establishment of 43 insurance and reinsurance companies in the KSA, in addition to 228 insurance service provider to support insurance service,[16] and the number continues to increase.[17]

The ongoing economic liberalisation and structural policy reforms currently underway in the KSA[18] create a need for effective legal

---

15 Office of the United States Trade Representative, 'National Trade Estimate Report on Foreign Trade Barriers (NTE)' (Office of the United States Trade Representative, 2009), www.ustr.gov/sites/default/files/uploads/reports/2009/NTE/asset_upload_file856_15503.pdf (accessed 30 July 2010). See 'Saudi Arabia': 431–7.

16 Values of exchange rate that are mentioned in this study (rounded to the nearest USD 10), according to OANDA Corporation website www.oanda.com/currency/converter and all USD approximations are to the nearest dollar.

17 SAMA (Research and Statistics Department), *Fifty-Third Annual Report – Saudi Arabian Monetary Authority* (2017) 87, www.sama.gov.sa/enUS/EconomicReports/AnnualReport/Fifty%20Third%20Annual%20Report.pdf (accessed 10 January 2018).

18 For example, 42 new trade-related laws and regulations have been put into force; the judicial system has been reformed; and corporate taxation has been reduced from 45 per cent to a flat 20 per cent. For all reforms that have taken place, see 'Speech by H.E. the Governor for the Institute of International Finance Inc., MENA [Middle East and North Africa] Regional Economic Forum, Riyadh, 7 November 2007, www.sama.gov.sa/sites/samaen/OtherReportsLib/20071215speech_by_his_excellency_the_governor_en.pdf (accessed 30 July 2010). In addition, the Ministry of Commerce and Industry released commercial registers showing the establishment of 2831 new companies as compared to 2274 in the preceding year. There was an increase in the number and total capital of new companies by 24.5 per cent and 36.3 per cent respectively in 2008 as compared with the preceding year. By the end of 2008, the total number of companies existing in Saudi Arabia had increased by 13.2 per cent over the preceding year. The Ministry of Commerce and Industry issued 68,400 new commercial registrations of the establishment of new commercial proprietorship firms during 2008 in different regions of the Kingdom, raising their total number by 9.6 per cent to 763,600. See SAMA, *Forty Fifth Annual Report* (2009), above n17, 31: The

regulation for Saudi businesses in the new business environment. This will ensure that any negative effects arising from the operation of corporations and the detrimental effects of globalisation will be properly addressed.[19]

Criminal liability is one of the factors that can affect the activities of business entities. Planning by businesses to avoid incidents that result in criminal liability plays an important role in ensuring that business operations are carried out smoothly and within legal bounds at all times.[20] The existence of criminal liability influences the operational strategies of companies, by shaping their operational environment as well as the strategies they develop.[21] Liability improves not only a business's functionality but also its internal rules and regulations.[22] It is unfortunate, however, that generally the expansion of companies correlates with an increasing number of cases of corporate crimes, including corporate tax evasion, internal corporate investment violation or embezzlement.[23] To discourage corporate law violation, Solaiman asserts that stringent and comprehensive national laws and regulation on corporate criminal liability are needed.[24] Unlike corporations in the United States and in

---

number of intermediaries at the beginning of 2008 stood at 42, with that number rising to 110 by the end of 2008: at 31, 93.

19 AMEinfo.com, *Saudis Move to Modernise Legal System* (2007), www.ameinfo.com/134904.html; Maher Hammoud and Peter Vayanos, 'Promoting the Growth and Competitiveness of the Insurance Sector in the Arab World' in World Economic Forum ' in World Economic Forum, *Arab World Competitiveness, Report, 2006–2007*, Part 8/11 (2007) 97, 108.

20 S. M. Solaiman, 'Investor Protection and Criminal Liabilities for Defective Prospectuses: Bangladeshi Laws Compared with their Equivalents in India and Malaysia' (2006) 13(4) *Journal of Financial Crime* 467, 469, 470.

21 Pamela H. Bucy, 'Corporate Criminal Liability: When Does it Make Sense?' (2009) 46(4) *American Criminal Law Review* 1437, 1440, 1445; John Hasnas, 'The Centenary of a Mistake: One Hundred Years of Corporate Criminal Liability' (2009) 47(4) *American Criminal Law Review* 1329, 1340.

22 F. N. Baldwin, 'Exposure of Financial Institutions to Criminal Liability' (2006) 13(4) *Journal of Financial Crime* 387, 390.

23 Edward D. Diskant, 'Comparative Corporate Criminal Liability: Exploring the Uniquely American Doctrine through Comparative Criminal Procedure' (2008) 118(1) *Yale Law Journal* 126, 166.

24 Solaiman, 'Investor Protection and Criminal Liabilities for Defective Prospectuses', above n20, 485.

commonwealth countries such as Australia and Great Britain, those in the KSA are not subject to a wide range of strict liability criminal laws.[25]

II. CORPORATE CRIME IN THE KINGDOM OF SAUDI ARABIA (KSA)

The rapid industrial expansion of the KSA has been the result of oil exploitation, as well as growth in the sectors of agriculture, tourism and urbanism.[26] However, given the existing autocracy, which has been the traditional form of rule in the KSA, many opportunities for corruption and corporate crime arose.[27] Leaders in the KSA have been taking advice from councils, consisting of various elders and advisers, many of them from among the leader's family. As a consequence, decision taking procedures have not been transparent, not only in the public, but also in the private sector, where connections have played a most important role.[28] As a consequence, high ranking members of the hierarchy have been unwilling to be held accountable for business decisions.

It is worth noting that provisions of sections 211, 212, 213 and 214 of Companies Law 2015 (*Nizam Asharaikaat* / نظام الشركات) (CL'15)[29] deal with certain types of corporate misconduct. Moreover, there are other set of rules dealing with such cases – for instance, the Anti Bribery Law 1992 (*Nizam Mukafahat Arashwah* / نظام مكافحة الرشوة) (ABL'92).[30]

Although the KSA has not, to date, had a written penal code, companies can be held liable for wrongful misconduct, under criminal laws and regulations such as the ABL'92.

---

[25] Karen Wheelwright, 'Goodbye Directing Mind and Will, Hello Management Failure: A Brief Critique of Some New Models of Corporate Criminal Liability' (2006) 19 *Australian Journal of Corporate Law* 287, 288.

[26] Oxford Business Group, *The Report: Saudi Arabia 2010* (London: Oxford Business Group 2010) 16, 229, 293.

[27] Lawrence M. Salinger, *Encyclopedia of White-Collar and Corporate Crime* (Thousand Oaks: Sage 2005) 45, 70.

[28] Shahid N. Bhuian, 'An Empirical Examination of Market Orientation in Saudi Arabian Manufacturing Companies' (1998) 43(1) *Journal of Business Research* 13, 15.

[29] The *Companies Law 2015* (*Niz}a>m Asharaikaat*/ نظام الشركات) (CL'15) was enacted by Royal Decree No. M/3 issued on 28 *Muharam* 1437 AH (11 November 2015).

[30] *Anti Bribery Law 1992* (ABL'92) was issued by Royal Decree No. M/36 of 29 *Dhul-h}ijjah* 1412 AH (30 June 1992).

Sections 19, 20 and 21 of the ABL'92 provide for a fine of an amount 10 times the value of the bribe for any company or artificial person, where employees are found guilty and where it is proven that the crime was committed in the interest of the corporation. There are also some consequential penalties that may be applied to the corporation under sections 19 and 21, as follows:

i. The company will be deprived of government procurement contracts, if its directors or any of its representatives are convicted of bribery.
ii. The Cabinet may take any further appropriate measure regarding the company.
iii. The conviction shall be made public in a daily newspaper.

This approach is illustrated at the criminal judgment of the Board of Grievance (*Diwan Al-Mazalim* / ديوان المظالم):[31] the financial and administrative manager in a company offered an amount of SAR 150,000 (approximately USD 40,000)[32] to a public official in one of the Ministries. The objective was to induce him to issue an illegal permit to operate a business to the said company. The public official refused to accept this bribe and informed the authority concerned of the matter. The accused, who appeared before the Board of Grievance, confessed that he had offered this amount to the public official in accordance with a verbal order from the manager of the said company. The Board of Grievance convicted him and passed its judgment based on sections 9, 15 and 19 of the ABL'92 as follows.

First, the financial and administrative manager of the company involved was found guilty of the charge filed against him, and sentenced to one year's imprisonment in addition to a fine of SAR 50,000 (approximately USD 13,000). Second, the amount of the bribe was to be confiscated. Third, the company was fined SAR 300,000 (approximately USD 80,000), because the employee who offered the bribe was acting in the interest of the company, since his aim was to obtain the permit requested by the company. The employee involved was also a member and representative of the company. This case demonstrates that the court held the company – as a legal person in the KSA – *vicariously* liable under the ABL'92 for the commission of a criminal offence, for the following reasons: (i) the company had an interest in obtaining the certificate requested; (ii) the said employee was a mere representative of

---

[31] Judgment of the Third Criminal Circuit in Riyadh No. 12/D/G/14 of 1418 AH (1998).

[32] Note: all USD approximations are to the nearest dollar.

the company and executing its will in offering the bribe to obtain the said certificate; and (iii) the said employee had no personal interest in the matter and that the sole party who had an interest was the company. Therefore, the company deserved to be punished by application of the ABL'92. Thus, this case proves that a company in the KSA can be held responsible for a criminal act by one of its employees, if this act took place within the scope of his/her employment, and if the company stood to gain from the employee's actions.

Further offending conducts may be punished, if they fall under the regulatory field of laws that regulate environment, such as the General Environmental Law 2001[33] and the Labour Law 2005.[34]

Corporate Crime Rate in the Kingdom of Saudi Arabia (KSA)

There are no exact statistics that reflect corporate crimes rate in the KSA. Even without exact statistics, however, corporate crime (such as embezzlement of funds, drug trafficking, business fraud and bribery) is of serious concern to the KSA.[35] In addition, the country faces a problem difficult to combat with regards to money-laundering used to finance

---

[33] Section 1(6) of the *General Environmental Law 2001* indicates that the provisions of this law apply to both natural and legal persons, including individual companies and institutions. Thus, a company may be held liable for environmental offences, depending on whether the actions of its directors, officers or representatives are meant to be in the company's interests or not. Under section 14 of the *General Environmental Law 2001* any trafficking of a pollutant, hazardous or radioactive substance is a crime, with a penalty of imprisonment not exceeding five years or a fine not exceeding SAR 500,000 (approximately USD 133,000), or both. The person who commits the said offence is obliged to remove the causes and impacts of the offence, and the entity involved (a company) may be closed permanently or temporarily. *General Environmental Law 2002* was enacted by Royal Decree No. M/34 of 28 *Rajab* 1422 AH (16 October 2001).

[34] Section 222 of the said law states that 'no case shall be accepted by the commissions provided for in this law, involving a claim of the rights provided for in this law, or arising from a work contract after twelve months following termination of the work relation'. With regards to *Labour Law 2005*, related claims are lapsed (will be time-barred) after 12 months from the date of violation as provided in section 222. In addition, the said section states that any right provided in *Labour Law 2005* will be time-barred after the lapse of 12 months from the date of termination of employment. *Labour Law 2005* was enacted by Royal Decree No. M/51 of 23 *Sha'ban* 1426 AH (27 September 2005).

[35] Salinger, above n27, 45.

terrorism, and other corporate crimes.[36] Moreover, the KSA itself has acknowledged that the country has also become a transit centre for organised arms smuggling.[37]

It is important to point out that there are companies in the KSA that commit corporate crimes. For example, Saudi Arabia-based Tamimi Global Company Ltd (TAFGA) paid a fine on account of its corporate criminal activity.[38] As result of corporate crimes, the KSA has closely worked with many countries to combat them. Furthermore, the country established programs to deal with the problems associated with organised crime. Therefore, there seem to be a tentative acceptance of corporate criminal liability for illegal act such as money laundering and bribery in the KSA. With a view to better combating forms of corporate crime, according to this writer's view, there is a need for strict liability offences.[39]

Is a Penalty Justifiable for Corporate Crime?

The criminal sanctions for a corporate crime can be on both individuals and corporate entities. The penalties include imprisonment, fines and denial of certain legal privileges (such as a licence) and so forth.[40] Hence legal sanctions may terminate the business.[41] However, the penalties should depend on the type of illicit activity committed.[42]

---

[36] Lawrence Malkin and Yuval Elizur, 'Terrorism's Money Trail' (2002) 19(1) *World Policy Journal* 60, 68.

[37] Salinger, above n27, 46.

[38] *US v Tamimi Global Co.*, 11cr40083, US District Court, Central District of Illinois (Peoria). Also, see Federal Bureau of Investigation (Springfield Division), *Saudi Arabia-based Tamimi Global Company to Pay US $13 Million to Resolve Criminal and Civil Allegations of Kickbacks and Illegal Gratuities: KBR Sub-contrator Provided Dining Services in Iraq and Kuwait* (Media Release, 16 November 2011), www.fbi.gov/springfield/press-releases/2011/saudi-arabia-based-tamimi-global-company-to-pay-u.s.-13-million-to-resolve-criminal-and-civil-allegations-of-kickbacks-and-illegal-gratuities.

[39] Jay S. Albanese, *Organised Crime in Our Times* (6th ed.) (Elsevier 2010) 3.

[40] Roger LeRoy Miller and Gaylord A. Jentz, *Fundamentals of Business Law: Excerpted Cases* (2nd ed.) (Boston, MA: Cengage Learning 2009) 134.

[41] For example, deprivation of commercial/business activities, a penalty found in section 26 of the *Law of Companies Operating in the Field of Pooling and Receiving Funds for Investment, Law No. 146 of 1988 (Egypt).*

[42] Peter-Jan Engelen and Marc van Essen (eds), 'Reputational Penalties in Financial Markets: An Ethical Mechanism?' in *Responsible Investment in Times of Turmoil* (Dordrecht: Springer 2011) 60.

Many corporations like Costain Coal Inc, C R Bard Inc and Odwalla Inc have caused deaths, yet the penalties that have been imposed on them were limited to a fine.[43] Although corporate crime has continuously been increasing, governments have not been taking drastic steps to combat such crimes.

Instead of complying with the relevant laws and supporting the legislators' and governments' recommendations, policies and solutions that attempt to ensure the support and protection of people's rights,[44] many companies either in the KSA or overseas have committed corporate crimes such as bribery, false advertising, fraud, use of unsafe manufacturing processes and adopted practices that comprise an abuse of human rights.[45]

In order to protect their own advantage around the world, governments may ignore human rights, preferring instead to maintain trade advantages. This naturally means the presence of less government support to address corporate crime.[46] It is evidenced that many corporate crimes are compensated by fines alone, depending on many factors such as strength of evidence, seriousness of the crime, and the availability of other types of penalties, while criminal sanctions may be last resort for serious violations of corporate regulations.[47]

III. CRITICISMS

Despite economic development and the liberalisation of the market, the Saudi government has not revised the relevant law to take into account new trends. Therefore, current legislation fails to provide sanctions for

---

[43] Russell Mokhiber, Top 100 Corporate Criminals of Decade, *Corporate Crime Reporter*, www.corporatecrimereporter.com/top100.html#Annotated.

[44] Florian Wettstein, 'The Duty to Protect: Corporate Complicity, Political Responsibility, and Human Rights Advocacy' (2010) 96(1) *Journal of Business Ethics* 33, 42.

[45] John Ruggie, 'Protect, Respect and Remedy: A Framework for Business and Human Rights', Report of the Special Representative of the Secretary-General on the issue of Human Rights and Transnational Corporations and Other Business Enterprises (www.mitpressjournals.org/doi/pdf/10.1162/itgg.2008.3.2.189) 203–10.

[46] Ibid., 193–208.

[47] Michael Jefferson, 'Regulation, Businesses, and Criminal Liability' (2011) 57(1) *Journal of Criminal Law* 37, 37 and 42; Anthony S. Barkow and Rachel E. Barkow, *Prosecutors in the Boardroom: Using Criminal Law to Regulate Corporate Conduct* (New York: New York University Press 2011) 14.

some forms of activities that elsewhere would be punishable as crimes as these activities (whether they are difficult to detect or not) are not identified within the relevant legislation.

The absence of comprehensive guidelines and robust legal provisions, along with outdated private commercial legislation, has been identified as the primary reason for the Saudi government's failure to effectively regulate the activities of corporations in the KSA. In fact, the Kingdom's main corporate law, the Commercial Court Law 1931 (CCL'31),[48] which was made by the Royal Decree No. M/6, is considered outdated as it was promulgated in the mid-1960s. While this particular legislation has been amended a number of times, it continues to have shortcomings, in particular in regard to measures to regulate company activities.[49] Not only is the Commercial Court Law outdated and inefficient, the rest of the regulatory instruments merely provide basic guidelines without having any legal or mandatory requirements. Notable in this respect are the Corporate Governance Regulations 2006 (CGR'06) introduced by the Kingdom's Capital Market Authority (CMA) in 2006.[50] It could be argued that even though the KSA is a

---

[48] The *Commercial Court Law 1931* (*Nizam Almahkamah Atijaryah* / نظام المحكمة التجارية) (CCL'31) enacted by Royal Decree No. M/32 of 15 *Muh}arram* 1350 AH (2 June 1931), the *Law of Handling Public Funds 1975* (*Nizam Mubasharat Alammwal Al'amah* / نظام مباشرة الأموال العامة) issued by Royal Decree No. 77 of 23 *Shawwal* 1395 AH (29 October 1975), *Arbitration Law 1983* (*Nizam Atahkym* / نظام التحكيم) issued by Royal Decree No. M/46 of 12 *Rajab* 1403 AH (24 April 1983), and *Law of Commercial Books 1989* (*Nizam Adafatir Atijaryah* / نظام الدفاتر التجارية) issued by Royal Decree No. M/61 of 17 *Dhul-h}ijjah* 1409 AH (27 June 1989).

[49] Muhammad Asayed Arafa, 'Control of Joint-Stock Companies Has Become a Pressing Issue at Present Time', *Saudi Economic Newspaper* (Riyadh, Saudi Arabia), 28 December 2006, 10.

[50] The CGR'06 were issued by the Board of Capital Market Authority by Resolution No. 1/212/2006 of 21 *Shawwal* 1427 AH (12 November 2006) based on the *Capital Market Law 2003*. It is noteworthy that according to section 1(b) of the CGR'06, these regulations merely provide basic guidelines for all companies listed on the Exchange without having any legal or mandatory requirements except paragraph [c] of section 1 related to disclosure in the Board of Directors' Report. Then the Board of the Capital Market Authority issued Resolution No. 1-36-2008 of 12 *Dhul-'l-qi'dah* 1429 AH (10 November 2008), making section 9 of the *Corporate Governance Regulations 2006* mandatory for all companies listed on the Exchange effective from the first board report issued by the company following the date of the Board of the Capital Market Authority resolution mentioned above. Also, the same resolution made paragraphs [c] and [e] of section 12 of the CGR'06 mandatory for all companies listed on the

leader of the GCC[51] and OPEC,[52] and a member of the WTO, its rules and regulations dealing with companies are outdated, and many restrictions inhibiting commercial activities still apply to the Saudi economy.[53] These have arguably contributed to the failure to effectively enforce the law. Considering the importance of legal certainty about subjects' rights and obligations together with their effective enforcement, the current CL'15 undermines the effectiveness of the domestic legal framework. Moreover, the shortcomings in the CL'15 create obstacles to the country's economic development.

Hand by hand with ambiguous or obsolete laws there comes a possibility of the existence of legal lacunae, or misinterpretation or circumvention of laws. With regard to corporate crimes it is then very difficult to maintain a high standard of compliance with legal provisions. Application of unamended outdated rules on new forms of crimes that have accompanied new technologies can never cover all the aspects of malicious acts and identify the persons responsible. Problems with interpretation and application of the respective laws by judges consequently cause difficulties with enforcement. Therefore, it can be seen that the current version of the CL'15 has been ineffective in dealing with increasing corporate crime.

The basic regulatory frame of the penal law of corporations is contained in sections 211 to 214 of CL'15. According to the writer's view, the main drawbacks of its legal provisions are weak correlation

---

Exchange effective from the year 2009. This resolution also made section 14 of these regulations mandatory for all companies listed on the Exchange effective from the year 2009. See Capital Markets Authority, *Corporate Governance Regulations* (2009), www.cma.org.sa/cma_cms/upload_sec_content/dwfile19/convE.pdf.

51 Andrys Onsman, 'Dismantling the Perceived Barriers to the Implementation of National Higher Education Accreditation Guidelines in the Kingdom of Saudi Arabia' (2010) 32(5) *Journal of Higher Education Policy and Management* 511, 518; M. S. Rafiq, 'The Optimality of a Gulf Currency Union: Commonalities and Idiosyncrasies' (2011) 28 *Economic Modelling* 728, 730.

52 Douglas B. Reynolds and Michael K. Pippenger, 'OPEC and Venezuelan Oil Production: Evidence Against a Cartel Hypothesis' (2010) 38(10) *Energy Policy* 6045, 6047.

53 John Hooman Donboli and Farnaz Kashefi, 'Doing Business in the Middle East: A Primer for U.S. Companies' (2005) 38 *Cornell International Law Journal* 413, 434; Mohamed El Hedi Arouri, Amine Lahiani and Duc Khuong Nguyen, 'Return and Volatility Transmission between World Oil Prices and Stock Markets of the GCC Countries' (2011) 28(4) *Economic Modelling* 1815–17, 1823.

with the needs of today's society, inadequate theoretical and legal judicial process, the lack of clear identification of the persons that can be held liable, ineffective sanctions and a lack of public confidence in the legislation.

Outdated Character and Weak Correlation with the Needs of Today's Society

The CCL'31 was enacted in 1931 with a view to boosting a healthy competitive environment in the KSA market. However, the formation, management and supervision of today's companies differ from those of 1931. According to this writer's view, the current penalties, which in the CL'15 cannot deter the new corporate crimes, and the law does not provide for any supplementary penalties, such as publication of the crime committed and its penalty, as well as deprivation of the ability to conduct commercial/business activities. Moreover, the CCL'31 was issued in 1931. Both the CCL'31 and the CL'15 are no longer able to deter corporate crimes and should be replaced by effective new legislation under one law, which should be named Commercial Law.

Lack of Sufficient Theoretical and Legal Process and Lack of Trust

The commercial courts in the KSA still lack public confidence. In the writer's view, one of the reasons for this lack of confidence is that the judges and lawyers are not properly qualified for the tasks in hand. In addition, there are a lot of delays with regards to the issuing of the decisions. Such delays can be measured either by the average length of the trial, or by the percentage of the lawsuits concluded in one year out of the total number of lawsuits. Moreover, the laws related to corporations are outdated; and there are no professional judges for, nor a body of specialised practitioners in, company disputes; nor specialised commercial courts.

Individual Liability

The CL'15 does not provide for a clear explanation for persons who are held criminally liable for the crime of offering company shares for subscription, under the scope of the application of section 211 of the CL'15. This, the writer considers, is another flaw in the CL'15.

Ineffective Sanctions

The study has revealed the weakness of the CL'15 in terms of the penalties for crimes related to formation of company capital during the phase of its incorporation as compared to those sanctions provided under company laws of some members of the Gulf Cooperation Council (GCC). Sanctions in other member countries include imprisonment and fines. In comparison, however, the KSA fines are very low. The CL'15 imposes a fine on the company based on section 217; it may be imposed on an individual if he or she committed a crime under section 211 of the CL'15. However, some opponents of the imposition of substantial fines may argue that the effects may be disproportionate. There have been cases where the Court itself has reduced the fine, in order not to have negative consequences on the corporation.[54] Those arguing against heavy fines may also point out that such fines will further adversely affect the innocent, that is, excessive fines can have perverse effects that may have to be borne by innocent shareholders, creditors, employees or consumers. However, penalties in terms of both imprisonment and fine are very low in the KSA compared to the ones imposed by the legislation of other countries.

IV. CONCLUSION

Taking into account the analysis attempted with regards to the KSA, the following could be underlined as far as the country's legal framework is concerned with regards to corporate criminal responsibility.

Firstly, the relevant legislation should be amended. The CL'15 should be revised, particularly the sections related to corporate crimes, namely, section 213. The CCL'31 (enacted some 80 years ago) should be updated. A number of its sections have already been cancelled due to the issuance of other laws.

Secondly, the KSA must create independent and specialised commercial courts with qualified and trained judges and prosecutors to hear only commercial cases.

Thirdly, the database of commercial cases and the commercial statistics, in particular corporate cases and statistics, should be published in

---

[54] For instance, in the case *R v Wattle Gully Gold Mines NL*, in which the Supreme Court of Victoria reduced a fine from AUD 20,000 to AUD 500 so as not to have a very high fine 'fall on the innocent' [1980] 4 ACLR 959.

the KSA. Such publication would help judges, investors, companies, lawyers and researchers.

Fourthly, an official English translation of the legal database and statistics should be available. This would avoid any misunderstandings that might otherwise arise due to a lack of an officially recognised text or use of a poor translation.

Fifthly, the length of judicial proceedings should be appropriate, and the problem of unreasonable delay in judicial proceedings should be tackled. To this end, unnecessary postponing of any claim against a corporate entity should be avoided; judges should be specialised; and decisions should be published in such a way that a large number of consumers will be aware of the crime. Moreover, modern technical means should be adopted in all courts. A network linking all courts and the ministry could be facilitated as well as easy communication and interaction among judges and staff, lawyers and disputants encouraged, with a view to easier transfer of the new legislation, amendments to laws and any other important information.

Sixthly, the system of sanctions also needs to be reformed in order to better address the current corporate reality and address corporate crimes in a more punitive way. To this end, fines should be higher and length of imprisonment longer.

To achieve this, it is crucial that breaches of corporate law should be prosecuted and those who are convicted for their criminal behaviour should be duly penalised. This principle must be applied irrespective of whether the convicted is a natural person or a company. The CL'15 does not prefer the imposition of criminal liability against a company and consequently most prosecutorial activities are directed towards individual wrongdoing. A framework for corporate criminal liability that reflects corporate behaviour should be developed. Similarly, to this end, and with a view to better deterring corporate crimes, such crimes should be reported to the appropriate authority in the appropriate time.

In order to develop a strong market, complex supportive mechanisms are necessary. To this end, the analysis in the chapter adheres to the proposition that the laws of the jurisdiction should be more supportive. In addition, rules imposing corporate criminal liability should be strict. Companies are real entities, which possess immense power and may perform actions that can harm individuals as well as society. In this context, regulatory authorities and governments should possess a full range of legal tools that will allow them to combat the various forms of corporate crime more effectively.

Within the context of better enhancing growth and competitiveness in the market, corporate law plays a very important role. It provides, in particular, the means whereby companies can develop their functional role with a view to forming the conditions and the rules for economic transactions in the market. This objective should be specified by a coherent and solid legal framework for corporate criminal liability.

Corporate crimes occur at high frequency across the globe. High level personnel often take decisions that are driven by their will to achieve for their company the best results in terms of market dominance or profit maximisation. In this context, the question of discerning 'who to blame' becomes a difficult task. Employees may claim that 'I was following the rules' with a view to reducing the individual's responsibility within the corporate institution.

The provisions of the legislation, such as that in force in the United States, impose penalties on the companies for the corporate crimes they commit.[55] These penalties may be fines and/or an imprisonment. During the past decades, however, praxis has demonstrated the strength of penalties that may be needed to create a truly effective deterrent preventative system, such as in the UK system.[56] Corporate lobbying and their ability to influence legislative frameworks are so well developed that such entities are still able to commit severe crimes and often escape with relatively small fines.

There exist countries and parts of countries which have become politically sensitive to such kinds of crime. In Australia, for instance, the Law Reform Commission of New South Wales has pointed out that:

> Corporate crime poses a significant threat to the welfare of the community. Given the pervasive presence of corporations in a wide range of activities in our society, and the impact of their actions on a much wider group of people than are affected by individual action, the potential for both economic and physical harm caused by a corporation is great.[57]

Other countries, however, such as continental law countries, have failed to integrate corporate criminal law into their legal system.[58]

---

55 Daniel Huynh, 'Preemption v. Punishment: A Comparative Study of White Collar Crime Prosecution in the United States and the United Kingdom' (2010) 9(1) *Journal of International Business and Law* 105, 133.

56 Ibid., 133–5.

57 See Law Reform Commission of New South Wales, *Sentencing: Corporate Offenders*, Issues Paper 20 (2001), www.lawlink.nsw.gov.au/lrc.nsf/pages/ip20chp01.

58 Manfred Möhrenschlager, 'Development on an International Level' (paper presented at the International Colloquium on Criminal Responsibility of Legal and Collective Entities, Berlin, Germany, 4–6 May 1998) 1.

With regards to the implementation of legal schema for corporate criminal liability, the KSA has included provisions related to corporate criminal liability in their legal system. There are many provisions related to criminal liability in the KSA; however, they are not confined to general criminal law but are scattered over a plethora of statutes with specific provisions, such as the CL'15 and the ABL'92.

Corporations can commit the same offences as natural persons. Given, however, the fact that governments rely on them for the economic development of their countries, the question of how to regulate corporate behaviour becomes highly complicated due to intrigues and conspiracies elaborated by the elite networks of strong multinational corporations.[59] As a result, many perpetrators of corporate crimes often believe they will not be detected.[60]

Corporate criminal liability is one of the significant tools governments can use to prevent corporate crimes.[61] By imposing corporate criminal liability by adopting legislative, judicial, administrative or other effective measures, each government can tackle this growing problem. International cooperation should be enhanced to ensure that an integrated and concerted effort is made by States to eradicate this crime.

Corporate crime is still an obscure subject, especially in the KSA. Moreover, there are neither exact statistics that reflect corporate crime rates, nor official data that has been gathered in the KSA on the harm and cost caused by corporate crime. Thus, more qualitative and quantitative analyses of corporate crime are needed in the KSA.

---

59 Laura L. Hansen, 'Corporate Financial Crime: Social Diagnosis and Treatment' (2009) 16(1) *Journal of Financial Crime* 28, 34.

60 Barkow and Barkow, above n47, 70.

61 Ibid., 71.

9. Blasphemy and apostasy laws in the Muslim world: a critical analysis

Faisal Kutty

Apostasy and blasphemy have been at the forefront of the news from the Muslim world in too many instances over the past few years.[1] To outside observers, it appears that Muslims are constantly on the lookout for blasphemers and apostates. Indeed, a Pew Research Center survey found widespread support for the death penalty as a punishment for apostasy in a number of Muslim countries including Egypt (86 per cent), Jordan (82 per cent), Afghanistan (79 per cent), Pakistan (76 per cent), Malaysia (62 per cent) and the Palestinian Territories (66 per cent).[2] Similar intolerance is evident in the context of blasphemy, with almost 70 per

[1] Whether it is a Court of Appeals decision from Malaysia barring non-Muslims from using 'Allah,' arrests and charges (Egypt, Sudan, etc.), or murders and death sentences under Pakistan's blasphemy laws, the Muslim world is in the news. See Krishnadev Calamur, 'Top Malaysian Court Upholds Ruling on Who Can Use "Allah"', *NPR* (23 June 2014, 12:01 PM), www.npr.org/blogs/thetwo-way/2014/06/23/324870230/top-malaysian-court-upholds-ruling-on-who-can-use-allah; 'Egyptian Christian Teacher Sentenced for Blasphemy', *Al Arabiya News* (16 June 2014), http://english.alarabiya.net/en/News/2014/06/16/Egyptian-Christian-teacher-sentenced-for-blasphemy.html; 'Sudan Orders Release of Christian Convert', *Aljazeera* (23 June 2014, 2:06 PM), www.aljazeera.com/news/middleeast/2014/06/sudan-orders-release-christian-convert-2014623132755108280.html; see also Asad Hashim, 'Living in Fear under Pakistan's Blasphemy Law', *Aljazeera* (17 May 2014, 12:12 PM), www.aljazeera.com/indepth/features/2014/05/living-fear-under-pakistan-blasphemy-law-20145179369144891.html; Faisal Kutty, 'Why Blasphemy Laws Are Actually Anti-Islamic', *The Huffington Post* (15 April 2014, 5:48 PM), www.huffingtonpost.ca/faisal-kutty-/blasphemy-laws_b_5149380.html [hereinafter Kutty, *Blasphemy Laws*]; Haggag Salama, 'Egyptian Christian Sentenced to 6 Years in Prison for Contempt of Religion', *U.S. News* (24 June 2014, 7:53 AM), www.usnews.com/news/world/articles/2014/06/24/egyptian-christian-jailed-for-contempt-of-religion.

[2] Pew Research Ctr., 'Beliefs about Sharia', *The Pew Forum on Religion & Public Life* (30 April 2013) (last visited 30 August 2014), www.pewforum.org/2013/04/30/the-worlds-muslims-religion-politics-society-beliefs-about-sharia. Authorities in six gulf countries – Saudi Arabia, UAE, Oman, Qatar, Bahrain and Kuwait – did not permit Pew Research to survey their population on apostasy.

cent of nations in the Middle East and North Africa criminalizing blasphemy.[3]

Consistent with such a narrow religious, social and legal worldview, alleged apostates, blasphemers and even their defenders or advocates are harassed, maimed and sometimes killed with impunity.[4] Many jurisdictions that have witnessed death, destruction, persecution, mayhem and abuse in the name of defending religious sensibilities have done very little, if anything, to punish such vigilantism. On the contrary, in some of these nations, legislation, policies and practices appear to tolerate if not encourage mob justice. Based on observing the facts on the ground, it would not be far-fetched to conclude that Islam sanctions severe restrictions on free expression and imposes cruel and unusual penalties for blasphemy and apostasy, at least from a modern human rights-oriented perspective. The reality is much more nuanced. In this chapter, I highlight the growing chorus who argue that these laws and practices are antithetical to the Qur'anic view of freedom of expression and religious liberty.

This chapter analyses the disconnect between the ground realities, the more forgiving outlook of the *Qur'an* and the more sophisticated and nuanced approach advocated by certain iterations of *fiqh*, some of which are contemporary but are rooted in historical practice or precedent.[5] The

---

[3] Angelina Theodorou, 'Which Countries Still Outlaw Apostasy and Blasphemy', *Factank, News in the Numbers* (29 May 2014), www.pewresearch.org/fact-tank/2016/07/29/which-countries-still-outlaw-apostasy-and-blasphemy. The focus of this article is on blasphemy as offensive and not at inciting hatred.

[4] Hashim, *supra* n1.

[5] Shari'ah and Islamic law will be used throughout the paper though the two do not have the same meaning. Some writers inaccurately use them interchangeably. There is also confusion and conflation of the terms Shari'ah and *fiqh*. Shari'ah encompasses the broad and overarching values, objectives, principles and methodologies while *fiqh* is used to refer to the body of derivative rules formulated by jurists. *Fiqh* and Islamic law may be closer in terms of meaning but the two may also be different depending on context and use. See M. H. Kamali, 'Source, Nature and Objectives of Shari'ah' (1989) 33 *Islamic Q.* 211, 233. Islamic law is far broader and includes those rules and laws that have been derived using the sources and methodologies for deriving laws sanctioned by Islamic jurisprudence, as well as all the quasi-Islamic laws in existence in Muslim countries as a result of colonization and secularization. In other words, Islamic law encompasses *fiqh* (from pre-modern times to contemporary times) as well the state sanctioned derivatives. While Shari'ah 'includes legal norms, it goes beyond just legal injunctions and includes aspects of good behavior, aesthetics and also personal responsibility, derived from Islam's rich 1400 year old history'. See Sabith Khan, '5 Myths About Sharia Law', *Policy.Mic* (21 July

chapter argues that the *Qur'an*, and the thrust and spirit of prophetic teachings, supports the protection of human dignity by, *inter alia*, guaranteeing the right to freedom of expression and religious liberty. This chapter also argues that this tolerant outlook was narrowed over the course of history through the imposition of limitations to address particular political and social exigencies that were specific to the historical context. Part 1 provides an overview of the Pakistani blasphemy laws and their misuse, and a discussion of references to the *Qur'an* and prophetic practices and teachings. Part II explores the Malaysian context around the issue of apostasy and offers an Islamic critique. In Part III, the chapter provides some parting thoughts and recommendations to reconcile the ground realities with the broader Qur'anic vision. The chapter then concludes. In essence, this piece posits that, while the *Qur'an* protects these fundamental rights, most iterations of *fiqh* and societal practices over time restricted the scope of these freedoms in the interest of advancing certain immediate policy objectives.[6] These decontextualized rulings are now being relied upon and used by various factions and stakeholders to advance their own goals and ostensibly to respond to what is perceived as a global attack on Muslims, Islam and its symbols.

I. BLASPHEMY LAWS – THE PAKISTANI LANDSCAPE

> Whoever by words, either spoken or written, or by visible representation or by any imputation, innuendo, or insinuation, directly or indirectly, defiles the sacred name of the Holy Prophet Muhammad (peace be upon him) shall be punished with death, or imprisonment for life, and shall also be liable to fine.
>
> Pakistan Criminal Code Article 295-C

Restrictive laws and extreme penalties, which as applied today are contrary to current human rights norms, are on the books in far too many Muslim nations when it comes to a number of offences, including

---

2013), www.policymic.com/articles/55727/5-myths-about-sharia-law. For a detailed discussion of Islamic law and the distinction between Shari'ah and *fiqh*, see Part 5 of Faisal Kutty, 'The Myth and Reality of 'Shari'a Courts' in Canada: A Delayed Opportunity for the Indigenization of Islamic Legal Rulings' (2010) 7 *U. St. Thomas L.J.* 559 [hereinafter Kutty, 'Myth and Reality'].

[6] Abdullahi Ahmed An-Na'im, 'Towards an Islamic Reformation: Civil Liberties' (1990) *Human Rights and International Law* 38.

blasphemy.[7] Of all Muslim nations, the Pakistani blasphemy laws have attracted the most attention both within the country and outside. Titled *Of Offences Relating to Religion*, Chapter XV of the Pakistan Penal Code provides the basis for much of the abuse and religious persecution taking place in the country. The provisions are a legacy of colonial rule.[8] Indeed, the existing blasphemy laws date back to 1860 British laws against insulting religion.[9] These laws were 'inherited' by Pakistan in the 1947 partition.[10] Though arguably blasphemy laws were originally conceived to uphold religious orthodoxy, modern formulations shifted the focus to 'preventing offence to religious believers and sympathizers and to maintaining public order'.[11]

It can be argued, given its secular orientation, that the British drafted Indian Penal Code had the goal of maintaining law and order and social

---

7 The Freethought Report, issued in 2013 by the International Humanist and Ethical Union (IHEU) found that 13 nations in the world (all Muslim) impose death for apostasy and blasphemy. See 'Malaysia Among Nations with Harshest Apostasy Laws, Study Shows', *Malaymail Online* (10 December 2013, 8:50 AM), www.themalaymailonline.com/features/article/atheists-face-death-in-13-countries-global-discrimination-says-study.

8 In fact, this is borne out by the fact that the laws in India are similar to the laws in Pakistan, including the section numbers. See Narendra Nayak, 'India's Blasphemy Law: Section 295A of IPC', *cārvaka 4 india* (6 May 2012), www.carvaka4india.com/2012/05/indias-blasphemy-law-section-295a-of.html. This colonial link is evident from the fact the language and even the relevant section number is the same.

9 Launching of Report *Blasphemy Laws in Pakistan: Historical Overview*, Ctr. for Research & Security Studies (7 September 2012), http://crss.pk/story/3349/launching-of-report-blasphemy-laws-in-pakistan-historical-overview/ [here inafter *Blasphemy Laws in Pakistan*]. The full report can be downloaded from http://crss.pk/reports/research-reports.

10 Id; Martin Lau, 'Sharia and National Law in Pakistan', in Jan Michiel Otto (ed.) *Sharia Incorporated: A Comparative Overview of the Legal Systems of Twelve Muslim Countries in Past and Present*, 376 (Leiden University Press 2010). The most controversial provisions are contained in Articles 295–8 under the heading *Of Offences Relating to Religion*, Pakistan Penal Code (Act XLV of 1860) Act XLV of 1860, 6 October 1860, as amended from time to time, available at www.fmu.gov.pk/docs/laws/Pakistan%20Penal%20Code.pdf, with one of the most abused provision being Article 295-C.

11 Ian Leigh, 'Damned if They Do, Damned if They Don't: The European Court of Human Rights and the Protection of Religion from Attack' (2011) 17 *Res Publica* 55, 58.

cohesion.[12] The need for such legislation was obvious given the multi-religious and religiously sensitive nature of Indian society. Indeed, this focus on maintenance of public order (at least in the context of religious insults) may partly explain the minimal use of the laws in the days immediately before and after partition. In fact, according to the Center for Research and Security Studies (CRSS), an independent think tank based in Islamabad, 'when the British ruled this region and the hatred between the Muslims and Hindus was at its peak, there were only seven blasphemy-related incidents' from 1851 to 1947, while from 1953 to July 2012, there were 434.[13]

A number of factors may have impacted on the increase in prosecution under the blasphemy provisions after partition. Two possible significant considerations may be: (1) the shift in purpose of such legislation from preserving public order to upholding religious orthodoxy or purity of Islam; and (2) changing political landscape as a result of increasing clout of Islamic oriented parties.[14] Both of these are evident from General Muhammad Zia-ul-Haq's expansion of blasphemy laws between 1977 and 1988 in his attempts to establish his piety and win support from orthodox parties and the masses.[15] In his quest to woo the conservative Islamic segments, General Zia enacted a number of martial law legal amendments adding or amending five new provisions (295-B, 295-C,

---

[12] Osama Siddique and Zahra Hayat, 'Unholy Speech and Holy Laws: Blasphemy Laws in Pakistan – Controversial Origins, Design Defects and Free Speech Implications' (2008) 17 *Minn. J. Int'l L.* 303, 337.

[13] *Blasphemy Laws in Pakistan*, *supra* n9.

[14] Javaid Rehman and Stephanie Berry, 'Is "Defamation of Religions" Passé? The United Nations, Organisation of Islamic Cooperation, and Islamic State Practices: Lessons from Pakistan' (2012) 44 *Geo. Wash. Int'l L. Rev.* 431–72; Siddique and Hayat, *supra* n12.

[15] General Zia recognized from the very beginning that appeals to Islamic symbols and idioms were powerful political tools. See Omar Noman, *The Political Economy of Pakistan 1947–85*, 150–56 (Kegan Paul Int'l. 1990); Mohammad Waseem, *Politics and the State in Pakistan* 349–420 (1st ed., Progressive Publishers 1989). Indeed, the masses always insist on harsh penal legislative changes as a sign of orthodoxy and commitment to the faith. Moreover, there is a growing consensus among scholars that appeal to Islam was a popular legitimacy-gaining strategy. See Charles H. Kennedy, 'Islamization and Legal Reform in Pakistan, 1979–1989' (1990) 63 *Pac. Aff.* 62, 72 (arguing that Zia's Islamization programme was partly designed to provide an Islamic justification for his regime); Ann Elizabeth Mayer, 'Islam and the State' (1991) 12 *Cardozo L. Rev.* 1015, 1042–47.

298-A, 298-B and 298-C) to the existing legislation.[16] These provisions collectively make up what are known as the blasphemy laws, although the latter three provisions appear to specifically target the minority Ahmadiyya community.[17]

According to Osama Siddique and Zahra Hayat, in addition to creating procedural inadequacies, General Zia's changes to the inherited laws involved eliminating 'any requirement of intent, deliberate or malicious', from various sections despite the fact that proof of intention on the part of the accused to 'insult[] the religion of any class of persons' was a prerequisite to the application of the blasphemy sections.[18] Indeed, as Siddique and Hayat sum up nicely:

> A new brand of Islamic obscurantism and, to many, a facile, opportunistic use of religion to legitimize realpolitik, brought about the introduction of flawed and highly controversial personal morality and blasphemy laws, the empowerment of courts to declare any law un-Islamic, and the concurrent curtailment of courts' jurisdiction in matters concerning fundamental rights and civil liberties. These steps caused jurisdictional and doctrinal confusions in many areas of law.[19]

The change in focus from a general law to maintain social and religious order to one privileging Islam and maintaining religious purity (whatever that may mean) created a multitude of other issues. Indeed, as Dimitria Petrova articulated: '[L]aws prohibiting the defamation of religions could easily be turned into a licence for the authorities to persecute not only religious dissent but also any opposition to the regime by bringing to trail not actions but ideas.'[20]

The abuse of blasphemy laws in Pakistan gives credence to this assertion. Pakistan has witnessed a proliferation of death, destruction, mayhem and abuse arising from these blasphemy laws over the years.[21]

---

[16] Siddique and Hayat, *supra* n12, at 337. For the wording of each of the provisions, see http://crss.pk/reports/research-reports at 22–23.

[17] The Ahmadiyya are a persecuted minority community in Pakistan who are considered deviant and non-Muslim by the majority of Sunni and Shia communities. It is beyond the scope of this chapter to delve into this in greater detail though they have borne the brunt of the blasphemy persecution and prosecutions.

[18] Siddique and Hayat, *supra* n12, at 340.

[19] For a thorough discussion and critique of Pakistani blasphemy laws, please see Siddique and Hayat, *supra* n12.

[20] Dimitrina Petrova, 'Smoke and Mirrors: The Durban Review Conference and Human Rights Politics at the United Nations' (2010) 10 *Hum. Rts. L. Rev.* 129, 133–4.

[21] Kutty, *Blasphemy Laws*, *supra* n1.

There appears to be a direct correlation with drives to 'Islamize' and return to orthodoxy. According to the 2013 CRSS report, in contrast to the seven cases from 1851 to 1947, during General Zia's rule from 1977 to 1988, 80 such cases were filed.[22] Consistent with the return to orthodoxy thesis, the numbers grew to a phenomenal 247 from 1987 to 2012.[23]

The Human Rights Commission of Pakistan reports that 34 people were charged with blasphemy in 2013, while 27 were charged in 2012. Nineteen people are now on death row for blasphemy, while another 20 are serving life sentences.[24] Moreover, dozens have died as a result of riots, extra-judicial killings and mob 'justice'. The CRSS, for instance, documents more than 52 people killed extra-judicially since 1990 while awaiting trial for the charge.[25]

The list of victims not only includes alleged blasphemers, but their supporters, journalists, lawyers representing accused, and even politicians calling for amendments to the law.[26] That last category includes former Punjab Governor Salman Taseer[27] and former Federal Minister Shahbaz Bhatti,[28] who were both killed for their opposition to blasphemy laws. In 2014 alone this has resulted in two accused blasphemers murdered by vigilantes, and three Christians – a couple and another unrelated man – being sentenced to death and fined.[29] A paralysed church school worker, Shafqat Masih, and his wife, Shagufta, were also sentenced for sending text messages against the Holy Prophet,[30] while Sawan Masih, a road sweeper from Lahore, was condemned to death after a friend accused him of making blasphemous remarks during an argument.[31] Human rights activists are counting on a *de facto* death penalty moratorium in

---

22 *Blasphemy Laws in Pakistan*, *supra* n9.

23 Id.

24 Kutty, *Blasphemy Laws*, *supra* n1.

25 Id.; Nasir Habib, 'Dozens of Christian Homes Set on Fire by Muslim Mob, Pakistani Authorities Say', *CNN* (9 March 2013), www.cnn.com/2013/03/09/world/asia/pakisan-unrest.

26 Hashim, *supra* n1.

27 'Pakistan's Punjab Governor Killed', *Al Jazeera* (4 January 2011, 12:25), www.aljazeera.com/news/asia/2011/01/201114115730846269.html.

28 'Pakistan Minorities Leader Killed', *Al Jazeera* (2 March 2011, 7:56), www.aljazeera.com/news/asia/2011/03/20113271659294319.html.

29 Kutty, *supra* n1.

30 Id.

31 Id.

place since 2008 to keep them from the hangman's noose,[32] though Prime Minister Nawaz Sharif has attempted to lift the moratorium. 'This is a travesty of justice,' said David Griffiths, Amnesty International's Deputy Asia Pacific Director, commenting on the Masih case.[33] Indeed, these cases are not only travesties of justice but also make a mockery of Islam.

Blasphemy, most accurately defined with reference to Christian teachings as making a mockery of God, has no exact equivalent in Islamic tradition, though a number of terms come quite close. Aslam Abdullah and others have argued: 'The idea of blasphemy is foreign to Islam. It was justified by many medieval Muslim scholars on the basis of their understanding of Christian and Jewish texts supporting laws against those who blaspheme and vilify their religions.'[34] Indeed, the *Qur'an* and many teachings of the Prophet characterized irreverence to God and religious symbols as hatred, provocation and acts of ignorance.[35] The closest Qur'anic phrase to blasphemy would be *Kalimat-al-kufr* ('word of disbelief').[36] The most common Arabic verbs for blasphemy are *sabba* (to abuse, insult) and *shatama* (to abuse, vilify), with the subject being God, Prophet Muhammad, or any part of divine revelation.[37] The concept evolved to become associated with denying the truth, insulting the divine and even inventing falsehoods.[38] *Shatama* does not occur in the *Qur'an*, and *sabba* appears only as part of a commandment to Muslims not to insult the idols of polytheists (Q6.108): 'Do not abuse those to whom

---

[32] Waqar Gillani and Salman Masood, 'Pakistani Gets Death Penalty for Blasphemy', *New York Times* (27 March 2014), www.nytimes.com/2014/03/28/world/asia/pakistani-gets-death-penalty-for-blasphemy.html?_r=0.

[33] 'Pakistan: Christian Man Sentenced to Death under Blasphemy Law', *Amnesty Int'l* (27 March 2014), www.amnesty.org/en/news/pakistan-christian-man-sentenced-death-under-blasphemy-law-2014-03-27.

[34] Aslam Abdullah, 'Apostasy – A Crime or an Exercise in Free Will', *IslamiCity* (22 December 2011), www.islamicity.com/articles/articles.asp?ref=IC1112-4959&p=2.

[35] Id.

[36] Carl W. Ernst, 'Blasphemy: Islamic Concept', in Lindsay Jones (ed.) *Encyclopedia of Religion*, 974–7 (2nd ed., Vol. 2. Detroit: Macmillan Reference USA 2005), www.unc.edu/~cernst/pdf/BLASPHEMY.pdf.

[37] Abdullah Saeed and Hassan Saeed, *Freedom of Religion, Apostasy, and Islam* (2004); Lutz Wiederhold, 'Blasphemy Against the Prophet Muhammad and his Companions (*sabb al-rasūl, sabb al saḥābah*): The introduction of the topic into *Shāfi'ī* legal literature and its relevance for legal practice under Mamluk rule' (1997) 42:1 *Journal of Semitic Studies* 39–70.

[38] Id.

they pray, apart from God, or they will abuse God in revenge without knowledge.' Additional teachings around this issue revolve around *takdhīb* (giving the lie, denial), and *iftirā'* (invention).[39] All of this suggests that in theological terms, this concept of blasphemy overlapped with the deliberate rejection of God and his revelation through his messengers (*kufr*), the idea of heresy (*zandaqah*), and irreverence and insulting language to God, his messengers and religious symbols.[40]

The *Qur'an, seerah* (biographies of the Prophet) and *hadith* (reports of the teachings, sayings and tacit approvals and disapprovals of the Prophet) literature are replete with verses and stories describing blasphemous utterances by hypocrites and disbelievers against the Prophet. Indeed, the *Qur'an* even points out that all of God's messengers were mocked:

> Then We sent Our messengers in succession. Every time there came to a nation its messenger, they denied him, so We made them follow one another [to destruction], and We made them narrations. So away with a people who do not believe.[41]

> How regretful for the servants. There did not come to them any messenger except that they used to ridicule him.[42]

According to the *Qur'an*, blasphemous speech was even uttered against Jesus and his mother Mary, who was called unchaste.[43] Prophet Muhammad himself was repeatedly mocked by the unbelievers. The *Qur'an* points out that his opponents claimed he was a madman,[44] and that 'in him is madness'.[45] Indeed, many of the disbelievers claimed that he was

---

39 Id.

40 See Ernst, *supra* n36.

41 *Quran* 23: 44.

42 *Quran* 36: 30.

43 'And [We cursed them] for their disbelief and their saying against Mary a great slander.' *Quran* 4: 156.

44 'And they say, "O you upon whom the message has been sent down, indeed you are mad."' *Quran* 15: 6.

45 'Or do they say, "In him is madness?" Rather, he brought them the truth, but most of them, to the truth, are averse.' *Quran* 23: 70.

merely a magician[46] and treated him as a liar. Furthermore, he was labelled a fabricator by the disbelievers.[47]

The attacks and insults did not stop with the messengers but extended to the *Qur'an* itself, which was called a book of 'Legends of the former peoples'.[48]

Yet despite the fact that the *Qur'an* confirms that all prophets have been subject to attacks by others, there is no unequivocal evidence that any of the offenders were ever ordered to be punished. Early Islam is replete with stories about insults to the Prophet, God, and Islamic symbols, with the rare instances of any worldly punishment.[49] This view is reinforced and consistent with the Qur'anic teachings. The *Qur'an* not only documents instances of insult, ridicule and attacks on Islamic icons and personages, but appears to provide guidance on how one should behave when faced with such conduct. Instead of mandating any physical worldly punishment, believers are directed to leave their company:

> And it has already come down to you in the Book that when you hear the verses of Allah [recited], they are denied [by them] and ridiculed; so do not sit with them until they enter into another conversation. Indeed, you would then be like them. Indeed Allah will gather the hypocrites and disbelievers in Hell all together.[50]

> Indeed, those who abuse Allah and His Messenger – Allah has cursed them in this world and the Hereafter and prepared for them a humiliating punishment. And those who harm believing men and believing women for [something] other than what they have earned have certainly born upon themselves a slander and manifest sin.[51]

A literal reading of this verse suggests that the 'humiliating punishment' for blaspheming God and his Messenger rests with God alone, and it is up to him whether he punishes such persons in this world or in the

---

46 'We are most knowing of how they listen to it when they listen to you and [of] when they are in private conversation, when the wrongdoers say, "You follow not but a man affected by magic."' *Quran* 17: 47.

47 'And when We substitute a verse in place of a verse – and Allah is most knowing of what He sends down – they say, "You, [O Muhammad], are but an inventor [of lies]." But most of them do not know.' *Quran* 16: 101.

48 'And when it is said to them, "What has your Lord sent down?" They say, "Legends of the former peoples."' *Quran* 16: 24.

49 Even these instances are subject to possible different interpretations as to the reason for the death punishment. See our discussion below on Ka'b bin Al-Ashraf.

50 *Quran* 4: 140.

51 *Quran* 33: 57–58.

hereafter. Moreover, despite the ill-treatment, disrespect and sometimes even physical interference with his person and Islamic symbols, God instructed the Prophet not to retaliate, because, says God: 'Indeed, We are sufficient for you against the mockers.'[52] In other words, God himself is sufficient to deal with those who commit blasphemy against him, the Prophet and religious icons. This view is reinforced when the Prophet is counselled by God: 'And do not obey the disbelievers and the hypocrites but do not harm them, and rely upon Allah. And sufficient is Allah as Disposer of affairs.'[53] These verses appear to foreclose any worldly physical punishment in this regard. Yet such conduct is clearly a sin and punishable by God in the next, and possibly even in this, world, but there is no directive to human beings to carry out any punishment. There is certainly no clear instruction to put someone to death.

So on what authority do iterations of Islamic law – and many Muslim nations – impose such stringent penalties for insults to Islam, its icons and personages?

The answer lies in the fact that Islamic law is derived not only from the *Qur'an* but also from the *sunnah* (prophetic practices), as well as the secondary sources and methodology of Islamic jurisprudence.[54] Traditionally jurists mined the *seerah* and examine *hadith* literature to deduce prophetic practices.

An incident from the Prophet's life, to which many point as supporting the death penalty for blasphemy, involves the assassination of a poet.[55] Ka'b ibn al-Ashraf was a Jewish Medinan poet from the Tayy tribe.[56]

---

[52] *Quran* 15: 95.

[53] *Quran* 33: 48.

[54] For a detailed explication of the sources and methodology of Islamic jurisprudence see Part 5 of Kutty, 'Myth and Reality', *supra* n5. See also Faisal Kutty, *The Kutty 'Islamic Law' Flowchart* (24 September 2014). Available at SSRN: https://ssrn.com/abstract=2501095 or http://dx.doi.org/10.2139/ssrn.2501095.

[55] Ctr. For Muslim-Jewish Engagement, Translation of Sahih Bukhari (M. Muhsin Khan trans.), *available at* www.usc.edu/org/cmje/religious-texts/hadith/bukhari (last visited 22 September 2014) [hereinafter Translation of Sahih Bukhari]. Assuming one accepts the reliability and authenticity of the report. See Kutty, 'Myth and Reality', *supra* n5, for a detailed elaboration of *hadith* evaluation.

[56] Norman Stillman, *The Jews of Arab Lands: A History and Source Book* 13 (Philadelphia: Jewish Publication Society of America 1979); Montgomery Watt, *Ka'b ibn al-Ashraf*, in P.J. Bearman, Th. Bianquis, C.E. Bosworth, E. van Donzel and W.P. Heinrichs (eds) *Encyclopaedia of Islam Online* (Brill Academic Publishers (ISSN 1573-3912) 2000).

According to a report appearing in the collection of *hadith* by Sahih al-Bukhari, he wrote poems satirizing Muhammad, defaming and scandalizing Muslim women with obscene songs, and eulogizing Quraish (the enemies of Islam). Ka'b was also reportedly upset with the Muslim victory in the Battle of Badr, in March 624, and at the executions of a number of Meccan notables of the Quraish tribe who had been captured after that battle.[57] Ibn Hashim records Ka'b as saying that 'if Muhammad has indeed struck down those people, then it were better to be buried in the earth than to walk upon it!'.[58]

Ka'b even travelled to Mecca to provoke the Quraish and instigate them to take up arms to regain lost honour. The *Seerah* records the Prophet as stating: 'He (Ka'b) has openly assumed enmity to us and speaks evil of us and he has gone over to the polytheists (whom the Muslims were at war with) and has made them gather against us for fighting.'[59] Some sources also suggest that during this visit to Mecca, Ka'b concluded a treaty with Abu Sufyan, stipulating cooperation between the Quraish and Jews against the Muslims.[60]

The Prophet was reportedly infuriated and gathered his men and asked if any were prepared to carry out an assassination: 'Who will kill Ka'b bin Al-Ashraf? He had maligned Allah, and His Messenger.' Muhammad ibn Maslamah said: 'O Messenger of Allah, do you wish that I should kill him?' The Prophet responded: 'Yes.' Maslamah then retorted: 'Permit me to talk (to him in the way I deem fit).' The Prophet replied: 'Talk (as you like).'[61]

Ka'b was later assassinated by a group that included Muhammad ibn Maslamah, 'Abbad bin Bishr, Al-Harith bin Aws, Abu 'Abs bin Hibr and Salkan bin Salamah, Ka'b's foster brother.[62] On the surface, this appears to justify the death penalty for speaking against the Prophet and God. However, upon closer examination of the historical, political and social context surrounding the incident, this explanation does not stand up to scrutiny. Blasphemy implies a religious offence. It is quite evident from the facts that Ka'b's opposition to Muhammad was not exclusively or even primarily religious in nature. There were numerous other factors and

---

57 Watt, *supra* n56.

58 Ibn Hisham, *Al-Sira al-Nabawiyya* (The Life of The Prophet). English translation in Stillman, *supra* n56, at 124.

59 Id.

60 Uri Rubin, *The Assassination of Kaʿb b. al-Ashraf*, 32 Oriens, 65–71 (1990).

61 Translation of Sahih Bukhari, *supra* n55.

62 Id.

considerations that may have played into settling on assassination as the solution. Indeed, it is only natural to assume that the political and social dimensions also influenced the Prophet's decision. Ka'b was an ardent political opponent of the Muslim community of Medina and had even attempted to assassinate the Prophet. The treacherous speech and conduct clearly makes him an enemy of the state and not just a religious critic.

The social and cultural context of the insult to Muslim women also needs to be considered. In fact, Norman Stillman, a scholar on the intersection of Jewish and Islamic culture and history, suggests that we cannot discount the fact that the Prophet may also have been acting in accordance with the norms of the Arab society of that period that demanded retaliation for a slight to a group's honour.[63]

Other accounts that may be relied upon to justify the death penalty in the *sunnah* would be a number of other prophetic sayings (*ahadith*). There are various accounts from the prophetic tradition that appear to justify death for those who insult the Prophet and certain religious icons.[64] Though, as noted earlier, two caveats are in order: (1) the authenticity and reliability of these reports would need to be considered and weighed; and (2) there may be more than one interpretation of the report possible as we highlighted with the discussion on the Ka'b bin Al-Ashraf incident.

These reports became the legal justification for the death penalty for both apostasy and blasphemy in traditional Islamic law. Jurists built on these reports to develop and elaborate the conditions and nature of a new crime of blasphemy in the loose sense of the word. Speaking against the Prophet had become regarded as an intolerable act within the Muslim empire by the third Islamic century. In fact, certain interpretations of Islamic Law even take a more severe view towards reviling the Prophet than they do towards reviling God, ostensibly because the Prophet is no longer in a position to avenge the abuse.[65] By the beginning of the fourth Islamic century, a consensus had developed among the scholars that the one who insults the Prophet of Islam must be put to death.[66]

---

63 Stillman, *supra* n56, at 13.

64 For a compilation of reports and stories relied upon to institute serious punishment for blasphemy, see www.khilaafah.com/Articles/07/sep/REVELATION %20FOR%20BELIEVERS.html.

65 Liyakat Takim, Blasphemy 3, www.ltakim.com/articles/Blasphemy.pdf.

66 *Id.* See also Fierro Marie Isabel, 'Andalusian "Fatawa" on Blasphemy', in *Annales Islamologiques* (1990); 'Abd al-Rahman al-Jaziri, Min Kitab al-Fiqh 'ala Madhahib al-Arba'ah (n.d.); 'Abd Allah b. Wahb al-Muranyi, Kitab al-Muwatta (1992). Abu Muhammad 'Abd Allah b. Ahmad b. Muhammad Ibn Qudama,

Two points are worth noting here. First, in addition to the primary sources (*Qur'an* and *sunnah*) discussed above, the secondary sources (*ijma*, *qiyas* and *ijtihad* tempered and influenced by other legal maxims and principles) of Islamic jurisprudence also factor into the evolutions and formulation of Islamic law. Given this central role of interpretation, inevitably the various schools of Islamic jurisprudence (be they *Sunni* or *Shi'a*) would have differences in terms of definitions, nature and punishments for blasphemy, much like they have on every other issue. Moreover, it also opens up the possibility that differences can be exaggerated and abused, as Liaqat Takim notes:

> Given that the exact definition of the terms that denoted blasphemy are not specified in the Qur'an and sunna, sectarian and doctrinal disputes among early Muslims provided subsequent jurists and theologians the opportunity to explore the implications of blasphemy even further. Jurists, scholars and ordinary Muslims who claimed that their own position on Islam was normative, began to characterize dissenting Muslims as apostates, blasphemers, hypocrites, or unbelievers. Thus, a charge of blasphemy and apostasy was often used to impose or refute certain doctrines or theological positions.[67]

The second major point to note for our purposes is that Islamic legal scholarship and debate on the question of blasphemy (whether against the Prophet, his companions, God, or religious symbols and icons) increasingly had to rely on the concept of apostasy (*riddah*) and unbelief (*kufr*), and active opposition or threat to the Muslim community, because the primary source, the *Qur'an*, was not very instructive, particularly when it came to worldly punishment for mere disbelief or insult. In fact, for instance, the Hanafi school defined blasphemy as an act of infidelity (*kufr*) while the Malikis treated it as apostasy. Indeed, there is diversity and tension on this issue between and even within all four major *Sunni* schools and the *Shi'a* schools.[68]

While the *Qur'an* was silent on worldly punishment for both apostasy and blasphemy, the *sunnah* projected mixed messages and the consensus of juristic opinion began to move towards backing the death penalty for both those who commit apostasy and those who commit blasphemy, with varying definitions, conditions and justifications. Clearly, apostasy and blasphemy are not the same, though many jurists confused and conflated

---

al-Mughni (Riyadh: Maktabat al-Riyad al-Hadithah, n.d.); and Muhammad b. Ahmad al-Sarakhshi, Kitab al-Mabsut vol. 10, (Beirut: Dar al-Ma'rifah, n.d.).

67 Id. at 5.

68 Id.

them. Blasphemy usually implies publicly insulting religion, while apostasy can take the form of a purely private renunciation of religion, in which case it would not be blasphemy. However, a Muslim who blasphemes in public may be legally deemed an apostate, and so the one offence can morph into the graver offence of apostasy. Much of the juristic discussion took this for granted and the foundations were laid to perpetuate this confusion.

In fact as we noted at the outset, even the terminology of blasphemy itself was not uniformly accepted by classical jurists, and this is evident from the Islamic legal discourse. As Intisar Rabb explains, with the exception of Hanafi jurists who expanded the Islamic doctrine of defamation to a new crime of blasphemy, jurists from the three other *Sunni* schools and the leading *Shi'a* school 'usually declined to hold even intentional jabs at the Prophet or his family to be criminally blasphemous, unless they constituted explicit denials of faith of the type outlined in the apostasy laws that meant departure from the laws and war against the community'.[69]

Ironically, during the medieval Islamic period, proving blasphemy required meeting the high evidentiary standards of the rest of Islamic criminal law. As Rabb notes:

> ... the elements required to declare speech to be blasphemy ... meant dealing with an internally coherent system of laws and folded in cultural, temporal, and jurisdictional standards of propriety and treasonous intent. The implication is that, for most jurists, the blasphemy laws formulated in classical Islamic legal writings could apply only to a Muslim society of earlier times and particular places of shared moral norms according to a narrow set of justifications.[70]

The evident disconnect between the Qur'anic message of tolerance and reservation of punishment to God and the juristic extrapolations and deviations from this has enabled contemporary jurists and scholars to question the classical positions on blasphemy. As Aslam Abdullah writes: 'It is time that Muslim scholars from all over the world revisit issues such as blasphemy and apostasy in the light of the *Qur'an* and *sunna*

---

[69] Intisar A. Rabb, 'Negotiating Speech in Islamic Law and Politics: Flipped Traditions of Expression', in M. Emon, Mark S. Ellis and Benjamin Glahn (eds) *Islamic Law and International Human Rights Law: Searching for a Common Ground?* 144, 158–61 (Anver 2012).

[70] Id. at 162–3.

rather than falling victim to positions that cannot be substantiated by the divine writ.'[71]

Indeed there is now a growing chorus of scholars arguing against the death penalty for blasphemy and apostasy. 'These blasphemy laws have no justification in Islam. These ulema [council of clerics] are just telling lies to the people,' argues Javed Ahmad Ghamidi, a Pakistani scholar and popular television preacher who had to flee the country for his own safety for his views on this issue.[72] A former leader of the Jamat-e-Islami Islamic party, Ghamidi, said that it has no foundation in either the *Qur'an* or the *Hadith* – the sayings of the Prophet Muhammad. 'Nothing in Islam supports this law,' he told a newspaper.[73]

This position is echoed by Indian-based scholar Maulana Wahiduddin Khan[74] and prominent Islamic legal scholar Mohamed Hashim Kamali, among others.[75] Kamali, as we discuss below, notes that there is an assumption that one who blasphemes the essentials of Islam also becomes an apostate. 'The offence of blasphemy is therefore subsumed under apostasy,' he explains.[76] However, he points out that there is no Qur'anic injunction or *hadith* that says that blasphemy is subsumed by the offence of apostasy, but jurists made the extrapolations based on their social, political and historical considerations.

With an appreciation of the involvement of human agency in determining the divine will on this question and the significance of the relationship between blasphemy, apostasy and disbelief in the minds of many pre-modern or classical jurists, we can move on to a discussion of

---

71 Abdullah, *supra* n34.

72 Declan Walsh, 'Salmaan Taseer: Islamic Scholar Attacks Pakistan's Blasphemy Laws', *The Guardian* (20 January 2011, 11:43 EST), www.theguardian.com/world/2011/jan/20/islam-ghamidi-pakistan-blasphemy-laws. See also Jāvēd Ahmad Ghāmidī, Punishment for Blasphemy Against the Prophet, www.ghamidi.net/article/Punishment%20for%20Blasphemy.pdf.

73 Jāvēd Ahmad Ghāmidī, 'Punishment for Blasphemy Against the Prophet', www.ghamidi.net/article/Punishment%20for%20Blasphemy.pdf.

74 Maulana Wahiduddin Khan, 'Renowned Indian Islamic Scholar on Blasphemy: "At No Point in the Koran Is It Stated That Anyone Who Uses Abusive Language About the Prophet Should Be Stopped From Doing So … [or] Should Be Awarded Severe Punishment"', *The Middle E. Media Res. Inst.* (30 September 2012), www.memri.org/report/en/print6714.htm.

75 Mohammad Hashim Kamali, 'Freedom of Expression in Islam' (1994) [hereinafter Kamali, 'Freedom of Expression'].

76 Mohammad Hashim Kamali, 'We Need to Rethink Blasphemy Law: UK Scholar', *The Express Trib.* (5 February 2011), http://tribune.com.pk/story/114452/we-need-to-rethink-blasphemy-law-uk-scholar.

apostasy. The discussions below on apostasy and *hudud* are therefore also relevant to the issue of blasphemy in Islam.

II. APOSTASY – THE MALAYSIAN LANDSCAPE

The Federal Constitution of Malaysia declares Islam as the 'official religion' of the Federation.[77] While freedom of religion is constitutionally guaranteed, there are significant restrictions arising from general laws relating to public order, public health and morality.[78] Restrictions also result due to the primacy given to Islam, particularly in the context of blasphemy and apostasy. This is best illustrated by analysing the *Syariah Criminal Code (II) Kelantan Enactment* (known as the *Hudud Bill*), which has been on the backburner in Malaysia since the State Legislative Assembly of Kelantan enacted it in 1993.[79] It has attracted increased attention over the last few years. Many religious leaders and politicians have now instigated efforts to speed up the implementation of the law in the state, which, among other things, introduces the death penalty for apostasy (and blasphemy by implication).

The Federal Constitution divides legislative power between the Parliament and State legislatures.[80] Islam and Islamic law fall under state jurisdiction.[81] Without getting into the technicalities, this jurisdictional tension from the division of is one of the reasons that the *hudud* enactment has been stalled for so many years. However, as noted above, segments of Malaysian society are now calling for its implementation.[82] Section 23 of the *Hudud Bill* addresses apostasy and defines it as:

---

[77] Min Choon Lee, *Freedom of Religion in Malaysia* 133, Article 3(1) (Kairos Research Centre 1999).

[78] Abdullah Saeed and Hassan Saeed, *Freedom of Religion, Apostasy and Islam* 1st ed. (Routledge 2004).

[79] For an overview, see Syariah Criminal Code (II) Enactment 1993 (August 2014), www.krisispraxis.com/wp-content/uploads/2014/08/Syariah-Criminal-Code-Hudud-Bill-Kelantan-summary.pdf; for an Islamic critique see Mohammad Hashim Kamali, 'Punishment in Islamic Law: A Critique of the Hudud Bill of Kelantan, Malaysia' (1998) 13 *Arab L.Q.* 203, available at www.jstor.org/discover/10.2307/3382008?uid=2&uid=4&sid=21104199869931 [hereinafter Kamali, 'Punishment'].

[80] Id.

[81] Id. at 134. The dual system of law is provided in Article 121(1A) of the Constitution of Malaysia. Article 3 also provides that Islamic law is a state law matter with the exception for the Federal Territories of Malaysia.

[82] Letter from Sisters in Islam to The Honorable Prime Minister Datuk Seri Dr. Mahathir Mohamad (25 December 1993), available at www.sistersinislam.

> ... any act done or any word uttered by a Muslim who is *mukallaf*, being an act or word which according to *Syariah law*, affects or which is against the *aqidah* (belief) in Islamic religion, provided that such act is done or such word is uttered intentionally, voluntarily and knowingly without any compulsion by anyone or by circumstance.[83]

Anyone found guilty of apostasy is required to repent within a period of three days, failing which the court can pronounce the death sentence. The punishment for apostasy in the *Hudud Bill* raises the question whether the classification of apostasy (and blasphemy by implication) as a *hudud* offence punishable by death, is justified according to the foundational texts of Islam and modern Islamic scholarship.

Scholars have identified numerous problems with the *Hudud Bill*, but this chapter only addresses the two major criticisms touching upon the issues of apostasy and blasphemy. First, the *Hudud Bill* is problematic in that it neglects the view that apostasy may not be a *hudud* (prescribed) but a *ta'zir* (discretionary) offence. This is a body of opinion among the *ulema* that has existed ever since the early days of Islam, and it is founded on the fact that the death punishment for apostasy is not a Qur'anic mandate. Secondly, the punishment fails to differentiate between apostasy simpliciter, which is neither hostile nor contemptuous, and apostasy combined with treason (*hirabah*).

Consistent with the classical view, the *Hudud Bill* incorporates apostasy as one of the six *hudud* offences.[84] Several prominent modern Muslim thinkers, such as Mohammad Hashim Kamali and Salim el-Awa, have argued that apostasy should not be part of the *Hudud Bill* at all, as it is a *ta'zir* (discretionary) rather than a *hadd* (prescribed) offence. The word *hudud* is the plural of the Arabic word '*had*', which means prevention, restraint or prohibition.[85] It is a restrictive and preventative ordinance of Allah concerning things lawful (*halal*) and things unlawful (*haram*).[86] According to Abul A'la Maududi (d. 1979), the *hudud* consist

---

org.my/news.php?item.32.121. See 'ABIM Calls for Dr. Mahatir to Retract Statement on Hudud Law', *Astro Awani* (22 April 2014), http://english.astroawani.com/news/show/abim-calls-for-dr-mahathir-to-retract-statement-on-hudud-law-34439; 'Kelantan Deputy MB: No Need to Test the Waters with Hadud', *Malaymail Online* (23 April 2014 10:43 AM), www.themalaymailonline.com/malaysia/article/kelantan-deputy-mb-no-need-test-the-waters-with-hudud.

[83] Syariah Criminal Code (II) (Kelantan) Enactment § 48 (1993).

[84] Kamali, 'Punishment', *supra* n79, at 203.

[85] Id. at 214.

[86] Id.

of certain principles, checks and balances, and specific injunctions in different spheres of life, that have been prescribed in order that man may be trained to lead a balanced life.[87] These ordinances are intended to lay down the basic framework within which man is free to legislate, decide his own affairs and frame subsidiary regulations of his conduct.[88]

Over the course of Islamic history, a basic development occurred in Islamic *fiqh* with respect to *hudud* whereby the term *hadd* came to signify a fixed and unchangeable punishment.[89] For *hudud* offences, the penalty was thought to be explicitly prescribed, either in the *Qur'an* or *Hadith*, and therefore there was little room for interpretation.[90] Consequently, the foundational texts of Islam, the *Qur'an* and *sunna*, must be consulted to analyse the categorization of apostasy properly as a *hadd* offence.

As we noted above in the discussion on blasphemy, the *Qur'an* sets out basic principles, not detailed legislative prescriptions. In the *Qur'an*, apostasy (*al-riddah*) is often mentioned expressly and occasionally by import.[91] According to juristic consensus (*ijma*), it is not possible to derive the death penalty for apostasy from a study of the *Qur'an* alone.[92] In fact, a study of the relevant verses suggests that punishment is postponed to the Hereafter, in the same way as that for original disbelief.[93] There is absolutely no mention in the *Qur'an* of temporal punishment for defection from the faith, except in the form of deprivation of the spiritual benefits.[94] It is revealed, for example, that 'Surely those who disbelieve after their (profession of) belief and then increase in disbelief; their repentance will not be accepted. These are they who have gone astray.'[95] Commentators note that the words of this verse are inclusive of Muslims who renounce Islam and then, by insistence on their disbelief, intensify it.[96] Not only does this specific provision fail to

---

87 Id.

88 Saeed, *supra* n78, at 99.

89 Id.

90 Id. at 100.

91 Nurjaanah Abdullah, 'Legislating Faith in Malaysia' (2007) *Singapore J. Legal Stud.* 264, 265.

92 Id.

93 Sheikh Abdur Rahman, 'Punishment of Apostasy in Islam' (1972) *Institute of Islamic Culture* 13.

94 Id. at 16.

95 *Qur'an* 3:91.

96 *Rahman*, *supra* n93, at 37.

prescribe any temporal punishment for an apostate, it envisages a natural death in his condition of disbelief.[97]

Other verses in the *Qur'an* even contemplate repeated apostasies and reversions to the 'true' faith on the part of an individual:[98] 'Those who believe, then disbelieve, and then (again) believe, then disbelieve, and then increase in disbelief, Allah will never pardon them nor will He guide them the (right) way.'[99]

This is a striking pronouncement that is almost conclusive against the thesis that an apostate must be put to death after his defection from the faith. It lends support to the opinion that the act of apostasy is a sin and not a crime, for if an apostate had to be killed for his first defection, he could not possibly have a history of renouncements and reacceptance.[100]

There is strong basis to argue that in matters concerning the individual conscience, the *Qur'an* places no fetters on free choice.[101] The appeal of the *Qur'an* is to history, observation and reason, in support of its invitation to the path of faith and rectitude.[102] Even to those who deny the truth, the *Qur'an* issues a challenge to adduce evidence to sustain their assertions:[103] 'Say: Bring forth your proof, if you are truthful.'[104] This rational approach runs like a golden thread throughout the fabric of the Qur'anic teachings.[105] To compel allegiance by force runs counter to these directives and admonitions.[106]

The principle *hadith* advanced to support death for apostasy is narrated by Ibn' Abbas: 'Whosoever changes his religion, slay him.'[107] To this *hadith* reported as authentic in *Sahih-al-Bukhari* is annexed the story of Ali burning to death a number of heretics, and Ibn 'Abbas, on being informed of the incident, reportedly remarked that he would not have burnt them but merely killed them, for the Prophet had forbidden the

---

97 Id.
98 Id. at 38.
99 *Qur'an* 4:138.
100 *Rahman, supra* n93, at 16.
101 Id.
102 Id.
103 Id.
104 *Qur'an* 1:112.
105 *Rahman, supra* n93, at 16.
106 Id. at 14.
107 This version of the *hadith* is given by al-Bukhari in his *Sahih*: 'Kitab al-Jihadi fi Istitabat al-Murtaddin.' See generally, *Rahman, supra* n93, at 59.

burning of human beings.[108] Although classical jurists accepted the authenticity of this *hadith*, there are differences between them as to its meaning.[109] This difference is rooted in the fact that this *hadith* was a general (*'amm*) command that was in need of specification (*takhsis*).[110] According to the rules of interpretation, as expounded in *usul al-fiqh*, once a decisive (*qat'i*) has been specified in some respect, the part which remains unspecified becomes speculative (*zanni*) and, as such, becomes open to further interpretation and specification.[111]

Imam Shafi'i and Ibn Hazm are reported to have expressed the view that the words of the *hadith* being general, it would apply even to a disbeliever who changes his faith.[112] On the contrary, the majority of the *ulema*, including Imam Malik, held the opinion that it is confined to Muslims who become renegades from Islam.[113] In support of this opinion, it is pointed out that the logical result of the view held by Imam Shafi'i and Ibn Hazm would lead to the absurd proposition (from the perspective of Muslims) that even a disbeliever who adopts Islam ought to be killed for his change of faith. Consequently, this *hadith*, according to better opinion, cannot be interpreted in its literal sense because it would be susceptible to being used to prevent non-Muslims from embracing Islam.[114]

Considering the nature of the evidence emanating from the *Qur'an* and *hadith*, there is considerable difference of opinion among jurists as to whether the punishment for apostasy is prescribed (*hadd*) or discretionary (*ta'zir*).[115] Shafi'is and Zahiris believe there are seven types of crime for which there is a *hadd* punishment, one of which is apostasy (*riddah*).[116] On the other hand, a number of prominent *ulema*, across the centuries, have subscribed to the view that apostasy is not a *hadd* offence because *hudud* (prescribed) penalties cannot be established on the basis of a *Ahad* (solitary) *hadith*, like the one reported by Ibn Abbas.[117]

---

108 David A. Jordan, 'The Dark Ages of Islam: Ijtihad, Apostasy, and Human Rights in Contemporary Islamic Jurisprudence' (2003) 9 *Wash. & Lee Race & Ethnic Anc. L.J.* 51, 55.

109 Id.

110 Id.

111 Mohammad Hashim Kamali, 'Freedom of Religion in Islamic Law' (1992) 21 *Cap. U. L. Rev.* 63, 72 [hereinafter Kamali, 'Freedom of Religion'].

112 Saeed, *supra* n78, at 52.

113 Id.

114 Id. at 56.

115 Id.

116 Id.

117 Id.

Moreover, according to the renowned Hanafi jurist, Shams al-Din al-Sarakhsi, apostasy is not an offence for which there is a prescribed punishment, because the punishment for it is suspended when the apostate repents.[118] Penalties for *hudud* offences are generally not suspended because of repentance, especially when they are reported and become known to the head of state.[119] Al-Sarakhsi goes on to recount the punishments for all the *hudud* offences, but leaves apostasy out altogether from the list.[120]

The Maliki jurist, al-Baji (d. 494 A.H.), also observed that apostasy is a sin that carries no prescribed penalty (*hadd*), and that such a sin may be punished only under the discretionary punishment of *ta'zir*.[121] The renowned Hanbali jurist, Ibn Taymiyyah, also categorically agrees on this latter punishment for apostasy.[122]

By incorporating apostasy as a *hudud* offence, the *Hudud Bill* completely neglects the view that apostasy may not be a *hudud* (prescribed) but a *ta'zir* (discretionary) offence. In the case of apostasy therefore, the *Fuqaha* (jurists) acknowledge generally that no punishment is prescribed in the *Qur'an*.[123] Their principle evidence for the view that apostasy must be punished with death is on a *hadith* that was a general ('*amm*) command and that was in need of specification (*takhsis*).[124] Based upon an interpretation of these sources, a number of prominent *ulema*, across the centuries, have subscribed to the view that apostasy is not a *hadd* offence because *hudud* (prescribed) penalties cannot be established on the basis of *Ahad* (solitary) *hadith*.

Moreover, prominent scholars such as Al-Sarakhsi and Ibn Taymiyyah have subscribed to the view that apostasy is a sin that may only be punished under the discretionary punishment for *ta'zir*.[125] This conclusion finds further support in the *sunnah*, as neither the Prophet himself nor any of his Companions ever compelled anyone to embrace Islam or convicted anyone to death for mere renunciation of faith. In fact, the practice of the early leaders of Islam, particularly the Pious Caliphs, was

118 Kamali, 'Freedom of Expression', *supra* n75, at 6.
119 Id.
120 Id.
121 Id. at 8.
122 Id.
123 Abdullah, *supra* n91, at 265.
124 Kamali, 'Freedom of Religion', *supra* n111, at 72.
125 Id. at 71.

consistently guided by the Qur'anic norms that seek to protect the integrity of the individual conscience.[126]

Given the dearth of evidence supporting the punishment for apostasy in the *Qur'an* and the debateable position based on *Hadith*, the *Hudud Bill* can essentially be viewed as a product of undiluted imitation (*taqlid*). By categorizing apostasy as a *hudud* rather than a *ta'zir* offence, and thereby failing to make necessary adjustments to the pre-modern position on apostasy, the *Hudud Bill* poses an unnecessary impediment to the realization of religious freedom. The very philosophy of *ta'zir* is that the government is within its rights to introduce legislation that might seek to regulate the proper application of punishment, when and where necessary. By giving discretion to the sovereign with regard to the appropriate combination of deterrent and reformative measures, *ta'zir* facilitates the possibility of true religious freedom and tolerance.

The second major criticism of the *Hudud Bill*'s treatment of apostasy is that it fails to differentiate between apostasy simpliciter and apostasy combined with high treason (*hirabah*) or severance of allegiance to the state. Mohammad Hashim Kamali, for instance, argues that apostasy was a punishable offence in the early years of Islam 'due to its subversive effects on the nascent Muslim community of the state'.[127] The law of apostasy was developed at a time and in circumstances that differ radically from today. Arguably, apostasy in early Islamic history was closely associated with the security of the Muslim community. At the time, communities were organized strictly according to their religious affiliations. Moreover, inter-group relations were governed strictly by religious laws. People were divided into two major groups: believers who, by definition, supported Islam and were actively engaged in the faith (*dar-al-Islam*), and unbelievers who were at war with Muslims (*dar-al-harb*).[128] Anyone who became a Muslim joined the believers, and anyone who rejected Islam became hostile to it. According to Kamali, any tradition from the Prophet indicating that apostates should be killed needs to be understood within this broader political context.[129]

This broader political context was also considered by several prominent Muslim scholars in the twentieth century, including Abul A'la Maududi, Rashid Rida and Yusuf al-Qaradawi, and many of these scholars attempted to introduce limitations to the pre-modern position.

---

126 Id. at 70.

127 Mohammad Hashim Kamali, *Islamic Law in Malaysia: Issues and Developments* 219 (Kuala Lumpur: Ilmiah Publishers 2000).

128 Id.

129 Id.

The most obvious limitation introduced by these thinkers was that apostasy was punishable by death only where it was accompanied by treason, hostility towards the Muslim community or severance of allegiance to the state.[130] In fact, the Pakistani scholar Abul A'la Maududi (d. 1979), in his major work on the punishment of apostates, justifies the punishment of death on the grounds that the *Qur'an*, *hadith* and the *ulema* all regard apostasy as an act of high treason (*hirabah*).[131] For Maududi, belief in Islam is not simply a personal matter. Rather, it suggests membership in the social order implemented by the state. Thus, a change of faith is tantamount to treachery, making such a traitor an enemy of the state.[132] In this respect, Maududi argues, Islam prescribes capital punishment for apostasy just as many modern nation states consider high treason a major crime punishable by death.[133]

Maududi addresses the moral difficulty of executing the apostate for privately rejecting the religion of Islam for another by expanding the definition of religion. In doing so, he transforms the concept of religion by equating religion with the state. For Maududi, Islam is a complete ordering of life. As such, the organizing of society and the shape of government are all part of Islam. According to Maududi, an organized society that has chosen the form of a state can hardly provide a place within its sphere of activity for people who differ from it in fundamental matters, such as the foundations on which the order of the society and the state are established.[134]

It is true that Maududi's view of Islam as a state makes it difficult to accommodate the apostate within it. At the same time, however, Maududi appears to concede that when the state is not based on Islam, or where the act of apostasy cannot be equated with treason, the apostate should not necessarily be punished, for it is the rejection of a 'divine' socio-political order that amounts to high treason. Maududi, therefore, considers the historical context in which the punishment for apostasy was developed and his analysis is sharper than those who simply follow the rulings of pre-modern thinkers (*taqlid*) on apostasy in its entirety.

Rashid Rida makes a similar distinction between the apostate who abandons Islam privately and one who revolts against Islam or otherwise poses a danger to the *ummah*. According to Rida, the latter should be put to death, if captured, while the former should not. Rida's position is

---

130 Saeed, *supra* n78, at 91.
131 Id.
132 Id. at 92.
133 Id. at 93.
134 Id.

established on the grounds that the pre-modern *ijma'* (consensus) on the execution of the apostate is not based on a clear text of the *Qur'an*; therefore, it does not need to be binding, but may be persuasive given the existing facts.[135]

Yusuf al-Qaradawi, one of the most prominent neo-revivalist scholars, has similarly argued that apostasy is a crime punishable by death only where the apostate subsequently declares an open revolt against the state in such a manner that threatens the solidarity of the Muslim community.[136] However, the death penalty can be implemented only by the proper authorities after due process of law prescribed by Shari'ah.[137]

The *Hudud Bill* defines apostasy as 'any act done or any word uttered by a Muslim who is a *mukallaf*, being an act or word which according to *Syariah law*, affects or which is against the *aqidah* (belief) in Islamic religion'.[138] The *Hudud Bill* further provides that the acts or words that affect the *aqidah* must be such that concern 'the fundamental aspects of Islamic religion' and that are deemed to have been known and believed by every Muslim, pertaining to pillars of Islam (*Rukum Islam*), pillars of belief (*Rukum Iman*) and matters of *halal* or *haram*.[139]

The expressions used to define apostasy in the *Hudud Bill* are problematic insofar that they are too imprecise and broad to form the basis of definition.[140] In fact, the definition of apostasy in the *Hudud Bill* is confusing because it includes a variety of different concepts such as blasphemy, apostasy, disbelief (*kufr*) and heresy (*bid'ah*), all under the same definition.[141] There exists substantial overlap between these terms, which is rooted in the fact that the *Qur'an* and *Hadith* did not provide specific definitions for such terms.[142] Specific definitions for these terms were subsequently developed through the use of interpretation, including *ijtihad*. As a result, many Muslim scholars of the early period were naturally reluctant to declare other Muslims to be unbelievers and to

---

135 Albert Hourani, *Arabic Thought in the Liberal Age: 1798–1939*, 237 (Cambridge University Press 1983).

136 Yusuf al-Qaradawi, *The Lawful and the Prohibited in Islam* 78–9 (Al-Falah Foundation 1997).

137 Id. at 79.

138 Syariah Crim. Code (II) (Kelantan) Enactment (1993) § 23(1).

139 Id.

140 Kamali, 'Punishment', *supra* n84, at 214.

141 Id. at 215.

142 Id.

exclude them from the community on the basis of differences of opinion often based on *ijtihad* alone.[143]

The definition of apostasy in the *Hudud Bill* is also vague and imprecise, and does not differentiate between apostasy simpliciter and apostasy combined with high treason (*hirabah*). The sum total of this approach is that there is no difference, for the purpose of enforcing the death penalty under this bill, between a simple conversion that is neither contemptuous nor hostile and one that inflames the masses of Muslims and is capable of causing bloodshed and uncontrollable civil strife. In this regard, the *Hudud Bill* functions as a product of undiluted imitation (*taqlid*), adhering blindly to the pre-modern position on the punishment for apostasy. It relies on the *ijtihad* of pre-modern jurists, without giving adequate consideration to either the degree of authoritativeness of this pre-modern *ijtihad* or the changed conditions of the modern period.

The punishment for apostasy was developed at a time where the world was essentially divided into *dar-al-Islam* and *dar-al-harb*. In theory, *dar-al-harb* was permanently in conflict with *dar-al-Islam*;[144] during the early years of Islam, those who abandoned the faith often became hostile towards the fledgling Muslim community. Over time, however, these distinctive features of *dar-al-Islam* and *dar-al-harb* have changed radically.[145] Unlike the communities that existed during the advent and early expansion of Islam, modern nation states are not politically organized strictly on the basis of religion. Moreover, among Muslims, the centrality of Shari'ah to today's Muslims' State ranges from absolute to non-existent.[146] As such, it is considered acceptable for individuals to remain loyal citizens of the political unit regardless of their religious affiliation. In this context, pre-modern Islamic law on apostasy, premised upon the symbiosis of religious identity and political community, loses much of its meaning. Therefore, by failing to differentiate between apostasy simpliciter and apostasy combined with high treason (*hirabah*), the punishment for apostasy potentially conflicts not only with the foundational sources of Islam and modern Muslim scholarship, but also with the contemporary realities of Malaysian society and even international norms.

---

[143] Id. at 216.

[144] Shaheen Sardar Ali and Javaid Rehman, 'The Concept of Jihad in Islamic International Law' (2005) 10:3 *J. Conflict & Security L.* 321, 334.

[145] Id. at 337.

[146] Sherman A. Jackson, 'Shari'ah, Democracy, and the Modern Nation-State: Some Reflections on Islam, Popular Rule, and Pluralism' (2003) 27 *Fordham Int'l L.J.* 88.

III. THE WAY FORWARD

Despite the fact that there is irrefutable evidence to conclude that blasphemous speech and apostasy are sins, the undisputed primary and only infallible source (according to a majority of scholars) of Islamic theology, philosophy and laws, the *Qur'an*, mandates no worldly punishment for blasphemy or apostasy, and certainly not death. Yet our review of the ground realities in Pakistan and Malaysia in the respective context of blasphemy and apostasy reveal that there are serious tensions in these societies. The main conflict revolves around the Islamic legitimacy of existing laws or proposed laws (in the context of the *hudud* enactment in Malaysia). As societies aiming to be rooted in Islam, there is a groundswell of interest and support to ensure that laws are consistent with Shari'ah or the divine will. Indeed, surveys have documented widespread support for a return to Islam and Shari'ah. Although there is obvious agreement at this general level, differences undoubtedly emerge as one begins to define Shari'ah. *Fiqhi* differences and even theological differences ensure that these mean different things to different people.

As a number of scholars have argued, the apostasy laws in Malaysia and the blasphemy legislation in Pakistan are the 'product of undiluted imitation (*taqlid*) failing to acknowledge the contemporary realities' of modern society.[147] Blindly abiding by classical rulings on such issues does a disservice to Islam and Muslims. Moreover, they fail to take into consideration the universal and ethical vision imagined by the *Qur'an* bounded by the *maqasid al Shari'ah* (higher objectives of Shari'ah). As Shaikh Jamal Badawi noted in the context of apostasy: 'As religious opinions (fatwas) change with the changing time, place, custom, and circumstances, this issue should be reexamined within the basic boundaries of Islamic jurisprudence …'[148]

How can we help change the status quo? This chapter proposes three recommendations to help alter the present direction and ground realities in the Muslim world. These are set out in summary form here, but will be developed further elsewhere.

---

[147] Kamali, 'Punishment', *supra* n84, at 214.

[148] Dr. Jamal A. Badawi, *Is Apostasy a Capital Crime in Islam?*, World Muslim Congress (26 April 2006), http://worldmuslimcongress.blogspot.com/2007/03/apostasy-dr-jamal-badawi.html.

A. Education about the Role of Human Agency in the Development of Islamic Law

First, the Muslim community needs to be educated on the distinction between Shari'ah and many of the technical legal rules derived from the *Qur'an* and *sunnah* through *Uṣūl al-fiqh*.[149] A *faqih*,[150] or jurist, derived these rules and thus the decision is not eternal and is open to reinterpretation in light of, *inter alia*, new social, economic, educational and political circumstances.[151] Too many Muslims are under the false pretence that *fiqhi* positions and views are the divine word of God. As trite as it may sound, the existing body of juristic opinion is just human opinion, not divine directives. Indeed, it is imperative that the Muslim world be educated about the reality that most of what is today treated as divine law is the product of human juristic agency.

This fact, combined with the evolutionary and dynamic nature of Islamic jurisprudence, provides much hope in rethinking *fiqh* broadly, and more specifically for our purposes in the context of blasphemy and apostasy. Indeed, even a cursory examination of the ways in which classical *fiqh* works from any of the jurisprudential schools will reveal how the exigencies of political, social, economic and theological controversies that arose over the course of Islamic history factored into their rulings. As a result, while the *Qur'an* clearly implies the right to entertain such religious beliefs as one chooses, juristic opinion (*fiqh*) severely restricted the scope of religious freedom and expression.[152]

Until the Muslim masses striving to establish Islam distinguish between the eternal universal message of the *Qur'an* and the juristic

---

149 Kamali, *supra* n127, at 216.

150 Abdul Ghafur Muslim, 'Islamic Laws in Historical Perspective: An Investigation Into Problems and Principles in the Field of Islamization' (1987) 31 *Islamic Q.* 69. ('A Faqih means a jurist; an expert in the field of law, who possesses outstanding knowledge of revealed sources and methodology, and the intelligence to make use of the basic sources through independent reasoning and the principles provided by the Shari'a.'); see Ismail R. Al Faruqi and Lois Lamya Al Faruqi, *The Cultural Atlas of Islam* 34 (Macmillan 1986) ('The great jurists of Islam-Shafi'i, Abu Hanifah, Malik and Ahmad ibn Hanbal-all understood the compound term usul al fiqh not as the general principles of Islamic law, but the first principles of Islamic understanding of life and reality ... The faqihs [sic] of the classical period were real encyclopedists, masters of practically all the disciplines from literature and law to astronomy and medicine.').

151 Kamali, *supra* n127, at 216, 224.

152 See generally Kamali, 'Freedom of Religion', *supra* n111; see also An-Na'im, *supra* n6, at 38.

attempts to articulate this, the world will continue to witness calls to return to rules of a bygone era, devoid of its context and spirit.

B. Encouraging Scholars and Jurists to Speak Out Against Blind *Taqlid*

Leading scholars and jurists must continue to speak out against blind *taqlid* (particularly without regard to context).[153] There is a relatively small but growing group of scholars who are pointing to the *Qur'an* and even examples from the life of the Prophet which documents silence as to any worldly punishment for blasphemy and apostasy (other than that classified as treason). It is high time that other prominent and populist scholars speak out, just as Shaikh Ghamidi, Shaikh Badawi, Prof. Kamali, Maulana Khan, Shaikh Ahmed Kutty[154] and others have done, and challenge the existing juristic rulings in a contemporary context. Indeed, this chorus must grow and continue to reiterate that the *Qur'an* and the thrust of prophetic teachings vindicate the right to freedom of expression and religious liberty. They must continue to proclaim loudly that while these are serious sins, apostasy (with or without treason) and blasphemy do not positively have to carry *hudud* penalties.

Unfortunately, for a very long time, traditional scholars have helped to perpetuate an aura of infallibility and mystery surrounding religious knowledge. This has enabled some to maintain their entrenched positions as guardians of 'sacred' knowledge, which is supposedly inaccessible and cannot be even commented upon except by those who are deemed 'authorized' to do so by opaque bodies or individuals that are as numerous and transient as there are groups. This has served some of them well by enabling them to maintain their hierarchical positions and monopolies over the 'correct' interpretations of Islam without having to justify, explain or even make such knowledge relevant to modern realities. The disconnect between the theoretical formulations and lived realities is starkly evident in most Muslim societies, and risks making

---

[153] For a simple definition, see *Taqlid*, Encyclopaedia Britannica, www.britannica.com/EBchecked/topic/583236/taqlid ('the unquestioning acceptance of the legal decisions of another without knowing the basis of those decisions. There is a wide range of opinion about taqlid among different groups or schools of Muslims').

[154] 'Heresy, Homosexuality, and Other Issues', *onislam*, www.onislam.net/english/shariah/special-coverage/460362-on-muslim-minorities-live-fatwa.html (Live Fatwa session with Sheik Ahmad Kutty).

Islam effectively irrelevant in the lives of the newer generations. Prominent Islamic jurist Ibn al-Qayyim al-Jawziyya, for instance, notes:

> Whoever issues rulings to the people merely on the basis of what is transmitted in the compendia despite differences in their customs, usages, times, conditions and the special circumstances of their situations has gone astray and leads others astray. His crime against the religion is greater than the crime of a physician who gives people medical prescriptions without regard to the differences of their climes, norms, the times they live in, and their physical conditions but merely in accordance with what he finds written down in some medical book about people with similar anatomies. Such is an ignorant physician; the other is an ignorant jurisconsult but more detrimental.[155]

C. International Initiative to Combat Islamophobia and Promotion of Hate

The third recommendation is aimed at the international community. In addition to the political climates in Muslim nations, part of the increased attention on blasphemy and apostasy among the Muslim masses can be linked to the global attacks on Muslims and Islam, and the symbols associated with these.[156] Arguably, the increased sensibilities among Muslims are due to the perceptions of siege and attack many Muslims feel today. Globalization and the reach of international media have made the world a much smaller place. Many Muslims believe that promoting hatred and scorn for Islam and its sacred symbols has become one of the few socially and legally acceptable modern prejudices on a global level. Indeed, this new growth industry of Islamophobia is the new anti-Semitism.[157] Today, numerous studies have documented the rise in Islamophobia around the globe, including one by the British Runnymede

---

[155] Ibn Qayyim al-Jawziyyah, I'lam Al-Muwaqqi'in 'an Rabb Al-Alamin: *cf.* Muhammad Faruq Abdullah, 'Creativity, Innovation, and Heresy in Islam', in Vincent J. Cornell (ed.) 5 Vols. *Voices of Islam* 13 (Greenwood Publishing Group 2007).

[156] Islam and many of its symbols are increasingly attacked around the world. These range from banning of the hijab, to movies attacking the Prophet and religious icons, to calls to burn the *Quran*, etc., all contributing to marginalize and create fear of Islam and Muslims. Nathan Lean, *The Islamophobia Industry: How the Right Manufactures Fear of Muslims* (London: Pluto Press 2012).

[157] Daniel Luban, 'The New Anti-Semitism', *Tablet* (19 August 2010), www.tabletmag.com; Haroon Siddiqui, 'Islamophobia: The New Anti-Semitism', *The Star* (16 September 2012), www.thestar.com.

Trust in 1997 and a more recent study by the European Monitoring Centre on Racism and Xenophobia released in 2002.[158] Moreover, Islamophobia was recognized as a form of intolerance alongside xenophobia and anti-Semitism at the 'Stockholm International Forum on Combating Intolerance'.[159] Indeed, even the University of California Berkeley School of Race and Gender's Islamophobia Research and Documentation Project recently launched the *Islamophobia Studies Journal* to focus on emerging research on and analysis about the nature of Islamophobia and its impact on culture, politics, media, and the lives and experiences of Muslim people.[160]

The frustration felt by many in the Muslim world was summarized by Malaysia's foreign minister Anifah Aman, who told the General Assembly that the creators of the anti-Islam film, *Innocence of Muslims*,[161] and those behind the publication of lewd caricatures of the Prophet by French satirical weekly *Charlie Hebdo* had shown 'blatant malicious intent' toward Muslims.[162] 'When we discriminate against gender, it is called sexism. When African Americans are criticized and vilified, it is called racism. When the same is done to the Jews, people call it Anti-Semitism. But why is it when Muslims are stigmatized and defamed, it is defended as "freedom of expression"?' Aman rhetorically asked the General Assembly.[163]

The calls to punish blasphemy and apostasy are partly rooted in this belief that Muslim sacred symbols are being attacked and violated. Muslim masses have directed their energy at both real and perceived threats to their sensibilities. Indeed, this reactionary response is bound to grow and entrench itself unless the discourse is changed. The seriousness

---

158 European Union Agency for Fundamental Rights, 'Highlights of EUMC Report "Muslims in the European Union: Discrimination and Islamophobia"', online: *FRA*, www.fra.europa.eu; Runnymede, Commission on British Muslims, online: Runnymede Trust www.runnymedetrust.org.

159 Declaration of the Stockholm International Forum Combating Intolerance (Declaration delivered at the Stockholm International Forum, 30 January 2001) (unpublished).

160 University of California, Berkeley: Centre for Race & Gender, *Islamophobia Studies Journal*, online: Centre for Race & Gender, http://crg.berkeley.edu.

161 Statement by the Honourable Anifah Aman, Minister of Foreign Affairs of Malaysia, General Debate of the 67th Session of the United Nations General Assembly (29 September 2012), http://gadebate.un.org/67/Malaysia.

162 David Stringer, 'Algeria Demands UN Pass Laws Limiting Free Speech', *Telegram* (30 September 2012), www.thetelegram.com.

163 Id.

with which the Muslim world treats this issue is evident from the long campaign by the Organization of Islamic Cooperation (OIC)[164] in favour of an international defamation of religion/incitement of hate law.[165]

Indeed, what is and is not tolerable in terms of restrictions on free speech will vary from state to state, even between those with democratic outlooks. Discussions about setting the limits must be open to the community of nations and must allow all stakeholders to have an equal say. Rather than hysterically dismissing the OIC calls as simply leading us down the slippery slope of banning any critical discussion of religion, it would serve us well to engage with the OIC and its supporters in addressing their valid complaints about Islamophobia[166] and then move

---

[164] The Organization of Islamic Cooperation (OIC) – formerly known as the Organization of the Islamic Conference – is the second largest inter-governmental organization in the world, with a membership of 57 states. From 1999 to 2011, UN members representing OIC annually put forth controversial resolutions proposing the banning of the 'defamation of religions'. Louis Charbonneau, 'UN Condemns Religious Intolerance, Drops "Defamation" Line for First Time in Years', *Reuters* (19 December 2011), available at http://blogs.reuters.com/faithworld/2011/12/19/un-condemns-religious-intolerance-drops-defamation-line-for-first-time-in-years. The first resolution was the Commission on Human Rights Res. 1999/82, Defamation of Religions, 62d mtg., U.N. Doc. E/CN.4/RES/1999/82 (30 April 1999).

[165] See Hannah Allam, *Outrage Over Anti-Islam Video Threatens to Reignite Blasphemy Debate at U.N.*, McClatchy DC (20 September 2012), www.mcclatchydc.com/2012/09/20/169211/outrage-over-anti-islam-video.html. See also Jon Boone, 'Pakistan Drops Blasphemy Case Against Christian Girl', *The Guardian* (20 November 2012, 4:52 AM), www.theguardian.com/world/2012/nov/20/pakistan-drops-blasphemy-case-christian; 'Christian Boy in Pakistan Arrested for Blasphemy', *BBC News* (11 October 2012, 10:20 AM), www.bbc.com/news/world-asia-19906528; 'Death Only Penalty for Blasphemer: Shariat Court', *The News* (5 December 2013), www.thenews.com.pk/Todays-News-13-27076-Death-only-penalty-for-blasphemer-Shariat-Court; Brandon Jones, 'Pakistan Changes Blasphemy Laws, Increases Likelihood of Death Penalty', *Global Dispatch* (12 December 2013), www.theglobaldispatch.com/pakistan-changes-blasphemy-laws-increases-likelihood-of-death-penalty-19367.

[166] 'Islamophobia is a contrived fear or prejudice fomented by the existing Eurocentric and Orientalist global power structure. It is directed at a perceived or real Muslim threat through the maintenance and extension of existing disparities in economic, political, social and cultural relations, while rationalizing the necessity to deploy violence as a tool to achieve "civilizational rehab" of the target communities (Muslim or otherwise). Islamophobia reintroduces and re-affirms a global racial structure through which resource distribution disparities are maintained and extended.' *Defining Islamophobia*, Univ. of Cal. Ctr. for Race & Gender, http://crg.berkeley.edu/content/islamophobia/defining-islamophobia.

from the points of agreement to areas of disagreement and work towards developing a new international consensus.

IV. CONCLUSION

In conclusion, the laws of apostasy and blasphemy in their current forms and their respective punishment by death in Islamic law are untenable in the modern period. As we demonstrated above, these laws conflict with a variety of foundational teachings of Islam and with the current ethos of human rights, in particular the freedom to choose one's religion and the freedom to express oneself. It is arguable that the early development of the law of blasphemy and apostasy were largely driven by political, historical and social realities of the time. It is high time that the aspirational, theoretical/legal and ethical vision of Islam is squared with the rules and practices in the area of blasphemy and apostasy.

For a good discussion of the evolution of the term, see Şerif Onur Bahçecik, 'Internationalizing Islamophobia: Anti-Islamophobic Practices from the Runnymede Trust to the Organization of Islamic Cooperation' (July 2013) 5 *Ortadoğu Etütleri* 141 – available at www.orsam.org.tr/en/enUploads/Article/Files/201395_makale6.pdf.

10. Restorative justice in Islamic law: application in Malaysian legal history and the criminal justice system

Hanifah Haydar Ali Tajuddin, Nasimah Hussin and Majdah Zawawi

I. INTRODUCTION

Malaysia has a unique blend of legal systems, civil and Shari'ah; it is a multi-religious country with the majority of its population being Muslims. Both civil and Shari'ah law are conferred with criminal jurisdiction. Nevertheless, the latter's jurisdiction is limited to dealing only with certain offences committed by Muslims, and the crimes listed under the jurisdiction of the Shari'ah court can be categorised as non-serious crimes, which some might interpret as morally wrong kinds of crimes.[1] On the other hand, civil court covers wider categories of crimes, including those that are serious in nature[2] and those that are non-serious.[3]

Being a country that upheld retributive or punitive justice, the legislature sees punishment as the appropriate response for crimes committed and that criminals deserve to be punished.[4] The same view is shared by Malaysians, in general. Thus, both believe that punishment alone can educate or teach criminals. Due to this 'favourite' view, stories about convicted offenders top the list of daily news. Knowing that offenders have 'rightly' been sentenced somehow satisfies the crowd, as they

[1] The matters that fall under the jurisdiction of the Shari'ah Court are listed under the State List of the Ninth Schedule of the Federal Constitution. As far as criminal jurisdiction of the court is concerned, its jurisdiction covers only the crimes that are against the precepts of Islam committed by Muslims. Such jurisdiction excludes matters under the Federal List.

[2] Which include offences that are punishable with imprisonment for a term more than ten years – section 52B of the Malaysian Penal Code.

[3] Punishable with imprisonment of not more than ten years – section 52A of the Malaysian Penal Code.

[4] Nasimah Hussin, 'Punitive Justice in the Malaysian Criminal Law: Balancing the Rights of Offenders with those of Victims' (2011) 7 (13) *Journal of Applied Sciences Research* 2399, 2401.

believe justice has then been served. But on whom is such justice served, technically? If being punished is about locking offenders behind bars, about paying to the government certain fines and so on, where are the victims in this context? Furthermore, a crime under the retributive system is treated as a crime against the state, which in a way forgoes the victim's right of having a say in the processes – for example, in determining an appropriate punishment on a criminal or even obtaining compensation or restoration for the losses suffered.

However, these downsides started to get noticed due to the development of criminal justice system in other countries. This development in the criminal justice system acknowledges the loss that victims suffer in acts of crime and looks at restoring it. The development also sees that the appropriate way to reform a criminal is to let him know of the effect and impact that he has caused due to his crime and to take responsibility. With these developments in mind, the government started creating initiatives, to include a few if not all of these new insights.

With the view to see the possibility of incorporating a different perspective of looking at the criminal justice system, research is being carried out. In 2011, Datuk Seri Shahrizat Abdul Jalil, the then Minister of Women, Family and Development of Malaysia, called for a study into the restorative justice system and stated that a taskforce would be established in order to carry out such a study.[5] Even though, at that time, she was only referring to restorative justice in dealing with juvenile offenders, her call was a base for some research carried out to examine the possibility of establishing restorative justice as an alternative to the current criminal justice system in Malaysia. Some researchers are looking at the possibility of establishing restorative justice by identifying similarities between this and the principles in Islamic law; they believe that Malaysia should consider restorative justice as the country is a Muslim country and it does currently recognise Shari'ah jurisdiction to some extent.[6] This view is further strengthened when the country's legal history is examined, where the application of Shari'ah is traced in one of the early legal texts in the country, *Undang-undang Melaka* (the Laws of

[5] N.a 'Shahrizat Jalil: Taskforce to look into restorative justice system' *The Star*, Malaysia (22 October 2011).

[6] An ongoing PhD research by one of the contributors of this chapter on 'Restorative Justice as an Alternative Disposal of Criminal Cases: A Comparative Appraisal between Malaysian, Australian and Islamic Laws'.

Malacca). Others also examined the possibility by looking at the readiness of the society, victims, lawyers, court officials and enforcement bodies to be included in this new 'justice'.[7]

As the intent of this chapter is to highlight the resemblance of restorative justice principles with the principles of Islamic law, and the idea that Malaysia should consider it, being a Muslim country which recognises Shari'ah jurisdiction, currently and historically, the focus of the discussion is three-fold: (1) to analyse the existing restorative principles in the Islamic law; (2) to examine the relevance of incorporating restorative justice into the country's criminal justice system based on the fact that Islamic law has always been the law of land according to its legal history; and (3) to see how far the country's criminal justice system has developed since the call for restorative justice was made back in 2011. Thus, the chapter is divided as follows: Section II analyses principles of restorative justice that resemble the principles of Islamic law; Section III traces the application of Islamic law in the Malaysian legal history; and Section IV examines current practices that are restorative and pro-victim, to a certain extent in the country's criminal justice system.

II. RESTORATIVE JUSTICE IN ISLAMIC LAW

Upholding justice is an essence in Islamic law: Muslims are encouraged to be just and fair in carrying out their affairs. Justice in Islam goes deeper than the surface; it is a moral virtue and an attribute of human personality.[8] As being just includes putting something in its rightful place, deciding a dispute by restoring any losses is one of the main features and objectives of Islamic law.

---

7 See Mohd Taufik Mohamad, 'The Readiness of Stakeholders in the Criminal Justice System on the Implementation of Restorative Justice in Malaysia' (PhD dissertation, University of Science, Malaysia, 2015).

8 Abdullah Yusuf Ali explained in verse 16:90 that justice is a comprehensive term, and that other than putting something in its rightful place, Muslims are encouraged to do more than that, something warmer and more humane. This includes 'returning good for ill, or obliging those who have "no claim" on you; and of course the fulfilling of the claims of those whose claims are recognised in social life'. See Abd Ar-Rahman I. Doi, *Shariah: The Islamic Law* (London: Ta-Ha Publishers 2008) 24.

The three categorizations of crimes and punishments under Islamic criminal law include *hudud*, *qisas* and *ta'zir*.[9] Previous research in this area has highlighted the similarities between *qisas* and restorative justice.[10] Nevertheless, analysis of the principles of Islamic criminal law uncovers the fact that some principles applicable in *hudud* and *ta'zir* are also found to be restorative.

Some of the principles include treating the victim as a stakeholder who is given the authority to decide on treatment and punishment of the offender. The community is also regarded as a stakeholder, but the role actually begins even before a crime is committed and continues after that. Other interesting principles of Islamic criminal law include pardon (*al-'afw*), compensation (*ad-diyyah*), repentance (*at-tawbah*), reconciliation and negotiation (*as-sulh*) and repentance (*at-tawbah*). Below are brief discussions on these principles.

A. Victim as Stakeholder

The victim is regarded as central in the prosecution of *qisas* crimes.[11] *Qisas* crimes affect and breach individual rights – for example, taking a person's life intentionally or unintentionally and injuring a person's body intentionally or unintentionally. In other words, a victim is considered as the stakeholder in *qisas*, and has the authority to decide on the kind and amount of 'punishment' of the offender. The 'punishments' include three basic options in terms of recourses: to retaliate; to ask for compensation; or to forgive. Such authority awarded to the victim of a *qisas* crime is because the life of a person is the most precious gift from Allah, and as such it needs to be preserved and maintained.

---

9 *Hudud* are 'crimes punishable with fixed punishment imposed as the rights of public'; *qisas* are 'crime punishable with fixed punishment imposed as the right of individual'; and *ta'zir* are 'crimes punishable with penalties that are discretionary, i.e. discretion of the judge'. See Hussin et al., 'Should Fines Also Benefit Victims? An Evaluation of Fines as a Form of Punishment in Malaysia with Special Reference to Islamic Law' (2015) 25 (1) *Intellectual Discourse* 185–200, at 192.

10 See Susan C. Hascall, 'Restorative Justice in Islam: Should Qisas be Considered as a Form of Restorative Justice?' (2011) 4 (1) *Berkeley Journal of Middle Eastern & Islamic Law* 35–78; Mutaz M. Qafisheh, 'Restorative Justice in Islamic Penal Law: A Contribution to the Global System' (2012) 7 *International Journal of Criminal Justice Sciences* 487–507.

11 Susan C. Hascall, 'Restorative Justice in Islam: Should Qisas be Considered as a Form of Restorative Justice?' (2011) 4 (1) *Berkeley Journal of Middle Eastern & Islamic Law* 35–78, at 73.

The right of the victim or his/her heir to choose and decide on the three recourses of *qisas* is sourced from the *Quran*:

> And do not kill any one whom Allah has forbidden, except for a just cause, and whoever is slain unjustly, We have indeed given to his heir authority, so let him not exceed the just limits in slaying; surely he is aided.[12]

The empowerment of the victim in *qisas* shows the flexibility in the administration of Islamic criminal justice. Nevertheless, such empowerment is regulated so as to prevent individuals from taking the laws into their own hands. In other words, the authority will still regulate the processes such as determination and payment of *diyyah*, discussion between parties, execution of retaliation and grant of pardon. This is evident from a *Hadith* of the Prophet (*pbuh*) who, when acting as a mediator and a judge who supervised the communication between the victim or his/her heirs and the offender, determined the option as favoured by the victim and ordered for the execution of the option opted by the victim. The same Hadith also proved the special treatment of the victim or his/her heirs in prosecuting the offender where the authority to opt is given solely to the victim. The *Hadith* is as follows:

> Narrated by Wa'il ibn Hujr: 'I was with the Prophet (ﷺ) when a man who was a murderer and had a strap around his neck was brought to him. He (the Prophet) then called the legal guardian of the victim and asked him: do you forgive him? He said: no. He (the Prophet) asked: will you accept blood money? He said: no. He (the Prophet) asked: Will you kill him? He said: yes. He (the Prophet) said: take him (the murderer). When he (the Prophet) turned his back, he said: do you forgive him? After repeating all this (four times), he said: if you forgive him, he will bear the burden of his own sin and the sin of the victim. He (the guardian) then forgive him.'[13]

B. Community as Stakeholder

Islam emphasises the unity of Islamic nations and holds that all the nations constitute a single community, termed *al-Ummah*.[14] Among the community members, all Muslims should be like brothers and they

---

[12] *Quran* (Al-Isra') 17:33.

[13] Abu Dawud, *Sunan Abu Dawud*, Book 41, No. 4484, available at https://sunnah.com/abudawud/41 (accessed 20 August 2015).

[14] Farhad Malekian, *Principles of Islamic International Criminal Law* (Brill 2011) 46.

should live in tranquillity and be entitled to equal justice.[15] This signifies that members of the community should be entitled to any legitimate rights religiously and under the law. A community is also duty-bound to look after each other so that the objectives of the community are achievable – for example, to create a peaceful atmosphere and to prevent conflicts.[16] One distinct feature of *qisas* is the liability of a group of people to pay compensation (*diyah*) on behalf of a criminal when he/she is unable to pay from his/her money or when he/she died. This group of people is termed as *'aqilah.* Initially during the prophethood, *'aqilah* consisted of family members from the father's side (*'asobah*). This is evident from a numbered *Hadith* that reported that the Prophet (*pbuh*) obliged *'asobah* to pay *diyah.* One of the *Hadith* is:

> Narrated by Abu Hurairah r.a: 'Allah's Messenger (pbuh) gave a verdict regarding an aborted foetus of a woman from Bani Lihyan that the killer (of the foetus) should give a male or female slave (as a *diyah*). But the woman who was required to give the slave, died, so Allah's Messenger (pbuh) gave the verdict that her inheritance be given to her children and her husband and the *diyah* be paid by her *'asobah.*'[17]

The concept of *'aqilah* continued until the reign of the first Caliph. During the reign of the second Caliph, Umar al-Khattab changed and extended the usage of *'aqilah.* He noticed a change in the structure of society during his reign in that Muslims were no longer attached to their tribe, but rather to the members of organised bodies.[18] The members of such bodies may comprise of people who have a common interest, based

---

[15] Ibid., 47. Such relation is mentioned in the *Quran*, where Allah says: 'The believers are but brothers, so make reconciliation between your brothers and fear Allah that you may have mercy.' *Quran* (al-Hujurat) 49:10. Nu'man bin Bashir reported Allah's Messenger (*pbuh*) as saying: 'the similitude of believers in regard to mutual love, affection, fellow-feeling is that of one body; when [a] limb of it aches, the whole body aches, because of sleeplessness and fever.' Muslim, *Sahih Muslim*, Book 45 No. 2586, available at https://sunnah.com/muslim/45 (accessed 27 November 2015).

[16] Ibid., 46.

[17] Al-Bukhari, *Sahih al-Bukhari*, Book 87, Hadith 6909, available at https://sunnah.com/bukhari/87 (accessed 6 June 2017).

[18] Syed Ahmad S. A. Al-Sagoff, *Al-Diyah as Compensation for Homicide Wounding in Malaysia* (Kuala Lumpur: International Islamic University Malaysia 2006) 340–1.

on their work or minority to which they belong.[19] Umar al-Khattab created registers (*diwan*) for members of the military in every district. Thus, the *diwan* would be the *'aqilah*, that is, the group of people who would be responsible for paying *diyyah* when a criminal who belonged to the same *diwan* committed *Qisas* and was unable to pay his/her *diyyah*.[20] This revolutionised the concept of *'aqilah* to include not only the *'asobah*, but also extended families, residents in the same neighbourhood, co-workers and members of the society.[21]

C. Pardon (*al-'Afw*)

Pardon or granting forgiveness also forms an important component in Islamic criminal law. It is discussed in detail under *qisas* as it is known as the category of Islamic criminal law that empowers victims. However, pardon is actually applicable in all categories of crimes, including *ta'zir* and *hudud*. This is especially the case in crimes that violate individual rights. The jurists agreed that pardon is one of the factors that remit the execution of *qisas* punishments on convicted criminals.[22] In *ta'zir* and *hudud*, principally, the ruler or judge is given the exclusive right to pardon criminals, by considering the interest of the public.[23] Some jurists, nevertheless, have opined that it is possible that if the victim chooses to pardon the criminal, the judge should also grant a pardon to the criminal, if he/she considers it necessary.[24] However, this only applies in *ta'zir* offences that violate the rights of individuals, not the public.

---

[19] Qafisheh, above n10, 489. Mutaz further illustrated as follows: the *diwan* for a policeman is the police force, for a judge it is the judiciary, for a businessman it is the chambers of commerce, etc.

[20] Al-Sagoff, above n18, 340–1.

[21] Qafisheh, above n10, 489–90.

[22] Abdul Qadir Oudah, *at-Tashri' al-Jina'I al-Islami Muqarinan bil Qanun al-Wad'I*, 776 ('Legislation of Islamic Criminal Law Comparison with the Modern Law'). See also Abdul Karim Zaidan, *Al-Qisas wa ad-Diyyat fi Syariat al-Islamiyyah* ('Concept of Retaliation (*Qisas*) and Compensation (*Diyyat*) in Islamic Law') (Muassasah al-Risalah 2007) 114.

[23] Abdul Qadir Oudah *at-Tashri' al-Jina'I al-Islami Muqarinan bil Qanun al-Wad'I* ('Legislation of Islamic Criminal Law Comparison with the Modern Law') 777.

[24] Mohammad Shabbir, *Outlines of Criminal Law and Justice in Islam*, 349. The stand is agreed by Al-Mawardi, who observed that in crimes affecting the rights of individuals, a judge should not dismiss a victim's right over the case, and if the victim chooses to pardon then the judge should take it into consideration in deciding whether to punish the criminal in order to teach him/her a lesson or to grant him/her a pardon, as the victim did. *See* Al-Mawardi,

D. Compensation (*ad-Diyyah*)

Diyah is an amount of compensation payable due to crimes committed involving death or injury.[25] Although at present monetary compensation is mostly a remedy for civil loss which can include injuries, Islamic law has for a long time allowed such compensation for homicide and murder cases. Compensation is a right of the victims of crime and their heirs; thus, it is compulsory and this is based on the sources from the *Quran* and *Hadith*. Allah says:

> And it does not behove a believer to kill a believer except by mistake, and whoever kills a believer by mistake, he should free a believing slave, and blood-money should be paid to his people unless they remit it as alms.[26]

The Prophet (*pbuh*) said:

> The blood-money for unintentional murder which appears intentional, such as is done with a whip and a stick, is one hundred camels, forty of which are pregnant.[27]

E. Reconciliation, Negotiation and Mediation (*as-Sulh*)

Reconciliation or mediation is formally known in Shari'ah as *sulh*. It originates from the word *salaha*, which means 'to do good deeds'.[28] The process of *sulh* itself can be defined as a process of restoring something, be it a relationship or a loss suffered.[29] Nonetheless, the parties must be

---

The Ordinances of Governments, translated from Arabic by Uthman bin Hj. Khalid (Percetakan Majujaya Indah Sdn Bhd 1993) 384.

25 Abdul Karim Zaidan, *Al-Qisas wa ad-Diyyat fi Syariat al-Islamiyyah* ('Concept of Retaliation (*Qisas*) and Compensation (*Diyyat*) in Islamic Law') 185.

26 *Quran* (An-Nisa') 4:92.

27 Abu Dawud, *Sunan Abu Dawud*, Book 4, No. 4531, available at https://sunnah.com/abudawud/41 (accessed 2 August 2017).

28 Ramizah Wan Muhammad, '*Sulh* (mediation) in the Malaysian Syariah Courts', in *Mediation in Malaysia: the Law and Practice* by Mohammad Naqib Ishan Jan and Ashgar Ali Ali Mohamed (eds) (Kuala Lumpur: Lexis Nexis 2010) 416.

29 Raihanah Haji Azhari, 'Sulh dalam Perundangan Islam: Kajian di Jabatan Kehakiman Syariah, Selangor Darul Ehsan' ('Mediation in the Islamic Legal System: A Research at the Syariah Judiciary Department of Selangor Darul Ehsan') (PhD dissertation, University of Malaya, 2005) 57, cited by Hanis

agreeable to this mediation, due to the amicable nature of the process that is required. According to Article 1531 of the Mejelle, '*Sulh* is a contract of removing a dispute by mutual consent.'[30] In criminal cases, *sulh* is an agreement between two disputants to reach a settlement, or an agreement to compromise between two disputing parties.[31]

Unlike litigation, where one party wins and the other loses, reconciliation or mediation is a platform where it is possible for both parties to win, be it monetarily or emotionally. In Islamic criminal law, reconciliation or mediation is viewed as a mechanism that enables parties to achieve positive outcomes, by compromising, reconciling and forgiving each other.[32] The positive outcomes can include easing of the animosity between parties where victims would be able to forgive, and promoting a better rehabilitative process of the criminals. Islam encourages mediation (*sulh*) in almost all types of disputes except for disputes that relate to permitting the prohibited matters or prohibiting the permitted matters in Islam. For example, Allah says in the *Quran*:

> If two parties among the believers fall into a quarrel make you peace between them: but if one of them transgresses beyond the bounds against the other then fight ye all against the one that transgresses until it complies with the command of Allah; but if it complies then make peace between them with justice and be fair, for Allah loves those who are fair (and just). The believers are but a single Brotherhood: so make peace and reconciliation between your two (contending) brothers: and fear Allah that you may receive Mercy.[33]

The Prophet (*pbuh*) in one of the Hadith encouraged Muslims to practise *sulh*:

> Kathir bin Abdullah bin 'Amr bin 'Auf narrated from his father that his grandfather said: I heard the Messenger of Allah (pbuh) said: 'Reconciling

---

Wahed, '*Sulh*: Its Application in Malaysia' (2015) 20 (6) *IOSR Journal of Humanities and Social Science* 71.

[30] C. R. Tyser (trans.), *The Mejelle* (Lahore: Law Publishing Company 1980) 254.

[31] Muhammad Iman Jabiri, *As-Sulh ka Sabab li Inqida' ad-Da'wa al-Jina'I* ('Mediation as a Factor of Waive of Criminal Charge') (Dar al-Jami'ah al-Jadidah 2011) 17.

[32] Norjihan Ab Aziz and Nasimah Hussin, 'The Application of Mediation (*Sulh*) in Islamic Criminal Law', (2017) 24 (1) *Jurnal Syariah* 116.

[33] *Quran* (Al-Hujurat) 49:9–10.

between is permissible, except reconciliation that forbids something that is allowed, or allows something that is forbidden.'[34]

F. Repentance (*at-Tawbah*)

Al-Qurtubi defined repentance as 'having a feeling of penitence to God with good faith and sincere piety by performing good deeds to counteract the effect of bad deeds'.[35] It is interesting to note that Islamic criminal law is the only criminal law that accepts repentance as a factor to remit one's punishment.[36]

Repentance is regarded as one of the factors that remit punishments in Islamic criminal law. The difference between repentance and pardon is that repentance is applicable in crimes affecting public rights, while pardon is applicable in crimes affecting private or personal rights. Thus, remittance of punishment due to repentance can only be granted by a judge or a ruler.

The discussion on the position of acceptance of repentance as a factor that remits punishment is primarily based on a Quranic verse where Allah explains that he who repents after committing the crime of *hirabah* (burglary) is forgiven, and thus his punishment is remitted, provided that the repentance happens before he is apprehended. This is related to the fact that the law is sourced from the religion and morality that promote humans to be better, and repentance is basically the option that one has in order to regain the mercy of Allah, and thus be better. Jurists hold on to the validity of repentance as a defence based on Quranic verses:

> Say: O my servants! Who have acted extravagantly against their own souls, do not despair of the mercy of Allah; surely Allah forgives the faults altogether; surely He is the Forgiving the Merciful.[37]

In the verse where Allah explains the punishments that await those who commit *hudud* crime of *hirabah*, Allah then mentions in the following verse that criminals of such crime can be forgiven if they repent:

---

[34] Ibnu Majah, *Sunan Ibn Majah*, Book 13 No. 2353, available at https://sunnah.com/ibnmajah/13 (accessed 7 August 2017).

[35] Al-Qurtubi, *Al-Jami' li Ahkam al-Quran*, cited by M. Shokry El-Dakkak, *Repentance as a Defence Comparative Study under Islamic Law, Common Law and Continental Law* (Kuala Lumpur: A. S. Noordeen 1994) 3.

[36] Ibid., 3.

[37] *Quran* (Az-Zumar) 39:53.

> Except those who repent before you have them in your power; so know that Allah is Forgiving, Merciful.[38]

The above discussion discovers the resemblances between restorative justice and Islamic law, specifically its criminal law. It can be submitted that the restorative values can be encompassed if Islamic criminal law is applied in accordance with its principles.

The next discussion focuses on the research attempt to trace the application of Islamic law in the legal history of Malaysia. This is to prove the fact that Islamic law has been applied since the fifteenth century and that its application can be traced back to the Sultanate of Melaka. Thus, this proves that Islamic law in general, and Islamic criminal law in particular, has partly set the base upon which the legal system of Malaysia is founded.

III. ISLAMIC LAW IN MALAYSIAN LEGAL HISTORY

Malaysia is a Muslim country because the majority of its population are Muslims. Another reason is because of its long-standing history, which records the arrival of Islam to the land and the application of *Syariah* (Islamic laws) by its sultans who ruled the land hundreds of years ago. The Malay Peninsula or the *Tanah Melayu* was recorded to have accepted Islam as early as the twelfth century. The first physical evidence of the influence of Islam was found in the state of Terengganu, where a set of writing in Arabic letters was found crafted on a rock called *Batu Bersurat* (the lettered rock). This rock is dated 22 February 1303 AD.[39] Discussion on the spread of Islam in the Malay Peninsula usually revolves around the establishment of the state of Melaka.

The history records that first ruler who found Melaka and embraced Islam is Parameswara (his Muslim name is Iskandar Shah). Parameswara was a Javanese Hindu prince who ruled Singapura (presently known as Singapore) in the thirteenth century. Manuscripts such as *Undang-undang Melaka*, *Undang-undang Johor*, *Undang-undang Pahang* and *Undang-undang Kedah* were found to be the early legal texts that uphold the principles of Islamic criminal law, Islamic family law and other civil

---

[38] *Quran* (Al-Maidah) 5:34.

[39] Syed Naquib al-Attas, *The Correct Date of the Trengganu Inscription* (1970) cited by Arba'iyah Mohd Noor, 'Perkembangan Pensejarahan Islam di Alam Melayu (Development of Islamic Historiography in Malay Archipelago)' (2011) 6 *Jurnal al-Tamaddun* 29–50, at 37.

matters. The manuscripts, however, were discovered to contain resemblances to *Undang-undang Melaka* as it came earlier, and thus it is recognised as one of the earliest Islamic legal texts of the country. Melaka did not only apply Shari'ah in its legal context; the influence of Shari'ah can also be traced in other aspects of its administration such as the usage of the term 'Sultan', which replaced the terms 'Maharajah' before that due to the Hindu influence, the use of '*Jawi*' alphabets which are the alphabets of Arabic language and the language of the *Quran*. For this very reason, Islamic law has been recognised as the law of the land. This was as decided in an old case of *Shaik Abdul Latif and Other vs. Shaik Elias Bux* and the case of *Ramah vs. Laton*.[40]

In acknowledging the importance of *Undang-undang Melaka* as one of the earliest legal texts of Islamic law in the country, it is pertinent that its contents, which are based on the principles of Islamic law, as the context of this chapter, are briefly highlighted.

Undang-undang Melaka, also known as *Hukum Kanun Melaka*, was compiled during the rule of Sultan Muzaffar Shah (1446–59).[41] The set of laws which manifested the strong influence of Islamic laws in the administration of justice of Melaka, showed the impact of education on *hukm fiqh* (Islamic legal rulings) in the state.[42] The set of laws has been a subject of research by many researchers who are interested to see how Melaka functioned legally. Liaw Yock Fang had analysed the contents of *Undang-undang Melaka* by taking into account the various versions of the set of laws. He claimed that laws found in other states in the Malay Peninsula, including Pahang, Johor and Kedah, had some striking resemblance with *Undang-undang Melaka*; this suggested the strength of Melaka as a strong Islamic state then.[43]

The influence of Islamic laws in the *Undang-undang Melaka* is reflected in the provisions and also the phrases used to elaborate the contents of the provisions. Phrases such as *Bismillahi-rahman-rahim*

---

40 *Shaik Abdul Latiff and Other v. Shaik Elias Bux* [1915] 1 FMSLR 204 and *Ramah binti Ta'at v. Laton binti Malim Sutan* [1924] 1 FMSLR 179.

41 Ashgar Ali Ali Mohamed, 'Implementation of *Hudud* (or Limits Ordained by Allah for Serious Crimes) in Malaysia' (2012) 2 (3) *International Journal of Humanities and Social Science* 237–46, at 237.

42 Arba'iyah Mohd Noor, 'Perkembangan Pensejarahan Islam di Alam Melayu (Development of Islamic Historiography in Malay Archipelago)' (2011) 6 *Jurnal al-Tamaddun* 29–50, at 34.

43 Liaw Yock Fang, *Undang-Undang Melaka, The Laws of Malacca* thesis published by Koninklijk Institut Voor-Taal-Land-En Volkenkunde (1976) at p. 1.

(with the name of Allah the Most Compassionate the Most Merciful),[44] *Wallahu-'alam-bis-sawab* (Allah Knoweth best what is true),[45] *mudda'I* (plaintiff), *mudda'a 'alaihi* (defendant), *bai'* (sale) and *ikrar* (admission) are found in the laws.[46]

Islamic laws that were applicable in *Undang-undang Melaka* consisted of *hudud* (limits ordained by Allah for serious crimes),[47] *qisas* (laws of retaliation) and *ta'zir* (laws set up by the ruler of state). Interestingly, the laws of *qisas* not only was applied in the aspect of retaliating against one's act of causing injury (for example), but also it was extended to apply the other components of the law which include compensation, pardon and repentance on the part of the offender. Nevertheless, the *adat* or customary law was also an integral part of the laws. Thus, it is observed that in provisions stating the punishments for acts of crime, two sets of punishments were mentioned: one under customary laws and the other under the Islamic laws. However, any departure from Islamic law was 'deemed worthy of notice'.[48] This again shows the strength and influence of Islamic law throughout *Undang-undang Melaka.* One of the examples of crimes where both sets of punishments were applicable was in the act of killing of a paramour who trespasses into one's marriage; this is pardonable according to the customary law,[49] and the paramour, however is killed according to the law of God as he who kills shall be killed.[50]

---

44 Ibid., 36.

45 Ibid., 34.

46 Ibid., 7.

47 As translated by Ashgar Ali Ali Mohamed, 'Implementation of *Hudud* (or Limits Ordained by Allah for Serious Crimes) in Malaysia' (2012) 2 (3) *International Journal of Humanities and Social Science* 237–46.

48 Liaw Yock Fang, *Undang-Undang Melaka, The Laws of Malacca* thesis published by Koninklijk Institut Voor-Taal-Land-En Volkenkunde (1976) at p. 33.

49 Section 5.3 'concerning the killing of a paramour: if he (a paramour) runs into someone's compound and is pursued by the husband, whereby the latter involved in a fight with the owner of the compound: if he (the owner of the compound) resists him and the pursuer is killed, the latter simply dies and there shall be no litigation. This is the custom of the country. But according to the law of God, he who kills shall also be killed. For this is in accordance with what is stated in the *Quran* and is in pursuance of (its teaching): (God bids us) to do good, and forbids us to commit sin.' See Liaw Yock Fang, *Undang-Undang Melaka, The Laws of Malacca* published thesis by Koninklijk Institut Voor-Taal-Land-En Volkenkunde (1976) at p. 71.

50 Ibid.

The application of the law of *qisas* is stipulated in section 5.1 of the *Undang-undang Melaka*, where it is specified that a person who kills shall be killed as his punishment.[51] However, section 5.2 elaborated on the circumstances where punishment for killing another person is substituted with certain amount of compensation. In this particular section, it is explained that such killing is substitutable with compensation when it has not reached the knowledge of the ruler or ministers. This suggests that the family of the murdered is entitled to give pardon and ask for compensation instead.[52]

Another interesting aspect of *Undang-undang Melaka* is the inclusion of punishment of shaming. Section 11.1 prescribed the punishment of crime of theft. The section detailed three circumstances; first, the actions that can be taken by the owner of premises; second, the punishment when the theft is committed by one person and when it is participated by more than a person but only one of them entered the premises; and third, the punishment for the thieves who did not enter the premises. For the first circumstance, the owner has the right to kill the thief who entered his/her premises while in the course of pursuing the thief. On the other hand, if the owner is unable to pursue the thief immediately after the theft was committed, and only meets the thief days after that, the owner is not entitled to kill the thief any more. The second circumstance stated that the punishment for crime of theft committed by one person is amputation of his right hand. The same punishment is sentenced on one thief who entered the premises if the act is participated by a group of them. The

---

[51] Ashgar Ali Ali Mohamed, 'Implementation of *Hudud* (or Limits Ordained by Allah for Serious Crimes) in Malaysia' (2012) 2 (3) *International Journal of Humanities and Social Science* 237–46, at 237. Section 5.1 of *Undang-undang Melaka* states: 'Even if he kills without any fault (on his part, i.e. if he is provoked), he is to be put to death by the law of God. This is what is understood by *'adil* (justice).'

[52] Section 5.2 explained where killing is pardonable and substituted with an amount of compensation. It states: 'To kill without knowledge of the ruler and ministers (is pardonable) under four circumstances. First, the killing of a paramour; second, the killing of a ruffian; but one must first try to arrest him and then bring him to justice, then it is customary to fine him (the ruffian) 1¼ *tahil*. If he cannot be arrested and is dangerously cunning, then it is fitting that he should be executed. Third, killing of a thief who cannot be captured. Fourth, killing of a person who brings disgrace on others, for instance (by slapping someone or by any other humiliating act, that is, if (the case) has not reached the ministers. If it has reached the ministers, and he (the killer) still does the same, he (the killer) shall be fined 10¼ *tahil*. This is the law.'

third, where the shaming concept is applicable, elaborated the punishment for the rest of the thieves. The punishment is termed *ta'zir* and it prescribed that the offender will be placed on a white spotted cow, decorated with hibiscus flowers and his head is dish-covered; his face will be smeared with lime, charcoal and turmeric, and he will be carried throughout the country with a beating gong as a means to announce his crime. In addition, if the stolen property is discovered, it is hung around the thief's neck (if possible). If the offender is a slave, the master compensates the owner, and if the thief is a free man, he becomes a debt slave of the owner.[53]

Another feature of *Undang-undang Melaka* is the implementation of *Sulh* or mediation. Mediation during this period of time was community mediation where a headman of a village (*penghulu*) or a religious leader (*imam*) was given the authority by the Sultan to handle and decide disputes. However, they did not carry such duty alone; they were assisted by a few assistants consisting of *Ketua Adat, Tok Siding* or *Tok Empat* and the elders.[54] Their duties, other than heading a village or religious ceremonies and looking after the welfare of the villagers, included educating the villagers in precepts of both law and religion, mediating disputes and enforcing sanctions against offenders, including fining

---

[53] Section 11.1: 'if the owner of the compound comes to know (about the thief), then he kills him (the thief) or pursues him between two compounds, and then kills him (the thief), the killer has committed no offence. But, if (the owner of property) meets the thief some days later and only then kills him (the thief), the killing is not legal and (the killer) is liable for prosecution.

> 'He who steals from a house shall have his (right) hand amputated. But if there are many thieves and only one of them breaks into the house, only the thief's (right) hand shall be amputated. As for the rest, (they will) undergo the *ta'zir* punishment, i.e. the offender will be placed on a white-spotted cow, adorned with hibiscus flowers and dish-cover on his head; his face shall be smeared with lime, charcoal and turmeric, and thus he will be carried around the country while a gong is being beaten (to announce his crime). If the (stolen) property is discovered, it shall be hung around his neck. If the (stolen) property is completely consumed, his master must make amends (to the owner). If the thief is a free man, he becomes a debt slave of the owner of the property.'

[54] Hanna Ambaras Khan, 'Community Mediation of Malaysia: A Journey from Malacca Sultanate to the Department of Unity and Integration Malaysia (DNUI)', paper presented at the International Conference on Islam in Asia and Oceania: Historical, Cultural and Global Perspectives 2012 held at the International Institute of Islamic Thought and Civilization (ISTAC) Kuala Lumpur.

thieves, flogging adulterers and even killing murderers.[55] Thus the appointment of a headman was based particularly on his religious background and show of piety by observing his religious duties.[56]

The explanation above signifies the influence of Islamic law over *Undang-undang Melaka.* It is undeniable that the customary laws had as well influenced the drafting of such laws; but then again, the punishments under the customary laws could fall under the category of *ta'zir*, in which such punishment does not go against Islam as long as it is in line with Shari'ah. The way the punishments were carried out suggests the informality of the authorities in ensuring the aspects of restoring, repairing and rehabilitating. The community mediation, prescription of compensation on the victim and the shaming that include not only the aspect of rehabilitating the offender, but also securing the peaceful living and safety of the members of society and educating them of the effects that could befall those who commit crimes, are observed to share some similarities with today's concept of restorative justice.

IV. CURRENT PRACTICES IN THE MALAYSIAN CRIMINAL JUSTICE SYSTEM

Looking at the current practices, as mentioned in the early part of this chapter, there was a call by the government to examine restorative justice for the purpose of applying some, if not all, of its principles and practices. This call, which was made in 2011, has not been fully realised as restorative justice until now so is yet to be incorporated into the country's criminal justice. Furthermore, the government has not officially looked at the possibility of applying restorative justice principles as contained in Islamic law. Nevertheless, the court through community service and bonds of good behaviour has unofficially included the elements to trigger repentance from incarcerated offenders.[57] The call to

---

[55] Hanna Ambaras Khan, 'Community Mediation of Malaysia: A Journey from Malacca Sultanate to the Department of Unity and Integration Malaysia (DNUI)', paper presented at the International Conference on Islam in Asia and Oceania: Historical, Cultural and Global Perspectives 2012 held at the International Institute of Islamic Thought and Civilization (ISTAC) Kuala Lumpur.

[56] Ibid.

[57] Nasimah Hussin, 'Alternative Punishment to Imprisonment in the Malaysian Shariah Court: Prospects for Reforms' (2017) 3 (5) *International Journal of Management and Applied Science* 70–3, at 72.

establish a Shari'ah Detention Centre, for example, is viewed as further embodying the objective of rehabilitating Muslim inmates by incorporating religious values.

Nevertheless, many are hopeful that amendments that could recognise and restore the lost rights of victims of crimes can at least be made to the Criminal Procedure Code and to a few other provisions. However, the developments are being made at a slow pace, as the government has been careful in studying the possible risks and effects. This is because restorative justice where victims are the centre of prosecution, offenders are to accept liability and make amends for the victims, and in so doing, the community is also to play a role, is regarded as a 'new thing' to the current criminal justice system of the country.

Starting from 2010, the country's Criminal Procedure Code was amended to bring in some changes that seemed to be in favour of the victim. Amendments such as victim impact statements and compensation for victims were introduced. Furthermore, the Domestic Violence Act was also amended in 2017; among other things, it provides more and immediate protections for victims against their abusers. Although imprisonment is still the 'favourite' kind of punishment, the government is making active efforts to find more effective measures to rehabilitate inmates.

A. The Criminal Procedure Code

Among the amendments that are considered as pro-victim in the country's Criminal Procedure Code are the victim impact statement and the awarding of compensation to victims of crime.

The victim impact statement is a statement of a victim regarding the impact of a crime committed by the offender against the victim. Included in the Criminal Procedure Code in 2012 where it allows victims to express grievances using a 'systematic mechanism' before the court.[58] Section 183A of the Criminal Procedure Code deals specifically with victim impact statements.[59] Subsection 183A (1) states that the court may

---

[58] Nasimah Hussin, 'Punitive Justice in the Malaysian Criminal Law: Balancing the Rights of Offenders with those of Victims' (2011) 7 (13) *Journal of Applied Sciences Research* 2403.

[59] Section 183A of the Criminal Procedure Code: (1) Before the Court passes sentence according to law under section 183, the Court shall, upon the request of the victim of the offence or the victim's family, call upon the victim or a member of the victim's family to make a statement on the impact of the offence on the victim or his family. (2) Where the victim or a member of the victim's family is

only grant such a statement to be made by the victim or his/her family member upon their request and that such a statement must be presented before the court passes the sentence. However, the section does not detail how the court should regard the statement; through an informal interview with a court official, it appears that some judges regard the statement as an aggravating factor, while others do not. Subsection 183A(2) further explains that in cases where the victim or his/her member of family failed to appear before the court after requesting to present such a statement, the court may admit a written statement detailing the impact.

Section 426 (1A) of the Criminal Procedure Code allowed a certain amount of compensation to be paid to the victims of crimes. Such compensation is only awarded through application made by the public prosecutor and not the victim. Furthermore, the amount of compensation could be considered small, and in most cases it is awarded to replace value of stolen property, such as in cases of theft. The previous position was that a victim could only obtain compensation through a personal civil suit filed against the offender, and this remains the case if the victim is attempting to obtain compensation for anything other than the value of his/her stolen property, such as fear, physical pain, trauma, loss of income or medical costs.

Another practice that was inserted into the Criminal Procedure Code in 2012 is that of plea bargaining. Nevertheless, lawyers and public prosecutors are of the opinion that plea bargaining has been in practice for several years already, albeit unofficially. The practice, which is basically a form of mediation, was officially recognised with the insertion of section 172C; this lays out the procedures in conducting plea bargaining. Essentially, plea bargaining is viewed as a practical method to reduce backlog of criminal cases where the accused's acceptance of the proposed sentence or charge would definitely save the court's time and public's expenses, compared to if a trial were to be conducted, which would probably be time-consuming.[60] Moreover, some judges considered that such a practice led to the accused pleading guilty, though to a lesser charge or punishment, thus encouraging honesty on the part of the accused to plead their guilt and that it might indirectly influence other

for any reason unable to attend the proceedings after being called by the Court under subsection (1), the Court may at its discretion admit a written statement of the victim or a member of the victim's family.

[60] Malia Afzan, 'The Case for Plea Bargaining in Malaysia', (July 2016) available at www.inhousecommunity.com/wp-content/uploads/2016/07/v8i2_Jur_Malaysia.pdf (accessed 19 October 2017).

criminals to do the same as well.[61] In *PP v. Jessica Lim Lu Ping*, the judge observed that expediting the disposal of criminal cases and sentencing the accused who pleads guilty with a lenient punishment are in the public interest.[62]

B. The Domestic Violence Act 1994

The Domestic Violence Act is a provision that mainly protects victims of domestic violence against their abusers. Taking into consideration the increase of domestic violence cases in the country, amendments to the provision were tabled before Parliament through the Ministry of Women, Family and Development of Malaysia. One of the amendments introduced, which has satisfied the NGOs, is the Emergency Protection Order (EPO). The EPO admits the urgency of protection that a victim requires when faced with an angry abuser. The EPO can be approved by the Welfare Department Officers within two hours of the application being made.[63] The provision also refers to a rehabilitation programme, where the court can make an order to refer the abuser and victim, if the victim agrees to a rehabilitation programme provided by the ministries responsible for welfare services for the purpose of family and community development.[64]

V. CONCLUSION

Restorative justice is undoubtedly a viable solution in dealing with the issue of victimization in crimes, as it focuses on restoring losses of victims of crimes, and the victim is allowed to play a role in the court procedure in adjudicating the crime committed against him/her. However, the development has yet to include laws that allow offenders to take responsibility and restore losses that they have caused personally to victims, other than paying some small amount of compensation. Nevertheless, the future remains uncertain; it is hoped that further research in

---

61 See *PP v. Jessica Lim Lu Ping* [2004] 2 CLJ 763.

62 Ibid.

63 Section 3A (5) of the Domestic Violence Act (Amendment 2017) provides that 'upon receipt of the application for an emergency protection order, the application shall be heard by the authorised social welfare officer immediately and the issuance of the emergency protection order, if any, shall be made, where practicable, within two hours after the application is made'.

64 Section 11 (1) and (4) of the Domestic Violence Act 1994 (Amendment 2017).

the area of restorative justice that is being carried out in Malaysia may encourage the government to make the move to effectively introduce it in the country's criminal justice system. In doing so, it is hoped that the principles of Islamic law can also be benefited, as there have been ongoing efforts to harmonise the two jurisdictions (civil and Shari'ah), and this can be regarded as part of developing the country's criminal justice system, both civil and Shari'ah.

PART 4

ETHICS, HEALTH AND SCIENCES

11. Genetic engineering and ethics in Muslim communities: case studies from Tunisia and Saudi Arabia

Nurussyariah Hammado

I. INTRODUCTION

Presently, the position of women in Islam is one of the most debatable and controversial topics, in both Western media and Islamic jurisprudence. This chapter will look at areas of Islamic law that affect the reproductive health and decisions of Muslim women. These include adoption, medically assisted reproduction, abortion, child marriage and female genital mutilation. The chapter will compare the situation in strongly religious Saudi Arabia, with Tunisia, where a more liberalist view prevails. The ultimate aim of this chapter is to discover how Islamic law differs in Saudi Arabia and Tunisia by discussing their respective positions on the reproductive needs of women today.

While women have traditionally had few rights under Islam and have been oppressed for centuries, their reproductive rights in Muslim countries such as Tunisia have greatly improved. In other countries, such as Saudi Arabia, women still lack many fundamental rights. Suggested reasons for this disparity are the impacts of colonisation and Westernisation in Tunisia that have allowed for a continual adaptation to modern society. In Saudi Arabia on the other hand, the culture remains more intact, with a strict adherence to Shari'ah persists and a lack of Western influence is evident.

It will be argued in this chapter that religion is not the source of all discriminatory treatment of women, but rather that it stems from the traditional cultural and social norms of a particular society. However, as religion informs and shapes cultures, such practices are the indirect consequences of religion, in this case, Islam.

As there is no central authority figure like the pope in Islam, there is an assortment of beliefs on every aspect of life.[1] Furthermore, as the primary sources of Islamic law – the *Quran* and *Sunna* – have continually been reinterpreted and adapted to society over time through *ijtihad*, *qiyas*, *ijma'* and the issuing of fatwas, it is almost impossible to find agreement on any topic throughout the Muslim world. This discussion will therefore refer to just some of the views held on reproductive health issues.

II. WOMEN IN THE ISLAMIC WORLD

While men and women are considered equal under the *Quran*, Muslim women in the twenty-first century are still being burdened by conservative and patriarchal interpretations of the *Quran*.[2] According to Hajjar, 'in many contexts Sharia provides a potent justification for states to deny or limit women's rights.'[3] However, Gbadamosi argues that it is culture that is employed throughout the world to justify discrimination and violence against women,[4] as opposed to religion. In a country such as Saudi Arabia where religion and culture are so closely interrelated, it is hard to distinguish the two.

While many Islamic countries have signed treaties that protect women's rights such as the Convention on the Elimination of All Forms of Discrimination against Women (CEDAW), many have made reservations to these treaties, limiting their scope and enforceability. Both Tunisia and Saudi Arabia have imposed reservations on core articles of CEDAW, such as articles 2, 16 and 28, on the grounds that they cannot implement CEDAW provisions if they are inconsistent with Islam or Shari'ah.[5] The effectiveness of international treaties is thus very limited.

Tunisia, however, became the first country in the Middle East/North Africa region to lift all specific reservations to CEDAW. On 16 August

---

[1] Nicholas Dunn, 'Abortion, *Ijtihad*, and the Rise of Progressive Islam' (2011) 37 (1/2) *Human Life Review* 53, 54.

[2] Olaide Abbas Gbadamosi, 'Intersection between Shari'a and Reproductive and/or Sexual Health and Human Rights' (2012) 36 (1) *University of Western Australia Law Review* 31, 36.

[3] Ibid., 32.

[4] Ibid., 38.

[5] Ibid., 47.

2011, the Tunisian Council of Ministers adopted a Decree to lift the reservations that limited women's equality within their families.[6]

An example of unfairness against women in Islamic law relates to the issue of *zina*, or adultery. Some Shari'ah courts have accepted the evidence of pregnancy as proof of the offence of *zina*, which clearly discriminates against women, as only women can be convicted on the basis of pregnancy.[7] *Zina* was referred to by Santillana in 1926 as 'any sexual relationship between a man and a woman who is not his wife or slave'.[8] This attitude of almost a century ago illustrates the proprietary nature of women back then; they were seen as mere chattels to be owned and controlled by men. While the status of women has improved in many Muslim countries since that time, the subjection of women to men still resonates today in countries such as Saudi Arabia in the form of guardianship.

Traditionally, and as viewed by the Western media, women in Islam are oppressed and discriminated against. This external perception of Islamic law views Saudi Arabia as one of the most oppressive towards women. However, as will be demonstrated, viewed internally from within Saudi Arabia, women's rights are advancing.

A. Saudi Arabia

Saudi Arabia is an independent Muslim country that has not 'received' any system of foreign law.[9] Saudi family law, or 'the Law of Personal Status', is based on the Islamic Shari'ah, which derives its authority from the *Quran* and *Sunna*.[10] The Kingdom has adopted the Hanbali School to govern its laws.[11] Unlike most other Muslim countries, Saudi Arabia has not codified its law, despite increasing pressure to do so.[12] In Saudi

---

[6] Ibid., 48.

[7] Ibid., 47.

[8] Dariusch Atighetchi, 'Islamic Tradition and Medically Assisted Reproduction' (2000) 169 (1–2) *Molecular and Cellular Endocrinology* 137, 138.

[9] J. N. D. Anderson, *Islamic Law in the Modern World* (New York: New York University Press 1959) 83.

[10] Zainah Almihdar, 'Human Rights of Women and Children Under the Islamic Law of Personal Status and its Application in Saudi Arabia' (2008) 5 (1) *Muslim World Journal of Human Rights* 1.

[11] Ibid.

[12] Frank E. Vogel, 'Shari'a in the Politics of Saudi Arabia' (2012) 10 (4) *Review of Faith & International Affairs* 18, 22.

Arabia, Shari'ah is the constitution of the state and the single formal source of political legitimacy.[13]

In Saudi Arabia, there is a 275-year history of adherence to the Wahhabi tradition, resulting in a differing interpretation of the Shari'ah than in other Muslim countries. As, unlike many other Muslim countries, Saudi Arabia has not been subjected to over a century of Western colonisation,[14] the Kingdom instead relies solely on Shari'ah for its legal, cultural and religious teachings. So while in other countries, Shari'ah is merely a body of legal rules acting as an alternative to the statutory scheme already in existence, in Saudi Arabia, it is the primary law which binds all citizens in their everyday lives.[15]

It is argued that the more closely Shari'ah is followed, the more it restricts women's social mobility and rights.[16] This is the case in Saudi Arabia, as the only puritanical Kingdom that practises strict separation of the sexes,[17] and where the daily activities of women are highly regulated by Shari'ah. Saudi women are banned from driving and are legally subject to male chaperones for almost all public activities. Under Shari'ah, women are 'imprisoned behind veils', justified by men to control a woman's sexual impulses.[18] Women are thus deprived of personal autonomy as well as the ability to express themselves and exercise their sexuality.

Vogel argues that restrictions on women in Saudi Arabia are more widespread and rigorous than what is required by Shari'ah, and that they instead 'appear to have evolved through a cross-breeding of *fiqh* rules with local customs and traditions'.[19]

Saudi Arabia has ratified four of the United Nations Human Rights treaties including the Convention on the Elimination of All Forms of Discrimination against Women (CEDAW) and the Convention on the Rights of the Child (CRC).[20] However, it has made both general and specific reservations to these treaties,[21] meaning their effect and enforceability in the Kingdom are negligible, if effective at all.

---

13 Ibid., 18.
14 Ibid.
15 Ibid.
16 Gbadamosi, above n2, 45.
17 Ibid., 46.
18 Ibid.
19 Vogel, above n12, 24.
20 Almihdar, above n10, 1–2.
21 Ibid., 1.

In addition to these international instruments, Saudi Arabia has adopted various regional instruments and is a member of the Arab League. However, the effect of these instruments in promoting human rights is also questionable, as they have been criticised for being 'so broad and vague as to give Member States only limited responsibility in their protection of human rights'.[22]

Authority in the family in Saudi Arabia is given to males over women and children.[23] This authoritarian relationship can be described by the term men's *qiwama*, or guardianship.[24] Under Saudi administrative and family law, guardianship gives male relatives the legal power over almost every aspect of women's lives, including their movements, work and children.[25] Saudi women thus need permission from a male relative to conduct everyday activities.[26] For this reason, opportunities for Saudi women can depend greatly on the men with whom they live, in terms of whether they are controlling and tyrannical or compassionate and progressive.[27]

While Saudi women have previously been deprived of the right to vote, drive and work with men, advancements have been made in these areas. Following a 2006 labour law provision, women can now work in a mixed workplace with men as opposed to being previously hidden away,[28] and in September 2011 the King announced that women would be able to vote in the 2015 municipal council elections.[29] Furthermore, various protests have been staged by women by driving vehicles in Saudi Arabia, and King Abdullah is trying to advance women's legal status and rights in the Kingdom.[30]

A new development has occurred. It was reported widely in September 2017 that the current Saudi King, Salman, had issued a decree giving women the right to drive for the first time from 2018. This would end a ban seen by human rights activists as an emblem of the conservative

---

22 Ibid., 2.
23 Vogel, above n12, 19.
24 Ibid., 24–25.
25 Ibid., 24.
26 Ibid., 25.
27 Ibid.
28 Ibid.
29 Ibid., 24.
30 Ibid.

Saudi Arabia kingdom's repression of women.[31] These progressions indicate an improvement in women's rights in Saudi Arabia and support the view that '[h]owever regressive and traditionalist Saudi Arabia appears from outside, viewed internally the country seems to be on a path of rapid change and evolution'.[32]

B. Tunisia

Unlike Saudi Arabia, Tunisia has been influenced by external sources. French civil law has had a substantial influence on the legal system in Tunisia and the court system introduced by French colonials was a major international influence.[33] The dominant school of law in Tunisia has been the Malikis, while the Hanafi school is also followed.[34] In January 1861, Muhammed Es Sadiq promulgated a Constitution[35] which specified the contours of a nationwide bureaucracy limiting the powers of the head of state.[36]

Habib Bourguiba led Tunisia to independence from the colonial powers, which resulted in a series of laws that recognised equal social responsibility between men and women.[37] Upon this gaining of independence in 1956, the Constitution was enacted.[38] Following independence, Islam was declared as the state religion and was deemed to be compatible with the guarantee of equal rights and duties for all. Furthermore, the Code of Personal Status made men and women equal in their rights and duties, giving each the right to marry and each the right to divorce, but imposing an obligation to be loyal to only one partner (prohibiting polygyny), and requiring divorce to be finalised in a court of justice.[39]

The law of Tunisia, however, is not and has not always been perfect in the arena of women's rights. The Code of Personal Status falls short in

---

31 See 'Saudi Arabia to allow women to drive, under decree issued by King Salman' *ABC News*, 26 September 2017, available at www.abc.net.au/news/2017-09-27/saudi-king-issues-decree-allowing-women-to-drive/8991486.

32 Ibid., 26–27.

33 Christina Jones-Pauly and Abir Dajani Tuqan, *Women under Islam: Gender, Justice and the Politics of Islam* (London: I. B. Tauris 2011) 71.

34 Ibid., 3.

35 Ibid., 17.

36 Ibid., 18.

37 Ibid., 1.

38 Ibid., 72.

39 Ibid.

the area of inheritance law, as women receive only half that of men.[40] Furthermore, there is a history of *dar jawad* (house of discipline), where disobedient women would be restricted physically.[41] There was no equivalent for disobedient husbands.[42]

Tunisian leaders derived their political discipline not from the military but from the socialist workers' movement, which could accommodate women's interests more easily than a political movement controlled by the male-dominated military.[43]

III. ADOPTION

Adoption was widespread among the Arabs before and during the early days of Islam. However, the practice was expressly forbidden under the *Qur'an*, which says: '... nor has He made your adopted sons your real sons ... Call them [adopted sons] by [the names of] their father's [names, call them] your brothers in faith ...' (33:4–5).[44]

While simply looking after a child is permitted (*kafala*), the prohibition on formal adoption has been kept by virtually all Muslim countries, including Saudi Arabia .[45] Tunisia, on the other hand, grants the right of adoption to every adult who is married and of sound character, mind and body, possesses civil rights and is capable of looking after the child.[46]

As the role of women in Islamic society is primarily one of reproduction and nurturing the family, infertility in Islam poses major problems for women.[47] Furthermore, under the *Qur'an*, offspring are considered to be a 'divine blessing', so the importance of reproduction is paramount.[48]

IV. POLYGYNY AND DIVORCE

The problem of infertility was thought to be adequately solved by resorting to repudiation and remarriage by the husband, or turning to

---

40 Ibid.

41 Ibid., 28.

42 Ibid., 34.

43 Ibid., 70.

44 Jamal J. Ahmad Nasir, *The Status of Women under Islamic Law and Modern Islamic Legislation* (3rd rev. ed.) (Leiden: Brill 2009) 180.

45 Atighetchi, above n8, 139.

46 Nasir, above n44, 180.

47 Atighetchi, above n8, 138.

48 Ibid.

polygyny.[49] While this may appear to be a perfectly acceptable solution for men, who are allowed to have up to four wives under the *Qur'an*[50] and to divorce their wives unilaterally (*talaq*),[51] women do not have this recourse. They cannot marry more than one man and it is much more difficult for them to divorce their husbands.[52] These patriarchal solutions to sterility thus perpetuate the gender inequality present in Islamic society and provide no plausible solution for infertility in women.

In Tunisia, polygyny was criminalised in 1956 based on the understanding of the *Qur'an* at 4:129 that no husband can treat his wives equally.[53] In Saudi Arabia, the practice still occurs.[54] Tunisia also outlawed divorce and repudiation by men in 1956, allowing women to divorce without stipulating any ground.[55] However, women in Saudi Arabia are still faced with many social, legal and financial barriers to divorce.[56]

V. MEDICALLY ASSISTED REPRODUCTION

Due to the prohibition on adoption in most Muslim countries, infertile couples are turning to other methods to have children. Medically assisted reproduction (MAR) is now used throughout the Islamic world.

Muslim jurists were initially critical of different methods of MAR, as many feared these methods would be used in defiance of Shari'ah.[57] Furthermore, unnatural methods of reproduction were avoided as fertility and sterility were considered to be the result of divine will (*Quran* 42, 49–50). Additionally, doctors carrying out the procedures would have to see parts of a woman's body that only her husband should see. Based on these views, some religious leaders prohibit all artificial methods of reproduction.[58]

---

49 Ibid.

50 Ann Black, Hossein Esmaeili and Nadirsyah Hosen, *Modern Perspectives on Islamic Law* (Cheltenham: Edward Elgar Publishing 2013) 121.

51 Ibid., 132.

52 Ibid., 132–8.

53 Gbadamosi, above n2, 39.

54 Black, above n50, 123.

55 Jones-Pauly, above n33, 8–9.

56 Almihdar, above n10, 3–4.

57 Atighetchi, above n8, 138.

58 Ibid.

MAR has become increasingly accepted, as it contributes to the stability and continuance of marriage and the family.[59] While there is disagreement about most aspects of MAR, the general position in Islam today is that only homologous techniques are allowed.[60] All heterologous techniques involving a third party who is extraneous to the couple, whether it is a sperm or egg donor or a person implanting the embryo into the woman, are classified as acts of *zina*.[61]

Reproduction (and contraception) by unnatural instruments are not considered an infringement of divine will as it is thought that the reproductive or contraceptive technique will only be effective if God wishes it.[62] While some argue that the recourse to semen banks comes under masked forms of *zina* and is thus not allowed,[63] in 1997 the National Committee for Medical Ethics of Tunisia noted that sperm banks are accepted, for example, in order to 'preserve the gametes of young people who are to undergo operations resulting in sterility'.[64]

In polygamous relationships, 'the implant of the embryo which was the result of the gametes of the husband and of one of his wives into a second wife maintains the reproductive relationship within the same family nucleus',[65] making it a homologous technique. This further displays the interchangeability of wives, and their lack of power and individual rights.

Most Muslim states do not have specific legislation regulating MAR practices. In Saudi Arabia, ministerial regulations are applied and the authorisation for the centres comes from government authorities,[66] whereas Tunisia is the only Arabic-speaking country that has legislated on the issue of IVF. Here, the law states that 'assisted reproduction treatment for infertility should be performed with gametes of a married couple, and frozen gametes or embryos are only to be used if the couple is alive and the marriage contract is valid and with valid consent'.[67]

---

59 Ibid.

60 Ibid.

61 Ibid.

62 Ibid.

63 Ibid., 139.

64 Ibid., 140.

65 Ibid., 139.

66 Ibid., 140.

67 Mohamed Aboulgar, 'Ethical Aspects and Regulation of Assisted Reproduction in the Arabic-speaking World' (2007) 14 (1) *Reproductive Biomedicine Online* 143, 145.

The law further provides that cryopreservation of embryos is allowed for five years, which can be extended for another five years, and any patient can ask for destruction of cryopreserved embryos if they are filing for a divorce.[68] Cryopreservation of embryos does not take place in Saudi Arabia, while multiple pregnancy reduction is practised in the Kingdom.[69]

There is also the issue of sex selection technologies, which have been condemned on the basis that they discriminate against female embryos and foetuses, 'perpetuating prejudice against the girl child and social devaluation of women'.[70] While some scholars accept sex selection and some oppose it, both agree that family, as the core of Islamic society, should be maintained.[71]

Due to the uncertainties and risks involved with MAR, it is tolerable only in cases of extreme necessity and in the absence of any better alternatives.[72] In summary, it appears that no one form of MAR is allowed throughout the Islamic world, and that each case must be considered on its merits.[73] Clearly, however, the more liberal Tunisia offers a much broader range of options for women.

VI. ABORTION

The Muslim theological position on abortion is more moderate than the Roman Catholic condemnation of the practice.[74] The abortion debate in the late twentieth century moved from the theological to the political. Decisions on abortion are made by the state, religious leaders and physicians, while '[n]owhere is the woman herself given a voice in deciding the suitability of abortion to her needs'.[75]

---

68 Ibid.

69 Atighetchi, above n8, 140.

70 G. I. Serour and B. M. Dickens, 'Ethical and Legal Issues in Reproductive Health: Assisted Reproduction Developments in the Islamic World' (2001) 74 *International Journal of Gynecology & Obstetrics* 187, 190.

71 Jonathan E. Brockopp, 'Islam and Bioethics: Beyond Abortion and Euthanasia' (2008) 36 (1) *Journal of Religious Ethics* 3, 6.

72 Atighetchi, above n8, 139.

73 Serour above n70, 191; Brockopp, above n71, 7.

74 Donna Lee Bowen, 'Abortion, Islam, and the 1994 Cairo Population Conference' (1997) 29 (2) *International Journal of Middle East Studies* 161.

75 Ibid.

Discussions around abortion tend to focus on the health of the mother and the issue of when the embryo becomes a human being, or 'ensoulment'. The time of ensoulment is considered to be anywhere between 40, 90 and 120 days.[76] Abortions carried out before ensoulment are not considered murder and as there is no human being to kill.[77] However, the general consensus is that once ensoulment has occurred, abortion is prohibited.[78]

In Tunisia, however, the Hanafi treatise didn't try to determine the occurrence of ensoulment in terms of months or days; instead, midwives were prohibited from aborting once formation was 'evolved'.[79] Abortion in Tunisia is believed to be a biological issue that is closely tied up with the bodily integrity of the woman, not the foetus, as opposed to a theological issue of predicting when something will become a soul or a life.[80] This point of view purports that women and the foetus are one, so that the woman is the determining factor when the issue of abortion arises, making the health of the woman the most important. If they are divided, on the other hand, the woman loses importance and the foetus takes precedence.[81] The latter is the position accepted in Saudi Arabia and in Christianity. An analogy with *azl* (withdrawing the penis before ejaculation) was utilised in Tunisia, demonstrating that if men are allowed to prevent pregnancy by practising *azl*, then women should be allowed to have an abortion.[82]

In Saudi Arabia, abortion is only permitted to save the life of the mother and to preserve her physical health,[83] and only if the pregnancy is less than four months old and it is proven beyond doubt that continued pregnancy would gravely endanger the mother's health.[84] In Tunisia, on the other hand, abortion is available on request, and is permitted on all grounds, including:

---

[76] Leila Hessini, 'Islam and Abortion: The Diversity of Discourses and Practices' (2008) 39 (3) *Institute of Development Studies Bulletin* 18, 23.

[77] Dunn, above n1, 53.

[78] Ibid., 55.

[79] Jones-Pauly, above n33, 92.

[80] Ibid., 93.

[81] Ibid.

[82] Ibid., 92.

[83] UN Department for Economic for Economic and Social Information and Policy Analysis: Population Division, *Abortion Policies: A Global Review: Volume III: Oman to Zimbabwe* (New York: United Nations 1995) Sales No. E.95.XIII.24, 74.

[84] Ibid., 75.

- to save the life of the mother;
- to preserve the mother's physical and mental health;
- rape or incest;
- foetal impairment; and
- economic or social reasons.[85]

Furthermore, in Saudi Arabia the government has placed major restrictions on contraception use,[86] while in Tunisia, the government directly supports contraception use.[87]

In Saudi Arabia, a legal abortion must be performed in a government hospital, a panel of three medical specialists must sign a recommendation before it is performed, and the written consent of the patient *and* her husband or guardian must be obtained.[88]

In Tunisia, in contrast, consent is only required from the patient herself. Married women have never been required to obtain the consent of their husbands.[89] Under section 214 of the Penal Code as amended in 1973, abortion is permitted on request within the first three months of pregnancy, and must be performed during this period by a legally practising physician in a hospital, healthcare establishment or authorised clinic.[90] Beyond the third month, abortion is allowed if the mother's health or mental equilibrium would be endangered by continuing the pregnancy or on the grounds of foetal impairment.[91]

Up until 1965, Tunisia prohibited abortion. In that year, Tunisia was the first Muslim country to liberalise its abortion law as part of its population policy. The 1965 amendment decriminalised abortion if a couple had at least five living children and the woman had been pregnant for less than three months. A further amendment of the Penal Code in 1973 removed this family size requirement, allowing abortion on request for all women.[92] This amendment was deemed urgent, as in the first years of independence, 25 per cent of all beds in gynaecological clinics were

---

85 Ibid., 137.

86 Ibid., 74.

87 Ibid., 137.

88 Ibid., 74.

89 Jones-Pauly, above n33, 94.

90 UN Department for Economic for Economic and Social Information and Policy Analysis: Population Division, *Abortion Policies: A Global Review: Volume III: Oman to Zimbabwe* (New York: United Nations 1995) Sales No. E.95.XIII.24, 138.

91 Ibid.

92 Ibid.

filled with women (including married women) who had developed complications as a result of unprofessional abortions.[93]

Although there was little religious opposition to the liberalisation of abortion in 1973, it is still difficult for a woman to seek a legal abortion openly, despite it being subsidised by the government and performed free in public hospitals for those entitled to free healthcare. Furthermore, abortion for unmarried women continues to be a taboo subject in traditional communities. Illegal abortion thus continues to be practised in Tunisia, especially for extramarital pregnancies and in rural areas.[94] These reasons may explain why Tunisia has the lowest abortion rate in the Middle East and North Africa, despite having the most liberal abortion law.[95]

VII. CHILD MARRIAGE

Another serious issue that negatively impacts on women is child marriage, which violates a number of human rights guaranteed in international human rights instruments.[96] The practice perpetuates gender discrimination by placing women in an inferior position, 'disempowered to participate equally in their marriage, sexual and reproductive choices'.[97] There is now medical evidence that early marriages could have adverse effects on a child's mental health and physical health.[98] This includes poor sexual and reproductive health, which often results in maternal mortality and morbidity as a result of early pregnancies.[99]

There is no minimum age for marriage set out in the *Qur'an*, so jurists established the position that once a child becomes an adult, they can marry.[100] Childhood under Islamic law is not defined by age, but instead is characterised as anyone who has not yet reached puberty.[101] Most child

---

93 Jones-Pauly, above n33, 94.

94 UN Department for Economic for Economic and Social Information and Policy Analysis: Population Division, *Abortion Policies: A Global Review: Volume III: Oman to Zimbabwe* (New York: United Nations 1995) Sales No. E.95.XIII.24, 138.

95 Hessini, above n76, 19.

96 Gbadamosi, above n2, 44.

97 Ibid., 42.

98 Almihdar, above n10, 10.

99 Gbadamosi, above n2, 42.

100 Black, above n50, 116.

101 Almihdar, above n10, 6.

marriages are forced marriages,[102] as in most cases, there is no consent of the child.

To counteract this problem, the CEDAW Committee suggested that 'no marriages shall be entered into before the age of 18 for both spouses'.[103] Further, article 16(2) of CEDAW holds that 'child marriages shall have no legal effect'.[104] However, as earlier stated, both Tunisia and Saudi Arabia imposed reservations on this article. Since Tunisia lifted all reservations, it is now obliged to comply with the article. In Saudi Arabia, however, child marriage continues.

Under Hanbali law, a father or guardian has the right to contract his previously unmarried wards into marriage without their consent.[105] While this is generally stated as the position of the Hanbali school, another opinion states that the consent of both parties is essential for a marriage contract, and numerous hadiths say a virgin should not be given into marriage without her consent.[106]

Two recent decisions to annul child marriages in Saudi courts have been praised as landmark judgments, as they were given around the same time a number of *fatwas* were issued declaring that there should be no set minimum age for marriage and it is permissible for young girls to wed.[107]

A court in Qatif annulled the marriage of a 14-year-old girl who had been contracted into marriage to an elderly man by her father without her consent. The court considered the girl's best interests and found that the marriage resulted in a deterioration of her education and psychological health.[108] This was the first known case where a Saudi judge annulled a child marriage to an elder.[109] Similarly, in March 2009, the Court of Appeal in Riyadh reversed a judgment that had held that 'the marriage of an 8-year-old girl to an elderly man was legal, despite the fact that she had been contracted into marriage by her father without her knowledge'.[110]

---

[102] Black, above n50, 129–31.
[103] Almihdar, above n10, 6.
[104] Ibid.
[105] Ibid., 3.
[106] Ibid.
[107] Ibid., 10–11.
[108] Ibid., 10.
[109] Ibid.
[110] Ibid.

VIII. FEMALE GENITAL MUTILATION

Female genital mutilation (FGM), which discriminates against women and causes significant reproductive health problems, is defined by the World Health Organization (WHO) as encompassing 'all procedures involving partial or total removal of the external female genitalia or other injury to the female genial organs for non-medical reasons'.[111]

While religion is commonly provided as a basis for FGM, there is little evidence that the practice is a religious obligation.[112] The practice, believed to have existed for at least 5,000 years, is not mentioned in the *Qur'an* and it is also practised in Christian communities,[113] suggesting that its origins may lie elsewhere. In a 1997 decision, Egypt's highest court upheld a ban on FGM which rejected an argument that FGM is a religious issue, ruling that the practice is not mandated by the *Qur'an*.[114] Despite this, evidence suggests that the practice is more commonly carried out in Muslim societies.[115]

The practice has been legitimised by some religious authorities who refer to the Hadith in which Prophet Muhammad said it is *Sunnah* 'if you cut, do not overdo it … , because it brings more radiance to the face, and it is more pleasant for the husband'.[116] Further, *fatwas* that stated that *khifad* (one type of FGM) is *Sunnah* led to the belief that all types of FGM are *Sunnah* and thus justified.[117]

Reasons put forward for FGM include the prevention of promiscuity and the regulation of the moral behaviour of women in society.[118] Such reasoning reflects the oppression of women in Muslim societies[119] and perpetuates male control of Islamic women.[120]

---

[111] Abdulrahim A. Rouzi, 'Facts and Controversies on Female Genital Mutilation and Islam' (2013) 18 (1) *European Journal of Contraception and Reproductive Health Care* 10.

[112] Maria Kontoyannis and Christos Katsetos, 'Female Genital Mutilation' (2010) 4 (1) *Health Science Journal* 31, 33.

[113] Ibid., 32.

[114] Margaret Brady, 'Female Genital Mutilation: What Every Nurse Needs to Know' (1998) 28 (9) *Nursing* 50, 51.

[115] Rouzi, above n111, 11.

[116] Ibid., 12.

[117] Ibid.

[118] Kontoyannis, above n112, 32.

[119] Ibid., 35.

[120] Ibid., 33.

Some of the serious immediate and long-term complications resulting from FGM[121] include the transmission of HIV and hepatitis B virus. Many girls also die of shock, haemorrhage, sepsis or infection.[122] In the long term, infertility and complications during pregnancy and childbirth are also common.[123]

FGM has not been documented in Saudi Arabia or Tunisia;[124] however, there is widespread medical evidence of the practice amongst Saudi women.[125]

IX. CONCLUSION

In comparing Saudi Arabia and Tunisia, we see the broadest range of attitudes regarding the treatment of women and their rights in the Islamic world. Tunisia offers legal abortion, divorce and access to IVF, while Saudi Arabia still demands male consent for the simplest procedure. Abortion and divorce are still unavailable there, and women remain at the mercy of men, even in regard to decision-making about their own bodies, particularly health and reproduction. Genital mutilation and the taking of child brides still occurs, but cautionary precedents are becoming evident.

It is worth noting, however, that while the West sees Saudi Arabia as rigidly fundamentalist and archaic in its treatment of women, changes are occurring within the Kingdom, which has until recently been almost devoid of Western influence. Although slow, when compared to the more progressive Tunisia, the general trend is towards liberalism. The Arab Spring, the internet and the emergence of Muslim feminism are all factors contributing to the reforms throughout the Muslim world, and Saudi Arabia cannot help but be affected.

---

121 Ibid.

122 Brady, above n114, 50.

123 Ibid., 50–1.

124 Rouzi, above n111, 12.

125 A. A. Rouzi, 'Epidermal Clitoral Inclusion Cysts: Not a Rare Complication of Female Genital Mutilation' (2010) 25 (7) *Human Reproduction* 1672–4.

12. Collective *ijtihad* on health issues in Indonesia

Nadirsyah Hosen

I. INTRODUCTION

The nature of the *Qur'an* and *Sunnah* as religious, non-legal texts ensures their status as the primary sources of Islamic law. The structure of Islam and the divinity of law within that structure necessitates that the *Qur'an* and the *Sunnah* remain the primary legal texts for Muslims. The anachronistic nature of the texts and the 'rule by law' (as opposed to the 'rule of law') become problematic when reconciling more modern concepts. Consequently the non-legal nature of the texts, and more recently their anachronism, has instigated interpretation, and a lack of a central, authoritative hierarchy has allowed a plethora of interpretations to arise over the centuries.

As Islam was a spiritual religion before becoming a complete political, legal and military force in the state of Medina,[1] the societal aspects of the teachings of Islam are considered Divine Will, along with the religious teachings. In fact, 'Islam is the only religion whose followers believe that the Qur'an is the word of God, and therefore that Qur'anic laws are God's direct commands.'[2] The *Qur'an*, being the word of God revealed to the Prophet, is a product of the phenomenon of Revelation and is indisputable for Muslims. While there are disputes as to the nature of the content in the *Qur'an* and scholars debate whether the Qur'an is the word of God verbatim or if the teachings were revealed to the Prophet who then spoke them in his own words, all scholars agree that the Qur'an is the product of Divine Revelation.[3] The death of the Prophet Muhammad arrests the process of Revelation, limiting the known will of God to the content of the Qur'an with Muslims being unable to access fresh Divine

[1] Ann Black, Hossein Esmaeili and Nadirsyah Hosen, *Modern Perspectives on Islamic Law* (Cheltenham: Edward Elgar 2013) 6.

[2] Ibid.

[3] Ibid., 8.

Will. The Qur'an is therefore entrenched as the primary legal source, being the final word of God, following the end of Revelation.

The nature of the Qur'an as a non-legal text is problematic because it does not expressly provide the solution to every legal quandary. The Qur'an, as a book about the relationship between God and people, deals predominantly with religion. While it does include verses that prescribe rules, only about 2 per cent of all Qur'anic verses relate to what is considered to be law in the Western legal tradition.[4] This relatively small amount of Divine Law is supplemented by the Sunna, or prophetic reports, that document what the Prophet of Islam said, did or consented to during his prophesying, yet this second text is also not a strictly legal text as only 10 per cent of the sayings of the Prophet (*Hadith*) relate to proper law.[5] The *Hadith*, compiled after the death of the Prophet based on what was passed down through the oral traditions of Islam, are also considered Divine Law because they are the product of the Revelation of the will of God to the Prophet. While it is accepted that the Qur'an is the word of God revealed to the Prophet Muhammad and because of its divine source cannot be questioned, it has been the function of Muslim jurisprudence to discover the terms of that command.[6] The relatively few legal verses in the Qur'an and the *Hadith* necessitate the interpretation of the two texts in order that Islamic law can be applied to situations not expressly considered in the texts.

Although earlier scholars took the view that Islamic law became increasingly rigid and set in its final mould,[7] the challenge for contemporary Muslim scholars is to use the institution of the *ijtihad* as a tool through which a society can adjust itself to internal and external social, political and economic change. Historically, *ijtihad* in Islamic tradition refers to the exercise of Islamic legal reasoning by a single Muslim scholar (*Mujtahid*). However, since the nineteenth century there has been a new development that *ijtihad* is exercised by a group of Muslim scholars. This activity is called *ijtihad jama'i* (collective *ijtihad*). As a result, through the institution they produced what we call a collective *fatwa*.

This chapter will examine the establishment of such institutions that exercise collective *ijtihad*. First, I will briefly explain the rules on *ijtihad* from a historical perspective. Second, I will discuss the concept of

---

[4] Ibid., 11.

[5] Ibid.

[6] Ibid., 7.

[7] Joseph Schacht, *An Introduction to Islamic Law* (Oxford: Clarendon Press 1998) 75.

collective *ijtihad* based on the 1964 decision of *Majma' al-Buhuts al-Islamiyah* in Cairo. Finally, I will provide examples of collective *ijtihad* on health issues. I would argue that collective *ijtihad* should be considered as a tool for modern Muslim scholars to meet the requirement of Mujtahid in a collective way and for providing better answers to the problems faced by Muslims in contemporary time.

II. THE RULES ON *IJTIHAD*

Ijtihad in Islamic law can be defined simply as 'interpretation'. It is the most important source of Islamic law next to the Qur'an and the Sunnah. The main difference between *ijtihad* and both the Qur'an and the Sunnah is that *ijtihad* is a continuous process of development whereas the Qur'an and the Sunnah, as mentioned above, are fixed sources of authority and were not altered or added to after the death of the Prophet.[8]

Ijtihad literally means 'striving, or self-exertion in any activity which entails a measure of hardship'.[9] According to a classical Muslim scholar al-Amidi, *ijtihad* is defined as 'the total expenditure of effort made by a jurist to infer, with a degree of probability, the rules of Islamic law'.[10] In this sense, al-Ghazali defined *ijtihad* as 'the expending, on the part of a *Mujtahid*, of all that he is capable of in order to seek knowledge of the injunctions of Islamic law'.[11]

Interpretation the Quran and the Sunna is not a new concept in Islamic law and is used to overcome the abovementioned limitations of the texts. The Prophet Muhammad himself sent one of his Companions (Mu'adh Ibn Jabal) to act as a judge of sorts based on the principles of the Quran and Sunna, and charged him to employ *ijtihad* if an answer could not be found expressly in those texts. They engaged in the following dialogue before the latter's departure:

> What will you do if a matter is referred to you for judgement?' Mua'dh said, 'I will judge according to the Book of Allah'. The Prophet asked, 'What if

---

[8] Mohammad Hashim Kamali, *Principles of Islamic Jurisprudence* (Cambridge: The Islamic Text Society 1991) 366.

[9] Ibid., 367; Hans Wehr, *A Dictionary of Modern Written Arabic* (London: Macdonald & Evans LTD 1974) 142–3.

[10] Sayf al-Din al-Amidi, *al-Ihkam fi Usul al-Ahkam*, Vol. 4 (Cairo: Dãr al-Kutub al-Khidîwîya 1914) 218. Also see Muhammad Taqi al-Hakim, *al-Usul al-'Ämmah li al-Fiqh al-Muqarin* (Beirut: Dar al-Andalas 1963) 561–2.

[11] Abu Hamid al-Ghazali, *al-Mustasfa min 'Ilm al-Usul*, Vol. 4 (al-Madinah al-Munawwarah: al-Jami'ah al-Islamiyah n.d.) 4.

> you find no solution in the Book of Allah?' Mua'dh said, 'Then I will judge by the Sunnah of the Prophet'. The Prophet asked: 'And what if you do not find it in the Sunnah of the Prophet?' Mua'dh said: 'Then I will make *ijtihad* to formulate my own judgement'. The Prophet patted Mua'dh's chest and said: 'Praise be to Allah Who has guided the messenger of His prophet to that which pleases him and His Messenger.[12]

However, it should be stressed that the concept and the meaning of *ijtihad*, as used in the conversation above, is different to *ijtihad* in its current context. Throughout history the meaning of *ijtihad* has altered according to place and circumstance. During the times of the Prophet and his Companions, it should be noted that *ijtihad* was still very much an abstract rather than a generally applied or apprehended concept.

In the period of the leaders of *Maddhab* (school of thoughts), Abu Hanîfah (d. 150 AH/767 CE) was reported as having said:

> I follow the book of Allah, and if I find no solution there, I follow the Sunnah of the Prophet, peace be upon him, If I find no solution in either the Qur'an or the Sunnah, I follow whichever of the pronouncements of the *Sahabah* (the Prophet's companions) I prefer, and leave whichever I wish. If there is a pronouncement on a particular matter by any of the *Sahabah*, I would not adopt any other opinion made by any other scholar. But if I found a solution only in the opinions of Ibrahim, al-Shu'bi, Ibn Sirrin, al-Hasan, or Sa'îd ibn al-Musayyab [all were Muslim scholars in the era of Tabi'un, or after companions' era] I would make *ijtihad*, just as they did.[13]

Abu Hanifah, the founder of the Hanafi school, here not only describes his method of issuing *fatwa* and the procedure to be adopted in the case of *ijtihad*, but also defines the procedure of *ijtihad*.

It is instructive to explore the meaning of *ijtihad* in the *Muwatta'* of Imam Malik (d. 179 AH/795 CE), since this book is usually considered to be amongst the earliest of Islamic juristic works.[14] Ahmad Hasan explained that Malik used the term *ijtihad* generally, for cases where he could find no definite answer from the Prophet or in commonly agreed practice and, therefore, left the matter to the discretion of the Imam to

---

12 Abu Dawud Sulaiman, *Sunan Abi Dawud* (Beirut: al-Maktabah al-'Ashriyah, n.d.) Hadith Number [HN]: 3,119.

13 See Muhammad Salam Madkur, *Manahij al-Ijtihad* (Kuwait: al-matba'ah al-Ashriyah 1974) 57–8.

14 See the analysis on *al-Muwatta'* in Norman Calder, *Studies in Early Muslim Jurisprudence* (Oxford: Clarendon Press 1993) 20–38.

decide.[15] An examination of the term *ijtihad* in *Muwatta'* lends support to Hasan's opinion. Several examples of how *ijtihad* is used in *Muwatta'* are outlined below:

1. Malik was asked about bonuses and whether they were taken from the first of the spoils, and he said, 'That is only decided according to the *ijtihad* of the Imam [the leader]. We do not have a known reliable command about that other than it is up to the *ijtihad* of the Sultan. I have not heard that the Messenger of Allah, may Allah bless him and grant him peace, gave bonuses in all his raids. I have only heard that he gave bonuses in one of them, namely the day of Hunayn. It depends on the *ijtihad* of the Imam whether they are taken from the first of the spoils or what is left after that.'[16]
2. Yahya said that Malik was asked whether someone who killed one of the enemy could keep the man's effects without the permission of the Imam. He said, 'No one can do that without the permission of the Imam. Only the Imam can make *ijtihad*. I have not heard that the Messenger of Allah, may Allah bless him and grant him peace, ever said, "Whoever kills someone can have his effects", on any other day than the day of Hunayn.'[17]

At the time of Malik who lived in Madinah, according to Ahmad Hasan, scholars of Iraq used the term *hukumah 'adl* (fair arbitration) in cases where Malik used the term *ijtihad*. Hasan believed that the term *ijtihad* was not in frequent use in the Iraqis' writings, except for Al-Shaybani, who wrote *Kitab Ijtihad al-Ra'y*.[18]

In the second century (eighth century CE), after the era of Malik, *ijtihad* was gradually dissociated from *ra'y* (opinion) as the latter (*ra'y*) increasingly fell into the category of objectionable practices.[19] Muhammad bin Idris al-Shafi'i (d. 204 AH) was the first to make a clean break from *ra'y* and to adopt *ijtihad* as a methodology synonymous with *qiyas*

---

15 Ahmad Hasan, *The Early Development of Islamic Jurisprudence* (Islamabad: Islamic Research Institute 1970) 116.

16 Malik bin Anas, *al-Muwatta'* (Beirut: al-Shirkah al-Alamiyyah 1993), HN: 865.

17 Ibid., HN: 864.

18 Hasan, loc. cit.

19 Wael B. Hallaq, 'Ijtihad' in John L. Esposito (eds), *The Oxford Encyclopedia of the Modern Islamic World*, Vol. 2 (Oxford: Oxford University Press 1995) 179.

(analogy). He said, 'They (*ijtihad* and *qiyas*) are two names for the same thing (*innahuma ismani li ma'na wahid*).'[20]

Defining *ijtihad*, Shafi'i says that if a Muslim is faced with a given situation, he/she should follow the express binding injunction, if available; otherwise he/she should try to seek by *ijtihad* the indications that lead to truth. Shafi'i says that *ijtihad* is nothing but *qiyas*.[21]

One of Shafi'i's followers, two centuries after the Shafi'i era, al-Mawardi (d. 448 AH/1058 CE), believed that it was Ibn Abî Hurairah (d. 345 AH/956. CE) who said that *ijtihad* is *qiyas*. Hurairah attributed this to al-Shafi'i. Actually, according to al-Mawardi, al-Shafi'i wrote only, '*anna ma'na al-ijtihad ma'na al-qiyas*' (verily, the meaning of *ijtihad* is the meaning of *qiyas*). The context of this writing was that al-Shafi'i took the view that both are used when there is no answer in the *Qur'an* and the *Sunnah*. So, al-Mawardi distinguishes between *ijtihad* and *qiyas*. For him, although *ijtihad* and *qiyas* are different, *ijtihad* is the introduction to *qiyas* (*al-ijtihad muqaddimah li al-qiyas*).[22]

Despite the fact that several of his followers took the point that *qiyas* is not the same as *ijtihad*, but is a part of *ijtihad*, since the Shafi'i era the word *ijtihad* has come to mean more than an abstract concept. At that stage, *ijtihad* was used as a technical word in Islamic law which required method and procedure in order to be performed. As Wael B. Hallaq explains:

> In the eight century *ijtihad* was also used in the sense of 'technical estimate' or 'fair judgment', particularly 'an effort at setting the value of a thing', as in estimating due compensation or damages. This meaning of the term was to persist for centuries in the realm of substantive law. With the elaboration of legal theory (*usul al-fiqh*) toward the beginning of the tenth century, the meaning and scope of *ijtihad* finally became defined. *Ijtihad* now came to signify the utmost intellectual effort of the *Mujtahid* to reach a solution or a rule (*hukm*) on a religious matter.[23]

The forming of schools in Islamic law launched the issue of whether anyone at all could perform *ijtihad*, or only a limited number of people. Al-Amidi (d. 631 AH/1233 CE) and al-Baydawi (d. 685 AH/1286 CE)

---

[20] Muhammad bin Idris al-Shafi'i, *al-Risalah* (Cairo: Dar al-Saqafah 1973) 209.

[21] Ibid.

[22] Abu al-Hasan, 'Ali bin Muhammad bin al-Mawardi, *al-Hawi al-Kabir fi Fiqh Maddhab al-Imam al-Shafi'i*' Vol. 16 (Beirut: Dãr al-Kutüb al-'Ilmiyah 1994) 118.

[23] Hallaq, 'Ijtihad', loc. cit.

agreed that only people who satisfy specific requirements can apply *ijtihad*. According to them, there were two main conditions of *Mujtahid*: firstly, to be an adult and believer in Allah and the Prophet; secondly, to be an expert in all aspects of Islamic law (*al-ahkam al-syar'iyah wa aqsamuha*).[24]

Furthermore, when discussing the requirements of *ijtihad*, Imam al-Ghazali maintained that in order to reach the rank of *Mujtahid*, additionally to the two conditions mentioned above, the individual jurist must:

1. know the 500 verses needed in law – committing them to memory is not a prerequisite;
2. know the way to relevant *Hadith* literature; the jurist needs only to maintain a reliable copy of Abu Dawud's or Bayhaqi's collection rather than memorise their contents;
3. know the substance of *furu'* works and the points subject to *ijma'*, so that the jurist does not deviate from the established laws. If he/she cannot meet this requirement, he/she must ensure that the legal opinion arrived at does not contradict any opinion of a renowned jurist;
4. know the methods by which legal evidence is derived from the texts;
5. know the Arabic language – complete mastery of its principles is not a prerequisite;
6. know the rules governing the doctrine of abrogation (*naskh*). However, the jurist need not be thoroughly familiar with the details of this doctrine; it suffices to show that the verse or the *Hadith* in question had not been repealed; and
7. investigate the authenticity of the *Hadith*. If Muslims have accepted the *Hadith* as reliable, it may not be questioned. If a transmitter was known for probity, all *Hadith* related through him/her are to be accepted. Full knowledge of the sciences of *Hadith* criticism is not required.

Al-Ghazali concluded that the jurist must have expertise in the science of *Hadith*, the Arabic language (*'ilm al-lugah*) and Islamic legal theory (*usul al-fiqh*).[25] The question is: do we still have scholars who can meet

---

[24] Sayf al-Din al-Amidi, Vol. 3, above n10, 139; Abu Nur Zuhair, *Muzakkirah fi Usul al-Fiqh li Ghair al-Ahnaf*, Vol. 4 (Egypt: Matba'ah Dar al-Ta'lif n.d.) 225.

[25] Al-Ghazali, above n11, 5–15.

all the requirements above? I have briefly examined the historical term and concept of *ijtihad.* We now move to our main discussion on collective *ijtihad.*

III. COLLECTIVE *IJTIHAD*: A NEW DEVELOPMENT

The term *Mujtahid* refers to a single scholar. Since the tenth century it has been hard to find one individual who fulfilled the requirements to be *Mujtahid.* If there has been a *Mujtahid,* he stands at the lower ranking. This situation has led to a new development in Islamic law, namely *ijtihad jama'i.* Since the nineteenth century, there has been a new development, in terms of using two expressions: *ijtihad fard* and *ijtihad jama'i. Ijtihad fard* refers to the exercise of *ijtihad* by a single scholar. If a group of scholars exercise *ijtihad* collectively, this activity is called *ijtihad jama'i.* This means that all the conditions to be *Mujtahid* will be held collectively by jurists acting together, not just a single jurist. A jurist who is expert only in *'Ulum al-Qur'an* (Qur'anic sciences) has the right to perform *ijtihad* in Islamic law if he/she performs it together with other jurists, who have expertise in other aspects. Through this combined effort, *ijtihad* is not as difficult or as exclusive as was previously the case.

Another supporting reason for the employment of *ijtihad jama'i* is that it allows modern and complex problems to be resolved, and tends to reduce the fanaticism of the schools of Islamic law.[26] As a result, a number of Muslim scholars advocate the performance of *ijtihad* not only individually but also collectively. For example, Yusuf al-Qaradawi has stated that 'the *ijtihad* which we need in our era is *al-ijtihad al-jama'i.* It is also considered as an apt solution for the crisis of thought in the Muslim world'.[27]

However, the term *ijtihad jama'i* has no single meaning. Historically, this term began to be used in referring to *ijma'* (consensus). Mahmud Shaltut, for example, used this term in respect of *ijma'* in the 1950s.[28] At this stage, there had not been any recent new development in the meaning of the term *ijtihad jama'i,* as *ijma'* had been used since the fourteenth century. A new development occurred when *Majma' al-Buhuts*

---

26 'Abd al-Halim Uwes, *al-Fiqh al-Islami baina al-Tatawwur wa al-Tsabat* (Madinah: Shirkah al-Madinah al-Munawwarah n.d.) 158.

27 Yusuf al-Qaradawi, 'al-Ijtihad wa al-Tajdid baina al-Dawabit al-Shar'iyyah wa al-Hajat al-Mu'ashirah', interview in *al-'Ummah,* Qatar, 31 May 1984, 48.

28 See Mahmud Shaltut, *Al-Islam Aqidah wa Shari'ah* (4th ed.) (Cairo: Dar al-Shuruq 1988) 536.

al-Islamiyah[29] in 1964 held its first *mu'tamar* (conference), which was attended by scholars from many Islamic countries. The conference announced that:

> *Mu'tamar* has decided that the Qur'an and the Sunnah are the main sources of Islamic law, and performing *ijtihad* is the right of every jurist who fulfills the requirements in the field of *ijtihad.*
>
> The procedure to maintain the *maslahah* (benefit) when facing new cases or problems is by choosing laws from the schools of Islamic law which are suitable for that case, and if there is still no answer by doing that, then by performing *al-ijtihad al-jama'i al-maddhabi* (collective *ijtihad* by following the rule of the school dependently), and if this way is not enough (to solve the problems), then by performing *al-ijtihad al-jama'i al-mutlaq* (collective *ijtihad* independently).
>
> This institution *(Majma' al-Buhuth al-Islamiyah)* will organise or manage the efforts to perform *ijtihad jama'i* in both categories [dependent and independent] when needed.[30]

It was unfortunate that the *mu'tamar* did not specify what it believed *ijtihad jama'i* to be.[31] It is interesting that in the proceedings of the *mu'tamar*, found in *al-Taujih al-Ijtima'i fi al-Islam min Buhuth Mu'tamarat Majma' al-Buhuts al-Islamiyah*, Vol. 1, 1971 (seven years after the first *mu'tamar* was held in 1383 AH/1964 CE), no single article from eleven discusses *ijtihad.* The question is, how did the *mu'tamar* reach the conclusion about *ijtihad jama'i* if it did not discuss that theme during the first *mu'tamar*?

However, in 1983, al-Azhar University published a book, *Majma' al-Buhuth al-Islamiyah Tarikhuh wa Tatawuruh*, which explains the history and the development of this institution. Unlike *al-Taujih al-Ijtima'i fi al-Islam*, this book consists of only the title and a summary of each article presented at the *mu'tamar.* Surprisingly, two articles about *ijtihad* are found in the latter book. Both have the same title, 'al-*Ijtihad: Madih wa Hadiruh*' (*ijtihad*: Past and Present). One article was written

---

29 *Majma' al-Buhuth al-Islamiyah* is formed by Law No. 103, 1961 in Cairo. See Ahmad Muhammad 'Uf, *al-Azhar fi Alf 'Am* (Cairo: Majma' al-Buhuth al-Islamiyah 1982) 134–41. It consists of 50 scholars from different *Maddhab*, 30 of whom are from Egypt. See al-Azhar al-Sharif, *al-Azhar Tarikhuh wa Tatawwuruh* (Cairo: al-Azhar 1983) 193–4.

30 See the conference proceeding, Majma' al-Buhuth al-Islamiyah, *al-Taujih al-Tashri'i fi al-Islam min Buhuth Mu'tamarat Majma' al-Buhuth al-Islamiyah*, Vol. 2 (Cairo: al-Azhar 1972) 167.

31 See al-Azhar al-Syarîf, above n29, 369.

by al-Sheikh Muhammad Nur al-Hasan and the other by al-Sheikh al-Fadil bin 'Ashur. Unfortunately, as has been said, the book does not include all the texts of the articles. The implication is that it is hard to understand the background of why the *Majma'* come to the conclusion of *ijtihad jama'i*.

It is also hard to understand what the definition of *ijtihad jama'i* is, according to the *Majma'*. As far as can be determined, from the explanation of the *mu'tamar (bayan al-mu'tamar)*, one should find that the idea of Islamic unity became the focus of the *Majma'* to solve in problems Muslim societies. For example, the *Majma'* would act for the unity of Islam, by eradicating the friction between Muslims over the cases in which schools of Islamic law may differ from one another.

If this is the reason why the *Majma'* reached its conclusion about *ijtihad jama'i* (to eradicate the *Asbab al-Khilafat al-Maddhabiyah*), it is unclear whether the term *ijtihad jama'i* refers to the *ijma'* or not, since the first *mu'tamar* suggested the performance of *al-ijtihad al-jama'i al-Maddhabi* (see the decision of the first *mu'tamar* above) which means that it recognised the existence of the schools, and it did not want to eradicate the schools.

Further, one may observe that although at the first *mu'tamar, majma'* announced that it would organise and manage the implementation of *ijtihad jama'i*; however, at the following *mu'tamar*,[32] this institution neglected to provide technical guidance for collective *ijtihad*. From the proceeding of the next conference, it appears that the *Majma'* sees itself as an upholder and proponent of Islam confronted with aggressive Western Spiritual Neo-Imperialism, especially in its Zionist garb. Meanwhile, Dr Yusuf al-Qaradawi takes the view that from its very inception the *Majma'* has been a failure; there has been too much political meddling, it failed to attract the most important foreign Islamic personalities and stayed essentially Egyptian. Since the 1970s its work has come to a halt and now it is but a building, with no meaning, which ought to be demolished.[33]

---

[32] See the results of the *mu'tamar* from the first *mu'tamar* until the fifth in *al-Taujih*, Vol. 2, above n30, 167–74. See the difference in title between the first volume and the second one: *al-Taujih al-Tashri'i* and *al-Taujih al-Ijtima'i*. The results of the sixth, seventh and eight *mu'tamars* can be found in al-Azhar al-Sharif, *Majma' al-Buhuth al-Islamiyah: Tarikhuh wa Tatawuruh* (Cairo: al-Azhar 1983) 416–48.

[33] See Yusuf al-Qaradawi, *Risalat al-Azhar bayna al-Ams wa al-Yawm al-Ghad* (Cairo: Maktabah al-Wahdba 1984) 121–2.

Subsequently, Dr Nadiyah Sharif al-'Umari of al-Azhar University has provided some technical guidance on how to practise *ijtihad jama'i* in the Muslim world. Firstly, the qualifications to be *Mujtahid* are to be organised by Muslim governments. Afterwards, those governments should choose their representatives to attend an international meeting. Secondly, in addition to the scholars on Islamic law, the meeting should invite other scholars from various disciplines of science. Thirdly, if there is disagreement in reaching a conclusion, the decision should be made by a majority vote. Fourthly, Muslim governments should follow that decision. Thus, Islamic societies will follow too.[34]

If the technical guidance by al-'Umari is considered, then the second meaning of *ijtihad jama'i* emerges; that is, *ijtihad* which is performed at the international level. Actually, *ijma'*, as the first meaning of *ijtihad jama'i*, is also held at the international level. The differences between the first meaning and the second are, firstly, *ijma'* does not require secular scholars to attend and, secondly, a decision of *ijma'* must be reached by the consensus of all Muslims scholars (*Mujtahids*), not by a majority vote.

Harun Nasution, the late Rector of the State Institute for Islamic Studies in Jakarta, argued that *ijtihad jama'i* should be at the national level, not the international. His reasons were: firstly, each community has special problems which might be different from those of others. Secondly, there are different interpretations and implementations of Islamic law in each community. Thus, he suggested that the institution of *ijtihad jama'i* should be present in every Muslim government.[35] This suggestion leads to the third meaning of *ijtihad jama'i*.

The first meaning, which equates the term with *ijma'*, as has been mentioned, is not a proper meaning in the context of new developments in Islamic tradition. The second meaning (collective *ijtihad* at the international level) and the third (collective *ijtihad* at the national level) are already implemented in the Muslim world.

At the international level, there is a Fiqh Academy (*Majma' al-Fiqh al-Islamiy*), which was created at the decision of the second summit of the then Organisation of Islamic Cooperation (OIC) 1974 and inaugurated in February 1988. It consists of all sheikhs and scholars from 57 state members of OIC. The Fiqh Academy is based in Jedda, Saudi Arabia, and headed by Sheikh Ahmad Khalid Babakr (b. 1940).

---

[34] Nadiyah Sharif al-'Umari, *al-Ijtihad fi al-Islam* (Beirut: Mu'asasah al-Risalah 1986) 265–6.

[35] Harun Nasution, 'Ijtihad, Sumber Ketiga Ajaran Islam', in Haidar Bagir and Syafiq Basri (eds), *Ijtihad dalam Sorotan* (Bandung: Mizan 1988) 115–16.

The following can be seen as *Mujtahid jama'i* in the third meaning (at national level). In Egypt, for instance, the *Dar al-Ifta* is a government agency, established since 1895, charged with issuing Islamic legal opinions on any question to Muslims who ask for *fatwas*. The agency issues around 5,000 *fatwas* a week, including both official *fatwas* that the Egyptian Mufti crafts on important issues and more routine *fatwas* handled via phone and internet by a dozen or so subordinate muftis. In Saudi Arabia, in 1971 King Faisal established the Permanent Committee for Islamic Research and Fatwas (*al-Lajnah ad-Da'imah li al-Buhuth al-'Ilmiyyah wal-Ifta*) whose task is to issue *fatwas*. Currently, its Chair is Sheikh 'Abd al-Aziz (b. 1940). He is named Grand Mufti of Saudi Arabia.

In addition to those performances at international and national levels, there are many Islamic organisations in several countries that perform collective *ijtihad*. Indonesia is one example. Instead of the performing of collective *ijtihad* at the national level, there have been three main Islamic organisations that perform *ijtihad* collectively. One of them is the Nahdlatul Ulama, which has performed collective *ijtihad* since 1926, and which is even older than most international institutions mentioned above. This phenomenon leads to the fourth meaning of *ijtihad jama'i*: collective *ijtihad* at the organisational level.

Despite the four different meanings of collective *ijtihad*, shared characteristics can be observed: Firstly, it is performed collectively. The justification for collective *ijtihad* comes from the Qur'an (3: 159 and 42: 38) which advocates *shura* (consultation). It also refers to the sayings of the Prophet:

> I ('Ali bin Abi Talib) said to the Prophet, 'O, Prophet, [what if] there is a case among us, while neither revelation comes, nor the Sunnah exists'. The Prophet replied, '[you should] have meetings with the scholars – or in another version: the pious servants – and consult with them. Do not make a decision only by a single opinion.'[36]

Secondly, the meetings are attended by jurists (*fuqaha*) and other scholars from various backgrounds. This procedure is followed since Muslim scholars appreciate and apprehend that problems in the modern era are far more complex than at the time of the Prophet 15 centuries ago. Accordingly, Muslim communities today expect Muslim scholars to provide broad answers to their problems, not only from Islamic law viewpoints, but also from other perspectives.

---

[36] See Uwes, above n26, 159.

Thirdly, the meetings are assembled basically to confront new issues, which did not exist 15 centuries ago, and to reinterpret old judgments from modern perspectives. The current situation is completely different from that faced by Abu Hanifah, Malik, al-Shafi'i and Ahmad bin Hanbal (the founders of four main maddhabs). It is a collective attempt to show that Shari'ah is adaptable to social change.

Performing collective *ijtihad* at the organisational level leads to the plurality of *fatwa*. It is possible that a method, process and sources of *fatwa* from one organisation may differ from those of the other Islamic organisations, although they are in the same country, Therefore, it is possible to have many *fatwas* in one case. This is clearly a new development in the production of plurality of *fatwas* in the Islamic world.

IV. CASE STUDIES: COLLECTIVE *IJTIHAD* ON HEALTH ISSUES

Until the beginning of the twentieth century, *ijtihad* in Indonesia was performed by individual Muslim scholars. In the second quarter of the twentieth century, the practice of *ijtihad* as performed by the scholars in groups began. In 1926, traditionalist scholars founded the Nahdlatul Ulama (NU) organisation, and it began issuing *fatwas* as early as its first congress. The modernist Muhammadiyah organisation, which was founded in 1912, did not concern itself with *fatwa* until 1927 when it created a special committee called Majelis Tarjih to deal with religious issues in general and Islamic law in particular.[37]

Although *fatwas* issued by certain individual scholars could still be observed, the tendency was for more and more scholars or clergies to identify themselves with one of those two poles: with the Nahdlatul Ulama or the Muhammadiyah. A new development emerged when in 1975 the Council of Indonesian Ulama (Majelis Ulama Indonesia or MUI) was established. Both the traditionalist and the modernist are represented in the MUI, through which they issue joint *fatwas*.[38]

The three Indonesian Islamic organisations who practise collective *ijtihad* have responded to medical and health issues. The *fatwa* on medical science on matters such as vasectomy and tubectomy, cornea

---

[37] Mohamad Atho Mudzhar, 'Fatwās as of the Council of Indonesian Ulama: A Study of Islamic Legal Thought in Indonesia 1975–88' (PhD dissertation, UCLA 1990) 6.

[38] Ibid., 15.

transplant, euthanasia, pills for menstrual prevention and IUD was issued. The nature of 'collective' in the process of issuing *fatwas* is as follows:

1. The Islamic organisations received questions from the Islamic communities or government on health issues.
2. They will have early discussion amongst their internal scholars.
3. If they require clarification or more explanation from doctor, practitioners or related parties, they will invite those people to the next meetings.
4. The *fatwas* are issued after they have considered all Islamic legal arguments, along with other considerations provided by medical doctors and other stakeholders.

As discussed above, a *fatwa* from one organisation may differ from those of other organisations. A *fatwa* issued from the national organisation my also be different from one given by the provincial organisation. Again, a *fatwa* from one provincial branch may be at variance with one from another province, even though both belong to the same organisation. Therefore, it is possible in Indonesia to have many *fatwas* covering one case.

A. On AIDS

The MUI has been involved in a campaign against Acquired Immunodeficiency Syndrome (AIDS). The Minister of Health, Adhyatma, said in November 1991 that cooperation with the MUI was important as the council could help enhance the people's awareness of the dangers of AIDS through a religious approach. However, KH Hasan Basri, the General Chairman of the MUI, expressed his disagreement with an official anti-AIDS campaign, recommending the use of condoms in free sexual intercourse, because this implied that the government condoned the sort of sexual behaviour that was abhorrent to Islam. He said that the policy could incite people to commit adultery.

B. On Sterilisation

From 25 to 28 November 1989, the NU held its 28th Congress in Pesantren al-Munawwir, Krapyak, Yogyakarta. The great interest attracted by the organisation was apparent from the fact that the Congress was opened by President Soeharto and addressed by several ministers and the Chief of the Armed Forces (1988–93), General Try Sutrisno.

The Congress had to make pronouncements on the Islamic legal aspects of several modern phenomena. Thus it decided that *tayammum* (dry ritual ablution with dust or sand), as practised on board aeroplanes, is not legal, nor is inter-religious marriage (mixed marriage) from the viewpoint of Islamic law. Sterilisation for the purpose of birth control is allowed as long as the anatomy of the body is not destroyed. Transplantation of organs is allowed, but bequeathing one's organs is not recognised. In addition, euthanasia is forbidden by Islamic law. Due to the complexity of the matter, however, the discussion of issues like the legality of economic conglomerations, the stock market and *in-vitro* fertilisation were left to forthcoming seminars.

It should be noted here that in meetings held in June 1979 and October 1983, the MUI stated that vasectomy and tubectomy are forbidden in Islam, except in emergency cases such as to prevent the spread of disease or to save the life of the person undergoing vasectomy or tubectomy. However, the NU stated in November 1989 that these procedures are allowed as long as the anatomy of the body is not destroyed and the procedure can be reversible. This 1989 NU *fatwa* differed from a previous one (April 1960) of the NU which stated that 'if family-planning is done by destroying the possibility of having children, then it is not permitted, except in an emergency case'.[39] The Muhammadiyah issued a *fatwa* on this matter in 1968, which stated firmly that sterilisation is forbidden.[40]

C. On Cornea Transplant

The MUI issued a *fatwa* on corneal transplants in June 1979. This was requested by the Red Cross, and the MUI ruled that cornea donation was lawful, provided that firstly, it was agreed to and witnessed by close relatives, and secondly, the removal of the cornea was carried out by qualified surgeons.[41]

The NU had earlier issued a *fatwa* in 1962 that corneal transplants were not permitted. This *fatwa* was very forthright in stating that the

---

[39] Azis Masyhuri (ed.), *Masalah Keagamaan Hasil Muktamar dan Munas Ulama Nahdlatul Ulama 1926–94* (Surabaya: PP RMI & Dinamika Press 1997) 216.

[40] Muhammadiyah, *Himpunan Putusan Majelis Tarjih*, 3rd ed. (Jakarta: PP Muhammadiyah, n.d.) 309.

[41] Majelis Ulama Indonesia, *Himpunan Keputusan dan Fatwa Majelis Ulama Indonesia* (Masjid Istiqlal Jakarta: Sekretariat MUI 1995) 165.

fatwa of the Egyptian Mufti in this case was not right.[42] In 1981, approximately two years after the *fatwa* of the MUI, a similar case was again put before the Muslim scholars. After having enough information on the new technology, the NU reviewed its 1962 *fatwa*, providing two answers: firstly, it is not permitted, based on two books of fiqh: *Ahkam al-Fuqaha*, Vol. III, p. 59 and *Hashiah al-Rashidi 'ala Ibn al-'Imad*, p. 26; and secondly, it could be *mubah* (permissible) provided that the cornea transplant was needed and the donor and the recipient were Muslims. This rule was based on seven books: *Fath al-Jawa*, *al-Mahalli*, *al-Bujairami 'ala al-Iqna'*, *Mugni al-Muhtaj*, *al-Muhazzab*, *al-Qalyubi* and *al-Bujairami 'ala Fath al-Wahab*.[43] Unfortunately, the NU did not make a decision regarding which opinion was based on the stronger argument, although the second opinion was supported by more classic books of *fiqh*. Unlike the NU, the Muhammadiyah, after consulting with the experts, decided in 1980 that principally, organic transplantation (not only of the cornea) was *mubah* (permissible). However, the Muhammadiyah suggested that the implementation of the transplantation should be done carefully.[44]

D. On a Pill for Preventing Menstruation

Another example showing how *fatwas* relate to social issues is the *fatwa* on the use of pills for preventing menstruation. Many Muslim women complain that because of menstruation, they cannot complete their performing of the *Hajj* (pilgrimage) or fasting in Ramadan. According to Islamic law, women who are having their period must not engage in fasting, prayer and pilgrimage. However, there is a new technology to delay menstruation for a while by taking appropriate pills. Many Muslim women have asked the MUI for a ruling on the use of the pills in this situation.

The MUI at its meeting, held on 12 January 1979, decided that the use of pills to prevent menstruation for the purpose of completing the performance of the *Hajj* was *mubah* (permissible). The use of pills to prevent menstruation for the purpose of completing fasting during the month of Ramadan was *haram* (forbidden). However, for women who have difficulty of performing fasting on days other than those during the month of Ramadan, the use of the pills is *mubah*. The lawfulness of the

---

42 See Masyhuri, above n39, 248.

43 Ibid., 289.

44 Muhammadiyah, Himpunan Putusan Tarjih ke 20 di Garut, 21 di Klaten, 22 di Malang (Jember: Muhammadiyah 1993) 230.

use of pills for purposes other than those described above depends on the motivation of the users. If it is intended to do things that can lead to violations of Islamic laws, it is *haram*.[45]

E. On IUD (Intra-Uterine Device)

The IUD as a form of birth control is popular, being used by millions of women worldwide. This reversible form of contraception has a high success rate. The *fatwa* on the permissibility of the use of IUDs was a revocation of a *fatwa* issued in 1971 by a group of 11 leading Indonesian clergies, stating that the use of IUDs was forbidden in Islam. Ibrahim Hosen, the chairman of the MUI's Fatwa Committee, explained, as quoted by Mudzhar, that the *fatwa* of 1983 was not a revocation of the one of 1971 but rather a correction of the bases of the arguments presented in that *fatwa*.[46] In the 1971 *fatwa*, the use of IUDs was prohibited on the grounds that the insertion involved the sight of the woman's genitalia, and the prohibition was classified methodologically as *Hurrima li dzatih* (forbidden for the essence).

Hosen believed that this argument had to be corrected, because the seeing of the woman's genitals is itself not forbidden, if it is done by her husband. Thus the seeing of the genitals is forbidden not because of the seeing itself but as a precautionary measure, to prevent adultery. In other words, the prohibition of the seeing of the woman's sexual organs should be classified as a forbidding for preventive purposes (*hurrima li sadd al-dzara'i*).[47]

According to Hosen, in the science of *usul al-fiqh* there is a difference in the degree of enforcement between prohibition based on *hurrima li dzatih* and those based on *hurrima li sadd al-dzara'i*. What is prohibited on the basis of the former cannot become permitted except in emergency circumstances which endanger the life of human beings (*ma hurrima li dzatih ubiha li darurah*). For example, pork is not permitted for the essence, but may be consumed by a Muslim only in a life-threatening emergency situation where there is no other food.[48]

Conversely, what is forbidden for preventive purposes can become permitted if the need arises without resort to emergency measures (*ma*

---

[45] Majelis Ulama Indonesia, above n41, 36.

[46] Mudzhar, above n37, 232.

[47] Wahbah al-Zuhailli uses the terms *haram li dzatih* and *haram li ghairih*. However, the meaning of these terms is similar to those used above. See Wahbah al-Zuhaili, *Usul al-Fiqh al-Islami*, Vol. 1 (Beirut: Dar al-Fikr 1986) 81–3.

[48] Mudzhar, loc. cit.

hurrima li sadd al-dzara'i ubiha li hajah). Hosen said that in the case of the use of IUDs for family planning in Indonesia, the need is already obvious. He concluded that it was on the grounds of such a need that the 1983 *fatwa* on family planning was issued, in which the prohibition of the use of IUDs by the *fatwa* of 1971 was lifted. Therefore, the MUI issued a *fatwa*, in 1983, that using IUDs is now permitted.[49]

V. CONCLUSIONS

Collective *ijtihad* has been practised widely in the contemporary Islamic world. From the time of the Prophet until the end of the nineteenth century, *ijtihad* was performed individually. In 1964, the concept of *ijtihad jama'i* was introduced formally in the Islamic world by *Majma' al-Buhuth al-Islamiyah* in Cairo. This chapter has shown that there are four meanings of *ijtihad jama'i* as practised by Islamic communities. One of them is *ijtihad jama'i* performed at an organisational level.

Having performed *ijtihad* collectively, Muslims scholars have provided the solution for the debate of 'the closing of the door of *ijtihad*' where the requirements to be *Mujtahid* can be met not at an individual level, but as a group of Muslim scholars. This chapter has provided some examples from the Indonesia case studies of how Muslim scholars have responded to modern health issues. This is to illustrate that collective *ijtihad* have been used as instruments to cope with modern developments. Inviting 'secular' scholars to join the discussion also indicates a collective attempt to answer complicated problems from many different perspectives.

As a final note, one may observe from the case studies that *fatwas* in Indonesia can be revised, particularly where previous rulings have proven no longer suitable to the situation. It can be stated safely that the institution of collective *ijtihad* is a viable tool through which a society can adjust itself to internal and external social, political and economic change.

---

49 Ibid.

13. Halal and other codes: can religion, science and ethics guide legal regulation?*

Richard Mohr

I. INTRODUCTION

This chapter explores some issues at the intersection of regulation and religion, as they apply to food. It examines the regulations and values that affect choices at food and drink outlets in an inner suburban street in Sydney. In exploring questions around community relations in a culturally and religiously diverse society, it focuses on the ways religious, ethical and scientific considerations interact with regulatory regimes, whether those of government, industry, or religious bodies.

Three case studies explore this range of intersecting claims and responsibilities. Religious requirements may be regulated by a religious council, Beth Din or Ulama; food safety is monitored by government and industry bodies; while consumer and animal rights organisations may be involved in demands for particular standards and the reliability of various claims for food. There is continuous negotiation between government, industry, religious or ethical bodies and consumer advocates over labelling and other regulations. Since food is ultimately a matter of consumption (indeed, it is the ultimate form of consumption), even religious regulation has much in common with other forms of consumer protection. The consumer wants to know, with some guarantee of the reliability of the certification or labelling, whether their food is safe, free range, halal, healthy, and so on.

While this may be seen as a fairly straightforward exercise in regulation for consumer protection, at another level it casts light on one of the most contentious issues of our time: the relations between reason, religion and law. These have been questioned anew, with the recent

* An earlier version of this chapter can be found in Richard Mohr, 'Rethinking the Secular: Religion, Ethics and Science in Food Regulation' Working papers of the Centre for International Governance and Justice, RegNet, Australian National University, 2013 (republished with permission).

challenges to the 'secularization thesis' which suggest that it is 'overly simplistic and grossly inadequate'.[1]

> [C]an we reconcile the enduring presence of religion in western societies with the dominant assumption that law is a logical, rational and objective enterprise, free of any connection to spiritual belief?[2]

This question is often put in terms that reflect or question the traditional separation between faith and law, or church and state: an ideology of secularism. Does religion have any role to play in establishing public norms? Does religion pose a challenge to a rational or scientific administration of public affairs? Indeed, can science or reason, any more than religion, be a guide to law and regulation?

Underlying my interest in the interaction of various (perhaps competing) value systems in the development of regulation is the hope that I can cast some light on the contemporary problems of secularism. I respond to the challenge of the secular, prompted by several recent themes and concerns in the discourse on secularism.

We hear a certain nostalgia, or worse, from many liberal or secularist scholars. The very aggression of the secularist counter-offensive has prompted me to explore new ways of conceiving secularism, whose purported neutrality and peaceful promise have been compromised by the divisive diatribes of authors like those whom Terry Eagleton (2010) has called, collectively, 'Ditchkins'.[3] This militant secularism may accept religion confined to the private sphere, but is more likely to identify it as a troublesome irrational force which is to be excluded from public life lest it corrupt impartiality and sow seeds of unrest and conflict. The very diversity of contemporary societies is invoked in support of this view. In once-Christian societies which are now home to substantial minorities of non-believers and believers in other religions, the very notion of religion is seen as inflammatory and potentially divisive. It plays the role in the politics of fear that ethnic identification of Australian soccer clubs was supposed to have when they were called 'Croatian', 'Serbian' or 'Hakoah'. Names like 'Melbourne Victory', 'Brisbane Roar' or the 'Sky Blues' are presumed to be sufficiently neutral to overcome the threat of

---

[1] Eve Darian Smith, *The Disenchantment of Secular Discourse* (Cambridge, MA: Harvard University Press 2010) 286.

[2] Ibid., 10–11.

[3] Terry Eagleton mischievously applied this name collectively to Richard Dawkins and Christopher Hitchens; see 'The God Debate' *The Gifford Lectures*. University of Edinburgh, 2010, www.giffordlectures.org/lectures/god-debate.

religious conflicts and ethnic brawls. In the same way, criteria for choice of public goods compete to be secular and innocuous, 'evidence-based' and perhaps even 'value-free'.

Elsewhere I have questioned the universalism of secularism in light of its Christian origins.[4] While that is not an argument against secularism as such, it does prompt further inquiry into the role of secular values as an alternative to religious ones in an ethnically and religiously diverse world.

Another response to the crisis of secularism is the view that it has been superseded by a 'post-secular' age, in which religious motivations and spirituality are rediscovered. This approach questions whether the secular universe of reason and science provides sufficient grounds for making hard moral and ethical choices. Thinkers as diverse as Jürgen Habermas (2008), Rosi Braidotti (2008) and Steven D. Smith (2010) welcome a 'post-secular' polity (in the case of the first two), or one in which religious values are admitted as a ground for ethical or even political claims (in the case of Habermas and Smith).[5]

I am sceptical about such alternatives. I have already expressed my concerns over a militant and divisive secularism. Likewise, we need a more nuanced approach to value choices in public life than those put forward in the name of competing established religions. In this I agree with feminists like Braidotti or Margaret Davies (2011),[6] who both advocate a richer framework for ethical debate than those sanctioned by traditionally accredited religious or political leaders. I am also interested to understand the legitimate role that might be played by rational and scientific discourse if they were to enter into the stimulating arena of

---

[4] Richard Mohr, 'The Christian Origins of Secularism and the Rule of Law' in N. Hosen and R. Mohr (eds) *Law and Religion in Public Life: The Contemporary Debate* (Abingdon, Oxon: Routledge 2011), and Brian Tierney, *Religion, Law and the Growth of Constitutional Thought 1150–1650* (Cambridge, UK: Cambridge University Press 1982).

[5] Jürgen Habermas, *Between Naturalism and Religion: Philosophical Essays* (Cambridge, UK: Polity Press 2008); Rosi Braidotti, 'In Spite of the Times: The Postsecular Turn in Feminism' (2008) 25 *Theory Culture Society* 1–24; and Steven D. Smith, *The Disenchantment of Secular Discourse* (Cambridge, MA: Harvard University Press 2010).

[6] Braidotti, above n5, or Margaret Davies 'The Future of Secularism: A Critique' in N. Hosen and R. Mohr (eds) *Law and Religion in Public Life: The Contemporary Debate* (Abingdon, Oxon: Routledge 2011).

public debate as engaged and valued participants and not just 'conversation stoppers'.[7]

II. THE RESEARCH

Having outlined some of my epistemological and ethical interests, I will report on a research project which, despite its modest dimensions, I hope will illuminate a number of these issues. The subject and site of this research was prompted by a concern to discover the roots and conditions of an inclusive and tolerant multiculturalism, in explicit opposition to the divisive and intolerant views of some conservative politicians, atheist crusaders or religious zealots.

It proceeded in three stages: a formulation of some very rough questions about how law, religion and 'scientific' or rational values and institutions may interact in private and public decisions regarding food. Then there was a period of empirical research, focussed on the semiotic presentation of food options and regulation in a multicultural Sydney neighbourhood (described in the following paragraphs). Finally, that data has been analysed through a number of lenses. Early oral presentations of the work focussed on social and religious implications, with particular interest in food, culture and identity. Pending further development of that side of the study, the present report focuses on the specific issues of law, religion and science in food regulation. The data from the empirical and regulatory study was analysed by identifying references to ethics, religion or science. Realising that this came down to the intersection of several institutions or movements based on particular systems of values, I went back to the literature on these issues, in order to interpret and trace the implications of the data. The empirical and regulatory research, into three specific issues, is outlined in the section on the case studies. The analysis of the intersecting value systems follows, in the concluding section.

The initial research (in June–August 2012) mapped all 117 food outlets in Marrickville Road, which forms the central spine of the Marrickville Local Government Area (LGA) about four miles (six km) south-west of

[7] Smith (above n5, 218) turns the tables on Rorty's claim that religion is a 'conversation-stopper': 'Rorty's opponents are not telling him: "Stop talking secular." Rather it is Rorty and like-minded thinkers who issue the injunction: "Don't talk religion."'

the Sydney CBD.[8] It runs through the middle of the suburb of Marrickville, from Sydenham station in the east to Dulwich Hill in the west. The area was for a long time one of the first stops for new immigrants who, over the decades, have been Greeks, then Vietnamese, Chinese and Pacific Islanders. Portuguese and Italians, from a relatively early stage of post-World War II immigration, are also conspicuous at the Dulwich Hill end of the street. The area is rapidly gentrifying,[9] but it is still home to many immigrants: at the 2011 Census, one in three households spoke more than one language at home (compared with one in four in New South Wales, and one in five in Australia). The main languages spoken are Greek, Vietnamese, Arabic, Portuguese and Cantonese.[10]

Religious affiliation in Marrickville is less to the dominant churches than in other parts of NSW, while the greatest proportion profess no religious affiliation (33 per cent). Eastern Orthodox and Buddhist adherents are respectively three times and twice as prevalent in Marrickville as in Australia as a whole. There are Anglican, Catholic and Baptist churches within the study area, and a Greek Orthodox church and a Lebanese Marronite complex within a hundred or so meters of it. There are no mosques or synagogues within the study area. The local government area is adjacent to two important Muslim localities, Arncliffe (in the Rockdale LGA) to the south and the Canterbury LGA to the south west.

Politically, the local council is dominated by Labor and Greens, while the parliamentary representatives are left Labor. The local Federal Member is the Labor Minister Anthony Albanese, who, during parliamentary debate of a controversy about sacred Aboriginal beliefs in the Hindmarsh Island case some years ago, taunted conservative members by questioning their reaction if the inquiry were to be 'into your beliefs; into

---

8 Local government boundaries have been redrawn since this research was carried out, and there have been changes in the businesses on the street. This report describes the situation at the time of the survey in 2012.

9 Beatriz Cavia et al., 'Crisis of the Social and Emergence of Sociality in the New Scenarios of Identity. The San Francisco District of Bilbao' (2008) *Papeles de CEIC* 39 (Centro de Estudios sobre la Identidad Colectiva, Universidad del País Vasco) effectively problematise this concept: 'the process of gentrification is not so much an explanatory factor as the condition of possibility of new social relationships' (p.8).

10 Census data in this and the following paragraph are from ABS, 2011 Census of Population and Housing, *Expanded Community Profile Based on Place of Usual Residence* (Catalogue number 2005.0).

whether you can prove the Holy Trinity exists'.[11] Local council elections held in September 2012 saw two Liberal councillors elected for the first time in Marrickville. One of them, the vice president of the synagogue in neighbouring Newtown, had been vocal in the campaign against the council's boycott, divestment and sanctions policy towards Israel.[12] The Greens' influence diminished at that election. Religion is entwined in indirect and distant ways in Marrickville local politics. The religious conflicts tend to be elsewhere: the Middle East or Hindmarsh Island.

The study area of this project covers the full 1.7 miles (2.7 km) length of Marrickville Road, and one block either side of that street.[13] It includes fruit shops and supermarkets, cafes and restaurants, butchers and bakers, takeaway food shops and convenience stores. The food preparation factories (of which there are many in the municipality, and a number in the study area) were excluded unless they specified sales direct to the public. The research identified any signs on the food outlets displaying any ethnic or national affiliation, as well as any regulatory regimes under which they operate. In addition to English language signs, 17 different cultures were identified, the most common being Vietnamese, Chinese, Greek, Thai, Italian and Turkish. The food shops and restaurants are regulated by the council's Local Environmental Plan as well as various industry, consumer, government and religious codes.

In the following section I explore three of the regulatory regimes that are acknowledged in signage on the various premises, devoting a brief case study to each of the following:

- free range
- halal
- food safety.

---

11 Marion Maddox, *God Under Howard: The Rise of the Religious Right in Australian Politics* (Crows Nest, Australia: Allen and Unwin 2005) 133.

12 Henry Benjamin, 'A Jewish Voice at Marrickville Council', *J-Wire* 14 February 2011, www.jwire.com.au/news/a-jewish-voice-at-marrickville-council/15073 (accessed 4 February 2013).

13 The side streets were sampled as far as pedestrians could walk on them without any vehicular road or lane crossing the footpath. The only significant concentrations of shops are in New Canterbury Road (east side only was sampled) and Illawarra Road, south of Marrickville Road.

III. CASE STUDIES

A. Free Range

Free range claims are made in advertising on takeaway food shops, as well as on eggs and poultry products in the various supermarkets. A large poster for Lilydale chickens displayed on the Classic Food Bar in Marrickville is headed 'Free to roam' above a photograph of chickens on grass under gum trees. 'Free range chicken' is written at the bottom.

Vague or misleading descriptors such as 'barn raised' and 'free to roam' have become the subject of legal action. The Australian Competition and Consumer Commission (ACCC) has taken action in the Federal Court of Australia against three poultry suppliers including Baiada Poultry Pty Limited, the supplier of Lilydale Free Range Chickens, for misleading and deceptive conduct. The ACCC alleged that phrases such as 'free to roam' are misleading and deceptive because the chickens 'do not, as a practical matter, have substantial space available to roam around freely'. The Court found that two of the firms, Baiada and Bartter, and an industry body had made false representations and engaged in misleading and deceptive conduct.[14]

Consumer demands for free range poultry products, based on ethical concerns for animal welfare, have become increasingly apparent. Egg and poultry producers have responded by increasing the supply. One way to do this is to redefine 'free range'.

There are a number of competing certifications, with different stocking densities (indoor/outdoor), some prohibiting beak trimming. Bodies sponsoring these certifications range from Australian Certified Organic and state free range farmers' associations (with some of the strictest limits at around 1,000 birds per hectare) through the RSPCA to the Australian Egg Corp Ltd (AECL).

The AECL sets very low standards for 'free range' and argues that densities under the Model Code of Practice for the Welfare of Animals should increase to 20,000 birds per ha. In support of this, they cite Scottish Agricultural College research, and they commissioned their own survey of consumers. Consumer advocates *Choice* have disputed AECL's use of this research, and carried out their own survey.

> When [*Choice*] asked consumers what they'd consider to be a reasonable maximum outdoor stocking density ... 65 per cent of respondents said they

---

[14] *Australian Competition and Consumer Commission v Turi Foods Pty Ltd* (No 5) [2013] FCA 1109.

> didn't know. This reinforces our belief that a maximum stocking density shouldn't be predominantly based on consumer research, but rather on a broader body of independent, scientific research in conjunction with consumer research.[15]

Choice campaigns for clarity and standardisation of labelling, so that consumers may make informed choices about the food they buy. This leads to demands for standards, regulations and well-understood terms on which to base buying choices. In any of these debates, there are disputed criteria, based on different interests and values. Poultry farmers may have economic interests that are at odds with those of humanitarians, or even chickens (if they can be said to have interests). These interests may be fought out in the name of various values (to paraphrase Marx).[16]

If we were to argue, with some secularists or certain Marxists, that these values are essentially arbitrary, irrational, or an ideological smokescreen for material interests, it may be difficult to find a way through such disputes. And yet the welfare of sentient beings can be seen to require that animals be allowed to express natural behaviours and be protected from suffering. Such values are held by many people, and can be defended on a variety of ethical, political or religious grounds.[17] They are subject to rational and ethical debate.

However, as *Choice* finds when surveying consumers who would choose free range products, it is difficult to know just where to set specific standards. Serious public debate on matters of values should be informed by scientific research and even philosophical analysis. If the average consumer has no idea what stocking densities are necessary to allow chickens to walk, scratch and peck, then ethological and veterinary research can be informative.

B. Halal

Two shops in the study area advertise that their food is halal. On the other side of Marrickville Road from the 'Classic Food Bar' that sells cooked 'Free to Roam' chickens there is Chicken Fantasy, which

---

15 R. Clemons, 'A Cagey Business' *Choice* July 2012: 20–22.

16 Karl Marx, *A Contribution to the Critique of Political Economy* (Moscow: Progress Publishers 1970) 21.

17 See, for example, the work of philosopher Peter Singer on animal rights (*Animal Liberation: A New Ethics for Our Treatment of Animals*, NY, Random House 1975), or the Papal Encyclical, *Laudato Sì*, 2015 ('We have only one heart, and the same wretchedness which leads us to mistreat an animal will not be long in showing itself in our relationships with other people' § 92).

advertises that their cooked chicken is halal. Just off Marrickville Road in New Canterbury Road is the Orange'O convenience store and halal butchery. While some consumers decide their choice of food according to the ethical principle of animal welfare, others apply the religious criterion that it should be halal.[18]

Just as we saw in the case of free range certification, halal certification may be awarded by a number of different bodies. These are not associated with industry but rather with various Islamic organisations. Eighteen certifiers across Australia are listed by the Commonwealth Department of Agriculture, Fisheries and Forestry (DAFF), according to whether they are recognised by particular export markets in Muslim countries.[19] Four of them are in New South Wales, including two widely recognised bodies, the Australian Federation of Islamic Councils and the Supreme Islamic Council of Halal Meat in Australia. It is not known how many other bodies may purport to certify halal products sold in the study area.

While these certifying bodies may compete in a market sense, offering their services to various producers, they must also compete for theological credibility. Bodies with a range of respected Islamic scholars gain wider acceptance than do more commercial organisations. More liberal Muslims may prefer certain authorities, while other sects may have their own preferences. *The Economist* (2013) quoted a restaurateur in the London Borough of Tower Hamlets saying he did not bother with certificates, but that 'he knows and trusts his suppliers and his customers know and trust him'.[20]

As in ethical considerations, acceptance that a product is halal (like free range) requires some known and accepted standards, and trusted and consistent authority or authorities. In the absence of government certification or adjudication, religious, like ethical consumers must simply determine which authority or supplier they trust. Consumer demands for

---

[18] It would be interesting to explore the similarities and differences between religious and broader ethical values. From a sociological point of view, it appears that religious positions are more associated with institutional hierarchies and codified texts. Ethical positions may move in that direction over time. There is little room for further developing this theme here.

[19] www.daff.gov.au/aqis/export/meat/elmer-3/list-islamic-halal-certification (accessed 12 February 2013).

[20] 'Food and Religion: A Meaty Question' *The Economist*, www.economist.com/news/international/21571419-who-should-regulate-kosher-and-halal-food-meaty-question (accessed 12 February 2013).

guidance and credibility, informed by ethical, scientific or religious debate, may require more transparent regulation.

The research has not remarked any local conflict – political or religious issues – associated with halal food. Nationally there have, of course, been several egregious instances of populist and intolerant politicians denigrating halal food.[21] There are also areas where religious and other ethical requirements may come into conflict. It is of interest to this study of religious, ethical and scientific bases of regulation to note debates over whether the ethical demands for humane treatment of animals conflict with religious demands for halal slaughter.

This debate often centres on possible conflicts between an ethical demand that an animal be stunned before slaughter and a religious demand that the animal be alive until it is slaughtered correctly. In the Australian context, the live export of animals to Indonesia and the Middle East, for halal slaughter at their destination, adds another dimension to the debate.[22]

The animal welfare arguments are based on minimising animal suffering. Stunning renders animals unconscious, to anaesthetise them so they do not feel pain, or possibly so they are not aware of their fate. The anaesthetic motivation needs to be tested against the methods used for stunning: whether they are less painful or traumatic than the method of slaughter. The pain of either should surely be minimised. The question of awareness is a difficult one in the case of animals which, while they obviously feel pain and may be stressed by certain methods of handling, may not have a conception of life, death or the future.

Animal Liberation (South Australia) has advocated halal slaughter within Australia as a humane alternative to live exports, which cause suffering and death to animals crowded into ships. Liaison between Australian and overseas governmental and religious authorities, such as those listed on the DAFF website, can assist in this move.

---

[21] For example, Senator Cory Bernardi, see Steve Lewis, 'Tackle Extreme Islam Before it's too Late, Liberal MPs Warn' *Herald Sun*, 9 February 2011, www.news.com.au/national/liberal-mps-warn-of-islam-danger/news-story/2d7448 4ee0e03792fc7149f6e79d11dc (accessed 16 February 2011); and W. A. Liberal MP Luke Simpkins, www.perthnow.com.au/news/western-australia/we-are-unknowingly-being-converted-to-islam-says-cowan-mp-luke-simpkins/story-e6fr g13u-1226206404318 (accessed 23 February 2013).

[22] See Nadirsyah Hosen, 'Live Cattle Export Ban from Australia to Indonesia: how does "social television" impact on law and religion?' paper presented at the International Symposium: Technologies of Law and Religion: Representation, Objects and Agency, Faculty of Law, Monash University, held in Monash Prato Centre, Italy, 13–15 June 2016.

> The answer is to increase the number of Halal slaughterhouses in Australia so that animals are handled and killed according to Australian standards … There are already Halal slaughterhouses in Australia with religious officials present. Stunning has been accepted as long as does not mark the carcass (electrical or non-penetrating captive bolt stunning). There is already a robust trade in chilled and frozen meat to both the Middle East and Indonesia.[23]

Other religious considerations concern the definition of stunning and death. Some Islamic scholars accept stunning as long as it is reversible: the animal should not be so damaged by the stunning that it cannot return to life and normal consciousness.

There is scope for detailed investigation into these matters, both from an ethological point of view and in regard to the physical impact (infliction of pain) of different methods of stunning or slaughter. Islamic scholars and thoughtful animal rights advocates could work with scientific, philosophical and empirical research on methods of slaughter to reach more rigorous and well-founded conclusions on questions of animal welfare and halal slaughter.

C. Food Safety

'Victoria Yeeros', on the corner of Marrickville and Victoria Roads, sells take-away spit grilled *yeeros* (or *gyros*, in an alternative transliteration from Greek used in Melbourne), and has a *yeeros* meat supply premises next door on Victoria Road. Its sign specifies 'Quality assurance through HACCP', 'NSW Food Safety Authority' and 'Authorised by NSWMIA'. These three certifications point to a maze of interlocking codes, authorities and industry organisations. All are focused on the safety of food from the point of view of the health of the consumer, and specifically on its freedom from bacteria and other infectious diseases.[24]

All premises that supply food are subject to regulation by the NSW Food Safety Authority (FSA, whose motto is 'safer food, clearer choices') and the local council. The council enforces food safety standards, through regular inspections, under the coordination and regulation of the state government's FSA. FSA publicises adverse findings through a 'name and shame' website that maintains notices for 12 months from the first notification. Only one business in the study area was 'named and

---

[23] http://animalliberation.org.au/national-rallies-against-live-export (accessed 16 February 2013).

[24] Infectious diseases are the target of the 'old public health', initiated in the nineteenth century. Though tempted, I cannot deal here with the 'new public health' focused on 'lifestyle' diseases, e.g. obesity.

shamed' on that website during the study period (June–July 2012). In February 2013,[25] four more premises in Marrickville Road, Dulwich Hill had been added (a butcher, a baker and a Chinese restaurant) and five in Marrickville Road, Marrickville (a fish shop, two bakers, an Indian takeaway and a cake shop).

The Hazard Analysis Critical Control Point system (HACCP) was developed from the international Codex Alimentarius as a means of ensuring food safety. It is promoted by the World Health Organization and implemented and accredited through national private companies (e.g. HACCP Australia).

The FSA classifies 'potentially hazardous foods', to which a '2 hour – 4 hour' rule applies: such food must be consumed immediately or thrown away if it has been stored above 5 °C and below 60 °C for two hours (four hours if it is in and out of refrigeration or hot storage). The Chinese practice of hanging roast duck and pork in shop windows at room temperature became contentious under this principle, so further study led to new guidelines being adopted, based on studies by the Victorian Food Safety Unit:

> traditionally prepared BBQ pork, duck and chicken on the day of preparation are low risk products until they are cut up for sale. After carving the protection provided by scalding, surface drying and roasting in a salty-sugary glaze is lost and the products become perishable and potentially hazardous.[26]

So the freshly roasted and glazed products can be hung at normal temperatures for longer periods, and only become 'potentially hazardous' when cut.

The NSW FSA recognises that traditional practices may be safe in their original context. Yet they point out that modern methods, such as centralised processing and larger batches may require more modern approaches (such as refrigeration). New foods (e.g. sushi) and the transfer of practices in food preparation from immigrant cultures require a clear understanding of those practices, as well as scientific analysis of the hazards. Authorities need to review the application of traditional

---

[25] It is presumably coincidental that these were generally added after the relevant council inspector was contacted in regard to the research. But if Heisenberg's principle can apply in physics, it can as easily apply in social research too!

[26] New South Wales Food Safety Authority, 'Potentially Hazardous Foods: Foods that Require Temperature Control for Safety' (Sydney, 2008), 10–11, available at www.foodauthority.nsw.gov.au/aboutus/science/food-risk-studies/potentially-hazardous-foods.

standards to introduced techniques. Assumptions made on the basis of traditional Anglo-Australian standards may need to be challenged and checked against scientific evidence, as in the case of Chinese barbeque products.

IV. CONCLUSIONS

A. Regulation and Values

In the case studies we have seen a variety of regulatory regimes. The notion of regulation, in broad terms, can be conceived as working from the top down, through the control and protection of populations.[27] We see this in the health standards of the Food Safety Authority and their application by council inspectors. We also see instances of regulation working from the bottom up, through the expression and codification of consumer demands. A traditional economic model of consumer action is that of supply and demand: if the consumers want free range eggs they will buy them, even if they cost more. But the consumer movement has become political, and makes demands of regulatory (as well as other) authorities. Consumers become consumer activists, or *consum'acteurs* in the French version, which emphasises consumption as eating more than buying.[28] Contemporary consumers – eaters – may no longer have a one-to-one relation of trust with their supplier, but instead group together, conscious of their common interests as consumers. Whether they are environmentalists, animal liberationists, or observant Muslims or Jews, they demand guarantees of the provenance of what they eat. Ethical, health or religious demands can gain political traction through lobbying or organising, or may be expressed in legal terms as rights: the right to informed choice, or animal rights.

In these case studies, consumer requirements and demands for particular food standards have led to wide-ranging debates. Those standards may be regulated or enforced by state and local government; the ACCC and the Federal Court; or industry, consumer or religious bodies. They demonstrate a wide range of legal mechanisms, from formal to informal law.

---

27 Michel Foucault, 'Governmentality' in G. Burchell, C. Gordon and P. Miller (eds) *The Foucault Effect: Studies in Governmentality* (London: Harvester Wheatsheaf 1991) 87–104.

28 Geoffrey Pleyers, La consommation critique: Mouvements pour une alimentation responsable et solidaire (Paris: Desclée de Brouwer 2011).

Controversies and debates have been carried out in various public and official forums: a consumer magazine, media, court, and the technical reports of food regulating agencies. They invoke legal, ethical, scientific, cultural and commercial arguments, which are typically intermingled in public debate. And yet, when the bigger issues of secularism and religion, science and law are discussed in academic terms, they take on the appearance of self-contained universes, rotating in their own self-referential spheres.

In concluding this work in progress, I take a step back to the broad terms in which I began, in order to try to understand the interaction of those overarching discourses. Law is characterised by rights and rules. Science invokes reason and evidence. Religion draws on ethics and the traditional ties of community, while there are also important ethical considerations that do not draw on any specific liturgical or scriptural tradition.

Teubner (1989), coming from a German tradition that emphasises the self-referentiality of law, compares it to religion. Both are discourses that are separate from science, but which attempt to make their constructs 'at least compatible with recent developments in the sciences'.

> Obviously, scientific facts collide with legal facts, but we are used to living with this collision, rationalizing it by invoking higher values, like legal certainty, or appealing to the relativism of our cultural provinces.[29]

This suggests that, while institutional barriers isolate disciplines (in Foucault's sense) or institutional modes of deliberation, channels of communication may open up between them at other levels, such as that of values. This is a pervasive theme in studies of law, religion and science.

B. Rights and Rules: Law

In this study I have taken a broad approach to law, constantly noting the spectrum from the formal law of state and courts to the informal laws of self-regulation and religion. That spectrum is found in conceptual critiques, as well as in empirical studies of law. Luhmann[30] or Teubner identify the formal self-referentiality, or autopoiesis of law, even as they

---

[29] Gunther Teubner, 'How the Law Thinks: Toward a Constructivist Epistemology of Law' (1989) 23 *Law and Society Review* 727–57.

[30] Niklas Luhmann, 'Law as a Social System' (1989) 83 *Northwestern University Law Review* 137–8.

try to explain, or explain away, the wormholes by which other social influences or values may interpenetrate with law. Critics (e.g. from a critical legal studies tradition) emphasise the ideological functions of this reified symbolic power 'that can be exercised only through the complicity of those who are dominated by it'.[31] Formalism is the height of this reified system, which treats law as 'entirely distinct from all political, moral, and social values and institutions'.[32]

The value of a fine-grained study such as the present one is that it may explore those interstices and interpenetrations, to find out a little more of how it is that law can take account of scientific or ethical considerations. The mechanisms we see emerging in food regulation (both formal and informal) illustrate some of the critiques of formal reliance on deterministic rules. Schauer follows Wittgenstein's warning that rule-following is 'deeply problematic' and underdetermined.

> But again as with any inductive process, the problem of underdetermination does not make induction in reality impossible. It does, however, make the inductive result dependent on contingent values lying outside the particulars around which the inductive generalization is constructed.[33]

If rules do not determine outcomes, it is through the application of 'contingent', extra-legal (Teubner's 'higher') values that we again find the possibility of a circuit breaker, a wormhole that frees legal deliberation from the tyranny of rules.

To see some of these operations in practice in a multicultural context, we can turn to the Bouchard-Taylor report commissioned by the government of Québec, on 'accommodation practices related to cultural differences'. The sociologist Gerard Bouchard and the philosopher Charles Taylor were reporting within the framework of the Canadian Charter of Rights and Freedoms on the accommodation of minority cultural practices within a dominant québécoise society, which is concerned to maintain its own distinctive character in an Anglo-dominated North America. The legal language of the Charter emphasises 'rights' and 'reasonable accommodation', which implies that the dominant society should 'accommodate' foreign difference, leaving the 'right' intact.

---

[31] Pierre Bourdieu, 'The Force of Law: Toward a Sociology of the Juridical Field' (1987) 38 *Hastings Law Journal* 844.

[32] Judith N. Shklar, *Legalism* (Cambridge, MA: Harvard University Press 1964) 33.

[33] Frederick Schauer, *Playing by the Rules. A Philosophical Examination of Rule-Based Decision-Making in Law and in Life* (Oxford: Clarendon Press 1991) 185.

Bouchard and Taylor emphasise the need for dialogue and work on both sides to help overcome deadlocks of competing rights and zero-sum games. Their more constructive term is 'concerted adjustment': all parties need to understand each others' practices and beliefs, and find means by which they may be expressed.[34] This shifts the paradigm from that of law to that of discourse, within and among communities.

'Concerted adjustment' is a further illustration of the possibility and need to reach across legal categories, like rights and rules, to find ways in which their intention may be worked out in practice. Similar approaches were identified in the case studies, as potential if not yet always actual solutions to ethical and cultural disputes over food. Consumers, animal rights activists, religious scholars, regulators, the courts and various branches of the food industry can draw on veterinary and ethological research and ethical, as well as legal, debate. These deliberations can help to apply and to define more widely accepted standards and to devise improved animal welfare practices. Food scientists and regulators can work with cooks to study cultural practices in food preparation. This can be combined with their knowledge of bacteria and risks of contamination to improve food handling guidelines. In each case advances are made, not through application of rules and invocation of rights, but through the vigorous interplay of values that are open to debate.

C. Rules and Reason: Science

The notion of 'values' plays an interesting role in the dubious terms of the secularism vs religion debate, mentioned in opening this discussion. On the one hand militant secularists tend to associate 'values' with subjectivity and religion, and hence view them with some suspicion. On the other hand, there are certain values that are privileged by secularists. Brooke (2007) points to the increased incidence in the British media of the phrase 'Enlightenment values' since the terrorist attacks of September 2001.

> The term appears most frequently in articles discussing the challenge posed to Western societies by varieties of Islamic fundamentalism. On the whole, it is

---

[34] Gerard Bouchard and Charles Taylor, 'Building the Future: A Time for Reconciliation. Abridged Report'. Québec: Consultation Commission on Accommodation Practices Related to Cultural Differences, 2008, 51–2.

> the more muscular liberals who are keen on this particular political language, with its connotations of sturdy opposition to religious fanaticism.[35]

But which Enlightenment values are being promoted here? Brooke implies that liberalism, of a 'muscular' variety, is attractive to his interlocutors, and points to the importance of 'sharp scepticism' as an alternative preferred 'Enlightenment value'. Suskind, reporting a conversation with a White House aide of the George W. Bush era, pairs 'enlightenment principles' with empiricism.[36] These invidious distinctions and arguments over who is more 'enlightened' than whom simply illustrate the problem that Foucault called 'Enlightenment blackmail'.[37] The question 'what is Enlightenment?' raised so 'imprudently two centuries ago'[38] continues to exercise philosophers and commentators alike. The blackmail inherent in invoking the Enlightenment requires one to be either 'for' or 'against' it. Against what? If Foucault must sum this up in a word, it is 'rationalism' or 'rationality'. This is further problematised, of course, by noting that various schools are for or against that, too, when they buy into this discourse.[39]

At least now we have three concepts that might be associated fairly reliably with this Enlightenment talk, or blackmail, if you prefer: liberalism, empiricism and rationality. Let's leave the first to one side: 'liberalism' is too partisan, too political to engage everybody. But empiricism and reason, surely, are values that can be widely supported and enlisted in public debate. Well, yes *but* ... They in turn need to be interrogated, and of course they must be given more than passing attention in any appreciation of the role of science in public life.

Brenner points out that philosophy of science has in the last one hundred years made a journey from questions of justification (how induction and experiment are used and criticised) to questions of discovery and invention (how we choose between competing theories); in short, first empiricism was problematised, then rationality was. Attention has more recently 'focussed on rational values attendant on theory choice.

---

[35] Christopher Brooke, 'Light from the Fens?' (2007) 44 *New Left Review* 151.

[36] Richard Mohr, 'Identity Crisis: Judgment and the Hollow Legal Subject' (2007) 11 *Law Text Culture* 106–7.

[37] Michel Foucault, 'What is Enlightenment?' in M. Foucault (ed.) *Ethics: Subjectivity and Truth* (London: Penguin 2000) 315.

[38] Ibid., 304.

[39] Ibid., 315.

This leads to a richer model of scientific rationality.'[40] When Kuhn (1970) went down this path fifty years ago, he pointed out that we do not choose between scientific theories according to some *rules*, but according to particular *values*.[41] The terms are familiar from our earlier discussion of legal formalism, and the parallels with a critical approach to law are even more striking as Brenner goes on:

> [T]he criteria of choice are not rules, but values. No one of our values has primacy, and there is no order that prescribes their application. It is necessary to judge case by case.[42]

Rationality has value in itself, but to say so simply draws attention to the very fact that rationality is a value. Yet if it is to be operationalised as a means for choosing between theories, between preferred science and obsolete or 'bad' science, it requires more specificity. Brenner breaks down the rational values into particular criteria for rational choice: coherence (or consistency), precision, simplicity, completeness and fecundity (or generativity). These are the judgements of value on which scientific reason itself rests. They were not determined by some empirical process, were not discovered in nature, are not 'evidence-based', are not adjudicated by 'rules'. They are values that we, the human authors of the scientific, and all the other enterprises, agree are worthwhile. How they are applied is worked out depending on the context, 'case by case'.[43]

> Rationality is at the same time a product of the mind (l'esprit) and a combination of words and signs; it is formulated in the context of a specific discussion.[44]

D. Religion: a Repository of Values?

The turn to 'post-secularism', which I introduced at the outset, takes values seriously. The danger in religious versions (and that is what seems

---

40 Anastasios Brenner, 'A Problem in General Philosophy of Science: The Rational Criteria of Choice' in A. Brenner and J. Gayon (eds) *French Studies in the Philosophy of Science* (Netherlands: Springer 2009) 86.

41 Thomas S. Kuhn, *The Structure of Scientific Revolutions* (Chicago: University of Chicago Press 1970).

42 Anastasios Brenner, *Raison scientifique et valeurs humaines: essai sur les critères du choix objectif* (Paris: Presses Universitaires de France 2011) 16. Translation is mine.

43 Ibid., 4.

44 Ibid., 97. Translation is mine.

to be implied by 'post-secular') is that, just as rights live in law and – in a narrow view – reason lives in science, an equally narrow view may claim religion as the home of values. Steven D. Smith (2010) deplores the exclusion of a values discourse in the modern polity. He sums up the problem with that polity, and the discourse on which it is based, in the word 'secular'. Smith denies juxtaposing 'secular' with 'religious' discourse,[45] yet this is disingenuous when he has chosen a word that arose in a theological context, and currently refers to the separation of religion from matters of state. When he identifies the illicit 'smuggling' of ideas based on a 'purposive cosmos' or 'providential design',[46] his argument rests on the embeddedness of values in great views of the cosmic order. Yet values need not derive from grand cosmic or theological narratives. They can inhere in simple ethical precepts, from the humanistic bottom up, as well as from the theological top down.

What distinguishes religions from other ethical positions, even constellations, is their institutional, traditional and communal structure. This is a strength of religions: they offer membership of a bigger group and a rich body of lore, law and discourse. They are also hierarchical, and usually dominated by a professional class of priests, rabbis or imams. None of these characteristics is dangerous to the social fabric or the well-being of the believers. Yet their very institutional qualities, their self-referential, professional and hierarchical character, can make them difficult models for open public discourse. Just as law must pronounce what is legal and illegal, cleaving normative reality, purportedly according to rules, so religious institutions must cleave the halal from the haram, the kosher from the terefah, according to internal referents. Formal religion, like formal law, tends to self-referentiality.

Davies (2011) and Cox (1965) have both conceived secularization as a process rather than an end point.[47] Their positions emphasise the multiple parties and identities that may be involved in decisions over matters of faith and the polity. This can extend to law-making based on religion within limited communities. However, on Davies's account this would clearly be a space for open debate and multiple voices to be heard. By pluralizing involvement in religious, cultural, political and legal discourse, a diverse society may be more fully democratised than by simply accommodating religious and political hierarchies within a corporatist

---

[45] Steven D. Smith, above n1, 37–8.

[46] Ibid., 26.

[47] Davies, above n6; and Harvey Cox, *The Secular City: Secularization and Urbanization in Theological Perspective* (London: SCM Press 1965).

decision-making apparatus.[48] Religion and secularism are not two opposed alternatives. Nor is religion (any religion) the legitimate guardian of values. Values, to reprise a cliché, are too important to be left to the priests.

E. Last Observations on Law, Science and Religion

Throughout this study we have seen the interactions of values and scholarship, whether science, jurisprudence, animal welfare, ethology or vegetarianism. The study seeks an alternative way to understand the links between reason and religion, science and ethics, law and culture. Each is in dialogue with the other, so that regulatory regimes can be informed by a three way conversation between science, ethics and law. In this bottom-up model, driven by ethical, political or religious communities of consumers, there is potential for negotiation and effective communication. None of these systems need dominate the others. Neither science nor religion are 'conversation stoppers' in Smith's or Rorty's terms. Each has a perspective as well as investigative and communicative methods to bring to the table, to continue the conversation.

Neither law, nor science, nor religion is a stand-alone, 'rational and objective exercise'.[49] Each is connected to other discourses within a matrix of values and conditions derived from ethics, religions, and social and material circumstances. Law, science and religion are all informed by values, such as truth, ethics and how the world is (now[50]). Reason itself is one value (among others) and is in turn constituted by other, more fundamental, values that guide our rational choice.

Law, religion and even science are often expressed as sets of rules. Yet rules do not tell the whole story; they do not apply themselves. Whether applying regulatory standards, choosing among scientific theories, or discerning good from evil, the context is as important as the rule. Each case is different, deliberations must always refer to contingent values,

---

[48] This paragraph has been adapted from Richard Mohr and Nadirsyah Hosen, 'Da Capo: Law and Religion from the Top Down', in N. Hosen and R. Mohr (eds) *Law and Religion in Public Life: The Contemporary Debate* (Abingdon, Oxon: Routledge 2011) 10.

[49] Eve Darian Smith, above n1, 10–11.

[50] Given the deep traditional roots of most religions, and the antiquity of their texts, it is sometimes necessary to remind the clerics of this little word.

and we need to recognise the specificity of corporeality and the other.[51] Any important decision about what we eat and how to regulate food should draw on legal, scientific and ethical arguments, which are only as useful as their capacity to engage with each other, and to respect cultural and religious diversity.

51 Charles Taylor, 'To Follow a Rule ...' in C. Calhoun, E. LiPuma and M. Postone (eds) *Bourdieu: Critical Perspectives* (Cambridge, UK: Polity Press 1993) 49.

PART 5

ARTS AND EDUCATION

14. Finding the Islam in Islamic art: the relationship between Islamic law and artistic practice

Mia Corbett

> In every age and in most religious matters, people are caught between those ultra-conservatives who interpret the law strictly so as to forbid, prohibit, restrict the scope of what is permitted, and moderates who constantly seek to enlarge the scope of what is permitted …
>
> Taha Al-Alwani,
> President of the Islamic Jurisprudence Council of North America (2000)[1]

I. INTRODUCTION

The relationship between law and art in Islam varies greatly between temporal, geographical and political boundaries. Scholarly attempts to define this relationship often construct definitions which ignore contemporary art practice or simply refer to the dominant discourse that use the interpretive lens of the West to show points of difference and similarity between what is produced by the contemporary 'us' and the backward primitive 'them'. These approaches hugely oversimplify the problem of defining Islamic art, which is not a stagnant or historicised concept confined to the pre-modern Middle East, but a dynamic and subjective cultural product informed by different interpretations of the Divine law. Any assertion to the contrary exhibits an ignorance of the diversity of cultural approaches to Islamic law, ignoring both that the making and reception of art does not take place in an intellectual

---

[1] Quote taken from Ismail Ozgur Soganci's essay, 'The Place of Figurative Representation in Islamic Art: A Multi-dimensional Attempt to Question Some Unjust Claims' (2006) 24 *Journal of Cultural Research in Art Education* 135, 140.

vacuum[2] and the receptivity of art to intellectual developments in cultural practice.

This chapter aims to explore the nature of the relationship between Islamic art and Islamic law, and debunk some common misconceptions, particularly with respect to the legality of the use of the human figure in artistic representation. The following discussion will also examine the way in which law influences and governs the production of art and how artistic practice can be understood as a tool for assessing the way in which legal principles are interpreted and applied as a result of the values and dominant *ijtihad* methodologies of the cultural context in which it was produced.

II. FINDING THE 'ISLAM' IN ISLAMIC ART

In order to define 'Islamic' art, a person must first have an understanding of the omnipresence of Shari'ah law in the lives of practising Muslims. For those of Islamic faith, religion is not something that is tied to institutional or church worship, but instead is present at all times and governs of all aspects of life – whether political, economic, public, private or artistic. Many art historians have referred to the indistinguishable relationship between a Muslim's personal and religious life as authority for suggesting that all art created by Muslims in inherently 'Islamic'.[3] This definition is condescending because it suggests that Muslim artists are unable to conceive or engage with the world in their artistic practice outside of the boundaries of religion. It is also incorrect to assume that Muslim art that engages with widely known tropes of Islamic art, such as arabesque patterns and abstract geometric forms does so for religious purposes. Often such designs are simply employed for decorative purposes on domestic items such as vases and tapestries and are not intended to convey religious meaning. It should also be noted that 'Islamic art' is not exclusively 'Middle-Eastern art', a distinction that is often overlooked by contemporary commentators on the practice of iconoclasm. In fact, Islamic art is 'more easily defined by what it is not:

---

[2] This opinion is fully informed by the definition of Islamic art in Asli Gocer's article 'A Hypothesis Concerning the Character of Islamic Art' (1999) 60 (4) *Journal of the History of Ideas* 683, 687.

[3] See, for example, Titus Burckhardt, Sheila Blair and Jonathon Bloom, 'The Mirage of Islamic Art: Reflections on the Study of an Unwieldy Field' (2014) 85 (1) *The Art Bulletin* 152, 158.

neither a region, nor a time period, nor a school, nor a movement',[4] but a visual culture that spans centuries and continents and which transcends the practice of individuals. To confine any discussion of Islamic art to practices which are exclusive to Middle East is to disregard the diverse qualities of Islam and the widespread Muslim populations in countries including India and Indonesia.

The problem of finding an appropriate definition for Islamic art is also heightened by the absence of an international Islamic authority that can provide clarity on the legal issues surrounding the portraiture and the artistic adaptation of the holy text. The lack of a central authoritative religious body derives from the Islamic belief that Muslims are not required to answer to any legal authority other than God. Although this creates legislative issues on a state level, it also allows for communities to adapt and diversify their approaches to art based on interpretations of the law that can be understood to give the artist creative license to the extent allowed by their cultural context. Law as a product of cultural context can mean that in some cases, Muslims from different schools of thought may disagree over what constitutes 'Islamic art'. For example, the Taj Mahal, arguably the most famous piece of Islamic architecture, was commissioned by an Indian Muslim as a tomb for himself and his wife, and is considered by some fundamentalists to breach Islamic law because it is an 'icon' which commemorates the dead.[5]

Perhaps the best way of determining whether art is 'Islamic' is to determine whether it engages with Islamic law through the representation of religious themes or content. Islamic law, primarily derived from the holy texts of the Qur'an and Hadith, has a unique role to play in the production of art. This is because unlike other cultures that are built on the foundation of religion, Islamic law is highly proscriptive of all areas of life. By defining Islamic art in terms of its relationship to law, problematic definitions that are incompatible with the practice of artists living outside a particular geography of place and time can be overcome.

Oleg Grabar, a highly regarded academic in the field, has attempted to understand Islamic art in a similar way, suggesting that it includes art made by Muslims and non-Muslims 'that is created for the spiritual, intellectual and physical usage or enjoyment of [people] living within the sphere of Islamic thought and civilisation'.[6] Thus, not all art created by Muslim artists is necessarily Islamic, even if the work engages with

---

4 Ibid., 153.

5 Ibid., 177.

6 Soganci, above n1, 19.

traditional tropes usually associated with Islamic art including arabesque patterns and abstracted figuration.[7] However, this definition does not go far enough to rule out art that engages with tropes of Islam for visual rather than religiously motivated purposes. Whether or not art is 'Islamic' should therefore be determined by reference to the engagement with principles of Islam, otherwise it is simply inspired by Islamic aesthetics.

III. DECONSTRUCTING THE LEGAL MISCONCEPTION

Perhaps the most pervasive misconception of Islamic art is the notion that portraiture and the representation of human features is expressly prohibited by Islamic law. Islamic art is often understood as being unwaveringly iconophobic and iconoclastic in its approach to portraiture and figuration. Iconoclasm is a practice whereby the representative qualities of a human portrait are removed or destroyed in a way that declassifies the human characteristics of the figure, often through the disfigurement or obliteration of the facial features. It is widely believed that iconophobia is a central component of Islamic art practice, a fallacy which is attributed to supposedly explicit restrictions on artistic representation in the primary texts of Islamic law. This misunderstanding of Islamic art is ill informed and completely ignores both that there is no express prohibition on figurative representation in the Qur'an[8] and historical evidence that shows that portraits of the Prophet Muhammad have been commonplace in Islamic artistic practice since the seventh century. It is unclear why the myth that portraiture in Islamic art is considered, by both Muslims and non-Muslims, to be *haram* under Islamic law, although it is likely to be a product of a number of sources; including the extremist iconoclasm of the Taliban in the Middle East (and the Western media's coverage of the events), literal and strict interpretations of the Hadith, *ijma* and *'urf* giving rise to *al-'adah muhakkamah*, and periods of frenzied image destruction throughout history. The following dialogue seeks to put debate as to the legality of the image in Islamic art to rest.

Because the Holy Qur'an – the primary source of Islamic law – does not make reference to the use of images in Islamic art, jurists must turn

---

[7] See Ismā'īl R. al-Fārūqī, 'Islām and Art' (1973) 37 *Studia Islamica* 81, 99 for more information on the popular mischaracterisation of art that is 'Arabic' as 'Islamic'.

[8] Taha Jaber al-Alwani '"Fatwa" concerning the United States Supreme Courtroom Frieze' (2000–01) 15 (1–2) *Journal of Law and Religion* 28, 6.

to the explanatory *ahadith* to derive the legal principles on images. The hadith that contain reference to the use of human likeness in art are often contradictory and difficult to reconcile. The use of hadith to declare binding legal doctrine is a significant point of contention for scholars, and opinion varies greatly across different schools of thought in contemporary jurisprudence. Sunni Muslims, for example, generally interpret hadith as strict legal doctrine, while Shia Muslims are generally more liberal in their approach, taking into consideration issues of context and reliability. The *sanad* of various books of the hadith that deal with the issue of the human figure in Islamic art can also be called into question, with some schools of thought favouring particular books over others, an issue which greatly contributes to different approaches to Islamic art across the schools of thought.

However, Moderates from both divisions of Islam believe the rule of the Hadith is open to interpretation by *ijtihad* which has resulted in diverse applications of the law in practice as variously informed by the understanding of the Divine as elucidated in the Qur'an. In his *fatwa* concerning the legality of a representation of the Prophet Muhammad in a sculptural frieze in the Supreme Court of the United States, Taha Jaber al-Alwani notes that although the use of images of the Prophet conflict with some of the more objectively anti-image passages, hadith must be interpreted with respect to the cultural context in which an image is produced.[9] He also cites the need to take a holistic approach by considering the legal ratio of the hadith on images, and the purposive approach of the Prophet to representations of the human figure, rather than the matter of the representation itself.[10]

Commonly cited hadith that deal with the representation of the human figure in Islamic art often include accounts of the Angel Gabriel refusing to enter houses where images are displayed in places of honour, and passages that relate interactions between the Prophet Muhammad and his wife 'A'ishah with respect to figurative images on items of her clothing, motifs on décor and her dolls. In total, there are between thirteen and fifteen *ahadith* that deal with the production of images. These can be classified into four categories according to their legal message. The first category of hadith, and the legal maxim most commonly accepted and applied, prohibit the use of images in art where artists seek to emulate the creation of God. One such hadith appears in the book of Sahih Muslim, who recalls the Prophet's words: 'those who make images will be

---

9 Ibid., 7.

10 al-Alwani, above n8, 8.

punished by God and it will be said to them: 'Breathe soul into what you have created' and they would not be able to.'[11] The hadith of Sahih Al-Bukhari also transcribes this incident, stating: 'the most grievously tormented people on the Day of Resurrection will be those who try to emulate the creation of God.'[12]

When taken literally, this hadith can be understood as an express prohibition on the creation of images in art. However, when looked at critically, it is clear that the true issue of the image in the hadith lies in the intention of the artist to create an image that rivals God's creation, rather than the use of the image itself.[13] This is a violation of one of the central messages of the Qur'an, that of the 'Oneness' and sole creativity of God embodied in the first *shahada*: 'There is no God but Allah.'[14] This belief that the divinity of Allah transcends what can be understood and replicated has contributed to the notion that in the process of image making, an artist competes with the creative power of God, and thus his sole authority.[15] A simple example of the widespread practical application of this law is evidenced through the fact that Islamic art almost never bears the signature of the artist. This ensures that the artist remains anonymous, and provides a safeguard against any accusation that he or she wishes to divert worship and praise from God onto themselves. Often, artists are only uncovered by considerable historical research and analysis by conservators. By refusing to acknowledge their own creation and protecting their anonymity, the artists submit that they are not to be considered as figures of skill and talent that could rival the creationary power of God. This is a significant point of division between Islamic and Western art practice, wherein the culture of the artist as celebrity is rife in the visual arts.

The second category of hadith that regulate the production of imagery are those warning against the power of images to distract the mind from focussing on the only true object of devotion, God. Warnings against the deceptive danger of 'idols', a term which refers to alternative, and therefore false, figures of adolation is also a strong theme in the Qur'an.[16] The concern with human and animal portraiture in art as a manifestation of an 'idol' arose from the Pagan, Jewish and Christian

---

[11] Hadith *Sahih Muslim* no. 1687.

[12] Hadith *Sahih Al-Bukhari* no. 5610.

[13] al-Alwani, above n8, 14.

[14] *Qur'an* 2:163.

[15] Finbar Barry Flood, 'Between Cult and Culture: Bamiyan, Islamic Iconoclasm, and the Museum' (2002) 84 (4) *The Art Bulletin* 641, 643.

[16] *Qur'an* 4:51, 4:76, 5:3, 5:60, 5:90.

tradition of praying to artistic representations of their Gods in places of worship. This is closely related to the third category of hadith, which warns against the overvaluing and worshipping of items of luxury and wealth, such as expensive commissioned portraits. These two maxims of law are clearly manifested in the architecture of Islamic places of worship, where both imagery and elaborate ornamentation are absent in severe juxtaposition to Christian churches.

The fourth and final category of hadith express concern for the power of images to diminish the ability of the mind to conceive of the abstract and unknowable greatness of God. This issue is particularly important to Islamic art because it supports the contention that the use of geometry and linear pattern is not a decorative necessity but a conscious aesthetic decision that promotes contemplation of the infinite earthly transcendance of God. This will be discussed further in the context of aversionary artistic practices.

It is important to note that all of these hadith deal with the way in which images are intended to be used, rather than the use of images themselves. By analysing these hadith, it is clear there is little evidence that a prohibitive ban on all images is justified or required under Islamic law. Further evidence that image making is, at worst, *makruh*, can be inferred by reference to an artistic tradition of portraiture in Islamic art which can be traced back through history.[17]

IV. PORTRAITURE IN ISLAMIC ART

Early interpretations of religious texts understood warnings about idol worship in the Qur'an and hadith solely as a deterrent against sympathy for the Gods of other religions. This broad interpretation of the law meant that pictorial representations of the Prophet Muhammad were not considered to be heretical, because they did not encourage the worshipping of false idols. As a result of this understanding of Islamic law, images of the Prophet Muhammad were considered to be completely legal, as they did not represent false Gods. The practice of figurative illustration in religious manuscripts was particularly prominent in the Persian school of painting. For example, Abu-l-Faraj's famous manuscript of *The Book of Songs* (*kitāb al-aghānī*) (completed in AD 967) contains a figurative embellishment on the opening page of each volume,

---

[17] Oleg Grabar, 'The Story of Portraits of the Prophet Muhammad' (2003) 96 *Studia Islamica* 19, 19.

which are now known collectively by art historians as the Aghānī Miniatures.[18]

The use of images in Islamic art was so prominent at this time that a literary genre of explanatory hadith developed in the ninth century known as *Shamā'il al-Rasūl* or 'Features of the Prophet', which acted as a manual for artistic representations of Muhammad the Messenger.[19] This consisted of a compendium of information about the character and physical features of the Prophet as they were recalled by his friends and Companions, and provided a foundation for the black beard, turban, robe, long dark plaited hair and round cheeks that came to provide a visual cue for recognising his presence in artworks.[20] One example of this is Sa'di's *Bustān* (Fruit Orchard), which was painted in 1292 and is currently in the collection of the Metropolitan Museum of Art in New York. The artist's unconcern for the representation of the Prophet is reaffirmed by the image's accompanying text, which explains his desire to create as close a portrait as possible. Referring to the Prophet, the artist asks: 'How shall I eulogise you acceptably?' and 'How can I [imperfect as I am] describe you justly?'[21]

It is important here to note that although the artist does attempt to visually replicate the Prophet's image, his reference to the impossibility of such a venture can be read as an attempt to demarcate his work from a perceived attempt to compete with God through the creation of the human image. This goal is further achieved by the intentional stylization of the figure, a trope characteristic of Islamic art which involves devoiding figures of character and personality such that they are identifiable only by aforementioned visual cues. The Islamic miniatures also display the artist's intention to self-consciously avoid realism by refraining from giving their figures a three-dimensional quality through the use of depth and shadow.[22] This is often incorrectly and condescendingly interpreted as artistic 'ignorance'[23] by Western historians. However, this

---

[18] D. S. Rice, 'The Aghānī Miniatures and Relgious Painting in Islam' (1953) 95.601 *The Burlington Magazine* 128, 129.

[19] Christine Gruber, 'Between Logos (Kalima) and Light (Nūr): Representations of the Prophet Muhammad in Islamic Painting' (2009) 26 *Muqarnas* 229, 234.

[20] See, for example, the image of the Prophet Muhammad's ascension in Nasrallah Munshi's *Kalila va Dimma* ca. 1350–1500, Bibliotheque nationale de France.

[21] Sa'di, *Morals Painted and Tales Adorned* lines 85, 53.

[22] Gocer, above n2, 690.

[23] al-Fārūqī, above n7, 100.

methodology is not indicative of an intellectual primitivism, but is instead a fulfilment of the artist's purpose, that is, to avoid giving the figure a distinctive quality that could deem it an attempt to replicate the diversity of Gods creation.[24]

Over time, the use of figurative representations of the Prophet evolved with the changing influence of certain passages of the Qur'an on Islamic thought, especially in the practice of Sufi mystics. After 1400 AD, representations of the Prophet began to reject the use of *Shamā'il* to describe the Prophet visually. Instead, artists began to prefer the use of what Gruber describes as *kalima* or *nūr Muhammad* portraits, whereby the Prophet's facial features were replaced with either a word or symbol.[25] *Kalima* (meaning 'graphical' or 'word') portraits, for example replaced the face of the Prophet with a circular disc inscribed with the words '*Yā Muhammad!*'[26]

It is important to note that this development did not arise out of a fear or prohibition of creative representation of the human figure, but rather an attempt to more effectively portray the spiritual quality of the Prophet as a quasi-Divine being that transcended his human body, and was unable to be truly captured in Islamic art by representation in human form. In other words, obscuring the Prophet's face with a graphic or word sought to convey the essential nature of the Prophet as the manifestation of the Divine word of Allah.[27]

Another way in which symbolism is used to more accurately represent the Divinity embodied by the Prophet is through the use of a flaming disc of light to obscure his facial features. This approach to the figurative realisation of the Prophet is largely inspired by two verses of the Qur'an[28] where it is stated that God sent a light (*nūr*) or an illuminating torch (*sirājan munīran*) to lead his people through darkness.[29] This sentiment also appears in the hadith of al-Bukhari: 'Wherever he went in darkness, [the Prophet] had light shining around him like the moon-light.'[30] Thus, these approaches to figuration in Islamic art were not the consequence of a prohibition on images, but an attempt to apply religious law as it understood the essence of the Prophet Muhammad through the visual translation of the message of the Qur'an and Hadith. In a way, the

---

24 Ibid.
25 Gruber, above n19, 231.
26 Gruber, above n19, 240.
27 Ibid.
28 Gruber, above n19, 247.
29 *Qur'an* 5:15, 33:46.
30 Hadith *al-Bukhari* 4:229.

use of bodily representations of the Prophet 'proves that a putative ban on figural imagery has not historically constituted the principle driving force behind the non-figural elements used in representations of the Prophet'.[31] These figurative practices have also manifested themselves in contemporary Islamic art, including in the propagandistic graphic art of the Islamic Republic on paintings and billboards in Iran.[32]

However, it is not only the Prophet who was the subject of images in early Islamic art. Portraits of kings, heroes and princes were common motifs in the 'picture galleries' of royal residencies, as well as on coins, medals, floor paintings and in sculpture.[33] These images also employ the use of intentional stylization, and often showed 'no likeness to the person they were supposed to represent',[34] perhaps in an attempt by the artist to defer any accusation that he had attempted to exercise the power of God by exactly replicating his creation. Baer, in her article *The Human Figure in Early Islamic Art*, also draws attention to the growing trend in the sixth century for artists to employ elements of satire and caricature in their figurative portraiture, which enabled the images to be lifelike and personified without necessarily imitating life. There is even evidence of at least one case where realism in an early Iranian painting was used for the purpose of creating a portrait of a man who had been issued with an arrest warrant.[35] Evidence of this relaxed contextual approach to the image also comes from the renowned Persian epic poet Nizami Ganjawi, who, known for his realistic style, is recorded as noting that as men can only be created by God, the painted image bears no threat to his power as it itself has no corporeal power and cannot match his creation.[36] This more liberal and rational approach to the legal position on the image was common in the regions of Persia and Mesopotamia, which, removed by geography from the centre of Islam in Mecca and Medina, were also removed from compliance with the proscriptive laws of the Caliphates, and were free to pursue their own legal interpretations of the holy texts.

[31] Gruber, above n19, 252.

[32] Kishwar Rizvi, 'Religious Icon and National Symbol: The Tomb of Ayatollah Khomeini in Iran' (2003) 20 *Muqarnas* 209, 214.

[33] Eva Baer, 'The Human Figure in Early Islamic Art: Some Preliminary Remarks' (1999) 16 *Muqarnas* 32, 33.

[34] Ibid.

[35] Baer, above n33, 38.

[36] Baer, above n33, 41.

V. ICONOCLASM

The proliferation of images of the Prophet Muhammad in Islamic art continued until around the fifteenth century AD despite edicts issued from devout individual political leaders, most notably that of the Caliph Yazīd (Abd al-Malik) in 721 AD, which had limited cultural effect outside the geographical region under his direct control near his residence in Jordan.[37] It is with Yazīd's edict that the first records of a practice known as iconoclasm emerged. Early Islamic iconoclasts generally restricted themselves to the removal of Christian and Jewish images as icons of other Gods, however, in later years, cultural understanding of the law expanded to include the representation of any human figure.

Generally, iconoclasm can be reduced to two forms; instrumental iconoclasm, where action is taken for the purpose of achieving a greater religious goal, and expressive iconoclasm, in which a desire to express a belief or feeling is achieved by the act itself.[38] Instrumental iconoclasm seeks to solve the problem of idol worship identified in the Qur'an by 'de-animating' or neutralising the images by removing the features that make them recognisable as icons or replicates of God's creation. This usually takes the form of defacement by burning or chiselling depending on the artistic medium used, but also includes less aggressive manifestations of censorship such as the painting of a white veil over the *shamā'il* of the Prophet when his facial features are represented in artworks.[39] These practical manifestations of instrumental iconoclasm are undertaken by persons who believed that such action is sanctioned by Divine law. A purposive distinction can be drawn here between *kalima* or *nūr Muhammad* portraits and those portraits which are the censoring practice of instrumental iconoclasm. Whilst the former constitutes an artistic attempt to more accurately represent the qualities of the Prophet as man who transcends his earthly body, the latter is an act that takes a strict objective approach to the legal texts by replicating the Prophet's proactive removal of images, rather than seeking to understand the law purposively by analysing the reasons behind his actions.

Expressive iconoclasm, on the other hand, has no legitimate legal grounding. Often overrepresented and exaggerated by Western media, contemporary expressive iconoclasm is singularly practiced by Muslim

---

[37] G. R. D. King, 'Islam, Iconoclasm, and the Declaration of Doctrine' (1985) 48.2 *Bulletin of the School of Oriental and African Studies, University of London* 267, 276.

[38] Flood, above n15, 646.

[39] Gruber, above n19, 241, 249.

fundamentalists of the Wahhabi and Salafi school revivalist movements of the nineteenth century, and includes such acts as the infamous destruction of the Bamiyan Buddhas, the response to the publication of caricatures of the Prophet Muhammad in the Danish newspaper *Jyllands-Postern* in 2005 and the attacks on French newspaper *Charlie Hebdo* in 2011 and 2015. The leaders and proponents of these movements claim legitimacy for their actions by taking a strict interpretative approach to the Qur'an, ignoring and denying value in the traditions of *ijtihad* that defines what has historically been the accepted practice for determining Islamic law contextually, with reference to changing social and cultural values.[40]

Their approach to figuration in Islamic art is almost anarchic, and utilises *fatwa* and doctrinal edicts as 'instruments for legalising un-Islamic behaviour'[41] without reference to any legal authority that validates their ideology. In 2001, for example, the Taliban issued an edict validating the destruction of the Bamiyan Buddhas in Afghanistan.[42] The publication of this edict was not motivated by religious piety, but was intended as a public statement of rebellion against the international community of the Western world through an elaborate performance[43] of expressive iconoclasm that served a political purpose. The fact that this act was politically motivated is confirmed by evidence that the Taliban rejected offers forwarded by the MET Museum in New York to pay for the statues to be moved to a different location[44] and by the fact that the statues had already been beheaded by early iconoclasts in the fifth or sixth century,[45] and thus presented no threat as icons of worship at the time they were destroyed by the Taliban in the new millennium. Thus, despite the official edict that stated the action was taken 'on the basis of religious judgements of the *'ulama* (clerics) and rulings of the Supreme Court of the Islamic Emirate of Afghanistan',[46] the destruction of the Bamiyan Buddhas had no basis in Islamic law.

---

40 Wendy M. K. Shaw, 'The Islam in Islamic Art History: Secularism and Public Discourse' (2012) 6 *Journal of Art Historiography* 1, 24.

41 Tamara Albertini, 'The Seductiveness of Certainty: The Destruction of Islam's Intellectual Legacy by the Fundamentalists' (2003) 53.4 *Philosophy East and West* 455, 464.

42 Flood, above n15, 655.

43 Ibid., 651.

44 Ibid.

45 Flood, above n15, 648.

46 Flood, above n15, 655.

In contemporary Western discourse, iconoclasm is used to create an image of Islam as inherently brutal and irrationally aggressive, furthering the narrative of the primitive 'other'. The reduction of Islam to the practical application of Islamic 'law' by fundamentalist schools of thought is a continuing problem that contributes to the perceived ideological divide between Islamic and Western cultural practice. It is also important to understand that iconoclasm as a whole is a cultural phenomenon geographically restricted to Islamic practice in the Middle East. Thus, by applying the iconoclastic narrative to Islam as a whole is to ignore that Islam, like any system of law, 'is not constituted solely by its "fundaments" … but is enacted within cultural products that can alter how those fundamental are understood within any given context'.[47]

VI. ANICONISM

One of the most recognised characteristics of Islamic art is its use of abstract linear or vegetative patterns and geometric forms, which are widely considered to be the only aesthetic form available to Islamic artists. However, the notion that this artistic practice developed to circumnavigate the legal prohibition on the image is a theory perpetuated by academics that misunderstand the use of non-figurative forms as a way of complying with a legal prohibition on the image, rather than a conscious cultural movement aimed at representing the Divine presence accurately. Aniconism, often referred to as the 'classical' Sunni artistic tradition, uses the infinite and unbroken line to represent the essential nature of God as infinite, transcendent, and unable to be understood or conceived through pictorial representation,[48] for, as the Qur'an expressly acknowledges, 'nothing is like unto Him'.[49] Thus, aniconism does not derive from a strict legal interpretation of the religious texts, but rather as a way of visually representing the underlying principle of Islam, that is, the nature of God as the one true and unknowable being from whom Holy law derives.

In order to appreciate the purpose of aniconism in Islamic art, one must first understand the historical context of Islam and its relationship to images in the art of Christianity. Islam explicitly rejects both the notion that God is present in the holy trinity and the belief that the human body

---

47 Shaw, above n40, 31.

48 Edward H. Madden, 'Some Characteristics of Islamic Art' (1975) 33 (4) *The Journal of Aesthetics and Art Criticism* 423, 425.

49 al-Fārūqī, above n7, 88.

is made in God's own image as a narcissistic fallacy that is 'an obstacle to human imagination'[50] and a barrier to comprehending the Divine. To Muslims, God is a being beyond all earthly presence: even the Prophet Muhammad does not represent or embody God but rather is the ideal of man on earth. The strong visual tradition in Christianity of creating portraits and sculptures of Jesus and other important religious figures as points of reference for prayer and worship is thus highly offensive to some Muslims who consider it an attempt to humanise God as earthly and finite. In fact, much of the early evidence of iconoclastic practices show that they were directed against Christian iconography rather than Islamic images. The practice was especially aggressive toward symbols like the Christian cross, which represented the holy trinity. Thus, the shirking of figurative images in Islamic art has the dual purpose of expressing an objection to the iconography of other religions, and ensuring that the viewer conceives of a Divinity that lies beyond human perception and experience, and ensuring that the viewer focuses its worship on God, rather than false human idols that made it 'impossible to draw attention away from the limited, the historical, and the parochial'.[51]

The almost universal practice of abstraction over figuration in places of religious worship can also be attributed both to the fact that aniconism was the officially sanctioned approach to artistic representation of the Caliphates prior to the fourteenth century.[52] This was because it was believed that the use of geometric forms was a metaphor for expressing the Divine whose perfection is 'synonymous' with the 'repetitive patterns, exactness of proportion and symmetry' of Islamic art.[53] Thus, by inundating the viewer's sight with a visually unending display of complex and interwoven pattern, Islamic art does not attempt to imitate Divine creation but invoke contemplation in the observer of the inhuman and transcendent quality of God.[54] The use of this 'infinite pattern' can be observed not only in decorative wall designs, but also in the most celebrated architecture of the Islamic world, including the Great Mosque of Cordoba in Spain,[55] where over 800 columns form a seemingly infinite forest of double horseshoe arches that are intended to elicit in the viewer

---

50 Rasheed Araeen, 'Preliminary Notes for the Understanding of the Historical Significance of Geometry in Arab/Islamic Thought, and its Suppressed Role in the Genealogy of World History' (2010) 24 (5) *Third Text* 509, 510.

51 Madden, above n48, 427.

52 Ibid., 425.

53 Above n2, 691.

54 al-Fārūqī, above n7, 109.

55 Madden, above n48, 425.

a feeling of awe and contemplation of the divinity of God as eternal and everlasting. The practice of aniconism and its religious purpose is not restricted to the art of the historical Islam, but is also found in the practice of modern artists in Malaysia, including Sulaiman Esa and Khatijah Sanusi, both of whom utilise arabesque infinity patterns as symbols of their belief in the transcendence and unity of God as the Original Source.[56]

VII. QUR'ANIC VERSE IN ISLAMIC ART

The holy text of the Qur'an is considered to be the most valuable and pure source of Islamic law. As God's express words, the text of the Qur'an is believed to be Divine, and the validity of its proscriptive verses are generally considered to be closed to *ijtihad*. The purity of the word of God has been retained through an oral tradition of memorisation and recital that prioritises the intricacies and subtleties of the language of the verses. Thus, the original Arabic text, unaltered by translation or interpretation, is extremely important to the notion of the Qur'an provides the first and most authoritative source of Islamic law.

Historically, Islamic culture has favoured the use of word over image as a means of self-expression, and as the mechanism most suited to expressing the values of a culture by enabling 'intellectual faculties and human consciousness to incorporate certain meanings ... while leaving room for new interpretations, explanations and comprehension'.[57] This 'culture of the Word' is at odds with the Western 'culture of the image' inherited from the Greek and Roman artistic practices from which a progression toward the most accurate embodiment of the human figure in Western art practice can be traced. It has also been argued that the departure from the use of the image in Islamic art was also a conscious attempt to demarcate Islamic art and the Islamic message from the proliferation of Christian art that dominated the visual culture of the eighth century.[58]

The use of Qur'anic verse in Arabic writing has long been considered synonymous with the Arabesque. Its widespread use in artistic practice is largely thanks to the development of calligraphic styles where each letter

---

[56] Virginia Hooker, 'Mindful of Allah: Islam and the Visual Arts in Indonesia and Malaysia' (2013) 33 (1) *Artlink* 70, 72.

[57] al-Alwani, above n8, 4.

[58] Oleg Grabar, 'From the Icon to Aniconism: Islam and the Image' (2003) 55 (2) *Museum International* 46, 51.

and word could be legibly and aesthetically joined together in one continuous line through the ordered manipulation of letters and words into a form of religious expression.[59] This had the dual effect of stating the will of God through the text while expressing His unknowable, infinite qualities through symbolic representation,[60] with the continuous line acting metaphor for his ceaseless existence throughout time.

Attitudes toward the use of the holy legal text of the Qur'an in artistic practice vary greatly across geographical boundaries. Controversy surrounding the use of Qur'anic verse in contemporary art, is, perhaps surprisingly, uniquely concentrated in Asian Islamic countries. This can be largely attributed to the fetishisation of the language of Arabic by Malaysian and Indonesian Muslims as the sacred language of Divine law.[61] That is not to say that the use of Qur'anic verse in contemporary and commercial art is prohibited, but rather that it is considered to be an unethical use of text of the Divine revelation. After all, Muslims have a duty that is steeped in generations of Islamic tradition to act as custodians of the language of the Qur'an,[62] and to ensure God's word is respected and protected for future generations.

Concerns about the appropriateness of using the holy text in art are usually voiced by Indonesia's religious communities, including radical street organisations such as the Islamic Defenders Front, who are opposed to the moderate approach to Islamic law exhibited in academia and broader society,[63] and act as a watchdog for the misuse of Arabic language and Qur'anic verse.[64] One example of this was the uproar from the Islamic community in response to the designer fashion label Chanel's show in January 1994 which unveiled a dress bearing the Qur'anic phrase 'and they are rightly guided' in its original Arabic in an upward direction across the model's bust.[65] This prompted the head of the Indonesian Council of Islamic Scholars, Hasan Basri, to persuade his organisation to file an official complaint of protest. In a response indicative of the

[59] Ibid.

[60] Madden, above n48, 427–8.

[61] Kenneth M. George, 'Ethics, Iconoclasm, and Qur'anic Art in Indonesia' (2009) 24 (4) *Cultural Anthropology* 589, 603.

[62] Ibid., 600.

[63] George, above n61, 608.

[64] See for example, the complaint made regarding the use of the word Allah written in Arabic script on the album cover of the band 'Dewa' www.thejakartapost.com/news/2005/04/26/fpi-reports-rock-group-dewa-police-blasphemy.html (accessed 26 June 2015).

[65] This phrase appears twice in the *Qur'an* at 36:21 and 6:82.

universal Western understanding of Islamic approaches to legally prohibited art as requiring iconoclastic elimination, Chanel burned the dresses and destroyed all photographs of them.

Another example of the practical relationship between Qur'anic art and Islamic law is through an understanding of the contemporary art practice of A. D. Pirous, who has a moderate liberal approach to religious law, states:

> The Holy Qur'an itself must not be changed, but to understand it, you must be free to interpret it ... So I take a verse and I try to animate it with my personal vision, with my personal understanding ... When I express it in visual language that's when I use aesthetic knowledge in composition, colour, texture, line, rhythm, everything ...[66]

In this approach, Pirous applies his own personal process of *ijtihad* to derive personal meaning from religious texts, conveying his relationship and understanding of the passages of the Qur'an through an expressive use of technique and materials. His use of Qur'anic verse has been subject to extensive scrutiny and even censorship when exhibiting his work. After an *'ulama* accused him of marring the Qur'an when a painting he exhibited suffered some scratches in installation,[67] Pirous changed his approach to public exhibitions to comply with cultural standards. Prior to an exhibition in Indonesia in 2002 which showcased a retrospective of his career, he had all his paintings checked by an Arabic expert and made adjustments where they were recommended, despite having previously exhibited and sold works without issue or alteration to Muslims in the Middle East to whom Arabic was an everyday language. This decision of self-censorship was largely ethically and culturally motivated by the expectations of the Islamic community, rather than by his own relationship and understanding of religious law.

These examples show that there is significant concern for the way in which misrepresentation of Islamic law in art can result in a denigration of the holy texts. Academic Kenneth George not only appreciates the value of understanding approaches to Islamic art as reflective of ethical understandings and ideologies of the religious texts, but also lists three ways in which these incidents of censorship show an understanding of the relationship of Islamic art as inextricable from Islamic law. Firstly is the concentration of authority in the religious elite (rather than artists and designers) for determining how the Qur'an can be used in artistic

---

66 Hooker, above n56, 70.
67 George, above n61, 602.

practice. Secondly is the ability of religious communities to 'weigh in' on Islamic art as it contributes to the discourse of Islamic law and the third is the use of objections to global Islamic art practice as a platform for expressing and instructing Muslims across the world in religious ideology.[68]

Although this notion of religious censorship can be alarming from a Western perspective where freedom of expression is a core value of contemporary artistic practice, it is important to remember the importance of the contextual legal environment in which the art is being produced. In the United States, many non-Muslims are engaging with Quranic verse in ways that would be illegal to many conservative religious elites, but which prompts a debate about the use of the Qur'an in a modern context. For example, in Sandow Birk's creative project 'American Quran', the artist transcribes passages from the holy text in contemporary graffiti script, illuminating the text with cartoon images of twenty-first-century life to invite the viewer to consider the Qur'an as a 'universal message to humankind'.[69] In many cases, works which are censored for breaching the established legal and cultural boundaries for Islamic art are still accessible over the internet, and successfully promote discussion across the developing transnational Islamic public[70] (assisted by the proliferation of internet *fatwa*) about how the law can be interpreted and applied to contemporary artistic practice.

VIII. CONCLUSION

Although some Muslims consider imagery and Qur'anic verse in contemporary and historic Islamic art as a threat to the integrity of Islamic law,[71] such approaches do not represent the understanding of the interdependent relationship between Islamic art and Islamic law by most Muslim communities. As Grabar states, 'it is foolish, illogical and historically incorrect to talk of a single Islamic artistic expression. A culture of thirteen centuries which extended from Spain to Indonesia is not now and was not in the past a monolith, and to every generalization

---

68 George, above n61, 596.

69 See this work and more by Birk at www.sandowbirk.com/paintings/recent-works (accessed 18 August 2015).

70 Armando Salvatore, 'The Exit from a Westphalian Framing of Political Space and the Emergence of a Transnational Islamic Public' (2007) 24 (4) *Theory, Culture & Society* 45, 50.

71 George, above n61, 603.

there are dozens of exceptions.'[72] Thus, by subscribing to the singular primitive and iconoclastic narrative of the West we do not allow ourselves to imagine Islam and Muslim culture complexly, and are blinded to the true nature of the relationship between artistic and legal practice as culturally and historically varied and diverse.

The lack of figurative representation in Islamic art is often also subjected to the Western understanding of art as a cultural movement toward the most accurate representation of the human figure, which is considered to parallel the development of civilisation. This narrow view of the relationship between artistic progression and social development has resulted in the denigration of Islamic art, and therefore Islamic law and civilisation, as primitive and backward for its perceived aversion to the development of figurative style. The reality is that Muslims are constantly changing and evolving their understanding and relationship with religious law. Like any other culture, 'Muslims ceaselessly rethink and rework their art as they respond to the shifting currents of culture, politics and history, and as they negotiate identifications with nation, ethnicity, and ideology.'[73] This reflects the contention of this chapter that the primary texts of Islamic law are living, dynamic texts that are open to different interpretations across contemporary nation states, religious communities and individuals, including as they apply to Islamic art.

72 Shaw, above n40, 29.
73 George, above n61, 591.

15. The lawfulness of music in contemporary Indonesian debate

Neneng Yanti Khozanatu Lahpan

I. INTRODUCTION

In early 2009, Ahmad Heryawan, the new governor of West Java, Indonesia, gave comments on *jaipong*[1] dancers that triggered controversy and debate among West Java citizens, especially Sundanese artists.[2] He criticised *jaipong* dance as an erotic, impolite and non-Islamic performance genre, especially for its performers' dance movements known as '3G' (*gitek*, *geol*, *goyang*, referring to types of hip movements). He also called attention to *jaipong* dancers' costumes and their transgression of moral values. The governor's statements immediately became a controversial issue, especially among Sundanese artists, by whom a *jaipong* dance has long been considered 'a cultural icon' of the West Java region. The case became all the more sensitive given the governor's political background with the Justice and Prosperous Party (*Partai Keadilan Sejahtera*/PKS), known for its strong Islamic basis. Although this case has been solved in 'a political way' following a meeting between the governor and local artists, it remains emblematic of the problematic issues that can arise between Islam and performing arts.[3]

---

[1] *Jaipong* is a popular traditional Sundanese dance of West Java.

[2] Sundanese is the second biggest ethnic group in Indonesia, after Javanese, occupying West Java province with the population 42,631,198 people with 97.29 per cent of its population being Muslim, and its local language, Sundanese, is used by about 29 million people. See Leo Suryadinata, Aris Ananta, and Evi Nurvidya Arifin (eds), *Indonesia's Population Ethnicity and Religion in a Changing Political Landscape* (Singapore: Institute of Southeast Asian Studies 2003), 103; Cece Sobarna, 'Bahasa Sunda, Sudah di Ambang Pintu Kematian Kah?' (2007) 11 (1) *MAKARA, Sosial Humaniora*.

[3] Indonesian media has covered this issue widely. See, for example, http://m.inilah.com/news/detail/82601/gubernur-jabar-jaipong-dan–seniman; http://nasional.republika.co.id/berita/nasional/pemprov-jabar/12/10/25/mcg5hj-polemik-soal-jaipong-di-jawa-barat-tuntas (accessed 15 February 2015).

Among different types of performance, music has been placed as a particular issue, which has attracted long debate in Islamic jurisprudence as well as its important position in cultural expressions of Indonesia, as this chapter will be discussed.

The way in which music is defined reflects how Islamic life is portrayed in Muslim-majority nations in which music is considered as one of the most debatable issues.[4] To explore how music is defined and contextualised in contemporary Indonesia, I provide discussion into four sections. First, I provide the picture of music debate in Indonesia, especially by describing how the lawfulness of music is used to support the development programme of the country. Second, I present particular views how music among Islamic communities (*pesantren*) is perceived in which they are considered as a place where Islamic music is rooted.[5] Third, I discuss the concept of 'Islamic music' (*musik Islam*) and 'music inspired by Islam' (*musik Islami*) that are defined in the Indonesian context. And fourth, I provide discussion on how the concept of *musik Islami* is discussed in the specific context of West Java.

As noted, discourses about music are inseparable from discussions on the lawfulness of music. In the Indonesian setting, this lawfulness of music is also placed and contextualised in broader themes, including academic opinions that support government programmes, as I shall explore in the next section.

II. THE LAWFULNESS OF MUSIC IN THE INDONESIAN CONTEXT

The question of the lawfulness of music in Islamic jurisprudence does not capture much attention from the majority of Indonesian Muslim

---

4 See Amnon Shiloah, 'The Status of Traditional Art Music in Muslim Nations' (1980) 12 (1) *Asian Music* 40–55; 'Music and Religion in Islam' (1997) 69 (2) *Acta Musicologica*; 'Enchanting Powers: Music in the World's Religions' (1999) 44 (1) *Ethnomusicology* (Lawrence E. Sullivan, Editor).

5 *Pesantren* communities are not always specifically linked to those in Islamic schools area, but also defined in broader context which refer to groups of society who are practising Islam as Muslim observant. In Bahasa Indonesia its people is called *masyarakat santri* (Islamic society). Ekadjati positions *pesantren* is not only as the centre for Islamic education, but also the centre for cultural activities. See Edi S. Ekadjati (ed.) *Masyarakat Sunda dan Kebudayaannya*, Cet. 1. ed. (Jakarta: Girimukti Pasaka 1984). Meanwhile Wahid categorises *pesantren* as 'sub-culture'. See Abdurrahman Wahid, *Menggerakkan Tradisi, Esai-Esai Pesantren* (Yogyakarta: LKIS 2001).

listeners. Their listening habits are at a distance from Islamic law. This happens because of the proximity of musical traditions with Indonesian cultural practices in general. However, in particularly Islamic milieu such as in *pesantren* communities, this discourse is very important. Apart from that, the acceptance of music is also supported in other areas, such as academic discourse and religious faith.

Becker states that music in Indonesia is strongly related to religious faith. Consequently, musical genres associated with Islam are readily noticeable in public awareness as well as in political discourse.[6] This concurs with van Zanten's claim that music in traditional Sundanese society has an important position as a medium to speak with God, as commonly occurs in monotheistic religions.[7] This does not reflect any creedal orthodoxy in Islam. Nettl has pointed out that music does not need to be put in an important place as a medium to speak with God, because Muslims can speak and pray directly to the God without need for any medium.[8] In this regard, Indonesia is unique because Islam is taken as a primary religious identity, and in the meantime music in its traditional setting is also a very important aspect of the cultural practices. At the same time, the popularity of the Islamic music genre dramatically increases in various forms.[9] This happens in accordance with the increase of Islamic symbols in the public sphere in contemporary Indonesia.

This conjunction means that discussion on the lawfulness of music has occasionally emerged in academic discourse and Islamic jurisprudence. Even though the general public may not pay much attention to the issue, legal determinations do have influence in some settings, and academically oriented clerics consider the question a serious one. In this case, the majority of Indonesian Muslims adhere to the orthodox Sunni denomination, which refers to four popular schools (*madzhab*) in their

---

6 Judith Becker, 'Epilogue', in David Harnish and Anne K. Rasmussen (eds) *Divine Inspirations Music and Islam in Indonesia* (Oxford and New York: Oxford University Press 2011), 325.

7 Wim Van Zanten, *Sundanese Music in the Cianjuran Style Anthropological and Musicological Aspects of Tembang Sunda* (The Netherlands: Foris Publications Holland 1989); 'Social Qualities of Time and Space Created in Performing Arts of West Java: The Implications for Safeguarding Living Culture' (2012) 14 (1) *Wacana*.

8 Bruno Nettl, *The Study of Ethnomusicology: Thirty-One Issues and Concepts* (Urbana: University of Illinois Press 2005).

9 David D. Harnish and Anne K. Rasmussen (eds), *Divine Inspirations Music and Islam in Indonesia* (Oxford and New York: Oxford University Press 2011).

religious practices.[10] Among those schools, Indonesian Muslims refer mostly widely to the Syafi'i school. Historically, the Syafi'i school has developed a tolerant view among modern Indonesian Muslims, and this tolerance has harmonised with state goals. The state has generally been unwilling to interfere directly in cultural preferences, and this gives the issue, as I show below, a political resonance.

An important example for analysis is the case of Taha Omar Jahja, an Islamic jurisprudence expert, who in 1964 produced an authoritative Islamic statement on the topic of lawfulness of music. The event was the first anniversary of the State Islamic Institute (IAIN) of Jakarta, at which he delivered an important speech titled 'The Law of Musical Art, Sound Art and Dance in Islam'. This academic event was held in conjunction with the Sukarno era's desire to promote the national revolution, which shaped the event as a moment to spread national values in supporting the development of national culture for the young state. This was also stated in the preface of the book written by state officials such as Saifuddin Zuhri (Minister of Religious Affairs), Hazairin (Rector of the Islamic University of Jakarta) and Idham Chalid (curator of IAIN Jakarta). They linked the theme of the speech to the development of the nation state, especially in terms of finding and shaping the national culture. For example, the Islamic scholar, Hazairin, stated his endorsement of the lawfulness of music by saying:

> Let's think, if we are still affected by an old concept … which forbids girls from doing sport and dancing, prohibits us from drawing human beings, bans sculptures and musical arts, and only permits frame drum (*rebana*) and *kasidah*.[11] Does not this become a major obstacle for the improvement of our nation in relation to its cultural development?[12]

---

[10] These are the Syafi'i school, Hambali school, Maliki school and Hanafi school.

[11] *Kasidah* or qasidah is Indonesian word rooted from Arabic, *qasidah*, which refers to Islamic pop songs accompanied by frame drums (*rebana*). In Arabic, *qasidah* refers to religious poetry in classical Arabic in specific metre. *Kasidah* is the most popular Islamic music playing in *pesantren* community. Almost every *pesantren* has a *kasidah* group. For further discussion about the Islamic music genre in Indonesia, see Anne K. Rasmussen, *Women, the Recited Qur'an, and Islamic Music in Indonesia* (Berkeley: University of California Press 2010).

[12] Taha Omar Jahja, *Hukum Seni Musik, Seni Suara Dan Seni Tari Dalam Islam* (Jakarta: Penerbit Widjaja 1964).

Further, he commented that this old concept (the prohibition of music in Islam) was a hindrance for development. Indeed, Chalid also argued that this understanding was a demand of the revolution for forming and developing Indonesia's national culture at the time.[13]

By providing arguments from the main sources of the hadith (tradition of the Prophet Muhammad) from both those who supported and those who opposed the lawfulness of music in Islam, Jahja concluded that among *Imam* (leaders) of four schools (*madzhab*), music is categorised as permitted (*mubah*) in its original law, as long as it is not followed by non-Islamic behaviour. Moreover, from the hadith he provided, he explained that the opposing position relied upon hadith that were weak (*dhoif*) and did not talk about the essence of music itself, but rather its consequences.[14] Commenting on the opposing position, he states that 'The illegitimate of musical art, sounds of art, and dance is based on the principle *amrun ariidiyyun laa dzaatiyyun*, which means "something caused by other things (its consequences) and not by its essence"'.[15] This means that the reason of abandoning music keeps debatable.

However, among those who support the permissibility of music there were at the same time differences in recommending which music was to be permitted. In relation to instruments, for example, some Islamic scholars only permit songs without instruments; others argue that some instruments are permitted, such as *rebana* (frame drums) and *kendang* (drums), while stating that other instruments such as flute, piano, and guitar are not. Also, some state that this music was permitted only in celebrations, such as wedding and circumcision ceremonies, as well as for welcoming guests following the Prophet examples as narrated in some hadith.[16] Most traditional Muslims, including those in *pesantren*, refer to these rules in defining and understanding music.[17]

---

[13] Ibid., xiv–xv.

[14] In general, there are three levels of hadith based on the narrator's quality, the number of narrators, and the text itself of which the final resource is the Prophet Muhammad, these being *shahih, hasan*, and *dho'if*. The level will affect the quality of the hadith and its strength as a legal reference for religious practice among Muslims. The *shahih* and *hasan* hadith are accepted as a source of Islamic jurisprudence, whereas hadith *dho'if* are rejected. For an overview, see Tengku M. Hasbi Ash Shiddieqy, *Sejarah dan Pengantar Ilmu Hadits* (Semarang: Pustaka Rizki Putra 2001).

[15] Jahja, above n12, 56.

[16] Ibid., 52–6.

[17] Discussion about the lawfulness of music in Indonesian Islam scholarship can also be found in Ingwuri Handayani (ed.) *Kiai, Musik, dan Kitab Kuning* (Jakarta: Desantara 2009).

For Muslims closer to the mainstream of Indonesian Islamic sensibility, music has been widely accepted as a part of cultural expression. At the same time, Indonesian Muslims also generally find it easy to adjust their music tastes.[18] For example, in the month of Ramadhan, over the course of the month all Muslims will change their genres of music into the *musik Islami* (music inspired by Islam) genre. Regardless of where the music group comes from, what the genre is or who the singer may be, it is acceptable as long as it includes the usage of Islamic symbols in their song and presentation. Moreover, the music industry supports this extensively. The market provides for all audiences' needs to feel more Islamic during the sacred month of Ramadhan. This also brings many pop singers to change the 'colour' of their music to include religious songs. Harnish and Rasmussen assert that in a current Muslim debate:

> The style of music is sometimes less relevant than its intention or content. Popular music, however, is a viable and effective vehicle for religious messages, and it has potential to unite still larger mass audiences into an 'imagined community' that is also at the same time religious and modern.[19]

This statement confirms the argument that Islamic music has been largely commodified by popular culture in contemporary Indonesia.[20] Correspondingly, these Islamic symbols have become more salient in recent years of the post-Reform era.

---

[18] There are some controversial cases when Indonesian singers were boycotted by certain Islamic groups due to their actions on stage being considered as immoral, such as in cases of *dangdut* performers Inul Daratista, Dewi Persik and Annisa Bahar. Inul's case was the most controversial issue at the national level. For further reading, see Andrew Weintraub, 'Morality and Its (Dis)Contents: *Dangdut* and Islam in Indonesia', in David D. Harnish and Anne K. Rasmussen (eds), *Divine Inspirations Music and Islam in Indonesia* (Oxford and New York: Oxford University Press 2011), 318–36. *Dangdut* is a genre of Indonesian popular music that is rooted in Malay, Arabic, and Hindustani musical elements.

[19] Harnish and Rasmussen, above n9, 26.

[20] For further readings about Islam and popular culture, see Weintraub, above n18; Timothy P. Daniels (ed.) *Performance, Popular Culture, and Piety in Muslim Southeast Asia* (New York: Palgrave Macmillan 2013).

III. MUSIC AMONG *PESANTREN* COMMUNITIES

Scholars noted that Indonesia's *pesantren* communities are centres for the performance of music genre called Islamic music (*musik Islam*).[21] Hence, it is important to discuss how Islamic scholars in this specific area perceive and understand music and its particular genres. In contrast to the public at large (see above), *pesantren* are considered as spaces in which a strong stance in relation to Islam jurisprudence is taken, and where the Qur'an, Hadith (Tradition of Prophet) and classical Islamic books (*kitab*) bear direct authority. In this regard, *pesantren* have a unique position in their stance toward music. In contemporary Indonesia, *pesantren* are often considered as being divided into two categories: modern and traditional. This difference registers, amongst other ways, in the nature of the pedagogies.[22]

Traditional *pesantren* are for the most part considered as more conservative because of their reliance on traditional classical books originating from the early centuries of Islamic history. In this type of *pesantren*, teachers and students take more care in ensuring that their religious practices are based on valid sources. In relation to music, most traditional *pesantren* take a rigid position and treat it as forbidden (*haram*). *Sulam Taufiq* (The Way of Success) is a classical book used as a main reference in all traditional *pesantren*. One of its chapters explains that *alaatul malaahi* (musical instruments) are not allowed (*haram*).[23] However, I found exceptions to this: there are examples of *pesantren* and prominent clerics who indeed have a close relationship with music. These examples are important to discuss in order to show how and why music is frequently accepted in a context where it is, according to influential texts, 'forbidden'. These cases also show the complexities as well as

---

[21] Sumarsam, 'Past and Present Issues of Islam within the Central Javanese Gamelan and Wayang Kulit', in David Harnish and Anne K. Rasmussen (eds) *Divine Inspirations, Music and Islam in Indonesia* (Oxford and New York: Oxford University Press 2011); Judith O. Becker, *Gamelan Stories: Tantrism, Islam, and Aesthetics in Central Java* (Tempe, AZ: Arizona State University, Program for Southeast Asian Studies 1993); Arthur Simon, 'Southeast Asia: Musical Syncretism and Cultural Identity' (2010) 57 (1) *Fontes Artis Musicae – Journal of the International Association of Music Libraries, Archives, and Documentation Centres*.

[22] For further explanation, see Zamakhsyari Dhofier, *The Pesantren Tradition: The Role of the Kyai in the Maintenance of Traditional Islam in Java* (Tempe, AZ: Monograph Series Press, Program for Southeast Asian Studies, Arizona State University 1999).

[23] See Handayani, above n17.

particularities of Islamic life in Indonesia. Likewise, discourses or examples that emerged in *pesantren* communities, which are considered as the most authoritative place in Islam, have a great impact on their followers.

An illustrative example of this comes from Pesantren Tegalrejo in Magelang, Central Java.[24] There is a very interesting story about how its founder, the late prominent and charismatic cleric KH Chudlori, dealt with religion and cultural issues within his milieu. The story is that there were two groups of people in Tegalrejo village who became involved in a dispute about spending money generated from donations (*uang kas*). One group insisted on spending the money to renovate a mosque, while the other wanted to use it for buying a *gamelan* (a Javanese traditional orchestra). They could not come to an agreement. They eventually decided to come to Kyai Chudlori's house to get his advice. Unexpectedly, the Kyai's suggestion was to ask the people to spend the money to buy the *gamelan* instead of renovating a mosque. 'The most important thing is that people can stay in harmony,' he said. 'If the people are unified and in harmony, the mosque will come later by itself.' It was a strange decision for some people, but it turned out to be a prophetic one. After those people ended their dispute and became harmonious, they then collected money to build a mosque.[25]

This is an unusual story in the Indonesian context. Kyai Chudlori's charisma and his ability to bring people together in harmony by respecting each other implied a special relationship between the *pesantren* and its surrounding residents. This example reflects an important aspect of everyday life of Indonesia: Islamic authority directly faces complex problems among society. The dialogical reflexivity between textuality and embodied reality displayed by Kyai Chudlori is also found in different places in various forms in Indonesian religious practice.

After KH Chudlori passed away, his descendants in Pesantren Tegalrejo continued to maintain good relations between *pesantren* and local arts. Once a year, when the *pesantren* celebrates the annual graduation

---

[24] Pesantren Tegalrejo is a unique *pesantren* located in the Merapi hills near Magelang, Central Java. Its community includes Muslims mingling with villagers retaining their old beliefs, called *Kejawen*. A number of traditional art groups are active there.

[25] Shohib Masykur, 'Epilog: Wajah Lain Dari Tegalrejo', in Heru and Ingwuri Handayani Prasetia (eds) *Agama dan Kebudayaan, Pergulatan di Tengah Komunitas* (Jakarta: Desantara 2010) 59–60.

called *khataman* (Quranic reading in congregation),[26] its leader invites traditional performance groups to perform in the *pesantren*, playing various arts genres such as *reog* (a kind of dance drama), *jathilan* (a kind of trance dance) and puppet shows. Performing arts and *khataman* are performed together on the same evening from stages close to each other. The event continues for the entire night. Audiences can move from one event (*pengajian*) to another (performance) and back.[27] This unusual combination shows an alternative way of building a relationship between the two different communities, by giving empathy and being respectful of each other. However, for Pesantren Tegalrejo itself it is not easy to maintain that situation, because many Muslim traditionalists and modernists will find this unacceptable, and say that it reflects poorly on the institution. Moreover, traditional arts have a bad stigma among the society, including the contention that performers are distant from God, and that they practise non-Islamic behaviours (alcoholism, prostitution, gambling and so forth).

In response to common understanding among *pesantren* communities *alaatul malahi* (musical instruments) that are categorised as *munkarot* (things related with immoral acts) are forbidden (*haram*), due to their power to cause people to neglect God. Yusuf Khudori, one of Kyai Chudlori's children, has a different opinion:

> *Munkarat* exist not only in art, but can also happen in any activities. The activity of Islamic study (*pengajian*) can be *munkarat* if its content is to blaspheme others. For example, the Friday sermon, when used to scoff and condemn other Muslim as *kafir* (unbelievers in Allah), spreads hatred among Muslims. So, it's relative. We cannot generalise that art/music is *haram* [forbidden].[28]

This statement strengthens the *pesantren*'s position in embracing local culture. Khudori has some authority on his side; this is an approach to Islamic proselytisation (*dakwah*) that has its precedent in the deeds that

---

[26] *Khataman* is a very important moment for students in the *pesantren*, symbolising the hard efforts of learning by both *kiai* and students in the previous year. In this event, the students show their learning achievements to the public, especially their parents or guardians. This event is very festive and eagerly awaited by all people in the *pesantren* (teachers, students, parents) and interested neighbours.

[27] Masykur, above n25, 152–3.

[28] Ibid., 164.

the Walisanga (nine saints) are popularly held to have carried out in the history of Islam in Indonesia.[29]

Another aspect that encourages moderate views towards music is Sufism. Differing from those Islamic scholars in jurisprudence who take a hard position against music, Sufism has embraced music in its ritual activity. An interesting example on this is the figure of KH Ahmad Siddiq (1926–91), who for decades held an important position as a NU (Nahdhatul Ulama) leader.[30] As a charismatic cleric favourably disposed to Sufi practices, Kyai Siddiq had amazingly diverse tastes in music, including not only famous Middle Eastern singers such as Ummi Kulthum, but also Western pop music stars such as Michael Jackson, as well as Mandarin and Japanese songs.[31] 'Human beings have a feeling of beauty, and art as one of humanity's activities cannot be separated from the religion's (Islam) rules and aesthetics. Therefore, the appreciation of art should be raised in its quality,' he says, believing that 'music is a universal beauty'. He also explained about art in different categories: preferred arts, such as literature and calligraphy; recommended arts, like instrument and vocal music; limited arts, such as dance; and arts to be avoided, such as sculpture and lustful art.[32]

---

[29] See Sumarsam, above n21; Kees Van Dijk, 'Dakwah and Indigenous Culture: The Dissemination of Islam' (1998) 154 (2) *Bijdragen tot de Taal, Land – en Volkenkunde*; Simon, 'Southeast Asia: Musical Syncretism and Cultural Identity'.

Walisanga are the famous nine saints who played roles as key Islamic figures in spreading Islam in Java Island in the fourteenth century and after. They were Maulana Malik Ibrahim, Sunan Ampel, Sunan Giri, Sunan Bonang, Sunan Drajat, Sunan Kudus, Sunan Kalijaga, Sunan Muria and Sunan Gunung Djati.

[30] NU is the largest religious mass organization in Indonesia: its followers total over 40 million people and its basis is in villages. Most traditional *pesantren* are affiliated with this organisation. From 1984, Kiai Siddiq was an NU leader together with his outstanding colleague, Abdurrahman Wahid [Gus Dur] (1940–2009), another prominent figure in NU, who led NU over two periods. Gus Dur was also well known as having been a music lover from various genres, from *dangdut* to classical music, and his favourite music was Beethoven's Symphony No.9. See Greg Barton, *Abdurrahman Wahid: Muslim Democrat, Indonesian President, a View from the Inside* (Sydney: UNSW Press 2002).

[31] See http://majalah.tempointeraktif.com/id/arsip/1991/02/02/OBI/mbm.199 10202.OBI13022.id.html and http://darussholahjember.blogspot.com/2011/05/kh-achmad-shiddiq.html (accessed 6 January 2012). Also Saifullah Ma'shum (ed.), *Kharisma Ulama, Kehidupan Ringkas 26 Tokoh NU* (Jakarta-Bandung: Yayasan Saifuddin Zuhri & Mizan 1998).

[32] Ibid., 363–9.

This classification, in which he tried to present a concept of art based on Islamic boundaries that he understood, and which arranges genres in line with Islam, is very interesting. This also confirms his unique position as a moderate cleric, a pious religious person and a music lover all at the same time. He practised *tarekat* (Sufism) on one side and enjoyed music on the other. He had a *tarekat* study group called *Majlis Dzikrul Ghofilin* (*dhikr* group for those who ignored God), which in the 1990s had 20,000 followers. He asked its followers to pray to God together by repeatedly chanting verses and prayers. On the other hand, in his house he had music collections of various genres.[33]

A current example in interpreting the lawfulness of music I found when I conducted research in Cikeusal village, Tasikmalaya in 2013. In interpreting the lawfulness of music (arts), local Islamic authorities that I interviewed gave some opinions about their position on supporting traditional musical performances, not opposing them. The close ties between Islamic figures and artists' families in the village are another reason why local people could actively negotiate different interpretations of Islam related to the performances. This has produced an interesting dialogue between Islamic leaders and local musical performances. The well-known Islamic leader of the village, Ajengan Entoy, explained his views on local music in the village.[34]

Ajengan Entoy's interpretation on the lawfulness of music is similar to those Islamic scholars in traditional *pesantren*. He argues that the basic rule of music in Islam is *munkarot* – in other words, whether the music incites people to immoral behaviour or not. His interpretation of when music is allowed (*mubah*) and when it is forbidden (*haram*) is similar to that of many moderate Islamic scholars, as discussed above. When the music is categorised as a pursuit for health reasons, then it is allowed, whereas if it is only used to follow lust (*lahw* – Arabic, *hawa nafsu* – Indonesian), for pleasure, then it is not allowed. In Cikeusal village, Ajengan Entoy prefers to avoid restricting music in a harsh way. In his words, 'Islamic rules, if they are used in a strict way, will not be easy to accept.'[35] This approach, popularly employed by traditional Islamic leaders, is similar to that attributed to the nine saints as mentioned. Thus, the interpretation is in harmony with the social realities in which Ajengan Entoy dwells. Here, he defers textuality to the context of social reality in society. Most *ajengan* are confident that to perform *dakwah* is to

---

[33] Ibid.

[34] *Ajengan* is a Sundanese word for *kiai* (Indonesian), which refers to a leader of Islamic community group (*pesantren*).

[35] Interview with Ajengan Entoy, 8 January 2013.

understand the socio-cultural background of society and to approach it in an appropriate way.

Another *ajengan* I interviewed was Ajengan Akub. He has a similar explanation – if anything, more moderate – to Ajengan Entoy's.[36] He quoted a fragment of verse in the al-Qur'an: 'And prepare against them whatever you are able of power.'[37] He explained that the background of this verse was when the Prophet was going to war and no one among his companions could ride a warhorse. He makes an analogy between the arts and sport, which makes music and other performances genre in the village less debatable. Moreover, to respect different interpretations among Muslims regarding the lawfulness of music, he refers to the Prophet's words, 'My companions are like stars, whoever you go with, you will get guidance.'[38] 'Companions' in this sentence refer to the Prophet's followers (*sahabah*), permitting Muslims to follow any standpoint held among his followers about in Islamic law.

From the description above, music discourse in Indonesian Muslim debate takes various meanings and interpretations following social, cultural and political changes. Islamic clerics' comments and responses to textual interpretations of music are adapted to the situational context. There is no single meaning. In its permissibility there are limitations, and in its prohibition there are some exceptions. The position of *mubah* (permitted) music has brought it into different interpretations, and at a certain point it serves as a negotiation tool, as happens in Pesantren Tegalrejo. As my examples have illustrated, some of the most authoritative persons among Muslims have an outstanding appreciation of music, while at the same time a prohibition of music is also very strong among them.

One thing to be noted here is that Islamic figures who get involved in Sufism are much more moderate in their attitude to music than those who do not. In contrast, among conservative *fiqh* (Islam jurisprudence) experts, where all guidance of religious practice is referred to, they tend to consider music as something not useful but rather as something that can bring people to bad behaviour, for which reason it is forbidden. It can bring people to neglect God; therefore it is forbidden (*haram*). However, *fiqh* for a moderate Islamic group is dynamic and dialectic; it can be changed to suit developments of Muslim life. In this situation, Muslims can choose where they will stand, in terms of whether to forbid music or

36 Interview with Ajengan Akub, 14 January 2013.
37 *Waa'iddu lahum mastato'tum min quwwah* QS. Al-Anfal verse 60.
38 *Ashabi kannujum, biayyihim iqtadaitum ihtadaitum.*

permit it. Judging by the reality that many Indonesian Muslims enjoy music, it is most likely that they have a preference for the moderate side, allowing music to enter their daily lives.

The contextualization of the interpretation of the lawfulness of music in Indonesia as described above has bear different concepts of music associated with Islam. In Indonesian music vocabularies, there are two terms used to refer to specific genre of music related with Islam: *musik Islam* and *musik Islami*, which give a specific resonance in Indonesian Islam. The terms are defined in a particular context, as I will explore below.

IV. *MUSIK ISLAM* AND *MUSIK ISLAMI*

Islamic music for many Indonesian Muslims is identical with Arabic. Despite understanding of Islam undergoing changes in contemporary Indonesia, the concept of Islamic music is still idealised in its Arabic lyrics. However, the concept has flourished as the genre of Islamic music has evolved enormously.

From its origin in the Middle East, Islamic music is now defined in specific ways among Indonesian Muslims. In this section, I particularly draw attention to discuss Islamic music discourse and how the concept is defined in Indonesian contemporary context. There are two main terms used in the vocabulary of Indonesian music to name Islamic music: *musik Islam* (Islamic music) and *musik Islami*. The latter term needs explanation. *Islami* is an Arabic adjectival construction; hence *musik Islami* literally means Islamic music, the same as *musik Islam*. However, drawing on the context of usage, which I describe below, it is more accurate to translate *musik Islami* as 'music inspired by Islam' or 'music with Islamic characteristics'. My explanation of these different terms in referring to distinct musical genres of Islamic music shows the riches of musical vocabularies as well as the complexity that arises in understanding Islam in relation to music in Indonesia.[39]

Limitations and boundaries of what we call *musik Islam* and *musik Islami* are not merely identified from musical elements. Socio-cultural meanings are also a crucial aspect of interpretation. In the discussion below, I address some key arguments and theories that have emerged in defining *musik Islam* and *musik Islami*.

---

[39] A brief discussion on this issue has also appeared in Neneng Lahpan, 'From Sundanese Traditional Music to Islamic Pop Genre: Cultural and Aesthetic Transformations' (2013) 23 (1) *SPAFA Journal*.

Rasmussen points out that the main characteristic of *musik Islam* in Indonesia is the Arabic elements that are strongly embedded in the music.[40] She begins her discussion with the primary source of the Arabic musical aesthetic that Indonesian Muslims know, namely the Qur'anic styles. However, as Shiloah[41] states, in the Arab world Qur'anic chant (*qiroat*), the call for prayer (*adhan*), remembrance (*dhikr*) and other religious music are not considered to be music. While some Indonesian Muslims probably also do not consider them as music but rather as ritual practices, Rasmussen contends that for their musical properties, these are considered as music. She refers to other musical forms, such as *qasidah*, *gambus*, *akapella* and so on, as *musik Islam*. She also emphasises that social and political aspects of music have a significant patronage from government. This also brings to inclination that new middle and upper classes of society enjoy this music. This is also supported by mass media and the recorded music industry, for *musik Islam* is considered very important in the Indonesian market. However, this trend has not been followed with the entry of Arabic music or its culture to the Indonesian music market.[42] Meanwhile, what Rasmussen calls Islamic musical arts (*seni musik Islam*) consist of a combination of foreign musical aesthetics (Arabic and Western) with local music, through which new Indonesian Islam identities are contested.[43] In referring to similar meaning, I use the term *musik Islami* as it is used widely among Indonesian Muslims in contemporary context. While most Indonesian Muslims seem to associate *musik Islam* with Arabic music, *musik Islami* is defined in a more debatable way.

The mixed understanding between *musik Islam* and *musik Islami* is shown in Berg's study of the Arabic music called *gambus*.[44] *Gambus* is one example of music with strong Arabic idioms that signify as *musik Islam* in Indonesia. In general, there are two groups of people in Indonesia with different perspectives on whether *gambus* is Islamic or not. First, members of the public generally look at *gambus* as *musik Islam* because of how the performance is displayed, and for its claims to being as *halal* or permitted under Islamic law. This includes the Arabic

---

40 Anne K. Rasmussen, 'The Arab Musical Aesthetic in Indonesian Islam' (2005) 47 (1) *World of Music (Wilhelmshaven)*.

41 Shiloah, above n4.

42 'Rasmussen, above n11.

43 Harnish and Rasmussen, above n9.

44 Birgit Berg, 'Presence and Power of the Arab Idiom in Indonesian Islamic Musical Arts' in *Conference on Music in the World of Islam, Assilah 8–13 August 2007* (2007).

style of clothing that performers wear, which is mostly regarded as 'Islamic' and has become an important symbol of Islam in Indonesia. They also tend to generalise the 'Arab sound' as the 'Islamic sound'. Second, those who understand the texts argue that *gambus* cannot be classified as 'Islamic' when its texts are mostly secular, non-Islamic and in pop song format, and only for entertainment. Concerning this, one of the most popular Indonesian Islamic singers, Hadad Alwi, rejected the term of *musik Islam* to point out that music is universal. He asserts that genre definitions are not important and as long as music can bring people to a better understanding of Islam (*dakwah* purpose), it is acceptable.[45]

However, in Indonesia the number of people who understand the meaning of Arabic lyrics in the music is much smaller than those who do not. Thus, people's perception on the concept of *musik Islam* in the case of *gambus* is similar to people's understandings of other Arabic musical expressions I observe from the daily life of Muslims in general. Therefore, although not all Arabic songs are *Islami*, many people still conceive of them as such. This is because of the similarity of musical elements they usually hear in Arabic music, added to which there is a perspective that 'Arabic' means 'Islamic'.

This parallels the explanation offered by Sundanese ethnomusicologist, Deni Hermawan. He distinguishes the concept of *musik Islam* and *musik Islami* based on their musical elements including lyrics, vocals, instruments, music scales and tonal systems. He defines *musik Islam* as 'music developing in countries with Islamic traditions', and refers to music in the Middle East, especially Egypt and its surrounds.[46] In this respect, he differentiates the concept of *musik Islam* as applied in the Middle East and in Indonesia. According to Hermawan, *musik Islam* in the Middle East is the music which uses Middle Eastern music scales with various themes and not only religious ones. Meanwhile, *musik Islam* in Indonesia is seen as music that uses a wide range of musical scales (depending on the regional culture) but with a single, Islamic religious theme. He concludes that, based on these characteristics, what is called Islamic music (*musik Islam*) in Indonesia is actually more suitably termed *musik Islami*.[47]

---

45 Ibid., 224.

46 Deni Hermawan, *Etnomusikologi, Beberapa Permasalahan dalam Musik Sunda* (Bandung: STSI Press 2002) 188–9.

47 Ibid.; 'Musik Etnik Sunda Islami Ath-Thawaf: Sebuah Kajian Terhadap Nilai-Nilai Musikal, Kultural, dan Religius', *PANGGUNG STSI Bandung* XXXV (2005).

Hermawan's differentiating of *musik Islam* in the Middle East from that of Indonesia is problematic, especially in arguing that themes of *musik Islam* in the Middle East are varied, including love songs.[48] Do Middle Eastern people call love songs *musik Islam*? Or is Hermawan's understanding of this categorisation based on his observation of what Indonesian people perceive as *musik Islam*?

Musik Islam in the Middle East was originally used as religious songs to glorify God, to praise the Prophet and his family, or to evoke Islamic spirit among Muslims. All those themes were imported and sung in Indonesian Islamic communities. However, communities in the Arab and Middle Eastern areas developed genres of music that are broader than religious songs. Thus, love songs and other secular songs thrive in Indonesia and are called *musik Islam* merely because they use Arabic language.

The Central Java-based Islamic cleric Kyai Adib Masruhan, a supporter of Islamic musical genres, gives an interesting example about his favourite Arabic love song entitled *Magadir*, a very popular song in many Islamic schools (*pesantren*) in Indonesia, and one which he heard when he was in Saudi Arabia. He says that:

> it is a love song. Thala'al Maddah [the singer] is a male singer, while *Magadir*, the title of the song, is a female's name. But, when the song entered Indonesia, many people misunderstood. Maybe because of its Arabic language, some people thought that listening to it is *sunah*, just like listening to *solawat*.[49]

This statement reflects another facet of Indonesian Muslims conception of 'Arabic sound' as 'Islamic sound', including in *pesantren* both for Islamic students and their teachers who understand Arabic language very well. It is also noteworthy that, based on my observations over several years, in most traditional *pesantren* Arabic music with secular content is considered acceptable. For example, a modern *kasidah* group, such as *Nasida Ria*, which was popular in the 1980s–90s, is very popular in *pesantren.*

This complexity also occurs in *rateb meuseukat performance* of Aceh. Although texts of *meuseukat* portray love, politics and other secular themes, it is categorised as 'art (that breathes) with an Islamic flavour

---

48 *Etnomusikologi, Beberapa Permasalahan dalam Musik Sunda* 188–9.

49 Handayani, above n17, 22. *Sunah* means receiving blessings from the Prophetic Tradition. *Solawat* is a sung text to praise the Prophet. Muslims believe that reading or listening to *solawat* will give them blessings from the Prophet, and following *sunah* is one of the Muslim obligations.

(*kesenian yang bernafaskan Islam*)'.[50] According to Harnish and Rasmussen, these categorizations reveal the ways that various cultural and political discourses define and identify the music as *Islami*, ultimately giving it 'an acknowledged place in Indonesian Islam'.[51] These categorizations have brought up another debate in which *musik Islam* (Islamic music) or songs in Arabic language are always regarded as *halal* (permitted) because of the Arabic symbols embedded within them. Meanwhile *musik Islami* is more contentious. In the Indonesian context, *musik Islami* tends to cover wider audiences and genres than those under *musik Islam*. It creates *musik Islami* as a diverse body of genres all of which are more or less acceptable and which enable blending of various genres as found in contemporary music forms in Indonesia. *Musik Islami* refers to any kind of music, both traditional and modern, with a single theme, which is about Islam, while for *musik Islam*, people commonly refer to Arabic music regardless of its content. This definition and understanding of *musik Islami* show the uniqueness of interactions between Islam and local culture in Indonesia.

This distinction is important, for it opens the space for Islamic musical expression that draws deeply on other indigenous and non-Islamic genres. It also signals the field as a polemical one. No better example exists than that of *dangdut*, which in some cases is also considered as *musik Islami*, while at the same time other *dangdut* songs are categorised as incompatible with Islam norms.[52]

Not only has *musik Islam* in Indonesia been widely accepted, it has also flourished in various forms, especially in the genre of *musik Islami* including in West Java. Following the above discussion on how *musik Islam* is defined in the Indonesian context, in the next section I shall particularly pay attention to how *musik Islami* is situated in West Java.

V. *MUSIK ISLAMI* IN THE CONTEXT OF WEST JAVA

The concept of *musik Islami* in West Java is contested through various meanings following social political changes in the region. Regional autonomy is one factor that has given a political resonance to many

---

[50] Margaret J. Kartomi, '"Art with a Muslim Theme" and "Art with a Muslim Flavor" among Women of West Aceh,' in David D. Harnish and Anne K. Rasmussen (eds) *Divine Inspirations Music and Islam in Indonesia* (Oxford and New York: Oxford University Press 2011).

[51] Harnish and Rasmussen, above n9, 26.

[52] See Weintraub, above n18.

aspects of society in the post-Reform era. In response to this situation, the Sundanese in West Java, has sounded the jargon 'Islam is Sunda, Sunda is Islam' to show the close relationship between Islam and Sundanese culture, that has been popularly uttered by an Islamic scholar, Endang Saefuddin Anshori in 1966.[53] However, people respond to this statement with different arguments. Firstly, as a result of political change, Islamic symbols become salient in the public sphere and have been politically reinforced by government programmes in various forms including the issue of *perda syariah* (sharia regional regulation); on the other hand, some people give opposing views by localising the Islamic values in Sundanese perspective. In this regard, they tend to avoid any Arabic symbols rather to show the Sundanese feature to be paralleled with Islam. This is noticeably shown in the case of music, especially in interpreting *musik Islami.*

A striking example for this contestation is found in the Institute of Indonesian Arts and Culture (*Institut Seni Budaya Indonesia*/ISBI) Bandung. I discovered some paradoxical views regarding the term. Some scholars and musicians tended to avoid Arabic symbols in their art works, and considered Islam as an inspiration in producing their creative works, opening their works to local traditions as a result. In this case, they would prefer for example *tembang Sunda* (Sundanese classical music) as *Islami*, claiming that it is *Islami* because of its substantive meaning rather than its external meanings or surface symbols.

Furthermore, the controversial case of the West Java governor and *jaipong* dance mentioned in the introduction exemplifies tension between Islam and performing arts. In the area of music, this invites further questioning over what *musik Islami* is and how far it extends. For some performers and musicians, *musik Islami* is defined in a wider context, not only in relation to the instruments, tonal systems or Islamic song themes, but as an inspiration for the whole musical arts. In this view, everything that can suit Islamic values can be categorised as *Islami.*

Those people dedicated to the preservation of traditional genres, such as my colleagues at ISBI Bandung, believe that traditional values of Sundanese in arts are in accordance with Islamic values, and as such can be called *Islami.* This is what can be found in *tembang Sunda*, as far as Yus Wiradireja (*tembang Sunda* singer and the founder of Ath-Athawaf group) is concerned. He argues that *tembang Sunda* songs contain Islamic values, such as human relationship with God (*hablum minallah*),

---

[53] Cik Hasan Bisri, Yeti Heryati and Eva Rufaidah (eds), *Pergumulan Islam dengan Kebudayaan Lokal di Tatar Sunda* (Bandung: Kaki Langit 2005).

human relationship with others (*hablum minannas*) and human relationships with the environment.[54] This statement is also strengthened by the fact that *tembang Sunda* was created in an Islamic environment; its performers, audiences and patrons are all considered to be Muslim.[55]

However, according to the categorisations created within Sundanese music, *tembang Sunda* cannot be categorised as *musik Islami* because no specific Islamic idioms are used; furthermore, the work is not intended as 'Islamic' or 'to be Islamic'. In this way, *Islami* in music need to register in any kind of Islamic symbols, including those displayed visually on stage. This is the reason why Yus Wiradireja was motivated to form the Sundanese Islamic music group 'Ath-Thawaf'. He argues that he needed to express his *tembang Sunda* inspiration, which he believes still has contextual meaning in the present era, through another medium of expression. By doing this, this inspiration could be recognised by the younger generation for whom *tembang Sunda* might no longer be attractive.[56]

Yus Wiradireja transferred the spirit of *tembang Sunda* to a new form of musical expression called *musik etnik Islami* or ethnic music inspired by Islam, a form that combines traditional and modern idioms of music in his musical works: Ath-thawaf. He tried to deliver religious messages with easy-listening music, so that wider audiences could enjoy it. In this case, Yus perceives an understanding of *musik Islami* in both ways: Islam as an inspiration, which means it does not need to be explicitly symbolised, as in the case of *tembang Sunda*, yet he also appreciates the value of Islamic symbols in music, as he shows in Ath-Thawaf music.

This example brings more clarity to the use of the term *musik Islami* in Sundanese music. Users of this term use it not in order to confront other traditional musics as non-*Islami*, but rather to differentiate it from Arabic music (*musik Islam*). They use the term *musik Islami* not to reject another kind of music, but rather to differentiate it from other Islamic (Arabic) music idioms. For example, *shalawat*, *rebana*, *barzanji* and *kasidah* are

---

[54] Neneng Y. Lahpan, 'Ath-Thawaf: Dari Tembang Sunda Cianjuran Ke Pop Sunda Religius (Perspektif Cultural Studies)' (2009) 21 (2) *Panggung Journal STSI Bandung*.

[55] Sean Williams, 'Current Developments in Sundanese Popular Music' (1989) 21 (1) *Asian Music*; Sean Williams, *The Sound of the Ancestral Ship: Highland Music of West Java* (New York: Oxford University Press 2001).

[56] Lahpan, above n54.

musik Islam, while various forms of Islamic-pop songs including contemporary *nasyid* and Islamic-traditional songs are *musik Islami*.[57] When Yus made a new form for his musical expression, Ath-Thawaf, he did not mean to oppose it to the *tembang Sunda* of his musical background, but rather to use it as a reference in his creative processes. For these reasons, *tembang Sunda* is not to be categorised as non-*Islami* music because of the absence of Islamic symbols; at the same time, this traditional music is also associated with Islam in its general values.

VI. CONCLUSION

Although the lawfulness of music is not particularly polemical in contemporary Indonesian Islam, its permissibility remains ambiguous. While music in many cultures is to be used for enjoyment, in Islamic rules this is not allowed. Music should bring people to good deeds. On the other hand, examples show that some Islam leaders are also very close to music. The broad interpretation of music in Indonesian Islam has been shown in the use of the term Islamic music itself. *Musik Islam*, which is associated with Arabic, is likely to be more preferred among the *pesantren*/Muslim community, whereas *musik Islami* in its broader meanings lives in wider communities, both traditional and modern Muslim societies.

In the context of Sundanese music in West Java, the contestation of *musik Islami* goes further beyond symbolic representations of Islam in the public sphere in Indonesia. It is also contested to drive new understanding of local identity of Sundanese, which emphasises on the parallel between Islam and Sundanese values. Everything in Sundanese values that is compatible with Islam is considered as Islamic. However, it does not imply opposition against other musical genres, but is differentiated from Arabic (Islamic) music idioms. Finally, in the wider context, the term *Islami* in music becomes an important symbol for making the

---

57 *Sholawat* is a praise song to the Prophet Muhammad considered as a very important aspect of Islamic rituals in Indonesia. *Rebana* is another name for *kasidah*. *Rebana* refers to its instrument, frame drums in various sizes. *Kasidah* is an Islamic music genre developed mainly in Indonesian *pesantren* community. The main instrument is the frame drum (*rebana*). *Barzanji* is Arabic text, in the form of prose-poem recited and sung in Arabic on ritual occasions in West Java and other parts of Indonesia. Its reading activity is called *marhabanan*. *Nasyid* is Islamic religious songs. In Indonesia, it is a popular Islamic music genre to propagate Islam. See also above, n11.

music acceptable, acknowledgeable and distinguishable from Arabic and local Islamic arts in the repertoire of music in West Java.

These distinctions become significant when we observe how they intersect with political and social discourses of Indonesia. The distinctions have renewed importance in the social and political changes taking place in West Java in the new era of regional autonomy, as exemplified in the case of the West Java governor. These have brought music into a complex interplay with social and political contestations of Indonesia.

16. Educational rights for women in Saudi Arabia

Maan Abdul Haq Khutani

I. INTRODUCTION

In the last five decades, women's rights have made immense gains worldwide. The degree to which they are accepted, however, varies from country to country. Women's rights have not evolved uniformly because of religious, political, social and economic differences. In particular, Islam has often been cited as the main factor inhibiting the development of women's rights in Muslim countries.[1] The chapter will explore the rights of women in Islam to education, and also how those rights have been implemented and maintained in a Muslim country, with special reference to Saudi Arabia.

The Kingdom of Saudi Arabia ratified the Convention on the Elimination of All Forms of Discrimination against Women (CEDAW) on the basis of Royal Decree No 25 (28 August 2000), and committed itself to establishing an association for women's rights to follow up and implement the United Nations (UN) convention.[2] The importance of the issue lies in finding ways to understand the purposes of Islamic law that are not inconsistent with the fundamental purpose of human rights in

[1] Simona Drenik, 'Human Rights of Women and their Acceptance in Muslim Societies' (2004) 1 (1) *Human Security Perspectives* 58, 60; Manoucher Parvin, 'On the Synergism of Gender and Class Exploitation: Theory and Practice Under Islamic Rule' (1993) 51 (2) *Review of Social Economy* 201, 201; Linda Cipriani, 'Gender and Persecution: Protecting Women Under International Refugee Law' (1993) 7 *Georgetown Immigration Law Journal* 511, 514.

[2] Committee on the Elimination of Discrimination against Women, 'Consideration of Reports Submitted by States Parties under Article 18 of the Convention on the Elimination of All Forms of Discrimination against Women: Combined Initial and Second Periodic Reports of States Parties, Saudi Arabia' UN Doc CEDAW/C/SAU/2 (29 March 2007). For text, see www.bayefsky.com/reports/saudiarabia_cedaw_c_sau_2.pdf. Hereafter CEDAW, Initial and Second Periodic Reports, Saudi Arabia, UN Doc CEDAW/C/SAU/2.

general. In fact, the absence of women's rights in some Muslim countries, caused by the customs and traditions in those countries, does not mean that Islamic law supports that particular individual country's stance.[3]

This chapter also explores the relationship between the educational rights of women and their duties in the home. It considers how these rights, as protected under Islamic law and international human rights law, can and should be recognised and promoted within the Saudi Arabian legal system.

II. SAUDI ARABIA AND WOMEN'S RIGHTS

The *Qur'an* and the *Sunnah* of His Messenger, Muhammad, are the basic texts from which all laws and regulations in force in the Kingdom of Saudi Arabia are derived. In the *Qur'an* and *Sunnah*, many stipulations prohibit various forms of discrimination, including discrimination on the basis of race, colour, or gender (in various circumstances). Moreover, they encompass many rulings regarding gender-based discrimination, with rulings that 'give women the same rights and duties on the basis of equality'.[4]

The Basic Law of Governance addresses the protection of human rights generally. Article 26 stipulates: 'The State shall protect human rights in accordance with the Islamic Shari'ah.' This Article prohibits discrimination against women in the manner that such that there is no conflict with the *Qur'an* and *Sunnah*.[5] Again, Article 8 of the Basic Law provides for 'government ... based on the premise of justice, consultation, and equality *in accordance with the Islamic Shari'ah*'.[6] The intersection of faith and justice is clear, and the rights of the people and the responsibilities of both the people and State are also given expression in the Basic Law of Governance.

---

[3] Abdul-Rahman Al-Sheha, *Women in Islam and Refutation of Some Common Misconceptions* (Abu Salman Deya ud-Deen Eberle trans, World Organisation for Presenting Islam, 1997) 10.

[4] CEDAW, Initial and Second Periodic Reports, Saudi Arabia, UN Doc CEDAW/C/SAU/2, 7.

[5] Some remain unimpressed at progress in women's rights in Saudi Arabia: see e.g. Radio Free Iraq, 'Activist Shrugs Off "Cosmetic" Improvements in Saudi Women's Rights' (transcript of interview of Wajeeha al-Huwayder by Karam Mnashe [trans: Ayad Al-Gailani]) (20 March 2011) www.rferl.org/content/interview_saudi_womens_rights_wajeeha_huwayder/2344307.html.

[6] Basic Law of Governance 1992 (Saudi Arabia) art. 8 (emphasis added).

The Basic Law of Governance provides for the principle of equality before the law. Article 47 stipulates: 'The right of litigation shall be guaranteed equally for both citizens and residents in the Kingdom. The law shall set forth the procedures required thereof.' Furthermore, equal access to justice is encouraged by the Basic Law of Governance which guarantees that litigation before all courts.[7] The Basic Law of Governance includes a body of rights it considers fundamental to Saudi society, such as unity,[8] the centrality of Islam,[9] and the sanctity of private property.[10] It contains provisions pertaining to the other fundamentals of Saudi society, such as the health[11] and welfare of the family and all its members,[12] and education.[13] Further, it addresses the freedom and inviolability of private property;[14] public confiscation of property cannot occur without 'fair compensation' and only when in the interests of the State.[15] Public confiscation of money is prohibited and the penalty of private confiscation is to be imposed only by a legal order,[16] though compensation can be sought.[17] The imposition of taxes and fees is forbidden unless necessary and on a reasonable basis.[18]

The Basic Law of Governance gives security in addition to freedom of communication to all people residing within the Kingdom, whether citizens or residents (within the bounds of the need for national security or unity, politeness (not slanderous) and in so far as is supported by

---

7 Ibid., art. 47.

8 Ibid., arts 11–12, 39.

9 See e.g. ibid., arts 6–11, 13, 17, 21, 23, 26, 33–4, 45–8, 57.

10 Ibid., art. 18.

11 See e.g. ibid., art. 31 (provision of healthcare for all citizens).

12 See e.g. ibid., art. 27 (welfare – social security – provision for citizens).

13 See e.g. ibid., arts 30 (provision of public education), 13 (education: its role to instil the Islamic faith and provide members with knowledge and skills to prepare them to be useful members of society).

14 Ibid., art. 18. (MOFA trans refers to inviolability of private property and the 'sanctity of public property' (art. 16), whereas the Arabic Translators International version refers to the 'sanctity' of private property and note that public money is sacrosanct, i.e. secured by religious sanction (art. 16). In either case, the inviolability appeared to be accorded public property is greater than that accorded private property, reinforcing perhaps the importance of the collective over the individual.

15 Ibid. See also art. 14.

16 Ibid., art. 19.

17 Ibid., art. 18.

18 Ibid., art. 20.

Shari'ah).[19] Saudi Arabian citizens and their families enjoy full rights in cases of emergency, sickness, disability, or aging.[20] Furthermore, the Basic Law of Governance supports the social security system and encourages both institutions and individuals to take part in charitable work.[21] The authorities in the Kingdom of Saudi Arabia have made great efforts in terms of securing social and economic development for the community in general and for women in particular. This has been done with the conscious involvement of women, as they are seen to play a vital role in shaping future generations.[22] Socially, several governmental organisations have been established by the State that encourage and support charitable and civic organisations to be committed to social development and the implementation of State policy in the area of social solidarity.[23] This attention has resulted in considerable and continuing efforts in regard to women's welfare. The State plays a vital role in affirming women's key role in the welfare of the family, and in protecting women against poverty, particularly in the event of the death, incapacity or imprisonment of the husband, or in the event of divorce, and has done

---

[19] However, the need for unity may mean that criticism of leading figures or policies etc. may not be well received, curtailing freedom of expression taken for granted to a varying extent elsewhere in the world (both in terms of freedom of the press and of individuals). Transgression may result in imprisonment: see e.g. Reporters without Borders website 'Internet Enemies: Saudi Arabia' (on net censorship etc) *Internet Enemies* (20 March 2011) http://en.rsf.org/internet-enemie-saudi-arabia,39745.html. The category (entered on a per country basis is updated at least annually, hence an updated version is now available for 2012: http://en.rsf.org/saudi-arabia-12-03-2012,42052.html (http://en.rsf.org/IMG/pdf/arabie_saoudite__ar__pdf.pdf). See also Reporters without Borders, *Repressive Regulations Target Internet Freedom of Expression* (8 January 2011) http://en.rsf.org/saudi-arabia-repressive-regulations-target-08-01-2011,39243.html. Freedom of speech in relation to religion may also be extremely limited given the interlocking roles of the State and monarchy to uphold and cultivate Islam, and Islam of a particular persuasion as the sole authentic model, rejecting others. See e.g. the ban on proselytism and the building of churches.

[20] This is limited in relation to residents (e.g., foreign workers) as it is in most states worldwide.

[21] Basic Law of Governance 1992 (Saudi Arabia) art. 27.

[22] See e.g. CEDAW, Initial and Second Periodic Reports, Saudi Arabia, UN Doc CEDAW/C/SAU/2, 7.

[23] For example: Women's Charitable Society, Association Faisaliah Charitable Women, Association of Charitable, Services and Care of Cancer Patients, Friends of the Heart Foundation, and the Bir Society.

so by promulgating laws in this regard.[24] In terms of efforts to prevent the dissolution of families, the State 'has created reconciliation sections in the country's courts within the framework of its desire to spread mutual support, tolerance, and cooperation among people in furtherance of the common good'.[25]

The Kingdom of Saudi Arabia ratified CEDAW in 2000 using the following wording:[26]

> 1. The Kingdom's accession to the Convention on the Elimination of all Forms of Discrimination Against Women adopted by United Nations General Assembly resolution 34/180 (18 December 1979), in the attached wording, is approved with the reservation that, in case of contradiction between any term of the Convention and the norms of Islamic Law, the Kingdom is not under the obligation to observe the contradictory terms of the Convention.
>
> 2. The Kingdom does not consider itself bound by Article 9, paragraph 2 and Article 29, paragraph 1 of this Convention.

That the general content of the Convention is consistent with the country's approach to conserving women's rights led to its acknowledgement by the Kingdom. This shows the Kingdom's desire to abide by the provisions of the Convention and indicates its determination to bear its responsibility to protect the human rights of women in the country while taking into consideration the reservations that it has expressed. These reservations are consistent with Articles 19–23 of the Vienna Convention on the Law of Treaties[27] concerning reservations, especially as they accord with the subject of the Convention and are not incompatible with its purpose.

It is difficult to discuss the philosophy of local and international law and its application within Saudi Arabia in any way separately from Shari'ah. In the Islamic State, law-making stems from Shari'ah. This is

---

[24] See Social Security Law 2006 (Saudi Arabia), promulgated by Royal Decree No M/45 (7/7/1427 H, 2/8/2006) arts 1, 2. See also Social Insurance Law 2000 (Saudi Arabia), promulgated by Royal Decree No M/33 (3/9/1421 H, 30/11/2000).

[25] CEDAW, Initial and Second Periodic Reports, Saudi Arabia, UN Doc CEDAW/C/SAU/2, 7–8.

[26] Royal Decree No 25 Concerning the Kingdom's Accession to the Convention on the Elimination of All Forms of Discrimination against Women (28/5/1421 H, 28 August 2000). For text, see CEDAW, Initial and Second Periodic Reports, Saudi Arabia, UN Doc CEDAW/C/SAU/2.

[27] Vienna Convention on the Law of Treaties, opened for signature 23 May 1969 (entered into force 27 January 1980).

self-evident in the Kingdom, where Article 1 of the Basic Law of Governance stipulates:

> The Kingdom of Saudi Arabia is a fully sovereign Arab Islamic State. Its religion shall be Islam and its constitution shall be the *Qur'an* and the *Sunnah* of His Messenger …

Therefore, the legislation, regulation and policy adopted within the country cannot breach the framework of Shari'ah. As a result, the country's laws cannot be expected to be altered or developed by the legislative authority in such a way as 'may lead to the creation of new principles, inconsistent with the bases of the *Shari'ah*, in letter and spirit'.[28] Indeed, there is 'no distinction between church and State in the theory of Islamic Law',[29] just as there is no distinction in life. 'People' and 'congregation' are essentially a single entity; with both ruler and ruled subject to the provisions of Shari'ah. The role of the courts,[30] and the position of the monarch and the allegiance owed him, are also supported by reference to the *Qur'an*, as is the role of government.[31] There is no separation, therefore, between Shari'ah and the State with its various laws, nor can there be (according to the traditional understandings adopted in the Kingdom).[32] Therefore, the legislative authority 'is obliged to abide by the totality of the sources of Islamic *Shari'ah*',[33] a point that is made clear in the Basic Law of Governance:

> The regulatory authority shall have the jurisdiction of formulating laws and rules conducive to the realization of the well-being or warding off harm to State affairs in accordance with the principles of the Islamic Shari'ah …[34]

---

28 CEDAW, Initial and Second Periodic Reports, Saudi Arabia, UN Doc CEDAW/C/SAU/2, 10.

29 Ibid.

30 Basic Law of Governance 1992 (Saudi Arabia) art. 48.

31 Ibid., arts 6–8. The religious title of imam which was early accorded to rulers of Saudi Arabia further emphasises the links, though in this theocracy there remains some tension (actual and potential) between ruler and religious leaders in regards to certain matters.

32 See e.g. CEDAW, Initial and Second Periodic Reports, Saudi Arabia, UN Doc CEDAW/C/SAU/2, 2, 5–6.

33 CEDAW, Initial and Second Periodic Reports, Saudi Arabia, UN Doc CEDAW/C/SAU/2, 10.

34 Basic Law of Governance 1992 (Saudi Arabia) art. 67.

This is the basis of the Kingdom's reservation to the provisions of the Convention, namely the Convention will be adopted in so far as it does not conflict with the principles of Shari'ah.

If there is discrimination and injustice against woman, then the Kingdom's laws that are taken from the *Holy Qur'an* and the *Sunnah* of Muhammad must be reformed to tackle women's issues and promote equality. Thus, the relevant bodies of State are obliged to apply the principles of equality in exercising their legal competence. They must not discriminate concerning the human rights within the framework stipulated in Article 26 (human rights in accordance with Shari'ah) and accorded under Article 27 (social security provision), Article 28 (employment opportunity to be provided by the State),[35] 30 (education and literacy provision), Article 31 (healthcare), Article 35 (treatment of nationality/citizenship other than as defined by Statute), Article 36 (freedom from arrest other than as provided by law), Article 37 (freedom from unlawful search of home, privacy provision), and Article 38 (legal penalties as provided by law) of the Basic Law of Governance.[36] There are a number of women's rights, elsewhere taken for granted, that are omitted.[37] The right of women to vote in municipal elections, for example, is still being considered, but then it must be understood that the first ever such elections were held in 2005 in the Kingdom of Saudi Arabia, where the King is a real and powerful (rather than merely titular) head of State.[38]

---

[35] Though this may be restricted in practice by lack of appropriate (single sex or relative provided) transport provision, childcare facilities, even the lack of provision of separate entrance doors or eating or working areas. The recent uproar over mixed gender university indicates the level of community opposition to such arrangements: Compare Henry Meyer and Glen Carey, *Mixed-Sex Saudi University Hits Clerical Opposition (Update1)* (6 April 2011) www.bloomberg.com/apps/news?pid=newsarchive&sid=az4zDJ6nTVEg.

[36] See CEDAW, Initial and Second Periodic Reports, Saudi Arabia, UN Doc CEDAW/C/SAU/2, 8. See also Saudi Arabian Ministry for the Interior SAMIRAD, *Questions of Human Rights* (24 March 2011) www.saudinf.com/main/x004.htm.

[37] Generally this is under Personal Status laws relating to child custody, divorce, property division, inheritance etc., also freedom for adult to travel (without spouse/father's permission).

[38] 'Women Remain Barred from Voting as Saudi Arabia Announces Elections' (7 April 2011) www.thenational.ae/news/worldwide/middle-east/women-remain-barred-from-voting-as-saudi-arabia-announces-elections. Other rights are not enjoyed by both men and women: e.g., the right of association in the

III. HISTORY OF WOMEN'S EDUCATION IN SAUDI ARABIA

The education of women in Saudi Arabia has a relatively short history. Prior to 1960, formal State-provided education did not exist for women and girls. In common with education for boys, any education was generally faith-centred.[39] Families wanting to educate their daughters sent them to *kuttabs* (small *Qur'anic* schools usually attached to a mosque) for classes (boys too were sent to these schools for a religious studies education). They may also have been sent to one of the very few private schools that were then available but only in a few of the large cities (see further below).[40] Other families sought professional Qur'anic readers for instruction of their daughters at home,[41] or employed non-Saudi women tutors or teachers to give them private lessons at home.

Education (outside the home and often inside it) for girls stopped at puberty 'when strict seclusion at home began and veiling in public became mandatory'.[42] A few wealthy families retained tutors, who continued to teach but often combined the role with that of governesses or companions. A tiny group were educated abroad.[43]

In the 1950s, the Ministry of Education, the governmental bureaucracy founded as recently as 1954[44] and originally responsible solely for the education of boys, first permitted girls to sit for the intermediate and secondary school examinations as external students and earn officially

---

workplace (for reasons such as union representation) is limited to those workplaces with over 100 employees: See Carnegie Endowment for International Peace, *Arab Political Systems: Baseline Information and Reforms* (6 April 2011) www.carnegieendowment.org/publications/index.cfm?fa=view&id=16918.

39 Nagat El-Sanabary, 'The Education and Contribution of Women Health Care Professionals in Saudi Arabia: The Case of Nursing' (1993) 37 (11) *Social Science and Medicine* 1331, 1332 ('The Case of Nursing').

40 Ibtissam A Al-Bassam, 'Institutions of Higher Education for Women in Saudi Arabia' (1984) 4 (3) *International Journal of Educational Development* 255.

41 ARAMCO, *Saudi Arabia – A Country Study* (24 March 2011) www.country-data.com/cgi-bin/query/r-11593.html.

42 Soraya Altorki, *Women in Saudi Arabia: Ideology and Behaviour Among the Elite* (New York: Columbia University Press 1986) 19.

43 See e.g. London Middle East Institute, 'Profile: Mai Yamani, Author, Broadcaster and LMEI Advisory Council Member' (24 March 2011) www.maiyamani.com/pdf/17_yamani.pdf ('Profile: Mai Yamani').

44 SAMIRAD, *Background to the Development of Education* (24 March 2011) www.saudinf.com/main/j1.htm.

recognised school certificates. It is worth recalling that in Saudi Arabia at this time there were few schools provided by the State even for boys but a huge effort had been being made since the early 1950s to correct that situation (and improve the nation's appalling literacy rate)[45] but even boys' primary education was not mandated until 1958, while the number of schools and their inspection was insufficient to guarantee boys' attendance.[46] That primary education for girls was mandated just three years later in 1961 represents quite an achievement.[47]

The first attempt to give Saudi girls (beyond the royal family) formal education within Saudi Arabia was the *Dar Al-Hanan*[48] ('House of Affection') school, a small privately funded residential school for girls that had been founded in 1955 by the Turkish-educated – and teacher-trained and qualified – Queen Iffat, who saw the 'dire need' for girls' education.[49] The aim of the School was to provide an education that would enable the girls to secure a higher standard of living than might otherwise have been the case.[50] First, upper nursery and primary education was provided where girls followed the curriculum of the Ministry of Education (with which it was registered from 1957) and took the same final examinations as the boys. The first group of *Dar Al-Hanan* pupils completed their primary school education in 1959/60, and in 1960,

---

45 Though this was slow to improve until the 1970s–2000s for just some of the reasons cited: 1970 male literacy 15 per cent, women 2 per cent; 1990 male 73 per cent, women 40 per cent; 2001 male 71 per cent, women 56.2 per cent: 'Saudi Arabia. Education' Encyclopaedia of the Nations website ARAMCO, *Saudi Arabia – A Country Study* (24 March 2011) www.country-data.com/cgi-bin/query/r-11593.html.

46 Indeed, according to the UN, in 1952 the country had just 306 primary schools (up from just two in 1925) but an illiteracy rate of 92–95 per cent: see State University, *Saudi Arabia – Educational System-Overview* (24 March 2011) http://education.stateuniversity.com/pages/1302/Saudi-Arabia-EDUCATIONAL-SYSTEM-OVERVIEW.html.

47 Ibid.

48 'Dar Al-Hanan is still in existence and expanding on a new site: Maha Akeel, Dar Al-Hanan to Reopen in New Location' (30 November 2005) *Arab News* http://archive.arabnews.com/?page=1&section=0&article=73948&d=30&m=11&y=2005.

49 Iffat Al Thunayan, King Faisal's wife, pushed enthusiastically for the education of women in the Kingdom of Saudi Arabia. See e.g. *Important Saudi Women of our Times* (25 March 2011) www.oocities.org/urfriendanne/saudiwomen.html; Patrice Flynn, 'A Slow Evolution: Saudi Educational Non-profits Push Reforms for Women', *Non Profit Times* 1 July 2010 www.nxtbook.com/nxtbooks/npt/npt060110/index.php?startid=12.

50 Ibid.

intermediate classes were opened, with this first cohort receiving their intermediate school certificates in 1963. Secondary school classes were begun that same year 'despite a lack of qualified teachers, a shortage of equipment, and the limitations of the building it then occupied'.[51] Also in 1963, *Dar Al-Hanan* girls were the first to graduate from a regular school in Saudi Arabia and with secondary school certificates.[52]

Formal education for girls was officially recognised in 1960, when King Faisal announced in a royal speech that it had been decided upon the wish of the *Ulama* (religious scholars) to open schools for girls under a committee responsible to the *Mufti*.[53] That same year that committee was replaced by the General Presidency of Female Education (GPFE),[54] which was responsible for girls' education at every level throughout the entire country. All private girls' schools came under its supervision in 1960, as did the girls' State-funded schools which had been opened across Saudi Arabia.

An early writer noted, however, that the GPFE remained 'effectively, a ministry staffed by men whose training and experience [were] entirely in religious sciences' (that is, religious scholars, reflecting what is still today the primary purpose of education).[55] Girls' education remained under the Department of Religious Guidance (rather than the Ministry of Education) until amalgamated with the Ministry of Education in 2002 (further on this below). Although the GPGE president had the same status as a minister and was a member of the Council of Ministers, the area of female education was comparatively poorly funded compared to boys' education with girls' schools therefore tending to be ill-equipped and often located in older, unsafe buildings.

---

[51] Ibid.

[52] This is the same year as the secondary section was opened – their graduation was made possible by girls returning to Saudi Arabia having already received part of their education elsewhere.

[53] *Mufti*: Jurist capable of giving, upon request, an authoritative although nonbinding opinion are generally based on precedent and compiled in legal reference manuals. In some contexts, *Muftis* are appointed by the State and serve on advisory councils.

[54] GPFE is one of the three official organisations which control education in Saudi Arabia, the other two being the Ministry of Education, founded in 1953, and the Ministry of Higher Education, founded in 1975.

[55] Basic Law of Governance 1992 (Saudi Arabia) art. 13, together with eliminating illiteracy (art. 30) and building knowledgeable and skilled citizens able to contribute to the nation and be proud of its history (art. 13).

Although King Faisal supported the right of women to reach their goals, he was not able to convince the public at the beginning.[56] Opposition could be quite formidable in local communities: he had to send an official force to *Buraydah* in 1963 to keep the girls' school there open. Although he ruled that girls' schooling was mandatory and obligatory (a ruling that continues in force to the present day), he did not force the parents to take their daughters to school; rather, he ensured that those who wished their daughters to obtain an education were able to do so. He rejected the idea that in order to modernise Saudi Arabia, the country would have to break from its past; rather, he believed that slow and steady change was better than violent, disruptive attempts to force change and that its traditions could be harnessed to provide the basis for and to give effect to that change. Respect for the King's position can be similarly utilised.

King Faisal would cite the *Qur'an* and Islamic teachings to support the concept of women's education. When he faced resistance, for example, he would ask, 'Is there anything in the *Holy Qur'an* which forbids the education of women?' Moreover he has been reported as saying (and quoting a well-known Hadith),[57] 'We have no cause for argument; Allah enjoins learning on every Muslim man and [woman].'[58]

While non-religious education for boys was considered of secondary importance to that of holy learning related to the *Qur'an*, secular knowledge (trade training and other non-religious learning) had gained increasing status as it related to the role of the male in his role as provider for his family and in relation to their role in driving the nation forward, rather than relying on increasing numbers of imported foreign nationals; however, non-religious education of girls was, at least initially, considered useless and even, according to certain conservative religious scholars, dangerous. While women centuries before, in the earliest days

---

[56] Many members of the general public have also indicated that they believe that a Saudi woman's place is in her home. As a result, Saudi women continually encounter limitations and restrictions on both an educational and professional level. According to the 1999 census, just 5 per cent of women work outside the home, and these women are concentrated in the teaching and health sectors.

[57] Ibn Majah, *Sunan Ibn Majah* (Dar Ehi'a Al Kutob Al Arabiah 1401) in the book of *Al Muqaddemah* hadith no 224; and Muhammad N. Al-Albani, *Sahih Al Targheeb* (Maktabat Al Ma'arif 1421) includes it in his collection of *hadith* as no 3913: see also M. H. Al Khayat, 'Women in Islam and Her Role in Human Development' (WHO-EM/CBI/022/E/G, World Health Organization 2003) 7.

[58] See Robert Lacey, *The Kingdom: Arabia and the House of Sa'ud* (Harcourt Brace Jovanovich 1998) 368.

of Islam, had reportedly been traders (including Khadijah,[59] the first wife of the Prophet), translators, administrators, scholars, jurists and persons whose valued advice could be sought, farmers, even warriors, as well as carers (including nursing and surgery)[60] of the injured and ill, this model had been lost in the intervening years and women had become ever more closely 'enclosed' as particular understandings regarding women and their roles rose to prominence.

Over time, however, the public took a generally and increasingly more favourable position toward the enrolment of girls in school. The continued support by both King Faisal and Queen Iffat, and the royal family generally, for education of women and girls contributed to that change.[61] By 1989, the number of girls (1.2 million) enrolled in schools was almost equal to the number of boys (1.4 million). This represented a considerable improvement on the 1981 figures where 81 per cent of boys and just 43 per cent of girls were enrolled).[62] An immense programme of school building (both schools for boys and schools for girls) continued apace. (Over 900 schools were opened in 1988/89, for example.)[63]

Administration of girls' education remained under the control of the General Presidency of Female Education, an organisation staffed by conservative religious scholars. The purpose of educating a girl, as stated by the Director General, was 'to bring her up in a proper Islamic way so as to perform her duty in life, be an ideal and successful housewife and a

---

59 Khadijah Bint Khuwaylid (dec. ca. 618) was the first wife of Muhammad and his only wife until her death. The mother of Fatimah and other sons and daughters of Muhammad, and the first person to believe in Muhammad's prophethood, she was a wealthy widow who hired Muhammad to oversee her commercial transactions. She married him when she was around 40 and he was 25. She is revered as a good and faithful wife, mother, and Muslim. See Abdul Ahad Alig, *The Honourable Wives of the Prophet* (Darussalam 2004) 11.

60 Fatimah Naseef, *Huqwq Almra'ah wa Wajibatuha fi Da'wa Alkitab wa Alsunnah* (Tuhamah, 1992) 178 [trans: Fatimah Naseef, *Women's Rights and Duties in the Light of Qur'an and Sunnah* (Tuhamah 1992)] ('Women's Rights and Duties'). See Muslim, *Sahih Muslim* (Dar Ehi'a Al Kutob Al Arabiah 1374) in the book of (*Aljihad*) hadith no 4659.

61 This has continued into the twenty-first century. See e.g. the founding of the King Abdullah University for Science and Technology. See also the activities of Queen Iffat's daughter: Kay Hardy Campbell, *Effat's New Roses* (25 March 2011) www.saudiaramcoworld.com/issue/200701/effat.s.new.roses.htm.

62 Helen Chapin Metz, *Saudi Arabia: A Country Study* (25 March 2011) http://countrystudies.us/saudi-arabia/31.htm.

63 Abdella Eleanor Doumato, 'Women and Work in Saudi Arabia: How Flexible are Islamic Margins?' (1999) 53 (4) *The Middle East Journal* 568, 370 ('Women and Work').

good mother, ready to do things which suit her nature as teaching, nursing, and medical treatment'.[64] Thus employment outside the home, though in roles particularly 'suited to [a woman's] nature' was explicitly recognised.

While upholding the centrality of Islam, the approach adopted by Queen Iffat also had much in common with early Western justifications for female education. She counselled women to learn about their faith, but added that every girl should get an education, because education enlightens human beings, who should know how to use their brains. Furthermore she emphasised the importance of an educated mother in the upbringing of a family, in the formation of children and the nation.[65] Again, the emphasis was on 'one woman at a time', on evolution of an education system that recognised women's abilities and rights and consolidated them, rather than a 'revolution' where wholesale and sudden change that risked a devastating backlash, damage to the society as a whole and to women in particular. Queen Iffat continued to open educational institutions for women, at an increasingly higher level of attainment and an increasing breadth of learning.

School education was not automatically accompanied by higher education for women. In the 1960s, women who aspired to earn a university degree without leaving the country enrolled as external students in the small undergraduate programme which was then offered to women by Riyadh University (now the King Saud University) and the King Abdul-Aziz University. A few women went to universities in other Arab countries or in the West, and they were sponsored either by their families or by the Saudi government. With girls' schools opening on a large scale across the country, and girls' education rapidly growing in scope, the need for qualified female teachers was pressing. This led to the opening of the Riyadh College of Education in 1970.[66] Its main goal was to train Saudi teachers for intermediate and secondary girls' schools. The Riyadh College of Education was the first institution of higher education for

---

64 See Alireza Moattari, 'Women of Arabia' (1987) 172 (4) *National Geographic* 423.

65 See e.g. 'Educate your [selves], be good mothers, bring up perfect Saudis, build up your country', a quote attributed to her by her daughter Princess Loulwa Al-Faisal.

66 See also Abdullah Saeed, 'Islamic Religious Education and the Debate on its Reform Post-September 11' in Shahram Akbarzadeh and Samina Yasmeen (eds), *Islam and the West* (Sydney: University of New South Wales 2005) 68 ('Islamic Religious Education').

women in Saudi Arabia. Later, seven more institutions of higher education for women were opened in the country: a college of education in *Jeddah* (1974), a college of education in *Makkah* (1975), an institute of social work in *Riyadh* (1975), a college of arts and sciences in *Dammam* (1979), a college of arts in *Riyadh* (1979), a college of education in *Madinah* (1981), a college of education in *Buraydah* (1981) and a college of education in *Abha* (1981).

These are all four-year degree awarding institutions, offering university-level education, and are governed by a department of GPFE known as the 'Vice-Presidency of Colleges' and headed by a vice-president. Education in women's institutions of higher education is free, as it is in all universities and State schools in Saudi Arabia. The colleges offer degrees in Islamic Studies, Arabic Studies, English, Geography, History, Home Economics, Mathematical Sciences, Physics, Botany, Zoology and Education. Their chief objectives are:

1. to train enough qualified female Saudi teachers and administrators for the nation's girls' schools and colleges;
2. to train girls to be good Muslims, accomplished house-keepers, ideal wives, good mothers and highly qualified scholars;
3. to provide higher education for Saudi women as well as to non-Saudi Muslim women living in Saudi Arabia; and
4. to give scholarships to a few women from other Muslim countries to study Islamic studies in Saudi Arabia.

Women's schooling at all levels – elementary, secondary, high school and university – remained under the Department of Religious Guidance until 2002, while the education of boys was overseen by the Ministry of Education. This supervision was to ensure that women's education did not deviate from the original purpose of female education, which was to make women good wives and mothers, and to prepare them for acceptable employment such as teaching and nursing that were believed to suit their nature. The GPFE did not enjoy the same prestige as the Ministry of Education, and was heavily influenced by conservative religious scholars, which resulted in course offerings remaining restricted, education chronically underfunded and buildings overcrowded. In 2002, the GPFE and the Ministry of Education were amalgamated as a result of requests from both the general public and the government.[67]

---

[67] Amani Hamdan, 'Women and Education in Saudi Arabia: Challenges and Achievements' (2005) 6 (1) *International Education Journal* 44. This followed a

The gender segregation of students prompted the growth of teacher and nursing training for women, but such segregation also had ramifications at institutions of higher education, which are also necessarily gender segregated. Until the 2010 foundation of the King Abdullah University, gender segregation prevailed in all tertiary institutions, and this remains the case for the overwhelming majority of institutions. The vast majority of the tertiary education providers are State institutions, these universities and similar State colleges do not possess any capital, nor do they accept revenues in their own right, and their finances are the responsibility of the government. The academic and administrative staffs are all civil servants. While UNESCO indicated that by 2003, there were some private tertiary education providers, with more planned,[68] another (domestic) source noted that there was just one private institution, the Arab Open University, affiliated with UK institutions.[69]

Men and women are generally strictly segregated in Saudi Arabia. There are very few exceptions (other than the King Abdullah University of Science and Technology, which opened in late 2009).[70] Men may, however, be allowed to teach women by closed circuit television at other institutions. Nevertheless, all the administrative and teaching staff of the girls' colleges are women. As men and women in Saudi Arabia do not generally meet unrelated members of the other gender, meetings are never held between the male and female administrators, and all communication is carried out through two channels: by telephone and official letters. The resulting system of administration is highly bureaucratic.[71]

---

notorious incident where religious police who were variously reported as discouraging fire brigade members from entering or actually instructing students to re-enter the building (in flames) as they were not deemed to be dressed correctly for public places: BBC News, 'Saudi Police "Stopped" Fire Rescue', 15 March 2002 http://news.bbc.co.uk/2/hi/1874471.stm.

68 UNESCO, *Portal on Higher Education Institutions* (25 March 2011) http://portal.unesco.org/education/en/ev.php-URL_ID=58276&URL_DO=DO_TOPIC&URL_SECTION=201.html.

69 Hend Suliman Al-Khalifa, 'The State of Distance Education in Saudi Arabia' (27 March 2011) www.elearnmag.org/subpage.cfm?article=101-1&section=articles.

70 Ulf Laessing and Asma Alsharif, 'Saudi Arabia Opens First Mixed-Gender University' (28 March 2011) http://in.reuters.com/article/2009/09/23/us-saudi-education-kaust-idINTRE58M65R20090923>. It is outside the supervision of the religious police and has a majority foreign student base.

71 For example, the colleges are not allowed to communicate with any official organisations (libraries, universities, ministries), even if the communication entails no responsibility of any kind. Such communication is done on

This research is not about stressing the patriarchal nature of Arab society in general and Saudi society in particular; rather, it is about explaining the *consequences* of excluding women from public life and constraining their educational choices. Women's issues in Saudi society are often mistakenly connected to Islamic teaching, with a failure to distinguish between the teachings of Islam and the survival of pre-Islamic values or their re-emergence subsequent to the life of the Prophet.[72] Women's issues in Saudi society and obvious gender inequalities in its educational system are institutionalised and difficult to dislodge through individual action. Women's inequality is traditionally structured in the society. The rationale for needing to focus on women's achievements in higher education is considered a key social development indicator that measures the status and condition of women in any country.[73]

IV. FINDINGS AND RECOMMENDATION

Although the United Nations and the government have exerted painstaking efforts to develop women's rights, there has been and continues to be broad discrimination against the women in all social, economic and cultural aspects of life. This constitutes a violation of their rights. Although the Kingdom of Saudi Arabia is a signatory to CEDAW, there remain problems relating to the implementation of some of its provisions. CEDAW has not in fact had a large effect.

Undoubtedly, Saudi Arabia has witnessed remarkable improvements in relation to women's rights and clearly also in regards to women's status because the government took steps in that field. For example, it encouraged the promotion of women to leadership positions, such as university

behalf of the colleges either by the vice-president, or by the general directors. Thus, for instance, if a college requires certain information from a certain ministry, the procedure is as follows: the department requiring the information writes a detailed letter to the dean, who sends it with a covering letter to the vice-president or a general director, who, in turn, writes a letter to the ministry requesting its cooperation. The ministry's reply is then sent to the president or general director, who writes to the college requiring the information.

[72] Al-Sheha, *Women in Islam*, above n3, 63.

[73] Goli M. Rezai-Rashti, *Women and Education in Post Revolutionary Iran* (2003) 2.

manager[74] and higher appointments in the Ministry of Education.[75] In addition, Saudi women have the opportunity to represent the Kingdom at the international level as well as participate in works of a number of international organisations.[76] Some new specialisations are also now offered to women in some universities. We hope that these steps continue, and are translated into facts 'on the ground' by the competent authorities, rather than being stymied. The latter can occur in situations where systems and legislation are in place to ensure women's rights but the relevant provisions are either not implemented (perhaps due to a lack of relevant regulations or required policies), or they are implemented, but are wrongly interpreted. With respect to the educational policy in Saudi Arabia, there is clear discrimination against women. Therefore, women's rights must be a focus in educational policy because the policy contains general provisions having broad application and impact on the multiple levels of education in the Kingdom. All provisions and educational regulations must be reviewed, especially those which decrease or restrict the eligibility of the women or their legal character in a form which contradicts Shari'ah and violates international laws.[77]

The interviews with Saudi women in different fields revealed that the main obstacles to women's education were legal and administrative. In addition, the data analysis showed that there is great difference between the theory and the practice of Saudi law.

---

[74] Dr Huda Mohammad Al Ameel, Rector of Princess Nora Bint Abdul Rahman University. See Stephen McBride, 'Princess Nora University Installs Banner by Ellucian' (8 October 2012) www.itp.net/mobile/590762-princess-nora-university-installs-banner-by-ellucian.

[75] Nora Al Fayez is the first woman to be named Deputy Education Minister for Women's Affairs, the highest position reached by a female in this conservative country. See Jumana Al Tamimi, '*Nora Al Fayez: A Role Model for Saudi Women*' (21 February 2009) http://gulfnews.com/news/gulf/saudi-arabia/nora-al-fayez-a-role-model-for-saudi-women-1.52726.

[76] Dr Thoraya Obaid, the Executive Director of the United Nation Population Fund and Under-Secretary-General of the United Nation, also Ms Sulafa Al Bassam, Chief, United Nation Regional Economic Commissions (level D1), Ms Fatima Al Mani, Economic and Social Commission for Western Asia (ESCWA), Beirut (level P4). See CEDAW, Initial and Second Periodic Reports, Saudi Arabia, UN Doc CEDAW/C/SAU/2.

[77] Constitution of Saudi Arabia, art. 26 (Human Rights): 'The state protects human rights in accordance with Islamic Shari'ah.' Hence the general reservation to CEDAW and a number of other human rights conventions. This does not, however, mean that the maximum permitted freedom and equality allowed by Shari'ah and the *Qur'an* should not be sought.

This study shows that there is a lacuna between women's rights in general and women's educational rights in particular. The results include the following matters that cause women to be unable to pursue their learning.

A. Dominance of Guardians

The securing of the permission of a woman's guardian is crucial in regard to education. A woman cannot take decisions in all matters relating to her without having permission from her guardian. This permission is required for her to be able to pursue her education and in regard to her choice of specialisation. This allows guardians (whether father or husband) to prevent their daughters and wives from pursuing their education because there are not written rules or formal decisions clarifying the legislative and legal boundaries in relation to the issue of guardianship, and this causes the suffering of women in different areas (education, employment and so on). Currently, the requirement for a guardian's permission affects many areas of women's lives. For example, some hospitals demand the guardian's permission before allowing women to have medical operations or enter or leave hospital.[78] Such excessive dominance of women and curtailment thereby of their legal capacity violates Article 15 of CEDAW which stipulates:

> States Parties shall accord to women, in civil matters, *a legal capacity identical to that of men and the same opportunities to exercise that capacity*. In particular, they shall give women equal rights to conclude contracts and to administer property and shall treat them equally in all stages of procedure in courts and tribunals.[79]

The parties are required to:

> Agree that all contracts and all other private instruments of any kind with a legal effect which is directed at restricting the legal capacity of women shall be deemed null and void.[80]

---

78 See for example, Saudi Women for Reform, 'The Shadow Report for CEDAW' (20 November 2007) 27 http://www.arabhumanrights.org/publications/countries/saudi/shadowreports/swr-sr-07e.pdf, 2–3; Human Rights Watch, *Saudi Arabia: Women's Rights Promises Broken* (8 July 2009) www.hrw.org/news/2009/07/08/saudi-arabia-women-s-rights-promises-broken.

79 CEDAW art. 15(2) (emphasis added).

80 Ibid., art. 15(3).

Women who have not legal capacity cannot dispose of their private affairs. In order to avoid this problem, the following solutions are suggested:

1. Issuance of legislation clarifying the limits of men's dominance[81] of women in all fields as well as clarifying the legal and legislative boundaries and following up on the execution of laws by the institutions.[82]
2. Cancellation of all regulations, systems and instructions that require the permission of the guardian (in terms of the appropriate limitation of dominance) needs to be executed systematically and legislatively.
3. Issuance of provisions in the penal law relating to aggression against women or violation of their rights where the aggressor/violator is the guardian and if the action is beyond the limits of dominance stipulated in the law or legislation.
4. Utilisation of the mass media to increase awareness of women's rights and of protections legally available for them in regards to aggression.

---

[81] In relation to CEDAW, it should be recalled that Saudi Arabia entered a general reservation: '1. In case of contradiction between any term of the Convention and the norms of Islamic law, the Kingdom is not under obligation to observe the contradictory terms of the Convention.' On the interpretation and definition of such law rests Saudi women's and men's rights. Such limits are to be those consistent with Shari'ah.

[82] Indeed, critics would say that any such dominance is unwarranted unless a similar imposition is made in regard to other adult spouse. For example, if a married woman is unable to enter a contract without her husband's permission then a reciprocal right must exist, that is the husband cannot enter a contract without his wife's permission. Another example, in relation to surgery would be that just as a husband's permission is required for a wife's surgery so a wife's permission is required for a husband's surgery. A husband may deal with property matters if a court has deemed the wife incompetent due to mental incapacity (injury or illness); and a wife may likewise administer her husband's affairs if he is similarly deemed incompetent. Article 15 would appear to demand nothing less than equality, rather than a form of 'limited dominance'.

B. Lack of Available Specialisations for Women

Although the Saudi government finances university education in full for men and women,[83] traditionally there have not been any separate programmes available for women's education in a number of areas, particularly in the fields of engineering, political sciences, geology and petroleum and so on, and extremely few in others, such as the pharmaceutical field (where the few female graduate pharmacists there are, for example, find their employment severely restricted, as is also the case for opticians).[84] Since the interviews for this research were conducted, a number of areas have been formally opened to women, at least at some universities,[85] and announcements have been made heralding change in an additional number of areas of study (see further below).[86]

Women's education is restricted in the number and types of programmes offered to female students in the vast majority of teacher colleges. There are still no public university programmes in engineering, architecture or political science, and women are prohibited from studying these disciplines in the male colleges.

The restrictions on woman's education in terms of access to various specialisations has undoubtedly caused (and continues to cause) higher unemployment among educated women than might otherwise have been the case both, because it causes an oversupply of graduates in the permitted areas, no possibility of employment in the areas where study is not permitted, and underemployment in areas where study is permitted but employment is either officially obstructed or informally frowned

---

[83] CEDAW, Initial and Second Periodic Reports, Saudi Arabia, UN Doc CEDAW/C/SAU/2, 31.

[84] To pursue specialisations some women have previously gone overseas. For example, the first female chemist was overseas educated at University College of Wales (UK). Suhad Maatoug Bahijri is now a professor in the Department of Clinical Biochemistry, Faculty of Medicine, King Abdulaziz University: http://sbahijri.kau.edu.sa/CVEn.aspx?Site_ID=0000889&Lng=EN. (Her father was the first chemist in the Kingdom and had been educated at Cairo University (then Fouad I University).

[85] See Clinical Pharmacy at Abdulaziz University: http://pharmacy.kau.edu.sa/Content.aspx?Site_ID=166&lng=EN&cid=108970.

[86] See *The Chronicle of Higher Education*, 'Saudi Arabia to Allow Women to Study Political Science' (16 April 2012) http://chronicle.com/blogs/global/saudi-arabia-to-allow-women-to-study-political-science/32855; see also *Al Arabiya*, 'Saudi Women to Study Politics at National Universities' (15 April 2012) http://english.alarabiya.net/articles/2012/04/15/207856.html.

upon.[87] The lack of various specialisations generally, as well as the lack of their local availability,[88] are considered an indirect cause of women leaving school, failing to enter the tertiary sector, or curtailing their education at higher level. Whilst the number of secondary school graduates is high, this number decreases in universities because of the scarcity of available specialisations. This contradicts CEDAW, which stipulates that:

> The same conditions for career and vocational guidance, for *access to studies* and for the achievement of diplomas *in educational establishments of all categories* in rural as well as in urban areas; this *equality* shall be ensured in pre-school, general, technical, professional and higher technical education, as well as *in all types* of vocational training.[89]

It should be kept in mind that the education is essentially the transmission of a message and the message does not determine whether its receiver is either men or women or both. But we see a large number of pretexts supplied for limiting the transmission of the message, such as unavailability of specialisations which do not meet the needs of the job market. This talk is without logic because the job market reflects different needs over the years; in fact, education creates the possibility of being able to satisfy employment opportunities as they arise and opens avenues for innovation to meet the nation's needs. The following solutions and new plans are recommended:

1. Opening new fields and educational specialisations for women, such as in commercial and industrial fields. Access by both men and women to courses, and the distribution of places are to be agreed upon after careful consideration.
2. Limiting the 'social' and 'theoretical' specialisations which have no value on the job market and are simply increasing the number of unemployed women. The majority of such women (as well as those contemplating studying at tertiary level) need to be encouraged/required to join technical specialisations or courses that will help them to increase their chances of gaining employment.
3. Supporting a greater variety of training courses. Women suffer from a scarcity of courses and the majority of training courses available

[87] In the case of fields not open to women formally or informally, many such jobs are filled by imported labour, as well as by male Saudi nationals.

[88] This is further complicated by lack of access to employment even when a woman is qualified.

[89] CEDAW art. 10(a) (emphasis added).

are in cooking, design and photography, as these are the only fields perceived as suited to women. There is a need to open other courses to women that are open to men.

4. Increasing vocational guidance. There is a need for increased availability of vocational guidance about which professions are needed by the society and encouraging students to take such courses to the benefit of society. Scarcity of direction (or negligence in terms of giving accurate advice) results in students entering the fields that they themselves are not attracted to but merely join as they are the courses available. Such students may form negative views of themselves, and although female students may enter these fields only to find work (and not a specialisations they require or personally prefer), their choice may not result in employment due to oversupply or lack of suitable local work opportunities.
5. Better academic coordination. There is a necessity for more and improved coordination among Saudi universities in regard to the programmes available for women in order to avoid the unnecessary course duplication. There is a need to create a development plan for the workforce based on the scientific fundamentals and according to the actual need for these specialisations.

C. Unemployment of Saudi Women

Lack of available employment is one of the greatest factors that deter women from pursuing their education or lead them to discontinue their course. The restriction of employment to mainly such as fields as teaching leads to an increase in the number of unemployed women. Those already trained are unable to work due to a lack of positions for which they have been trained and for which educational institutions took so much time to prepare them. Those who are deterred from enrolling in the field or from continuing their studies in the area because of the excess of graduates then lack any educational qualifications, as they have been unable to enrol in any suitable alternative course.

Unemployment has increased, especially in the field of accountancy and computer science, because the jobs that are available in highly specific specialisations for which training is not generally available to women. For the small number of women who have been trained in the field, when an area become highly competitive or subject to a downturn or other pressure, in Saudi Arabia as elsewhere, men tend to be prioritised over women. This results in a job market that is closed to women. It also deprives them of the opportunity of being hired in the private sector.

The education available to women generally has been based on rules determining outcomes in specific specialisations that theoretically offer the impression that they are suitable for women by their nature. Hence women have traditionally been restricted to education and health. In fact, tens of thousands of women cannot enrol in university education institutions, nor can they look for jobs as these are rare and the women are not sufficiently qualified to apply. In addition, women who are unemployed due to the lack of available employment for women become liable to be subject to abject poverty, frustration and depression. Currently women are the main recipients of unemployment benefits, an indication of the extent of the problems related to the employment of women in the Kingdom.[90] The 'right to work' is a principal right for women, as provided in Article 11 of CEDAW:

> a) The right to work as an inalienable right of all human beings.
>
> b) The right to the *same employment opportunities*, including the application of the *same criteria for selection* in matters of employment.[91]

The State has already moved to allow teaching contracts of foreign teachers in the public sector to lapse, thus increasing the employment opportunities for women in the sector.[92] The policy of Saudisation is being consciously adopted to absorb more, young secondary school leavers and tertiary graduates into the workforce. Where the government cannot exert direct control in the private sector, other means have been adopted to encourage greater local employment.[93] With an estimated

---

90 It has been reported that women now are the largest proportion of beneficiaries of unemployment relief in Saudi Arabia with some 85 per cent being women: see *POMED Notes*, 'Saudi Arabia's Race against Time' (18 September 2012) http://pomed.org/blog/2012/09/pomed-notes-saudi-arabias-race-against-time.html. Low wages in the private sector are also reported to be an obstacle as well as less ability to influence policy in that area.

91 CEDAW art. 1(a, b) (emphasis added).

92 See www.tatweer.edu.sa/Ar/TatweerProjects/Pages/default.aspx.

93 This includes reportedly 'withholding foreign worker visas for companies who employ a high number of foreigners in the hopes of raising the percentage of Saudis employed in the private sector to between ten and 37-percent': See *POMED Notes*, above n90. Unfortunately the skill mix is not always a clear match, and the results are not as positive as anticipated. Lower public sector wages, poorer conditions and relatively high unemployment benefits also reduce uptake in the sector.

one million persons unemployed, the task is enormous.[94] To tackle this problem further, I have come up with the following suggestions:

1. A campaign needs to be adopted to satisfy the necessity of enhancing awareness of women's abilities and the contributions of working women to society and their families. Positive accounts of how working women should be shared, that tells of how they have been able to overcome social and economic difficulties, to make that contribution, and also demonstrate how they confronted challenges and faced them seriously.
2. The Ministry of Work, the Ministry of Education and the Department for the Establishment of Technical Training and Human Resources, together with businessmen, should make strategies for training for all qualifying unemployed persons and seek to bridge the gaps in order to help learning outcomes meet the needs of the job market. In addition, the Ministry of Finance, Ministry of Civil Services and other competent authorities must meet all needs of all sectors for overcoming the shortage of different jobs.
3. I also propose the creation of a fund to which all governmental authorities should contribute as well as the private sector and businessmen. The monies in this fund should be used for qualifying and training unemployed persons to meet the needs of the job market as is necessary. The fund would work towards ensuring the mix of trained personnel meets the demands of the job market, particularly as the policy of Saudisation takes place. This fund would be supervised by the Ministry of Work and the Ministry of Social Affairs and the Establishment of Technical Training and Human Resources.
4. Finally, I suggest creating a website for registration of the data of those who desire to be hired and their particular area/s of specialisation, and also data related to the needs of the competent authorities. The website must be updated daily in order to facilitate the applicants gaining access to the authorities that are in need of workers. This could occur under the supervision of the Ministry of Social Affairs and Human Resources.[95]

---

[94] See e.g. Angus McDowall, 'More Than 1 Million Saudis on Unemployment Benefit' (28 March 2012) www.reuters.com/article/2012/03/28/us-saudi-unemployment-subsidy-idUSBRE82R0L320120328.

[95] Ibid.

D. Driving

The obstacles facing women in all walks of life and educational fields in particular include transportation. Until recently, the Kingdom of Saudi Arabia had been the sole country in the world which prevented women from driving because of religious opinions or *fatwa* had been issued to deprive women of the opportunity to drive.[96] In addition, the Minister of the Interior has supported this decision, giving as his reason for the decision that the Saudi society is not ready at the current time. It has created controversy between groups who oppose or support the move.[97] This research neither supports the right of a woman to drive or desire to prevent her, but rather is concerned about the means of giving the woman her rights and maintaining her dignity where she is travelling for education or training or work.

Traffic jams in the Kingdom are one of various severe problems[98] which must be taken into consideration, as must the poor driving levels generally in the Kingdom[99] (and the resulting atrocious accident rate). This is a matter of concern when considering whether to decide that women should drive. In addition, an appropriate traffic system (that is, proper licensing and road laws) does not yet exist in Saudi Arabia as it does in advanced countries. The Kingdom lacks provisions in its penal codes which would impose sanctions on those who violated of women's rights in instances where women were disturbed or harassed while driving. This is something that could be addressed, though not all women

---

[96] The General Presidency of Scholarly Research and Ifta, Fatwas of Permanent Committee No. 6412. However, a new development has occurred. It was reported widely in September 2017 that the current Saudi King, Salman, had issued a decree giving women the right to drive for the first time from 2018. This would end a ban seen by human rights activists as an emblem of the conservative Saudi Arabia kingdom's repression of women. See 'Saudi Arabia to allow women to drive, under decree issued by King Salman' *ABC News*, 26 September 2017, available at www.abc.net.au/news/2017-09-27/saudi-king-issues-decree-allowing-women-to-drive/8991486.

[97] Ruth Pollard, 'Women Ready to be Saudi Arabia's New Driving Force' (18 June 2012) www.smh.com.au/world/women-ready-to-be-saudi-arabias-new-driving-force-20120617-20i76.html.

[98] '*Procedure for Obtaining Driving License in Saudi*' (17 June 2008) http://workinginsaudiarabia.blogspot.com.au/2008/06/procedure-for-obtaining-driving-license_17.html.

[99] Manal Soliman Fakeeh, *Saudization as a Solution for Unemployment; The Case of Jeddah Western Region* (PhD thesis, University of Glasgow Business School, 2009) 125, 129–30, 133.

actually want to drive, as has been shown in the interviews. Therefore a number of solutions need to be adopted that preserve a woman's dignity while giving her increased access to the transportation necessary for greater access to education and employment.

Over the last few years, the Saudi government has slowly taken a number of decisions concerning woman's education and employment in different fields and the extension of their activities in so many areas will create the need for greater access to transportation. Alternative solutions must be provided that facilitate the balance between women's rights to move and the need to prevent her from driving. These solutions include the following:

1. Compensation should be provided in the form of an allowance for women if they are students or employees for the financial costs of transportation.
2. Each university or company or ministry should provide minibuses for the women who work for them.
3. General means of transportation should be provided, such as buses for women or setting particular sections aside for women in such buses or similar transport. Such transportation must be an improvement on the existing services because these are not at the level needed even now.
4. A network of clean and air-conditioned trains inside towns should be provided.
5. Private companies should provide vehicles and buses for female employees.
6. Academic studies and strategies should be undertaken for reaching practical solutions for ensuring the rights of women in regard to movement generally, and meeting their transportation needs in a manner in keeping with their dignity.

E. Childcare Centres

The provision of childcare centres can have a great effect on women and the children and the society because they enable women to attend university and participate more widely and effectively in the workplace by relieving them of some of their caring responsibilities for the part of the day or evening while they work. Childcare centres also seek to develop the abilities of the children in the absence of mothers, and with trained staff and fully equipped facilities, they are preferable to leaving children with babysitters without education. However, women, either students or mothers, suffer from the scarcity of childcare centres, and they are sometimes forced to discontinue their education out of concern for their children. Most women face difficulties in balancing education and work with their concern for household affairs. The country decided in both the old and new Saudi Labor Law that:

> An employer who employs fifty working women [or] ... more shall provide them with [a] suitable place with [an] adequate number of nannies to look after the children under the age of six years, if the number of children reaches ten and above.[100]

This decree is clear and applied to each governmental and national establishment in regard to providing the care needed for the children. In fact, the decree has yet to be implemented as is the educational policy in the Kingdom of Saudi Arabia which provides encouragements in Articles 116 and 117 to establish preschools and kindergartens for the care of children. In addition, the competent authorities should plan for building preschools and kindergartens as well as their supervision by the competent bodies. Actually, the systems are largely inactive and the private sector has even fewer individuals who are interested in childcare provision. The effective experience that we have witnessed in advanced countries strongly encourages us to put into practice the existing laws which would support the spread of these centres across the Kingdom of Saudi Arabia, because these centres would have positive effects on women and children and society. Because childcare centres provide children with the educational and recreational environment required to develop their understanding and abilities, a woman can undertake and complete her study and ensure the care of her children by confidently using these centres for that care while she is studying. The society will benefit from these centres in other ways, as they will employ appropriately educated but hitherto unemployed women, thereby decreasing the rates of unemployment among women, which is currently adding significantly to the nation's budgets.[101] In respect to this, I suggest the following:

1. Execute orders and decisions issued for establishing preschools and childcare centres as well as following up the implementation of these decisions.

---

[100] Old Saudi Labor Law 1969 (Saudi Arabia) art. 158(1). New Saudi Labor Law 2005 (Saudi Arabia) art. 159(1).

[101] Women comprise some 85 per cent of unemployment relief beneficiaries in Saudi Arabia.

2. Declare clear plans for building childcare centres around Saudi Arabia.
3. Support the private sector in its efforts to compete in presenting services and establishing childcare centres as well as providing necessary facilities needed to establish these centres.
4. Refuse issuance of building permits for building these centres unless they comply with medical and health specifications and educational and social standards that will meet the goals of parents.
5. Develop regulations and systems for kindergartens and what this entails for technical and administrative organisations. Develop employment in the preschool environment as well as the environment of preschools by bringing experts in the field to prepare all that is needed for the delivery of education for children up to the age of four years, including setting conditions and assigning tasks for all childcare employees.
6. Benefit from the experiences of developed countries which have experience in that field as well as developing these experiences in a manner that is compliant with Saudi development and Saudi society.

F. Early Marriage

Early marriage is one of the problems suffered by the women who, despite a diversity of opinions relating to that issue, all agree that the marriage of minors to those who are aged 60 years or more is a violation of women's rights. In any case, 'early marriage' as intended in this research refers to the marriage of girls who are aged between 15 and 18, which prevents the women from pursuing their education. From my point of view, women should get married at an age suited to bearing the responsibility entailed by marriage and having the knowledge required to run a house holding and the ability to raise children and care for them. The age of 18 is the minimum age at which a woman can complete her secondary school education. From a statistical point of view, higher numbers of cases of divorce result in marriages where there the age of the couple are not equivalent or the woman is under the age of 18. This is because majority of women are not yet intellectually mature and have little or no ability or the skills required to shoulder the responsibility of the home and family. Article 1 of the Convention on the Rights of the Child also stipulates that:

> For the purposes of the present Convention, a child means every human being below the age of eighteen years unless under the law applicable to the child, majority is attained earlier.[102]

A woman at that age has more knowledge and education, as well as the physical and psychological maturity in order to be qualified for responsibility.

All countries decided to determine the marriage age in the light of the application of local and of international laws when they became signatories to and ratified international covenants, as referred to in Article 16 of CEDAW, which provides that:

> The betrothal and the marriage of a child shall have no legal effect, and all necessary action, including legislation, shall be taken to specify a minimum age for marriage and to make the registration of marriages in an official registry compulsory.[103]

Saudi Arabia is still examining an issuance decree determining age of marriage for both sexes. Although there have been promises over the last few years, the fulfilment of which both women and the society are waiting for, I suggest the following:

1. commission and submission of academic and scientific studies about the effects of early marriage so as to increase awareness of its dangers;
2. issuance of the law that prevents the marriage of minors under the age of 15 and provides for severe punishment for everyone who commits this action or is associated with its commission (that is, the relevant guardian);
3. acceleration of the issuance of the decree preventing the marriage under the age of 18 or 17; and
4. raising the awareness of the society of the importance of women's education before marriage, especially the importance of completing secondary school as a minimum.

G. Ignorance of Rights

Although national and international law guarantees women's rights, women are often ignorant of their rights and existing systems, which prevents them from demanding their rights. This brings them a great

---

[102] Convention on the Rights of the Child art. 1.

[103] CEDAW art. 16(2).

many problems, which represent daily concerns especially in the field of education and work.

Every individual, whether male or female, should be acquainted with the general principles of law for the protection of his/her rights. Knowledge of the laws issued are spread via mass media. Hence, ignorance of laws does not exempt the individual from legal responsibility. Thus every woman should be aware of the systems that organise her rights in all fields such as education, work and justice.

The main problem is ignorance of the law and lack of development of the legal culture. This knowledge is close to zero. Interviews showed that 90 per cent of women have no knowledge of CEDAW. The average Saudi woman does not know the mechanisms supporting women's rights and how women can obtain these rights. In addition, the women do not deal with the various systems because they lack the knowledge and/or ability to defend or demand their rights as decided by the law.

The most important causes beyond the immediate problems include the following:

- Dominance of habits and traditions inherited from the society: these prevent women from demanding their rights because they think that these traditions must be not be violated, even if they appear to contradict Islamic law.
- Scarcity of awareness in mass media: the viewers who watch the mass media feel that the issue of women's rights has been put aside.
- Weakness of women's nature if compared with that of men in some societies, because the guardians exploit the weakness of the women in order to prevent them from demanding their rights. In addition, some women prefer silence to demanding their rights, in order not to incur greater problems.

I therefore suggest the following to deal with the problem:

1. Make systematic and national regulations for women's rights in order that these may be a reference for governmental and national authorities in dealing with women's issues.
2. Create or nominate an effective mechanism for deciding women's rights to enable the women and each individual to perform the role assigned in life making.
3. Examine academic curricula and consider the addition of issues relating to the women in order to make them aware of their legislative rights. This is especially needed in the intermediate and

secondary syllabus, as is the teaching of compulsory law materials within university specialisations.

4. Increase awareness of women's rights by using visual and audio mass media and presenting special programmes about women on television channels and radio programmes to spread knowledge of the issues relating to women's affairs.
5. Create training courses in schools and training centres to spread knowledge of women's rights and methods of dealing with the problems facing them.

V. FINAL WORDS

It is clear that although progress has been achieved by Saudi women in the areas of education and work, there are some obstacles and difficulties that are faced by the women in these two areas. This requires a review of the philosophy and the objectives on which these two sectors are based as well as reviewing the systems and policies concerning the natural participation of women in the fields of education and work.

In summary, the average Saudi woman cannot obtain her rights in full in education and be promoted to higher positions in education unless great efforts are made in relation to the applicable systems and Saudi laws derived from the *Holy Qur'an* and the prophetic sayings, as well as application of international laws that are compliant with the Islamic laws.

My research has revealed the structural gaps in institutions concerning women's education which seem to be clear that this is one of the causes behind overcrowding in the job market. There is a necessity to review all philosophical and social basics and domestic laws relating to women's education in the Kingdom of Saudi Arabia. Its objectives need to be reviewed, and its suitability examined in regard to the modern changes which have changed each woman's vision of herself and society's vision of her. This, in turn, requires radical change in educational and vocational services, opening them to women in order to increase their opportunities and create future strategies for investment of feminist ability and power in economic and educational activities. This may be done on condition that the basics shall be changed to achieve the expectations of the women.

The activities of the main traditional roles of the women, namely in being a wife and a mother, are human powers that present positive returns for both society and the economy. The woman has the right to get work when she wants it. In fact, not all women are in need of work and women cannot work at all stages of their lives, but empowerment to choose and obtain suitable opportunities for the training and educational levels are the objectives of this research. It is difficult for this to be available without radical change in relation to visibility of women as productive human beings who have potential and educational abilities like men. This cannot be done without the government and the institutions that care for women's rights formulating and implementing policies and systems as well as appropriate programmes being applied in schools and universities and across mass media to help women change their perceptions of themselves as well as the attitudes of others towards them.

Societal change on a broader level is necessary for the broader implementation 'on the ground' of any policies and legislation that are enacted. Education and employment are inextricably intertwined, and must be mutually supportive for maximum benefit development in Saudi Arabia. Women's largely untapped potential has been revealed through education; it must not be allowed to languish for lack of employment. If employment requires a degree of extra training to suit it better to labour market demands, then such training must be offered, as outlined above. However, employment opportunities must not be denied on spurious rather than genuine religious grounds. Needless obstacles in education and employment must be removed. Means must be explored and adopted to ensure that women can make their contribution to the national economy and to their families, if they so desire, with neither women nor their families suffering. This study has suggested a number of ways in which this can be facilitated.

PART 6

COMMUNITY AND PUBLIC SPHERES

17. Progressive Islam in Europe: a critical analysis of the unique nature of Bosnia and Hercegovina's Islamic practice

Richard Burgess

I. INTRODUCTION

Among the explosion of emerging states in the post-communist era was Bosnia and Hercegovina. What made this State of particular significance within a European context was the absence of an allegiance to Christianity. Suddenly, the traditional religious uniformity across the continent had been broken. No longer were European Muslims simply a minority existing within established nation-states. They now were politically represented under the Republic of Bosnia and Hercegovina.

Historically, Islam had tended to be a private affair among Bosnians. Often conveniently defined as 'European Islam', it preaches the tolerance of Sufi mysticism in regards to religious pluralism and has had 150 years of co-existence within Christian or secular Western states. However, while the West struggled to come to terms with an Islamic territory contained by 'Christian Europe', the Islamic heartland of the Middle East sought to guide this emerging nation on its path towards a more traditional and conservative Islamic revival. Through military and financial aid, Saudi Arabia reconnected with its long lost brother-in-faith during the early 1990s Bosnian war, in turn introducing to the Balkans the Salafi approach to Islamic jurisprudence.

This Chapter will demonstrate that the state of Bosnia and Hercegovina has acquired a unique concept of Islam which is both compatible and sustainable within a Christian and laic Europe. Through an examination of Bosnia and Hercegovina's Islamic history, it will expound how the gradual osmosis of various religious traditions, accompanied by the continual reformation of Shari'ah law, has resulted in a confident, democratic nation guided by Islam. This will be contrasted to the Saudi Arabian sponsored Salafism in order to demonstrate the direction that Shari'ah has taken in this society. The result: a national community where (among other things) the social participation of women is expected and inter-faith dialogue is endorsed. While domestically serious tensions regarding national identity remain, the Bosnian model rests as an example as to how the faith may be practiced throughout Europe.

II. ISLAM IN THE BALKANS

Bosnia and Hercegovina is religiously incomparable to other European countries. Its Islamic presence is not a modern conception, a product of the increased movement and displacement of peoples during the twentieth century. Nor is it purely the remnant of the Ottoman frontier, a European window into Anatolian life. Undoubtedly, the late fourteenth century military incursions into the region, and resulting Ottoman occupation, play a vital role in the Bosniak[1] genesis. Yet its true origin is far more subtle, and its composition far more complex. Islam in this Balkan state is the product of a rich and turbulent 500-year history characterised by invasion, isolation and assimilation.

Rather than 'by the sword', this Semetic faith began first to filter through to the Balkan population via roaming spiritual leaders (*shaykhs*) who preached the Sufi Islamic philosophy.[2] Sufism is a unique order within Islam. It is considered a mystical dimension of the faith which focuses on the power of meditation and asceticism. Sufis seeks the internal (*hatin*) view of Islam while contemplating the concealed mystery of the Qur'an. The combination of these elements endeavours to achieve inspiration from a divine perspective.[3] This tends to draw religion into the introspective private sphere and, as a result, Sufism maintains a prominent following throughout secular countries such as America and Australia.[4]

Upon the arrival of the Turkish authorities to the region, Sufi missionaries set about establishing a permanent religious presence through the

---

1 The term 'Bosniak' (Bošnjak) is used to refer to Bosnian Muslims and is not to be confused with the term 'Bosnian', which is used to describe all inhabitants of Bosnia and Hercegovina.

2 The documentation and preservation of shines to the thirteenth-century Sufi saint Sari Saltik throughout Bosnia, Romania, Macedonia and Albania stand testament to this past.

3 John Hinnells and Jamal Malik, *Sufism in the West* (New York: Routledge Press 2006) 3.

4 Celia A. Genn, 'The Development of a Modern Western Sufism' in Julia Day Howell and Martin van Bruinessen (eds), *Sufism and the 'Modern' in Islam* (London: I. B. Tauris 2007) 257.

construction and legacy of hospices and religious lodges (*tekkes*).[5] Reports of the condemnation of Sufi practice by Serb, Greek and Sunni Islamic institutions during the late nineteenth century show that this faith continued to exist throughout the Ottoman period in parts of the population.[6] Its impact is not inconspicuous. Sufism has been attributed with bridging many of the initial gaps between Christianity and Islam while permitting the adoption of local beliefs into the theology. As a package, this facilitated Islamic conversions and, barring recent complications, religious tolerance. In addition to the Sufis, Shi'a refugees are also known to have sought sanctity within Eastern Europe during this period; their legacy is confirmed through Persian practices[7] which have today filtered into the Bosniak tradition. This demonstrates that, with the official arrival of Islam through Ottoman forces in 1463, this region became a religious 'mosaic rather than monolith',[8] already a unique representation of merging Islamic faith and ideals.

Meanwhile, under the supervision of the Ottoman Empire from the fifteenth century, the majority of Bosnia's Islamic population subscribed to the Hanafi School of jurisprudence.[9] Developed by Abu Hanifa during the early to mid-eighth century, this school fervently supports the concept of independent reasoning (*ijtihad*) in the revealing of Shari'ah law.[10] The fact that this is achieved through the use of both personal judgement (*ra'y*) and analogy (*qiyas*) means that it shares many similarities with the British common law system: the two relying on highly educated judges to interpret the legislation and use analogy, reasoning and legal precedent to decide new cases before them. While the element of individuality in decision making has sometimes come at the cost of uniformity (as those in common law countries will recognise), this school of jurisprudence has contributed to the progressive development of Shari'ah in the various

---

5 Ines Aščerić-Todd, *Dervishes and Islam in Bosnia: Sufi Dimensions to the Formation of Bosnian Muslim Society* (Leiden: Brill 2015) 66.

6 Isa Blumi, 'Political Islam among the Albanians: Are the Taliban coming to the Balkans?' (Policy Research Paper No. 2, *Kosovar Institute for Policy Research and Development*, June 2005) 4.

7 For example, the celebration of the coming of spring (Sultan Nevruz).

8 Harun Karčić, 'Islamic Revival in Post-Socialist Bosnia and Herzegovina: International Actors and Activities' (2010) 30.4 *Journal of Muslim Minority Affairs* 519, 522.

9 Ibid.

10 Irshad Abdal-Haqq, 'Islamic Law: An overview of its origins and elements' (2002) 7 *Journal of Islamic Law and Culture* 27, 69.

situations that the expanding Ottomans encountered.[11] Bosnia and Turkey, two countries potentially vying for European Union membership, both continue this progressive practice today.

Nevertheless, the Islamic development of Bosnia and Hercegovina had its limits under Ottoman rule. For one, local inhabitants were afforded limited autonomy in respects to the interpretation and a practice of Islam through *ijtihad*; this religious science was instead confined to Istanbul, 620 miles (1,000 km) away.[12] Surprisingly, the acquisition of the Balkans by the Catholic Habsburg Empire in 1878 saw Bosniaks assume a greater control over religious institutions through the platform of the Islamic Community (*Islamska zajednica*). Led by the chief cleric (*re'is ul-ulema*), this organisation, under the tutelage of the Hapsburgs, established the first exclusively Balkan religious hierarchy, education institution and system of pious endowments (*waqf*).[13] This cultural and religious renaissance continued through the redevelopment of Shari'ah courts and the foundation of the Mekteb-i Nuwwab School in Sarajevo: the former incorporated into the Hapsburg state judiciary for handling personal matters such as marriage and inheritance; the latter was to provide modern education for future Shari'ah judges in Bosnia.[14] While discontent endured, particularly in regards to the appointment of Islamic religious posts by the Catholic monarchy, any such grievances were comparatively insignificant to those in the years to come.

Bosnia's 1918 absorption into the Kingdom of Serbs, Croats and Slovenes saw religious control wrested from the Islamic Community by the King, who assumed control of all religious affairs. Then, with the advent of communism following World War II, Shari'ah courts were abolished, elementary religious schools were closed, *waqf* was nationalised and the veils worn by Muslim women forbidden.[15] Consequently, the

---

[11] Etim Okin, 'The sources and schools of Islamic jurisprudence' (2012) 3.3 *American Journal of Social and Management Sciences* 106.

[12] Juan Carlos Antúnez, *Wahhabism in Bosnia-Herzegovina* (Bosnian Institute, 16 September 2008).

[13] Ina Merdjanova, *Rediscovering the Umma: Muslims in the Balkans between Nationalism and Transnationalism* (New York: Oxford University Press 2013) 30.

[14] Fikret Karčić, *From Law to Ethics: The Process of Modernization and Reinterpreting the Shari'a in Bosnia* (Lecture Paper, Bosnischer Islam fur Europa, Stuttgart-Hohenheim, Akademie der Diözese Rottenburg-Stuttgart, 16–17 November 2007) 2.

[15] Karčić, above n8, 522; Merdjanova, above n13, 31.

religion went underground and, without the courts, Shari'ah law transformed into a code of religious and ethical norms in an endeavour to remain relevant to the Bosniak population.[16]

As a consequence of the miscellany of religions and cultures prevalent in the Yugoslav state, reform through the form of *ijtihad* re-emerged in Bosnia. One of the initial proponents, Ibrahim Fejić in his work *Nešto o šerijatu* (A few words about Shari'ah) argued for a Bosnian reinterpretation of Shari'ah principles to allow, among other things, modern banking methods. He believed that the ultimate purpose of Shari'ah was to regulate human relations and needs. The conclusion stood, therefore, that when these relations and needs changed, the rules should likewise adapt.[17] This underlying principle would prove to be a fundamental difference between the Islam of Bosnia and the traditional approach promoted by Middle Eastern institutions during the 1990s.

Following on from Fejić, the 1960s saw imam Husein effendi Djozo publish *fatwas* under the title 'Pitanja i odgovori' (Questions and Answers) to provide further guidance to his Bosnian fellowship. His *fatwas* related to religious obligations such as prayer times, dietary issues and financial donations, all of which promoted a greater freedom of exercising religious obligations within the confines of Yugoslavia.[18] The next 20 years also saw the introduction of a constitution for the revived Islamic Community, the opening of the Faculty of Islamic Studies, and an increase in the dissemination of Islamic literature by the El-Kalem publishing house. However, in spite of these reforms, Islamic culture began to stagnate. The years of living underground had taken their toll on the education of the next generation of Islamic scholars. Few were religiously equipped to lead Bosnia towards the twenty first century.

This scenario stands as a stark warning. The institutionalisation of religious education for Islamic minorities within the European nation-state is essential in ensuring that the conditions and pressures of Western society are appropriately addressed through *ijtihad* and *fatwas*. An un-educated population is open to the injection of conservative doctrines which vehemently oppose many modern practices as sinful vices. Were Bosnia and Hercegovina to have suffered through 20 more years of

---

16 Karčić, above n14, 3.

17 Ibid., 5.

18 Jamal Malik, 'Muslims in the West – A Muslim "Diaspora"?' in Stefan Schreiner, *Religion and Secular State. Role and Meaning of Religion in a Secular Society from Jewish, Christian, and Muslim Perspectives* (Zurich: European Abrahamic Forum 2008) 149. Also see Karčić, above n14, 6.

religious isolation, the arrival of Saudi Arabian academics might have had more of a contagious and permanent impact.

III. THE ARRIVAL OF SALAFISM

It has been said that the Bosniak tragedy of the 1990s lies in the fact that they were too Muslim for the West and not Muslim enough for the Islamic world.[19] Surfacing amongst the crumbling communist chaos, much of the population had, over the course of Tito's reign, come to see their religion more like an ethnicity, something which separated them from the Serbs, Slovenes and Croats. They would have felt more at home in the secular societies of Western Europe as opposed to the Islamic Middle East, having spent over 100 years mixing with European institutions. Yet the West continued to regard these peoples' plight with suspicion. The delay in international intervention in their ethnic-religious civil war, between March 1992 and December 1995, reinforced this feeling of abandonment by Europe. With its hand forced, Bosnia and Hercegovina opened up to a new wave of assistance.

While Turkey preferred to play a financial footnote in the affair of its former province, support for Bosnia and Hercegovina came willingly from the Middle East in the form of troops and aid. Men like Khalid Suliman al-Jhari became involved when they 'saw footage of the Bosnian war and felt impelled to help [their] fellow Muslims'.[20] However, the troops, known as the *mujahidin*, found the post-socialist Bosnian community to be clasping on to un-Islamic practices brought about following decades of repressive rule. With little direction in their Islamic faith, there are reports that the ordinary Bosniak had begun to smoke, drink and even consume pork.[21] This was in stark contrast to the faith that the *mujahidin* had nurtured in their homelands and consequently they began to encourage what they termed the country's 're-Islamisation'. In fact, a report from the Bosnian Army Centre for Analytics and Security stated that the 'El-Mujahid commanders and soldiers [were] showing less interest in combat but instead increased their activity in persuading

---

19 Aydin Babuna, 'National Identity, Islam and Politics in Post-Communist Bosnia-Hercegovina' (2005) 39.4 *East European Quarterly* 405, 412.

20 David Aaronovitch, 'Remember Bosnia, seedbed of radical Islam: The people of Syria wonder why the West will not help. Twenty years ago, jihadis stepped into a similar breach' *The Times* (31 May 2012).

21 Kenneth Morrison, *Wahhabism in the Balkans* (Defence Academy of the United Kingdom: Advanced Research and Assessment Group, February 2008) 4.

Bosnian Muslims in central Bosnia to practice radical Islam'.[22] Originally this met staunch opposition within the Balkan community. However, the poor economic and unemployment situation following the war seems to have promoted some disenfranchised sections towards the more conservative theology.[23]

In addition to the presence of the *mujahidin*, re-Islamisation came in the form of financial aid. Saudi Arabia, in particular, offered governmental support through the Saudi High Committee for Assistance to Bosnia and Hercegovina.[24] This assistance included the translation and dissemination of Islamic texts and scholarships to study at Saudi Arabian universities. Through both these avenues the traditional Salafism fostered in the Middle East found its way into Eastern Europe. With Islamic institutions in the doldrums following the war of succession, graduates of Middle Eastern universities, who promoted the Salafi views of conservatism and a discontinuity with modern Islamic developments, were accepted into the Bosniak community as a beacon around which to found the revival of Balkan Islam.[25]

Salafism is a movement within Sunni Islam initiated by Muhammad ibn Abd al-Wahhab and developed in the mid to late nineteenth century by intellectuals at the al-Azhar University in Egypt.[26] It is closely associated with the Hanbali Madhhab and based upon patriarchal and exclusionary foundations.[27] Followers of Salafism blame the demise of the Islamic Empire throughout the eighteenth and nineteenth centuries on innovations within the faith (*bidah*), a result of the new technological and cultural frontiers encountered by the Ottomans and Western-colonised Islamic communities. To counter this, Salafism rejects many of the rational and mystic concepts of Islamic religion and aims to realise the

---

[22] Karčić, above n8, 526. See also Harun Karčić, 'Globalisation and Islam in Bosnia: Foreign Influences and their Effects' (2010) 11.2 *Totalitarian Movement and Political Religions* 151, 157.

[23] Babuna, above n19, 419.

[24] Karčić, above n22, 156.

[25] Karčić, above n14, 9.

[26] There is great debate surrounding the use of the titles Salafism and Wahhabism. While both are often used synonymously, various global communities argue that certain stigmas are attached to either term. For simplicity's sake, the term Wahhabism, often championed by the West and progressive Muslims to refer to this ideology, will be replaced uniformly in this paper with the term Salafism.

[27] Adis Duderija, 'Islamic Groups and Their World-views and Identities: Neo-traditional Salafis and Progressive Muslims' (2007) 21.4 *Arab Law Quarterly* 341, 350.

return to the 'essential values' of the faith as they were practiced originally by the Prophet and the *al-salaf al-salih*, or righteous predecessors (*Salaf*). While the Salafi movement is in no means monolithic, generally participants retain a romanticised vision of life in the seventh- and eighth-century Arabian Peninsula of which they aspire to somewhat recreate through very literal interpretations of the Qur'an and the Sunnah.[28] Professor Adis Duderija explains that adherents to Salafism consider revelation to be the 'first source of human knowledge and the indisputable complete final source in which human beings are torn between two extremes, command and prohibition'.[29] This excludes the rational approach of the Hanafi School and will be shown below to create friction between the distinct communities within Bosnia and Hercegovina. As mentioned, much of the Salafi view arose in a response to liberating Muslim communities from Western colonialism or intervention and the un-Islamic practices that they had subsequently acquired.[30] This made Bosnia, which has existed now for over a century outside the guidance of the Ottoman Islamic Empire, a prime target for Salafi preachers.

IV. INTRA-RELIGIOUS RELATIONS

There remain several Salafi communities in Bosnia and Hercegovina, particularly around the north-eastern rural regions of Gornja Maoca and Bocinja. These communities are known not to adhere to the domestic legislature and secular constitution,[31] often declaring that their villages are governed by their own Shari'ah law. Under this localised legal system, veils and headscarves are compulsory, men are separated from women (women are forbidden from working if it means mingling with men), and the 'lewd temptations' of Western society are to be avoided.[32] This has encouraged the destruction of shops which sold alcohol or

---

[28] Karčić, above n8, 525.

[29] Duderija, above n27, 351.

[30] Ibid., 348.

[31] Zlatan Music, *Encountering the Wahhabi Movement in Bosnia: The Benefits of Social Network Analysis in Intelligence Management and Police Harmonization* (Thesis for a Masters of Arts in Public Policy, Central European University Budapest, 2012) 12.

[32] Gyorgy Lederer, 'Islam in East Europe' (2001) 20.1 *Central Asian Survey* 5, 13.

pornography, the harassing of men who failed to grow beards and of women who refused to meet the Salafi social expectations.

While the resurgent mainstream Islam of Bosnia and Hercegovina shares Salafism's disapproval of some of these 'lewd' practices, the tolerance indoctrinated by both the Sufi and years under Western leadership has ensured a more moderate and restrained approach. Up until recently, this has been led by the now retired *re'is ul-ulema*, Mustafa Cerić. During his time as *re'is*, Cerić's primary focus had been on returning the post-socialist Bosnian population back to their religious roots. He has stressed that:

> [a] Boshnyak without Islam would be 'a spiritually illegitimate child' and without Bosnia would be 'a physically illegitimate child'. Consequently he must have his mother and father: his father is Islam, his mother is Bosnia, and he has been indolent to his parents so far.[33]

This demonstrates an acceptance of the prior half-hearted practice of their faith as pointed out by the *mujahidin* in the 1990s. However, while appreciating the assistance of the Saudis, Cerić credits both the rationality of Maturidi's theology (*kalam*)[34] and the practicality of the Hanafi jurisprudence (*fiqh*) with the Islamic reformation in Bosnia.[35] Both of these doctrines were instead imported during the Ottoman occupation and highlight a fortitude to continue to interact with the West rather than adhere to the Salafi conservativism. This emphasis of rationality and practicality is highlighted by the Gazi Husrev-bey madrasa in Sarajevo. The motto of this school is that students should learn 'all that is required by time and place'.[36] Established in the sixteenth century, Cerić believes that throughout all of the challenges encountered by his homeland, this motto has ensured Islam's compatibility in each and every scenario. It

---

[33] E. F. Focho, 'Exclusive interview with Reis-ul-Ulema Professor Dr Mustafa Ef. Ceric', *Gazi Husrev Beg*. (Magazine of the Bosnian Islamic Culture Study Group, Kuala Lumpur—English version, 1994).

[34] Maturidism is considered to be a key variation of Islamic theology in Sunni Islam focused on deriving the existence of God through reason alone. Established in the tenth century by Abu Mansur al-Maturidi, it was overwhelmingly accepted by the Turkish tribes who eventually introduced it to the Balkans.

[35] Mustafa Cerić, 'History of the Institutionalized Training of Imams in Bosnia-Herzegovina' in Willem Drees and Pieter Sjoerd van Koningsveld, *Study of Religion and the Training of Muslim Clergy in Europe: Academic and Religious Freedom in the 21st Century* (Leiden: Leiden University Press 2008) 285.

[36] Ibid.

echoes the twentieth-century reform propagated by Fejić regarding the adaption of Shari'ah rules to changing circumstances.

Known for adopting an Islamic realist approach, Cerić has identified that a policy of Islamic pluralism is an essential safeguard against future atrocities, such as genocide, which have historically plagued this region. Accompanying this policy, he calls for an inclusive theological approach whereby no religious community has the monopoly of the 'Truth'.[37] This course of action is displayed through the Fatwa Council ('Vijeće za Fetve') of Bosnia and Hercegovina.[38] The Council endeavours to be inclusive of all Sunni schools of thought (*madhhabs*), except in respect to devotional matters, where the Hanafi school will be given precedence.[39] The benefits for pursuing the Hanafi course within Europe have been explained above. However, this acknowledgement by the Council that there is no 'one truth' is a significant step forward towards an inclusive Islamic society.

Uncertainty remains in Bosnia regarding the Salafi influence. Generally, Bosniaks finds this conservative approach confronting and a slight against their more liberal European culture and identity. They view Salafism as a form of 'Arab' or 'desert' Islam – an extension of Arabian culture, which has no place in the Balkans. A popular Bosnian phrase emphasises this point of view: 'a palm tree cannot grow in Bosnia any more than a plum tree can in Arabia.'[40] Rešid Hafizović, a professor of Islamic sciences in Sarajevo, has gone so far as to describe Salafism as 'a potentially fatal virus' for Bosnian Islam.[41] However, one must caution against being drawn in by unfounded paranoia and the West's generic fear and association of Salafism with terrorism. There are followers of the Salafi school who defend their ability to cooperate with the larger Islamic community if such interaction will benefit Islam and Muslims in general.

---

[37] Simonetta Calderini, 'Islam and Diversity: Alternative Voices within Contemporary Islam' (2006) 89.1021 *New Blackfriars* 324, 335.

[38] 'Pravila o radu Vijeća za Fetve-Fetve-i-Medžlis u Bosni i Hercegovini', (2005) 3.4 *Glasnik*, 415.

[39] Harun Karčić, 'Applying Islamic Norms in Europe: Is Bosnia a good example?' (Lecture Paper, Bosnischer Islam fur Europa, Stuttgart-Hohenheim, Akademie der Diözese Rottenburg-Stuttgart, 15–16 November 2013).

[40] Andreja Mesarič, 'Muslim Women's Dress Practices in Bosnia-Herzegovina: Localizing Islam through Everyday Lived Practice', in Arolda Elbasani and Olivier Roy, *The Revival of Islam in the Balkans: From Identity to Religiosity* (New York: Palgrave Macmillan 2015) 109.

[41] Nidzara Ahmetasevic, *Insight: Emissaries of militant Islam make headway in Bosnia* (The Sofia Echo, Bulgaria, 9 April 2007).

Semir Imamović is one such Salafi representative. He openly encourages the need for dialogue between Islamic scholars and religious leaders of other faiths. Semir believes that religious tolerance is rooted in the Qur'an and Sunnah and has previously published *fatwas* issued by the European Council for Fatwas and Research in Salafi magazines.[42] He has also openly outlined arguments for Salafis to engage with Bosnian politics, to vote and to take part in elections.[43] In the wake of renewed Islamic radicalisation, these messages of integration and cooperation are particularly important. Only recently, an informal leader of the Salafi community in Bosnia, Husein Bilal Bosnić was sentenced to seven years in prison for public incitement of terrorist activities and recruitment of terrorists for Daesh. Further, around 150 Bosnians are confirmed to have left to fight in Syria since 2013. The international attention that this information attracts has only intensified the desire of some Bosnians to see the 'foreign' Salafis relocated. Yet the reality is that the vast majority with Salafist beliefs in Bosnia are locals to the region, often war veterans who fought alongside the *mujahidin*.[44] This is not something which the Balkans can escape.

Through his time as a leader of the Bosnia and Hercegovinan Islamic Community, Mustafa Cerić had gathered around him not only the traditional Bosnian Muslim believers but also Salafi reformists who wanted to distance themselves from their more radical brethren.[45] In a 2006 interview, Cerić described the current Salafi paranoia to that of the seventeenth century Salem witch hunts or McCarthy's communist scare of the 1950s.[46] He argued that the West has grouped any concept of Islam that they consider extremist under the 'Salafi' banner and, in doing so, reject the beneficial contribution of people such as Imamović. However,

---

[42] Sunnah as reported by Al-Khatib: 'Whoever hurts a non-Muslim person under protection, I am his adversary, and I shall be an adversary to him on the Day of Resurrection.'

[43] Juan Carlos Antúnez, *Wahhabism in Bosnia-Herzegovina* (Bosnian Institute, 16 September 2008).

[44] Andreja Mesarič, 'Muslim Women's Dress Practices in Bosnia-Herzegovina: Localizing Islam through Everyday Lived Practice', in Arolda Elbasani and Oliver Roy, *The Revival of Islam in the Balkans: From Identity to Religiosity* (New York: Palgrave Macmillan 2015) 107.

[45] Juan Carlos Antúnez, *Wahhabism in Bosnia-Herzegovina* (Bosnian Institute, 16 September 2008).

[46] Orahovac Luckin, 'Islamic leader believes Wahhabism "problem" in Bosnia is exaggerated' (BBC Monitoring European, London, 30 December 2006).

he does counsel against leaving these isolated communities to their own devices.

> Unfortunately, we have individuals disturbing us with their attitude toward our Bosnian tradition. Furthermore, there are those who are in the area of takfir (disparaging others in faith) and hijrah (isolation), meaning that they are exclusivist in religion and inaccessible in communication. We must put an end to such practice.[47]

Cerić requests that Salafi followers within the Balkans respect the Bosnian principles of co-existence and tolerance and condemns the Salafi promotion of *takfir* and *hijrah*. In his words, '[n]o-one has the right to play with what the Bosnian Muslims have for centuries been building in patience and dedication in order to stay and survive in this part of the world'.[48] This approach by Cerić equally applies beyond the Balkans. It presents an important unifying message to the broader Islamic community, while encouraging those Muslims living within Western societies to engage rather than reject. It sets an example for all religious and political leaders to interact and cooperate with non-violent conservatives so as to encourage integration.[49] To this end, the prominent Islamic American author and journalist Stephen Suleyman Schwartz has issued a timely reminder: while it is true that a Salafist can be an Islamic 'extremist' or 'fundamentalist', the reciprocal association cannot be freely made since Islamic fundamentalism is not homogenous.[50] Fear and reactions based on unfounded categorisations are sure to hurt and ostracise any minority to which they are directed.

V. WOMEN AND ISLAM IN BOSNIA-HERCEGOVINIAN SOCIETY

One issue that has been particularly polarising between the Salafi and progressive Bosniaks is the status of woman and their position in society with regards to Shari'ah law. Janet Afary considers that this is a common disparity between many of the schools of jurisprudence as women play 'a

---

[47] Ibid.

[48] Ibid.

[49] International Crisis Group: working to prevent conflict worldwide, *Bosnia's Dangerous Tango: Islam and Nationalism* (Europe Briefing No. 70, 26 February 2013).

[50] Stephen Schwartz, *The Two Faces of Islam: The House of Saud from Tradition to Terror* (New York: Random House 2002) 131–4.

vital role in the (re)-construction of Muslim religio-cultural identity'.[51] It is therefore an appropriate litmus test in gauging the nature of Islam in the Balkans. Unfortunately there continues to be reports of harassment and abuse of women within the rural Salafi communities.[52] Salafism considers the female body as inherently moral and socially corrupting. On account of this, it imposes a number of rules and regulations on women such as the wearing of the niqab, the seclusion of women and the segregation of the sexes (as mentioned above).[53] In relation to the niqab, there are several verses in the Qur'an and Sunnah from which the Salafi draw their position. One such example is in the Súra Núr which states that women 'should not display their beauty and ornaments except what (must ordinarily) appear thereof; that they should draw their veils over their bosoms and not display their beauty except to their [male relatives]'. Some conservative Muslims, including the Salafi, argue that the message conveyed by verses such as this is one of avoiding temptation. They consider the face to be the ultimate source of male temptation and therefore the first body part that must be hidden.[54] Consequently, this understanding finds the onus in temptation resting predominantly on the woman.

Bosnia and Hercegovina's Muslim community maintains that the traditional Islamic perception of female gender and sexuality is socio-culturally contingent.[55] Thus, they reject the classical view of feminine sexuality and moral corruptibility. Rather, they believe that the verse of the Súra Núr states only that the bosom must be covered and that 'what must ordinarily appear' refers to the face and hands.[56] Based on this interpretation, Bosnians argue that the traditional concept of complete covering relates instead to the cultural and patriarchal nature of the ancient Arabic communities. This consequently has no traditional basis in Bosnian Islam and is considered inappropriate in the south-eastern European climate. Further, it may not fulfil the desired cultural intention, as wearing the niqab in the Balkans attracts more attention than it deflects. Rather, these moderates regard modesty as the key message that

---

[51] Duderija, above n27, 360–1.

[52] Kenneth Morrison, *Wahhabism in the Balkans* (Defence Academy of the United Kingdom: Advanced Research and Assessment Group, February 2008) 6.

[53] Duderija, above n27, 361.

[54] Ann Black, Hossein Esmaeili and Nadirsyah Hosen, *Modern Perspectives on Islamic Law* (Cheltenham: Edward Elgar Publishing 2013) 356.

[55] Ibid.

[56] Ibid.

Allah wished to convey. This is something which must be adhered to by all, irrespective of gender.

Amra Babić's election as mayor of the small town of Visoko in 2012 made her perhaps the first European mayor to wear the hijab. This raised the ire of conservative adherents to Islam who consider the participation of women in the public sphere as resentful, provocative and offensive. The verse '[a]nd stay in your houses'[57] is but one example of evidence on which these conservatives rely. However, most Bosniaks are unconvinced. They point to the fact that women led a very active social life during the early Muslim community in Medina, frequently appearing in public and attending the mosque. Their unwavering insistence on female social involvement is (like many things) tied to the Bosniak past, where under Tito's administration women were given complete civil and political rights as well as access to Islamic educational institutions (*madrasas*) and prominent leadership positions.[58] In evidence of their social commitment to this cause, the Bosnia and Hercegovinian government passed a law in 2001 requiring 33 per cent of election candidates to be female.[59] In Bosnia, women are considered autonomous beings with an equal standing to men. The religious identity of Bosniak women is something they obtain themselves through *taqwa* (consciousness of God) and not through the obedience of their male counterparts.[60] This aligns with the contemporary push for greater equality between genders in all facets of life.

The media surrounding Amra Babić's rise to power has provided a rare insight into the position of women in Bosnian society. Most of all, it has begun to challenge the perception that the veil is a repressive practice that is incompatible with moderate Islam. Many Bosnian Muslims contend that the reintroduction of the veil after its prohibition under Tito

---

57 Qur'an 33:33.

58 Catharina Raudvere, 'Textual and Ritual Command: Muslim Women as Keepers and Transmitters of Interpretive Domains in Contemporary Bosnia and Herzegovina' in Masooda Bano and Hilary Kalmbach, *Women, Leadership and Mosques: Changes in Contemporary Islamic Authority* (Leiden: Brill 2012) 260.

59 Drude Dajlerup, 'Increasing Women's Political Representation: New Trends in Gender Quotas' in Julie Ballington and Azza Karam, *Women in Parliament: Beyond Numbers* (Stockholm: International Institute for Democracy and Electoral Assistance 2005), 146.

60 Duderija, above n27, 362.

represents a resurgence of moderate religious practice as a counterbalance to the conservative forms applied by the rural Salafi.[61] While the majority of Muslim women continue not to wear the veil regularly, some have adopted it as a means of openly professing their faith. However, it remains an individual choice. An attempt by the Islamic Community to implement a dress code in its offices requiring women to cover their hair and body except for the face, hands and feet was met with opposition by many female employees. Consequently, the community has not vehemently stood by its religious policy, perhaps conceding that Islam must find its place in Bosnia's emerging cultural identity.[62] Yet the demise of some traditional Islamic practices does not of itself represent an apostate society. The numerous Bosnian language periodicals and websites, which distribute *fatwas* and religious opinions to the Balkan community, demonstrate that Shari'ah continues to have relevance for Muslims living in a secular state. As under Socialism, Shari'ah endures as an ethical code of behaviour for the Bosniaks, while also acting as a set of criteria for the evaluation of secular laws and dominant social principles.[63] The absence of Shari'ah courts to enforce religious rules has not prevented Muslim citizens from observing an underlying ethical and religious code.

Marriage is an exquisite example of this. While Bosnian law does not allow for a Shari'ah marriage by itself to be valid, it does provide that religious marriages can be conducted after the civil marriage. The fact that many couples are returning to this practice is an evident illustration of how Shari'ah law may exist alongside democratic and secular institutions. Duderija writes that this progressive Islam is difficult to characterise: 'it is not a school of thought as it is more than a systematic theory of interpretation of the entire Muslim law, theology, ethics, and politics. It is at best a practice, a package of loyalties and commitments, a work in progress.'[64] Based on this synopsis, progressive Islam is a living religion. It is capable of cohabiting with secular institutions while continuing to evolve through study, debate and social change.

---

[61] Michael Birnbaum, 'Rise of Bosnian Mayor with a Head Scarf Challenging Assumptions about Islam' *Washington Post* (9 March 2013).

[62] Ahmet Alibašić, 'Bosnia and Herzegovina', in Jocelyne Cesari, *The Oxford Handbook of European Islam* (New York: Oxford University Press 2014) 456.

[63] Fikret Karčić, *Main Trends in the Interpretation of the Shari'a in Bosnia and Herzegovina 2000–05* (Copenhagen University Islam Lecture Series, 15 September 2010) 7.

[64] Duderija, above n27, 344.

The broader issue of marriage is also a subject of debate in Bosnia and Hercegovina. At the end of the socialist reign and revival of religion, over 25 per cent of all marriages in Bosnia were between mixed ethnicities, and therefore mixed faiths. A number of senior leaders spoke out as representatives of the Islamic Community against this practice, condemning it as a 'betrayal of one's faith and culture'.[65] This argument has a religious grounding. In Islam, it is generally agreed that a Muslim woman is prohibited from marrying a non-Muslim man. The basis for this is the *Súra Baqarah*, which states 'nor marry (your girls) to unbelievers until they believe'.[66] While some adherents consider men to equally be bound by this condition, other verses in the Qur'an are often thought to permit men to marry from among the 'People of the Book'.[67] Children are put forward as the primary justification for this gender inequity. Since, under Islamic law, the children of an interfaith marriage will be Muslim, it has traditionally been thought that a Muslim woman is not individually equipped to raise them in accordance with her faith.[68]

Similarly to discussion on the veil, some Bosniaks consider that the above Qur'anic passage must be read in light of its historical context. It was developed at a time when the survival of Islam was rightly feared and when women did not enjoy the same freedom of self-determination as they do in Bosnia and Hercegovina today. This explains the difference in male and female obligations; historically a man could simply forbid his wife from performing her religious duties. In current Bosnian society, where freedom of religion is expressly protected in the Constitution, a woman has the opportunity to carry out her religious duties irrespective of marriage.[69] That is not to say that interfaith marriages are common within Bosnia, only that the rationale for not doing so may differ to that traditionally preached. Many Bosnians point instead to past and present ethnic tensions and family expectations as reasons for maintaining matrimony between those of the same faith.[70]

---

[65] Merdjanova, above n13, 88.

[66] Qur'an 2:221.

[67] See Qur'an 5:5. In addition, the Prophet Muhammad is believed to have had wives of both Christian and Jewish faiths.

[68] Ann Black, Hossein Esmaeili and Nadirsyah Hosen, *Modern Perspectives on Islamic Law* (Cheltenham: Edward Elgar Publishing 2013) 113.

[69] Edien Bartels and Mieke van Dijk, '"European Islam" in Practice – in the Bosnian City of Sarajevo' (2012) 32.4 *Journal of Muslim Minority Affairs* 467, 476–7.

[70] Ibid., 476.

Whether or not Bosniak women choose to marry within their faith, more and more have the opportunity and capacity to provide spiritual instruction to their children. Today, Bosniak women are exposed to religious education through the *madrasas* (which operate very similar to a private high school supervised by the Ministry of Education). As with many of the unique aspects of Bosnian religion, this theological empowerment stems back to the rights obtained during the socialist years.[71] However, in spite of this exposure, few female graduates of the *madrasas* have gone on to higher religious education at the Faculty of Islamic Sciences in Sarajevo. Instead, these educated women mostly gravitate towards roles in the schooling system or small associations and networks.[72]

This observation is not meant to demean or devalue the importance of Bosnian women in these occupations. The fact that women can interpret the Qur'an and take theological stands is a recent and commendable step forward. However, by not advancing towards higher education, women do not attain the influential roles and prominence in which to make their voice publicly heard (of course there is a strong argument that women would not receive these opportunities irrespective of their training). On this basis, Catharina Raudvere notes that '[i]f female religious leadership (or management of activities) is defined in terms of women being in charge of formal prayer, preaching or executing public Qur'an exegesis, it will only be found to a limited extent in contemporary Bosnia'. However, she accurately acknowledges that 'other genres stand out as women's tools: oral narratives, songs, informal spiritual charge, not to mention networks with the focus of social interaction and welfare'.[73] For one, a number of organisations have developed in recent years to publicly promote female issues. Nahla is one such NGO which aims to improve the quality of life for Bosniak women through domestic violence programs and women shelters, at the same time as offering general religious and life education. While the influential roles, either in the Islamic Community or at the local mosques, are still overwhelmingly populated by men, Bosniak women are playing a significant role in the religious and social development of their communities.

The place of women in Islamic societies is often denounced by the West on the grounds of human rights and gender equality. It is therefore no surprise that a nation that purports to share these Western values

---

71 Raudvere, above n58, 260.

72 Ibid., 262.

73 Ibid., 275–6.

observes Islam in a distinct way. Generally speaking, Bosnian women are afforded the right to express their faith individually and better acquaint themselves with religious texts and teachings. By virtue of their cultural history, they are actively aware that their world is not defined by simple right or wrong answers. To this end, it is through questioning and reflecting that these women seek personal spiritual guidance. Armed with these tools, they are continuing to develop the composition of 'European Islam'.

VI. THE SECULAR STATE AND RELIGIOUS DIVERSITY

As discussed, Bosniaks have existed in a secular state for over a century. Yet the independence following the wars of succession did not lead to loud calls for an Islamic Republic. Rather, it was perceived that the only way for the Muslim leadership to integrate non-Muslim Bosnians was to maintain the secular state principle. While this has encountered problems of its own, the further devolution of states within the former Yugoslavia was the most probable alternative outcome. Today, the state of Bosnia and Hercegovina is made up of three regions: Bosnia, Hercegovina and the Republika Srpska. Since the ethnic cleansings of the 1990s, the population has become largely segregated into separate ethnoreligious areas based on these three regions: the majority of Bosniaks live in Bosnia, the majority of Catholics in Hercegovina and the majority of Orthodox in the Republika Srpska.[74] The Bosnian Constitution reflects and protects this division; Articles IV and VI ensure equal representation for each region and ethnicity in the Parliamentary Assembly and Constitutional Court.[75]

Most Bosniaks are not troubled by the secular status of their nation. The Islamic Community itself has repeatedly affirmed its commitment to the separation of religion and state[76] and there remains no reason why Islam cannot continue to flourish in this environment. Fikret Karčić is a scholar and professor of law and Shari'ah in Sarajevo. One of his main

---

[74] U.S. Department of State, *International Religious Freedom Report 2009 – Bosnia and Herzegovina.*

[75] Constitution of the Federation of Bosnia and Herzegovina.

[76] Ahmet Alibašić, *The Profile of Bosnian Islam and What West European Muslims Could Benefit from It* (Lecture Paper, Bosnischer Islam fur Europa, Stuttgart-Hohenheim, Akademie der Diözese Rottenburg-Stuttgart, 16–17 November 2007) 4.

focuses has been on ways to adapt Shari'ah to the secular state; he believes this can have a number of positive influences on an Islamic community. Admittedly, this secularisation has meant that some traditional religious privileges have been lost; yet, as a result, communities have become free to manage their own affairs and apply their resources to the needs of their members.[77] Ahmed Alibašić adopts a similar view to Karčić. He considers that the neutrality provided by a secular state is required to deliver a free and open space for debate without marginalising the meaning of religion for individuals or communities.[78] It stands to reason that laicity establishes a forum for the continual development of religion.

In considering Islam's place in a secular society, Karčić conceives that there are two domains of human life in which Shari'ah should always remain significant: the relationship between an individual and God, and the relationships between other individuals and communities. Karčić assures his reader that, in regards to the application of Shari'ah, there is no conflict between the relationship with God and the present separation of church and state. This relationship is a private affair outside the realms of appropriate political control. However, he recognises that secularism may inhibit the ability of Shari'ah to actively govern interpersonal relations. In order to preserve these laws, Karčić insists that they be assigned the status of 'ethical laws' which 'need no enforcement by the state, but would influence people's actions and decision through appealing to their conscious'.[79] It is to this conclusion that Bosniaks naturally gravitated during the twentieth century.

As the ethnicities of Bosnia and Hercegovina's population are principally founded on religion, it is hardly surprising that the state law on religious freedom reaffirms the right of every citizen to religious education. The law calls for an official representative of the various religious communities to be responsible for teaching religious studies in all public and private schools, usually twice a week.[80] These teachers are accredited

---

77 Xavier Bougarel, 'Bosnian Islam as "European Islam": Limits and Shifts of a Concept' in Aziz Al-Azmeh and Effie Fokas, *Islam in Europe: Diversity, Identity and Influence* (Cambridge, UK: Cambridge University Press 2007) 102–3.

78 Bartels and van Dijk, above n69, 472.

79 Ibid., 473–4 (Discussing Fikret Karčić, *Islam u sekularnoj državi: primjer Bosne I Hercegovine* [Islam in Secular Countries: The Example of Bosnia and Herzegovina], Draft paper, Sarajevo: University of Sarajevo, 2008.

80 U.S. Department of State, *International Religious Freedom Report 2013 – Bosnia and Herzegovina.*

by the governing religious denomination but perform as employees of the schools in which they teach. Interestingly, religious instruction is not bound by the ethnic borders within Bosnia and Hercegovina. When a sufficient number of students (between 15 and 20) of a minority religious group attend a school, it is a requirement that the school organise religion classes on these students' behalf. The ability of the Bosnian education system to accommodate all religious faiths demonstrates that, unlike in some other European countries, a secular state does not come at the cost of state sponsored theological education.

There are many other examples within Bosnia and Hercegovina of compromise for the sake of religious harmony. For example, agreements between Bosnia, the Holy See and the Serbian Orthodox Church in 2007 and 2008 recognised the legal personality of Bosnian churches and granted a number of rights, including official recognition of Catholic and Orthodox holidays. Both of these agreements notably advanced the basic human right of freedom of religion.[81] The status of public holidays is particularly telling as these are often founded on deeply significant religious and cultural events. Currently, different counties, municipalities and regions celebrate religious public holidays as they apply; only a small number apply universally across the country. This is not simply a token recognition. The labour laws of the Federation of Bosnia and Hercegovina (the area made up of the regions of Bosnia and Hercegovina) obligate all employers within the Federation to permit an employee four days off in a calendar year for the purpose of religious or traditional needs, two of which must be paid.[82]

The environment created by this inclusive compromise is an accurate microcosm of Bosnian society. While plurality and cooperation exist at heart, the actions of some can be antagonistic, based on ulterior motives. For example, Republic Day is celebrated in the Republika Srpska to commemorate its declared 'independence' from Bosnia and Hercegovina in 1992. Understandably, many ethnic groups within the Federation view this as a direct provocation.[83] Governments at the local level have also been known to restrict minority religious services and ceremonies. In 2007, the eastern Republika Srpska municipality of Bratunac repeatedly

---

[81] Constitution of the Federation of Bosnia and Herzegovina.

[82] U.S. Department of State, *International Religious Freedom Report 2010 – Bosnia and Herzegovina.*

[83] Svein Mønnesland, 'Disputes over National Holidays: Bosnia and Herzegovina 2000–10' in Ljiljana Šarić, Karen Gammelgaard and Kjetil Rå Hauge, *Transforming National Holidays* (Amsterdam: John Benjamins Publishing Company 2012) 262.

denied a permit for Muslims to build a cemetery and memorial on the property of a downtown mosque. Bosniaks had intended to bury 98 identified victims of a 1992 massacre in Bratunac in which more than 600 persons were killed.[84] Evidently, the wounds from the 1990s civil war have not closed. Similarly, Bosniaks have impeded the building of Catholic Churches, while the vandalising of religious sites for all faiths has been common. The fact that this increased in 2014 when the country's national football team competed for the first time at the FIFA World Cup highlights an ingrained mindset of ethnic superiority within a number of Bosnian subgroups.[85]

Due to the fact that religion and ethnicity are often closely linked in the Balkans, it is often near impossible to differentiate to which category each inflammatory act belongs.[86] Unfortunately, too often spiritual symbols are used in Balkan politics to achieve national objectives rather than religious ones.[87] While Bosniaks compose a majority of the populations (around 45 per cent, with the remaining 55 per cent split between Serbs and Croats), very few countries in the world exist in such a fine ethnic equilibrium. The guns may have stopped, but the struggle for supremacy and security remains. Bosnia's leaders have often spoken out against this perceived siege mentality. They preach of a *Harmonica Abrahamica*, based on the Qur'anic verse '[t]o each of you We prescribed a law and a method. Had Allah willed, He would have made you one nation.'[88] The former Bosnian vice-President, Rusmir Mahmutéchajić, spoke on this 'Harmonica Abrahamica':

> the three religions of Bosnia – Christianity, Judaism and Islam – can be seen as different but doctrinally complete exoteric expressions of one and the same Reality. Their single forefather, Abraham, the prophet, has an endless diversity of offspring.[89]

It follows that an idea of superiority has no place within Bosnian Islam. Amongst the historic friction exist a people who share similar cultural

---

[84] U.S. Department of State, *Bureau of Democracy, Human Rights and Labour – Report on Bosnia and Herzegovina 2007.*

[85] U.S. Department of State, *International Religious Freedom Report 2014 – Bosnia and Herzegovina.*

[86] U.S. Department of State, *International Religious Freedom Report 2013 – Bosnia and Herzegovina.*

[87] Alibašić, above n76, 4.

[88] Qur'an 5:48.

[89] Clinton Bennett, *In Search of Solutions: The Problem of Religion and Conflict* (London: Equinox Publishing Ltd 2008) 118.

evolutions. Should this seemingly historic and cultural antagonism be extinguished, there is no rational reason on the facts that religious harmony cannot be sustained.

VII. CONCLUSION

> One can understand Islam only as a grand and complex religious system defined not only by its metaphysical principles and ethical requirements but circumstances and conditions in which its followers – Muslims as individuals and their Communities as organised groups – live in today's world.[90]
>
> Dr Marko Babić, 2014

The rise of contemporary Islam in Bosnia has been a slow and eventful process. The tolerant, syncretic and liberal application of the faith seen today is the product of a number of factors:

1. the Hanafi school of *fiqh* and relevant Sufi orders;
2. the Ottoman Islamic culture and its strong religious authority;
3. the Islamisation of pre-Islamic Bosnian practice;
4. Islamic reform through *ijtihad*;
5. the Islamic Community religious institution; and
6. an existence within a secular state.[91]

While the Constitution promotes a secular government and legal system, Shari'ah continues to play a significant role in the life of Bosnian Muslims. It provides Bosniaks with a code of ethics by which to live their life as Bosnia continues to find its feet on the world stage. Furthermore, it is an avenue through which Muslims can openly demonstrate their religion.

While the Salafi minorities have at times caused disunity amongst the greater Bosnian community, they must be credited with kick-starting the initial revival. The *mujahidin* and Saudi instruction turned around the lives of those emerging from Yugoslavia with drug, alcohol or other like vices controlling their lives.[92] It is for this reason that the pluralist

---

[90] Marko Babić, 'Two Faces of Islam in the Western Balkans' in Marko Milosevic and Kacper Rekawek, *Perseverance of Terrorism: Focus on Leaders* (Amsterdam: IOS Press 2014) 135.

[91] Alibašić, above n76, 3.

[92] Stephen Schwartz, *Wahhabism and al-Qaeda in Bosnia-Herzegovina* (Center for Islamic Pluralism, 20 October 2004).

approach headed by Cerić has proven so effective. It encourages the integration and participation of all Islamic communities. It has shown that in the absence of state institutions and religious laws, an Islamic identity can and has been be preserved through simple but fundamental liberties and rights. This outcome can be replicated, with time, in other European States, particularly in the wake of increased migration from the Middle East and Africa. All that is required is an open mind. The acceptance that Islamic faith comes in all shapes and sizes is the first step in properly understanding and benefiting from Muslim participation within a secular society.

18. *Khutbahs* and *fatwas* in colonial Indonesia and Malaya

Muhamad Ali

I. INTRODUCTION

The present chapter will examine the sermon (*khutbahs*) and edict (*fatwas*), and the extent to which colonial contexts shaped their characteristics and development in colonial Indonesia, particularly South Sulawesi, and Malaya, particularly Kelantan. It will analyse how various *ulama* constructed sermons and edicts, what sources and languages they used, and what problems and issues they faced. In such an analysis, the flexibility of religious knowledge and the contending interpretations of the religious texts will reveal some of the tensions as well as the compromises that characterize the production of such knowledge. The sermons and the edicts are textual and contextual, persistent and changing according to the *ulama*'s interpretation and socio-cultural and political circumstances.

As preachers, the *ulama* conceive of their sermons and edicts as religious spaces and symbols despite preaching about socio-political and other secular issues. Faith precedes knowledge, and so the preachers try to link the ever-changing local and global issues to the fixity of religious texts. The preachers would interpret social reality in light of the Qur'an and the Prophet's tradition (Hadith) as their sacred and complete textual guidance. When this notion of 'returning to the Qur'an and the Hadith' is analysed more closely, however, one finds great variation among the groups. Most preachers are unaware of the importance in considering the context or the contingent elements that shape a belief and interpretation.

Sermons and edicts need to be situated within power/knowledge relations. For the religious establishment, the sermons and edicts function as an instrument of power for the strengthening of the Muslim collective identity, the preservation of religious authority, and the protection of Islamic knowledge from what they regard as heterodoxy and heresy. At the same time, the sermon in particular serves as a medium of resistance and contention. Because some of the colonial authorities were well aware of the importance of sermons and religious edicts, they rarely interfered with them. Although the colonial regimes did not exercise direct control on the content of the sermon and edict, they created new circumstances which forced the preachers to adapt. An important consequence of this indirect colonial interference was that sermons and edicts became a site of power contestation among different groups.

II. SERMONS, EDICTS AND THE RELIGIOUS SPACE

A sermon (*khutbah*) is a religious address delivered orally and directly to a specific audience, small or large, in the mosque and other religious spaces. A *fatwa* is an edict or a ruling on specific religious matters (*masail diniyyah*) that concern the community. From the early twentieth century the *fatwa* in British Malaya and the Netherlands Indies became institutionalized when Muslim communities facing with new problems in a colonial situation sought guidance from the *ulama* as the religious authority. While the *fatwa* tends to be issued in written form, it can also be delivered orally or made part of a sermon. The sermon is more popular than the edict because the former is delivered every Friday at a mosque, whereas the latter is only issued irregularly when required. But because of the infrequency of edict announcements, it is regarded as being more authoritative than a khutbah. In addition, the *fatwa* is issued by a *mufti* with certain qualifications such as a knowledge of the Qur'an, the Hadith, Arabic language, and the methodology of deriving rules from the sources (*istinbat al-hukm*), whereas a sermon can be delivered in theory by anyone who knows something about Islam, even if only a Qur'anic verse, and is able to convey it to others.[1]

---

[1] In Arabic, *fatwa* means edict or ruling; *ifta* is the process of delivering a *fatwa*; *mufti* is the *fatwa*-giver; *istifta* is the act of asking a *fatwa*, and *mustafti* is the *fatwa*-asker. The *fatwa* became institutionalized following the institutionalization of the *ulama*, whose main task is to issue the *fatwa*. Originally, *fatwa* referred to any opinion coming from any individual. The Prophet Muhammad is reported to have said to his companion, 'You could ask your own heart in deciding what is right and wrong.' In Kelantan, the journal *Pengasuh* had a section *sual jawab* (question and answer) but later called the section *fatwa*. The *khutbah* or more generally the *tabligh* (to convey) is the task of almost everyone capable and willing to spread Islam to the others, even if only one verse of the Qur'an. Although delivering a Friday *khutbah* requires certain qualifications, these are not as high as those for issuing the *fatwa*. Besides *fatwa* and *khutbah*, there are other forms of religious advice, which are commonly said to be less strict than the *fatwa*. These other forms include personal advice (*nasihah*, *taushiyah*), admonition (*tazkirah*), letters (*risalah*) and written articles

While the *khatib* or preacher who gives a sermon must seek to conform to the tradition of the Prophet Muhammad and the Qur'an, how successful he/she is in this endeavour of course depends upon circumstances and each individual.[2] The preacher's education and experience shape his or her way of preaching. In Kelantan and in South Sulawesi, the *pondok* (traditional boarding school)-educated preacher has greater training on and hence understanding of traditional Islamic knowledge such as the Qur'an, the science of the Qur'anic interpretation (*tafsir*), the science of Hadith, jurisprudence (*fiqh*), and Arabic, enabling him to be better versed than others in delivering sermons. In many of the pondok, how to deliver a sermon is regularly taught as it is also an act of communication and performance, not simply of possessing certain knowledge. Some preachers write down their topic and points beforehand, others rely on their memory and spontaneity, and still others use a combination of text and improvisation.[3]

(*maqalah*), which might contain religious knowledge and a mission (*da'wa*). In post-colonial Indonesia, new but more secular forms of advice emerged, such as position statements (*pernyataan sikap*), appeals (*himbauan*), contributions to opinion (*sumbangan pemikiran*), and instruction (*amanat*). See Nico Kaptein, 'The Voice of the *'Ulama*: *Fatwas* and Religious Authority in Indonesia', Institute of Southeast Asian Studies Working Papers, visiting research series, no.2, 2004; Aboebakar Atjeh, *Beberapa Tjatatan Mengenai Da'wah Islam untuk Perguruan Tinggi Agama Islam* (Semarang: CV Ramadhani 1971), pp. 6–7.

[2] Muhammad Zakaria, *Fadhilah Tabligh*, 2nd ed. (Kota Bharu: Pustaka Aman Press 1982), pp. 1–33.

[3] Most of the preachers probably did not make an outline; but they did have some idea about their audience and the choice of a subject. They also needed to accumulate the material and to meditate on the subject chosen. They tried to choose a text or texts, to write the introduction, the content, and the conclusion. Perhaps some did make some review, elimination and rejection of some points. One of the sermon manuals, for instance, suggested that the preacher should be well prepared, should have a wide intellectual horizon, be brave and wise, polite, not arrogant, calm not in a hurry, normal, should know the level of thinking of the listener, should be a good example, and dress appropriately. The sermons should not be too long, should be in accordance with time and place, constructive, not insulting to people, make sense, and interesting. In Christian tradition, sermons were also equally and in some cases more elaborate in terms of its aims, methods and content. In many aspects, however, Christian sermons shared many characteristics with Islamic ones. Dja'far Amir, *Teknik Chutbah (Pedoman bagi Para Chotib)* (Solo: AB Siti Sjamsijah 1965); Paul B. Bull, *Preaching and Sermon Construction* (New York: Macmillan Company 1922); Charles Reynolds Brown, *The Art of Preaching* (New York: Macmillan Company 1922); Ray C. Petry, *Preaching in the Great Tradition* (Philadelphia: Westminster Press 1946).

For sources, a preacher would select one or several out of more than 6000 verses of the Qur'an and/or one of or several of the thousands of the Prophet's sayings and tradition (Hadith) of six major collections.[4] Since the structure of the Qur'an is neither systematic nor thematic, the selection of verses may come from a major Hadith collection or from selections incorporated in religious books. A sermon can be delivered 'deductively', meaning that a preacher would speak of a phenomenon and then examine it in accordance with his/her interpretation of the normative values derived from particular verses. An 'inductive' sermon, on the other hand, is one where the preacher quotes from the Qur'an and the Hadith to explain a particular issue.

Apart from the Qur'an and the Hadith, a preacher may pick ideas from books in Arabic, in translation, or in the vernacular. The preacher may be influenced by works such as those of al-Imam al-Ghazzali (d.1111), to mention just one example.[5] Other sources of sermons may come from material gathered from international and local journals. In Kelantan, reform-minded preachers (*kaum muda*) might consult the international publications of *al-Urwat al-Wuthqa* (the Strong Bind) and *al-Imam* (the Leader), as well as the local ones, such as *Pengasuh* (the Bearer) and *al-Hidayah* (the Guidance). In South Sulawesi preachers found inspiration in the stories or commentaries found in the local bulletins such as *Suara As'adiyah* (Voice of As'adiyah), magazines of the Muhammadiyah, and *al-Wafd* (the messenger). One sermon manual mentions a book of Qur'anic exegesis entitled *Tafsir al-Jamal* (The Beautiful Interpretation)

---

[4] The Sunni six major Hadith collections are Shahih al-Bukhari (d. 870), Shahih Muslim (d. 875), Sunan al-Nasa'i (d. 915), Sunan Abi Daud (d. 888), Sunan al-Turmudzi (d. 892), Sunan Ibn Maja (d. 886) or Muwatta Imam Malik (d. 796). The first two were considered 'authentic' (that is why the two were often called '*shahih*'), and the other four were said to be simply 'Sunan', which contained the authentic, less authentic, and even the weak Hadith. Imam al-Bukhari and Ibnu Madjah were Persian, while Imam Muslim and al-Turmudzi were Arabs. The tradition of the science of Hadith (*Ulum al-Hadith*) discusses the history, validity and various dimensions of the Hadith. The Shiite Muslims rejected the claim of authenticity of these Sunni Hadith collections. The Shiite Muslims have their own Four Book collections, consisting of *Usul al-Kafi, Man La Yahdhuruhu al-Faqih* of Shaikh Shadud, *Tahzib al-Ahkam* and *Al-Istibsar* by Imam al-Tusi.

[5] The often-cited works by Imam al-Ghazali (d. 1111) included *Bulugh al-Maram* (Reaching the Honor)*, Riyadh al-Shalihin* (Garden of the Pious) and *Ihya Ulum al-Din* (Revitalization of the Religious Sciences). See Machfuzh Siddiq, *Pedoman Tabligh*, vol.1, 4th ed. (Jakarta: Pengurus Besar Nahdlatul Ulama 1955), first published in 1938.

and that of the legal philosophy of *fiqh* (entitled *Hikmat al-Tasyri' wa Falsafatuhu*, the Wisdom of Islamic Law and Its Philosophy).[6] During the colonial period, references from Western books in sermons were uncommon and mainly used to highlight shortcomings or emphasize favourable remarks on Islam, such as a statement by a Scottish scholar of Islam, H. A. R. Gibb (1895–1971), that Islam is both a faith and a civilization.[7] While sources consulted were wide-ranging, the materials selected were used solely for a religious aim.

In Kelantan during this time, the language of Friday sermons was predominantly local Malay (Kelantanese dialect) and usually written in *jawi*, a modified Arabic script used for the Malay language.[8] In South Sulawesi, sermons were delivered in the local vernacular language (Bugis, Makassarese, or Mandarese) and were sometimes written in the Arabic-script called *serang*, but more often in Latin script. The use of *serang* in South Sulawesi, however, was limited and not as popular as the use of *jawi* in Kelantan because Malayness and Arabic were intertwined. In South Sulawesi, while the majority preached in the vernacular, some gave Friday sermons in Arabic, as occurred in the mosque of As'adiyah in Wajo.[9]

---

[6] Siddiq, *Pedoman Tabligh.*

[7] Siddiq, *Pedoman Tabligh.*

[8] '*Jawi*' means people of Java, which were 'Malays' because the Arabs considered all the people in the Malay archipelago as Javanese; therefore the Malay writing using Arabic characters was called tulisan Jawi (Jawi script). 'Kitab' which literarily meant simply 'book', became to mean 'religious book' in Malay and Indonesian usage. The book of *jawi* (*kitab jawi*) were used by the Malays as a major source of Islamic knowledge because most ordinary Malays did not understand Arabic. Abdullah Munshi observed that Arabic was used by the Malays only in worship and prayers. The *kitab jawi* were mostly written during the period from the nineteenth to the early twentieth century. R. Roolvink, *Bahasa Jawi* (Leiden: Leiden University Press 1975), p. 2; Abdullah bin Abdul Kadir Munshi, *Hikayat Abdullah*, trans. A. H. Hill (Kuala Lumpur: Singapore 1970), p. 56; Mohd. Nor Bin Ngah, *Kitab Jawi: Islamic Thought of the Malay Muslim Scholars*, research notes and discussion papers no.33, Institute of Southeast Asian Studies, Singapore, 1983, pp.vii–viii.

[9] The As'adiyah had its *Da'wa* Department, organizing the training of the preachers and the journal *Risalah As'adiyah* in the Bugis language. In later years, the As'adiyah also had its radio station broadcasting the teaching, sermons and other information for the people around Wajo. Abd. Aziz Al Bone, *Lembaga Pendidikan Islam di Sulawesi Selatan (Studi Kasus di Perguruan As'adiyah Sengkang) Laporan Hasil Penelitian*, Departemen Agama RI, 1986, p. 16.

The Muhammadiyah in South Sulawesi urged their preachers to use the local languages or the national language of Indonesian.[10] But Arabic was used for the main part of the sermons, which included the recitation of the praise to Allah (*hamdalah*), the praise to the Prophets (*shalawat*), encouragement to do good (*wasiyyat taqwa*), the declaration of faith (*shahadat*), the quoted Qur'anic verses and Hadith, and the recitation of prayer (*do'a*).[11] Most of the ordinary people in Kelantan and South Sulawesi did not know Arabic, except in some pondok where Arabic was taught intensively and sermons were delivered in Arabic for educational purposes.

Fatwa is more formal than a *khutbah*. The *fatwa* uses different sources, including the Quran, the Hadith, and religious books regarded as 'acceptable' by the mufti. In Kelantan, during this period, *fatwa* were issued in the journal *Pengasuh*. The sources of the *fatwa* were various, but primarily Ahl al-Sunnah wa al-Jamaah books of Abu Hasan al-Ash'ari (873–975) in matters of belief, and books of Imam al-Shafi'i (767–820) for matters of ritual, legal and social matters.[12] South Sulawesi did not

---

[10] The Sixteenth National Congress of Moehammadijah issued a ruling that all sermons should be carried out in the vernacular (*bahasa Boemipoetera*). *Boeah Congres Moehammadijah XXIII* (Djogjakarta: Hoofdcomite Congres Moehammadijah 1938), p. 20.

[11] See Dja'far Amir, *Teknik Chutbah (Pedoman bagi Para Chotib)* (Solo: AB Siti Sjamsijah 1965), pp. 50–1; H. Muhamad Arsyad Sunusi, *Khutbah Jumat Lengkap Satu Tahun*, 6 vols (Makassar: Toko Buku Pesantren, n.d.); H.Muhammad Arsyad Sunusi, *Hotbah Jum'at Bahasa Makassar*, 2nd ed. (Makassar: Toko Buku Pesantren 2002); *Khutbah Jum'at Lengkap Satu Tahun Bahasa Bugis Tulisan Latin* (Makassar: Yayasan Pendidikan dan Penyiaran Islam 2002); Muhammad Jamil Hamid, *Mimbar al-Jumati Li 'Aamatil Muslimin* (Ujung Pandang: Toko Buku Pesantren 1968).

[12] It was little known that Abu al-Hasan al-Ash'ari was actually a Mu'tazalite follower until the age of forty and then turned against the Mu'tazalite theological thinking. Abul Hasan al-Ash'ari was then more known for his theological idea of 'compromise' between predestination of Jabariyya and free will of Mu'taziliyya. Abu al-Hasan al-Ash'ari wrote a number of theological books, including *Maqalat Islamiyyin, Kitab al-Luma* and *Al-Ibanah 'an Ushul al-Diyanah*. Imam al-Maturidi, another theologian of *Ahlu Sunnah*, had less impact in the Islamic world than Al-Ash'ari. Al-Ash'ari was a follower of Imam al-Shafi'i. Muhammad Idris al-Shafi'i stressed the four basic sources of Islam: the Qur'an, the Hadith, the *Ijma*' (scholarly consensus) and the *qiyas* (analogy). The Shafi'i *fiqh* has been prevalent in many parts of the Islamic world, such as Turkey, Iraq, Syria, Egypt, Somalia Yemen, and Southeast Asia. See Abu al-Hasan al-Ash'ari, *Al-Ibanah 'an Ushul al-Diyanah* (Lebanon: Dar al-Qutub al-Ilmiyya, n.d.); Muhammad Idris al-Shafi'i, *Islamic Jurisprudence; Shafi'i's Risala*, trans. by

have a state-supported *fatwa* and office of *mufti* as in Kelantan,[13] but the Muhammadiyah and the *Nadhlatul Ulama* (NU) branches circulated their nation-wide collection of religious rulings in the form of religious decisions (*tarjih, keputusan*) considered as *fatwa*. The Indonesian Islam Labor Party (PSII) also had a Council of *Shari'ah* and *Ibadah*, which organized the preaching and writing on Islam, as well as the issuance of *fatwa*, for its members.[14]

The NU as an organization did not penetrate into South Sulawesi until early 1950, although the Ahlussunnah wal-Jama'ah theological and Shafi'i legal school of thought was represented by Islamic schools, such as *Madrasah al-Arabiyyah al-Islamiyyah* (Islamic Arabic School) and *Darul Da'wah wal-Irsyad* (House of Mission and Guidance) and some other *pesantrens* in the island of Salemo and other districts in South Sulawesi. During the first half of the twentieth century, South Sulawesi did not have a collection of *fatwa*, but they had individual religious edicts, such as those issued by K. H. As'ad. Comparatively speaking, in Java, the NU organizational *fatwa*, collected later on, used about 160 religious books (*kitab kuning*) as references to the *fatwa* issued between 1926 and 1994. The *fatwa* are in the vernacular with references in Arabic without Indonesian translation, whereas the Muhammadiyah *fatwa* provide Indonesian translation for the references as well. The Muhammadiyah *fatwa* use the Qur'an and the Hadith more but Arabic books less than the NU *fatwa* collections. In matters ambiguously explained in the Qur'an and the Hadith, the Muhammadiyah uses the legal methodology of *ijtihad* (reasoning) and *ittiba* (following but knowing the reasons),

---

Majid Khadduri (Baltimore: Johns Hopkins Press 1961); Montgomery Watt, *Free-will and Predestination in Early Islam* (London: Luzac & Co., 1948); Muhammad Mukhtar bin Atharid al-Jawi al-Batawi al-Buqari, *Ushuluddin I'tiqad Ahl al-Sunnah wa al-Jama'ah* (Kota Bharu: Ahliyyah Sendirian Berhad 1978); Abdul Shukor Husin, *Ahli Sunah Waljamaah Pemahaman Semula* (Bangi: Universiti Kebangsaan Malaysia 2000); Michael E. Marmura, 'Ghazali and Ash'arism Revisited', *Arabic Sciences and Philosophy*, vol.12 (2002), pp. 91–110.

[13] Majlis Ugama Islam dan Adat Istiadat Kelantan, *Himpunan Fatwa Mufti Kerajaan Negeri Kelantan*, vol.1, 3rd ed. (Kota Bharu: Majlis Ugama Islam 1996).

[14] The organizational document was first written in 1933. 'Pasal 5: Madjlis Departemen Sjariat dan Ibadat', Putjuk Pimpinan PSII, *Anggaran Dasar Partai Sjarikat Islam Indonesia berikut Anggaran Rumah Tangga dan Peraturan Tata Tertib* (Djakarta: Partai Sjarikat Islam Indonesia 1952), pp. 33–4.

while the NU applies *taqlid* (following the established opinions of the *ulama* without necessarily knowing the reasons).[15]

With regard to sermons in South Sulawesi, local *ulama* individually and organizationally write down various aspects of their sermons in manuals or guidebooks for limited or wider circulation.[16] In Kelantan during the colonial period, the journal *Pengasuh* had a section devoted to religious rulings or edicts, but no section on sermons until the 1950s. Few books of sermons were written and published by individual preachers and/or the Council of Religion in Kota Bharu, and after independence published more manuals.[17] The khutbah, despite its simple form, is a complex practice. It constitutes drama and performance, involving various aspects of communication: language, dress, mimic, gesture and so

[15] The Muhammadiyah and the Nahdlatul *Ulama* issued their own collections of *fatwa* on a wide-range of issues using different methodologies. K. H. A. Aziz Masyhuri (ed.), *Masalah Keagamaan Hasil Muktamar dan Munas Ulama Nahdlatul Ulama Kesatu-1926 s/d kedua puluh sembilan 1994* (Surabaya: PT RMI and Dinamika Press 1997); Pimpinan Pusat Muhammadiyah, *Himpunan Putusan Madjlis Tardjih Muhammadijah* (Djakarta: P.P. Muhammadijah 1971).

[16] For example, Risalah Djum'ah by Ahmad Hassan (Bandung, 1931); Ta'jidil Islami fi Chutabil Chas wal'Am (Javanese; al-Chutabatul's Ashrijah by Muhammad Nur Idris (Indonesian language, Padang, 1931); Kitab Da'wah Djum'at dan Da'wah Hari Raja (Bandung, 1938); and Pedoman Muballigh Islam by Hamka (Medan, 1937). The Islamic organizations such as As'adiyah, the Muhammadiyah, the Nahdlatul *Ulama*, and Persatuan Islam, also published books on sermons. The As'adiyah had its own bulletin entitled 'Risalah As'adiyah' and the Darul Da'wa wal-Irsyad (D.D.I.) also had Risalah Ad-Dariyah, both of which contained religious knowledge and information, including sermon text samples for its students, teachers and the people. These sermon guidelines generally elaborated sermon requirements, ethics, preparation, suggested topics and models, for a period of one year. See Aboebakar Atjeh, *Beberapa Tjatatan mengenai Da'wah Islam* (Semarang: Ramadhani 1971), p. 30; Muhammad Shawir Dahlan, *Pedoman Khutbah Jum'at Praktis* (Ujung Pandang: Yayasan Pendidikan Ilmu Al-Qur'an al-Muzahwirah Sulawesi Selatan 1992); S. J. Soetan Mangkoeto, *Pedoman Penjiaran Moehammadijah* (Padang Panjang: Drukkerij Islamijah F.D.K., 1936); *Laporan Penelitian Naskah Khotbah pada Pelita II Tahun 1974–79 di Daerah Sulawesi Selatan dan Sulawesi Tenggar*, Balai Penelitian Lektur Keagamaan Ujung Pandang, Departemen Agama RI, 1981–82.

[17] With the increase in publishing technology and in the numbers of preachers, more manuals were produced and circulated in the postcolonial period. For example, Arifin bin Awang, *Pemimpin Tabligh* (Kota Bharu: Pustaka Dian 1959); Muhammad Zakaria, *Fadhilah Tabligh*, 2nd ed. (Kota Bharu: Pustaka Aman Press 1982); Majlis Ugama Islam dan Adat Istiadat, *Khutbah Jum'at*, 9 vols (Kota Bharu: Pustaka Aman Press n.d.).

forth. Unlike the edict, the sermon involves the use and manipulation of words, styles and sometimes illustrations and anecdotes.

This performative aspect of sermon is situated within a 'religious field' between the preacher and the audience. The stories are usually about the Prophet Muhammad, his companions, his four successors (*caliphs*), other prophets, and other exemplary figures. What was important for the preachers and the audience was not the factuality of a story, but rather the moral meanings behind the stories, such as patience, courage, fairness, devotion and other qualities that the preacher intends to emphasize. A Bugis preacher KH Muhammad Abduh Pabbaja, for example, said that when he was a boy he used to listen to the stories of the Prophet Muhammad, Ali bin Abi Talib, Khalid bin al-Walid, and Hamzah, which gave him lessons on courage.[18] The *ulama* see the moral values that govern the daily behaviour of such figures not as 'secular' and 'contingent', but as 'religious' and 'constant'. The sermon acts as a link between the past, the present, and the future by providing an occasion for the preacher and the listener to share in a common religious space where exemplary figures – prophets, saints, scholars – become living and real.

The preacher maintains the 'religious' character of the sermon by interpreting particular issues through his/her understanding of Islamic doctrine and practice.[19] Thus, to believe and to preach are intertwined.[20] Even while adhering to the belief in the absoluteness and universality of knowledge (*wahyu*), the preacher nevertheless conveys it through his/her individual interpretation. In religious sermons, pure thinking and reasoning without reference to the sacred texts are rarely made and would make them less authoritative for the congregation. References to the Qur'an and the Hadith are a sign of authoritative sermons and usually precede purely personal opinions.

The regular and the most frequent sermon is Friday sermon. The Friday sermon functions as a practical religious guide, source of religious information, a religious response to any problem, and as encouragement

---

[18] Rosehan Anwar and M. Yusrie Abady, *Laporan Penelitian dan Penulisan Biografi K.H. Muhammad Abduh Pabbadja di Propinsi Sulawesi Selatan*, Proyek Penelitian Keagamaan Departemen Agama Bagian Proyek Penelitian dan Pengembangan Lektur Agama, 1986/1987, p. 43.

[19] See *Laporan Penelitian Naskah Khotbah pada Pelita II Tahun 1974–79 di Daerah Sulawesi Selatan dan Sulawesi Tenggar*, Balai Penelitian Lektur Keagamaan Ujung Pandang, Departemen Agama RI, 1981–82, pp. 40–5.

[20] See for example, Ronald J. Allen, *Preaching is Believing: The Sermon As Theological Reflection* (Louisville and London: Westminster John Knox Press 2002).

to strengthen faith and deepen religiosity.[21] Sermons are by nature repetitive (daily, weekly, or annually) and therefore contribute to a sense of continuity. The Friday sermon is in reality not a space for dialogue or debate; it is one-way communication. One sermon manual suggests that the Friday congregation should be a space for those who seek spiritual peace and for uniting the heart and the mind of the Muslim community. The sermon is not intended to create friction and disunity among the Muslim community by highlighting errors committed by the people or imposing the preacher's political ideology. Public sermons, particularly those delivered in a public space or the electronic media, tend be more general in content to appeal to an audience that may include both non-Muslims as well as Muslims with varying theological and ritual orientations.[22] The main concern of sermons, however, continues to be the introduction, maintenance, and reinforcement of a sense of community among Muslims within a particular space – neighbourhood, village, city, country, etc.

Even though sermons and edicts are endowed with religious authority, they are not legally binding. In Kelantan in colonial times, sermons were often the business of the state and the Sultan through the Council of Religion. There were regulations that attempted to force attendance at Friday sermons, for instance. However, even though the Friday sermons were forcefully attended, the degree of reception by the audience during this time could not be exactly measured, as there was rarely direct feedback to a sermon by audience. The *ulama* hardly intended to measure the feedback from the audience they preached, neither did they examine if their *fatwa* were actually followed by the asker (*mustafti*), although there were sometimes letters from the audience sent to journals. For example, one reader of a *fatwa* sent his letter to the journal *Pengasuh*, expressing his agreement with the *fatwa* issued by the Council on the recitation of *basmalah* in the Surah of Fatihah of the Qur'an since it was according to the Shafi'i school of thought in the kitab *al-Um*.[23] In South Sulawesi, a local ruler in Bone discarded his membership of the Sufi

---

[21] For example, a preacher gives a guidance about how to do a formal prayer in right way, gives some information about the history of the Qur'an and its main teachings, a response to particular social issues, persuades the audience to improve knowledge, to pay the almsgiving, to go to the pilgrimage to Mecca when able, and so on. There could be any topics deemed important by the preacher.

[22] Dja'far Amir, *Teknik Chutbah (Pedoman bagi Para Chotib)* (Solo: AB Siti Sjamsijah 1965), pp. 42–5.

[23] '*Fatwa* Majlis Ugama Islam Yang Tersiar' (1930) 292 *Pengasuh*.

Order Tariqah Khalwatiyya after he heard in a meeting KH As'ad *fatwa* on the falseness of the Sufi Order. KH As'ad's *fatwa* about ritualistic matters such as Friday sermons in Arabic was followed by the preachers in the mosque of Sengkang, Wajo. But the Muhammadiyah preachers also gained a following since the 1930s when the khutbah began to be preached in local languages.[24] There was, therefore, some leeway among Muslims to choose which religious opinions to follow.

A *khutbah* is not inherently political if this means practical politics. M. B. Hooker has argued that the mosque and the *khutbah* are 'socially and even politically identified and the *khutbah* is the public expression of a specific identity'.[25] This view is true to some extent and in some cases. As mentioned earlier and demonstrated below, the preacher sees his or her sermon as 'religious', even though the topic is categorized as 'political', 'social' and 'non-religious'. The issues are theological and ritualistic, but when political and social concerns are the focus of the sermon, the preacher delivers judgments based on his/her try interpretation of the Qur'an, the Hadith, and other religious sources. In the sermon and the edict, the distinction between religious and the non-religious aspects of knowledge thus becomes blurred because the *khutbah* and the *fatwa* are viewed as being 'religious space'. This emphasis on the 'religious' character of the *khutbah* and *fatwa* and the constant return to the sacred texts explain why the secular, context-specific problems and issues tend to become 'de-secularized'.

III. THE CONTEXTUAL DIMENSION

The characteristic of *khutbah* and *fatwa* as being 'religious' should not lead us to suggest that there is not contextual dimension. De-secularization of worldly issues requires contextualization. If textualization is a process that involves the use of the sacred texts (the Qur'an, Hadith, religious books), contextualization is a process of making references to such religious texts relevant and meaningful to particular groups within specific contexts. Some preachers are more contextual than others, and suggest that the ideal preacher should possess not only religious knowledge but also 'general knowledge', especially of social and current

---

24 KH Daud Ismail, *Riwayat Hidup Almarhum K.H.M. As'ad*, pp. 19–20.

25 See M. B. Hooker, *Indonesian Islam: Social Change through Contemporary Fatawa* (Honolulu: Allen & Unwin and University of Hawaii Press 2003), pp. 87, 104–5, 127–9; Muhamad Ali, '*Fatwa* on Interfaith Marriage in Indonesia' (2002) 9 (3) *Studia Islamika: Indonesian Journal for Islamic Studies.*

issues of his or her time. As one preacher put it, 'human beings are the sons of their times.'[26] Thus they need to 'follow the times' (*mengikuti zaman*) by continuously reading current news and affairs through the available media such as the books, newspapers, magazines and other sources.[27]

One of the requirements of preachers is the ability to communicate by using appropriate speech and terminology because even the prophets were asked to 'speak to people according to their level of comprehension'.[28] As a result, preachers tend to adjust their language and ideas to the audience, whether it be courtiers, farmers, labourers, women or youth groups. In speaking to the Muhammadiyah Youth in Makassar, one local preacher chose as his subject the early life of Prophet Muhammad and his companions. Another preacher sought a rapport with his young audience by urging them to be physically healthy, strongly motivated to obey God, and aware of the danger of the 'women problem' resulting from a free intercourse between the sexes.[29] Current problems and challenges, including the colonial and the local, informed the sermons, and the preachers sought to address them directly.

In 1937 a local preacher named Hamka openly acknowledged that the contents of Friday sermons should be appropriate for this day and age and not for a society that lived hundreds of years ago. He observed that many preachers taught the disregard of the world (*dunia*) for the sake of the life after death (*akhirat*) and still used the Arabic language rather than the vernacular in the Friday sermons. As a result the audience became disinterested in the sermon and could not understand the message being

---

26 In Arabic, it reads, الانسان ابناءالزمان *al-insan abna'uz zaman*. See Djafar Amir, *Teknik Chutbah (Pedoman bagi Para Chotib)* (Solo: AB Sitti Sjamsijah 1965), pp. 23–4.

27 Djafar Amir suggested that ideally, a preacher should prepare the material for sermon; he should be polite, not hurry, be apt and normal, aware of the level of the intellectuality of the audience, motivating, be a model, attractive, not insulting people, reasonable, knowledgeable of the people's aspiration, and keeping the public order. Djafar Amir, *Teknik Chutbah (Pedoman bagi Para Chotib)* (Solo: AB Sitti Sjamsijah, 1965, pp. 13–14, 24–44.

28 A popular Prophet's saying is read: '*Umirna Ma'asyiral Anbiya an Nukallima al-Naasa bi qadri Uquulihim*'. See *Pedoman Chutbah* (Djakarta, Projek Penerangan, Bimbingan dan Da'wah/Chutbah Agama Islam (Pusat), 1971), p. 45; KH Mustafa Zahari, in H. Muhammad Arsyad Sunusi, *Khutbah Jum'at Lengkap Satu Tahun*, 6 vols (Makassar: Toko Buku Pesantren, n.d.), p. 3.

29 *Pemberita Makassar*, no.2, 3 January 1940.

conveyed.[30] By contrast, he cited an example of a Bugis preacher named KH Abdullah who maintained the interest of his congregation by speaking his mind about the colonial situation.[31]

Signs of both continuity and change are evident in the ideas contained in sermons and edicts from colonial South Sulawesi and Kelantan.[32] In South Sulawesi, K. H. As'ad commented on religious matters such as the religious status of paying a fee for a religious teacher for a substitute of a Muslim not performing the daily prayer (*salat*) during his life time.[33] In Kelantan, by the 1987 instruction of Sultan Ismail Petra, the Council of Religion published a collection of the *fatwa* that had been issued by the Council since its establishment in 1915. The new collection in 1997 simply added more *fatwa*, but did not modify the previously issued *fatwa*. The book contains a wide variety of religious matters, including belief (*tauhid* and *aqidah*), physical and spiritual cleanness and dirt, prayer for the traveller, prayer clothing for women, reciting the daily prayer in the Malay language, marriage procedures, man-woman relationships, gifts, food and drink, buying and selling, debt, endowment, sacrificed animals, jewellery, clothing, the messiah and the Prophet 'Isa (Jesus Christ), and religious innovation and superstition (*bid'ah* and *khurafat*). Under the section 'belief', topics include the question of passive imitation (*taqlid*) of the recognized schools of thought, the right and deviant paths, whether the sinful believer and the good unbeliever go to heaven, and men

---

30 Hamka, 'Pedoman Muballigh Islam' (Medan, 1937) in Aboebakar Atjeh, *Beberapa Tjatatan*, p. 31.

31 Hamka, *Muhammadijah Melaloei 3 Zaman*, p. 36.

32 For instance, in Java, the Ahlussunnah wal-Jama'ah Association, N.U., had its *fatwa* from 1926 to 1946, As we mentioned, NU did not come to South Sulawesi until the 1950; the NU *fatwa* contains a wide variety of social, cultural and political issues, such as drawing of animals, orchestra instruments for entertainment, playing chest, dances, firework, wearing Western tie, trousers, shoes and caps, using golden pen, cultivating a Muslim land to the *kafir* (interpreted as non-Muslim), offerings to the earth, the status of *tariqah*, and Friday prayer in prisons. The collection also deals with the issues of the studying the books authored by a *kafir*, the status of Muslim convert to Christianity until the death, the status of women as preachers, the name of Indonesia, depositing money in the bank, joining an Islamic organization, accusing the NU as *bid'ahh* (religious innovation, heresy), life insurance and Muslims joining organization not based on Islam. K. H. A. Aziz Masyhuri (ed.), *Masalah Keagamaan Hasil Muktamar dan Munas Ulama Nahdlatul Ulama Kesatu-1926 s/d kedua puluh sembilan 1994* (Surabaya: PT RMI and Dinamika Press 1997); pp. 1–196.

33 Daud Ismail, *Al-Ta'rif bi al-Alim al-Allamah al-Shaikh al-Hajj Muhammad As'ad al-Bugisi* (Sengkang: Yayasan As'adiyah 1989), pp. 16–17, 19.

reaching the moon.[34] These collections of edict indicate that different issues and contexts produced variant resolutions. In applying such textual and contextual methods, the *ulama* were able to do their duty in answering the 'religious' problems of the day.

The Muhammadiyah, even though they argued for the use of the vernacular, were stricter than the Ahlussunnah wal-Jamaah group in their attitude toward aspects of local culture which were regarded as being contrary or alien to Islam. In 1931, the Muhammadiyah Council of Scholars issued their ruling on the pillars of faith: belief in God, belief in angels, in holy books, in the messengers of God, in the hereafter and in the human fate. It concluded with a short explanation that such beliefs were of the *Ahl al-Sunnah wa al-Jama'ah*, based on the Qur'an, the reliable Hadith, and the work by the early generations of Muslims (the *Salafi*).[35] For the Muhammadiyah, the emphasis on the Qur'anic fundamental beliefs is directly related to the strict attitude toward local tradition (*adat*) deemed harmful to the purity of the belief in one God. Correcting the false *adat* became an important part of their preaching.[36] The Muhammadiyah *ulama* emphasized the purification of the faith (*aqidah*) and rejection of religious innovation (*bid'ah*) and superstitions (*takhayyul, khurafat*), often connected to animism and polytheism (*shirk*).[37] For the Muhammadiyah preachers, there is less toleration for cultural accommodation in matters of fundamental religious ideas because they regard the Qur'an and the Hadith as the primary references for judging what are true and false beliefs.

The *ulama* do not always recognize changing dimensions of their sermons and opinions when they believe that the fundamentals of faith

---

34 See Dato' Haji Ismail bin Yusuf, *Himpunan Fatwa Mufti Kerajaan Negeri Kelantan* (Kota Bharu: Majelis Agama Islam dan Istiadat Negeri Kelantan 1986), pp. 2, 184–96.

35 'Aqaidoel-Iman: Poetoesan Madjlis Tardjih', *Almanak Moehammadijah Tahoen Hidjrah 1351, Kitab Almanak ke-IX* (Djogjakarta: Taman Poestaka, 1931/32), pp. 124–33.

36 The twenty-third congress made a statement that the Moehammadiyah heads and consuls throughout the East Indies should examine the regulations to be followed in relation to the relationship between the local tradition and Islamic norms, but the twenty-forth congress amended this statement because without such statement the Muhammadiyah members should have understood this doctrine any way. *Boeah Congres Moehammadijah XXIII*, p. 23.

37 Later on, however, the Muhammadiyah added a phrase, 'without overlooking the doctrine of tolerance in Islam'. It is a matter of importance to examine why and when the word 'tolerance' emerged in the Muhammadiyah formal statement. This needs further research.

(the essence of Islam) should not be compromised. It is not commonly realized that in reality there is room for contending interpretations, and that there is localization of even what is believed to be fundamentals of the faith, as will be demonstrated in the following.

IV. ATTITUDES TOWARD MUSLIM DIVERSITY AND LOCAL NORMS

The issue of tolerance toward religious difference was sometimes brought up by the *ulama* in Kelantan and South Sulawesi. Again, the issue was not simply textual, but also contextual. Some preachers argued for Muslim unity while recognizing diversity in non-fundamental matters. In Kelantan, Haji Nik Muhammad Adeeb (1918–64), who studied in Mecca and then in an American University in Egypt where he learnt general knowledge and English, was asked about diversity in Islam to which he replied: 'If they prayed there would be no difference.'[38] Tok Khurasan, the *ulama* graduate from Deoband, India, was reported to have been not very interested in the then current debate on the issues of talqin and talfiq (see above). Instead, he focused on his teaching of the hadith and the school of thought of Imam Hanafi, rather than Imam Shafi'i.[39] Nik Muhammad Adeeb and Tok Khurasan were among those who did not see the need to worsen the existing internal schism on the issues they regarded as non-fundamental. In other words, they wished to adopt a 'moderate position' between or remain outside the *kaum tua* and *kaum muda* debate of the time.

In South Sulawesi, some preachers paid some attention to the issue of tolerance. The Muhammadiyah preachers recognized the diversity of Muslim organizations in the Netherlands Indies as part of global and local reality as long as they shared the commitment to preach and teach Islam according to the Qur'an and the Prophet's tradition. They interpreted the term *ummah* as not simply the Islamic community but also as Islamic organization, which meant that Islam could be preached by different organizations (*ummah*) in different local areas.[40] Here the

---

[38] Ismail Awang, 'Haji Nik Muhammad Adeeb (1918–64)', Ismail Che Daud (ed.), *Tokoh-Tokoh Ulama' Semenanjung Melayu*, vol.II (Kota Bharu: Majlis Ugama Islam dan Adat Istiadat Melayu Kelantan 1996), p. 84.

[39] Nik Abdul Aziz Hj. Nik Hassan, 'Tok Khurasan; Seorang Tokoh *Ulama* di Negeri Kelantan', *Malaysia in History*, vol.18, no.1, 1975, p. 32.

[40] H. Hasjim, 'Choetbatoel Arsj', '*Almanak Muhammadijah 1351* (Djogjakarta: Taman Poestaka, 1932/3), pp. 1–16.

Muhammadiyah tolerated organizational plurality. The local organization, Bone Islamic Association (Perhimpoenan Islam Bone, PIB) in established on 20 January 1940 in Watampone, also aimed to promote tolerance among Muslims particularly in Bone because of difficulties there. In their sermons, local Muslims were encouraged to counter backwardness, improve the economy, be more faithful to Islam and be tolerant toward different interpretations of Islam.[41] Here the P.I.B. promoted tolerance of more ritualistic orientations of Islam.

As for the local norms, many emphasized that Islam should coexist with these. For instance, in Bugis society, *siriq* is regarded as an important cultural belief. As I have discussed above, *siriq* is a fundamental concept which governs behaviour based on mutual respect.[42] Some preachers tried to explain the local norm of *siriq* in light of Islamic norms. Hamka, a Muhammadiyah preacher who preached and taught in South Sulawesi from late 1931 to 1934, realized the religious importance of *siriq* and the cultural importance of the religious norm of shame. In a public speech, Hamka suggested that *siriq* was actually in accordance with Islamic norms but should not be done in an excessive or exaggerated fashion. Dignity, he continued, should be based on true faith and moral moderation. Hamka then quoted Imam al-Ghazzali who said that 'the best dignity is one that is moderate'. What he meant by exaggeration was killing and violence that often resulted in the defence of *siriq*. In justifying his opinion, Hamka quoted an Arab poem translated as: 'If you

---

[41] The organization also aimed to introduce general knowledge (*ilmu-ilmu umum*) and Islamic knowledge (*pelajaran Islam*), to improve the economy by providing financial support to the members, to improve the peoples' health, and to disseminate Islam through public sermons. One of the speakers quoted a Qur'anic verse, 'God will not change the course of a group unless the group themselves are willing to change,' and explained it in the Bugis language. *Pemberita Makassar*, no.26, 31 January 1940.

[42] It is believed that violation of the norm will bring calamity to the region, such as drought, severe economic conditions, etc. Run-away couple, which was without familial consent, is an example of *siriq* that should be paid off. The family that had been brought shame become *tomasiriq* [meaning those who become *siriq*]. To remove this shame, the *tomasiriq* are thus obligated to remove the shame by killing the one who is responsible for causing *siriq*. The Makassarese have a saying: '*Ikambe Bugisi Mangkasara, nialle toddopuli, sipassiriqkia siagang sipacceia*' (We Bugis and Makassarese, We declare our oath, to respect each other, to show our solidarity). See Musda Mulia, *Ketaqwaan terhadap Tuhan Yang Maha Esa dalam Sistem Sosial Budaya Makassar di Kelurahan Mangasa Kecamatan Tamalate – Ujung Pandang* (Ujung Pandang: Badan Penelitian dan Pengembangan Agama, Proyek Penelitian Agama, 1988/89), p. 11.

do not defend your dignity then you undermine it, and others will undermine it even more; therefore respect yourself and if a place is narrow for it, then move to another place where respect is possible.' Hamka explained *siriq* by the Islamic terms *maru'ah* (self-dignity), *shaja'ah* (bravery) and *haya* (shame). An Islamic *siriq*, according to Hamka, is a reflection of individual liberty, national freedom, no fear but of God, no place with greatest protection but in God. *Siriq* could also mean respect for women and the dignity of religion. Hamka then quoted a Hadith saying: 'Whoever is killed in defense of his property dies a martyr (*shahid*); whoever is killed defending his life dies a martyr; whoever dies because he defends his religion dies a martyr; whoever dies in defending his family dies a martyr.' He then supported this with a hadith, 'shame is part of faith'.[43]

Hamka noted that a Bugis preacher, Haji Abdullah, preached at the Congress of the Muhammadiyah in 1932 at Makassar, emphasizing that 'to die in the defense of the religion of Allah is to die in the most honorable way and to idealize the implementation of Islam in the country is to live meaningfully'. Hamka then concluded his speech by saying, 'I am amazed by the bravery of the Bugis and Makassarese people in facing death over only small things, but I would encourage you to apply the *siriq* in reaching higher goals, such as the dignity of your country, your nation, and your religion, so your death will be worth it.'[44] Bugis scholars, such as Abu Hamid, later argued that *siriq* is equivalent to Islamic motivation (*niat*) because *siriq* serves as a motivating factor in social action.[45] Here Hamka and Abu Hamid tried to Islamize the traditional doctrine of *siriq* and to localize the Islamic norm of respect and dignity. Thus, in South Sulawesi, there was an attempt to synthesize and reconcile the local norms of *siriq* and the Islamic norms of shame, dignity and respect to form a single religio-cultural concept.

---

43 Hamka, 'Pandangan Islam terhadap Siriqk', in Andi Moen Mg., *Menggali Nilai-nilai Budaya Bugis-Makassar dan Siriqk Na Pacce* (Ujung Pandang: Yayasan Mapress 1988), pp. 66–74.

44 Hamka, 'Pandangan Islam terhadap Sirik', pp. 75–8.

45 Abu Hamid even speculates that the term *siriq* is derived from the Arabic *sirri*, meaning secret (*rahasia*), in the Arabic saying '*Allahu sirriy wa ana sirruhu*' (God is a secret and I am His secrecy). Yet Abu Hamid further contends that *siriq* belongs to shame culture, rather than guilt culture. Abu Hamid, 'Sistem Nilai Islam Dalam Budaya Bugis-Makassar', Aswab Mahasin et al. (eds), *Ruh Islam dalam Budaya Bangsa: Aneka Budaya Nusantara* (Jakarta: Yayasan Festival Istiqlal and Bina Rena Pariwara 1996), pp. 173–5.

In Kelantan, a similar melding of cultural and religious ideas was complicated because there was no consensus on what aspects of Malay culture were actually Islamic. However, the connection between Malayness and Islam was often emphasized in the sermons. If Malays were poor, Islam played a role; and if they were developed, Islam also played its role. In Kota Bharu, Friday sermons emphasized the close connection between the Islamic faith and the Malay community. Even while recalling the glories of the Melaka Sultanate, preachers were aware that the Malays remained poor and backward in comparison with other nations, especially the Chinese and the English. Haji Abdullah Nuh (1905–47) travelled through Kelantan to raise awareness among ordinary Malays of the continuing relevance of Islam.[46] For him, Malayness and Islam were an interlinked identity that could prove productive by emphasizing that Islam promotes progress, and therefore the Malay people as true Muslims must become modern.[47]

In addition to the effort by preachers to reconcile Islam with local culture, another of their concerns was to determine how they should interpret what the Qur'an and the Prophet's tradition said regarding the proper Islamic attitudes toward other religious communities. Both Kelantan and South Sulawesi had large religious minorities, and therefore this was an important problem facing the preachers. While some focused on religious books for a resolution of the question, others formed their interpretations by going directly to the Qur'an. In shaping preachers' views of other religions, elements of text and context, as well as exegesis and history, had a major role.

V. ATTITUDES TOWARD OTHER RELIGIONS

One common feature among Islamic preachers was the belief in the truth of Islam. Most, if not all were 'theologically exclusive', to use a contemporary term. They tended to see Islam as the only true religion without allowing some possibility about the truth in other religions.[48]

---

[46] Ismail Awang, 'Maulana Abdullah Nuh (1905–47)', in Ismail Che Daud (ed.), *Tokoh-Tokoh Ulama' Semenanjung Melayu*, vol.1, (Kota Bharu: Majlis Ugama Islam dan Adat Istiadat Melayu Kelantan 1992), p. 399.

[47] Ibid.

[48] Professor of religious studies in America, Diana L. Eck, for instance, offers her definition of exclusivism, a definition I follow here. An exclusive theology is when one believes that 'our own community, our tradition, our understanding of reality, our encounter with God, is the one and only truth,

However, preachers in South Sulawesi and Kelantan expressed their exclusivity differently. In 1928, the conference of the Nahdlatul *Ulama* issued their edicts in response to various questions concerning other religions and the practices deemed as foreign influences. One of the questions was: 'What is the opinion of the NU regarding wearing trousers, ties, shoes, and hats?' The NU general conference replied in the following manner, which then became its *fatwa*: 'If one wears these with the intention to imitate and to follow the path of the unbelievers (*kafir*) and to promote their unbelief, then the person becomes *kafir*. If he or she does not have an intention at all to imitate the *kafir* (simply wearing this or that) and to follow their path, then the act is not forbidden. Nevertheless, it is undesirable (*makruh*).'[49] In response to another question on the different kinds of *kafir*, the answer was: First, the one who does not believe in God (called *kafir inkar*); second, the one who believes in God in his heart, but does not proclaim this verbally, such as Satan and the Jews (called *kafir juhud*); third, the one who says he believes in God

excluding all others'. This exclusivism is in opposition to inclusivism which signifies the acceptance of multiple communities, traditions and truths, although one's own truth is superior to the others. The third position is the pluralist who believes that there are truths equally present in all religions. Diana L. Eck, 'Is Our God Listening? Exclusivism, Inclusivism, and Pluralism', Roger Boase (ed.), *Islam and Global Dialogue: Religious Pluralism and the Pursuit of Peace* (Burlington: Ashgate 2005), p. 23; Muhamad Ali, *Teologi Pluralis-Multikultural: Menghargai Kemajemukan, Menjalin Kebersamaan* (Jakarta: Penerbit Buku Kompas 2003), pp.viii–xix.

[49] This *fatwa* is written in Indonesian language, then with Arabic text. It is based on the *fiqh* books '*al-Fatawa al-Kubra*' by Ibn Taimiyyah (1263–1328) and 'Bughyatul Mustarsyidin' by Abdurrahman bin Muhammad bin Husain bin Umar al-'Alawi, a *mufti* at Hadramaut. Ibn Taimiyyah is the follower of Imam Hanbali rather than of Imam al-Shafi'i. This indicates some flexibility regarding the sources of *fiqh* in the *fatwa* of the NU. Yet in this matter of belief, the *fatwa* remains fixed. After this *fatwa* in 1927, there emerged a similar question in 1939, and the answer remained the same, with some additional explanation. To resemble (*menyerupai, tashabbuh*) a *kafir* that is forbidden is wearing anything that is specific to that particular religion such as the cross (salib) or for instance closing shop on Sundays following the Christians. 'Masail Diniyah Keputusan Muktamar Nahdlatul *Ulama* ke-2', Surabaya, 12 Rabiul Awwal 1346 H, 9 October 1927, in K. H. A. Aziz Masyhuri, *Masalah Keagamaan Hasil Muktamar dan Munas Ulama Nahdlatul Ulama Kesatu – 1926 s/d kedua puluh sembilan 1994* (Surabaya: PP RMI and Dinamika Press 1997), p. 25; 'Masail Diniyah Keputusan Muktamar Nahdlatul *Ulama* ke-14', Magelang, 14 Jumadil Ula 1351 H/1 July 1939, in K. H. A. Aziz Masyhuri, *Masalah Keagamaan Hasil Muktamar dan Munas Ulama Nahdlatul Ulama Kesatu – 1926 s/d kedua puluh sembilan 1994* (Surabaya: PP RMI and Dinamika Press 1997), p. 171.

verbally, but does not believe it in his heart (*kafir nifaq*); and lastly, the one who knows God in his heart, and says it verbally, but does not obey Him in practice, such as Abu Thalib (called *kafir 'inad*).[50] When asked if it is allowed to read the books authored by non-Muslims, such as an Arabic dictionary *al-Munjid* by Louis Maloef, the NU *fatwa* states: 'It is not allowed to read works by non-Muslims except for a Muslim who has adequate knowledge and can distinguish the truth from the untruth.'[51] Another *fatwa* proclaimed that 'a Muslim who converts to Christianity and does not return to Islam before death is not allowed to be buried in the Islamic way and in a Muslim cemetery'.[52] In another judgment, the NU decided that when a non-Muslim (*kafir*) says 'there is no god but Allah' right before death, but does not say that Muhammad is the messenger of Allah, then he/she remains a non-Muslim.[53] Also, there is a *fatwa* which states that a Muslim parent should not agree to allowing his/her child to become non-Muslim. Instead, a Muslim parent should try

---

[50] This is based on a book called *Syarah Safinah al-Najah* by al-Imam al-Nawawi al-Banteni. 'Masail Diniayah Keputusan Muktamar Nahdlatul *Ulama* ke-5, Pekalongan, 13 Rabiul Tsani 1349 H/7 September 1930, in K. H. A. Aziz Masyhuri, *Masalah Keagamaan Hasil Muktamar dan Munas Ulama Nahdlatul Ulama Kesatu – 1926 s/d kedua puluh sembilan 1994* (Surabaya: PP RMI and Dinamika Press 1997), pp. 61–2.

[51] This *fatwa* is based on a book called *Fawaid al-Makkiyah*, which referred to another kitab *al-Fatawa al-Haditsiyyah*. In the latter, it is stated that it is not allowed to read books such as *Nuzhah al-Majalis* because it contains the truth (*haq*) and the false (*batil*). This shows how the NU *fatwa* follows the other *fatwa* on similar matters, but interprets it for local questions and circumstances. 'Masail Diniyah Keputusan Muktamar Nahdlatul *Ulama* ke-9', Banyuwangi, 8 Muharram 1353, 23 April 1934, in K. H. A. Aziz Masyhuri, *Masalah Keagamaan Hasil Muktamar dan Munas Ulama Nahdlatul Ulama Kesatu – 1926 s/d kedua puluh sembilan 1994* (Surabaya: PP RMI and Dinamika Press 1997), p. 110.

[52] This *fatwa* is based on two books, *Sullam al-Taufiq* and *Tarsyikh al-Mustafidin*. Masail Diniyah Keputusan Muktamar Nahdlatul *Ulama* ke-9', Banyuwangi, 8 Muharram 1353, 23 April 1934, in K. H. A. Aziz Masyhuri, *Masalah Keagamaan Hasil Muktamar dan Munas Ulama Nahdlatul Ulama Kesatu – 1926 s/d kedua puluh sembilan 1994* (Surabaya: PP RMI and Dinamika Press 1997), p. 111.

[53] This is based on the religious book *Fath al-Muin* by Zainuddin al-Malabary. 'Masail Diniyah Keputusan Muktamar Nahdlatul *Ulama* ke-12', Malang, 12 Rabiul Tsani 1356 H/25 March 1937. In K. H. A. Aziz Masyhuri, *Masalah Keagamaan Hasil Muktamar dan Munas Ulama Nahdlatul Ulama Kesatu – 1926 s/d kedua puluh sembilan 1994* (Surabaya: PP RMI and Dinamika Press 1997), pp. 145–6.

to educate his/her children according to Islam.[54] In making all of these judgments, the NU sought justification in their interpretations of the previous religious books. In other words, there was no direct consultation nor a comprehensive reference to the Qur'an which shows various attitudes toward other religious communities.[55]

To the question whether Indonesia remained an Islamic country, the NU issued its *fatwa* in 1935, stating that 'Indonesia remains an Islamic country (*negeri Islam*) because it was governed by Muslim rulers although it has now been taken over by the infidel (*kafir*) colonizer; Indonesia remains an Islamic state and it will be so forever'.[56] One year after the proclamation of Indonesian independence in 1945, there was a question whether to fight against the colonizer was an obligation for every Muslim or only for some of them. The NU *fatwa* in 1946 stated that to fight against the colonizers and their collaborators is an obligation for everyone, male and female, old and young, within an area of 58 miles (94 km), and becomes an obligation beyond the area in order to assist those unable to undertake the fight alone.[57]

---

[54] Masail Diniyah Keputusan Muktamar Nahdlatul *Ulama* ke-13', Menes Banten, 13 Rabiul Tsani 1357 H/12 July 1938, in K. H. A. Aziz Masyhuri, *Masalah Keagamaan Hasil Muktamar dan Munas Ulama Nahdlatul Ulama Kesatu – 1926 s/d kedua puluh sembilan 1994* (Surabaya: PP RMI and Dinamika Press 1997), p. 163.

[55] For example, the NU *fatwa* does not say anything about some Qur'anic passages that say plurality of ways among humankind as God's will. 'If God had willed, He would have made you one nation.' (Q.S. 5:48). There was no mention of a Qur'anic verse saying, 'Verily, those who have attained to faith as well as those who follow the Jewish faith, and the Christians, and the Sabians – all who believe in God and the Last Day, and do righteous deeds – shall have their reward with their God, the Sustainer; and no fear need they have, and neither shall they grieve.' (Q.S. 2:62; 5:69). On this theological issue, see for example, Nurcholish Madjid, 'Interpreting the Qur'anic Principle of Religious Pluralism', Abdullah Saeed, *Approaches to the Qur'an in Contemporary Indonesia* (London: Oxford University Press and the Institute of Ismaili Studies 2005), pp. 209–22.

[56] The book contains the term *dar al-Islam* (Abode of Islam) translated in the NU *fatwa* as '*negara Islam*' (Islamic state). It also mentions the country of Batavia and Java as *dar al-Islam*, not as *dar al-harb* (Abode of War). 'Masail Diniyah Keputusan Muktamar Nahdlatul *Ulama* ke-11', Banjarmasin, 19 Rabiul Awwal 1355 H/9 June 1935, in K. H. A. Aziz Masyhuri, *Masalah Keagamaan Hasil Muktamar dan Munas Ulama Nahdlatul Ulama Kesatu – 1926 s/d kedua puluh sembilan 1994* (Surabaya: PP RMI and Dinamika Press 1997), p. 138.

[57] The *fatwa* is based on several books *Bajuremi Fathil Wahhab, Asna al-Mathalib Syarah Raudh al-Thalibin*, and *Fathul Qarib*. Masail Diniyah Keputusan Muktamar Nahdlatul *Ulama* ke-16', Purwokerto, 1946, in K. H. A.

The Muhammadiyah did not issue *fatwa* specifically regarding the attitude toward other religions. However, they had speeches and decisions in the conferences related to the issue. According to one speaker, the Muhammadiyah asked the Dutch colonial government to assure the security, peace and freedom to Muslim preaching and educational activities. The Muhammadiyah invited non-Muslim communities to return to the basic doctrine of belief in one God (*tauhid*) and to respect all prophets, and to help the Muhammadiyah to undertake these tasks since they were intended for all religions.[58] In Netherlands Indies, they interpreted the concept of *kafir* by associating it with the Dutch colonial power.[59] A Bugis Muhammadiyah preacher named Haji Abdullah expressed his hatred openly against the Dutch government and called them *kafir*: 'Think, my friends, Islam will not develop (in this country) if the Dutch kafir remains in control.'[60] For some preachers in South Sulawesi, the Dutch were regarded as *kafir harby* (infidels warring against Muslims), unlike the Japanese rules who were also *kafir*, but not engaged in a war against Muslims.[61] This is not the only attitude toward the Dutch among Muslims however.

In Kelantan, there was little attention paid in the sermons and edicts to Buddhism, let alone Christianity. The *fatwas* and sermons in the colonial era contained nothing on other religions. The possible reasons are that in Kelantan, the Malay Muslims were a large majority and did not see the Siamese or the Chinese as threats. Buddhist temples (*wat*) were erected without objection from the surrounding Malay community. The Buddhist monks had great freedom to preach in their temples and performed their

---

Aziz Masyhuri, *Masalah Keagamaan Hasil Muktamar dan Munas Ulama Nahdlatul Ulama Kesatu – 1926 s/d kedua puluh sembilan 1994* (Surabaya: PP RMI and Dinamika Press 1997), pp. 197–201.

[58] M. H. Mansoer, 'Choetbatoel-'Arsj', *Boeah Congres Moehammadijah Seperempat Abad* (Djogjakarta; Hoofdbestuur Moehammadijah, n.d.), pp. 9–10.

[59] The idea of Christians as the People of the Book (*Ahl al-kitab*) had not become popular in South Sulawesi and Kelantan during this time, despite the existence of such Quranic interpretation of the Christians, Jews and Muslims as being the Peoples of the Book with shared Father, Abraham. For most of the preachers, the term *kafir* had carried the notion of communal identity rather than quality of disobey and unthankful-ness which could actually apply to the Muslims too. They asserted the idea that all non-Muslims were inherently *kafir*, whereas all Muslims were never *kafir*.

[60] See Hamka, *Moehammadijah melaloei 3 (tiga) Zaman* (Padang Pandjang: Markaz Idarah Moehammadijah 1946), p. 36.

[61] See H. Ismuha, '*Ulama* Aceh dalam Perspektif Sejarah', Taufik Abdullah (ed.), *Agama dan Perubahan Sosial* (Jakarta: CV. Rajawali 1983), p. 11.

rituals without opposition. Despite the assertion of ethnic and religious difference, there were no reports of open conflicts in Kelantan between Buddhists and Muslims during the colonial period.[62] As for Christianity, the Kelantanese *ulama* hardly discussed it during this time, except when it related to the British. Although the preachers must have had strong views about Christianity as *kafir*, they did not express this view in their sermons and edicts, at least insofar as our sources allow us to infer. One possible explanation is that when an ethnic and religious group became an overwhelming majority, divisions arise within the majority group, rather than between a majority and a relatively insignificant minority. These decisions whether to engage certain issues in sermons and edicts were significant since these vehicles for transmission of Islamic knowledge were contested sites of power. To determine what the attitudes were toward other religions, therefore, required an examination of both texts and contexts. In short, Muslims in Kelantan and South Sulawesi had some shared but more different concerns.

VI. CONCLUSION

Sermons and edicts are different but complementary genres in the transmission of Islamic knowledge. Through these genres, the complexity and diversity of what is considered 'Islamic knowledge' have been revealed. The religious knowledge contained in the sermons and edicts in South Sulawesi and Kelantan in the European and Japanese colonial periods may be classified into the fundamentals of belief, rituals and social relationship. In assessing these categories of knowledge in terms of persistence and change, the more fundamental a particular knowledge is perceived, the less resistance it is to change. For example, the concept of one God has been relatively persistent across time and place, although the interpretation of the concept varies from one group to another group. The category in the middle is the one related to ritual. Muslims have shared forms of rituals based on the Prophet Muhammad's example, yet they disagree on certain ritual practices based on traditions, especially regarding divinity, spirits and healing.

---

[62] See Mohamed Yusoff Ismail, *Buddhism and Ethnicity: Social Organization in A Buddhist Temple in Kelantan* (Singapore: Institute of Southeast Asian Studies, 1993), pp. 1–5; Louis Golomb, *Brokers of Morality: Thai Ethnic Adaptation in A Rural Malaysian Setting* (Honolulu: University of Hawaii at Manoa 1978), pp. 1–8.

The most contingent category of religious knowledge is the one related to social and political issues, which mostly appear in public speeches rather than in the mosques and collections of edicts. The social issues are those such as progress, science and the status of women. The political issues of the time are colonialism and nationalism. South Sulawesi provides more data on views on Dutch policies than does Kelantan on the British Adviser. The term '*kafir*' has become more salient in South Sulawesi than in Kelantan because of their different kinds of relationship. The Japanese occupation shaped Muslim discourse regarding Islamic unity, the new age, and the worldly matter. In general, however, what issues are discussed and to what extent depends very much on how the preachers linked the text with the context.

Despite the different degree of persistence and change in the different categories of religious knowledge, it is undeniable that text and context are crucial. Muslims pay attention to the way the text is treated, translated, interpreted, and applied in local contexts. Contextualization is the process of making the text relevant to particular time and space by different agents, not only the so-called reformist, but also the conservative (*Islam kolot*). I agree with Abdulkader Tayob, who has studied sermons in South Africa. He argued that sermons must be studied in relation to the historical context and the discursive tradition employed, and go beyond the written word and the speech and the gestures of the preachers and the teachers.[63] However, such a historical study of Islamic discourse needs to delineate the dynamics of what is textual and what is contextual, and what is persistent and what is changing. This chapter is an attempt to posit sermons and edicts within the binary dimensions of text and context, and persistence and change.

---

[63] Ashraf Dockrat, book review essay, Abdulkader Tayob, 'Islam in South Africa: Mosques, Imams, and Sermons' (Gainesville: University Press of Florida 1999) (2004) 36 *International Journal for Middle East Studies* pp. 519–21.

Index

Aaronovitch, D. 410
Abady, M. 436
Abbas, A. 14, 18, 29, 32, 43, 46
Abdal-Haqq, I. 407
Abdalla, M. 42
Abdul Rahman, N. 28–9
Abdullah, A. 224, 231–2
Abdullah, N. 235, 238
Abiad, N. 147
ablution (*tayammum*) (dry ritual ablution) 303
  see also health issues
abortion 282–5
  and ensoulment 283
  see also contraception use; genetic engineering and ethics; women
Aboulgar, M. 281
Accounting and Auditing Organization for Islamic Finance Institutions (AAOIFI) 173, 175, 176
  see also banking practices, Bangladesh
ad-Diyyah (compensation), and restorative justice 257, 263, 266, 267
Adhar, R. 75
Admad, H. 147
adoption (*kafala*)
  colonial legacies and family laws, Singapore 29–30
  prohibition of formal 279
  see also children
adoption (*kafala*) application in the West 48–76
  change, adaptation and recognition 70–74
  Convention on the Rights of the Child (CROC) *see* Convention on the Rights of the Child (CROC)
  equality of access to orphans for care 76
  fraudulent activity and trafficking concerns 75–6
  future solutions 74–6
  Hague Convention on Intercountry Adoption 52, 66, 68–9
  inheritance issues 58, 60, 61, 74, 76
  and international law 68–9
  Islamic countries 55–67
  Islamic countries, post-colonial pragmatists and international migration 60–64, 76
  Islamic countries, strict compliance 56–9
  kafala definition 49–51
  migration and permanence 72–4
  naming considerations 74
  open and ethical adoption 70, 74, 75
  permanency issues 50–51
  permitting adoption via a purposive approach and influence of *urf* (custom) 64–6, 76
  Western constructs 51–5
  Western constructs, Australia 51–2, 71
  Western constructs, Canada 54–5
  Western constructs, France 53–4
ADR *see* alternative dispute resolution (ADR) and family law
adultery (*zina*) 274, 275, 281
  see also genetic engineering and ethics
Afary, J. 416–17
Afghanistan
  Bamiyan Buddhas 342, *see also* Islamic art
  kafala (adoption) interpretation 57–8, 59

African Charter on the Rights and Welfare of the Child 78, 79
Afzan, M. 267
Aghababaei, E. 181
Aghānī Miniatures 337–8
see also Islamic art
Ahmad, F. 163
Ahmed, F. 137
Ahmed, H. 168
Ahmed, M. 167, 174, 175
Ahmed, N. 149, 150, 151
Ahmed, W. 151
Ahmetasevic, N. 414
AIDS 302
see also health issues
Aisha, N. 16
Akub, A. 361
al-'Afw (pardon), Malaysia 256
Al-'Alim, A. 86, 88
Al-Alwani, T. 334, 335, 336, 345
Al-Attas, S. 260
Al-Bassam, I. 378
Al-din, A. 181
Al-Fārūqī, I. 334, 338, 343, 344
Al Faruqi, I. and L. 244
Al-Jawziyya, I. 246
Al-Julaydi, S. 84, 88
Al-Khalifa, H. 385
Al-Qaradawi, Y. 241, 296, 298
Al-Ramahi, A. 121
Al Sabiq, S. 191
Al-Sagoff, S. 255, 256
Al-Sheha, A. 372, 386
Al Tamimi, J. 387
Al-'Umari, N. 299
Al-Zahiriy, A. 108
Al-Zuhaily, W. 84, 91, 108, 116
Albanese, J. 208
Albertini, T. 342
Alexander, N. 201
Ali, A. 252
Ali, M. 8, 428–51
Ali, S. 242
Alibašić, A. 419, 422, 423, 425, 426
Alig, A. 382
Allam, H. 248
Allen, R. 436
Almihdar, Z. 275, 276, 280, 285, 286
Alsharif, A. 385
Alsubaie, M. 6, 201–16
alternative dispute resolution (ADR) and family law 120–38
classical Islamic thought and theory 120–23
personal autonomy 137
private arrangement concerns 137–8
alternative dispute resolution (ADR) and family law, Singapore 128–36
Administration of Muslim Law Act (AMLA) 129–30, 131, 132–3, 134, 135
Arbitration Act 134
fatawa opinions 129
Majlis Ugama Islam Singapura (MUIS) 129, 130, 133, 135
minorities and special position of Malays 128–9
Shari'ah Court 130–36
sulh-based practice 134–5
alternative dispute resolution (ADR) and family law, UK 123–8
Arbitration Act 123–4, 127
community-based Shari'ah courts 126–8
mediation and Shari'ah Law 124–8
Altorki, S. 378
Aman, A. 247
'American Quran' (Birk) 348
Amin, S. 188
Amir, D. 430, 439
An-Na'im, A. 80, 81, 219
Anderson, J. 275
aniconism (geometry and linear patterns) 337, 343–5
see also Islamic art
Antúnez, J. 408, 415
Anwar, R. 436
apostasy *see* blasphemy and apostasy
Araeen, R. 344
Arafa, M. 210
Ardic, N. 70
Aroney, N. 75
Arouri, M. 211
art *see* Islamic art
Arthur, J. 168

Aščerić-Todd, I. 407
Atighetchi, D. 275, 279, 280, 282
Atjeh, A. 430
Auda, J. 184
Australia
Australian Competition and Consumer Commission v Turi Foods 313
colonial legacies and family laws *see* colonial legacies and family laws, Australia
Concord MD v Coles 190
corporate crime 215
food regulation *see* food regulation and religion, Australia
H v H 21
kafala (adoption) application 51–2, 71
kafala (adoption) and migration 72–4
Mabo v Queensland 16
Mohamed v Mohamed 44–5
Mohammed Salah & Gastana 40
Oltman & Harper 22
R v Wattle Gully Gold Mines 213
Tahiri 73–4, 75
Wold v Kleppier 21, 23
Yanner v Eaton 180, 181
Ayman, S. 64
Ayub, M. 170
Azhari, R. 257–8
Aziz, N. 258

Babić, M. 426
Babuna, A. 410, 411
Badawi, B. and G. 154
Badawi, J. 243, 245
Baer, E. 340
Bahçecik, Ş. 249
Baiz, K. 165
Baldwin, F. 204
Bamiyan Buddhas 342
see also Islamic art
Bangladesh
Ain O Salish Kendra (ASK) v Government of Bangladesh 152
banking practices *see* banking practices, Bangladesh
corporate social responsibility and workplace *see* corporate social responsibility and workplace casualties, Bangladesh
Islamic Investment Company of the Gulf (Bahamas) Ltd. v Symphony Gems 168
banking practices 159–77
business in Islam 160–62
economic development focus 161–2
interest-based transactions, prohibition of 161, 162
ownership-oriented selling 162
profit-loss sharing (PLS) strategies 162, 164–73
banking practices, Bangladesh 163–73
Accounting and Auditing Organization for Islamic Finance Institutions (AAOIFI) standards 173, 175, 176
Banking Companies Act and Shari'ah principles 163
debt-based sale-lease transactions (DST) 164–73
equity based profit-and-loss-sharing (PLS) 164–73
failure of delivery and burden of proof 168–9
financing modes 164–5
implementing mechanism 173–6
interest rate utilisation 166, 167, 170–72
mark-up practice 166–7, 169–72
Musharakah and *Mudarabah* (partnerships or joint ventures) 164–5
price determination 169–70
risk-taking issues 167–9
Shari'ah Councils (SCS) 174–5
Shari'ah Supervisory Board (SSB) 173–6
Bano, S. 125
Bargach, J. 49, 56
Barkow, A. and R. 209, 216
Barratt, A. 78
Bartels, E. 420, 423

Barton, G. 359
Becker, J. 352, 356
Begum, A. 5, 159–77
Benjamin, H. 312
Bennett, C. 425
Bentham, J. 182
Berg, B. 363–4
Berkovic, N. 45
Berry, S. 221
Bhatia, A. 155
Bhuian, S. 205
Birk, S., 'American Quran' 348
Birnbaum, M. 419
Bisri, C. 367
Black, A. 4, 13–47, 52, 75, 122, 280, 285, 286, 289, 417, 420
blasphemy and apostasy 217–49
blasphemy and apostasy, future directions 243–9
  education about role of human agency 244–5
  international initiative to combat Islamophobia and promotion of hate 246–9
  Organization of Islamic Cooperation (OIC) and free speech issues 248–9
blasphemy and apostasy, in Islamic tradition 224–7, 235–8, 242
  death penalty support 227–9, 230, 232, 236–7
  divine law as product of human juristic agency 244–5
  interpretation differences 230–33, 235–9, 242, 243
  rulings of pre-modern thinkers (*taqlid*) and undiluted imitation 240, 242, 243, 245–6
blasphemy and apostasy, Malaysian apostasy laws 233–5, 238–42
  apostasy differentiation issues 239–40, 242
  death penalty 234, 238, 240–41
  Hudud Bill and apostasy definition 233–5, 238, 239, 241–2
  and treason 240–41, 242
blasphemy and apostasy, Pakistan blasphemy laws 219–24
  death penalty moratorium 223–4
  expansion of blasphemy laws and political motives 221–3
  Human Rights Commission of Pakistan 223
  Indian Penal Code effects 220–21
  opponents as victims 223–4
Blumi, I. 407
Boone, J. 248
Bosnia and Hercegovina and progressive Islam 405–27
  Fatwa Council 414
  Hanafi School of jurisprudence 407, 413
  history of Balkan Islam 406–10
  history of Balkan Islam, communism effects 408–9
  history of Balkan Islam, institutionalisation of religious education for Islamic minorities, effects of 409–10
  intra-religious relations 412–16
  rationality and practicality focus 413–14, 415–16
  religious public holidays and ceremonies 424–5
  Salafism 410–12, 414–16, 417
  Saudi financial aid 411
  secular state and religious diversity 422–6
  Sufism 406–7
  vandalism of religious sites 425
Bosnia and Hercegovina and progressive Islam, women and Islam 416–22
  domestic violence programs and women's shelters 421
  higher education 421
  marriage 419–21
  and niqab 417–19, 420
  religious education 421–2
Bouchard, G. 321–2
Bougarel, X. 423
Bourdieu, P. 321
Bowen, D. 282
Bowen, J. 127
Brady, M. 287, 288
Braidotti, R. 309

Branine, M. 202
Brenner, A. 323–4
Brockopp, J. 282
Brooke, C. 322–3
Brown, C. 430
Bryan, M. 196
Bucy, P. 204
Bull, P. 430
Burckhardt, T. 332
Burgess, R. 8, 405–27
Burman, S. 78
Bustān (Fruit Orchard) (Sa'di) 338
  see also Islamic art
Butt, P. 185, 188

Caeiro, A. 41
Cairo Declaration of Human Rights in Islam 156
Calamur, K. 217
Calder, N. 292
Calderini, S. 414
calligraphic styles 345–6
  see also Islamic art, Qur'anic verse
Campbell, K. 382
Canada
  Kaddoura v Hammoud 44
  kafala (adoption) application 54–5
  'limping' marriages 28
  Marcovitz v Bruker 44
  minority cultural practices, accommodation of 321–2
Carey, G. 377
Carroll, L. 61
Cavia, B. 311
censorship, Islamic art 341, 347–8
Cerić, M. 413–14, 415–16, 427
Chan, S. 13, 15, 30
Chan, W. 18
Chapra, M. 147, 161
children
  child marriage 22, 285–6
  childcare centres 396–8
  Convention on the Rights of the Child (CROC) *see* Convention on the Rights of the Child (CROC)
  and guardianship *see* Libya, 'best interests of the child' concept and guardianship
  trafficking 75–6
  World Declaration on the Survival, Protection and Development of Children 77–8
  see also adoption; guardianship; women
Chowdhury, A. 160, 163, 174
Chowdhury, S. 150
Chowdhury, Z. 150
Clemons, R. 314
Coelho, P. 146
cohabitation 24
  see also marriage
colonial legacies and family laws 13–47
  common legal heritage 13–14
  community acceptance versus community concerns 32–4
  consistency versus diversity 39–42
  convergence and divergence 30–46
  courts working together versus separately 42–5
  divorce 25–30
  historical context 15–18
  homogeneity versus heterogeneity 35
  indigenous peoples versus immigrants 31
  khuluk/khula (no-fault) divorce 25, 27, 28, 38–9
  mahr (dowry) provisions 19, 27, 44
  mandatory versus voluntary jurisdiction 36–9
  marriage 19–25
  unofficial versus professional 45–6
colonial legacies and family laws, Australia
  cohabitation 24
  divorce and Family Law Act 25–7, 37–8, 44–5
  fatwas, sources of 41–2
  'forced' or 'servile' marriages 23
  'limping' marriages 27–8, 38
  Marriage Act 21–2

Muslim Community Reference Group (MCRG) 37
Muslim ethnicities 355
'one law for all' 14, 24, 33–4, 35, 36
opt-in system concerns 37–8
same-sex marriage 24
Shari'ah adherence, voluntary 17
Shari'ah law experts 40
talak/talaq (pronouncement) divorce 23–4, 25, 26
terra nullus concept 16
underage and polygamous marriages 22
colonial legacies and family laws, Singapore
Administration of Muslim Law Act (AMLA) 17–18, 19–20, 24–5, 28–9, 32, 37, 39–40, 43
adoption 29–30
cohabitation 24
divorce 28–9, 38
divorce and maintenance and custody issues 29–30, 43
gross indecency acts and homosexuality 24
khuluk/khula (no-fault) divorce 38–9
legal aid 46
legal dualism and Shari'ah Court system 14, 15–16, 17–18, 31–2, 34, 36–7, 39
Majlis Ugama Islam Singapura (MUIS) 18, 32, 35, 36, 39–40
Majlis Ugama Islam Singapura (MUIS), *fatwas* 40, 41
Muslim Advisory Board 18
polygamous marriages 20
registration system (ROMM) for Muslim births, conversions and marriages 20, 24, 36
Registry of Muslim Marriages (ROMM) 20–21
Shari'ah Court's lack of powers of enforcement 42–3
talak/talaq (pronouncement) divorce 28
transparency and appellate review 45–6
wali position in marriage 20, 24
Women's Charter 18, 19, 24, 31
colonialism, sermon (*khutbahs*) and edict (*fatwas*), Indonesia and Malaya 428–51
contextual dimension 438–42
continuity and change, evidence of 440–42
fatwa sources 433–5
Friday sermon, functions of 436–8, 439–40
lack of legal enforcement 437–8
languages used 432–3
local traditions, attitudes towards 441
Muslim diversity and local norms, attitudes towards 442–5
other religions, attitudes towards 445–50
performative aspect of sermon 430, 436
political aspect 438
preacher's communication skills 439–40
and preacher's education and performance 430
preacher's individual interpretation 436
preacher's sources 431–2
and religious space 429–38
sermons published for wider circulation 435–6
unbelievers (*kafir*) types 446–8
see also fatwas
communication
languages used 432–3
preacher's communication skills 439–40
sermons published for wider circulation 435–6
see also colonialism, sermon (*khutbahs*) and edict (*fatwas*), Indonesia and Malaya; interpretation
community as stakeholder, and restorative justice 254–6

compensation (*ad-Diyyah*), and restorative justice 257, 263, 266, 267
consumer requirements and demands, and food regulation 319–20
contraception use 284, 305–6
  sterilisation for birth control 302–3
  see also abortion; genetic engineering and ethics; health issues; women
Convention on the Elimination of All Forms of Discrimination against Women (CEDAW)
  educational rights for women 371–2, 375, 377, 386, 388, 391, 393, 399, 400
  genetic engineering and ethics 274–5, 276, 286
Convention on the Rights of the Child (CROC) 58, 66, 69, 276, 398–9
  Libya, and 'best interests of the child' concept 77, 78, 79, 82–3, 87, 101–2
Conyon, M. 146
Corbett, M. 7–8, 331–49
cornea transplant 303–4
  see also health issues
corporate criminal liability, Saudi Arabia 201–16
  companies responsible for criminal act by employee 206–7
  corporate crime and lack of transparency 205–9
  crime rate 207–8
  criticisms 209–13
  economic liberalisation effects 203–4
  Gulf Cooperation Council (GCC) 202, 213
  individual liability 212
  judicial proceedings' delays 214
  outdatedness 212
  penalties 206–7, 208–9, 212, 215
  sanctions, ineffective 213
  Tamimi Global Company Ltd (TAFGA) 208
  trust, lack of 212
corporate social responsibility and workplace casualties, Bangladesh 141–58
  Cairo Declaration of Human Rights in Islam 156
  corporate social responsibility definition 146–7
  corporation, legal definition 145–6
  employment levels and exploitation 141–2
  Generalised System of Preferences (GSP) program suspension 151
  hierarchies in corporate management 153–4, 155
  International Covenant on Economic, Social and Cultural Rights 156
  legal system 143–4
  occupational health and safety 148–57
  Rana Plaza collapse 142, 149, 150, 155
  right to life as fundamental right 152–3, 156
  Shari'ah law, rights and obligations 143–5, 147–8, 151–6
  stakeholder theory of the corporation 146, 152
  Tazreen Fashions 142, 149–50, 155
  Universal Declaration of Human Rights (UDHR) 156
  Universal Islamic Declaration of Human Rights (UIDHR) 157
  see also employment levels
Coulson, N. 58
Cox, H. 325
criminal justice system research, Malaysia 251–2
criminal liability, corporate *see* corporate criminal liability, Saudi Arabia
Criminal Procedure Code, Malaysia 266–8
cryopreservation of embryos 282
  see also genetic engineering and ethics
custody issues and divorce 29–30, 43
  see also divorce

Dajlerup, D. 418
Daniels, T. 355
Davies, M. 309, 325–6
Davis, J. 145
death penalty 234, 238, 240–41
  moratorium 223–4
  support 227–9, 230, 232, 236–7
debt-based sale-lease transactions (DST) 164–73
  see also banking practices, Bangladesh
Dhofier, Z. 356
Dickens, B. 282
Diskant, E. 204
diversity, Muslim diversity and local norms, attitudes towards, Indonesia and Malaya 442–5
divorce
  colonial legacies and family laws 25–30, 38
  and Family Law Act, Australia 25–7, 37–8, 44–5
  khuluk/khula (no-fault) divorce 25, 27, 28, 38–9
  maintenance and custody issues 29–30, 43
  parental separation issues 104–5
  polygyny, divorce and gender inequality 20, 22, 279–80, 281
  talak/talaq (pronouncement) divorce 23–4, 25, 26, 28
  see also marriage
Doi, A. 252
domestic violence 268, 421
  see also women
Donaldson, T. 146
Donboli, J. 145, 211
Donohue, J. 169
Doumato, A. 382
dowry (*mahr*) provisions 19, 27, 44
Drenik, S. 371
driving rights, women's 277–8, 395–6
Duderija, A. 411, 412, 417, 418, 419
Dunn, N. 274, 283

Eadie, K. 4–5, 48–76
Eagleton, T. 308
Eck, D. 445–6
economic development focus, banking practices 161–2
economic liberalisation effects, corporate criminal liability, Saudi Arabia 203–4
edicts *see fatwas*
education
  higher 383–4, 385, 421
  human agency role, and blasphemy and apostasy 244–5
  preacher's education and performance, Indonesia and Malaya 430
  religious 409–10, 421–2
educational rights for women in Saudi Arabia 371–402
  Basic Law of Governance and human rights 372–6
  Basic Law of Governance and Shari'ah law 375–7
  childcare centres 396–8
  Convention on the Elimination of All Forms of Discrimination against Women (CEDAW) 371–2, 375, 377, 386, 388, 391, 393, 399, 400
  driving restrictions 395–6
  early marriage issues 398–9
  guardians' dominance 388–9
  ignorance of rights 399–401
  international organisations, women's involvement in 387
  leadership positions 386–7
  reform recommendations 386–401
  Saudisation employment policy 393–4
  specialisations, lack of available 390–93, 394, 400–401
  unemployment issues 392–4
  unemployment issues, job market fund proposal 394
  vocational guidance, need for 392
  women's rights as focus, need for 387
  women's rights overview 372–7
educational rights for women in Saudi Arabia, history 378–86

Dar Al-Hanan school 379–80
gender segregation issues 384–5
General Presidency of Female Education (GPFE) 380, 382–3, 384
higher education programme 383–4, 385
intermediate and secondary school examinations as external students 378–9
non-religious education 381–2
puberty, seclusion and veiling 378
public opposition 381
royal family support 381–2, 383
supervision 384
Egypt
collective *ijtihad* and *fatwas* 300
foster parents and child name changes 59
inheritance rights 58
kafala (adoption) interpretation 58–9
Ekadjati, E. 351
El Matrah, J. 31, 34
El-Dakkak, M. 259
El-Gamal, M. 148, 159, 164, 165, 170
El-Ghanim, W. 201
El-Ghattis, N. 159
El-Sanabary, N. 378
Elizur, Y. 208
Elkhatib, D. 161–2
Elsaman, R. 143, 145
employment levels
and duties of guardian 100, 102–3
Saudisation of employment policy 393–4
and workplace provisions, Saudi Arabia 277
see also corporate social responsibility and workplace casualties, Bangladesh
Engelen, P.-J. 208
ensoulment, and abortion 283
Entoy, A. 360
Ernst, C. 224, 225
Esmaeili, H. 5, 178–98
Esposito, J. 1
Esq, U. 159, 168
Essof, I. 28, 37, 38
ethics
adoption, open and ethical 70, 74, 75
food regulation and demands for humane treatment of animals, Australia 316–17
and genetic engineering *see* genetic engineering and ethics
European Court of Human Rights, *Harroudj v France* 49, 52–4, 64, 70, 75
euthanasia 303
see also health issues
Evans, M. 194

Fakeeh, M. 395
family laws
and alternative dispute resolution (ADR) *see* alternative dispute resolution (ADR) and family law
colonial legacies *see* colonial legacies and family laws
Fang, L. 261, 262
fatwas
alternative dispute resolution (ADR) and family law, Singapore 129
and collective *ijtihad* 299, 300
colonial legacies and family laws 40, 41–2
Fatwa Council, Bosnia and Hercegovina and progressive Islam 414
and sermons *see* colonialism, sermon (*khutbahs*) and edict (*fatwas*), Indonesia and Malaya
female genital mutilation (FGM) 287–8
see also genetic engineering and ethics
Ferdausi, F. 141, 142
figurative representations of the Prophet, evolution of 338, 339
see also Islamic art
fiqh (Islamic jurisprudence) 57, 243, 276, 413

cornea implants 304
as divine word of God 244
Hanafi school, Bosnia 426
hudud offences 235
impact of education on 261
and music 361–2
property law and trusts, Iran 181–2
Flood, F. 336, 341, 342
Focho, E. 413
Fontes, A. 58
food regulation and religion 307–27
consumer requirements and demands 319–20
and Enlightenment values 322–4
legal rights and rules 320–22
philosophy of science, and rules and reason 322–4
regulation and values 319–20
religion as repository of values 324–6
research project 310–12
and secularism 308–9, 322–3, 324–6
food regulation and religion, Australia
ethical demands for humane treatment of animals 316–17
food safety 317–19
food safety, traditional practices 318–19
free range certification in egg and poultry production 313–14
halal certification 314–17
halal certification, theological credibility 315
Hazard Analysis Critical Control Point (HACCP) system 318
live export of animals for slaughter 316–17
stunning of animals 317
'forced' or 'servile' marriages 23
see also marriage
Foster, N. 202
Foucault, M. 319, 320, 323
France
adoption and care arrangements 53–4
kafala (adoption) application 53–4
Freamon, B. 143
free range certification in egg and poultry production 313–14
see also food regulation and religion, Australia
free speech issues 248–9
see also blasphemy and apostasy, future directions
Friday sermon, functions of 436–8, 439–40
Friedman, M. 146

Gaffaney, K. 176
gambus Arabic music 363–4
see also music in contemporary Indonesia
Gbadamosi, O. 274, 276, 280, 285
gender inequality, polygyny and divorce 20, 22, 279–80, 281
see also divorce; genetic engineering and ethics
gender segregation issues, Saudi Arabia 384–5
Generalised System of Preferences (GSP) program suspension, Bangladesh 151
genetic engineering and ethics 273–88
abortion 282–5
abortion, and ensoulment 283
adoption, prohibition of formal 279
adultery (*zina*) 274, 275, 281
child marriage 285–6
contraception use 284
Convention on the Elimination of All Forms of Discrimination against Women (CEDAW) 274–5, 286
cryopreservation of embryos 282
female genital mutilation (FGM) 287–8
medically assisted reproduction (MAR) 280–82
polygyny, divorce and gender inequality 279–80, 281
sex selection technologies 282
sperm banks 281
women in Islamic world 274–9

genetic engineering and ethics, Saudi Arabia
  abortion 283–4
  child marriage 286
  contraception use 284
  Convention on the Elimination of All Forms of Discrimination against Women (CEDAW) reservations 276, 286
  Convention on the Rights of the Child (CRC) reservations 276
  employment and workplace provisions 277
  families and male authority (guardianship) 277
  female genital mutilation (FGM) 288
  Hanbali School of legal governance 275–6, 286
  human rights protection 277
  medically assisted reproduction (MAR) 281
  strict separation of the sexes 276
  voting rights 277
  Wahhabi tradition and Shari'ah interpretation 276
  women's driving rights 277–8
genetic engineering and ethics, Tunisia
  abortion 283, 284–5
  child marriage 286
  Code of Personal Status and equality 278–9
  contraception use 284
  Convention on the Elimination of All Forms of Discrimination against Women (CEDAW) 274–5, 286
  cryopreservation of embryos 282
  discipline and disobedient women 279
  Malikis and Hanafi schools of law 278
  medically assisted reproduction (MAR) 281–2
  polygyny criminalisation 280
  sperm banks 281
Genn, C. 406
geometry and linear patterns (aniconism) 337, 343–5
  see also Islamic art
George, K. 346, 347, 348, 349
Ghāmidī, J. 232, 245
Ghena, K. 26
Ghosh, P. 141, 142
Gibb, H. 432
Gigler, F. 158
Gillani, W. 224
Gillard, J. 13
Gleave, R. 2
Gocer, A. 332, 338
Golomb, L. 450
Grabar, O. 333–4, 337, 345
gross indecency acts and homosexuality, Singapore 24
Gruber, C. 338, 339, 340, 341
guardianship
  and children *see* Libya, and 'best interests of the child' concept and guardianship
  dominance, and educational rights for women in Saudi Arabia 388–9
  families and male authority, Saudi Arabia 277
  see also children
Gulf Cooperation Council (GCC) 202, 213

Habermas, J. 309
Habib, N. 223
Hachemi, S. 187
Hafizović, R. 414
Hague Convention on Intercountry Adoption 52, 66, 68–9
Hak, N. 132
halal certification 314–17
  see also food regulation and religion, Australia
Hallaq, W. 122, 293, 294
Hammado, N. 7, 273–88
Hamoudi, H. 159, 162, 173
Handayani, I. 354, 356, 365
Hansen, L. 216
Harnish, D. 352, 355, 363, 366

Hasan, A. 292–3
Hasan, J. 141
Hascall, S. 253
Hashim, A. 217, 218, 223
Hasnas, J. 204
Hassan, M. 162, 167, 173
Hayat, Z. 221, 222
health issues
  and *fatwas see ijtihad* (Islamic legal reasoning), health issues and *fatwas*, Indonesia
  guardian's health considerations and 'best interests of the child' 98–9, 101, 104
Hearn, B. 159
Helfand, M. 128, 137
Helli, M. 182, 191, 195
Hermawan, D. 364–5
Hessini, L. 283, 285
Higgins, D. 51
Hinnells, J. 406
Hirvonen, H. 57
Holden, K. 164, 173
homosexuality and gross indecency acts, Singapore 24
Homoud, S. 172
Hooker, M. 438
Hooker, V. 345, 347
Hosen, N. 1–9, 41, 42, 289–306, 316, 326
Hourani, A. 241
human rights
  Basic Law of Governance and human rights, Saudi Arabia 372–6
  Human Rights Commission of Pakistan 223
  right to life as fundamental right, Bangladesh 152–3, 156
Hunter, M. 160
Hussain, J. 87
Hussin, N. 6, 250–69
Huynh, D. 215
Hye, H. 149

Ibrahim, A. 148
iconoclasm 334, 341–3
  see also Islamic art
ijtihad (Islamic legal reasoning) 289–306
  interpretation process 291–6
  Majma' al-Buhuts al-Islamiyah conference 296–8
  Qur'an as undisputed word of God 289–90
ijtihad (Islamic legal reasoning), collective 296–301
  at organisational level 300–301
  international level and Fiqh Academy 299
  national level and *fatwas* 299, 300
ijtihad (Islamic legal reasoning), health issues and *fatwas*, Indonesia 301–6
  AIDS 302
  cornea transplant 303–4
  euthanasia 303
  IUD (intra-uterine device) 305–6
  mixed marriage 303
  organ transplant and donation 303
  pill for preventing menstruation 304–5
  sterilisation for birth control 302–3
  tayammum (dry ritual ablution) 303
  vasectomy and tubectomy 303
images and Islamic art 334–6, 338–9
Imamović, S. 415
Indonesia
  Chanel dress protest 346–7
  collective *ijtihad* at organisational level 300–301
  colonialism, sermon (*khutbahs*) and edict (*fatwas*) *see* colonialism, sermon (*khutbahs*) and edict (*fatwas*), Indonesia and Malaya
  health issues and *fatwas see ijtihad* (Islamic legal reasoning), health issues and *fatwas*, Indonesia
  music *see* music in contemporary Indonesia
inheritance issues and adoption 58, 60, 61, 74, 76
instruments, use of 354, 357, 358–9

see also music in contemporary Indonesia
intellectual property, Iran 193
interest-based transactions 161, 162, 166, 167, 170–72
see also banking practices
International Covenant on Economic, Social and Cultural Rights 156
international initiative to combat Islamophobia and promotion of hate 246–9
see also blasphemy and apostasy, future directions
international organisations, women's involvement in, Saudi Arabia 387
interpretation
differences, blasphemy and apostasy 230–33, 235–9, 242, 243
ijtihad interpretation process 291–6
preacher's individual interpretation, Indonesia and Malaya 436
Wahhabi tradition and Shari'ah interpretation, Saudi Arabia 276
see also communication
intra-religious relations, Bosnia and Hercegovina 412–16
Iran, property law *see* property law and trusts, Iran
Isabel, F. 229
Islam, M. 149, 150
Islamic art 331–49
Aghānī Miniatures 337–8
Bamiyan Buddhas, Afghanistan 342
censorship 341
definition problems 332–4
diverse qualities and widespread populations 332–3
figurative representations of the Prophet, evolution of 338, 339
finding Islam in 332–4
geometry and linear patterns (aniconism) and representation of Divine presence 337, 343–5
iconoclasm 341–3
iconoclasm, expressive and fundamentalism 341–2
iconoclasm, instrumental 341
iconophobia fallacy 334
images and hadith 334–6
images that rival God's creation 336, 338–9
Islamic law engagement 333–4
kings, heroes and princes 340
legal misconception 334–7
portraiture 337–40
portraiture, and early interpretations of Islamic law 337–8
power of images to distract the mind from object of devotion 336–7
Sa'di's *Bustan* (Fruit Orchard) 338
Shāma'il al-Rasūl (Features of the Prophet) manual 338
symbolism use 339–40
Islamic art, Qur'anic verse 345–8
appropriateness concerns 346–7
Birk's 'American Quran' 348
calligraphic styles 345–6
religious censorship 347–8
self-censorship 347
Islamophobia, international initiative to combat 246–9
see also blasphemy and apostasy, future directions
Ismail, M. 450
IUD (intra-uterine device) and contraception 305–6
see also contraception use; genetic engineering and ethics; health issues
Izutsu, T. 121

Jabiri, M. 258
Jackson, S. 242
Jacquot, N. 160, 161
Jahja, T. 353–4
jaipong dance 350, 367
see also music in contemporary Indonesia
Jamal, A. 4, 120–38
Jasimuddin, S. 201
Jefferson, M. 209
Jentz, G. 208
joint ventures 164–5

see also banking practices, Bangladesh
Jones-Pauly, C. 278, 280, 283, 284, 285
Jordan, D. 237

kafala see adoption (*kafala*)
kafalah (sponsorship), and guardianship 84–5
Kamali, M. 218, 232, 233, 234, 237, 238, 239, 241, 243, 244, 245, 291
Kaptein, N. 430
Karčić, F. 408, 409, 411, 419, 422–3
Karčić, H. 407, 408, 409, 411, 412, 414
Kartomi, M. 366
Kashefi, F. 145, 211
Katouzian, N. 190
Katsetos, C. 287
Kay, J. 148
Kennedy, C. 221
Keung, N. 54, 55
Kevin, C. 162
Khadduri, M. 182
Khan, H. 264, 265
Khan, L. 3
Khan, Maulana 232, 245
Khan, Muhammad 154
Khan, S. 218–19
Khayat, M. 381
khuluk/khula (no-fault) divorce 25, 27, 28, 38–9
see also divorce
Khutani, M. 8, 371–402
khutbahs (sermon) *see* colonialism, sermon (*khutbahs*) and edict (*fatwas*), Indonesia and Malaya
Khyeda, S. 202
King, G. 341
Kontoyannis, M. 287
Kuhn, T. 324
Kutty, F. 6, 49, 54, 70, 71, 217–49

la-dharar (no harm principle), property law and trusts, Iran 180
Lacey, R. 381
Laessing, U. 385
Lahpan, N. 8, 350–70
Lambton, A. 183
language *see under* communication
Lau, M. 220
leadership positions, educational rights for women in Saudi Arabia 386–7
Lean, N. 246
Lederer, G. 412
legal aid, Singapore 46
legal dualism and Shari'ah Court system, Singapore 14, 15–16, 17–18, 31–2, 34, 36–7, 39
legal misconception, Islamic art 334–7
legal reasoning *see ijtihad* (Islamic legal reasoning)
Leigh, I. 220
Leong, W. 15, 32
Lewis, M. 147, 151
Lewis, S. 316
Libya, 'best interests of the child' concept and guardianship 77–119
African Charter on the Rights and Welfare of the Child 78, 79
child definition 82–3
child versus guardian rights 88–92
Convention on the Rights of the Child (CROC) 77, 78, 79, 82–3, 87, 101–2
cultural effects 82
employment duties of guardian 100, 102–3
female assisting the male guardian 92, 96, 103
guardian's accommodation 117–18
guardian's health considerations 98–9, 101, 104
guardianship conditions 92–7
guardianship definition 83–8
kafalah (sponsorship) 84–5
lapse of guardianship 92
legal system 80–82
Libyan High Court (LHC) decisions 82, 83–5, 87, 89–106, 107, 110
Libyan High Court (LHC) discretion 111–14

maintenance expenses 82, 108, 111, 112, 115–17
mother's remarriage to stranger 104, 111–14
moving with the child inside the country 106–9
new-born babies 91
non-Muslim guardians 91, 92
ordering preference 87–8
parental rights 84
parental separation/divorce issues 104–5
reinstating guardianship right 114–15
Shari'ah law effects 81, 82
silence of prospective guardians 99–100, 105
trustworthiness considerations 107
upholding guardianship 106–9
visitation rights 109–10
World Declaration on the Survival, Protection and Development of Children 77–8
Lim, H. 185
'limping' marriages, Australia 27–8, 38
see also marriage
Lindsey, T. 129
local traditions, attitudes towards, Indonesia and Malaya 441
Luban, D. 246
Luckin, O. 415
Luhmann, N. 320
Luk, S. 137

McBride, S. 387
McDowall, A. 394
Macfarlane, J. 19, 28
Madden, E. 343, 344, 346
Maddox, M. 312
Maggs, P. 169
mahr (dowry) provisions 19, 27, 44
maintenance expenses, children and guardianship 82, 108, 111, 112, 115–17
Malaya, sermon (*khutbahs*) and edict (*fatwas*) *see* colonialism, sermon (*khutbahs*) and edict (*fatwas*), Indonesia and Malaya
Malaysia
apostasy laws *see* blasphemy and apostasy, Malaysian apostasy laws
PP v Jessica Lim Lu Ping 268
Ramah binti Ta'at v Laton binti Malim Sutan 261
restorative justice *see* restorative justice in Islamic law, Malaysia
Shaik Abdul Latiff v Shaik Elias Bux 261
Maldonado, D. 33
Malekian, F. 254
Malik, J. 406, 409
Malkin, L. 208
Mandhour, I. 180
Mannan, M. 184
Mannheim, K. 32
mark-up practice 166–7, 169–72
see also banking practices, Bangladesh
Marmura, M. 434
marriage
Bosnia and Hercegovina and progressive Islam 419–21
child marriage 285–6
colonial legacies and family laws 19–25
early marriage issues, Saudi Arabia 398–9
'limping' marriages, Australia 27–8, 38
Marriage Act, Australia 21–2
mixed marriage, Indonesia 303
mother's remarriage to stranger, Libya, and 'best interests of the child' concept 104, 111–14
polygyny 20, 22, 279–80, 281
registration system, Singapore 20, 24, 36
same-sex marriage, Australia 24
wali position, Singapore 20, 24
see also cohabitation; divorce; women
Ma'shum, S. 359
Masood, S. 224

Masud, M. 2
Masyhuri, A. 303, 304, 435, 440, 447
Masykur, S. 357, 358
Mattson, I. 70–71
Maududi, A. 234–5, 240
Mayer, A. 221
mediation (*sulh*) 124–8, 134–5, 264–5
medically assisted reproduction (MAR) 280–82
  see also genetic engineering and ethics
Menski, W. 62
menstruation, pill for preventing 304–5
  see also health issues
Merdjanova, I. 408, 420
Merritt, C. 28, 34
Mesarič, A. 414, 415
Mesrati, A. 5, 77–119
Metz, H. 382
Meyer, H. 377
migration and permanence, and adoption 72–4
Miller, R. 208
Min, C. 233
minorities and special position of Malays, Singapore 128–9
minority cultural practices, accommodation of, Canada 321–2
Mirdha, R. 150
mixed marriage, Indonesia 303
  see also marriage
Moattari, A. 383
Modarres, M. 195, 196
Mohamad, Maznah 20
Mohamad, Mohd 252
Mohamed, A. 159, 261, 262, 263
Mohr, R. 7, 307–27
Möhrenschlager, M. 215
Mokhiber, R. 209
Mønnesland, S. 424
Moradi, H. 184
Morocco
  adoption and care arrangements 53
  kafala (adoption) interpretation and guardianship 63–4, 72, 75
Morrison, K. 410, 417
Mortuza, G 149
Mudzhar, M. 301, 305
Muhammad, R. 257
Mulia, M. 443
Mulinge, M. 77, 78
Mullin Marta, J. 201
Munni, M. 149
Music, Z. 412
music in contemporary Indonesia 350–70
  and cultural development 353–4
  gambus Arabic music 363–4
  instruments, use of 354, 357, 358–9
  and Islamic symbols 352, 355, 366, 367, 368
  jaipong dance 350, 367
  lawfulness issues 351–5, 359–62
  musik etnik Islami (ethnic music) 368–9
  musik Islam (Islamic music) and *musik Islami* definitions and distinctions 362–6
  pesantren communities 351, 352, 354, 356–62, 365
  pesantren communities, and local culture, relationship with 357–9, 360–61
  pesantren communities, traditional 356–8
  Ramadhan and *musik Islami* 355
  and religion 352
  secular music and love songs 364–6
  social and political aspects 363, 366–9
  Sufism 359–60, 361–2
  Syafi'i school 353–4
  West Java and *musik Islami* 366–9
Muslim, A. 244

Naraghi, A. 180
Naseef, F. 382
Nasir, J. 279
Nasution, H. 299
Nayak, N. 220
Neighbour, S. 22, 26
Nettl, B. 352

New Zealand, adoption law changes 71–2
niqab wearing *see* veiling
Nizami, S. 164, 170
no harm principle (*la-dharar*), property law and trusts, Iran 180
Noman, O. 221
Noor, A. 261

occupational health and safety 148–57
  see also corporate social responsibility and workplace casualties, Bangladesh
O'Halloran, K. 50, 55, 58, 60–61, 62, 64
Okin, E. 408
'one law for all', Australia 14, 24, 33–4, 35, 36
Onsman, A. 211
opt-in system concerns, Australia 37–8
organ transplant and donation 303
  see also health issues
Organization of Islamic Cooperation (OIC) and free speech issues 248–9
Othman, A. 121
Otto, J. 201
Oudah, A. 256
ownership-oriented selling 162
  see also banking practices

Pakistan
  blasphemy laws *see* blasphemy and apostasy, Pakistan blasphemy laws
  inheritance rights 60, 61
  kafala (adoption) interpretation and guardianship 60–63, 64, 72, 75
  Mst. Irfana Shaheen v Abid Waheed 61, 62
pardon (*al-'Afw*), Malaysia 256
parental separation/divorce issues, Libya, and 'best interests of the child' concept 104–5
Parvin, M. 371
penalties, corporate criminal liability, Saudi Arabia 206–7, 208–9, 212, 215
Penzer, M. 161
performative aspect of sermon 430, 436
  see also colonialism, sermon (*khutbahs*) and edict (*fatwas*), Indonesia and Malaya
personal autonomy, alternative dispute resolution (ADR) and family law 137
pesantren communities *see under* music in contemporary Indonesia
Petrova, D. 222
Petry, R. 430
Pippenger, M. 211
Pirous, A. 347
plea bargaining, Malaysia 267–8
Pleyers, G. 319
political aspects
  music in contemporary Indonesia 363, 366–9
  sermon (*khutbahs*) and edict (*fatwas*), Indonesia and Malaya 438
Pollard, D. 202
Pollard, R. 395
polygyny 20, 22, 279–80, 281
  see also marriage
portraiture 337–40
  see also Islamic art
Possamai, A. 17
Preston, L. 146
price determination 169–70
  see also banking practices
Prodip, M. 141, 142
profit-loss sharing (PLS) strategies 162, 164–73
  see also banking practices
progressive Islam *see* Bosnia and Hercegovina and progressive Islam
property law and trusts, Iran 178–98
  absolute ownership of land and property by God 184–5
  Constitution 186–7
  cooperative ownership 187

Department of Hajj, Trusts and Charities 197
fiqh (Islamic jurisprudence) 181–2
industrial privatisation effects 187
intellectual property 193
la-dharar (no harm principle) 180
mal (property concept) 180–81
milk (relationship with a thing) 181
minerals ownership 192–3
public versus private ownership 183–5
Registration of Deeds and Properties Act 192
taslit (control) principle 180
Urban Land Act 192
waqf (trust) 194–7
property law and trusts, Iran, Civil Code 187–91
ahya mawat (working and cultivating the land) 191
hagh entefa (right to use) 189
hagh ertfagh (limited rights over another's land) 190
property classification 188
property interests 189–90
property ownership sources 190–91
public property 188–9
waqf 195–7
water ownership 191
puberty, seclusion and veiling, Saudi Arabia 378
see also veiling

Qafisheh, M. 253, 256
Qasaymeh, K. 162, 164, 172
qisas (laws of retaliation) 253–4, 262–3
see also restorative justice in Islamic law, Malaysia
Quartly, M. 51
Qudamah al-Maqdisiy, I. 90
Quraishi, A. 69
Qur'anic verse *see* Islamic art, Qur'anic verse

Rabb, I. 231
Rafiq, M. 211
Rahman, A. 16, 32, 43, 47
Rahman, N. 129
Rahman, R. 153
Rahman, S. 235
Ramadan, H. 3
Ramadhan and *musik Islami* 355
see also music in contemporary Indonesia
Rana Plaza collapse, Bangladesh 142, 149, 150, 155
Rane, H. 34
Rasmussen, A. 352, 355, 363, 366
Raudvere, C. 418, 421
Rehman, J. 221, 242
religion as repository of values, and food regulation 324–6
religious education, Bosnia and Hercegovina 421–2
religious public holidays and ceremonies, Bosnia and Hercegovina 424–5
religious space, sermon (*khutbahs*) and edict (*fatwas*), Indonesia and Malaya 429–38
repentance, Malaysia 259–60, 265–6
restorative justice in Islamic law, Malaysia 250–69
community as stakeholder 254–6
compensation (*ad-Diyyah*) 257, 263, 266, 267
criminal justice system research 251–2
Criminal Procedure Code 266–8
current practices 265–8
current practices, repentance 265–6
Domestic Violence Act 268
justice in Islam, significance of 252–3
legal history 260–65
mediation 264–5
pardon (*al-'Afw*) 256
plea bargaining 267–8
punishment seen as appropriate response for crimes 250–51
punishment of shaming 263–4
qisas (laws of retaliation) 253–4, 262–3

reconciliation, negotiation and mediation (*as-Sulh*) 257–9, 264–5, 267–8
repentance (*at-Tawbah*) 259–60, 265–6
Undang-undang Melaka manuscript 261–5
victim impact statement 266–7
victim as stakeholder 253–4, 266, 268
Reynolds, D. 211
Rezai-Rashti, G. 386
Rice, D. 338
Rida, R. 240–41
risk-taking issues 167–9
see also banking practices
Rizvi, K. 340
Roolvink, R. 432
Rouzi, A. 287, 288
royal family support, educational rights for women in Saudi Arabia 381–2, 383
Rozario, P. 80, 81
Rubin, U. 228
Ruggie, J. 209

Sabeeq, S. 194
Sa'di, *Bustān* (Fruit Orchard) 338
see also Islamic art
Sadiq, K. 45, 47, 52
Saeed, A. 2, 3, 34, 224, 233, 235, 237, 240, 383
Saeed, H. 224, 233, 235, 237, 240
Safaei, S. 190
Sahbeq, S. 195, 196
Sait, S. 185
Salafism, Bosnia and Hercegovina 410–12, 414–16, 417
Salama, H. 217
Salasal, S. 185
Salinger, L. 205, 207, 208
Salvatore, A. 348
same-sex marriage, Australia 24
see also marriage
Samuelson, P. 151
sanctions, ineffective, corporate criminal liability, Saudi Arabia 213
Sarker, A. 165, 166, 174, 175
Saudi Arabia
collective *ijtihad* and *fatwas* 300
corporate criminal liability *see* corporate criminal liability, Saudi Arabia
educational rights for women *see* educational rights for women in Saudi Arabia
genetic engineering and ethics *see* genetic engineering and ethics, Saudi Arabia
kafala (adoption) interpretation 57, 59
Saudi financial aid, Bosnia and Hercegovina 411
Schacht, J. 290
Schauer, F. 321
Schoenblum, J. 194
Schwartz, M. 146
Schwartz, R. 158
Schwartz, S. 416, 426
secular music and love songs 364–6
see also music in contemporary Indonesia
secularism
food regulation and religion 308–9, 322–3, 324–6
and religious diversity, Bosnia and Hercegovina 422–6
Serajuddin, A. 49–50, 61
sermon (*khutbahs*) *see* colonialism, sermon (*khutbahs*) and edict (*fatwas*), Indonesia and Malaya
Serour, G. 282
sex selection technologies 282
see also genetic engineering and ethics
sexual segregation, Saudi Arabia 276
see also women
Shabbir, M. 256
Shachar, A. 138
Shaltut, M. 296
shaming, punishment of, Malaysia 263–4

Shari'ah Councils (SCS), banking practices, Bangladesh 174–5
Shari'ah courts
  alternative dispute resolution (ADR) and family law, Singapore 130–36
  community-based, UK 126–8
  lack of powers of enforcement, Singapore 42–3
  and legal dualism, Singapore 14, 15–16, 17–18, 31–2, 34, 36–7, 39
Shari'ah principles, Banking Companies Act, Bangladesh 163
Shari'ah Supervisory Board (SSB), Bangladesh 173–6
Shaw, W. 342, 343, 349
Shibli, A. 141
Shiddieqy, T. 354
Shiloah, A. 351
Shklar, J. 321
Siddiq, K. 359–60
Siddiq, M. 431, 432
Siddique, O. 221, 222
Siddiqui, H. 246
Siddiqui, S. 164, 167, 169, 170–71
Silbertson, A. 148
silence of prospective guardians, Libya, and 'best interests of the child' concept 99–100, 105
Simon, A. 356
Singapore
  alternative dispute resolution (ADR) *see* alternative dispute resolution (ADR) and family law, Singapore
  colonial legacies and family laws *see* colonial legacies and family laws, Singapore
  Mohamed Yusoff bin Mohd Haniff v Umi Kalsom bte Abas (Attorney-General) 131
  Noor Azizan bte Colony v Tan Lip Chin 25
  Saniah Binte Ali & Anors v Abdullah Bin Ali 40, 129
  Shafeeg bin Salim Talib v Fatimah bte Abud bin Talib 129
  TMO v TMP 131–2
Singer, P. 314
Smith, E. 308, 326
Smith, S. 309, 310, 325
Sobarna, C. 350
social aspects, music in contemporary Indonesia 363, 366–9
Soganci, I. 331, 333
Solaiman, S. 5, 141–58, 204
Solomon, J. and A. 146
specialisations, lack of available, and educational rights for women in Saudi Arabia 390–93, 394, 400–401
sperm banks 281
  see also genetic engineering and ethics
stakeholder
  community as, Malaysia 254–6
  victim as, Malaysia 253–4, 266, 268
stakeholder theory of the corporation, Bangladesh 146, 152
Steiner, K. 129
sterilisation for birth control 302–3
  see also contraception use; health issues
Stillman, N. 227, 228, 229
Stringer, D. 247
Sufism
  Bosnia and Hercegovina 406–7
  music in contemporary Indonesia 359–60, 361–2
sulh (mediation) 124–8, 134–5, 264–5
Suryadinata, L. 350
Syafi'i school, music in contemporary Indonesia 353–4
symbolism use
  Islamic art 339–40
  music in contemporary Indonesia 352, 355, 366, 367, 368

Tajuddin, H. 6, 250–69
Takim, L. 229
talak/talaq (pronouncement) divorce 23–4, 25, 26, 28
  see also divorce

taqlid (pre-modern thinkers), and blasphemy and apostasy 240, 242, 243, 245–6
tayammum (dry ritual ablution) 303
  see also health issues
Taylor, C. 321–2, 327
Taylor, J. 143
Taylor, M. 159, 165
Tayob, A. 451
Tazreen Fashions, Bangladesh 142, 149–50, 155
terra nullius concept, Australia 16
Teubner, G. 320
Theodorou, A. 218
Thio, L. 30
Thomsen, S. 146
Tierney, B. 309
Towler, R. 32
tradition, attitudes towards local, Indonesia and Malaya 441
transparency
  and appellate review, Singapore 45–6
  corporate crime and lack of transparency, Saudi Arabia 205–9
treason 240–41, 242
  see also blasphemy and apostasy, Malaysian apostasy laws
trust, lack of, corporate criminal liability, Saudi Arabia 212
trustworthiness considerations, Libya, and 'best interests of the child' concept 107
Tunisia
  adoption and care arrangements 53
  genetic engineering and ethics *see* genetic engineering and ethics, Tunisia
  inheritance rights 74
  kafala (adoption) interpretation and *urf* (custom) 64–6, 71, 72, 75
Tuqan, A. 278
Turkey
  adoption and care arrangements 53
  kafala (adoption) interpretation and *urf* (custom) 66–7, 71, 72
Tyser, C. 258

UK
  alternative dispute resolution (ADR) *see* alternative dispute resolution (ADR) and family law, UK
  Beximco 125
  Bury v Pope 189
  Case of Mines 189
  Jivraj v Haswani 124
  Knight v Knight 197
  'limping' marriages 27
  Salomon v Salomon 145
unbelievers (*kafir*) 225, 230, 239, 241–2, 358, 420
  sermon (*khutbahs*) and edict (*fatwas*), Indonesia and Malaya 446–8
Undang-undang Melaka manuscript, restorative justice in Islamic law, Malaysia 261–5
underage marriage 22, 285–6
  see also children; marriage
unemployment issues, educational rights for women in Saudi Arabia 392–4
Universal Declaration of Human Rights (UDHR) 156
Universal Islamic Declaration of Human Rights (UIDHR) 157
US
  Prophet Muhammad in sculptural frieze in Supreme Court 335
  US v Tamimi Global Co. 208

Valiani, Z. 50, 74
Van Dijk, K. 359
Van Dijk, M. 420, 423
Van Essen, M. 208
Van Zanten, W. 352
vandalism of religious sites, Bosnia and Hercegovina 425
Vann, V. 196
vasectomy and tubectomy 303
  see also contraception use; health issues

veiling
niqab wearing, Bosnia and Hercegovina 417–19, 420
puberty, seclusion and veiling, Saudi Arabia 378
see also women
Vericat, G. 63
victim impact statement, Malaysia 266–7
victim as stakeholder, Malaysia 253–4, 266, 268
visitation rights, Libya, and 'best interests of the child' concept 109–10
vocational guidance, need for, Saudi Arabia 392
Vogel, F. 57, 123, 275, 276, 277
voting rights, Saudi Arabia 277
Voyce, M. 17

Wahed, H. 257–8
Wahhabi tradition, Saudi Arabia 276
Wahid, A. 351
wali position in marriage, Singapore 20, 24
Walsh, D. 232
Wanchic, F. 58
Waseem, M. 221
water ownership, Iran 191
Watt, M. 227, 228
Wehr, H. 291
Weintraub, A. 355, 366
Welchman, L. 67, 69
Wettstein, F. 209
Wheelwright, K. 205
Wiederhold, L. 224
Williams, G. 143, 152, 153, 155, 158
Williams, S. 368
Wiradireja, Y. 368–9
women
Bosnia and Hercegovina *see* Bosnia and Hercegovina and progressive Islam, women and Islam
contraception use 284, 305–6
domestic violence 268, 421
driving rights, women's 277–8, 395–6
educational rights, Saudi Arabia *see* educational rights for women in Saudi Arabia
genetic engineering and ethics 274–9
Women's Charter, Singapore 18, 19, 24, 31
see also abortion; children; marriage; veiling
workplace casualties, Bangladesh *see* corporate social responsibility and workplace casualties, Bangladesh
World Declaration on the Survival, Protection and Development of Children 77–8

Yaquby, N. 173
Yilmaz, I. 27
Yousuf, S. 163
Yusuf, A. 182

Zahraa, M. 132
Zaidan, A. 256, 257
Zakaria, M. 430
Zawawi, M. 6, 250–69
Zibakalam, S. 183–4, 192
zina (adultery) 274, 275, 281
see also genetic engineering and ethics
Zinkin, J. 143, 152, 153, 155, 157, 158